THE CAMBRIDGE HISTORY OF RUSSIAN LITERATURE

THE CAMBRIDGE
HISTORY OF
RUSSIAN LITERATURE

edited by

CHARLES A. MOSER

✱

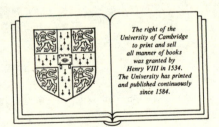

The right of the
University of Cambridge
to print and sell
all manner of books
was granted by
Henry VIII in 1534.
The University has printed
and published continuously
since 1584.

CAMBRIDGE UNIVERSITY PRESS

CAMBRIDGE

NEW YORK   PORT CHESTER   MELBOURNE   SYDNEY

Published by the Press Syndicate of the University of Cambridge
The Pitt Building, Trumpington Street, Cambridge CB2 1RP
40 West 20th Street, New York, NY 10011, USA
10 Stamford Road, Oakleigh, Melbourne 3166, Australia

Printed in Great Britain at the University Press, Cambridge

British Library cataloguing in publication data

The Cambridge history of Russian literature.
1. Russian literature, to 1979 – Critical studies
1. Moser, Charles A.
891.709

Library of Congress cataloguing in publication data

The Cambridge history of Russian literature / edited by Charles A. Moser.
p.   cm.
Bibliography:
1. Russian literature – History and criticism.   1. Moser, Charles A.
PG2951.C36 1989
891.709–DC19   88-25999 CIP

ISBN 0 521 30994 8

CONTENTS

v

PREFACE

This history presents in narrative form a survey of Russian literature from the beginnings to this decade, in sufficient but not overwhelming detail. Those who wish to pursue particular points in more depth will find guidance in the bibliography appended to the volume, which is also in effect an outline of the historiography of Russian literature for approximately the last century, though with emphasis upon studies in western European languages, and especially in English. In 1987, indeed, we marked the centenary of the publication of the first truly influential work on Russian literature in a western language: Eugène Marie Melchior de Vogüé's *Le Roman russe*, which initiated what has turned out to be a sturdy tradition of criticism and scholarship in western languages. In addition, we are approximately at a century's remove from the time when the great pioneer translators of Russian literature into English – Isabel Hapgood in the United States, whose first translations appeared in 1886, and Constance Garnett in England, who started publishing her translations in 1894 – began the careers which would do so much to bring Russian writers to the attention of the English-speaking world.

The beginning date of this study is a traditional and a political one: 988, the year of the official christianization of Kievan Rus, now a millennium in the past. The concluding date of 1980 has been chosen more or less as a matter of convenience and contributors have not been forbidden to speak of works published since then if it seemed appropriate. As general editor I have divided the history into ten chapters and chosen what seemed to me appropriate division points. All such division points are necessarily arbitrary to a degree, but I have sought to select years which were primarily of literary-historical significance. Of course one cannot altogether ignore politics in literary history, and one division point – the year of Stalin's death, 1953 – has been chosen for reasons both political and literary, in token of the unprecedented literary importance which politics assumed during the Stalinist era.

Each of this book's ten chapters has been written by a different hand, that of a specialist in the period for which he or she is responsible. Of the ten, one is a western European, two are former Soviet scholars now in emigration in the west (the general editor is responsible for the English translations of their chapters), three are British, three are American, one a long-term resident of the United States, and the general editor is American. The bibliography emphasizes scholarship in Russian and in western European languages. Thus the general editor has sought to bring an international perspective to this volume.

Though each chapter in this book has been composed by a different person, and thus invariably exhibits a different approach, the general editor has made some adjustments to ensure coverage of the material, and in addition has himself written brief introductions to each chapter outlining the nature of literary development during the period described in that chapter.

The general editor has stipulated that contributors dealing with Russian literature of the twentieth century should treat works written or published outside the Soviet Union on an equal footing with literature written or published within the Soviet Union since 1917. One of this volume's objectives is to promote the healing of the division between those two branches of Russian literature, a healing which has begun in recent years of a breach which – at least in western scholarship – never should have occurred in the first place.

Finally, a word about the always vexing problem of transliteration. Though the bibliography consistently employs the Library of Congress system for Russian transliteration, the body uses a slightly different system easier for those who know no Russian. First names are anglicized when they correspond to widely recognized forms in English, though when an individual of Russian origin is well known in the west under a name in a particular form, that form is used. In chapter one, dealing with the old Russian period, however, most Christian names have been Hellenized because of the close links prevailing at that time between Byzantine Greek and Russian culture.

The editor would like to express his gratitude to all the contributors to this volume for their cooperation in writing the chapters requested of them and their willingness to adjust portions of their contributions; to Terence Moore, literature editor of the Cambridge University Press; and to the staffs of the Library of Congress and the Gelman Library of George Washington University for their assistance in providing information needed for the editing of the manuscript and the compilation of the bibliography.

THE LITERATURE OF
OLD RUSSIA, 988–1730

The story of Russian literature begins with a date of great significance for Russian political and cultural history: the year 988, when the ruler of Kievan Rus officially accepted Christianity as the new faith of the principality. At that point there was no written literature in Rus, but by his action Prince Vladimir laid the foundations of what we now call medieval Russian literature, even though it would not come into real being – so far as we know from what has reached us after the destruction wrought by the Mongol invasion – for some years thereafter. But the eastern Slavs received an alphabet designed by SS. Constantine-Cyril and Methodius, and also fell heir to the rich Byzantine cultural heritage which had been and would be translated from the Greek.

When we speak of "literature" in the old Russian period, however, we must understand it as something quite different from our notions of "literature" in the twentieth century.

In the first place, most old Russian literature was not what we would consider fictional, or at least it presented itself as dealing with fact and reality. In the earliest period one of the leading literary genres was the chronicle (exemplified by the *Primary Chronicle*) which built upon the achievements of the Byzantine historians. This genre by its very nature claimed to be factual even though it contained some clearly fictional (or at least non-factual) elements. Another leading genre was hagiography, which dealt with biographical accounts of the lives of Russia's holy men and women: if a saint's life contained fantastic elements, they were meant to be taken seriously, and not regarded as fiction. Even works such as the epic *Igor Tale* purported to deal with historical matters, though the author obviously took literary liberties with his materials. To be sure, there were semi-fictional or fictional works in old Russian literature from very early on (the *Supplication of Daniel the Exile*, for example), and their importance increased as the old Russian period approached its end. But this does not alter the fact that "literature" in old Russia dealt primarily with the real world as medieval men saw it, and not with fictionalized accounts of it.

In the second place, old Russian literature was highly ideological.

From the beginning it was closely linked to the church, and indeed in its first few centuries hardly existed outside it. Among the leading literary genres of Kievan Rus were prayers and sermons, specifically ecclesiastical in nature, as well as hagiography; and the oldest original manuscript in our possession is the *Ostromir Gospel* of the mid eleventh century, a selection of texts from the Gospels. Since the church nurtured literature so carefully during the old Russian period, it was difficult for more secular works to be copied and to survive. This also meant that originality was suspect. Indeed, originality was even dangerous, for it could easily lead to heresy: the writer's chief task was to quote skilfully from those who had gone before him, or to express old and well-tested truths in a novel way. He was ill-advised to offer his readers anything startlingly original.

Since the church and the state were closely intertwined in medieval Russia, and since most literature was linked to the church, literature naturally supported the purposes of the state. Far from regarding themselves as antagonists of the state or the ruler, writers for the most part were at one with the objectives of their society and state. There were exceptions to this, of course, as with Prince Kurbsky and his polemic with Ivan the Terrible: but even here the fact that Ivan himself was a leading writer of the sixteenth century points to the closest possible connection between the state and literature. Indeed, in the broad sweep of the history of Russian literature it is only during the nineteenth century and down to the October revolution of 1917 that writers viewed themselves as fundamentally opposed to the state, or as social critics. Both before and after that interlude they have by and large supported the objectives of their society and the state in which they lived.

To this it may be added that in the medieval period there was little in the way of literary culture. Many works of the earliest period are anonymous – among them the greatest work of that time, the *Igor Tale* – or merely attributed to certain individuals, with greater or lesser certainty, on the basis of internal or external evidence. Most writers evidently worked in near isolation, deriving intellectual sustenance from the writings that had gone before them but not from any "literary community" in the modern sense of the word. Indeed there was scarcely anything resembling a professional writer in the medieval period: there were people who wrote, and sometimes very well, but they were really something else: priests or monks or government officials or even tsars. Toward the end of the seventeenth century this situation began to change, so that we may speak of two or three or four identifiable writers who lived at the same time and place and knew one another. Thus Feofan Prokopovich, one of the best writers of the early eighteenth century though he was in fact a high ecclesiastical functionary, could regard the government official and diplomat Antiokh Kantemir as a literary disciple of his. At this time not only did there begin to appear something resembling a community of literary men, there also emerged literary works in the modern sense (Kantemir's verse satires, for example), and at times which are important for literary history as distinct from political history. The year 1730 is more important in Russian literary history than it is in Russian political history, for it is a key year for the transition from the rich traditions of an ecclesiastically oriented medieval literature to a secular modern literature. Indeed, as a date in literary history proper it may be the most important one in the entire thousand-year sweep of Russian literature.

OLD RUSSIAN LITERATURE takes its origins from the work of the two Thessalonian brothers Constantine-Cyril (826–69) and Methodius (815–85), the Greek apostles to the Slavs. During their mission to Great Moravia, where they arrived as envoys of the East Roman Emperor in 863, they created a liturgical language enabling them to preach the Christian gospel in the vernacular of the Slavs. This language, today known as Old Church Slavonic, was based on the dialect spoken by the Slav population of the brothers' native Thessaloniki, but it was strongly influenced by Greek models in vocabulary, phraseology, syntax, and style. At the end of the first millennium, linguistic differences among the Slavs were still negligible, and Old Church Slavonic became the common literary idiom of all the Orthodox Slavs. After the death of Methodius, the Moravian church came under Frankish hegemony, and his disciples were exiled. The Cyrillo-Methodian tradition was preserved by Boris of Bulgaria and his son Simeon, whose reign (893–927) is still remembered as the golden age of Bulgarian literature. Ohrid and Preslav emerged as the new centers of Old Church Slavonic where the work of the two preceptors of the Slavs was preserved and a wide range of early patristic and Byzantine writings were translated or adapted from the Greek. From Bulgaria the corpus of Old Church Slavonic literature spread to Kievan Rus, and when Prince Vladimir in 988 finally decided to accept Byzantine Christianity, the Eastern Slavs soon developed a literature of their own on the foundation of the Cyrillo-Methodian and Bulgarian heritage.

The corpus of Greek texts translated into Old Church Slavonic by the brothers and their disciples was not arbitrarily chosen, but a hierarchically ordered group of writings, the most important being the books required for liturgical purposes. These included the *Leitourgikon* (*Sluzhebnik*) and the *Horologion* (*Chasoslov*), containing the prayers and hymns for the fixed yearly cycle; the *Triod katanyktion* (*Triod postnaya*), the *Pentekostarion* (*Triod tsvetnaya*), and the *Oktoechos* (*Oktoikh*), with prayers and hymns for the moveable cycle; the Lectionaries, drawn from the Gospels, from the Acts and Epistles of the Apostles, and from the Old Testament; the Psalter (*Psaltyr*); and the *Synaxarion* (*Prolog*), a collection of short exegetical sermons and saints' Lives. The oldest dated manuscript to have come down to us from old Russian literature, the *Ostromir Gospel* (*Ostromirovo evangelie*), belongs to this set of liturgical texts. It is a Gospel Lectionary copied from a Bulgarian translation for the Novgorod alderman Ostromir in 1056–7.

Second in the hierarchy of translated literature came the extended Lives of the saints and the writings of the Church Fathers, in particular the works of John Chrysostom, Basil the Great, his brother Gregory of Nyssa, and Gregory Nazianzen, the classics of Greek patristic literature. Their writings were either translated separately, or gathered in miscellanies with excerpts from various authors. From early Kievan literature two such miscellanies (*Izborniki*) have been preserved, copied in 1073 and 1076 for Prince Svyatoslav of Kiev, the former from manuscripts that had belonged to Tsar Simeon of Bulgaria. It also contains a treatise on figures of speech by the Greek rhetorician George Choeroboscus, and a list of twenty-five "secret" books on the Church's index, with a commentary that clearly shows that Church Slavonic literature could attract the reader for many reasons, even in Kievan times:

> If you want great stories, you may read the Books of Kings. If you crave exciting and edifying reading, you have the Prophets, the Book of Job, or Jesus Sirach. But if, finally, your demand is for song books, you may read the Psalter.

Next to the canon of liturgical, hagiographical, and patristic texts, the Russians received from their western and southern neighbors works belonging to such popular, "lowbrow" genres of Byzantine literature as the apocrypha, stories about the lives of the desert fathers, and chronicles. Among the Old Church Slavonic translations imported from Bulgaria by the beginning of the twelfth century were the Chronicle of John Malalas, a Syrian rhetorician of the sixth century, and the Chronicle of George the Monk, called the Sinner (Hamartolos), written in the middle of the ninth century. Both go from the creation of Adam down to their authors' own time. They relate the history of the Jewish people, the Oriental empires, Rome, and the Hellenistic world, culminating in an account of the Byzantine Empire and its role in the history of man's salvation. These chronicles contained a wealth of curious information culled from a variety of sources. Malalas is particularly interesting in this respect: his rambling narrative is interlarded with stories about pagan gods and ancient Greek heroes, sensational miracles and cruel disasters, so that it becomes a kind of Byzantine *Trivialliteratur*, in contrast to the Chronicle of Hamartolos, in which the monastic ideology is more evident. Byzantine chronicles had a decisive influence on the form and ideological content of old Russian historical writing.

The body of translated literature accumulated in Kievan Rus during the first century after Vladimir's conversion corresponds fairly accurately to the selection of books found in monastic libraries throughout the Orthodox world. In this selection there was no place for the classics of ancient Greek literature, still read and studied by educated "humanists" in Byzantium, or for "high-brow" historians like Procopius, Psellus, and Anna Comnena. Even such pseudo-historical works as the *Tale of Troy (Skazanie o Troe)* and the *Romance of Alexander (Khronograficheskaya Aleksandriya)* which might be seen as belonging, however marginally, to the classical tradition, were received in Rus in the context of the chronicles, and interpreted in terms of their Christian world view. Similarly, the sophisticated casuistry of Flavius Josephus' *History of the Jewish War*, translated by the beginning of the twelfth century, found no response with old Russian readers, whose interest focused on its account of events of biblical history, and on the striking imagery of its battle scenes, which provided original old Russian literature with a whole arsenal of military terms and martial metaphors.

The literary corpus received by the Eastern Slavs in Old Church Slavonic translations included the medieval *artes dictandi*, both in their metrical and in their non-metrical forms. Metrical discourse was first transposed into Old Church Slavonic by Constantine-Cyril, whose verse compositions in the new literary idiom closely

5

follow the patterns of Greek verse. His "Prologue to the Gospels" goes back to the Byzantine dodecasyllable, whereas the meter of his "Eulogy to Gregory Nazianzen" may have been based on Byzantine hexameters. The writing of verbal poetry seems, however, to have been confined to the Cyrillo-Methodian tradition in Moravia and Bulgaria, while in Russia the musical variant was taken up and developed into a national school of Church Slavonic hymnody. This musical poetry has been sadly neglected by historians of old Russian literature, and we are still waiting for the manuscripts to be properly edited and examined.

Apart from the hymns of the liturgy, the forms of discourse found in old Russian literature are all versions of the non-metrical *ars dicendi*, ranging from the highly elaborate rhetoric inherited from the Greek *logos epideiktikos*, regulated by rhythm as well as by rhyme, to the simple, unadorned style, oscillating between artistic prose and ordinary speech.

From Vladimir's conversion until the Tatar invasions in the first half of the thirteenth century, Kiev was the cultural and political center of Rus, the capital, and seat of the metropolitan of the new Russian church. Here, Prince Yaroslav Vladimirovich (ruled 1019–54) strove to emulate the splendor of Byzantine art in its manifold manifestations: architecture, icon painting, music, and literature. This imitation of Byzantine models was not mechanical but active. The artists and writers of old Russia showed their creative skills by taking the models apart into single motifs and elements, selecting certain ones, and recombining them into new configurations.

The literary masterpiece of this early Kievan court art is the *Sermon on the Law and Grace* (*Slovo o zakone i blagodati*), a work attributed to Metropolitan Hilarion, the first Russian to hold this office, appointed by Prince Yaroslav in 1051.

The sermon is written in the form of *logos epideiktikos* and addressed, as the author explicitly declares in the proem (preamble), "Not to the ignorant, but to those who have feasted most abundantly on the sweetness of books." In accordance with encomiastic rhetoric, its prose is regulated by *isocola* (couplings of period-members of equal length) and by *homoioteleuta* (like endings.) The compositional theme of the sermon is the triumph of the grace of Christ over the Law of Moses. In the first part, this theme is developed in a series of allegorical antitheses, in which events and characters from the Old Testament are seen as fore-shadowings and images of the truth revealed in the Gospels, beginning with the contrast between Hagar and Sarah, borrowed from Saint Paul (Gal. 4:21ff.). The central part of the sermon represents the triumph of divine Grace in a sequence of Christo-logical antitheses, seventeen in all (five referring to the birth of Christ, five to His public life, and seven to His Passion). The third and last part, with its final eulogy to Prince Vladimir, celebrates the entry of Rus into Christendom. What was prefigured in the first, allegorical part of the sermon has been fulfilled in the third through the Incarnation of Christ, the event around which the whole sermon is centered. Allegory and fulfillment here corres-pond to each other as *figura veritatis* and *veritas* in the conception of history that underlies the rhetorical technique of the sermon. In this conception, taken from the Church Fathers and from Byzan-tine theology, the Old Testament was seen as a series of prefigur-ations of Christ and the salvation of future nations, led into the promised land of the Heavenly Kingdom, not by the Law of Moses, but by the Grace of the Lord. History understood in this way does not seek to discover the causal links between events and characters, but rather to interpret them as images of a timeless, archetypal pattern designed by God before the foundation of the world. This conception of history also underlies the representation of Vladimir as the imitator of Constantine the Great. What the latter achieved among Greeks and Romans in subjecting his empire to God, the former has achieved among the people of Rus, and their heavenly glory is the same.

Whereas the encomiastic rhetoric of the *Sermon on the Law and Grace* is a mode of expression typical of the *logos epideiktikos*, its figural interpretation is not confined to the genre of the encomium. Figural interpretation is more than a rhetorical tech-nique. It is a way of thinking characteristic of early Kievan litera-ture as a whole.

The ornate discourse of the encomium was not unanimously accepted in old Russia. There were those who, like the anonymous author of the twelfth-century *Sermon to a Brother Stylite* (*Slovo k bratu stolpniku*), refused to write "in artfully interwoven words or in a covert style," preferring the unadorned mode of expression found in the homilies of Abbot Theodosius of the Kiev Caves Monastery and those of Archbishop Luka Zhidyata of Novgorod, written in the same period as the *Sermon on the Law and Grace*. The only extant work of Clement Smolyatich, the second Russian to become Metropolitan in Kiev (1147–55), the *Epistle Written to Thomas the Presbyter (Poslanie napisano Klimentom metropolitom ruskym Fome prozviteru)*, is a defense of allegorical exegesis.

The finest examples of the rhetorical sermon in twelfth-century Russian literature are the works of Cyril, Bishop of Turov (died about 1182). Cyril wrote epistles, parables, prayers, hymns, and sermons. A number of his sermons were included in the old Russian anthologies of Greek homiletics, the *Chrysostom (Zlatoust)* and the *Panegyrikon (Torzhestvennik)*, a sure sign of their popularity. Most widely admired were his eight Easter sermons. Their compilatory character and lack of originality have been heavily criticized by modern scholars, but Cyril's use of the texts of others does not preclude originality. Cyril would select a verse from the Bible, a passage from John Chrysostom, another from Cyril of Alexandria, a third from Simeon Metaphrastes, and bring them together in a collage of quotations, allusions, and paraphrases. Among Cyril's favorite rhetorical devices are isocolic antitheses and parallelisms, comparisons, and prosopopeia, i.e. fictitious recreations of the speeches and gestures of his personages, as when, for example, in the *Sermon on the Deposition*, the Mother of God bursts into a long lament while gazing upon her crucified Son. Like the *Sermon on the Law and Grace*, Cyril's sermons are Christocentric and inspired by an awareness of Christ's presence. But his allegories are less dogmatic and more intuitive, his rhetoric often verges on poetry.

The *Sermon on the Law and Grace* and Cyril's Easter homilies follow a common compositional scheme inherited from Greek epideictic oratory. According to this scheme, a *logos* may be divided into three main parts: a proem, a "narrative" or exposition of the subject matter, and an epilogue in the form of a eulogy ending in a prayer. In the epideictic oration, the narrative is shortened and concentrated on the elements that enable the author to extol the acts and personal traits of his heroes above their real dimensions by means of rhetorical amplification. But in other variants of the *logos epideiktikos* the narrative is also amplified in the linear dimension, with the result that the eulogy is transformed into an entire account of the life and deeds of the central hero.

Both types of amplification are found in hagiography, the most popular of all the literary forms that prospered in Kievan Rus. The models were derived from works translated from the Greek, and by saints' Lives and legends written by the disciples of Constantine and Methodius, whose *vitae* are among the earliest examples of original Church Slavonic hagiography.

The first notable hagiographer in old Russian literature is Nestor, a monk from the Caves Monastery, the monastic center of Kievan Rus. Nestor wrote the *Reading on the Life and Slaying of the Blessed Martyrs Boris and Gleb (Chtenie o zhitii i o pogublenii blazhennuyu strastoterptsu Borisa i Gleba)*, and the *Life of Our Holy Father Theodosius, Abbot of the Caves Monastery (Zhitie prepodobnogo ottsa nashego Feodosiya, igumena pecherskogo)*, the former belonging to the abridged type, the latter to the type with expanded narrative. Both works were probably written between 1079 and 1085. In the *Life of Saint Theodosius* Nestor refers to himself as the author of the *Reading*, which he had already completed before embarking upon the larger *vita*.

Nestor's *Reading* is one of three different, but textually interrelated, versions of the same story: the killing of Vladimir's youngest sons by their brother Svyatopolk in the power struggle that ensued upon Vladimir's death in 1015. The throne was first seized by Svyatopolk, but he was later ousted by another brother, Prince Yaroslav Vladimirovich of Novgorod, and died in exile in 1019. The other versions of these events are the chronicle account and the anonymous *Narrative and Passion and Eulogy of the Blessed Martyrs Boris and Gleb (Skazanie i strast i pokhvala svyatuyu mucheniku Borisa i Gleba)*. The basic story is identical in the various versions, but they differ in the rhetorical treatment of the material. Common to them all is a combination of two distinct modes of expression, one simple and artless, the other containing all the devices of panegyrical oratory. The former mode is used in relating the historical facts, the latter to amplify and interpret the historical narrative. The contrast between the two modes is most pronounced in the chronicle account and in the *Narrative*, whereas Nestor's style is more balanced. In the *Narrative* in particular, the martyrs' fictitious soliloquies are composed in the form of highly emotionalized laments, with strings of anaphoric *isocola*, scriptural quotations, and figural juxtapositions. Nestor views the misdeed within the context of universal history, in much the same way as the conversion in the *Sermon on the Law and Grace* is seen. Vladimir is the new Constantine, Boris and Gleb are compared to Joseph and Benjamin, Svyatopolk to Cain.

In spite of such divergences, the religious interpretation of the assassinations is fundamentally similar in all three versions. The brothers' acceptance of a violent death without resistance is represented as an *imitatio Christi* (imitation of Christ), by which they become partakers in the divine nature of Christ, exercising their powers of intercession in the Kingdom of Heaven as the celestial patrons of their brother Yaroslav and the Christian people of Rus.

This celestial aspect of their sainthood is symbolized in the mystical light that surrounds their earthly remains and their post-humous miracles. The light symbolism, less evident in the *Reading* and in the chronicle account, is a predominant feature of Nestor's miracle stories, in which their exhumed bodies "shone white like snow, and their faces were radiant like those of angels."

The use of light symbolism in order to bring out the *anagogical* dimension of the saints as images of the divine figure of Christ is characteristic of Nestor's hagiographical art, where this anagogical aspect is complementary to the representation of the saints' imitation of Christ's humbled, earthly figure.

This complementarity of the human and the divine in the saint's *imitatio Christi* also determines the structure of Nestor's *Life of Saint Theodosius*. Nestor never knew Theodosius personally: he entered the Caves Monastery only after the saint's death in 1074. The events forming the story line of his *vita* represent a selection from what others had told him about the life of his hero. A characteristic feature of the *Life of Saint Theodosius* is the strong emphasis on the abasement and sufferings of the saint in his childhood. We are repeatedly told that his mother, who objects to his becoming a monk, torments him, beats him to the ground, puts him in chains, and throws him into a dark dungeon. Although the account of the conduct of the saint's mother may seem strikingly realistic, this effect is only of secondary importance in the *vita*, where the primary function of the saint's humiliations is disclosed in his own interpretation of them in imitation of the suffering of Christ:

> Listen mother, I pray you, listen! The Lord Jesus Christ has abased and humbled himself and given us an example, so that we too should humble ourselves for his sake. Also, he was scorned, spat upon and beaten. And all this he suffered for our salvation. Must we not then with even greater cause suffer in patience, so that we shall gain Christ!

In inverse correlation to this imitation of Christ's suffering, the second part of Nestor's narrative is amplified by a series of mystical light visions, transfiguring the life of the saint as abbot of the Caves Monastery into an anagogical prefiguration of his celestial glory, anticipated by his illumination in the light of Christ, the Sun of Justice, in the vision that accompanies Nestor's account of the saint's baptism. Figural interpretation thus provided Nestor with the pattern underlying his rhetorical transformation of Theodosius into an image of Christ in both his human and in his divine aspects.

In his *Life of Saint Theodosius* Nestor recalls that Theodosius in his youth had wanted to join a group of pilgrims to the Holy Land, "where Our Lord had walked in the flesh." But God would not let him leave his own country, according to Nestor, and the pilgrims departed without him.

Russian pilgrimages to the holy places of Palestine began soon after the conversion, but the earliest account of such a journey extant in old Russian literature is the *Life and Pilgrimage of Abbot Daniel from the Land of Rus* (*Zhitie i khozhdenie Danila ruskyya zemli igumena*). We know little about the author, who was probably the abbot of a monastery in the principality of Chernigov. He spent sixteen months in the Holy Land in 1106–8, travelling with a large retinue and employing professional guides everywhere. In Jerusalem he was received by Baldwin I, King of Jerusalem, under whose protection he was able to go to places normally inaccessible to visitors. During the Easter Service at the Holy Sepulchre, the king placed Daniel next to himself.

The *Pilgrimage* is first and foremost a description of the holy places associated with the life story of Jesus Christ. Daniel sees these places both in their biblical context and in their natural environment, endeavoring to convey to his Russian readers the emotional effect they had on him. He walks along the banks of the river Jordan "with love," comparing it to the river Snov back in

Rus, kisses the place of Christ's Transfiguration "with love and tears," and exclaims at the first sight of Jerusalem that "no one can hold back his tears at the sight of this much longed-for land of these holy places, where Christ Our Lord endured sufferings for the sake of us sinners." The pilgrimage culminates in the celebration of the Easter Service, when Daniel kindles a light by the sacred fire "on behalf of the whole Russian land."

From the point of view of genre, Daniel's *Pilgrimage* represents a rather free version of the Greek *proskynetarion*, a form that emerged in the tenth century in imitation of the Latin *itinerarium*. As with the Latin variant, Daniel's itinerary displays a personal tone, in contrast to the *proskynetaria*, which provide impersonal descriptions of various places of worship in and around Jerusalem, meant as guides for pilgrims to the services arranged especially for them.

Whether Nestor the hagiographer also wrote the *Primary Chronicle* (*Povest vremennykh let*), we shall probably never know. Arguments have been advanced both for and against this attribution, based on a reference to "Nestor, the monk of Theodosius' Caves Monastery" in a sixteenth-century copy of the *Primary Chronicle* and on references in the oldest, twelfth-century part of the *Paterikon of the Caves Monastery* (*Kievo-pechersky paterik*) to Nestor "who wrote the Chronicle." Current scholarship commonly sees Nestor as the author of the first comprehensive redaction of the *Primary Chronicle*, compiled about 1113 on the basis of at least two earlier texts. This redaction was revised about 1117 by Abbot Silvester of the Kievan Monastery of Saint Michael, while another version was prepared for Prince Mstislav Vladimirovich in the Caves Monastery in 1118. Silvester's redaction is believed to have been preserved in the *Laurentian codex* of 1377, and the redaction of 1118 in the *Hypatian codex*, dating from the 1420s. These are the oldest surviving manuscripts of the old Russian chronicles. The *Laurentian codex* contains under 1096 the *Instruction* (*Pouchenie*) of Prince Vladimir Monomakh on Christian virtues and Christian behavior, addressed to his children. Modelled on Byzantine sources, the work draws heavily on Scripture, and was obviously meant as a practical manual for ruling princes in a newly converted Christian society.

In its basic outline this reconstruction of the development of the *Primary Chronicle* goes back to the investigations of Alexey Shakhmatov at the beginning of this century. With slight modifications, his hypothetical reconstruction is generally accepted in current scholarship.

From a literary point of view, the *Primary Chronicle* is an unusual work, an accumulation of very heterogeneous texts strung together according to a simple chronological principle. This form was probably taken over from the Paschal calendars, tables showing the dates of Easter for a number of years in succession with columns for the recording of important events under each year. This simple cumulative structure still shows through in places where the text is reduced to the mere enumeration of years, with no subsequent entry. However, all the events listed in this way are unique: they stand out against the background of the ordinary, that which is not worth recording. Expanded into narratives, these records retain their anecdotal, legendary form.

This annalistic cumulation of extraordinary events is theoretically unlimited: it has no beginning, and could go on forever. Only by inserting into his own annalistic recordings excerpts from translated Byzantine chronicles can the author of the *Primary Chronicle* provide his own work with a beginning, a middle, and an end.

The *Primary Chronicle* opens with a story about the division of the earth among the sons of Noah after the flood, when the northern and western lands, among them the land of Rus, went to Japheth, and of the building of the Tower of Babel, when God scattered His people over the face of the earth and the linguistic and ethnic unity of mankind gave way to a multiplicity of nations and languages. This story, known in Kievan Rus from works such as the Chronicle of George Hamartolos, is further combined with passages from an unidentified story about the migrations and early history of the Slavs, leading up to the legendary description of the foundation of Kiev and the emergence of Rus. The technique used by the author of the *Primary Chronicle* is identical with that employed in the *Sermon on the Law and Grace*. By bringing his domestic records together with passages quoted from other texts, the author of the *Primary Chronicle* likewise integrates the history of Rus into the context of world history, interpreted teleologically, as an eschatological process, beginning with the fall of Adam and the expulsion from Paradise, and moving towards the final Day of

Judgement, when history will come to an end. Furthermore, this linear conception of history is complemented by a spatial dimension, in which historical events and characters are transformed into a network of prefigurations and fulfillments centered around the Incarnation and expiatory Passion of Christ. In the *Primary Chronicle* this figural interpretation emerges in the "philosopher's speech," inserted into the chronicle under 986 in the form of a didactic dialogue between an anonymous philosopher "sent by the Greeks" and Prince Vladimir, on the eve of the baptism of Rus. Its sources have not been identified, but there can be no doubt of its Greek origin.

The philosopher's speech interprets events in the Old Testament as anticipations of the coming of Christ and the spreading of the Gospel to the "new nations." Similarly, the imminent conversion of Vladimir and his people is seen as a fulfilment of Old Testament prophecies. In his allegorical exegesis of the story of Gideon (Judges VI), the philosopher employs the very terms "prefiguration" (*preobrazhenie*) and "prefigured" (*preobrazi*) in order to bring out its hidden meaning: dew (on the fleece) prefigures the baptism of the new nations.

This figuration enables the chronicler to carry the method over into his own description of the Russians. With the help of biblical quotations he interprets the baptism of his own people as an *imitatio Christi*:

> Praised be our Lord Jesus Christ, who loved His new people, the kingdom of Rus, and illuminated it with holy baptism . . . Saint Paul says: "Brothers! All of us who have been baptized into Jesus Christ were baptized into His death." We were buried therefore with him by baptism into death, so that as Christ was raised from the dead by the glory of the Father, we too might walk in newness of life.

The "philosopher's speech" and the eulogy to Vladimir that follows belong to a group of texts that together represent the ecclesiastical strain in the early redactions of the *Primary Chronicle*. This group includes episodes such as the baptism and death of Olga, the martyrdom of the first Varangian Christians, the slaying of Boris and Gleb, and the eulogy to Prince Yaroslav under the year 1037. To this group may be added the introduction on the origins and history of the Eastern Slavs. Stylistically, these passages are characterized by a combination of crisp and simple narrative, verging on the vernacular, with rhetorical elements typical of the Church Slavonic encomium.

A very different style prevails in the episodes dealing with the coming of the Varangians and the history of the Varangian rulers in pre-Christian Rus. Told in the form of short, pointed independent anecdotes, often culminating in dramatic dialogues, these episodes reflect an oral epic tradition, and have been associated with the Varangian element in the retinue of the Kievan princes. Some of them are clearly based on motifs also found in old Norse literature. Well known examples are the combat tale of Mstislav and Rededya under the year 1022, the description of Olga's (Scand. Helga) murder of her suitors to avenge her dead husband Igor (Scand. Ingvarr) under 945 (which has its counterpart in the story about Sigrid Storrada in the *Olaf Tryggvasson Saga*), or the death of Oleg (Scand. Helgi), bitten by a snake which suddenly emerges from the skull of his favorite horse. In this part of the chronicle Prince Vladimir is no longer the Christian ruler but a Varangian warrior who ravishes Rogned (Scand. Ragnheidr), the daughter of the Varangian Prince Rogvolod (Scand. Ragnvaldr) of Polotsk. The story of her unsuccessful revenge occurs in another variant in the story of Gudrun, Ironbeard's daughter, in the *Olaf Tryggvasson Saga*.

Correspondences such as these have given rise to the theory that the Varangians brought their own oral epic tradition with them from Scandinavia to Rus. More plausible, however, is the explanation put forward by Adolf Stender-Petersen, who suggests that both the old Russian and the old Norse material reflect a Greek-Byzantine tradition passed on to Varangian merchants and mercenaries in Byzantium and carried back to Kiev and Scandinavia. From this perspective, the tales about Gudrun, Rogned and Sigrid appear as echoes of ancient Greek heroic tales.

One of the most enigmatic heroes of the *Primary Chronicle* is Prince Vseslav of Polotsk, whose birth is recorded under 1044. Conceived by magic, he was born with a caul which his mother was told by magicians to bind upon the child that he might bear it for the rest of his life. This he did, and so was "merciless in bloodshed," according to the chronicler. The figure of Vseslav is surrounded by ominous signs: a large star appeared "as if it were made of blood," the sun was "like the moon," and these signs "portended bloodshed." By combining the account of Vseslav given in the *Primary Chronicle* with the description of him in the *Igor Tale* and with the figure of Volkh (i.e. wolf) Vseslavevich of the *byliny*, it is possible to reconstruct an old Russian Vseslav epic about the prince-werewolf, based on an ancient werewolf myth also reflected in Serbo-Croatian epic poetry and deeply rooted in the Indo-European tradition common to both Slavs and Scandinavians (Roman Jakobson and Marc Szeftel).

Vseslav of Polotsk is the hero of an extensive digression in the *Igor Tale* (*Slovo o polku Igoreve*), in which the description alternates between his diurnal life as prince and warrior, and his nocturnal adventures as a werewolf:

> Vseslav the prince sat in judgement over men,
> as prince he ruled over cities;
> but at night he coursed as a wolf;
> running from Kiev to the ramparts of Tmutorokan,
> as a wolf he crossed the path of Great Hors.
> For him the bells rang early for matins in Polotsk at St.
> Sophia, but he heard the ringing in Kiev.

The folkloric character of this passage is reinforced by the reference to the Great Hors, an Iranian borrowing designating the radiant sun, another name for Dazhbog ("giver of wealth"), the sun god of the pagan Slavs. In the *Igor Tale* the old pagan deities have lost their cultic value. Like the werewolf myth, they seem to belong to an oral epic tradition exploited by the author of the *Tale* for purely poetic purposes.

When the *Igor Tale* was published in 1800, nine years after it had been acquired by Prince Alexey Musin-Pushkin, it was immediately regarded as an oral epic and even compared to the poems of Ossian. The correspondences between the *Tale* and James Macpherson's forgeries were subsequently used as an argument against the authenticity of the old Russian manuscript, which perished in the Moscow fire of 1812, so that the text only survives in the first edition and in a copy made for Catherine II in 1795–6.

The authenticity of the *Tale* has been challenged by a number of scholars, but the philological evidence supporting its genuineness is now overwhelming. It would not have been possible to reconstruct the old Russian and Turkic forms found in the *Tale* in

16

Catherine II's Russia, or in the sixteenth century, a date that has also been suggested for its composition. Furthermore, the *Igor Tale* no longer appears as an isolated work in pre-Tatar Rus. Parallels to its style and imagery have been found in Cyril of Turov's sermons and in the *Sermon on the Resurrection of Lazarus* (*Slovo o Lazarevom voskresenii*), an anonymous homily dating from the same period. Words and phrases once regarded as unique in the *Tale* have been identified with expressions found in texts such as the chronicles, Flavius Josephus' *History of the Jewish War*, and the old Russian *Digenis Akritas* romance.

The *Igor Tale* must have been composed in the years between 1185, when the events that form its subject matter took place, and 1 October 1187, the death date of Igor's father-in-law, Prince Yaroslav Osmomysl of Galich, referred to as still living in the *Tale*.

The *Igor Tale* describes a campaign against the Polovtsians, Turkic nomads who had appeared in the southeastern steppes in the middle of the eleventh century. The campaign, led by Igor Svyatoslavich, Prince of Novgorod-Seversk, was only an episode in the wars against this people but is recorded both in the Laurentian and in the Hypatian copies of the chronicle. On 23 April 1185, Igor set off with his son Vladimir and his nephew Svyatoslav Olgovich. In spite of a bad omen – a total eclipse of the sun – the Russians decided to cross the Donets river and attack the Polovtsians. At first they were successful, and the enemy fled. But when they decided to spend the night in the abandoned Polovtsian camp instead of retreating with their spoils, they were taken by surprise, and defeated. Igor was taken prisoner and spent about five weeks in Polovtsian captivity, from which he escaped in June 1185.

The basic sequence of events is roughly the same in the Kievan chronicle (the Hypatian codex) and in the *Tale*. The difference between them lies in the rhetorical treatment of the material. On the one hand, the anonymous author of the *Tale* has condensed his subject matter so greatly as to make it well-nigh incomprehensible to an audience unfamiliar with its historical context. On the other hand, he has amplified his condensed narrative by a series of digressions, creating a network of similarities and contrasts between the princes of his own troubled present, fighting each other in ruinous wars, and the heroes of a legendary, united past,

17

between his own style and the devices of Boyan, the "vatic singer" of old. Lyrical exclamations and emotional appeals, laments and eulogies interrupt the story. The poetic imagery transforms men and animals, plants and trees into a complex pattern of metaphoric and metonymic equivalences. The author has translated his troubled premonitions of the ruin of Rus into a poetic vision of tragic portent.

The intricate imagery of the *Igor Tale* has been compared to similar instances of enigmatic speech and ornament in other twelfth-century European literature, to scaldic poetry, and to Wolfram's epic. The corresponding old Russian mode of expression is the parabolic-figurative style inherited from Byzantine epideictic rhetoric. It is from the Byzanto-Slavonic *logos epideikti-kos* that the *Tale* derives its encomiastic composition: first a proem in which the author addresses his audience and introduces his theme, followed by the central part of the narrative, with digressions and interruptions characteristic of encomiastic glorification, and concluded by an epilogue in the form of a final hymn of praise celebrating the happy return of Igor, his son, and his brother.

The *Supplication and Address of Daniel the Exile (Molenie i Slovo Daniila Zatochnika)* is known in two versions, the *Supplication* and the *Address*, surviving in copies from the sixteenth and seventeenth centuries, both going back to an original believed to date from the last decades before the Tatar invasions. Neither the author of the petition, Daniel, nor its addressee, a certain Prince Yaroslav, has been identified, and it may well be that the work is pure fiction. Daniel has for unknown reasons fallen into poverty and been abandoned by his friends and family. He turns to the prince for material support, hoping that his wit will be rewarded. He begins his appeal to the prince with a sycophantic eulogy, which gradually changes into facetious satire centered around the two traditional motifs of evil wives and self-indulgent monks. The text is a patchwork of quotations from biblical and secular sources, aphorisms, and quasi-popular proverbs, ranging from a description of the prince in words taken from the Song of Solomon – "sweet is thy voice, thy lips drop as the honeycomb, ... thy cheeks are like a bed of spices ... thy countenance is as Lebanon, excellent as the cedars ... thy belly is like an heap of wheat..." – to misogynous adages ("I should rather take a fiery bull into my house than an evil wife") and sarcastic ribaldry ("I have never seen a dead man riding on a swine, nor the devil on a woman"). Though he boasts of his own wisdom, Daniel does not flinch from self-mockery: "I am not wise, but have only donned the robes of those who are, and put on their boots." His pompous onset – "Let us trumpet forth, o brethren, as on a trumpet of gold, on the wisdom of our wit" – sounds like a parody of an epic invocation. The whole petition is, in fact, a kind of parody, and it has been suggested that it belongs to the jocular folklore of the *skomorokhi*, the wandering minstrels of old Russia who were persecuted by the church and could only survive on the fringes of old Russian culture. The difficulty with this explanation is that the *Supplication* is not folkloric, but a written composition. Its generic origin is more likely to be found in Byzantine literature, in particular in satires such as the demotic verse supplications of the twelfth-century writer Theodore Prodromos, a nephew of the Metropolitan John of Kiev, and his contemporary, Michael Glykas. Addressed to the Emperor and other high-ranking persons, these poems combine coarse realism and a macabre sense of humor with malicious satire, flattery and shameless begging. Recurrent motifs in these supplications include the plight of a husband married to a cantankerous wife, an innocent suffering in jail, the scholar's wretched existence as opposed to the comfort enjoyed by ignorant artisans, and the contrast between simple monks, living in utter misery, and the meanness of wealthy abbots. Daniel's *Supplication* appears to be a unique example of this particular genre in Kievan Rus.

In 1223 a large army suddenly invaded the land of Rus from the south and dealt a crushing defeat to a coalition of Russian and Polovtsian armies on the Kalka River, before disappearing as quickly as they had come, leaving the Russians totally bewildered. This was their first reaction to the Mongols, or Tatars, as they were always called in Russia. In 1237–41 they returned to central Russia, ravaging towns and villages, massacring all who dared to resist them, but leaving the country's political institutions intact. The city of Ryazan was devastated in 1237, Vladimir in 1238, and in 1240 Kiev was sacked. The whole of northeast Russia and Novgorod became tributary lands of the Golden Horde, a branch of the Mongols' vast Asian empire controlled by Khan Batu, a grandson of Chingis Khan. The administrative center of the Horde was the city of Sarai on the lower Volga, where the Russian princes now had to go for their investiture, in order to pledge allegiance to the khan. Some of them even undertook the long journey to Karakorum in central Mongolia, the capital of the empire.

The Tatars established a rule in Russia based on tribute, which the local princes were obliged to pay under the threat of new reprisals, with only the Russian Church granted exemption from Tatar taxation: according to the Laurentian Chronicle, "abbots, monks, priests, members of the clergy and those who vow loyalty to the Holy Mother of God and the bishop" went free. Throughout the years of Tatar rule the Russian metropolitanate thus continued to exercise jurisdiction over the whole of Russia, and the Church remained the center of Russian civilization, the guardian of the religious and cultural values of the country. Metropolitan Cyril, who had first supported Daniel of Galicia's contacts with the papacy and the Catholic kingdoms of central Europe, eventually decided to transfer his allegiance to the khans at Sarai, and in 1250 travelled to Vladimir, where he established close ties with Alexander Nevsky, prince of Novgorod (r. 1240–52) and grand prince of Vladimir (r. 1252–63). Alexander, who in 1240 had defeated the Swedes on the Neva river and in 1242 won the battle against the Teutonic Knights on the ice of Lake Peipus, was confirmed by Khan Batu as a grand prince. In his anti-western, pro-Mongol policy, Alexander acted with the support of both the Russian metropolitan and the Byzantine patriarch, who saw in the Mongol ruler a safeguard against western expansionism while, they believed, the religious tolerance of the Tatars would guarantee the independence of the Orthodox Church. In 1299 the metropolitanate was moved from the southwest to the city of Vladimir, the capital of the northern grand princes.

The result of all this was that Russian civilization now survived and continued to develop in the north and east, in Novgorod and the principalities on the upper Volga, Moscow, Vladimir, Kostroma, Yaroslavl and Tver. Towards the end of the Tatar yoke, Moscow emerged as the new political and cultural center of Russia.

Hagiography remained a predominant genre in this period of old Russian literature, and a number of Lives were written to commemorate the monastery builders of the north, such as Saint

Leonty Rostovsky, Saint Nikita of Pereyaslavl-Zalessky, Saint Varlaam of Khutyn, and others. More interesting from the point of view of literary history, however, is the development of princely Lives and martyr passions in this period.

The cult of the ruler and the martyred prince was a characteristic feature of Kievan Rus. In the eleventh century this cult had found its literary expression in eulogies to Olga and Vladimir and their descendants, and in passion stories about Boris and Gleb.

In subsequent centuries both forms found their way into the chronicles. The appanage princes of Novgorod and Vladimir, for example, were glorified according to the hagiographical schemes developed in Kievan literature. One of the most moving princely martyr passions is the story of Igor Olgovich, recorded in the *Kievan Chronicle* under 1147. The central motif is the prince's *imitatio Christi* through suffering, and like Boris and Gleb, Igor is killed by his brothers in the struggle for power.

With the Tatar invasions, the princely Lives and passions acquired new significance. The *martyrologion* was chosen to represent the steadfastness of Russian princes tortured and killed by the henchmen of the khans, whereas the Life was used to glorify Alexander Nevsky, the secular hero embodying the policy of the Orthodox Church.

The new historical context engenders a marked change in the selection of motifs. The *imitatio Christi* motif disappears and the motif of fratricide is often suppressed, as the rivalry of the Russian princes for the khan's favor is played down.

A typical princely passion from this period is the *Story of the Murder of Prince Michael of Chernigov and his Boyar Feodor in the Horde* (*Skazanie ob ubienii v orde knyazya Mikhaila Chernigovskogo i ego boyarina Feodora*). The murder took place in 1246, when the prince had gone to Sarai, probably in order to receive his decree from the khan, even though the story gives as the reason for his journey his desire to expose the khan's deceit. As in the early martyr passions, the khan – or *tsar*, as he is called here, and was always officially called in Russia – represents the power of this world, whereas the two Russians stand for a higher, divine authority. In accordance with church teachings, the two Christians are prepared to accept the khan's superiority in secular matters, but they firmly refuse to take part in a pagan fire-ritual and to bow to the sun and the idols of the Tatars: "I bow to you, O tsar, for God has given you the tsardom and the glory of this world." Rather than betray their Christian faith, they suffer torture and a terrible death at the hands of the khan's people. The story thus has an ideological message, reflecting the *Realpolitik* of the Russian Church under Tatar rule.

A similar combination of political realism and hagiographical ideals appears in the *Tale of the Life and Valor of the Faithful and Grand Prince Alexander* (*Povest o zhitii i o khrabrosti blagovernogo i velikogo knyazya Aleksandra*), written shortly after his death in 1263 by an author who had known him personally. The Life makes no attempt to describe Alexander Nevsky's biography in detail, but rather concentrates on the main events of his political career, his victories over the Swedes, the Livonians, and the Teutonic Knights. His humiliating relationship with the khan, on the other hand, is glossed over. The style of the Life is a mixture of hagiographical and martial rhetoric. Alexander is compared to Joseph the Beautiful in appearance, to Samson in strength, to Solomon in wisdom, and in military prowess to the Emperor Vespasian, known from Flavius Josephus. Before the battle against the Swedes, a vision foreshadows the invisible assistance of Boris and Gleb heading a heavenly host of warriors. In the battle on Lake Peipus against the Teutonic Knights, Alexander's army is likened to the warriors of King David, and in his prayers the prince remembers the victories of Moses and Yaroslav. Heavenly hosts appear in the sky, and with their help Alexander conquers the German invaders.

These hagiographical elements create an otherworldly framework for the battle scenes, described with the precision of the military tales of the chronicles: "And when the sun rose, the enemies met. And there was a cruel fight. And a cracking of snapping spears. And a clanging of clashing swords. And it was as if the frozen lake was moving. And the ice could not be seen, covered as it was with blood."

The combination of two different stylistic registers within it has given rise to the theory that the Life was originally written in the form of a secular biography. As long as this notion is not corroborated by textological studies, however, there is no reason to assume that the hagiographical element is secondary. On the contrary, these elements give the *Life of Alexander Nevsky* its deeper significance, transforming its hero into a vehicle of God's will.

The traumatic effect of the Mongol invasions is reflected in the military tales, a group of texts composed in the second half of the thirteenth century and the early fourteenth. None of them survives as an individual work: they have been incorporated in larger compilations like the chronicles. The *Tale of the Battle on the River Kalka* (*Povest o bitve na Kalke*) interprets the first Tatar incursion as God's punishment for the sins of the Russian people, and sees in their sudden departure a sign that the end of the world is near. The style is simple and prosaic, as in so many of the military chronicle tales.

In contrast to the unsophisticated narrative of the battle on the Kalka, the *Tale of Batu's Sacking of Ryazan* (*Povest o razorenii Ryazani Batyem*) is a complex epic work of great poetic beauty. Using a lyrical mode of expression, the author recalls how the city was destroyed, and how its princes, the Ingvarevichi, were savagely killed, "all together emptying the same chalice of death." Passages cast in the martial style alternate with hagiographical rhetoric. In their laments, the *dramatis personae* give voice to their despair at the misfortune that has befallen the country. The author bewails the martyrdom of the young and beautiful princes Oleg and Feodor, of Eupraxia, who jumped from a tower to escape the khan's embraces, and Agrippina with all her daughters and daughters-in-law, killed in the church where they had sought refuge. In the central part, the boyar Evpaty Kolovrat, a true epic hero, gathers around him a small host of men "whom God had preserved" and sets out against the enemy. Echoing the folk epic, the tale describes how Evpaty kills one of the Tatar chiefs in single combat, and how the khan, when the Russians finally bring their dead hero before him, sends for his "mirzas, and his princes, and his snachuk-beys, and all were amazed at the courage, fortitude, and bravery of the Ryazan warriors." The tale ends with the burial of the dead princes, whose earthly remains have been collected and brought back to Ryazan by Prince Ingvar Ingorevich. Order has been restored, and Ingvar's lament for his dead brothers concludes with an invocation of Boris and Gleb for help against the enemy.

On 8 September 1380, a Russian army led by the Grand Prince

Dmitry Ivanovich of Moscow (Donskoy) defeated Khan Mamai and his army on the Kulikovo field on the upper Don, less than 200 miles south of Moscow. This was the first time the Russians had bested the Mongols, and the victory was undoubtedly of great psychological importance both to the Russians and to the Mongols: though the Tatar yoke would last for another century and more, it showed that the invaders were vulnerable. By 1393, the account of the victory had been turned into an epic composition by Sofoniya of Ryazan, of whom nothing is known but his name. His work is today called the *Zadonshchina* (*The Battle Beyond the Don*), a title it received in the earliest of its six extant copies, dating from the 1470s.

The *Zadonshchina* was composed in conscious imitation of the *Igor Tale*: the epic movement from initial disaster to final success for the Russians on the Don in 1380 mirrors the movement from triumphant victory to total surrender on the Kayala in 1185. According to Roman Jakobson's ingenious conjecture, this mirror symmetry is a deliberate device employed by the author in order to bring together in a diptych his own original Lament and Encomium and an old Lament "copied from books", i.e. the *Igor Tale*. Or, to quote from Sofoniya's proem: "First I wrote down the Lament of the Russian land and so forth, citing from books. After that I composed the Lament and Praise to Grand Prince Dmitry [. . .] let us adjoin Tale to Tale."

Like the author of the *Igor Tale*, Sofoniya refers back to the "vatic Boyan." But the archaic imagery associated with this legendary figure in the *Tale* is no longer understood by the author of the *Zadonshchina*. He reduces the nature symbolism of the older work to much simpler figures. The wolf-symbolism of the *Tale*, for instance, reappears in the *Zadonshchina* as a negative parallelism: "And the grey wolves [. . .] want to advance against the Russian land. Those were not grey wolves, but the pagan Tatars [. . .]" Moreover, Sofoniya's discourse is multistyled, with elements borrowed from the chronicles and the military tales, such as the contrast between pagans and Christians, the *topos* "God has punished the Russian land for its sins," the princes' prayers before the battle, etc. In spite of all these differences, however, the esthetic significance of the *Zadonshchina* depends on its relationship to the *Igor Tale*. The tragic vision of the ruin of Rus in the *Tale* is counterbalanced in Sofoniya's work by a new vision of "the glorious town of Moscow."

The rise of Moscow as the new center of Russian culture is due most of all to the influence of Metropolitan Cyprian. Little is known about Cyprian's early years. He probably spent some time as a monk on Mount Athos, where he was trained in the hesychast tradition of contemplative prayer. At the beginning of the 1370s, he was taken into the service of the pro-hesychast Patriarch Philotheos, and soon became one of his trusted men. In 1375 he was appointed metropolitan of Kiev and Lithuania, and in 1390 finally moved to Moscow, after a brief and unsuccessful stay there in 1381–2. An accomplished diplomat, theologian and man of letters, Cyprian was a typical representative of "political hesychasm," advanced by a group of ecclesiastical princes who, in the second half of the fourteenth century, worked together to restore and preserve the unity of the Orthodox Church under the patriarchate of Constantinople. To this group also belonged Patriarch Euthymius of Trnovo and his pupil Gregory Tsamblak, both friends and colleagues of Cyprian's, and in Russia such distinguished church leaders as Sergius of Radonezh and his nephew Theodore, Abbot of the Simonov Monastery and Grand Prince Dmitry Donskoy's confessor, later bishop of Rostov. Cyprian contributed actively to the spread of hesychast theology in Russia. He translated texts promoting hesychast doctrine from Greek into Church Slavonic, among them the *Ladder* of John Climacus and certain writings of Dionysius the Areopagite. Furthermore, he revised the Russian ritual in order to bring it more in accordance with Byzantine practice. In the years before his death in 1406, he was involved in the compilation of the first comprehensive Moscow chronicle, completed in 1408. His major works as a man of letters are his two versions of the *Life of Metropolitan Peter* (*Zhitie metropolita Petra*, ruled 1308–26), based on an earlier *Life* of Peter commissioned by Ivan Kalita in 1327 to commemorate Peter's translation of the metropolitanate from Vladimir to Moscow. Cyprian's first and shorter version may have been written in 1381–2, during his initial incumbency in Moscow, whereas the longer version was written after 1385, probably after Cyprian's return to Moscow in 1390.

In Cyprian's Life, Peter is depicted as the incarnation of

fourteenth-century hesychasm in both its aspects, the mystical and the political. During his years of monastic apprenticeship the saint spent his days

> in meditation, setting up a ladder of ascent in his heart [. . .] according to the instruction and teaching of Saint John Climacus [. . .] soon he had learnt the painting of Holy Icons [. . .] and through this all his spirit and mind were carried away from earthly things, and in spirit he was wholly deified [. . .] lifting his mind from these painted images to their archetypes.

The saint's mystical *theosis* and the Orthodox theology of the Holy Icons are here described with a precision which itself testifies to Cyprian's hesychast background. By the same token, his account of Peter's career as a church leader is accompanied by a vision of the saint as the servant of the Holy Mother of God and her Son and Lord, the heavenly archetype of the hesychast bishop. This relationship between Christ and his servant is extended to Cyprian himself, who in his concluding eulogy to Peter projects the main events of his own life onto the life story of his protagonist, emphasizing the correspondences between them. The eulogy ends with a depiction of "our glorious Orthodox princes" venerating the saint's relics. Receiving blessings with all the Orthodox, praising the Lifegiving Trinity, the secular princes are represented humbly kneeling before Metropolitan Cyprian, the image of the divine prototype of Christ.

Cyprian's expanded *Life* of Peter is commonly regarded as the first example in old Russian hagiography of a new hagiographical style, captivating the audience more by rhetorical embellishment than by reliable and sober narration. Cyprian's style is thus intermediate between the neo-Slavic rhetoric of fourteenth-century Bulgarian and Serbian hagiography, and its Russian counterpart, known as "word-weaving" (*pletenie sloves*), a Greek calque. In early Muscovite literature, "word-weaving" is usually associated with the hagiographical writings of Epiphanius the Wise and Pachomius the Serb.

The *Life of Saint Stephen, Bishop of Perm* (*Zhitie svyatogo Stefana, episkopa Permskogo*), written by the monk Epiphanius the Wise soon after Stephen's death in 1396, is known in an early sixteenth-century copy, believed to be identical with Epiphanius' original composition.

Saint Stephen brought the Gospel to the Finnish Zyrians (the Permians of the Life) and translated the Christian Scriptures into their language. The hagiographical significance of this is brought out in a comparison with the missionary work of the Apostles and with Constantine-Cyril. By these parallels, the conversion of the Permians is integrated into the history of salvation, seen as a linear progress beginning with the Fall and moving towards the Day of Judgement, a temporal process that has its spatial correlative in the expansion of the Russian Church to the land of Perm. A similar chronotope determines the representation of Stephen's ascent in the hierarchy of the Church in the form of a movement in time and geographical space. From his home town of Ustyug he moves to Rostov, where he is shorn a monk, ordained as deacon, and receives his priesthood, before proceeding to Moscow and to Perm, returning back to Moscow to become bishop. This idea of sanctification as an ascent in the ecclesiastical hierarchy is one of the two ways to divine knowledge described by Dionysius the Areopagite, the other being the way of spiritual ascent in contemplation of the divine mysteries. In the writings of the Areopagite the two ways are equal, one belonging to the personal sphere, the other to the sphere of the Church as a social institution. What is remarkable in the *Life of Saint Stephen* is the one-sided emphasis on social and political themes. Ideologically, the *Life of Saint Stephen* is a document of political hesychasm; its mystical, contemplative aspect has been suppressed.

By his own admission Epiphanius wrote the *Life of Saint Stephen* "to praise the preacher of faith, Perm's teacher, and the Apostles' successor." Thus the *Life* was conceived as an encomium. In a series of rhetorical amplifications, culminating in three final laments in commemoration of the saint, Epiphanius exploits the whole register of Church Slavonic devices, following the exemplars of Kievan oratory and of the neo-Slavonic *logos epideiktikos* of Serbian hagiography developed in the thirteenth and fourteenth centuries. This ornamental style of "word-weaving," with its paronomastic repetitions, synonyms, *isocola* and *homoioteleuta*, is brought to a flamboyant apex in Epiphanius' tirades.

Before his death about 1420, Epiphanius wrote the *Life of Saint Sergius of Radonezh* (*Zhitie svyatogo Sergiya Radonezhskogo*, 1314–92), the founder of the Monastery of the Holy Trinity north of Moscow, and one of the leaders of monastic hesychasm in early Muscovite Russia.

This *Life* was rewritten by Pachomius the Serb soon after his arrival in Russia about 1440, and has only been preserved in this revised version. Pachomius had received his education on Mount Athos, and was fully familiar with the ornate style of Serbian literature. For the next forty years Pachomius was active in both Novgorod and Moscow, revising old saints' Lives and writing new ones. Besides this, Pachomius composed a number of canons with which he laid the foundations of an original Muscovite hymnography. In the *Life of Saint Sergius*, the devices of "word-weaving" are used less conspicuously than in the *Life of Saint Stephen*, and there is more emphasis on narrative. At the same time, Pachomius introduces into his glorification of the saint a number of light visions, a motif not found in Epiphanius' eulogy to Stephen of Perm. The light visions reflect the inner ascent and mystical illumination of Sergius, creating a link between his figure and the illuminated figure of Nestor's Saint Theodosius. The correspondences between the two saints are hardly accidental. They are both depicted as *imitatores Christi*, though Theodosius' *imitatio* takes the form of a mystical re-enactment of Christ's suffering and an anagogical prefiguration of His celestial glory, whereas the prototype of Sergius' *imitatio Christi* is the Trans-figured Christ on Mount Tabor, the central image of mystical hesychasm.

With the fall of Constantinople in 1453, Moscow emerged as the new center of the Orthodox Church and heir to the imperial legacy of East Rome. In 1459 the Russian Church was declared auto-cephalous, and the marriage in 1472 of Ivan III to Princess Zoe, niece of the last Byzantine emperor, seemed to confirm Russia's new status. During the next century the Russian Church turned inward and developed the ideology of Moscow as the third and last Rome.

The idea that the grand princes of Moscow – the *tsars*, as they were now called – were the legitimate heirs of the Roman em-perors was developed in several pseudo-historical works dating from the reigns of Ivan III (1462–1505) and Vasily III (1505–33). One of the most popular was the *Tale of Constantinople* (*Povest o Tsargrade*), included in the *Russian Chronograph* (*Russky Khrono-*

graf) of 1512, and ascribed in one copy to a certain Nestor Iskander. In the final part, the tale describes the sultan's triumphant entry into the fallen city, concluding with a prophecy of Byzantium's liberation by a "fair people" (*rusy rod*), soon taken to mean that the Russians (*russky rod*) had been chosen by Providence to free Constantinople. A related idea is expressed in Spiridon Sava's *Epistle on the Crown of Monomakh* (*Poslanie o Monomakhovom ventse*), which traces the genealogy of the reigning Russian grand princes back to Caesar Augustus. In the *Tale of the Princes of Vladimir* (*Skazanie o knyazyakh Vladimirskikh*), Spiridon's genealogy, originally designed to glorify the princes of Tver, has been transferred to Grand Prince Yury Danilovich of Moscow and his descendants, as part of the new ideology.

From the literature of this period a number of tales have reached us, either in translations or in original Russian versions belonging to the international repertoire of medieval story telling. Among the translated works are the so-called *Serbian Romance of Alexander* (*Serbskaya Aleksandriya*) and Guido de Colomna's Latin *Tales of Troy* (*Troyanskie skazaniya*), originally completed in 1287, and translated from a printed late fourteenth-century German edition. Closer to the folkloric tradition are *Stefanit and Ikhnilat*, based on a tale from the Indian *Panchatantra*, and the *Tale of Solomon and Kitovras* (*Skazanie o Solomone i Kitovrase*). The *Dispute between Life and Death* (*Prenie zhivota i smerti*) was translated from Nicholas Mercator's German version, published in Lübeck in 1484, whereas the *Tale of Dracula* (*Povest o Drakule*) appears to have been written by a Russian familiar with the Dracula legend. These texts signalled a new trend in old Russian literature. A work apart is the *Journey beyond the Three Seas* (*Khozhdenie za tri morya*) by the Tver merchant Afanasy Nikitin. Hardly intended for publication, these travel impressions of Islamic India recorded by an Orthodox Russian in 1466–72 have more appeal to a modern reader than most of the period's official literature.

The end of the fifteenth century and the beginning of the sixteenth was a period of great religious unrest in Russia, in Novgorod and Moscow in particular. Critics of the official church could be found among both the laity and the clergy. Their most serious complaints had to do with the institutional hierarchy of the church, which they attacked in its foundations through a scrutiny of canon law. One of their most prominent leaders, Ivan Volk Kuritsyn, developed his ideas of "free will" and of the "spiritual church" of the early Christians from reading the official *Nomocanon (Kormchaya kniga)*.

Ivan's brother Fyodor wrote that "the soul has a free will and is defended by faith [. . .] wholly blessed in knowledge, whereby we arrive at the fear of God, the beginning of virtue." The reform movement reached the court of Ivan III, who initially supported it as part of his plans to confiscate the landed estates owned by the Russian Church and her monasteries. But when the reformers proved too dangerous, the Church launched a counterattack under the leadership of Abbot Joseph of Volokolamsk (1439–1515), a staunch defender of monastic property and head of the Possessors (*styazhateli*) in their struggle with the non-Possessors (*nestyaz-hateli*). The latter were headed by Nil Sorsky (1433–1508), a great mystic who insisted on monastic poverty and withdrew to the remote forests beyond the Volga in order to devote himself to solitary contemplation. However, the two antagonists joined forces in opposition to the reformers, and Joseph's main anti-heretical work, *The Enlightener (Prosvetitel)*, was written with Nil's assistance.

The religious unrest in early Muscovite Russia ended with the victory of the Josephites over the "heretics" as well as the non-Possessors. Prince Vassian Patrikeev, a disciple of Nil Sorsky, fought in vain against them, chastizing the property-owning monasteries for desecrating the tradition of the saints and describing the acquisition of property as the "new heresy." In 1531 he was arrested and imprisoned in Joseph's monastery at Volokolamsk, where he died about 1545. A similar fate befell his friend Maxim the Greek. Known in the world as Michael Trivolis, Maxim had in his youth been close to the Italian humanists, but under the influence of Savonarola's antihumanist sermons he became a monk on Mount Athos and later went to Russia. He died in 1556 after spending thirty-one years in prison for his opposition to the church and the secular establishment.

After 1547, when Ivan IV the Terrible proclaimed himself "Tsar," official Russian literature was characterized by an encyclopedic activity which paralleled the political centralization and unification of the country under its autocratic ruler. The chronicles were codified and brought up to date, the Church Council of 1551 affirmed the established ritual of the Russian Church and issued its decrees in a *Book of a Hundred Chapters* (*Stoglav*). Under the leadership of Metropolitan Macarius (in office 1542–63), the hagiographical and patristic legacy of old Russia, as well as more recent polemical writings, were collected in a vast compilation entitled the *Great Reading Menaia* (*Velikie cheti minei*). In *Household Management* (*Domostroy*), the rules of family life and everyday behavior were laid down once and for all. Among the original tales of this period is the *Tale of Peter and Fevroniya* (*Povest o Petre i Fevronii*) composed by the monk Ermolay-Erazm in mid-century. The legend is based on international fairy-tale motifs, such as the slaying of a dragon, and the "wise maiden." These folklore motifs are combined with hagiographical *topoi* and contemporary political themes in a work expressing the social ethos of the author, a reformer in the tradition of the trans-Volga elders.

The cult of the tsar was codified in the *Book of Ranks of the Tsars' Genealogy* (*Stepennaya kniga tsarskogo rodosloviya*), perpetuating the mythical link between Caesar Augustus and the Russian princes, now said to have been "tsars" even in Kievan times, and glorifying the house of Kalita, rulers by divine appointment and support. According to Ivan Peresvetov, an adventurer from Lithuania who became the mouthpiece of the new Russian service nobility, the tsar, in order to exert his "terrible power," should combine "Christian faith" with "Turkish order."

The terrible tsar and his policies are glorified in the *History of Kazan* (*Kazanskaya istoriya*), written in 1564–5, and in the *Tale of Stefan Batory's Attack on Pskov* (*Povest o prikhozhdenii Stefana Batoriya na Pskov*), written only after the death of the tsar.

There is little doubt that Ivan the Terrible was a cruel and mentally deranged tyrant. But he was also the author of some of the most original works of sixteenth-century Russian literature. Educated in the stern spirit of Josephite monasticism, Ivan mastered to perfection the rules of Muscovite rhetoric, at the same time demonstrating his despotic omnipotence by bringing into his rhetorical discourse elements of blasphemy and scorn associated with the buffoonery of the *skomorokhi* and court jesters, whose company he cherished, although their pranks had been banned by the *Hundred Chapters*. Ivan's hybrid style was a forceful instrument in his polemics against political opponents, but it proved a double-edged sword once the enemy discovered its unholy combination of apparent Christian piety and personal arrogance, of Scriptural quotations and foul-mouthed ribaldry.

The weaknesses of Ivan's style were probed mercilessly by his principal adversary, Prince Andrey Kurbsky (1528–83). A descendant of old princely families of Yaroslavl and Smolensk, Kurbsky had distinguished himself in Ivan's military campaigns as well as in administration, when, in 1564, during a war with Lithuania, he deserted to the enemy. From Lithuania he responded to the tsar's accusatory letters, and in 1573, during the Polish interregnum, compiled the *History of the Grand Prince of Muscovy* (*Istoriya o Velikom knyaze moskovskom*), produced for the explicit purpose of preventing the election of Ivan IV to the Polish throne.

The correspondence between Ivan and Kurbsky has been preserved only in seventeenth-century copies, and its authenticity has recently been questioned. The ideological positions of the two correspondents, however, coincide with views put forward in their other writings. Ivan defends his autocratic idea of tsardom, whereas Kurbsky favors limited princely power and shared governmental responsibility, a position he further developed in his *History*. Kurbsky is the first Russian writer to regard European civilization and secular knowledge as superior to the theological learning of the Orthodox Church and the traditions of old Russia. To Kurbsky Ivan represents cultural barbarism, whereas Ivan uses the same word to characterize Kurbsky's apostasy from Muscovite Christianity.

After the death in 1598 of Fyodor Ivanovich, the last tsar of the old dynasty, and of his successor Boris Godunov in 1606, the Muscovite state was thrown into a crisis that lasted until 1613, when Mikhail Fyodorovich, the first Romanov tsar, ascended the throne. The interregnum, known as the Time of Troubles, had shaken the foundations of the state. The country had been ravaged by civil unrest and by wars of succession in which Poles and Swedes had intervened in support of their respective candidates.

The Time of Troubles was a turning point in old Russian literature. During this period church and state lost control over the written word, Polish verse composition was imitated in Moscow, and oral poetry was transposed into writing. The country was swamped with the "alluring leaflets" of the false pretenders' Catholic supporters, and Church Slavonic rhetoric acquired a new role in the verbal battle with the enemy. Political pamphleteering was no longer the preserve of the tsar, as it had been under Ivan IV. In the ideological struggle of the interregnum, the authority of the written word had ceased to be absolute. It now depended on the individual author's ideological stance.

The new situation is clearly reflected in the memoirs written during or shortly after the Time of Troubles, such as Avraamy Palitsyn's *Narrative* (*Skazanie*, 1612–20), Ivan Timofeev's *Discourses* (*Slovesa dney i tsarey i svyatiteley moskovskikh*, 1616–24), Ivan Khvorostinin's *Chronicle* (*Vremennik*, 1616–19), and Semyon Shakhovskoy's *True Account in Memory of the Martyred and Faithful Tsarevich Dimitry, and of His Slaying* (*Povest izvestnoskazuema na pamyat velikomuchenika, blagovernogo tsarevicha Dimitriya i o ubienii ego*), probably composed in the 1620s.

In these works the old rhetoric is skilfully employed to express, and at times to camouflage, the authors' personal assessments of the events and characters of the period. In trying to understand the behavior of Ivan the Terrible and Boris Godunov, these authors went beyond the traditional character-drawing of old Russian literature, with its clear distinction between sinners and righteous men, between good and evil, and developed a literary technique for the representation of complex, or "strong" characters (Dmitry Likhachov). Whereas Kurbsky had explained the contradictory nature of Ivan the Terrible's personality diachronically, seeing the death of the Tsarina Anastasia as the watershed between the wise and brave ruler and the cruel tyrant who finally murdered his own son, the chroniclers of the interregnum try to depict the rulers of the period as products of an internalized struggle between good and evil in a contrastive technique where good and bad qualities are no longer mutually exclusive, but form a syndrome, modifying each other and creating a dramatic inner conflict. Boris Godunov's character, which to his contemporaries seemed so enigmatic, is explained as an interplay of many factors: human "nature," "free will," striving after fame, the influence of other men. The original contribution of these authors to old Russian literature lies in their invention of a rhetoric of complex characterization.

After the accession of Alexey Mikhailovich in 1645, Moscow

33

became the center of a spiritual revival, led by Stephen Vonifatev, the tsar's teacher and father confessor. Inspired by the *Hundred Chapters* of 1551, Stephen dreamed of a "lay monasticism" of small penitential communities headed by a priest or archpriest. Among the members of Stephen's "circle of zealots" were both Nikon, the future patriarch, and Avvakum, who was to become his most intransigent opponent when, upon his appointment in 1652, Nikon decided to bring "Russian Gallicanism" to an end and work for a closer relationship with the Ukrainian Church. After the union between Russia and the Ukraine in 1654 this became a matter of urgent concern, and the zealots' dream of reviving Muscovite religiosity was a lost cause. The schism following Nikon's liturgical reforms of 1653 split the whole Russian Church into two camps: the Old Believers, representing the ideals of the *Hundred Chapters*, and the Graecophiles, who accepted the necessity of putting an end to the cultural isolationism of Muscovite society. At their initiative, Ukrainian bookmen educated at the Kiev Academy were called to Moscow, bringing with them a culture strongly influenced by the educational system of the Polish Jesuits, on which the Kievan Metropolitan Petro Mohyla had modelled the curriculum of the Academy.

The decisive step toward a westernization of Russian literature was taken with the invitation of Simeon Polotsky (1629–80) to Moscow in 1663. Born in Polotsk in White Russia, Simeon was educated at the Kiev Academy, and he probably also studied at the Jesuit College at Wilno, where he learned Polish and Latin. In 1656 he became a monk and teacher at the Orthodox Brotherhood's School in his home town, where in the same year he twice attracted attention with verses he wrote on the occasion of Tsar Alexey's visits to the city. On his arrival in Moscow he opened a school for government officials where he taught grammar, Latin, poetics and rhetoric. In 1667 he was appointed tutor to Tsarevich Alexey, and later to Fyodor, Sofia, and Peter I. He was court preacher and one of the organizers of the Council of 1666–7, which officially deposed Nikon and condemned the Old Believers, whom he attacked in his *Scepter of Government* (*Zhezl pravleniya*). His sermons were published posthumously in two volumes: the *Spiritual Midday Meal* (*Obed dushevny*, 1681) and the *Spiritual Supper* (*Vecherya dushevnaya*, 1683). He wrote the first plays for the new court theater, *Comedy* on the *Parable of the Prodigal Son* (*Komediya pritchi o bludnom syne*) and the tragedy *On Nebuchadnezzar the King* (*O Navkhodonosore tsare*), both cast in the style of Jesuit school drama, the tragedy based on an old Byzanto-Russian liturgical play about the "three youths in the fiery furnace." Simeon's large collections of poems, *The Garden of Many Flowers* (*Vertograd mnogotsvetny*), and the *Rifmologion*, remained unpublished. The former contains satirical, panegyrical, narrative and didactic verse, the latter panegyric odes and occasional poems written to the tsar and his family. Simeon's verse translation of the *Psalter* (*Psaltyr rifmotvornaya*), printed in Moscow in 1680, was set to music at the end of the century.

In his panegyrical verse Simeon created an "imperial style" for the glorification of the new absolutist empire and its ruler. This style combines old Russian rhetoric and Byzanto-Russian imperial ideology with tropes and figures taken over from ancient and contemporary western European literature in the form of Jesuit school Baroque. With Simeon, a whole museum of ancient gods, muses, heroes, authors and philosophers entered Russian literature. But they had been lifted from their historical context and given a purely ornamental function in his tirades of syllabic lines.

Verbal poetry – verse composition regulated by meter – was unknown in Kievan and Muscovite literature. Verse composition was known in old Russia only in the musical poetry of the Church Slavonic hymns and in the spoken verse of brief oral genres, proverbs, riddles, incantations, etc. recited by the *skomorokhi*. Examples of *skazovy stikh* are to be found in Daniel's *Supplication*. From the beginning of the sixteenth century, the musical poetry of the liturgy was imitated outside its liturgical context in compositions known as "penitential verse" (*stikhi pokayannye*).

Syllabic poetry came to Russia from the west, through the Ukraine, Belorussia, and Poland. The first *virshi* (from Latin *versus*) were written in Russia in the early seventeenth century. Following Ukrainian and Belorussian patterns, they were either written in the form of isosyllabic couplets, or as couplets of lines with a varying number of syllables (relative isosyllabism). The latter variant – found, for instance, in the writings of Prince Khvorostinin – coincided with the old *skazovy stikh*, but they were soon differentiated functionally: "relative isosyllabism" was associated with serious poetry, *skazovy stikh* with popular, "low" rhymes.

35

According to Alexander Panchenko, the new art of verse writing was further developed by a group of Moscow government officials whose activity seems to have ended with the schism, when they sided with the Old Believers. Nikon favored the new art too, and at his patriarchal court hymns were written on the Polish model. But it was Simeon Polotsky who finally transferred the whole system of syllabic poetry to Russia. His work was continued by his favorite pupil, Silvestr Medvedev (1641–92), beheaded by Peter I for his support of the tsar's sister, the Tsarina Sofia, and Silvestr's friend, Karion Istomin (mid-17th century–after 1720), after 1698 head of the printing office.

From the end of the sixteenth century and throughout the seventeenth, a number of medieval adventure novels were translated into Russian, not from the originals but from the chapbook versions in which these works survived in German and Polish literature. The *Tale about Prince Bova* (*Povest o Bove Koroleviche*), which goes back to the Italian romance of Buovo d'Antona, *Peter of the Golden Keys and Queen Magilena* (*Povest o Petre zlatykh klyuchey*), derived from *Pierre de Provence et la belle Maguelonne*, the *Tale of Bruntsvik*, a chapbook version of an old Czech poem, the *Tale of the Golden Haired Czech Prince Vasily* (*Povest o Vasilii Zlatovlasnom, koroleviche Cheshskoy zemli*), and others.

Equally popular were the Russian counterparts of the German *Schwänke* and French *fabliaux*, sometimes translated from Polish *facetiae*, sometimes developed into original Russian versions of well-known international motifs. Among the most popular were the *Tale about Karp Sutulov* (*Povest o Karpe Sutulove*), the *Story of a Life in Luxury and Fun* (*Skazanie o roskoshnom zhitii i veselii*), the *Tale of Ersh Ershovich* (*Povest o Ershe Ersheviche*), and *Shemyaka's Trial* (*Shemyakin sud*), which project traditional denunciations of bureaucracy and corrupt judges onto the reality of seventeenth century Russian life. The original *Tale of Frol Skobeev* has been called both a Russian "picaresque novel" and the "masterpiece of Muscovite fabliaux." This rather cynical tale describes the devices by which the roguish hero seduces a nobleman's daughter, clandestinely marries her, is finally reconciled with her parents, and ends "in great fame, and rich." Both its tone and plot suggest that this story already belongs to the Petrine period.

Another group of seventeenth-century satires deals with the

clergy and monastic life. In stories like the *Tale about Sava the Priest* (*Povest o pope Save*) and the *Petition of the Monks from Kalyazin* (*Kalyazinskaya chelobitnaya*), the solemn world of monks and priests is turned upside down and parodied. The particular variant of spoken verse employed in these satires points to their oral origin. The existence of similar forms in Byzantine literature is an indication that this is an old oral tradition fixed in writing in the seventeenth century, the century when Russian folklore took permanent form for the first time.

Somewhat different from the merry, recreational parody of these tales are the satires in which laughter mingles with tears. Among them are such texts as the *Mass of the Tavern* (*Sluzhba kabaku*), and the *Abecedary of the Naked and Poor Man* (*Azbuka o golom i nebogatom cheloveke*), the former a parody of the vespers, concluding with the life story of a drunkard in the form of a mock-*vita*, the latter of a devotional abecedary, a genre common in Byzanto-Slavonic literature. In both works the comic inversion of official genres is combined with social satire. Like the prodigal son, so popular in Jesuit literature of the period, the heroes, or anti-heroes, of these works are described as social outcasts who act against the will of their parents and waste their patrimony in the company of the dregs of society. They are set in the inns and taverns of the slums. But there is a characteristic element of redeeming irony in them too. The first-person narrator of the *Abecedary* depicts his own abasement with an element of irony, as if in his humiliation he has broken away from the values of this world.

A central text in this group is the *Tale of Woe–Misfortune* (*Povest o Gore i Zlochastii*). Composed in the unrhymed lines of the folk epic, with four stressed syllables in each line, the work is clearly a literary transcription of an oral composition close to the genre of the "penitential songs," with a strong admixture of elements from popular apocrypha about the figure of Khmel, or Humulus, as the embodiment of the demon of drunkenness. The *Tale of Woe-Misfortune* is thus a hybrid work in which a nameless youth leaves his parents, strays from the right path, loses his possessions, and is pursued by Woe-Misfortune, his evil spirit and the incarnation of death, until he is saved at the monastery gates, where he is spiritually reborn and becomes a monk.

Underlying the *Tale of Woe–Misfortune* is a vision of life as tragic farce in which demons play tricks on men in a godforsaken world ruled by the forces of evil, by Satan and the Anti-Christ, or their henchmen. This same vision undergirds the autobiographical *Life* (*Zhitie*) *of Archpriest Avvakum*, the last great hagiographical work in old Russian literature.

The Hundred Chapters Council had envisioned a Russian Church encompassing the whole of society, extending church discipline to all spheres of human life. The center of this "lay monasticism" was to have been the "household church" under the supervision of a priest or archpriest. This idea found expression in the regulation of everyday life prescribed in the *Domostroy*, and it was revived by the circle of religious reformers around Tsar Alexey Mikhailovich in the 1640s.

One of the few literary expressions of this ideal is the *Life of the Holy and Pious Mother Juliana Lazarevskaya* (*Povest o svyatoy i pravednoy materi Yulianii Lazarevskoy*), written about 1625 by her son. The *Life* is composed on the traditional pattern, but now projected onto a secular life story, with the result that some of the well-known *topoi* have been distorted, or even turned upside down. Juliana did not go to church regularly, as a traditional saint would have done. She was more concerned with her duties towards the hungry, the poor, and the sick, than with ritual matters. Also, she obeyed her husband when he forbade her to enter a convent, and spent the rest of her days as a lay ascetic in constant "spiritual prayer."

The schism of 1653 wrecked hopes for a revival of household religiosity. The leaders of the reformist movement went over into opposition to the tsar and the patriarch, continuing their work as religious dissidents, persecuted by church and state, tortured, and finally burnt at the stake.

The *vitae et passiones* of these martyrs are the most significant seventeenth-century contribution to old Russian hagiography. These works include the anonymous *Life of Boyarina Morozova, Princess Urusova, and Maria Danilova* (*Zhitie boyariny Morozovoy, knyagini Urusovoy, i Mari Danilovoy*), and the autobiographical Lives of Archpriest Avvakum and his fellow sufferer, the monk Epiphanius.

Archpriest Avvakum (1621–82) wrote his Life at Pustozersk on the White Sea, where he spent his last fifteen years as a prisoner. The *Life* went through several revisions, with the hagiographical element becoming more pronounced in each new version.

Written in the form of an intimate "talk" (*beseda*) addressed to Epiphanius, the *Life* has a markedly dialogic structure. The author conducts a dialogue with his own past, trying to discover meaning in his suffering, be it in the patriarchal torture chambers or during the years of his Siberian exile. The memories of his suffering become meaningful only when he regards his own life as a re-enactment of Christ's Passion. Avvakum's theological thought is permeated by the symbolism of the Areopagite (Konrad Onasch): in his *Life*, people and events, even the flora and fauna of eastern Siberia, are "signs and miracles" of divine prototypes, revealing themselves in the immediate reality of his suffering. The interference of this supernatural world of prototypes transforms his humiliations into a series of symbols of the world to come, of his triumph over the arch-enemy, that Anti-Christ incarnate, Patriarch Nikon.

Avvakum's combination of ecclesiastical and colloquial language transposed into writing the pathos of his oral rhetoric, and has remained a source of inspiration to modern Russian literature ever since the *Life* was first published in 1861.

Ukrainian influence in Moscow, which had steadily increased during the reign of Alexey Mikhailovich, became all-pervasive during the reign of his son, Peter the Great. The Ukrainian-Orthodox imitation of Polish-Jesuit school Baroque, introduced into Russian literature by Simeon Polotsky, continued to flourish in the writing of his successors, the Metropolitan Dimitry of Rostov (1651–1709), Stefan Yavorsky (1658–1722), *locum tenens* of the patriarchal chair, and Feofan Prokopovich (1681–1736). All three were educated at the Kiev Academy, after which Yavorsky and Prokopovich temporarily converted to Catholicism and continued their studies abroad, the former at Polish and Lithuanian universities, the latter in Rome, where he became acquainted with Jesuit scholasticism. This he later rejected, together with the divinity of the Greeks, trying to revitalize Russian theology in confrontation with Protestantism, whose doctrines he also refused to accept. As distinguished men of letters, these ecclesiastics caught the attention of the tsar, whose reforms they regarded with various

feelings, from Yavorsky's open resistance and Dimitry Rostovsky's silent disapproval to the enthusiastic support of Prokopovich, who saw Peter as the embodiment of his own ideal of
enlightened despotism.

All three men were professional writers, trained according to the
rules of Jesuit school rhetoric, which Yavorsky summarized in his
Rhetorical Handbook (*Ruka retoricheskaya*), while Prokopovich
wrote his own Latin courses in both poetics and rhetoric.

Dimitry Tuptalo, later canonized as Saint Dimitry Rostovsky, is
known mainly for his *Reading Menaia* (*Minei-Cheti*, 1689–1705).
Written under the influence of the Jesuit Peter Skarga's Polish
Lives and the *acta sanctorum* of the Bollandists, the work replaced
Macarius's old *Menaia*, and became the hagiographical thesaurus
for generations and generations of Russian readers and writers,
right up to our own century. The highly ornate discourse of his
ecclesiastical oratory shows how well Baroque rhetoric and
Byzanto-Slavonic "word-weaving" could function together. His
plays *A Comedy for the Day of Christ's Birth* (*Komediya na Rozhdenie
Khristovo*), *A Comedy for the Dormition of the Virgin* (*Komediya na
Uspenie Bogomateri*), and others, are written in the tradition of
Jesuit school drama, while his poems, epigraphs and hymns reveal
a predilection for Baroque conceptism. In Rostov, Dimitry estab-
lished the first Russian theological seminary using Greek and
Latin.

To his contemporaries, Stefan Yavorsky was known first and
foremost as the author of the anti-Protestant treatises *Vineyard of
Christ* (*Vinograd Khristov*, 1698) and *Rock of Faith* (*Kamen very*,
1718). His sermons, written in the Baroque mannerist style, were
aimed at impressing the audience with exclamations such as "O
Noah, glorious admiral!" "O celestial pharmacist, how miraculous is Thine alchemy, how marvellous Thy pharmacy [...]."
Stefan's arguments against the Protestants were borrowed from
Catholic works. Like Feofan Prokopovich, Stefan was tri-lingual,
and wrote his poems in Latin, Polish and Church Slavonic. His
most accomplished verse composition is a Latin valedictory elegy
to his library, written in the tradition of the humanists.

Of all the Ukrainians active in Moscow under Peter the Great,
Feofan Prokopovich was the most prominent. He it was who
carried out Peter's church reforms, abolishing the old Byzanto-

Russian idea of a diarchy between church and state and subjecting the ecclesiastical hierarchy to the authority of the secular ruler as "high priest" and "supreme shepherd".

In his literary work Feofan glorified the tsar and the new absolutism in panegyrical *logoi*, such as the *Discourse on the Power and Dignity of the Tsar* (*Slovo o vlasti i chesti tsarskoy*, 1718), and the *Panegyrical Discourse on the Russian Fleet* (*Slovo pokhvalnoe o flote rossiyskom*, 1720). His tragicomedy *Vladimir* (1705), written in syllabic verse, is regarded by some historians as an allegorical satire on the opponents of Peter's reforms though on the surface it deals with Vladimir's Christianization of Rus. His *Epinikion* (1709), celebrating Peter's victory over the Swedes at Poltava, was written in Latin, Polish and Church Slavonic. The Slavonic version is composed according to the traditional scheme of thirteen-syllable lines, with the caesura after the seventh syllable, a fixed stress on the sixth and twelfth, and regular rhyme. After Peter's death Feofan's poetry became more experimental and varied, with imitations of the Italian *ottava rima* (a/b a/b a/b c/c), epodic couplets in which a long line is followed by a shorter one, more frequent use of non-grammatical rhymes, and a poetic diction closer to everyday speech. During these years he was surrounded by a "learned retinue," a circle of intimate friends, among whom were the historian Vasily Tatishchev (1686–1750) and the young Prince Antiokh Kantemir, whose first and most famous satire, "Against the Enemies of Education" ("Na khulyashchikh uchenie"), was directed against Feofan's enemies. In this work, the reign of Peter the Great is already viewed as a "golden age" of the past, nostalgically referred to by one of the harbingers of a new age in Russian literature.

According to the *Primary Chronicle*, in 980, only eight years before his official conversion to Christianity, Prince Vladimir set up a group of pagan idols on a hill near his castle at Kiev. The gods represented were Perun, Khors, Dazhbog, Stribog, Simarigl, and Mokosh. Perun is further mentioned in the Graeco-Russian treaties reproduced in the chronicle (907, 945, 971), where it is said that the non-Christian Russians swore by Perun and by Veles, the god of cattle.

Comparative studies have shown that the pagan deities of the eastern Slavs have their counterparts in the mythology of other Slavs, and that ultimately they are derivations of an Indo-European pantheon. A notable feature of Slav paganism is the strong Iranian influence still to be found in terms like *bog* ("god"), meaning "giver of wealth"; *vera* ("faith"), coinciding with the Iranian word denoting choice between good and evil; and *svyat* ("holy"). The Russian word *mir*, meaning both "peace" and "peaceful community," is connected with the Iranian god Mithra.

With the acceptance of Christianity, the old pagan beliefs were relegated to the periphery of old Russian culture, and the church began an endless struggle to eradicate the remnants of paganism. In spite of this, the old traditions survived in popular peasant cults, in folklore and decorative folk art, right up to the twentieth century.

In popular tradition, pagan and Christian elements often coalesced in hybrid forms, known by the church as "ditheism" (*dvoeverie*). Perun, for instance, the old thunder-god, whom the Varangians of the princely retinue identified with the old Norse Thor, found a Christian equivalent in Elijah, and Veles, the god of wealth and cattle, was transformed into Saint Blasius. But in the popular juxtaposition of Elijah and Blasius/Veles, modern scholars have detected traces of an archaic antagonism between the Indo-European thunder-god and a dragon-shaped cattle god, hiding from his opponent in trees, cliffs, animals, human beings, etc. Folkloric transformations of this deity are such epic heroes as the Serbian Zmaj Ognjeni Vuk (Dragon Fiery Wolf), Volkh Vselavevich in the Russian folk epic, and the magician Prince Vseslav of Polotsk in the *Primary Chronicle* and the *Igor Tale*.

In the old Slavonic version of the *Romance of Alexander*, Zeus is identified with Perun. Hephaistos and Helios are translated as Svarog and Dazhbog in the *Chronicle* of Malalas, and the two are described in the *Hypatian Chronicle* under 1114 as father and son. Khors is another name for the sun god, borrowed from the Iranian. Stribog, who comes next to Dazhbog in Vladimir's ensemble of idols, has been translated as "the apportioner of wealth" (Roman Jakobson), and Dazhbog and Stribog form a divine pair corresponding to the Greek Aisa and Poros, "Portion" and "Allotment," Vedic Aṃśa and Bhaga, all pointing to a common Indo-European prototype. In the *Igor Tale*, the Russians

42

are called, "Dazhbog's grandsons," and the winds are the "grandsons of Stribog," blowing from the sea with arrows against Igor's valiant hosts.

The genuine folkloric tradition of old Russia was transmitted by the *skomorokhi*, the Russian minstrels. Persecuted by the church and finally outlawed by Tsar Alexey Mikhailovich in the middle of the seventeenth century, they receded into the remote regions of northern Russia, where their art was taken over by peasant singers and tellers of tales. It was in the seventeenth century as well that the first Russian folk tales and ballads were recorded, the tales by an Oxford doctor of medicine, Samuel Collins, the ballads by another Oxford man, Richard James, at the beginning of the century chaplain to the English diplomatic mission in Moscow. He returned to England in 1620, bringing with him the first transcriptions of Russian secular folk songs.

An important event in the study of Russian folklore was the publication of Kirsha Danilov's *Drevnie rossiyskie stikhotvoreniya* (1804), a collection of epic songs, or *byliny*. The classical collection of Russian folk tales is the one published by Alexander Afanasev in 1855–64, containing about 600 texts.

In the Middle Ages the *byliny* were sung to the accompaniment of the *gusli*, a harp-like instrument. The line is the compositional unit: each line has a fixed number of stressed syllables, usually three, with the last stress falling on the antepenultimate syllable to give the line a dactylic ending. There is no end rhyme, and the lines are grouped into larger sections by means of repetitions and parallelisms. A single *bylina* usually consists of between 200 and 300 lines.

The *byliny* are divided into a Kievan and a Novgorod cycle. The central hero of the latter is the poor *gusli* player Sadko, who becomes a rich merchant with the help of the tsar of the underwater realm of Lake Ilmen. The Kievan cycle is centered around the legendary figure of Prince Vladimir and the banquets he arranges for his retinue; its heroes are the valiant knights Vladimir sends out to fight foreign invaders and internal foes. The most popular are Ilya Muromets, Dobrynya Nikitich, and Alyosha Popovich. They are all *bogatyri*, a Persian word meaning "athlete." Ilya, a hero of superhuman strength granted him by Jesus and two Apostles, first uses his power to clear the land on his parents' farm, and later in Vladimir's service. He destroys the Tatar Kalin Tsar and his army before descending into a Kievan cave, where he is turned into stone. Dobrynya and Alyosha Popovich are dragon slayers. The historical prototype of the latter may have been Alexander Popovich, mentioned in the chronicle under 1223 as one of the warriors killed by the Tatars. In the *bylina* historical elements are fused with mythological motifs. Thus Alyosha kills the dragon Tugarin, a poetic transformation of the Polovtsian chief Tugor Khan.

The heroes of the *byliny* moved easily into the fairy tales, a genre closely related to the epic songs in subject matter, but following different poetic patterns. Whereas the *bylina* glorifies the heroes of a distant historical past, the fairy tales conjure up a social utopia, a vision of the "other world." The *bylina* heroes belong to a golden age, while the folk-tale hero sets out in search of a "better place," "three years by a crooked way, or three hours by the straight – only there is no thoroughfare." When finally he finds it, the other world is very much like the one he has left: "The bed is wide and the pillows are of down."

Much of the charm of the Russian folk tales is due to their verbal artistry, in particular their use of dialogue and their incorporation of other, smaller folkloric genres: proverbs, riddles, and incantations. According to a traditional narrator, the talk of the tale is the most difficult: "If a single word is wrong, nothing will work out right."

2

THE EIGHTEENTH CENTURY: NEOCLASSICISM AND THE ENLIGHTENMENT, 1730–90

Although those who came first chronologically in the history of eighteenth-century Russian literature – Antiokh Kantemir and Vasily Trediakovsky – initially wished to effect a radical break with their medieval tradition, much as Peter the Great had done in the political sphere, they could not manage it immediately. They initiated the transition to a modern literature, but it would take some time to accomplish, for the greatest literary figure of mid-century, Mikhail Lomonosov, was not so anxious as they to jettison native ways, and indeed eventually Trediakovsky too reverted to a greater sense of his roots than he had displayed in his youth, when under strong western European influence.

Although the church ceased to nurture literature directly in those years, it still continued to do so indirectly – through its schools, for example, which Lomonosov attended – and took an active hand in developing culture generally. Although literature was evidently much more secular in the eighteenth century than it had been earlier, there was still a serious religious component to it, one which emerged, for example, in Lomonosov's "Morning meditation" and "Evening Meditation," in Trediakovsky's *Feoptiya*, and in Derzhavin's ode "God," promptly translated into many languages. Nor did it prove a simple matter to implant an understanding of literature as fiction: Kantemir had to explain carefully to the readers of his satires that his characters were but literary creations. There was also a continuing emphasis on history in the eighteenth century, both in the strict sense (even in the nineteenth century Karamzin's *History of the Russian State* would be seen as a great literary achievement), and in the literary sense: the ode, the leading literary genre of mid-century, dealt primarily with great historical events, though often contemporary ones, while the tragedy, another principal literary genre, for the most part described crucial moments of Russian history. On the other hand, the leading forms in the years immediately after 1730 (the year in which Kantemir's verse satires began to circulate widely) were poetic ones, which had not been the case for most of the old Russian period. In the minds of most readers, a work written in verse is clearly literary, whereas a literary work in prose may be confused with a piece of documentary writing. Thus the supremacy of poetry for several decades after 1730 may be regarded as an implicit affirmation that Russia indeed now had a modern literature.

After largely rejecting the legacy of medieval Russia, the creators of eighteenth-century Russian literature went back to classical models, and shaped a literature based upon its precepts. However, this approach represented no very radical departure from previously prevalent literary doctrine. Neoclassicism in literature dealt with that which was common to all peoples in all places at all times. Thus there was a serious internationalist component to neoclassicism, which went well with the internationalist – or, more precisely, universalist – perspective of the Christian culture which had preceded it: nationalism had not yet become a major element of the Russian cultural outlook. In addition, literature of the neoclassical period raised serious moral and social issues, problems affecting the society as a whole or in which the state was involved. The writer did not consider it appropriate to speak of himself or his own personal experiences: his gaze was fixed upon higher things. Several writers of the eighteenth century had quite pungent personalities, but they did not express them directly through their writing. To be sure, they were not so self-effacing as their medieval predecessors, but they were very far from their nineteenth-century successors, who tended to concentrate upon their own emotions and opinions. Literature in the eighteenth century thus tried to offer serious guidance to society as a whole on important questions.

There is yet another literary parallel with the medieval period to be detected in the eighteenth century: the close connection between literature and the objectives of the state, as well as between writers and the state. Most of the outstanding writers of the eighteenth century were also important government officials: Kantemir was a leading diplomat; Trediakovsky, though less successful in finding employment, still derived much of his livelihood from the state, as did Lomonosov, who in his numerous odes on official occasions such as coronations set out his ideals for Russian society; Fonvizin was a government bureaucrat close to the man responsible for Russian foreign policy in the 1770s; Derzhavin gave unsolicited advice to Catherine; Radishchev was employed in the St. Petersburg customs house; and Catherine herself had literary ambitions. Such examples could be multiplied to show that even during the eighteenth century there were almost no professional literary men. Rather, most writers derived their primary livelihood from the state (though not the church anymore), and tended therefore to feel considerable responsibility for its policies.

In creating the foundations of a modern literature, Russian writers after 1730 adapted the theories of western European neoclassicism to

Russian conditions. Trediakovsky and Sumarokov worked out detailed descriptions of an intricate system of literary genres which was rather different from that which had gone before, and promulgated rules which the serious writer was virtually obliged to follow. Trediakovsky and Lomonosov elaborated a new system of versification which replaced the classical scheme of syllables containing long or short vowels with syllables containing stressed or unstressed vowels (syllabo-tonic versification), rejecting the scheme of syllabic versification – when only the number of syllables in a line was regulated – which Kantemir had perfected in practice on the basis of Polish models, and which he also defended in theory before his death. Lomonosov adapted a variant of the classical system of three styles (high, middle and low) to the Russian literary language, in so doing providing it with a theoretical structure of great importance even if it was frequently honored in the breach. And all the writers of the decades following 1730 were much concerned with the problem of developing a modern Russian literary language, laying the foundations of a synthesis which would be brought to perfection by Pushkin and those who came immediately after him in the early nineteenth century.

During the eighteenth century the number of writers increased, and the rudiments of a literary society began to appear. In the first decades after 1730 the number of writers was small, and there were many antagonisms among the leading ones – Trediakovsky, Lomonosov and Sumarokov – but still they knew one another, and even antagonistic competition could be stimulating. In 1755 literary journals began to be founded, and with them literary groupings of an informal sort, so that writers could lend one another support and advice. Later on Derzhavin in particular seems to have had a powerful sense of the importance of literary society, and even at the beginning of his career gathered about him writers like Khemnitser and Lvov. Thus literature gathered momentum, and it is appropriate that the concluding date of this chapter – 1790 – should be the date of the appearance of a political book by a man who worked for the government, cast in an eclectic neo-classical literary form but with infusions of the new sentimentalism then coming to the fore, and yet one which clearly looked to the future, when the writer would regard himself as antagonist to the state: Radishchev's *Journey from St. Petersburg to Moscow*. The publication of the *Journey* would also establish a sad precedent for modern Russian literature: the persecution and jailing of a writer for an implicit and explicit political critique expressed in literary form. But at least this showed that Russian rulers regarded literature as a serious enterprise.

IN 1730, in both capitals, but especially in Moscow, where the Court and the Guards regiments were situated at the time – that is,

47

a large part of the nobility which had by that point become Europeanized – the verse satires of Antiokh Kantemir which had first appeared in 1729 continued to circulate in manuscript. In that same year of 1730, in St. Petersburg there appeared an allegorical novel in prose by Paul Tallemant entitled *A Voyage to the Isle of Love (Ezda vo ostrov Lyubvi)* in a translation by Vasily Trediakovsky, who had just returned from Paris. Thus two themes entered Russian literature which had had no place in it before: laughter and love. To be sure, Russian folklore had already developed the lyrical lovesong and various humorous genres, but all this existed on a level of everyday life and ordinary holiday amusement and did not reach the basic literary genres: the chronicles, the lives of the saints, and also polemical essays, which developed especially rapidly in the seventeenth century because of the schism within the Russian Orthodox Church leading to the departure of significant numbers of clergy and laypeople, the Old Believers.

The appearance in Russia of literature of the new, Europeanized type became possible only after a whole series of political and administrative reforms and cultural and educational legislation put through in the first quarter of the eighteenth century by Emperor Peter I. Peter's reforms were primarily subordinated to the requirements of politics. In order to create a state technologically equal to the most powerful states of Europe, Peter needed industry and trained specialists; and in order to create the latter he required appropriate institutions of learning. All this came into being in the course of unceasing wars which shaped the entire life of the state. Consequently Peter had little interest in the development of the humanities or the creation of a Europeanized artistic literature.

The culture which Peter as political leader required was a secularized one liberated from the control of the Orthodox Church. By subjecting the church to the state and depriving it of its role as the nation's ideological guide, Peter did a great deal to implant within the social consciousness of the ruling stratum, the Russian aristocracy, the ideas of European political thought in that variant which viewed enlightened absolutism as the most effective instrument of cultural and social progress.

When they made their debuts in literature – or more precisely, in their consciously and carefully calculated initial literary enterprises – neither Kantemir nor Trediakovsky drew upon any sort of

Russian literary tradition. With Kantemir and Trediakovsky the Russian literary consciousness acquired the conviction that the new literature of the European type could derive no benefit at all from the Russian literary experience of the eleventh to seventeenth centuries.

As Alexander Sumarokov, one of the most prolific of modern Russian authors, later phrased it in his "Eulogy to Emperor Peter the Great" ("Slovo pokhvalnoe o gosudare imperatore Petre Velikom," 1759):

> Until the time of Peter the Great Russia was not enlightened by any clear conception of the nature of things, by any useful knowledge or by any profound doctrine: our reason was submerged in the darkness of ignorance, sparks of intellect would be extinguished, because they lacked the strength to burst into flame [. . .] But when Peter became a man the sun arose; and the darkness of ignorance was dissipated.

Antiokh Kantemir (1708–44) was the son of Prince Dmitry Kantemir, a Moldavian ruler who went over to Peter's side during the Russo–Turkish war in 1711. Dmitry Kantemir was not only a statesman, but a writer as well, the author of satirical works and also of a *History of the Ottoman Empire,* later translated into major European languages. Since Antiokh was clearly the outstanding one among Dmitry's four sons, his father saw to his education with special care. Italian and Modern Greek were spoken at home, and Antiokh was taught Russian and Church Slavic by the poet and translator Ivan Ilinsky. In St. Petersburg Antiokh attended lectures by Academician Christian-Friedrich Gross, who was conducting a course on Cartesian *Naturphilosophie*. It was very likely Gross who stimulated his interest in French culture, which at that point still had not penetrated the Russian mind. Kantemir began his investigations of the spirit and forms of French poetry with translations of Nicolas Boileau's satires in 1726 and 1727. Since Kantemir wrote in syllabic verse (he was one of the last Russian writers to do so), the translations came out with equivalent numbers of lines.

Boileau's satires attracted Kantemir primarily because they contained elements not to be found in the Russian poetic tradition of the Simeon Polotsky school, which he knew quite well: their concern with literature itself, their support for a good and proper national literature and their opposition to literature that was not good and proper. Boileau's satires combined in literary form a typology of contemporary society with literary polemics and argumentation in favor of the literary principles which Boileau defended.

Kantemir was equally influenced in his intellectual development by Jean de la Bruyere's satirical prose and Justus Van Effen's French journals published in Holland. From these Western authors he could learn methods of transforming characterological satire into an instrument of political combat.

Kantemir's first original satire appeared in manuscript in 1729, at a time when the debates between the supporters and the opponents of the Petrine reforms were becoming more spirited. In 1730 he actively participated in attempts to gain influence with the new Empress Anna: he it was who wrote the first proposal in Russian history for a gentry constitution which would have established a parliament of the nobility and limited the monarch's authority. With the support of the gentry Anna rejected the attempts of the high aristocracy to gain power with their own oligarchical proposal, and would have no part of Kantemir's either. She reverted to the traditional system of unlimited autocratic authority. Kantemir was removed from the center of political life and dispatched as ambassador to London in late 1731. By that time he had already written five satires.

The first task with which the founders of modern Russian literature grappled was that of selecting a literary orientation. In view of his aspirations to make Russian poetry an active participant in the effort to educate the Russian intelligentsia in the spirit of the ideas of Peter's reign, Kantemir settled upon the verse satire – partly in its classical examples by Juvenal and Horace, but primarily on the model of the satires of Boileau, who had subsequently renewed the genre – as the most suitable genre for his purposes. Following Boileau's example, in his satires Kantemir combined the energy of current ideological debate with a precise depiction of Russian ways and Russian mores. Contemporary reality was poetically reflected within them; it became the object of conscious literary depiction.

Kantemir as well as those, like Trediakovsky, who started out with him, not to mention such writers as Lomonosov who came along later, faced the necessity of defining themselves in literary terms, that is, of comprehending their place in the literary context, both within Russian culture and on the stage of European culture.

When he addressed his readers in the satirical form, although his satires were read with interest, Kantemir discovered that in themselves his verse texts were difficult to understand. Consequently he felt compelled to equip them with prose commentaries, sometimes quite substantial ones. Kantemir turned to his readers directly to deal with that which was most complicated for them: his satires' literary form and devices connected with that form. In order to elucidate these devices, in many of his footnotes Kantemir would engage in vigorous arguments with his own characters.

In Kantemir's first satire (first version) the "envious man" ridicules and condemns the sciences:

> We lived, he says, without knowing Latin,
> Before a great deal better than now, though ignorant;
> In our ignorance we reaped much better harvests;
> After we adopted a foreign tongue, our harvests have gone down.

Kantemir adds the following note to these lines:

> *In our ignorance we reaped much better harvests.* One hears such things from many people quite frequently, that after we started to adopt foreign languages and customs we began to suffer from famine, as though that were the reason for it; but people do not want to see the truth, which is that this is caused by the idleness of our agriculturalists and the bad weather, signs of God's displeasure with us for our severe offenses against Him and our insults to our neighbors, the sorts of things we have no need to borrow from other nations because we have plenty of them at home.

This note informed the satire's readers that the satirist did not think the same way as his character, that he disagreed with his character, and that his character's opinions were precisely those convictions and ideas which the satirist opposed.

In this way readers comprehended both the structure of the verse satire, a new poetic genre for Russian literature, as well as the basic principle of the new literature: it acted not through direct didacticism but rather by juxtaposing various conflicting viewpoints, inviting the reader to select those which seemed to him rational and correct.

The novelty of Kantemir's satirical approach within Russian literature lay in the fact that for the most part he based it on the self-exposure of his negative characters. In speeches of ignoramuses, hypocrites and obscurantists which expose their motivations the reader can discern as it were through the text the images of positive heroes, honorable and virtuous people, enthusiastic supporters of science and enlightenment. In the name of a common and universal human morality Kantemir derides everything which cannot withstand the criticism of reason and feeling.

But if Kantemir's negative personages incorporate living elements of contemporary mores within themselves, to such an extent that we can sometimes guess at their actual prototypes, then his positive figures are created through contrast with his negative ones and emerge as ideal schemes without any genuine living content. This does not mean that in itself Kantemir's ideal as a satirist was concocted solely in his own imagination: that ideal was founded on his profound conviction of the absolute superiority of the new view of the world created during Peter's reign over the old, traditionally religious approach.

In London, where he spent six years, and then in Paris, where he was sent as ambassador in 1738, Kantemir continued to work on his satires, although the lack of any direct and living contact with a literary milieu made things difficult for him. As far as possible he compensated for that lack by making new acquaintances. In London he did not associate with the English particularly, but rather with Italian literary men and diplomats representing those north Italian states in which reforms along Enlightenment lines were being actively introduced in the 1730s (Parma, Lucca, and others).

In Paris Kantemir drew close to Montesquieu, whose *Persian Letters* he translated (although the translation has not survived), and to those around him; he became a familiar figure in Paris literary salons. In these years as well Kantemir reworked his first five satires, evidently planning to publish them in Russia. He also wrote new satires, which set forth his Enlightenment viewpoint, though they had no specific connection with the situation in Russia.

Kantemir died before his satires ever saw print, and in this sense the first modern Russian writer established a Russian tradition. His satires appeared initially in a French translation of 1749, next in a German version of 1752, and only then, finally, were they printed in Russia, in 1762.

Various literary impressions of the years 1727–30 found places in Vasily Trediakovsky's basic literary project implemented abroad: his translation of Tallemant's book. The dispute within French literature over the advantages of poetry in prose or in verse was not yet decided, and Trediakovsky, not adhering definitively to either side in the dispute, chose to translate a work written in both verse and prose, that is, he tested his readers' reactions to both possible resolutions of the debate.

In Paris Trediakovsky (1703–68) must have been even more greatly influenced by the arguments over the novel than he was by the disputes over verse and prose. In Russia there was no such thing as the novel as cultural phenomenon, the novel as a component part of the cultural surroundings of all levels of the population. It would acquire such popularity only in the nineteenth century.

French scholars call the years Trediakovsky spent in Paris the "golden age" of the French novel. Between 1725 and 1730 fifty-one new novels were published, and in the subsequent five-year period 129 appeared. The novel became the most popular genre, supplanting the tragedy and the comedy.

French novels of the late 1720s spoke of love as a law unto itself, a thing above all else in human existence. Novels undermined the official system of morality and were considered dangerous to religion.

The version of Tallemant's novel which Trediakovsky offered to the Russian reading public contains essentially two conceptions of love. Tallemant's novel is an allegorical one, and its prose text tells of romantic adventures and mishaps which conclude with a taking leave of love and a turning to Glory at the advice of Reason. Even the most adamant critics of the novel of the late 1720s could accept such a love story as that. But the book by Trediakovsky–Tallemant contains verse as well as prose. In his verse translations Trediakovsky abandons any sort of trivial literalness: he alters the structure of strophes, utilizes lines of varying lengths, and so forth. But the most essential alterations he introduces have to do with the treatment of love and romantic relationships. He systematically modifies Tallemant's verse descriptions of love relationships. He replaces abstract and periphrastic expressions in the original with concrete images and erotic situations.

Trediakovsky made such serious modifications of Tallemant's verse because he was attracted by the French school of free-thinker libertine poets, whose work at the time was not published but only circulated in manuscript (it gradually began to appear in print only after Louis XIV's death). Precisely that sort of philosophy of love and life made Trediakovsky the most popular poet and songwriter in Russian society of the 1730s.

In 1732 Trediakovsky became official translator for the Academy of Sciences in St. Petersburg. This position offered him new opportunities to influence literary life, but at the same time he was required to work in conformity with the demands of the Court, which regarded Academicians in the humanities as suppliers of solemn odes and eulogies for appropriate occasions, as planners of illuminations and firework displays, and as translators of texts for theatrical presentations by touring foreign troupes.

Trediakovsky's position as an Academy poet-bureaucrat was made more difficult by the fact that the new Empress Anna, Peter I's niece, had formed her tastes and outlook in Mittau, capital of the duchy of Courland, a vassal state of Russia's, which had been governed first by her husband and then by her. Anna's German sympathies and those of her favorite, Ernst Johann Biron, a stableman whom she had created a Duke, were reflected in the preferential treatment the Court accorded to Academy poets who wrote in German. Gottlob Friedrich Wilhelm Junker (1703–46) received special encouragement from the Court: invited to the St. Petersburg Academy in 1731, in 1734 he was made professor of poetry over Trediakovsky's head. Junker and Jakov von Stählin (1709–85), who replaced him in 1735, produced eulogistic odes and verse inscriptions for firework displays published in the German original and in Russian translation. That was the way Trediakovsky's "Solemn ode on the surrender of the city of Danzig" ("Oda torzhestvennaya o sdache goroda Gdanska," 1734) was printed: Junker did the German translation.

By 1734 Trediakovsky, in addition to Latin and French versification, had become fairly well acquainted with German verse (since he translated the odes of the German court poets); with

Italian poetry from the originals of comedies which he translated; with the poem "Tears of the Prodigal Son," written in trochaic meter, by the Croatian poet Ivan Gundulić. And then he was familiar with Russian folksongs as well. After comparing these different versification systems Trediakovsky came to the conclusion that Russian verse should be regulated in conformity with the nature of the Russian language, and that a versification reform was necessary.

On 14 May 1735 Trediakovsky gave an address at the "Russian Convocation" of the Academy of Sciences in which he presented a proposal for a species of "Petrine reform" of all contemporary literature. Among the various projects he urged one had already been carried out: a "science of versification."

Trediakovsky wished to replicate in literature that rupture with pre-Petrine Rus which the adherents of the Russian Enlightenment saw Peter as having effected on the level of the state. It was then that people became persuaded that the syllabic system as exemplified in "Polish verse" should be replaced by a system of versification which was more national and closer to the character of the Russian language. To be sure, Russian syllabic verse – by virtue of the very fact that it made use of another language than did Polish syllabic verse – had become Russian and not Polish, and could not really resemble its model. But the adherents of the Russian Enlightenment believed that if their campaign for a new poetry were to be successful they must declare syllabic verse "foreign," and not even poetry either, but rather prose. Trediakovsky elaborated on both these points in his *New and Brief Method for Composing Russian Verse* (*Novy i kratky sposob k slozheniyu rossiyskikh stikhov*, 1735).

Along with the "Ode on the surrender of the city of Danzig," which had appeared a year earlier and to which was appended a "Treatise on the Ode" ("Rassuzhdenie ob ode"), the *New and Brief Method* offered a complete exposition of a system of poetic genres, a new model done in verse. For the first time in the history of Russian poetry a unified principle had been established for constructing a hierarchy of poetic genres corresponding to the relationship of each to the general idea of the new poetry. Moreover, the system of Russian poetic genres was laid out synchronically, with appropriate French examples for comparison and contrast. As a man of the Enlightenment and a rationalist, Trediakovsky held that the poetry of any nation should express the great truths of the new science which were obligatory for all enlightened countries, and that Russian poetry was fully capable of carrying out this historical task once it had grasped the "rules" and adopted a new versification system more appropriate to its nature and consequently more "correct."

Trediakovsky's book did not contain merely a practical "poetics": it was essentially an exposition of a new esthetic system, a programmatic statement for Russian classicism for half a century to come. Later attempts to elaborate this program in more detail added nothing substantial to Trediakovsky's ideas. The notion of the generality and universality of ideas which are identical for all nations and peoples, the conviction that poetic perfection could be achieved by imitating recognized models both ancient and modern, and that imitation could be successful only if the rules of each poetic genre were strictly observed: such were the basic ideas of the new esthetics, at the basis of which lay the notion of human nature as a good and rational product of rational upbringing shaped by the combined powers of science and art.

Since Trediakovsky failed to find a wealthy patron among influential men at court, by the end of the 1730s his position had become not simply difficult, but unbearable. In early 1740 he was beaten up at the instance of Minister Artemy Volynsky; he received moral satisfaction and material compensation only after Volynsky was executed later that year. During the 1740s Trediakovsky abandoned poetry in the proper sense to busy himself with stylistic problems and questions of Russian grammar. In the 1750s he saw several quite extensive literary projects through to fruition.

In addition to a prose translation of 1751 of John Barclay's (1582–1621) Latin novel *Argenis* (1621) – an apologia for powerful and enlightened monarchical authority – in the early 1750s Trediakovsky also did a verse translation of the Psalms, and the poem *Feoptiya*, a poetic version of Fénelon's popular treatise *Démonstration de l'existence de Dieu* (1713). Neither of these poetic works of Trediakovsky's was published during his lifetime, nor for a very long time after his death: *Feoptiya* first came out in 1963, and the *Psalms* have even now been published only in very small part.

In 1730, like Kantemir, Trediakovsky declined to employ what he considered the obsolete Church Slavic language in which all literary works in the Muscovite state had been written down to the period of the Petrine reforms; but in the 1750s he began composing verse in extraordinarily archaic, slavonicized, and deliberately syntactically convoluted language. His final and perhaps most significant poetic work – *Telemakhida* (1765), a verse translation of Fénelon's prose novel *Les Aventures de Télémaque* (1699) – became for contemporaries a laughing stock and symbol of artistic incompetence. Later generations of literary men – Radishchev, Gnedich and Pushkin among them – looked on *Telemakhida* differently: they admired Trediakovsky's innovation in employing a dactylotrochaic meter in his poem as a substitute and analogue for the ancient Greek hexameter, considering this an important contribution to the development of Russian verse.

Mikhail Lomonosov (1711–65) studied at the Slavic-Greek-Latin Academy in Moscow a few years before Trediakovsky matriculated there, and later was sent to Germany to study mining engineering. After spending five years in Germany, he returned in 1741 to Russia, where he quickly garnered renown as a poet.

The experience of the first decade of Russian poetry's problematic existence (if we calculate from 1729, the year Kantemir's first satires appeared) had not produced a satisfactory solution to the problem of poetic style as a whole. Basing it solely upon the bookish Church Slavic tradition meant Russian poets would be mere epigones of the Simeon Polotsky school. But the exclusive use of the colloquial language might have submerged the new poetry and its ideas, quite novel for Russian culture, in a sea of unregulated linguistic currents with its great variety of social and regional dialects.

A national literature required a unified, common, normalized literary language.

Lomonosov founded his program, not on the notion of a break with the past, as Kantemir and Trediakovsky had advocated in the 1730s, but rather on the idea of incorporating within poetry everything genuinely poetic and genuinely artistic which Russian literature from the eleventh to the seventeenth centuries had to offer.

"Russian verse should be written in conformity with the natural character of our language," wrote Lomonosov in his "Letter on the rules of Russian versification" ("Pismo o pravilakh ros-

siyskogo stikhotvorstva," 1739). It followed from this fundamental principle that Russian versification should draw upon the
actual Russian accentual system, "as our natural pronunciation
shows us quite easily."

As Boris Tomashevsky has brilliantly noted, the essence of
Trediakovsky's reform lay in his making the actual alternation of
stressed and unstressed syllables, or the genuine rhythms of the
language which had been totally ignored by the syllabic poets, into
the metrics of the verse. But Trediakovsky was reluctant to extend
his understanding of the nature of verse to all its categories.
Lomonosov, having absorbed the experience of purely tonic
German verse, boldly declared all of Russian verse to be tonic.
Lomonosov then buttressed the theoretical correctness of his solution of the problem with his own poetic works, his odes of the
1740s, through which the Russian ode in fact defined its own
essence.

The ode did not develop so variously or become such an important poetic genre in any European literature of the ones with which
the creators of modern Russian literature competed and compared
themselves as it did in Russian literature. The ode was usually
written on the occasion of some official event (a birthday, an
anniversary of the coronation of a monarch) and was presented in
the name of the Academy of Sciences. This accounts for its com-
plimentary tone, its inevitable and obligatory praise of whoever
was in power at the moment. The presence of such obligatory,
ritual praise later caused some to accuse Lomonosov of flattery and
unjustified exaltation of the ignorant, trivial and indolent Elizabeth, during whose reign from 1741 to 1761 most of his poetic
works were produced.

Those who castigated Lomonosov for his "unjustified praises"
of the monarch – Radishchev, among others – did not realize that
Lomonosov's eulogies as a rule display a rather conventional
character and relate not so much to the present as to the future.
Fundamentally, each of Lomonosov's odes is not so much a eulogy
as a program elaborating those political and cultural initiatives
which he thinks the Russian government should undertake if it
genuinely has the nation's good at heart. All the way down to
Alexander Pushkin's "Liberty" ("Volnost," 1817) and Kondraty
Ryleev's "To Ermolov" ("K Ermolovu," 1822) the Russian ode

preserved that peculiar character with which Lomonosov had endowed it: it always set forth a political program and was oriented toward the future.

The thematic and linguistic structure of the Lomonosovian ode provides a special and original form to embody its content. Lomonosov does not limit himself to a simple, systematic exposition of his ideas or of any specific political program. He wants the reader to respond emotionally, and not just logically, to his feelings and ideas. He seeks to stir up his reader's emotions, not merely to make an impact upon his intellect. It is precisely for that reason that he develops the ode's poetic idea through conflict, through a clash of two polarities, two opposing concepts. Most frequently this is a clash between tranquility and destruction, war and peace, ending with the ultimate victory of the powers of reason and good.

The author's attitude toward the universe he depicts in the ode is expressed not only, and not so much, through his own direct evaluation as through his clearly expressed view of the conflicting forces within the ode. The poet as ode writer appears before us as the sole personage within the poetic drama whose task it is not only to express his opinions of the conflicting forces, but also to provide an objective picture of the scale and intensity of the conflict itself.

The basic contradiction within Lomonosov's view of things stemmed from the fact that he saw the world as divided, which meant that it could not be reduced to a single, all-embracing principle. Thus, while he discovered harmony and beauty in nature deriving from the movement of atoms, within society he found only conflict and contradictory interests. This pessimistic view of man in society emerged with particular force in Lomonosov's poetry in the theme of enemies and the theme of a destructive environment hostile to man.

The spiritual odes which make up the first subdivision of Lomonosov's *Collection of Various Works* (*Sobranie raznykh sochineniy*, 1751) are arranged in the following order. First come translations of the first, fourteenth, twenty-sixth, thirty-fourth, seventieth, hundred forty-third, and hundred forty-fifth psalms, each of which is a monologue with complaints and petitions addressed by man to God. The complaints have to do with the imperfections of this world, the intrigues and slanders of one's enemies, while the petitions are for the punishment of those enemies, vengeance upon them for all their crimes and evil deeds. Next comes the "Ode selected from Job" ("Oda, vybrannaya iz Iova"), cast as a monologue addressed by God to man. This subdivision is capped by the "Morning" and "Evening meditations" ("Utrennee razmyshlenie," "Vechernee razmyshlenie"), in which nature's perfection and complexity are praised in the name of man. That same idea – though now advanced in God's name – constitutes the basic content of the "Ode selected from Job."

There is an obvious demarcation line between the translations of the Psalms and the three subsequent spiritual odes (the "Ode selected from Job" and the two "Meditations"). The psalms depict man in society; they contain a passionate and furious denunciation of the imperfections of human life as life in society.

Although the themes running through the translations of the Psalms have a certain autobiographical character, they nevertheless remain a poetic treatment of the fate of man in general, of man in his loneliness foundering in a hostile world of human passions, of man with a burning desire to eradicate evil in the world. Lomonosov sees this evil as afflicting everything, even the throne, where the ruler stands at the head of the social order. Over against society he counterposes not only his ideal of man and citizen, but also the world of nature, the limitless variety and magnificence of the cosmos in which all is subject to unified and rational laws, in which the harmony of the world order in general is not threatened by the selfish or treacherous plots of man, of a cosmos through the study and contemplation of which man recovers confidence in his own powers and (as Lomonosov as deist was persuaded) belief in God the Creator, in the original impulse given Creation by its Great Master.

Although during the 1740s Lomonosov wrote only odes, both eulogistic and spiritual, in the 1750s he took up other poetic genres. At the command of the Court he wrote two verse tragedies: *Tamira and Selim* (1750) and *Demofont* (1752). Of these only the former was ever staged, and it had no success with the public.

In 1752, on his own initiative, Lomonosov composed a didactic poem entitled *Letter on the Use of Glass* (*Pismo o polze stekla*), addressed to Ivan Shuvalov. In it he mounted a strong defense of

contemporary scientific thought and, most especially, of the helio-
centric view of the solar system, in opposition to the Holy Synod,
which at the time sought to suppress any references to Copernicus
and his discoveries. A few years later Lomonosov entered into an
open conflict with the Synod in coming to the defense of his
student Nikolay Popovsky, who by that time had become a
professor at the newly founded Moscow University. A talented
poet, Popovsky had done a verse rendering from a French translation of Alexander Pope's *Essay on Man*. The Synod refused to
permit the translation to be published, and so in 1756 Lomonosov
composed a satirical poem entitled "Hymn to the beard" ("Gimn
borode") in which he attacked obscurantist church officials quite
mercilessly and without mincing words. The "Hymn to the
beard" circulated widely in manuscript, infuriating Lomonosov's
enemies. The Synod submitted an official complaint against
Lomonosov to the Empress (although no name was attached to the
"Hymn") and requested that he be given over for trial to an
ecclesiastical court. But Shuvalov was a favorite of the Empress,
and his protection rescued Lomonosov from any further persecution. The translation of *Essay on Man* was published as well,
although the most "harmful" lines within it were replaced by
others composed by a censor appointed by the Synod.

Lomonosov's largest poetic project was the epic poem *Peter the
Great* (*Petr veliky*, 1760–1), which remained unfinished. Taking
Voltaire's *Henriade* as his model, Lomonosov planned to depict
Peter I's entire life, including his struggle against the opponents of
his reforms and the difficult wars which he brought to successful
conclusions. Lomonosov managed to write only two cantos of the
poem, but even in that state it served for many years as a model for
Russian poets interested in the epic genre.

During his own lifetime Lomonosov was recognized as a classic,
as the creator of modern Russian literature. Even his literary
enemies – headed by Sumarokov during the 1750s – admitted that
the Russian ode was Lomonosov's creation. And he remained the
most widely recognized authority in Russian literature down to
Pushkin's day, although in the late eighteenth century Radishchev
condemned him for flattering the tsars and Karamzin criticized his
prose as outdated.

Even Pushkin could not avoid drawing upon the Lomonosovian

legacy in his artistic quest. For example, in his poem *Poltava* he consciously employed the stylistic devices of the Lomonosovian eulogistic ode. And the Russian romantics of the 1820s and 1830s were attracted both by his philosophical positions and by his life, which they admired for its heroic quality. After Pushkin's day interest in Lomonosov's poetry subsided, although, as Yury Tynyanov has put it, "Lomonosov flared up here and there in the poetic currents of the nineteenth century." These "flare-ups" occurred most often when Russia undertook a war and stood in need of Lomonosov's odic verses for the glorification of military heroism. That was the case, for example, during the years of the Crimean War (1853–6), when odes began to be written once more, and also in 1904–5, during the Russo-Japanese War, when such well-known poets as Valery Bryusov and Vyacheslav Ivanov produced odes.

The October revolution of 1917 and the period of totalitarian stabilization initiated in the mid-1920s saw no diminution of interest in the Lomonosovian ode in modern Russian poetry. On the contrary, reality in its official forms and official interpretations reproduced the basic historical situation of Lomonosov's day: the Poet in the presence of Authority, in the presence of the Leader and Master.

Alexander Sumarokov (1717–77), unlike Trediakovsky and Lomonosov, came from the hereditary gentry and studied from 1732 to 1740 at the Cadet School for the Nobility, an elite training ground which prepared young aristocrats to enter government service, and principally military service.

While still at the Cadet School Sumarokov began writing verses, initially imitating Trediakovsky; later he became a disciple of Lomonosov's. Along with his literary ally, he went up against Trediakovsky in a competition involving the translation of the hundred-forty-third psalm (1743). Trediakovsky did his translation in trochaic meter, while Sumarokov and Lomonosov used iambs for theirs. All three versions were published anonymously in a single booklet, and readers were invited to decide which version was best.

Sumarokov acquired notoriety within Russian society of the 1740s for his love songs, which his youthful admirers set to music and sang in private gatherings. These lyrics not only brought

Sumarokov an audience: through them he came to head an entire group of poets who specialized in songs. Intended for a popular audience, and not designed as great literature, Sumarokov's songs offered the public a novel conception of love as a genuine, profound, and unconquerable passion, and not as some sort of drawing-room flirtation, as it was presented in Trediakovsky's songs and in his translation of *Journey to the Isle of Love*. In Sumarokov's hands the song as it were goes beyond the limitations of the genre to become an original sort of dramatic concentrate which foreshadows his verse tragedies.

The first of these tragedies, *Khorev*, appeared in 1747, a crucial year for Sumarokov. In that same year he published his "Epistle on poetry" ("Epistola o stikhotvorstve"), the first Russian verse treatise on poetics based on the model provided by Boileau for modern European literature in his *L'Art poétique*. For all its resemblances to European treatises on poetics, the "Epistle on poetry" took proper account of the Russian literary situation and of Russian literature's future requirements as Sumarokov understood them. For example, aside from the verse tragedy, the "Epistle on poetry" treats the song and its stylistics in some detail, and emphasizes the importance of the verse fable as well. With the appearance of this treatise on poetics modern Russian literature declared, essentially and formally, its adherence to the dominant literary trend of the times, i.e. classicism, although this term came to be used only later, during the romantic war against eighteenth century literary traditions. Sumarokov took from classical literary theory its insistence upon norms, its system of rules and taboos, a particularly strict view of genres, and a painstaking distinction among stylistic devices corresponding to the genre hierarchy, from the highest (the epic poem) to the lowest (the fable).

At the same time Sumarokov advocated the principle of stylistic simplicity for the majority of poetic genres as well as for literature in general. On this basic point Sumarokov parted company with Lomonosov both in theory and in practice. Their formerly friendly relationship became quite hostile, and a vicious literary polemic sprang up between them in which Sumarokov and the young poets who followed him were on the attack.

In this literary controversy Sumarokov drew sustenance from his increasing popularity, for which his verse tragedies were primarily responsible. Sumarokov wrote nine tragedies in all: *Khorev* (1747), *Hamlet* (1748; he was acquainted with the Shakespearean tragedy in Laplace's French translation), *Sinav and Truvor* (1750), *Artistona* (1750), *Semira* (1751), *Yaropolk and Dimiza* (1758), *Vysheslav* (1768), *Dmitry The Impostor* (*Dmitry Samozvanets*, 1771), and *Mstislav* (1774). The playwright sets six of his tragedies in Kievan times, i.e. from the tenth to the twelfth centuries, while the action of *Dmitry the Impostor* occurs in the early seventeenth century, and thus is considerably closer in time.

The structure of Sumarokov's tragedies, their plots, the fact that their heroes are chosen only from among rulers and great nobles, the absence of realistic details of everyday life, and the obvious distance of the events described from the time of writing – all these things link them to the well-established general European tradition of the classical tragedy from Racine to Voltaire and Gottsched.

Sumarokov's tragedies had an immense esthetic and ethical impact upon Russian society. What was new and astounding for the viewers of these tragedies was his system of ethical precepts, that world of moral principles in which his heroes lived, principles for which they were willing to fight and to die. The system of ethical precepts set out in Sumarokov's tragedies was strictly defined by the time of the action, by the epoch in which they took place as Sumarokov understood it. In all Sumarokov's tragedies on old Russian topics the action takes place in the pre-Christian pagan era. The characters in his tragedy speak only of the gods, of fate and its influence on human destiny. However, the gods do not interfere in human affairs in any specific way in Sumarokov's tragedies. When his heroes address the gods in monologues or dialogues, they do so merely for emotional reasons: the gods take no part at all in the "plot." Rather the principal determinant of the heroes' actions is ethics and morality, condensed in the concept of honor.

The fundamental source of the conflict in Sumarokov's tragedies is the struggle between love and honor in the consciousness and behavior of the heroes. The playwright depicts this struggle as the chief motivation behind their behavior.

This notion of purely ethical motivations for the ideas and actions of the Russians before the Mongol invasions to which Sumarokov gave such artistic expression became established in

Russian tragedy and survived there until the mid 1820s. In this sense Sumarokov regarded the time of Kievan Rus as a special and heroic era of the nation's history. Sumarokov and his followers by no means set out deliberately to modernize the past. On the contrary, they knew very well that Kievan Rus was fundamentally different from the Muscovite state of the early seventeenth century and from the Russian Empire of the mid eighteenth century. But their conception of the moral consciousness of the Russian nobility in the pre-Mongol period made that epoch seem especially attractive to them in the esthetic sense; they found in it especially appropriate material for their tragic art.

Although he confirms his hero's unvarying obligation to heed the requirements of honor rather than the summons of passion, Sumarokov nevertheless views and depicts passion as a force just as powerful as honor. In fact, if there were no passions there would be no tragedy either. For that reason Sumarokov's contemporaries spoke of him as "tender," that is, as a poet most interested in depicting love and not honor. And it was precisely that "tenderness" – the depiction of love – which contemporaries valued most of all in Sumarokov.

Sumarokov's early tragedies made such an impression on Russian society that Elizabeth's government decided to create a Russian theater in Russia: it was founded in 1756, and Sumarokov became its first director. But his prose comedies had no great influence. One finds in them neither complex personalities nor an especially complete depiction of contemporary society. Sumarokov wrote a series of pamphlet comedies in whose characters contemporaries could easily recognize the author's personal or literary enemies.

Sumarokov's admiring contemporaries bestowed the title of "The Northern Racine" upon him for his tragedies. His fables brought him no less notoriety, as well as the title of "The Russian La Fontaine." In the dispute over various types of fables which engrossed European theoreticians of this genre in the middle of the eighteenth century, Sumarokov consciously sided with La Fontaine, the advocate of situational and linguistic humor within the genre, and not moralism.

Sumarokov went even further than La Fontaine by eliminating in his fables the distinction between the poet and the reader. The fable-writer no longer looks down on ordinary mortals from the Parnassian heights, but is rather alongside them, nearby; he does not instruct and berate his readers, but rather shares with them his thoughts, ideas, and life-experience. The narrator in his fables is in the very thick of things, alongside his characters. This proximity to the world of the fable is a special and important fundamental innovation of Sumarokov's, a manifestation of his artistic original-ity in developing an approach to the fable which led to an entirely independent variant of the fable as La Fontaine created it. At the same time, as a fable-writer Sumarokov does not hesitate to evalu-ate the actions of his fictional characters, even though he formulates his evaluations through a comic exposure of his heroes in a manner analogous to that employed by Kantemir in his verse satires.

In both Sumarokov's fables and Kantemir's satires there emerges a clear opposition quite typical for the psychology of the eighteenth-century Enlightenment, an opposition on the one hand between the author as the proponent of a scientifically rational approach to the world, as a "philosopher" in the sense in which that word was generally used during the Enlightenment, and on the other hand an "irrational," confused world of social and human relationships lacking any sort of natural, rational, moral criterion of human behavior.

The peculiarity of this sort of consciousness – which the litera-ture of Russian classicism counterposed to that universal fair of worldly vanity – lay in the fact that this consciousness was a poetic one, one which produced its impact not merely by the power of "rational thought," as Sumarokov had said of Kantemir, but rather through the energies of art, through laughter and the comic expo-sure of literary characters in the satirical genres.

As Grigory Gukovsky, that remarkable investigator and special-ist on Sumarokov's art, has pointed out,

> Sumarokov's contemporaries, who used to extol his fables to the heavens and who considered his tragedies among the finest achieve-ments of European literature, have almost nothing to say about his per-sonal, intimate and primarily love lyrics [...] and [...] about that extensive segment of his poetry which he called "spiritual" verse.

It was precisely in his lyric verse that Sumarokov exploited the possibilities of Russian syllabotonic verse which had escaped Lomonosov's and Trediakovsky's notice. He wrote in every sort of meter, reproduced classical strophic forms, wrote free verse and utilized *dolniki* (accentual verse), to which Russian poets reverted only in the twentieth century. In the area of versification Sumarokov was far ahead not only of his own time, but of the nineteenth century as well.

At mid-century it became clear that the efforts of the few enthusiasts who had labored in the 1730s and 1740s had made Russian literature a notable feature of Russian cultural life. The founding of the Russian theater in 1756 also had an impact on literary development.

The fledgling theater faced an immediate problem requiring immediate resolution: it had to stage plays without waiting for new Russian playwrights to appear in Sumarokov's wake. There was only one solution: translate those items from the popular European repertoire suitable for the Russian theater-goer of the 1750s and 1760s. We know exactly what sort of things St. Petersburg theater-goers wanted from contemporary memoirs. One memoirist wrote in 1765: "One segment of the audience, a very small one, likes plays dealing with characters, sentimental and filled with noble thoughts, while the larger segment prefers merry comedies." This means that most theater-goers wished to be entertained, they wanted to laugh and be amused, and not especially to be instructed.

These demands upon the Russian theater determined its history for half a century, if we confine ourselves solely to the eighteenth century. The chief questions which the founders of Russian comedy had to answer were first formulated in the mid 1760s in a circle of theatrical people and playwrights gathered around Ivan Elagin (1725–94), who took over the directorship of the St. Petersburg theater from Sumarokov. This group advanced the idea of adapting foreign comedies to Russian tastes. The approach developed by the Elagin circle was the first step toward the creation of a national comedy repertoire as opposed to a translated repertoire designed solely for entertainment. These playwrights gathered their theoretical ideas and their practical examples from the achievements of west European literature, and especially the French stage. In the early 1760s Denis Diderot's views on theatrical reform were very popular with Russian translator-playwrights, who accepted his doctrine of the comedy as a "serious genre."

Vladimir Lukin's (1737–94) programmatic work *A Wastrel Reformed by Love* (*Mot, lyubovyu ispravlenny*, 1765), written and staged with Elagin's enthusiastic approval, was a first attempt in the genre of the serious comedy, then quite novel for Russian literature. Lukin's basic dramatic device was self-narration, a character's account of himself, his self-analysis, his conclusions about himself, which were supposed to serve both as an authorial evaluation and also to let the viewer know quite definitely and entirely unhesitatingly what attitude he should adopt toward a particular character in the play, depending on whether the latter's behavior has been moral or immoral.

So far as dramatic characterization is concerned, in principle there is no difference between positive and negative personages in Lukin's serious comedy; they are all equally dedicated to self-analysis and to providing information on their actions, intentions and feelings to the audience. Lukin's efforts at creating a serious comedy yielded no significant artistic results because in rejecting Sumarokov's proposals for the creation of social satire he also ceased to employ humor as a special form for expressing the author's attitude toward his depiction, toward the object of his satirical exposure.

Along with the theater, another new departure for Russian literature was prose in its various forms, since for the preceding quarter-century poetry had been dominant, and all the founders of modern Russian literature had been poets first of all. Sumarokov was not only the editor and almost the sole author of the first Russian literary journal, *The Industrious Bee* (*Trudolyubivaya pchela*, 1759), he also wrote for its pages satirical prose which built upon the varied accomplishments of French and German satirical journalism of the eighteenth century.

Following Sumarokov's example, in 1760 a group of teachers at the Cadet School began issuing a literary and didactic journal entitled *Spare Time Put to Use* (*Prazdnoe vremya v polzu upotreblennoe*). This same group of writers also set about the systematic translation of English and French novels. For example, Lukin and Elagin translated Antoine Prévost's *Adventures of Marquis G., Or, The Life of a Nobleman Who Abandoned the World* (1756–61), and Semyon Poroshin translated the same author's *English Philosopher* (1761–7). The novels of Henry Fielding, René Lesage, Pierre

Marivaux, and Daniel Defoe's *Robinson Crusoe* were also translated. These translated novels provided the Russian public with entertaining reading in addition to acquainting it with those works which had already become part of the culture of every literate person in western Europe.

The first Russian novelist, Fyodor Emin (1735–70), also began publishing in the early 1760s. He was a man of astonishing background and of quite varied literary abilities. His most popular works were the adventure novels *Inconstant Fortune, or Miramond's Adventures* (*Nepostoyannaya fortuna ili pokhozhdeniya Miramonda*) and *Themistocles's Adventures* (*Priklyucheniya Femistokla*), both published in 1763. The action of the novels takes place in various European countries as their heroes undergo most unexpected experiences before their creator brings everything to a happy ending. Emin's later novel, *Letters of Ernest and Doravra* (*Pisma Ernesta i Doravry*, 1766), was the first attempt at a Russian epistolary novel and an open imitation of Jean-Jacques Rousseau's *La Nouvelle Héloïse* (1761), which had caused a stir in Europe at that time. Following Rousseau's lead, Emin acquainted his readers with the preromantic devices of psychologism which were new to them.

Mikhail Chulkov (1734–92) was an actor and then a servant at court before he finally became a literary man; but his financial circumstances compelled him to seek government employment, in which he rose to a sufficiently high bureaucratic rank to obtain personal nobility.

In cooperation with Mikhail Popov, Chulkov in 1767 compiled a *Brief Mythological Dictionary* (*Kratky mifologichesky slovar*), which offered the Russian reader, in addition to information on the gods of antiquity, a pagan Slavic pantheon of divinities drawn up on the basis of rather unreliable sources and partially simply concocted by the compilers. But Chulkov's and Popov's Slavic gods continued to figure in Russian literature down to the middle of the nineteenth century.

In 1770–4, again in cooperation with Popov, Chulkov published the first printed collection of Russian songs, the *Collection of Various Songs* (*Sobranie raznykh pesen*), containing some 800 literary and folk songs.

But Chulkov's most important literary work was the unfinished

novel *The Comely Cook, or The Adventures of a Debauched Woman*
(*Prigozhaya povarikha ili Pokhozhdeniya razvratnoy zhenshchiny*,
1770), a remarkable instance of a Russian rogue-novel. The book's
heroine, Martona, fights a desperate battle against all obstacles in
an effort to achieve worldly success without taking account either
of the law or of religious morality (it should be added that the
entire world as Chulkov sees it has no use for morality either).
Stylistically Chulkov employs living colloquial Russian with a
generous smattering of proverbs and folk sayings. In this regard
Chulkov's prose is immeasurably better than the prose of Emin,
whom Chulkov attacked unsparingly in his journals at the time.

The invigoration of literary life was not confined to St. Petersburg. In Moscow the first Russian university, founded in 1755,
became the center of the city's literary life. In 1760 Mikhail Kheraskov – one of the university's curators and himself a poet of the
Sumarokovian school – followed the example of the *Industrious Bee*
and began publishing a literary journal entitled *Useful Entertainment*
(*Poleznoe uveselenie*, 1760–2). This was followed by *Free Time*
(*Svobodnye chasy*, 1763), *Innocent Exercise* (*Nevinnoe uprazhnenie*,
1763), and *Good Intentions* (*Dobroe namerenie*, 1764). For the most
part these journals published poetry, although they offered philosophical and moralistic prose as well. These were the journals in
which those poets who considered themselves Sumarokov's followers made their debuts; in subsequent years those poets defined
the course of Russian literature. In addition to Kheraskov the
contributors included Ippolit Bogdanovich, Vasily Maykov and
others who have left less noticeable traces in the literature of that
time.

The new literary vigor of the early 1760s was not only the result
of the fact that the new Empress Catherine II considered herself
obliged in the eyes of her subjects and of all Europe to nurture
enlightenment and literature, but also of the fact that she wished to
function as an author herself. Catherine compiled a treatise, mostly
on the basis of the writings of Montesquieu and Beccaria, in which
she expounded the general principles of Enlightenment thought.
She published the treatise anonymously in major European languages under the title *Instruction to the Commission for the Compilation of a New Code of Laws* (*Nakaz dlya komissii po sochineniyu
novogo ulozheniya*). This publication was supposed to demonstrate

to the whole of Europe that in Russia, reputed to be a despotic state, a body of legislation could be passed which would be founded on the basic principles of western political thought. The Commission for the Compilation of a New Code of Laws, created in 1767, which had elected representatives from all segments of the population except the enserfed peasantry, seemed to many at the time to resemble a Parliament.

As a means of distracting public opinion, in early 1769 Catherine began the publication of a satirical weekly entitled *All Sorts and Sundries* (*Vsyakaya vsyachina*). In this connection she not only urged Russian writers to follow her example, but for a certain period freed editors from preliminary censorship. And several literary figures did follow the example of *All Sorts and Sundries*, which was under the direction of Catherine herself with her State Secretary G. Kositsky as its editor. Mikhail Chulkov began publishing a weekly, *This and That* (*I to i syo*), a title which duplicated the title of Catherine's journal in a different form; Emin began publishing the weekly *Miscellany* (*Smes*) and the monthly *Hell's Post* (*Adskaya pochta*); Nikolay Novikov brought out the weekly *Drone* (*Truten*). The prose works appearing in the satirical journals of 1769 were simultaneously a new literary phenomenon for Russian culture and a new form for the expression of public opinion.

Nikolay Novikov (1744–1818) had the task of establishing satirical journalism's right to treat such social phenomena as had formerly been within the sole jurisdiction of the bureaucracy in Tsarist Russia, which could be considered only in secret and then only with the knowledge and approval of the authorities. The appearance of the *Instruction*, however, made it possible for journalists to discuss questions of political life which had earlier been forbidden.

The Deputies to the Commission of 1767, for all their sharp differences on other matters, were agreed on the necessity of basing social relations as they had developed by the 1760s on the firm foundation of legality. The majority of the speeches by the deputies display a consistent desire for its establishment. The situation of the peasantry was not examined in and of itself, but rather as part and parcel of the general problem of arbitrariness and illegality from which all social classes, including the nobility, suffered to some degree.

The chief object of satirical treatment in Novikov's *Drone* was the Russian nobility, which refused to adopt the ideas of the Enlightenment or yield even a fraction of its privileges. This approach of *Drone's* generated a critical response in the pages of Catherine's *All Sorts and Sundries*. Catherine was evidently quite displeased at this dispute, for in any case the *Drone* was compelled to cease its polemics with her journal, and in general Novikov could renew his journalistic activity only in 1772, by which time Catherine had already made her debut as a playwright with the anonymously published comedy *Oh Time! (O vremya!)*. The very fact that the ruler should be participating directly in literary life was an astounding novelty in Russia.

In dedicating his new satirical journal *The Painter (Zhivopisets)* to the author of *Oh Time!*, Novikov asserted that his struggle against the moral barbarism of the aristocracy coincided with the aims of the Empress as comedy writer.

When public opinion shifted as a consequence of the Pugachov rebellion of 1773–4, Novikov ceased to publish any further satirical journals, confining himself instead to collecting the best articles from *Drone* and *The Painter* for reissue in 1775.

At this point Novikov's purely literary activity ceased. In 1775 he became a Freemason and an adherent of Rosicrucianism. In Moscow, with the assistance of his ideological allies, he organized a publishing house called the "Typographical Company," an immense enterprise for the time. Translations for it were supplied by the so-called "Friendly Society," which he also organized. At this stage Novikov published journals of masonic content such as *Morning Light (Utrenny svet)* and *Evening Light (Vechernyaya zarya)*. He also leased the newspaper *Moscow News (Moskovskie vedomosti)* from 1779 to 1789, transforming its *Supplement (Pribavleniya)* into a serious political and general publication which paid considerable attention to the American revolutionary war. Novikov's activity as a book publisher through the Typographical Company reached a scale unheard of at that point in the history of Russian culture. He published textbooks, books on agriculture, medicine, pedagogy, philosophy and theology as well as books for children, including the first Russian children's magazine *Reading for Children (Detskoe chtenie)*, which became a literary training ground for Nikolay Karamzin, that outstanding writer and reformer of Russian prose in the 1790s. As he expanded his publishing activity Novikov also created a book trade within Russia on a European scale in every province of the enormous country by making arrangements with local merchants to sell his books on a commission basis.

The scale of the educational enterprise upon which Novikov and his associates had embarked aroused Catherine's displeasure from the very first. In 1792, having come to suspect him and the other Moscow Freemasons of political connections with the heir to the throne, the future Emperor Paul I, Catherine destroyed everything Novikov had created. He was himself arrested and sentenced to fifteen years imprisonment in the Shlusselburg Fortress. When Paul came to the throne in 1796 he freed Novikov, but by that time he was both ill and completely ruined financially.

Denis Fonvizin (1745–91), who emerged from the Elagin–Lukin circle, concentrated his energies on developing methods for the comic depiction of contemporary mores, in which sense he became a literary ally of Novikov and his *Drone*. His first successful play was the comedy *The Brigadier* (*Brigadir*, 1769), in which "right-thinking" characters – i.e. reasonable and virtuous personages – are not the exception but rather the norm.

Fonvizin compensates for the small numbers of these adherents of intellect and virtue in *The Brigadier* by giving them a powerful ally – laughter. It is precisely laughter which overcomes and conquers the forces of unreason presented in such variety within the comedy. Sofya and Dobrolyubov, the virtuous heroes, adopt a neutral attitude toward the other characters. They are concerned primarily with their own affairs, and the most they permit themselves are cautious mockery and contempt. There is absolutely no link between them and the other characters in the play, not even a conflict.

In *The Brigadier* Fonvizin utilized a great deal from the theory and practice of the serious comedy, but that did not cause him to reject laughter or to cease searching for comic depictions of various types of human behavior. The special circumstances under which the characters in *The Brigadier* are placed – the intertwining of family and romantic relationships – gave the author the opportunity to display various personages in one and the same comic situation, to make them participants in a common dispute. For example, the humor in one of these disputes (over the limitations of God's omnipotence) derives from a collision between the phraseology of high literary style and its interpretation in everyday terms, from a reinterpretation of formulas translated from the Biblical world of images and concepts into the world of contemporary Russian life, into an everyday context, into the sphere of military and bureaucratic discourse and notions of life in which the official "Table of Ranks" is viewed as something unchangeably established by divine sanction. In such fashion the author's relationship to his comedy is not "eliminated," but does acquire a considerable internal complexity. It is not only the comic characters who fall within its field of gravity, but also in many instances that "serious" world which they parody.

In *The Brigadier* the social problem concerns solely the social elite: there are no servants in the play, and all its heroes are members of the nobility. This gives Fonvizin an opportunity to analyze the moral condition of the governing class, whose internal situation led him to conclude that social morality should be based upon a system of values outside the individual. In *The Brigadier* the conflict between intellect and stupidity is realized theatrically in the form of a dispute among idiots. "Our" morals – that is, the morals which existed at the time among the Russian nobility and the necessity of providing some sort of national definition for them – are displayed through the grotesque depiction of the Gallomania of Ivanushka and the Councillor's Wife. Gallomania and the Helvetian morality of the young taken to idiotic extremes are shown as inevitable consequences of the absence of any moral standards at all among the older generation.

Fonvizin's skepticism and pessimism in *The Brigadier* are balanced by his comic treatment of all the characters, for the author's laughter provides the viewer with the support he needs in the conflict between intellect and stupidity transpiring on the stage.

Fonvizin's philosophical development in the period between *The Brigadier* and *The Minor* (*Nedorosl*, 1783) bears the imprint of the intellectual battles and the diplomatic activity in which he was engaged at the time along with Count Nikita Panin. The internal struggles within the court gave him the opportunity to study at first hand the structure and mainsprings of the absolutist system in the variant which Catherine developed to preserve her own power and to strengthen her social base.

To absolutism and its practical morality of "luck" and success Fonvizin sought to counterpose the independent intellect of the nobility and a morality of social service based upon a concept of the social necessity of religion as a basis for such morality. Fonvizin's viewpoint on the role of religion as a force for socialization, in which are to be found "all the power and security of human law," was first set forth in his "Discourse on the recovery of the Crown Prince Paul" ("Slovo na vyzdorovlenie velikogo knyazya Pavla Petrovicha," 1771).

Fonvizin conceives of education as the basic instrument for the formation of the socially engaged personality grounded in religion, which he assembles as a system in the form of a particular variant of deistic stoicism ultimately stemming from the masonic idea of the soul as a concentration point of moral concepts and habits of behavior which meet the criteria of social reasonableness.

His return to a recognition of religion's social utility and even its necessity brought Fonvizin into conflict with the Encyclopedists and caused him to seek support from such moderate representatives of the French Enlightenment as Antoine-Léonard Thomas and even from Fénelon's humanitarian religious views, resurrected during the French ideological battles of the 1770s.

On the basis of a visit to France soon after the failure of Anne Robert Jacques Turgot's reforms, Fonvizin decided that the Encyclopedists were just as responsible as the reactionary clergy for the profound social and moral crisis which afflicted the country then.

A comparison of Fonvizin's letters to Panin of 1777–8 with his "Discourse on permanent laws of state" ("Rassuzhdenie o nepremennykh zakonakh"), written in 1783, makes it possible to comprehend Fonvizin's social and historical conception, constructed on the basis of a comparative analysis of the contemporary cultures of Russia and the west, in this case represented by France. In the "Letters to Panin" and the "Discourse on permanent laws" Fonvizin examined the social structure of France from the viewpoint of the elite class: for him the determining element in evaluating the state of the nation was the moral condition of the nobility, which he regarded as the "nation's representatives," the only ones who expressed its consciousness. If we used the terminology of Russian thinkers of the 1840s, we might say that in the thinking portion of the nobility Fonvizin saw a "self-consciousness" raised above "substance," a group counterposed to the benighted, uneducated masses, the body of the nation, which was incapable of absorbing ideology and thought. Far from weakening that belief, the Pugachov rebellion simply confirmed Fonvizin's conviction that "substance" was incapable of playing a conscious historical role, of acting in a rational social sense.

As Fonvizin depicted her in his letters to Panin, France was in an at least unhappy, if not actually catastrophic, situation as a consequence of the moral paralysis of the French nobility, which had lost any sense of its obligations to the nation and was selfishly interested merely in exercising its own rights. Absolutism had been transformed into despotism, and the nobility transformed into the pillars of that despotism, into its obedient servants.

As a consequence, in *The Minor*, whose action occurs in a distant province far from the capital, the "court" theme – references to the highest authorities and their malignant influence on morality – receives no less attention than the play's basic action: the conflict between the Prostakovs on the one hand and Starodum and his associates on the other. The "court" with its named and unnamed personages, Prostakova's father and Starodum's father, is represented offstage. The offstage characters create within *The Minor* the historical and social perspective necessary for the development of the comedy's basic ideological conflict. What Nikolay Gogol once called the Prostakov family's "coarse bestiality" is contrasted within the comedy with the high level of gentry self-consciousness and morality displayed by Starodum and his friends. Starodum's behavior and that of his friends is always ideologically motivated; all their actions, feelings and thoughts are permeated by their sense of moral obligation. Their consciousness has an ethical quality, and their code of ethics is quite conscious.

The opposing party in *The Minor* – Mrs. Prostakova, her family and relatives – live and act independently of any ideology: in their minds custom and habit substitute for it. Prostakova espouses no theories, no ideological systems, no religion or morality. Her behavior on stage is determined by her emotional assessment of any given situation, not a rational one. Her behavior is not guided by the logic of self-consciousness but by a logic of instinct.

In *The Minor* the opposing sides in the conflict are both intellectually and morally so *unequal* that there really can be no quarrel between them. No more can there be a quarrel among Starodum's friends, for they are all united in their outlook, "sympathizers," and therefore their stage conversations are make-believe dialogues in which they elaborate but a single thought which they all take for granted.

The actual dispute which Starodum conducts on stage and over the heads of his friends is a quarrel with the universe of false conceptions. He defends social and ethical truths from the distortions to which they are subjected by contemporary aristocratic society. Starodum steps forward as judge and prosecutor of this universe of distorted conceptions, and his associates support him in that struggle. As Fonvizin sees it, in the area of thought and ideology Starodum can make contact only with his associates and with the theater audience, at least if we assume that it shares the viewpoint of the author of *The Minor*.

By their ironic rejoinders and questions Starodum and his friends provoke Mrs. Prostakova, Mitrofan and Skotinin to make comic statements which have consistently evoked laughter from the Russian theatergoer to this day. As Fonvizin saw it, this was the form the victory of Starodum and his friends should take, the victory of the world of high ideas and moral truths over the world of ignorance and dark instincts, the victory of culture over ignorance, of reason over the unbridled forces of empirical existence, of conscious service to the cause of the nation's social progress over the world of selfishness and animal instincts.

The comic elements in *The Minor* appear only in the words and actions of Mrs. Prostakova and her relatives. The words and behavior of Starodum and his friends are serious. The most they permit themselves beyond the boundaries of absolute seriousness is to ironize at Prostakova's expense. *The Minor* displays with special force one of the most acute internal contradictions to afflict the Russian Enlightenment of the second half of the eighteenth century: the contradiction between abstraction, the idealization of certain concepts, and the real world of concrete phenomena, between a static notion of a deductively defined system of the rational and the obligatory, and a dynamic idea of empirical reality which develops of its own accord. In *The Minor* laughter and

77

comedy are always with Mrs. Prostakova and Mitrofan, and are never to be found in Starodum. The wild, unchannelled displays of blind vital energy in Prostakova turn out to be immeasurably more significant than the elitist system of values to which Starodum wants to subject history and life. The conflict between thought and life in *The Minor* – the conflict between beautiful, rational thought and monstrous, ridiculous life – is resolved ideologically by the victory of thought; but theatrically, artistically, it is Mrs. Prostakova, and not Starodum, who gains the victory. Life with its brute force and particularity emerges the victor, and not thought with its rationality and abstraction. It is the lines of Mrs. Prostakova and Mitrofan, their sayings, that people now remember, and not Starodum's noble arguments. They remember Mrs. Prostakova's sayings because "nature" speaks in them, not a role which the author has assigned the character to play. When Mrs. Prostakova, enraged at the news that her servant girl Palashka is ill, shrieks: "She's delirious, the beast! As if she were a noblewoman!" – her words are humorous because they combine absurd stupidity (as if only a nobleman, a member of the gentry, could be delirious) with Prostakova's own straightforward conviction that she is quite correct. Prostakova is not playing on a stage: she lives in the world of her own understanding, and never emerges from it. She is always serious. That is precisely what makes her humorous. Perhaps without realizing it himself, Fonvizin perceived in Prostakova's "undirected force" some sort of constant within the national character.

Starodum's beautiful and noble ideas are excessively burdened by the utopian optimism of the period immediately preceding the French revolution. The system of values they contain is excessively elitist. The wild and directionless outbursts of blind vital energy from Mrs. Prostakova have not become outmoded either in their essence or in their form. Such is the irony of history, and that Fonvizin could not have foreseen.

In the 1760s and 1770s certain writers who had been disciples and followers of Sumarokov's in their youth continued to develop those same genres in which Sumarokov had gained general recognition (the tragedy and the fable) as well as others to which he had paid no attention – which latter included the epic poem. Vasily

Maykov and Ippolit Bogdanovich boast the greatest achievements in this genre.

Vasily Maykov's (1728–78) poem *Elisey, or Bacchus Enraged* (*Elisey, ili razdrazhenny Vakkh*) was, after Sumarokov's fables, the most important example of Russian satirical poetry, conjoining as it did the force of satirical exposure with a vivid depiction of the mores of the urban underclass in the Russian capital. In addition to specifically poetic traditions (Sumarokov's depiction of the "life of the common people" in his fables and Kantemir's descriptions of popular entertainments), Maykov also made use of the accomplishments of Russian satirical journalism of 1769–70, which had worked out methods of depicting social vices and disorders. As Maykov first conceived of the poem – the adventures of the cabdriver Elisey and his wife, who finally ends up in a prison for streetwalkers – were to have reflected a development in Russian life which many journalists and economists of the mid 1760s had written about and which was typical of the increasing complexity of economic relations in a system based on serfdom, when economic growth was limited by the amount of labor available and the labor market had to be supplemented by peasants temporarily permitted to work in the cities for wages. Maykov depicts this movement from the country to the capitals as an unavoidable shift from healthful, productive labor to a slough of drunkenness, vice and crime. That is the chief journalistic line promoted in *Elisey*.

The work's plot is constructed on another economic topic, one no less important at the time: criticism of the system of farming out the sale of alcoholic beverages which was introduced in Russia in 1767 and which proved quite ruinous for the basic mass of the population. The struggle against these tax-farmers is the plot center of the poem's "fabulous," fantastic portion, which takes place among the gods of Olympus. Bacchus dispatches the cabdriver Elisey to wreak vengeance upon the tax-farmers for raising the prices of vodka and beer.

In his poem Maykov defends the interests of the peasantry to the extent that they coincide with the interests of the landowners who manage their estates rationally, but no further. Consequently, although he derives condescending enjoyment from the feats of the valiant cabdriver in the taverns, winecellars, and other dens of

79

iniquity in the big city, he remains of the opinion that only agricultural labor under the reasonable supervision of the landowner can keep the peasant within the bounds of healthy morality and social discipline.

Along with Maykov's hero we are introduced to a St. Petersburg of a sort no one had ever written about in eighteenth-century Russian poetry before him. This was not the St. Petersburg of palaces, churches, and parks, but rather the city of lower-class suburbs, of taverns and of lock-ups. The poem described what later came to be called urban lowlife. The city's entire geography in the poem is defined by the location of one point or another in relation to popular drinking establishments.

Aside from its purely journalistic aims, Maykov's poem was composed for a particular literary purpose. It was the first attempt at an original "heroic-comic" poem of the sort Sumarokov had described in such detail and with such taste in his "Epistle on poetry." In it the adventures of drunken hotheads or a fight between the peasants of Zimogorets and those of Valday is described in the high style of the epic poem, made even more humorous by the fact that it is Elisey who is recounting all this.

Maykov preserves the distinctions between the high and low style, and the poem's humor derives partially from the collision between the two, but it was not only that which made his poem so popular in literature as late as the 1820s. Maykov's humor often derives from the narrator's attitude toward his narration, and not only from the contrast between elements from differing stylistic spheres. Pushkin esteemed Vasily Maykov precisely for his unconstrained authorial attitude, for his natural and ironic approach to his heroes and their adventures.

In the 1770s new literary trends, new esthetic notions, new poetic worlds revealed to the European literary consciousness by sentimentalism and preromanticism, evoked a double response from the representatives of Russian classicism. Some of them simply unequivocally rejected everything new: genres, themes, and especially the new understanding of the principle of feeling which sentimentalism advanced. Sumarokov adhered to this position to the end of his life, as did Maykov; nor was Novikov as author of satires inclined to make any concessions to the new trends. But others thought it possible to absorb certain elements of "foreign" literary programs, to assimilate them, to subordinate them to the esthetic system they had already worked out for themselves. This position was adopted in the 1770s by Kheraskov, Bogdanovich, Ivan Khemnitser, and – at the end of the decade – Derzhavin. This ability to assimilate and digest new ideas demonstrated the enormous vitality of Russian classicism, the extent of its powers and resources still in reserve.

As preromantic tendencies penetrated the poetry of Russian classicism, there appeared as early as the 1770s a more definite interest than earlier in the national character, the national history, and folklore. At this time there emerged the first poetic attempts at reproducing historic events and folklore images.

As far as contemporaries were concerned, the most remarkable poetic work of the 1770s was Mikhail Kheraskov's poem *Rossiada* (1779), which astounded them by the grandiosity of its conception and the resolve with which it was pursued. Before it appeared Russian poetry had not known an epic poem so monumental in its national and historical scope.

Mikhail Kheraskov (1733–1807) took as his poem's subject the destruction of the Kazan Khanate by Ivan the Terrible in the sixteenth century, an event which contemporaries rightly perceived as the first step toward Russia's transformation into a powerful and independent state of the east European plain. The struggle between Russia and Kazan in Kheraskov's poem is the struggle between east and west, between Christianity and Islam. Moreover, in the poem Islam is presented not so much as a thing in itself as it is as a collection of all possible pagan superstitions and prejudices, as a creature of the forces of darkness and evil generally. These forces of evil assist the Kazanians in their struggle against the Russian forces, summoning first unbearable heat (seventh–ninth cantos) and then sudden winter frosts in the middle of summer (twelfth canto). Over against the enchantments, wizardry and demonic forces aiding Kazan there are counterposed the Orthodox Russian troops, Christian saints and martyrs who conquer the evil powers of pagan Islam. Thus events in the poem develop as it were within two spheres: the human and the superhuman. But the forces of good and evil intervene quite directly in human affairs as well, assisting their favorites or suggesting that they take particular actions. Kheraskov followed Tasso's example in linking political decisions and military undertakings of the warring camps with the actions of "unearthly" forces.

But what interested contemporaries most of all in *Rossiada* was neither religion nor politics. Kheraskov was the first Russian poet to offer extensive landscape descriptions in his work. Thus Kher-. askov paints nocturnal landscapes before presenting the moon, quite an obligatory element in Young's or Ossian's night scenes.

However, in his concept of "feeling" Kheraskov adheres, generally speaking, to classical positions, continuing to regard individual psychology as the sum of certain traits of character which can be rationalistically defined and comprehended.

The influence of Kheraskov's poetic portraits on poetry of the late 1770s and early 1780s is particularly noticeable in Derzhavin's work.

Ippolit Bogdanovich (1743–1803) became one of the most popular Russian poets in the final decades of the eighteenth century thanks to his long poem *Dushenka* (1783, first published in 1778 as *Dushenka's Adventures*). Using as his plot the story of Cupid and Psyche, one of the most poetic myths in classical Greek literature, Bogdanovich sensed the popular, folktale basis of the stylized ancient narration found in Apuleius and in La Fontaine's reworking of it, and therefore made an attempt, quite bold for his time, to insert some motifs from Russian folktales into his poem. Bogdanovich transferred the story of Dushenka, with its ancient origin, onto Russian soil; it took firm root there. This is not merely a matter of folktale motifs and personages: as Maykov had done before him, Bogdanovich boldly introduced everyday life into his poem. Thus, as Dushenka sets off on her journey to be wed, her servants bear after her, in addition to her "crystal bed," all the objects which a noblewoman of that period would require:

Sixteen men, placing them on cushions,
Bore along the Empress's embroidery and bobbins,
Which the Empress-mother had herself placed there,
Toilet articles for the journey, combs and pins,
And all sorts of other items of necessity.

All these scattered details of everyday Russian gentry surroundings link the poem with life to some degree. What happens within it ceases to be a folktale; the abstract personages of idylls and eclogues give way to Dushenka's captivatingly human image. Bogdanovich succeeded in breathing life into the conventional figure of La Fontaine's Psyche by presenting her as a living, modern girl from a gentry family of the middling sort. By her naturalness of behavior and liveliness of character Dushenka surpassed everything created in Russian literature before Zhukovsky's "Svetlana" and Pushkin's *Ruslan and Lyudmila.*

In his poem Bogdanovich adopts a characteristically ironic attitude toward his subject, toward the events he describes. He does not cease to be ironic even when his heroine is in peril or finds herself in difficult situations. The smile always on his lips as he recounts Dushenka's joys and sorrows, his jocular attitude, all create in the reader's mind a special "literary" image of the author, who becomes a character within the work: indeed that image may replace the real figure of the poet in the consciousness of later generations of readers. In *Dushenka* the poet Bogdanovich presented himself as the bard of the beautiful and the harmonious, but he did not endow the image of the poet (his own image) with any particular specificity or a historical perspective. The author of *Dushenka* lives solely in the world of beauty and poetry. Bogdanovich's poem was one of the fullest embodiments of Russian classicism's aspirations at the "esthetic" stage of its development.

The best-known playwrights of the Sumarokov school – Yakov Knyazhnin (1742–93) and Nikolay Nikolev (1758–1815) – made certain essential changes in the artistic structure of the tragedy and endowed it with a directly social resonance which had been missing earlier.

If Knyazhnin in *Vladimir and Yaropolk* of 1772 had worked out the problem of honor entirely in the spirit of early Sumarokovian tragedy, then in *Rosslav* (1783) he broke with his mentor's approach and took as the basic source of dramatic conflict the idea of the common good embodied within patriotic forms. That conscious civic patriotism which the "great soul" of the chief hero of Knyazhnin's tragedy exhibits is contrasted not only to various sorts of egotism and selfishness as embodied in Khristiern and Kedar, but even to such wholly positive heroes as Lyubomir, the Russian ambassador to Sweden, and the Russian prince who is prepared to sacrifice the territory he has taken from the Swedes in order to save Rosslav. Rosslav's firmness in all the trials to which fate subjects him may be explained by the special concept of honor by which he is guided. His notion of honor is quite different from that which inspired the heroes of Sumarokov's tragedies: as Rosslav sees it, patriotism consists of unconditional and absolute dedication to the fatherland, that is Russia as the fatherland, and not to a prince or to the authorities.

The philosophy of heroism which permeates Knyazhnin's entire tragedy is not founded on any well-defined historical conception, as in Sumarokov, but rather on an emotional and psychological image of the Russian citizen-patriot. As a consequence, the Russian political system which Rosslav represents so brilliantly is depicted rather fuzzily in the tragedy. It is indicated that Russia has already cast off the Mongol yoke, but no more precise definitions than that are given. The basic content of the dispute which continues for the entire course of the tragedy between Rosslav and all the other characters, whether positive or negative, is an emotional and psychological conception of the essence of the national character. Rosslav wishes to die for his fatherland and thus demonstrate his right to be called a citizen of Russia. The other characters in the play – for various reasons and from different points of view – seek to deflect him from his intention. Consequently the dispute is always over the same thing, although the negative heroes (the tyrant Khristiern and the traitor Kedar) fail to comprehend Rosslav's aspirations, while the positive heroes understand them but think one need not always be so morally rigid.

The tragedy's transformation from an internal to an external dispute, the displacement of interest in the hero's self-analysis by the depiction of a struggle which occurs outside him, led to a revision of the tragic style. Dialogue among characters was transformed into a dialogue between the hero and the audience over the heads of those to whom the hero seemed to be speaking directly.

Knyazhnin's eighth and last tragedy, *Vadim of Novgorod* (*Vadim Novgorodsky*, 1789), had a peculiar history. Knyazhnin took as his subject a rather vague legendary account – but quite a popular one in the eighteenth century – about a ninth-century conflict between the Scandinavian Prince Rurik and the Novgorodians under the leadership of Vadim, who fought in defense of his city's ancient liberties. In Knyazhnin's tragedy Rurik overcomes Vadim because the people are weary of the anarchy into which the aristocrats have plunged free Novgorod, and opt for peace and order under a tsar's firm authority. In view of the political tension which gripped Russia after the outbreak of the French revolution, Knyazhnin declined to have *Vadim of Novgorod* staged. It was first published only in 1793, after his death. However, terrified by the Jacobin dictatorship in France, Catherine regarded Knyazhnin's play as quite dangerous, and so the entire edition was destroyed ("burned at the executioner's hand"). It was reprinted only in 1871.

Nikolev also sought methods of reviving tragedy, but they did not coincide with the ones Knyazhnin adopted. Instead of Rosslav the heroic patriot, Nikolev depicted contemporary man as the victim of spiritual division. Nikolev is interested in the philosophical and political content of the conflicts of his day; he felt under no obligation to seek any historical explanation for them, and was satisfied with the same sort of communication with his audience and the same sort of system of declarative aphorisms with which we are familiar from Knyazhnin's plays.

Gavriil Derzhavin (1743–1816), the major Russian poet of the eighteenth century, began to follow the basic lines of poetic currents of his day only toward the end of the 1770s: it took him more than fifteen years to discover his own personal poetic approach. During the years when his younger contemporaries were publishing book after book, occupying prominent places on the Russian Parnassus, and being rewarded with detailed and approving estimates in Novikov's *Preliminary Historical Dictionary of Russian Writers* (*Opyt istoricheskogo slovarya rossiyskikh pisateley*, 1772), the first survey of Russian literature, Derzhavin had to be content with a rather dubious description of him as the author of satirical poems directed against the Guards regiments. Derzhavin did not absorb the theory and practice of Russian poetry through personal study with an older poet or recognized teacher; rather he had to make his own way among the complexities of contemporary literary currents, to test his powers in various genres and approaches, imitating Lomonosov at some times, at others Sumarokov. He sought answers to the questions which concerned him in the writings of Lomonosov and Trediakovsky which were available to him as well as in the works of popular classical theoreticians of the eighteenth century.

Derzhavin's attitude toward the published works of contemporary Russian poetry was molded by his theoretically developed view of poetry as a collection of exemplary works in all genres. The beginning poet needed only to study these models diligently and then imitate them.

The careful study of various exemplary works in the lesser genres did not prevent Derzhavin at the same time from writing odes and epistles in which he willy-nilly followed Lomonosov's lead, without concealing his dependence on the "Russian Pindar." But despite all his stubborn attempts to grasp its secret, Derzhavin never mastered the Lomonosovian "high style." On occasion Derzhavin seemed to feel that essentially there was no secret to it at all, and that one could write an ode in the high style even without using its Lomonosovian form.

At the end of the 1770s Derzhavin found himself as a poet, and selected another path in poetry, not the one Lomonosov had blazed. His new poet friends Nikolay Lvov, Vasily Kapnist, and Ivan Khemnitser contributed considerably to Derzhavin's poetic self-definition. They kept up with all the latest happenings in European literary and artistic life, and were brimful of the most daring literary enterprises. After Sumarokov, Khemnitser (1745–84) was the most prominent fable-writer in Russian literature of the 1770s: he published his first collection of fables in the same year of 1779 which marked the beginning of Derzhavin's own independent literary career. *Fables and Tales by N.N.* (*Basni i skazki N.N.*), as Khemnitser entitled his collection, was innovative within the confines of the genre.

In their fables Sumarokov and his followers mocked particular cases of the violation of rational and moral norms. The characters in Sumarokov's fables are sinful and stupid, although the laws which govern the world are rational and correct. In Sumarokov's world humor stems from a collision of the ridiculous, irrational and unnatural with the ideal of the rational and correct which exists in the writer's consciousness.

The world of Khemnitser's fables is quite different, with different interrelationships between ideas and things. Khemnitser does not attack particular cases of stupidity and unreason, but rather the general absurdity of things and the impropriety of life's structure overall. Khemnitser's fables are not so humorous as Sumarokov's, since their satirical targets are mostly widespread human traits,

shortcomings and habits common to all peoples and to all humanity. Consequently, Khemnitser's plots are a great deal less russified, and their social aspects less specific. His characters are often
"rich men" and "poor men," without any clearer definition of
their social origins. The satirical aim of Khemnitser's fables is to
expose the absurdities of human society as a whole from the
viewpoint of the progressive philosophical thought of the age. He
seeks to point out to his readers their "delusions" and errors, to put
across the truth in place of false conceptions of life: this is the task
which Khemnitser as fable-writer sets himself, and to which he
subordinates both the thematics and the stylistics of his works.

Khemnitser has no interest either in individualizing the speech of
his characters or in endowing them with any sort of individual
characteristics. All his characters speak one and the same fully
literary language. The authorial text in Khemnitser's fables stylistically is quite similar to the speeches of his characters. It is just that
the author is better informed than his heroes, a good deal is
obvious to him about which his characters cannot even guess.
Khemnitser very scrupulously avoids humorous incongruities and
unnatural combinations of human and animal traits. The animals
in the world of his fables in all their actions do not go beyond
general human limitations, and indeed there is very little of the
animal in them.

In the late 1770s Derzhavin destroyed the solemn ode's taboo on
the personal and the biographical. He appears in his odes addressed
to tsars not only as a poet, a singer of grandeur and beauty, but also
as a person, as a government bureaucrat, a family man, a victim of
the persecutions of high officials who dislike him, a fighter for
truth and justice both social and individual.

As Derzhavin sees it, poetry has a double countenance. The poet
"sings" "spiritual praises to the Creator" and "sings of" "good
[...] tsars," i.e. acts just as Lomonosov and all the other ode-
writers who followed in his footsteps had acted: he praises Catherine just as Lomonosov had praised Elizabeth.

After developing his own stylistic approach at the end of the
1770s, Derzhavin constructed his religious and philosophical odes
on quite different bases than had Lomonosov. He found no inspiration in the vast horizons offered by natural science in the
eighteenth century which Lomonosov had helped to create. The

basic question for which Derzhavin sought answers under the guidance of his religious convictions was that of man's fate in the universe and the degree to which it was predetermined.

In his ode of 1779 "On the death of Prince Meshchersky" ("Na smert knyazya Meshcherskogo") – ordinarily considered by Russian critics his finest poetic work – Derzhavin meditates on the relationship between time and eternity, on the irreversibility of time's flow and the dependence of individual existence upon it. Although Derzhavin was not a Mason, he included in this ode several motifs from *Night Thoughts* by Young, an author much esteemed by the Russian Masons of the Novikov circle. By means of this ode Derzhavin initiated a new theme in Russian poetry, becoming the teacher and forebear of Zhukovsky and Tyutchev.

In his ode "God" ("Bog," 1784) Derzhavin gave a poetic depiction of the idea of the Great Chain of Being, one common to all of religious and philosophical thought in the eighteenth century. Derzhavin believes that man as an individual, that man in general outside his historical and social context, is spiritually capable of overcoming his physical insignificance and drawing near to the Godhead, or even possibly coming to resemble the Divinity.

In these odes Derzhavin's poetic intuition took him beyond the limits of dogmatic Orthodox theology, but the criticisms of the theologians had no effect upon their enthusiastic reception by readers, either during the poet's lifetime or afterwards.

The poet as Derzhavin conceives of him expresses the living feeling of the nation – the "echo of the Russian people," as Pushkin would put it later – but he speaks not only in the name of the people or the nation but in his own name as well. The world of the exalted as it were diminished to create space in Derzhavin's work for the poet's private life, for his personal and professional relationships.

Thus in Derzhavin's poetry we find, on an equal footing with the traditional ideal of moral stoicism and dedication to virtue, the Horatian and epicurean ideal of the golden mean and of moderation in one's demands upon fate; in short, all the atmosphere of personal life with its domestic joys and consolations.

Of course "domestic," "everyday" themes could not expel the grand themes of citizenship, politics and the state from Derzhavin's poetry: they developed in his writing in complicated ways, now prevailing, now retreating to peripheral verse of an incidental character. The prevalence of personal motifs over general political and moral ones, observable in Derzhavin's poetry between the 1770s and the 1780s, beginning in the early 1780s and down to the mid 1790s yields to a new predominance of the solemn ode and the themes of historic events and political questions associated with it. After the mid 1790s personal and domestic subjects again come to the fore in Derzhavin's poetry: they are reflected in a particular collection, the *Anacreontic Songs* (*Anakreonticheskie pesni*) of 1804, although Derzhavin still considers it his definite duty to react to the course of contemporary political and military events.

Derzhavin received governmental recognition – i.e. Catherine's personal favor – upon the publication of his "Ode to Felitsa" ("Oda Felitse," 1782), which was dedicated to the Empress. In this ode Derzhavin violated all the canons of the genre by having Felitsa – or Catherine – behave like an ordinary mortal: she walks "on foot," eats, reads, writes, treats people nicely, and enjoys jokes. The significance of the Empress's simplicity and business-like behavior is emphasized by the contrast between the modesty of this great stateswoman who cares only for the "happiness of humankind," and the emptyheaded, egotistical behavior of her high aristocrats, their feasts and entertainments and the luxury of their dress, as well as by the contrast between the most ordinary amusements of the common people (boxing matches) and woodwind music, the most refined fancies of musical art in the eighteenth century.

However, despite the variety of aristocratic tastes, all the "murzas" (high officials) in "Felitsa" lack any serious civic interests and ideas: even those lines in which Derzhavin speaks of Potyomkin's political plans are ironic and present them more as the amusements of an idle mind than the thought of a statesman.

Against the background of Felitsa's modest way of life and businesslike activity, the idealized image of the Empress which Derzhavin creates is strengthened even further by an account of her everyday cares, which encompass the entire gamut of statesmanship, all the nation's needs. As Derzhavin depicts her, Felitsa does not demand civic heroism of her subjects, or any stoic negation of one's personal interests. The Derzhavinian formula "be a human being on the throne" in "Felitsa" turns out to mean that Catherine should condescend to human weaknesses and short-comings and not be a rigorous moralist.

The boundary between a "hero" in Lomonosov's poetic vocabulary, between a great man as bearer of the idea of enlightened absolutism and an ordinary mortal or common man, ceases to be eternal and unchangeable in Derzhavin. It vanishes because Derzhavin demands of the tsar, the ruler and lord, that before all else he recognize the legitimacy of not only the nation's interests as a whole, but of each individual in particular (what we would now call human rights).

Since he shared what was then a widespread faith in the Empress's talents and abilities, Derzhavin tried to show that her purely human traits provided the base for Catherine's positive qualities as a ruler. His Felitsa copes so successfully with her governmental obligations because she is herself a human being and comprehends every human necessity and weakness. It was precisely Derzhavin who created the poetic legend of Catherine, a legend which sustained itself in the Russian cultural consciousness for nearly a century.

In "Felitsa" and other odes linked to it ("The Murza's vision" ["Videnie murzy"], "To Reshemysl" ["Reshemyslu"]) Derzhavin discovered a new vantage point from which to view the high aristocrats around the Empress. Its novelty consisted of a combination of abstracting people and events (the fairytale world of the east) and concretizing the immediacy of hints and details of the everyday world. Contemporaries had no difficulty in recognizing which individuals the poet was writing about. Derzhavin's odes on the high nobility incorporated a system of hints and allegories brilliantly developed by Russian journalism of 1769–72, and especially in Novikov's journals.

In Derzhavin's long odes such as "The Image of Felitsa" ("Izobrazhenie Felitsy," 580 lines), "The Waterfall" ("Vodopad," 444 lines), "On the Capture of Izmail" ("Na vzyatie Izmaila," 380 lines), or "On Perfidy" ("Na kovarstvo," 320 lines), one can clearly perceive Derzhavin's break with the Lomonosovian idea of the high style: Derzhavin defined his stylistic principle as one of "equal choice of words." In "Felitsa" and the cycle of odes connected with it Derzhavin allocated a definite but rather strictly defined place to the low or colloquial style. The poet who is supposed to be the narrator in "Felitsa" is a "murza" who uses words and expressions which until then could have been encountered only in humorous poetry or in such genres as the fable and the heroic-comic poem.

And yet the system of "three styles" (high, medium, and low) which Lomonosov had created and which had become the basic stylistic rule of Russian classicism is still intact in Derzhavin, even within the bounds of a single genre. The hierarchical ranking of poetic subjects – from high to low, from God to worm – remains unquestioned even in Derzhavin. Only the poet's approach to reality has changed. The further Derzhavin's art develops, the more esthetic considerations determine both his choice of subjects and his stylistic treatment of them. With Derzhavin's poetry Russian classicism enters the highest phase of its development – the point at which esthetic principles become decisive, whereas earlier everything had been subordinate to politics and ethics.

In his odes of the 1780s and 1790s Derzhavin evaluated people and events from a viewpoint which seemed to him to express the general opinion of the nation: among the leaders of Russian society he sought those dedicated to duty and enthusiasts for the "common good." After the mid 1790s Derzhavin withdrew more and more into the poetry of personal life. He became increasingly terrified at the gap between his ethical ideals and contemporary political battles.

3

THE TRANSITION TO THE MODERN AGE: SENTIMENTALISM AND PREROMANTICISM, 1790–1820

From 1790 to 1820 the Russian Empire underwent tumultuous years beginning with the immediate aftermath of the French revolution, continuing through the rise of Napoleon and the Napoleonic wars which saw the French invasion of Russia in 1812 and the allied occupation of Paris, and ending with the intellectual ferment of the movement which would culminate in the abortive Decembrist uprising of 1825. No great fraction of the nation's energies at this time could be directed toward literature.

In literary terms this period begins with a work which faithfully reflects the political tensions of the time of the French revolution – Radishchev's *Journey from St. Petersburg to Moscow* – and ends with a narrative poem, Pushkin's *Ruslan and Lyudmila*, which expresses well the romantic sensibility then on the verge of a short-lived cultural triumph. In the intervening thirty years, a culturally chaotic period, a major alteration occurred in literature's approach to the world. As Arthur Lovejoy has so aptly put it, during the years of neoclassicism and the Enlightenment intellectuals looked to a single standard, "conceived as universal, uncomplicated, immutable, uniform for every rational being." But then a "momentous" shift in outlook occurred, and was completed by the time of the romantic period, "when it came to be believed not only that in many, or in all, phases of human life there are diverse excellences, but that diversity itself is of the essence of excellence." In short, the change in emphasis was from a unitary human standard to a belief in diversity for its own sake.

Where the classical mind had excluded individual experience and personal emotion from literature, writers of the sentimental era made a fetish of individual sensibility; where the classical eye had seen only events important to society as a whole, the sentimental author tended to concentrate on personal idiosyncrasies and even individual aberrations. The individual rather than society came to be at the center of literary perception: if in the classical period in the standard conflict between love and duty the latter must prevail, in the sentimentalist epoch love must win through if the entire conflict were not reduced to meaninglessness or shown to have been illusory in the first place. Thus, though Derzhavin was firmly grounded in the neoclassical tradition, his poetry of the turn of the nineteenth century required extensive notes for its comprehension, for he wrote of very personal experiences of which others could not be expected to know except by being told.

Amid such change there were also constants. One of them was the primacy of poetry: the reigning poetic genres altered, as the ode faded from view to be replaced by such shorter and less specific genres as the elegy, but poetry maintained its positions fairly well against the competition of prose, and would continue to do so until the end of the romantic period. A second constant was the linkage between writers and the state. Karamzin, for example, after a brilliant early career as poet and prosewriter, was appointed official historiographer, a position which enabled him to produce his classic *History of the Russian State* and also provided him access to the sovereign as an advisor. In the early part of the century Derzhavin was appointed Minister of Justice for a time; later on, during the Napoleonic invasion, Alexey Shishkov turned from his literary and linguistic activities to compose patriotic manifestoes to rally the Russian people against the invader. Zhukovsky was close to the royal family as tutor and advisor. Even Radishchev, jailed as a radical at the beginning of this period, was released after Paul I came to the throne and later for a while held a position of some governmental responsibility. Along with this, however, there appeared signs of political disaffection among writers, a disaffection which would bear fruit in the succeeding romantic period.

A phenomenon peculiarly characteristic of this period was the existence of extensive formal and informal literary circles, which sprang from Russian writers' sense that they were engaged in a common cultural enterprise. The most prominent such circle was the "Colloquy of Lovers of the Russian Word," which met at Derzhavin's home under Shishkov's leadership for some years. It was countered by the "Arzamas" literary society, which, though very informal, included many writers whose names are now writ large in the history of Russian literature. Authors were well acquainted personally with one another; they engaged in polemics which helped them to sharpen their own intellectual positions; they could be reasonably certain that whatever they wrote would have a resonance in cultured Russian society, even though that society was not very extensive. These personal contacts were important in preparing the ground for the flowering of nineteenth-century Russian literature which would begin with the work of Alexander Pushkin.

IN THE MIDDLE of the eighteenth century, approximately, new literary trends began to contest the place of classicism. This literary movement which had once been so powerful and influential began to abandon its former positions not only within writers' artistic consciousness, but also in the minds of readers.

It was natural that literary trends should arise in opposition to classicism, trends which viewed life in a different way in a country in which drama had never surrendered to the classical system and in which the traditions of the novel, a genre which classical theoreticians rejected, had long been well developed: in England, in the land of Shakespeare and Marlowe, of Ben Jonson and Smollett.

English literature nurtured a concept of personality quite alien to the one predominant under classicism. Classicism viewed man not so much as a personality, but as the bearer of a particular idea or feeling; it regarded the individual as a molecule within a particular hierarchically constructed social system (a hero in a tragedy, a gentle shepherd in an idyll, a military commander or ruler in the ode, and so forth).

The pioneer in the new depiction of man was Samuel Richardson, whose famous epistolary novels *Pamela, or Virtue Rewarded* (1740) and *Clarissa, or The History of a Young Lady* (1747–8) offered detailed depictions of the inner worlds of their heroes, ordinary people concerned with romantic experiences.

Laurence Sterne published two interconnected novels – *The Life and Opinions of Tristram Shandy, Gentleman* (1760–7) and *A Sentimental Journey Through France and Italy* (1768) – in which he undertook a painstaking investigation of the slightest spiritual experiences, feelings and sensations of his characters. He brought his analysis to perfection. Sterne's second book indeed bestowed its name upon an entire literary movement: sentimentalism. Needless to say, in actuality the formation of sentimentalism was quite complex, and involved many works of world literature, including such masterpieces as Rousseau's *Nouvelle Héloïse* (1761) and Goethe's *Die Leiden des jungen Werthers* (1774).

In the literature of sentimentalism man is viewed and depicted as an individual, as an independent personality of value in and of itself (and not acting under the influence of duty or its surroundings), defining its own fate and behavior (thus Sterne's heroes pay little attention to the rules of society but live according to their whims, their moods, attending to their various hobbies). Such an individual often turns out to be lonely and feeble in the threatening world around him: the reverse side of the coin of constant attention to man's inner life is man's fear of the world about him. A sense of horror at the thought of inevitable destruction, a feeling that the world was doomed, and fear of death were embodied very adequately in Edward Young's *The Complaint, or Night Thoughts on Life, Death, and Immortality* (1742–5). Gloomy depictions of the harsh northern landscape with its mists, rain and storms as well as melancholy descriptions of bloody battles, death and despair are to be found in the well-known *Poems of Ossian* (1762) by James Macpherson.

The *Poems of Ossian* reflected a heightened interest in all national cultures (and not just in ancient culture, as under classicism) which was characteristic of romanticism's early stages. For the romantics the culture of each nation within the context of other world cultures was just as particular and individual as was each human personality. As a consequence the romantics were consistently interested in the folklore and the history of their own people and also in the art of all other peoples and tribes, including primitive and undeveloped ones.

If sentimentalism treated the peaceful and slightly idyllic existence of the individual, preromanticism is generally seen as dealing with the exploration of man's tragic sense of the world. Thus preromanticism finds its expression in the description of death, natural catastrophes and other such things. Naturally enough, these two currents often intertwine in the work of a single author and coalesce with each other.

These developments in European literary life which we have just described so briefly and schematically began to have an impact on Russian cultural life toward the end of the eighteenth century. Richardson's novels were translated into Russian in 1790, and Sterne was translated at the same time. Young's *Complaint* was widely read as early as the 1780s, at which time there also appeared the first complete translation of that book done by Alexey Kutuzov, Radishchev's friend and a well-known Freemason. The Russian reader had become familiar with Ossian's works by the very end of the 1780s and the early 1790s, and in 1792 there appeared a complete two-volume prose translation of Ossian from the French. The translator was the talented poet Ermil Kostrov, who followed the latest literary trends very closely. The publication of his translation was a literary event at the time, and all later interpreters of Ossian drew upon it, including the young Alexander Pushkin.

We should also note that many Russian readers (writers and poets among them) became acquainted with contemporary preromantic literature in the original language – although not many people knew English in Russia at that point – and in French translation. Thus it is not surprising that preromantic and sentimentalist trends had acquired considerable resonance in Russian literature by the end of the 1780s and the 1790s. An outstanding figure in the development of Russian sentimentalism and preromanticism as well as the history of Russian literature as a whole was N. M. Karamzin.

Nikolay Karamzin (1766–1826) was born on his father's estate in the Simbirsk province on the middle Volga. He received a modest education at home before entering Professor Johann Schaden's boarding school in Moscow in 1778–81, where courses were given on the university level. During the last year of his studies Karamzin attended lectures at the university. Upon completing his boarding school course he was a well educated young man, with a knowledge of French and German.

Being in no position to continue his education, Karamzin was compelled to enter military service with a Guards regiment, although his military service was not very lengthy and was interrupted by frequent leaves. In 1783, upon his father's death, Karamzin left military service and returned to Simbirsk, where he began to write in the free time remaining to him after an active social life of balls and cardplaying. The eighteen-year-old Karamzin was strongly influenced at the time by a meeting with Ivan P. Turgenev, a prominent Freemason and director of Moscow University, who encouraged the talented young man to dedicate himself to serious intellectual work and received him at the "Golden Crown" masonic lodge.

In 1785 Karamzin moved to Moscow and joined the Friendly Literary Society, headed by the famous Freemason and promoter of Enlightenment ideals Nikolay Novikov. At this point Karamzin began a serious literary career, translating Gessner, Haller, Shake-speare, and Lessing, editing the journal *Reading for Children* along with his friend Alexander Petrov, corresponding with Lavater, and in 1789 setting out on an extensive trip abroad. His journey was apparently undertaken with the approval of his masonic friends, for they drew up a plan for it and may well have supplied him with a certain amount of money, even though Karamzin's masonic interests were never very profound and he parted company with them after his return.

Karamzin traveled through Germany, Switzerland, France and England for fourteen months. Upon his return to Russia he published an account of his journey under the title *Letters of a Russian Traveler* (*Pisma russkogo puteshestvennika*, 1792), a book which immediately made his reputation. The epistolary form pro-vided a framework for his spiritual effusions and a detailed analysis of his inner world, even though that form was fictional, for he wrote no letters to his friends and probably compiled the book upon his return to Moscow on the basis of brief travel notes no longer extant. The writer was clearly under Sterne's influence, for he never missed an opportunity to emphasize his links to his great predecessor: for example, in the first letter he bewails his separation from his beloved friends in the best sentimentalist style, and in the 130th he hastens to visit those places where Yorick had stayed.

However, as a matter of fact Karamzin does not imitate Sterne so much as derive his orientation from another type of travel literature, that which communicated new information to the reader and stimulated him to political and historical ruminations, like Charles Dupaty's *Lettres sur l'Italie en 1785*, Voltaire's *Lettres philosophiques*, or Jean Jacques Barthélemy's *Voyage du jeune Ana-charsis en Grèce*. The young traveler – he is not yet twenty-four – visits famous scholars and thinkers, including Johann Kasper Lavater and Christophe Martin Wieland, wanders about Paris during the days of the French revolution (it is even possible that he knew Robespierre at the time), praises the British political system, and provides sharp, interesting, vivid and entertaining descrip-tions of everything he sees. In the *Letters* one can already detect that moderately liberal to conservative political position of Karamzin's which with some further development formed the basis for the philosophical and historical conception underlying his *History of* the Russian State (*Istoriya gosudarstva rossiyskogo*). Karamzin always opposed despotism and tyranny of whatever origin, whether they stemmed from a monarch or from the rebellious people. An established legal system, he felt, was always preferable to anarchy or sudden political shifts.

Letters of a Russian Traveler appeared in the *Moscow Journal* (*Moskovsky zhurnal*), which Karamzin began to publish immediately upon his return from abroad and which came out in 1791–2. It was quite a successful publication, with 300 subscribers, more than any other such publication enjoyed in the eighteenth century. The fact that it was reprinted in 1801–2 is another indication of its popularity.

On the pages of *Moscow Journal* also appeared some of the short stories which brought Karamzin fame as a Russian writer. The most important among them was "Poor Liza" ("Bednaya Liza," 1792). Liza, a peasant girl, lost her father when she was very young. She falls in love with Erast, a handsome young aristocrat, who loves her tenderly in return. However, once Liza has given herself to her beloved the passion for a young peasant cools down within the inconstant young man. When she discovers her beloved has been unfaithful to her, Liza drowns herself in a pond near the Simonov Monastery. Afterwards Erast repents bitterly of his behavior and can find no solace for the rest of his life.

Karamzin offers a skillful depiction of the genesis and development of feeling within the lovers' souls, of the young girl's sufferings and her mother's blindness. Readers were captivated by the expressively romantic depictions of nature and by the endearing tenderness of the heroes' emotions transmitted through a sentimental vocabulary which up until that point had been little used either in life or in literature.

As Karamzin sees it, love places people on an equal footing: he wrote the famous formula "even peasant women are capable of loving" in the course of describing the grief of Liza's mother at her husband's death. The author sympathizes immensely with Liza, who falls in love to such a degree as to surrender her honor, but he understands Erast as well, seeing him as a good person but also inconstant and not very serious. The tale ends with a reconciling resolution: in Heaven Liza and Erast are no doubt joined once again.

At this time Karamzin is much concerned with the depiction of romantic experience and the inner life of women. Indeed he directs his writing toward his female readers. It is precisely women who, in his view, having finally begun to read and speak Russian rather than French, should help writers to create a Russian literary language, a subject on which Karamzin expounded in his article "Why is there so little writing talent in Russia?" ("Otchego v Rossii malo avtorskikh talantov?").

The short story "Julia" (1796), a high society variant of "Poor Liza," was no less successful with readers. The beautiful Julia (her name was intended to remind readers of Rousseau's *Nouvelle Héloïse*) falls in love with the intelligent, honest and good young Aris, but then the brilliant Prince N. appears and steals her affections. Unlike her predecessor, the peasant girl Liza, as well as the heroine of Rousseau's novel, Julia does not yield to the blandishments of her brilliant suitor and preserves her chastity. The Prince, lacking Erast's goodness, sincerity, and weakness, abandons the intransigent beauty, who returns to Aris and marries him. A short time later, however, she again becomes infatuated with Prince N. On discovering this Aris departs, leaving Julia to retire to the country to bring up her son and lead a lonely, virtuous life. A few years later Aris returns to her, and they find happiness together.

In both tales the reader was attracted by the depiction of the heroes' inner life and by the presentation of ordinary people who aroused sympathy by their very ordinariness and their excusable weaknesses, a characteristic of the sentimentalist movement as a whole. Karamzin demonstrates once again that he recognizes no social inequalities: all people are equal, and equally interesting.

Along with sentimental short stories Karamzin also produced typically preromantic tales, in the tradition of the "Gothic novel" of Ann Radcliffe, Matthew Lewis, Charles Maturin and others. The best of them is the famous "Island of Bornholm" ("Ostrov Borngolm," 1793), in which we find all the attributes of preromanticism: a gloomy island lost in the North Sea; an ancient castle; a beautiful young woman confined in a dungeon for an unknown crime (probably incest); and a plot line which suddenly breaks off, although it is not difficult for the reader to imagine how the story might end. All this makes the "Island of Bornholm" a masterpiece of Russian preromantic literature.

Karamzin also experimented with historical tales. "Natalya the Boyar's Daughter" ("Natalya, boyarskaya doch," 1792) transports the reader to the times of Tsar Alexey Mikhailovich. Natalya, daughter of an aristocratic boyar named Matvey, falls in love with a young stranger who turns out to be the son of a boyar currently in disfavor. The two escape to a forest retreat until they finally return to her father's roof after a victorious battle against the Lithuanians in which Natalya, disguised as a man, and her husband have both participated. Except for the names, there is nothing historical in the tale. A Russian boyar of the seventeenth century kisses a girl's hand, falls seriously ill and nearly perishes of love, sketches landscapes while his young wife does embroidery: in short acts exactly like a sentimental hero of the late eighteenth century. Still, this story bears witness to that interest in Russian history which a few years later would lead Karamzin to become a professional historian.

In 1792 Novikov was arrested and the Freemasons suppressed. By that time Karamzin had not only parted company with the Masons, but had also quarrelled with Novikov, whom he never liked. But that did not prevent him, with that profound decency which always characterized him, from publicly defending the victims of such persecution. In the *Moscow Journal* he published an ode entitled "To forgiveness" ("K milosti"), in which it is not difficult to detect a defense of the Freemasons then the object of governmental repression: Karamzin maintains that governmental stability is assured by the preservation of the rights of the people as a whole and of each individual in particular. The concepts of the Rousseauian "social contract" emerged here with unexpected force and emphasis.

No doubt Karamzin realized that the general intellectual situation in Russia in the 1790s was not conducive to the development of journalism and literature, so he gradually reoriented his publishing activities. Despite its popularity, the *Moscow Journal* ceased to appear in 1792. In 1794–5 Karamzin brought out two issues of a literary almanac, *Aglaya*, whose pages were filled primarily with his own works.

Here Karamzin published a sketch in the form of letters ("Melodor to Filalet" and "Filalet to Melodor") describing the tragic bankruptcy of the ideology of the Enlightenment: the flower of Enlightenment ideas has been destroyed in the "blood and flame" of the French revolution. To the melancholy present Karamzin counterposes merely an idyllic dream of the past, as he does in the sketch "Athenian life" ("Afinskaya zhizn") describing a typical day in ancient Athens in the manner of the young Anaharsis in Barthélemy's novel. The author describes Plato instructing his disciples, attends a performance of Sophocles's *Oedipus*, and goes to an evening feast, or symposium. It should be noted, though, that even this ancient Greek idyll is done in melancholy tints.

Emperor Paul I was assassinated on 1 March 1801. After his death and the beginning of liberalization under Alexander I, Karamzin intensified his literary activity. He started publishing the *Herald of Europe* (*Vestnik Evropy*), which soon became the finest periodical of its day. Here he printed the historical short story "Martha the Mayoress" ("Marfa Posadnitsa," 1803), an incomparably better work than its predecessor "Natalya the Boyar's Daughter."

"Martha the Mayoress" deals with the conquest of the Republic of Novgorod by Grand Duke Ivan III. In this tale Karamzin's view of history emerges in full panoply. He obviously sympathizes with the Novgorodians in their struggle for liberty, and he sketches the portrait of the heroic republican leader Martha with understanding and affection. Martha organizes the defense of her native state, summons her compatriots to the love of liberty, appoints the young Miroslav commander-in-chief, giving him her daughter Xenia to wife, and herself meets death on the scaffold courageously after the Novgorodians have been defeated and subjected to the power of the autocrat of all the Russias.

At the same time, however, Karamzin regards Ivan III's victory as historically justified and necessary for Russia's growth. Every nation has its own historical destiny. A republican system or a constitutional monarchy is appropriate for very small states like Switzerland or relatively small countries like England, but in France, say, the overthrow of the legal monarch led to senseless bloodshed. For Russia the monarchy is the most suitable form of state organization. Ivan makes an appearance at the place of execution where Martha gave her life and promises the Novgorodians order, justice and security. At first the people remain silent, but after an interval they cry: "Glory to the Russian tsar!" as they bid farewell to their liberties and accept a new form of governance.

Before much longer Karamzin abandoned literature altogether. By order of Alexander I, on 31 October 1803 he was appointed court historian at a modest salary of 2,000 rubles per year. Residing in Moscow, working in the archives, studying the chronicles, he became entirely absorbed in writing his history of Russia. Still, his scholarly commitments did not keep him from following current events attentively, and paying special attention to the rather rapid transformations which the young tsar had already effected or was preparing to effect: Alexander wished to alter the bureaucratic system, introduce constitutional limitations on the monarchy, and abolish serfdom. In view of the tragic course of the French revolution, Karamzin considered such radical transformations at the least premature and inappropriate to the established state structure. In 1811 Karamzin addressed to the tsar a "Memoir on Ancient and Modern Russia" ("Zapiska o drevney i novoy Rossii"), one of the most remarkable political documents of the nineteenth century. The "Memoir" dealt with basic problems of Russian history and current affairs with such honesty that it was published only once in pre-revolutionary Russia (in 1914) and has never appeared in the Soviet Union.

Karamzin's fundamental assumptions in the "Memoir" are consistently monarchist: he considers an enlightened monarchy the best form of government for Russia. Karamzin traces the genesis and development of the monarchy over the course of time, as the Russian state was gradually created. The people had peaceably given up their liberties and adored their rulers. In Karamzin's view any popular uprisings against the monarchy (the assassination of the False Dmitry, the Time of Troubles) were much more damaging to the state than the sins and deficiencies of rulers. But this does not justify rulers in anything they may wish to do, for they must meet, or seek to meet, the ideal of the enlightened monarch. With the scope and skill of a brilliant journalist Karamzin describes the cruelty and arbitrariness of Peter I as well as his hatred for his own people and his native culture, the sensuality and vice of Catherine II, and the extravagant behavior of Paul I. Then, taking up contemporary issues, Karamzin condemns the reforms which the present monarch has instituted or is considering introducing. He opposes rapid and showy transformations. The sudden abolition of serfdom would be a greater evil than was its introduction in the first place, and limitations upon the monarchy would lead to a new Time of Troubles: "Any innovation in the structure of the state is an evil [...] time alone provides the necessary stability to the laws."

Alexander I did not care for such fundamental criticism; it offended him. However, he managed to suppress his resentment, and personal relations between the historian and the tsar continued to be friendly until the latter's death. Along with many other factors, Karamzin's arguments played a role in the tsar's decision to abandon his reforms, and that in turn had a tragic impact on the entire subsequent course of Russian history even down to our day.

In the meantime Karamzin continued with his major work, the *History of the Russian State*. When the first eight volumes appeared in 1818 in an unprecedented printing of 3,000 copies, they sold out in twenty-five days. Karamzin kept working on the *History* to the end of his life. When he died in 1826, the last words he had written for volume thirteen were: "Oreshek would not surrender . . ."

Karamzin rendered his judgements on moral grounds, attempting to comprehend the inner motivations behind the behavior and actions of tsars. Thus he condemned the cruelty of Ivan the Terrible in words worthy of Tacitus. At the same time Karamzin adhered consistently to his conception of the state and the monarchy, and he relied honestly on his sources: half of each volume consists of references to the sources and extensive quotations therefrom. The *History* is written in beautiful and expressive Russian. Karamzin succeeded in overcoming the excessive emotionalism and sentimentality of his early works.

The *History*, then, was a worthy culmination to the career of Nikolay Karamzin, reformer of the literary language, poet, prose-writer, journalist and historian, a man whose fiction is read to this day and whose historical contributions still retain their value.

Karamzin gave rise to an entire pleiad of sentimentalist writers who imitated his themes, his plots and his language, overburdened with epithets, periphrases, detailed "sentimental" descriptions, and so forth. There was born a new genre of the sentimental tale, describing unhappy lovers, tragic deaths, the joys of country life, and so forth. Their titles speak for themselves: "Unhappy Maslov" ("Neschastny Maslov," 1793), by Alexander Klushin; "The Dark Grove, or A Monument to Tenderness" ("Temnaya roshcha, ili Pamyatnik nezhnosti," 1819), by Peter Shalikov; "A Russian Werther" ("Rossiysky Verter," 1801), by Mikhail Sushkov; "The Tale of Poor Marya" ("Istoriya bednoy Mari," 1805), by N. Milonov; "Poor Masha" ("Bednaya Masha," 1801), by Alexander Izmaylov; and the anonymous "Unhappy Liza" ("Neschastnaya Liza," 1810).

Also, Karamzin's *Letters of a Russian Traveler* engendered an entire literature of sentimental travelogues, whose authors generally did not even go beyond Russia's borders and who busied themselves not so much with recalling places they had visited as with exaggeratedly detailed descriptions of their own experiences and impressions. Such works include "My Journey, or the Adventures of a Single Day" ("Moe puteshestvie, ili Priklyuchenie odnogo dnya," 1803), by Nikolay Brusilov; "A Journey to Little Russia" ("Puteshestvie v Malorossiyu," 1804) and "Another Journey to Little Russia" ("Drugoe puteshestvie v Malorossiyu," 1817) by Peter Shalikov; "Journey to the South of Russia" ("Puteshestvie v poludennuyu Rossiyu," 1800–2) by Vladimir Izmaylov; and others.

The work of Alexander Radishchev (1749–1802), who wrote independently of Karamzin and a little earlier than he, belongs to another category of sentimentalism. Radishchev knew European literature at least as well as Karamzin, perhaps even better. Born in 1749, he studied initially at the St. Petersburg School for Pages, then at the University of Leipzig in 1766–71, where Catherine sent him along with twelve other students to obtain a legal education. Upon his return he worked in the Senate, then was a military procurator, and finally found employment at the St. Petersburg custom house, whose director he became in 1790.

Radishchev began his literary career with stylized "letters" and "diaries." It is likely that his "Diary of a week" ("Dnevnik odnoy nedeli"), a sentimental account of a separation from friends done in a Sternian mode, dates from the 1770s. The language of this brief work is a strange amalgam of sentimental, archaic Church Slavic with civic-journalistic vocabulary. This stylistic approach (with a considerable buttressing of archaisms) remained characteristic of

Radishchev's writing, setting him clearly apart from the Karamzinian school.

In 1782 Radishchev wrote a "Letter to a friend resident in Tobolsk" ("Pismo drugu, zhitelstvuyushchemu v Tobolske") describing the unveiling of the famous "Bronze Horseman," the monument to Peter I, and thoughts on the power of the monarch, who never abandons his authority voluntarily.

Afterwards Radishchev composed the "Life of Fyodor Vasilevich Ushakov" ("Zhitie Fedora Vasilevicha Ushakova," published in 1789). With typical stylistic insensitivity, Radishchev inappropriately selected the word *zhitie*, ordinarily employed only for saints' lives, for a biography of his friend and fellow student at Leipzig University. Ushakov was no doubt a capable and talented young man, but he was no saint, since he died while still a student as a consequence of excessive sexual indulgence.

The "Life" is filled with journalistic essays drawing upon the relationships between the students and their instructor, about the nature of state power, the links between the tsar and his subjects, etc. As Radishchev sees it, the absence of specific legislation to define (as in Rousseau's "social contract") the rights and duties of social groupings leads to rebellion and destruction, and ordinarily rulers who have exceeded their powers are to blame for this.

In the course of the 1780s Radishchev worked over his principal book, *A Journey from St. Petersburg to Moscow* (*Puteshestvie iz Peterburga v Moskvu*). The title, the basic plot line, and even the style (description of the experiences and feelings of the author-narrator) were suggested to Radishchev by Sterne's *Sentimental Journey*. However, in the realm of ideas and content Radishchev most emphatically parted company with his predecessor.

Radishchev wrote his book slowly and with great difficulty: he was not only devoid of any great artistic gift, but also had a feeble grasp of the rules of composition. He was obviously incapable of writing an extensive work, and so his book divides into various fragments, episodes, inserted verses, sketches, and meditations. The *Journey* consists of chapters bearing the names of towns and posting stations located between St. Petersburg and Moscow: Sofia, Lyubani, Torzhok, Tver, and others. These place names mark the author-traveler's progress between one capital and the other, but have no connection with the content of the sketches, each of which stands by itself, is dedicated to a particular social problem and, as a rule, consists of facts and authorial commentary combined with a detailed analysis of the traveler's feelings and experiences. The major topics to which Radishchev dedicates his descriptions and essays are state power, the situation of the serfs, governmental reform, and literary problems.

Radishchev is extremely critical of state authority. In the chapter "Spasskaya Polest" he depicts a ruler blinded by his own magnificence and the flattery of those around him. The ruler issues orders which are not carried out; his top officials deceive him while his unhappy subjects live in poverty and are unjustly persecuted. However, the author, raised as he is in the spirit of Enlightenment philosophy and enlightened absolutism, immediately offers a cure. The Holy Wanderer Pryamovzora (i.e. Truth) removes the cataracts from the tsar's eyes, and deceit is vanquished. Thus, from the author's point of view, if the tsar will seek truth, then proper order can be established within the state.

In this depiction of the tsar it is not difficult to detect traits of Catherine II, and in her courtiers certain outstanding high officials, including the famous Count Grigory Potyomkin. The depiction of the tsar was as far as Radishchev could go in exposing iniquity, but he also depicts local officials who abuse their authority: for example the governor who spends official funds on the purchase and delivery of oysters in "Spasskaya Polest," the officer who does not care about saving those who are perishing in "Chudovo," corrupt judges in "Spasskaya Polest," and others.

It should be added that in eighteenth-century Russia such criticism was not at all unusual. Novikov had engaged in open polemics with Catherine in his *Drone* in 1769, and in 1783 Denis Fonvizin had exasperated the Empress with sharply probing questions on the pages of her very own journal *Collocutor of Lovers of the Russian Word* (*Sobesednik lyubiteley rossiyskogo slova*).

Radishchev paid particular attention to describing the difficult situation of the serfs. A peasant might have to labor six days a week on the land of a cruel landowner. In order to keep himself and his family alive he would work for himself at night and on Sundays ("Sofia"). A cruel and libertine serfowner deprives his peasants of all their property, demands the right of first night for himself, and is ultimately assassinated by his peasants ("Zaytsevo"). An intelligent young peasant who has received a good education but has subsequently been humiliated by his young masters is overjoyed at being dispatched as an army recruit ("Gorodnya"). A poor peasant woman lives in a hut with no chimney, eats bread made of chaff, and has never tasted sugar in her life ("Peshki"). But let us again note that there was nothing unusual in this condemnation of the cruelty and monstrosity of the system of serfdom in eighteenth-century literature. Fonvizin had written about all this in *The Minor*, Novikov in his satirical journals, Krylov in his *Spirit Post* (*Pochta dukhov*).

However, unlike his immediate predecessors and contemporaries, Radishchev pays a great deal of attention to the likely consequences of cruel exploitation. He speaks directly to cruel serfowners, threatening them with the wrath of the peasantry ("Lyubani," "Peshki") and predicting a rebellion during which the slaves will smash their masters' heads with their chains ("Gorodnya"). And from Radishchev's point of view they would be justified in so doing, since cruel slavery violates the law, the peasant is not entitled to legal protection ("he is dead to the law"), and therefore has the right to violate a law which protects only the masters. On this basis Radishchev welcomed the American revolution which liberated the country from its subjection to the British crown, and was prepared to justify Cromwell, who, by executing Charles I, affirmed the right of vengeance for a people deprived of liberty (the ode "Liberty" included in the chapter "Tver"). From all this it does not follow, though, that Radishchev considered a popular revolution the best possible resolution of political problems. It could occur only as a result of illegitimate and excessively cruel exploitation.

Thus Radishchev makes various proposals for the improvement of the existing system. First of all, a ruler must know the truth ("Spasskaya Polest"), for then his governance will be useful and will make his subjects happy; in "Vydropusk" he proposes abolishing the system of Court ranks on the grounds that courtiers are parasites, and it is wrong to equate their servile accomplishments with genuine service to the fatherland. Unnecessary luxury merely offends the ordinary people in our enlightened and rational age.

In this age of reason, when the fatherland is flourishing (a compliment to Catherine on Radishchev's part), it is shameful to keep one's countrymen in the chains of bondage ("Khotilov"). Serfdom is harmful to the state from all points of view: it is dangerous (i.e. it may lead to political rebellion), it sets a bad moral example, and it hinders economic progress, since only free men work diligently. All these shortcomings afflict Russia, and a serf uprising may destroy her, as nearly happened during the Pugachov rebellion of 1773–4. So Radishchev urgently summons his compatriots to liberate "our brothers from the bonds of slavery," to undertake a selflessly humanitarian act: embrace the former serfs and "love one another sincerely." At the conclusion of the chapter Radishchev elaborates a gradual plan for the complete abolition of serfdom.

Literary questions, dealt with in "Tver," are kept somewhat separate from the social and political problems predominant in the *Journey*. In "Tver" Radishchev argues primarily that various different meters besides the customary iambs (spondees, dactyls, hexameters) should be used in poetic texts, and that poetic rhyme is not at all necessary: its constant usage is merely the result of blind imitation of French models.

The most interesting aspect of Radishchev's literary theories had to do with the notion of "difficult" verse, that is, poetic lines full of consonants, difficult to pronounce, rough and cacophonic. As Radishchev saw it, poetry ought to be "stiff and difficult to pronounce" if its poetic aims so required, as, for example, in his ode "Liberty," which depicts the difficult transition from slavery to freedom; or if the complex thought contained in the verse demands careful, slow reading and complicated, slow deciphering ("The eighteenth century" ["Osmnadtsatoe stoletie"], "Ode to my friend" ["Oda drugu moemu"]). In such cases harmony must be subordinated to the expressiveness of the verse.

Later on, in the last portion of his life, Radishchev developed his ideas on the hexameter as a complex and expressive meter in a treatise on Vasily Trediakovsky entitled "Monument to the dactylo-trochaic champion" ("Pamyatnik daktilo-khorei-cheskomu vityazyu," 1801). Nikolay Gnedich's translation of the *Iliad* done in the 1810s and 1820s, still the best rendering in Russian, was produced under the influence of Trediakovsky's experiments and Radishchev's theories.

Radishchev's ideas had a certain influence later on in the campaign of the so-called "archaists" against the Karamzinists: Radishchev's language, replete with archaisms, provided an excellent model for the struggle against the high-society frivolity of the Karamzin school's language. Literary men of the 1800s and 1810s were much more interested in Radishchev's literary views than they were in his political ideas, so that, paradoxically, his followers turned out to be political conservatives, the early Slavophiles and members of the "Colloquy of Lovers of the Russian Word."

When Catherine II came to power she issued several liberal ukases, one of which permitted citizens to establish "free printing presses" for the publication of anything their owners wished under only nominal censorship. In 1789 Radishchev established just such a printing press in his home, and there, in 1790, he printed his *Journey from St. Petersburg to Moscow* in 650 copies, an ordinary press-run for that time.

As we have seen, the book did not contain any especially subversive ideas, except for some clumsy remarks about the cruelties of peasant rebellions and the execution of the English king – and even these could easily have been regarded as mere lack of political tact. But this journalistic treatise on social and political questions came out at precisely the wrong time. Catherine was getting along in years, and as a result was becoming ever less tolerant and ever more persuaded of her own infallibility. Since she had usurped the throne in 1762, she feared her own son Paul, the legitimate heir to the throne. But the Empress was frightened most of all by events in France, where the revolution had broken out, a Constituent Assembly had been formed, and Louis XVI had abdicated his throne. All this caused the Empress to keep very close track of public opinion in Russia.

Upon a careful reading of Radishchev's book Catherine found it exceedingly dangerous, discovering in it "dissemination of the French infection," a call to rebellion and threats to rulers: she termed the author a "rebel worse than Pugachov." At Catherine's order Radishchev was arrested, tried, and condemned to death. But the Empress, as was her custom, lightened the sentence considerably and ordered the writer to be sent to Siberia for ten years.

Thanks to the assistance of his superior and consistent protector Alexander Vorontsov, Radishchev arrived safely at the distant

Siberian town of Ilimsk, where he purchased a home and lived with his family until the Empress died in 1796. The new Emperor Paul I, who had released Novikov from jail, permitted Radishchev to return from Siberia as well and settle on his ancestral estate at Nemtsovo near Moscow. Here Radishchev devoted the years of Paul's reign to literary endeavor. He wrote the beginning of a comic poem in the folk tradition entitled "Bova," several other poems, the beginning of a narrative poem entitled "Songs performed at competitions in honor of the ancient Slavic divinities" ("Pesni, petye na sostyazaniyakh v chest drevnim slavyanskim bozhestvam"), the treatise on Trediakovsky mentioned above, and so forth.

When Alexander I came to the throne in 1801, Radishchev was not only permitted to return to St. Petersburg, he was even invited to participate in the work of a Commission on the Laws. But imprisonment and exile had deepened the melancholy pessimism so characteristic of Radishchev in any case. As Alexander Pushkin tells it, the chairman of the Commission made some half-jocular reference to Radishchev's past political sins. The sensitive Radishchev was frightened by this, returned home, and took his own life. The date was 12 September 1802.

In addition to prose, Russian sentimentalist writers also produced poetic works. Karamzin and Radishchev, Shalikov and Izmaylov and many others wrote poetry. Karamzin was a superlative poet: his poetry is filled with profound meditations and often attains formal perfection. It also analyzes subtle facets of human emotions, which is quite characteristic of sentimentalism. Other sentimentalist poets of the time include Mikhail Muravyov (1757–1807), Vasily Kapnist (1738–1823), Nikolay Lvov (1751–1803), and Yury Neledinsky-Meletsky (1752–1818).

One of the most outstanding Russian sentimentalist poets was Ivan Dmitriev (1760–1837). A high government official (Minister of Justice), Dmitriev was a close friend of Karamzin's and a convinced adherent of Karamzin's poetic practice: thus he called his collection of verse of 1795 *My Trifles Too* (*I moi bezdelki*) in a demonstrative echo of Karamzin's *My Trifles* (*Moi bezdelki*, 1794).

In his writing Dmitriev broke with the traditions of classicism. In his famous satirical poem "What others say" ("Chuzhoy tolk," 1794), he mounted a witty attack on the solemn ode, the most important classical genre. He also reformed the classical fable. Instead of an undeviatingly didactic narration in a coarsely popular tone, Dmitriev created an elegant miniature done in the style of La Fontaine and written in light, refined language (later on Krylov would return to the traditions of the classical fable).

Dmitriev's sentimentalism emerges most clearly in his songs, many of which have become popular songs since. Dmitriev's songs are ordinarily melancholy romantic effusions in which he speaks of the happiness of life with his beloved, of the sorrows of parting, and so forth: "Without my loving friend I wander o'er the meadows..." ("Bez druga i bez miloy brozhu ya po lugam..."), "The consolations of love are measured in minutes..." ("Lyubovny uteshenya minutami letyat..."), "Friends, time is so short..." ("Drugi, vremya sko-rotechno..."), etc. Dmitriev's best-known song was "The grey dove moans" ("Stonet sizy golubochek," 1792).

Russian writers in the eighteenth century were not very numerous; as a rule they felt isolated, as though they were eccentrics involved in strange occupations quite incomprehensible to those around them. They tried to assure their few readers, the public generally, and themselves that literary work was a pleasant, entertaining, interesting and useful enterprise: so many journals were given names in that spirit, such as *Pleasant and Useful Pastime*, or *Pleasant, Interesting and Entertaining Reading*.

By the end of the eighteenth century that situation had changed. Writers by then regarded themselves as representatives of public opinion which, in the course of its development, became subdivided into different currents. That led to ideological conflict, and to the necessity of bringing ideological allies together in small circles on the basis of linkages of family and friendship, and later on in official and semi-official literary societies (for example, in St. Petersburg in the late 1770s there was a circle which included four poets – Derzhavin, Lvov, Kapnist, and Khemnitser; the first three of them were married to three sisters, all great beauties of the day).

In the early nineteenth century the director of the Public Library and the President of the Academy of Arts, Alexey Olenin, organized a brilliant literary salon at his home which was attended by Derzhavin, Batyushkov, Zhukovsky, Vyazemsky, and many others. The most faithful members of the circle, and those closest to Olenin, included Gnedich, Krylov and Batyushkov.

The introduction of Masonic ideas in Russia and the founding of numerous Masonic lodges provided ready-made organizational structures for more formal literary associations. So when such talented young people as Andrey Turgenev, Andrey Kaysarov, Alexey Merzlyakov, Alexander Voeykov, and Zhukovsky decided to meet for discussion of literary and social questions, they organized a "Friendly Literary Society" with a President, records of meetings, an archive, and so forth. Despite that the Society, which came into being in January 1801, had disintegrated by November.

The "Free Society of Lovers of Literature, Science and Art" existed for a considerably longer period, from 1801 to 1825 with some interruptions. It brought together primarily lesser known writers not of gentry origin: Ivan Born, Ivan Pnin, Vasily Popugaev, Alexander Vostokov, Nikolay Radishchev (Alexander Radishchev's son), and others. This society, which took up a middle position in the disputes between the Karamzinists and their opponents, the archaists, had no serious role in the history of Russian literature. Still, one should mention two members of the society, poets who played a certain part in the development of Russian preromanticism: Semyon Bobrov (1763–1810), author of over-weighty and tense philosophical odes and gloomily romantic nature descriptions; and Gavriil Kamenev (1771–1803), author of what might be considered the first Russian romantic ballad, "Gromval" (1802).

One of the Society's most important and influential members was Alexander Vostokov, not only a gifted poet but also an outstanding scholarly philologist, author of the classic *Experiment in Russian Versification (Opyt o russkom stikhoslozhenii*, 1812). He did a great deal for the development of Russian versification, expanding its metrical potential by the use of classical meters and folk rhythms.

The major literary grouping of the early nineteenth century was the "Colloquy of Lovers of the Russian Word" (Beseda lyubiteley russkogo slova, 1811–16), which had begun to meet unofficially as early as 1807. In March of 1811 the "Colloquy" inaugurated its regular monthly meetings in a beautiful and luxuriously appointed hall in Derzhavin's large home on the banks of the Fontanka in St. Petersburg. As many as 500 people – in a word, nearly all of educated St. Petersburg – might attend the meetings. The Society published its own journal, *Readings at the Colloquy of Lovers of the Russian Word* (*Chteniya v Besede lyubiteley russkogo slova*), which printed for the most part materials presented at the meetings. Nineteen issues of the publication appeared.

The Colloquy was controlled by conservatively inclined literary men opposed to Alexander I's liberal reforms. In literary matters the members of the Colloquy were against the Karamzinists. They looked to the Church Slavic language, folklore and national cultural traditions in an effort to create a cultural and historical utopia rooted in the past.

Interest in national history and culture and in popular folklore is quite typical of romanticism, which began to appear at the turn of the century and sooner or later permeated all the Western literatures: Herder, Brentano and the Brothers Grimm in Germany, Ossian and Walter Scott in England, James Fenimore Cooper in the United States, and so forth. In this sense the activities of the Colloquy may be linked to the early history of Russian romanticism.

The Colloquy of Lovers of the Russian Word was organized by Admiral Alexander Shishkov (1754–1841). He began his literary career as a poet: in his poem "Old and new" ("Staroe i novoe vremya," 1784) he contrasted an idealized pre-Petrine past with the present state of affairs in Russia. His book of 1803 *Essay on the Old and New Styles of the Russian Language* (*Rassuzhdenie o starom i novom sloge rossiyskogo yazyka*) sparked a great controversy, since in it Shishkov criticized the mannered style of sentimentalist Karamzinian prose. Shishkov argued that literature should take its direction from Church Slavic, which he termed the "root and foundation of the Russian language." Displaying the concern with medieval national history so characteristic of the romantics, he also composed an enormous commentary on the *Igor Tale* and produced a translation of the text which was rife with archaisms and Church Slavic elements.

In an "Address upon the inauguration of the Colloquy" ("Rech pri otkrytii 'Besedy'," 1811) Shishkov emphasized the importance of ancient church books and folklore for the development of the national culture, contrasting these helpful sources with malignant western influences. Shishkov developed these ideas in two more specialized works of the same year. One was a brochure entitled "On the eloquence of the Scriptures" ("O krasnorechii Svyashchennogo pisaniya"), in which he sought to demonstrate his favorite argument: that Church Slavic and Russian are one and the same language, and that familiarity with church books was a prerequisite for literary creativity in Russian. In his second book, *Conversations on Literature* (*Razgovory o slovesnosti*), Shishkov for the first time painstakingly worked out a poetics of Russian folklore.

In short order Shishkov received the opportunity to address his linguistic and literary ideas to as large an audience as any writer could ever hope for. In 1812 he was appointed State Secretary to Alexander I, and given the task of drafting all the official manifestoes, orders and rescripts issued during the war of 1812–13. Shishkov used these documents to elaborate his ideological and political program: he rejected the ideas of the Enlightenment and the French revolution, affirmed the principles of monarchism and Russian Orthodoxy (which he considered an integral part of Russian nationality from time immemorial), praised Russia's historic past, and so forth. In his manifestoes Shishkov employed solemn, lofty, and ponderously archaic language of the sort to which the Russians had long been accustomed from the liturgy and the Holy Scriptures. These manifestoes were very popular among the common people: as they listened to them people "wept and gnashed their teeth." After the war they were published in a separate book, and contemporaries – including Shishkov's literary opponents – recognized their indisputable positive qualities.

After the war, having aroused the Emperor's displeasure by his conservatism and his consistent defense of serfdom, Shishkov withdrew from government service and at his own request was appointed president of the Russian Academy. Later on, from 1826 to 1828, after Alexander's death, he served as Minister of Education. He died at an advanced age.

Another founder of the Colloquy was Gavriil Derzhavin, who retired in 1803 to dedicate himself wholly to literature. In Derzhavin's work of the final period (1803–16) one can easily detect

Shishkov's influence: Derzhavin wrote more frequently on Biblical subjects, and in a complicated and archaic style. Shishkov and Derzhavin were quite close politically, for Derzhavin was also a consistent monarchist and foe of all liberal reforms. It is not surprising that the Colloquy should have ceased to exist after Derzhavin's death.

The Colloquy opposed sentimental poetry with its interest in the trivialities of the inner lives of private individuals, holding that literature was a serious social matter. Consequently its adherents gave their primary attention to lofty and serious genres which had pretensions to influencing public opinion. The Colloquy was particularly interested in the heroic poem, a genre which, though well developed in the classical period, had become totally obsolete and considerably transformed in the romantic period, when the best example of the heroic poem was thought to be, not Virgil's *Aeneid*, composed according to all the rules, but Homer's *Iliad*, viewed as a spontaneous expression of Greek national culture and character. Homer newly interpreted in this sense could serve as a model for the creation of Russian national heroic works as well.

At the beginning of the nineteenth century there was no *Iliad* in Russian. The best translation extant, by Ermil Kostrov – done in six-foot iambic lines with paired rhymes, called Alexandrines – broke off at the ninth canto and was never completed. In 1807 the young poet Nikolay Gnedich (1784–1833) set out to translate the *Iliad*. At first he used Alexandrines to complete Kostrov's translation but later on, taking Trediakovsky's efforts and Radishchev's theories into account, he shifted to Russian hexameter (dactylotrochaic meter), which from that time to the present has been the Russian poetic equivalent of the ancient hexameter and the instrument for the embodiment of ancient culture in the Russian tongue. Gnedich worked at his translation for more than twenty years, completing it only in 1829. His version is still one of the finest renderings of Homer not only in Russian, but in any modern European language.

The members of the Colloquy (Gnedich did not formally belong, but he worked closely with it) were interested in Gnedich's efforts at creating a "Russian Homer," and sympathized with them. The young poet's translations were discussed enthusiastically at its meetings; there were polemics over Homeric metrics, and the *Readings* brought out a portion of the hexametric translation of the *Iliad* in its first publication.

However, even the most superlative translation of Homer could not take the place of a heroic epic created on a national foundation as the romantics understood it. Sergey Shirinsky-Shikhmatov (1783–1837), one of Shishkov's most dedicated disciples, accepted that task. He sought to extend the lofty, solemn style of the Lomonosovian ode to all literary genres, making consistent use of archaisms and Church Slavicisms, expelling foreign words from the literary language, and making syntactic constructions ever more complex.

In 1807, in compliance with his principles, Shirinsky-Shikhmatov wrote a narrative poem entitled *Pozharsky, Minin, Germogen, or Russia Saved* (*Pozharsky, Minin, Germogen, ili spasennaya Rossiya*) which depicts the Time of Troubles and the heroic efforts of Russia's best people to save their country from ruin. The author, however, has little interest in narrating the events of that time, as the classical narrative poem usually did. Instead Shirinsky-Shikhmatov's extensive work is an agitated monologue describing the author's own feelings and emotional experiences in connection with these great and dramatic events. The genre distinctions so obligatory under the classical system vanish here: the ode coalesces with the narrative poem to form a lyrical monologue more typical of the romantic narrative poem than anything else.

These same traits characterize Shikhmatov's second poem as well, his *Lyric Oratorio Peter the Great* (*Liricheskoe pesnopenie Petr Veliky*, 1810): here again it is the lyric rather than the epic element which predominates in the ecstatic enthusiasm for Peter's accomplishments. Both poems are composed in expressive and energetic verse completely free of verbal rhymes.

However, Shikhmatov's attempts at creating a new type of narrative poem on the basis of archaic language and a reformed classical esthetic system were doomed to failure, for the future belonged to the romantic poem of the Byronic type which Pushkin would create. Contemporaries wrote numerous epigrams criticizing his poems, and he himself was dubbed "verbless Shikhmatov."

Within the Colloquy another classical genre was also developed and modernized: the fable. We have already mentioned Ivan Dmitriev's reform of the fable along La Fontainean lines. The Colloquy sought to return the fable to its ancient sources, Aesop and Phaedrus, and to their successor Lessing.

Thus Dmitry Khvostov (1757–1835) rejected the La Fontainean approach of vividly literary narration in favor of emphasizing the fable's allegorical qualities and traditionally primitive moralizing. For the sake of this allegorical quality he eliminated the most important element of classical poetics, verisimilitude, as understood within a strictly defined genre system. Khvostov created a strange world containing doves with teeth and donkeys with claws and heels, where carp shriek from pain and ravens have mouths and lips. Contemporaries did not understand what Khvostov was trying to do and mocked his efforts, so that he has gone down in the history of Russian literature as a comic and pitiful graphomaniac.

The Russian fable reached its zenith at the hands of Ivan Krylov (1768–1844), whose literary achievements exceed the bounds of the Colloquy and also the chronological limits of the nineteenth century, and deserve especially careful consideration.

The son of an impoverished army officer, after his father's death Krylov, at the age of ten, began working in an office in a provincial city. Though he lacked formal education, he taught himself languages (in his old age he even learned ancient Greek so that he could read Homer in the original); in general he was an educated man, well acquainted with Russian and European literatures.

In 1782 Krylov made his way to St. Petersburg, where he wrote several dramatic pieces even as he continued his bureaucratic employment: these included the comic opera *The Fortune Teller* (*Kofeynitsa*) and the tragedies *Cleopatra* and *Philomela*. Distinguished as a young man by his boldness and independent judgment, Krylov used his comedies to mount sharp attacks upon contemporary mores, and that without stopping short at direct hints at particular individuals: for example in his comedy *The Pranksters* (*Prokazniki*) he made fun of the playwright Yakov Knyazhnin and his entire family. His comedies *A Frenzied Family* (*Beshenaya semya*) and *A Writer in the Anteroom* (*Sochinitel v prikhozhey*) contained sharp critiques of the morality of contemporary literary life. A quarrel with a theater director, who had at first assisted the young writer, made it impossible for his plays to be staged.

Krylov then turned to journalism, continuing on the one hand the Novikovian tradition of satirical journalism while on the other drawing upon the achievements of English satirical journalism (Addison and Steele) and French satirical epistolary novels (Montesquieu). In 1789 he published a monthly entitled *Spirit Post* in which spirits – undines, gnomes, sylphs, etc. – correspond with Malikulmulk the wizard, discuss philosophical problems, describe various everyday scenes, and laugh at people's weaknesses and failings (it has only recently been discovered that twenty-three out of forty-eight letters in the *Spirit Post* were translated from two novels by the Marquis Jean-Baptiste d'Argens, *Lettres cabalistiques* and *Lettres juives*). Thereafter Krylov and his friends in 1792 published the journal *Spectator* (*Zritel*), whose title was no doubt borrowed from Addison and Steele's English publication of the same name. In 1793 he published the journal *St. Petersburg Mercury* (*Sankt-Petersburgsky Merkury*).

All during these years Krylov worked within the traditions of late classicism and of eighteenth-century French philosophical prose connected with them. The tale "Kaib" (1792), describing the journey of a young eastern monarch traveling incognito, recalls Voltaire's so-called "eastern tales" – "The Princess of Babylon," "The White Bull" – and makes fun of pastoral idylls written in a sentimentalist spirit. In "Nights" ("Nochi," 1792), a narrative describing several of the hero's nocturnal adventures in a certain city, one can detect the influence of eighteenth-century French prose (Jean-Baptiste Louvet de Couvray, Antoine Prévost, Louis Sébastien Mercier).

As we have already seen, advancing age and the French revolution impelled Catherine II to intensify governmental supervision of literature and to persecute Radishchev and Novikov. Krylov suffered certain difficulties as well. In 1792 his printing house was searched, and he himself was placed under police surveillance.

In 1794 Krylov left St. Petersburg to wander about the country until 1804. During that time he wrote nothing at all except for a burlesque comedy entitled *The Nibbler* (*Podshchipa*), in which he attacked Paul I and German influence at court. Here one can discern that shift toward Russophile ideas which later brought him to membership in the Colloquy. The comedy was of course not published, and circulated only in manuscript.

After Alexander I's accession to the throne, Krylov returned to literature, coming back to St. Petersburg in 1806. His comedies of 1807 *The Fashion Shop* (*Modnaya lavka*) and *A Lesson for Daughters* (*Urok dochkam*) (the latter falls somewhere between an imitation and an adaptation of Molière's *Les précieuses ridicules*) won Krylov great notoriety, and had long runs in St. Petersburg and Moscow. His comedies attacked Gallomania and cosmopolitanism while praising Russian mores and the foundations of the national life.

In 1806 Krylov began writing fables. In his first published fables he entered upon a literary competition with Dmitriev by selecting some of the same subjects that the latter had borrowed from La Fontaine: the proud oak uprooted by a storm and the reed which bends but survives; the old man who plants a tree and outlives some young people who laugh at his supposedly pointless efforts. Dmitriev's elegant and nationally neutral narration becomes a living picture under Krylov's pen, a picture of Russian life not merely with its local color but even with its social system and its national consciousness. Krylov's fables deal with broad philosophical and ideological problems as well as the most immediate details of social and political life.

In the early part of the century Krylov was consistently reinforced in his conservative, monarchist, anti-western and anti-Enlightenment views. From his viewpoint, the French revolution had demonstrated the destructive nature of Enlightenment ideas. The poet does not reject the Enlightenment altogether, as Rousseau did, but demonstrates that a dedication to the ideas of the Enlightenment leads to the moral corruption of particular individuals and of entire states, just as an evil smell of wine remains forever in a barrel which has been filled even once with it ("The barrel" ["Bochka"]). The fable "The writer and the bandit" ("Sochinitel i razboynik") describes a France which has perished thanks to the spread of Enlightenment doctrine and Voltairianism along with the ideas of the Encyclopedists.

Krylov also opposed Alexander I's liberal reforms. In his fable "The lion's education" ("Vospitanie lva") he mocked the Emperor's French tutors who had trained the King of Beasts to "build nests," i.e. had alienated him from the needs and interests of his country by filling his head with worthless liberal ideas. Krylov also opposed the tsar's constitutional projects. In the fable "Horse and Rider" ("Kon i vsadnik") both characters perish because the Rider (the tsar) releases the reins and permits the Horse (the people) to gallop off wherever he wishes without caring where he is going. In "Leaves and Roots" ("Listy i korni") the Leaves fail to understand the Roots because they do not recognize their dependence upon the soil, the national sources of their being.

It is understandable that a man of such anti-western, anti-liberal and Russophile views as Krylov should have become a pillar of the Colloquy and a regular participant in all its activities. He also joined the Olenin circle, which resembled the Colloquy in its political, cultural and ideological viewpoints. With Olenin's assistance Krylov obtained a post at the Public Library, where he remained, with regular promotions, until he retired with the rank of general.

Krylov's fables are distinguished by their supreme artistic perfection. They contain astoundingly precise descriptions of the ordinary peasant's way of life along with witty characterizations of various human – but simultaneously Russian – types: the lazy miller, cardplayers, the hard worker, the braggart, the wastrel, and so on. Krylov's fables became incredibly popular within all classes of society, and especially among the common people. During the author's lifetime they appeared in eighteen editions; the pages of his books were read to shreds.

In bringing the Russian fable to such perfection, Krylov exhausted all the genre's comparatively modest resources. Thereafter the fable ceased to claim a serious place in the history of Russian literature.

Since they were drawn to social activism and sought to establish and expand their influence on public opinion by propagandizing their ideas extensively, the Colloquy naturally took a great interest in the theater. They promoted Krylov and his patriotic comedies *A Lesson for Daughters* and *The Fashion Shop*. Another member of the Colloquy was the playwright Alexander Shakhovskoy (1777–1846), who as early as 1805 wrote a very successful play, *A New Sterne* (*Novy Stern*), in which he made viciously wicked fun of Karamzin and his followers.

Still, the archaist circle was not the source of genuine innovation in the Russian theater. Vladislav Ozerov (1769–1816), the creator of the sentimental tragedy, did transform the Russian stage, and for a very short time became its leading figure. He first acquired fame through his *Oedipus in Athens* (*Edip v Afinakh*, 1804), a play on a subject drawn from antiquity. In it Ozerov exalted the liberal and constitutional policies of the young Alexander I, through the image of the Athenian king Theseus. In the sympathetic depiction of Oedipus, who unintentionally kills his father, one might detect a certain moral justification of the tsar, who had been indirectly responsible for the murder of his father Paul I. The play's most important theme, however, is Antigone's love for her blinded father, and not any political allusions. This love makes up the play's central content, transforming it into a sentimental tragedy emphasizing the depiction of the most refined elements of the heroes' emotions. The play was magnificently produced with Olenin as designer; the classical local color was retained, and the details of everyday life in antiquity were preserved to the greatest possible extent.

Ozerov's next play, *Fingal* (1805), based on Ossianic motifs, was no less successful. This time Scottish local color was depicted on the stage: the sets were steeped in the northern romanticism associated with the Scottish bard's songs; the play's monologues consisted of elegiac meditations on love and death while reproducing images of the gloomy natural settings of the north. The tragedy lacked action and genuine dramatic tension, but it did have a great many beautiful lines.

These same shortcomings were observable in Ozerov's next tragedy, *Dmitry Donskoy* (1806). Here the playwright once again resorted to a political topic and direct political allusions; in the viewers' minds Alexander I's struggle against Napolean was the subtext of Dmitry Donskoy's contest with the Mongols. As in *Oedipus*, so in this tragedy the author supported the tsar's liberal projects for the limitation of the monarchy. At the same time Ozerov introduced a love theme: Dmitry Donskoy is in love with Princess Xenia, and the playwright complicates the struggle against the common enemy with a rivalry between princes. The public was ecstatic about the play, but it was Ozerov's last success.

Ozerov's final play, and very possibly his best, was *Polyxena* (1808), which describes the ritual sacrifice of Hecuba's daughter

Polyxena at the grave of Achilles, who has been killed under the walls of Troy. Polyxena indeed desires her own death, for she hopes to be reunited with her beloved beyond the grave. Her passionate monologues contain some of Ozerov's finest poetry, but the public was completely indifferent to them. In the course of a few years the sentimental tragedy had reached its apogee and then embarked on its downward course.

Ozerov's own fate was tragic. He was dismissed from his employment without the pension he should have received and fell into obvious disfavor. No matter what the reason for this may have been, the playwright suddenly found himself living in a distant village under very difficult financial circumstances. The failure of *Polyxena* completely shook his mental stability: Ozerov went insane, burned all his papers, and died after six years of mental illness.

The archaists, Karamzin's enemies, bore a considerable responsibility for Ozerov's sudden failure as a playwright. Derzhavin, Shishkov and other future members of the Colloquy had done detailed and sharp critiques even of *Oedipus*, attacking the play's sentimental vocabulary and its liberal author's political views.

Shishkov and his allies found *Dmitry Donskoy* especially unacceptable. The Shishkov circle produced a nasty parody of it entitled *Mityukha Valdaysky* (1810), and Derzhavin sneered at the tragedy's hero for being in love like some adolescent and at the Princess, who on the eve of the bloody battle goes visiting the tents of various princes to tell them all about her unhappy love. Shishkov was also indignant over these same historical inaccuracies in the play.

Taking Ozerov's plays as a point of departure, Derzhavin tried to create his own historical plays, writing several on Russian topics: *Pozharsky* (1806), *Vasily the Blind* (*Temny*, 1808), *Eupraxia* (1809). These plays were clumsy and overwrought, replete with excessively direct hints at contemporary reality, and so never saw the stage. But there was a certain logic to them, an undoubted expressiveness of their heavy, archaic language, and they exerted some influence on the development of the Russian theater. Thus Shakhovskoy clearly took Derzhavin as his guide in writing his tragedy *Deborah* (1809), done on a biblical topic but with contemporary allusions, as for instance to Napoleon's attempt at marrying the Grand Duchess, the tsar's sister. The play was staged quite successfully.

One must note, however, that the Russian tragedy on lofty political themes turned out on the whole to have no future. As we have seen, the Ozerovian tradition soon came to an end, and without any consequences to speak of; the Derzhavinian tradition had some influence on the playwriting of the Decembrists (Fyodor Glinka, Paul Katenin, Wilhelm Küchelbecker), but their plays were almost never staged. With considerable mediation the overall tradition did re-emerge in Pushkin's *Boris Godunov*. To some degree that play may be regarded as the apex of the tradition of political tragedy in Russian literature.

By the early nineteenth century sentimentalism was on a down-ward trajectory. Its founder, Karamzin, abandoned literature. His overenthusiastic imitators, with the assistance of sharp and in many ways justified criticism from the Shishkovites, were grad-ually nudged to the periphery of literary life. A new generation of gifted, energetic and well educated writers arose to take their places. Since they were closely linked to Karamzin both personally and professionally, they blazed new trails in the history of Russian literature by developing their mentor's literary and linguistic ideas. These trails led to romanticism, which reached its apogee in the poems of Pushkin and Lermontov and Gogol's colorful, grotesque prose. But the poets of the first part of the century, treading their own paths, created works of very great esthetic value, so that it would be fair to term them early Russian romantics.

First place among them belongs to Vasily Zhukovsky (1783–1852), whose romantic life constitutes an astonishing parallel to his poetic work. Zhukovsky is Russian literature's Petrarch, a man who remained hopelessly and forever in love with his Laura.

Zhukovsky was the illegitimate son of a wealthy landowner named Bunin and a young Turkish woman, apparently from a pasha's harem, given to Bunin by a friend of his. He obtained his name from his godfather, a poor neighbor of Bunin's called Andrey Zhukhovsky. Zhukovsky's literary interests and talents developed quite early. As a youth he was already an educated man and a fine teacher, a tutor to his nieces Masha and Alexandra, daughters of his step-sister Catherine Protasova. Soon Masha, ten years his junior, and Zhukovsky fell in love. Masha, who had grown up under Zhukovsky's care and guidance, was a gentle, tender girl with a poetic nature. Zhukovsky rightly saw in her the happiness of his entire life, but her mother set herself resolutely against a marriage on grounds of their blood relationship (although the church permitted marriages of this type). Protasova was a firm-willed woman of rare stubbornness, and all attempts to change her mind failed. Zhukovsky's religious and moral principles, as well as Masha's, would not permit them to go against her mother's will. In 1817, at her mother's insistence and with Zhukovsky's assent, Masha married a professor. In 1823 she died in the Estonian city of Tartu, then Dorpat. Zhukovsky cherished her memory as long as he lived.

In the meantime Zhukovsky's literary and poetic fame was spreading. During the campaign of 1812 he composed a patriotic poem, "A bard in the camp of Russian warriors" ("Pevets vo stane russkikh voinov"), which every literate Russian soon knew by heart. In 1817 Zhukovsky was appointed Russian language tutor to the fiancée of the future tsar Nicholas I (she was German, as were most of the wives of Russian tsars). In 1823 he was appointed instructor to the heir to the throne, the future Alexander II. It was that pupil of Zhukovsky's who in 1861 abolished serfdom in Russia and introduced many other liberal reforms. A year after his retirement in 1840, Zhukovsky married the daughter of a German artist friend of his and settled in Germany for the remainder of his life. It was there he died in 1852, in Baden-Baden.

Zhukovsky made his literary debut with a translation of Thomas Gray's famous poem "Elegy written in a country churchyard" (1751), published in 1802 in Karamzin's *Herald of Europe*. This poem brought Zhukovsky some little renown, and also in large measure determined the course of his subsequent literary development: Zhukovsky's poetry is almost invariably linked to western originals. The poet himself used to say: "Everything I have done is foreign or *à propos* of something foreign, and yet it is all still mine." Thus Zhukovsky's lyric poetry, despite its foreign sources, is vividly autobiographical in nature. It is usually melancholy and elegiac.

At Zhukovsky's hands the individual word in Russian poetry for the first time becomes multivalent, and its shades of meaning often turn out to be more essential than its basic sense. The author seeks to describe not so much his physical environment as the world of his feelings and experiences, his subjective sensations. Consequently the basic components of Zhukovsky's lyrics are meditations on the passing of youth, regrets over an unhappy love or the death of a beloved (Zhukovsky was especially fond of this topic), or melancholy appreciations of natural beauty: he usually describes the evening, mists, the moon, and so forth.

By his pioneering experiments in the field of multivalency of the Russian poetic word, Zhukovsky paved the way for Russian symbolists such as Alexander Blok and Valery Bryusov, whose poetry dissolved the reality of everyday existence and summoned readers to the ideal worlds of Plato or of Vladimir Solovyov.

Ballads – that is, narrative verse commonly of fantastic content and sunk in a gloomy fairytale atmosphere – occupied an important place in Zhukovsky's art. Almost all Zhukovsky's ballads – and he wrote thirty-nine of them – are either translations or else, though more rarely, comprised of motifs taken from German and English ballads. Among the writers upon whom Zhukovsky drew were Schiller, Goethe, Gottfried Bürger, Walter Scott, and Robert Southey.

Zhukovsky became famous with his first translation of a German ballad, a rendering of Bürger's "Lenore" which he titled "Lyudmila." This ballad describes a dead man who rises from the grave to claim his bride and carries her off to the cemetery, straight into the tomb. The Russian author significantly softened the sharp expressiveness of the original and a certain coarseness found in it: Lyudmila's melancholy plaints are not at all like Lenore's curses and blasphemies. Later on Zhukovsky used motifs from this same ballad of Bürger's to assemble an entirely russified ballad entitled "Svetlana" (1812), which includes poetic descriptions of fortune-telling on the eve of Epiphany and other Russian customs. This ballad was one of his best literary creations.

In other ballads Zhukovsky depicts the ancient world as the preromantics understood it ("Cassandra," "Triumph of the con-querors" ["Torzhestvo pobediteley"], "The Eleusinian festival" ["Elevzinsky prazdnik"], all taken from Friedrich Schiller) or the romantic Middle Ages (Walter Scott's "The Eve of St. John" ["Zamok Smalgolm, ili Ivanov vecher"], "A ballad showing how an old woman rode double on a black horse and who rode before her" ["Ballada, v kotoroy opisyvaetsya, kak odna starushka ekhala na chernom kone vdvoem i kto sidel vperedi"] based on Southey's poem).

Russian culture is deeply indebted to Zhukovsky as a translator. He translated Byron and Schiller, acquainted Russian readers with the Sanskrit epic by rendering the story of "Nala and Damayanti" from the *Mahabharata*, and put the charming prose tale "Undine" by Friedrich de la Motte-Fouqué into elegant Russian hexameters. Zhukovsky also produced the finest extant Russian translation of Homer's *Odyssey*.

The other major poet of the early nineteenth century was Zhu-kovsky's contemporary Konstantin Batyushkov (1787–1855). Though his health was always frail, he was a fearless soldier who participated in three military campaigns. Though a pessimist by nature, he wrote energetic satirical epistles in which he defamed the Karamzinists' literary enemies. Victim of a cruel heredity, in 1822 Batyushkov went insane and thereafter spent half his life in a condition of mental incompetence. He died of cholera in the provincial city of Vologda.

The contradictions within Batyushkov's personality were reflected in his art. On the one hand there is the painful premo-nition of death with which the poet must deal against the back-ground of a gloomy northern landscape. The ghost of a dead friend appears to him in the Ossianic setting of the North Sea ("Ghost of a friend" ["Ten druga"], 1814), or he meditates on bards and skalds long dead, on Ossian's heroes, in "On the ruins of a castle in Sweden" ("Na razvalinakh zamka v Shvetsii," 1813). Batyushkov also speaks of the horrors of war in his epistle "To Dashkov" ("Dashkovu," 1813), saying: "I have seen a sea of evil."

At the same time, the poet describes the joys of a calm and peacefully sybaritic existence in an isolated cottage with a beloved woman, a glass of wine, and a stack of books by his favorite poets. That is the message of the famous "My Penates" ("Moi penaty," 1812), which had a great impact on Zhukovsky, Pushkin, Vyazemsky, and Denis Davydov.

Anacreontic motifs are also quite important in Batyushkov's work. He makes no attempt at re-creating antiquity as it really was, as his friend Gnedich had sought to do in his translations of Homer. Batyushkov finds his antiquity not so much in original

Greek texts as in the verse of Evariste Parny, Jean-Baptiste Gresset, Giovanni Casti, French translations of the *Greek Anthology*, and so forth. The antiquity which Batyushkov depicts most conventionally in his love lyrics is a fragile, elegant world of conventional eroticism whose vivid colors temporarily banish tragic thoughts of the inevitable end; it is useless to hope that one's experiences of love will continue after death in Elysium ("Elysium," 1810). In one of his last and finest poems Batyushkov laments the beauty of the ancient world now vanished forever as he views the porphyry columns of an ancient city inundated by the sea, a city destined never to appear to men's eyes again ("You awake, oh Baia, from the tomb . . ." ["Ty probuzhdaeshsya, o Bayya, iz grobnitsy . . ."], 1819).

Batyushkov's poetry had a great and fruitful influence upon the subsequent development of the anthological trend in Russian poetry in the verse of Pushkin, Fet, Apollon Maykov, Nikolay Shcherbina, Leo Mey, and many others.

Batyushkov's poetic language is remarkably melodic, flowing and euphonic; it is unique in Russian poetry. Possibly this is due to the influence of Italian poetry, of which Batyushkov was a connoisseur.

Zhukovsky, we recall, extended the semantic boundaries of the poetic word by endowing it with numerous supplementary shades of meaning. Batyushkov, to the contrary, made the word astoundingly precise by bestowing upon it within the poetic context the only possible objectified clear and definite meaning. Possibly it is for that reason that Batyushkov is so drawn to painterly color epithets: purple grape, yellow hops, lilac hands, leaden waves, and so forth. If Zhukovsky is a predecessor of Russian symbolism, then Batyushkov might be considered a forerunner of the acmeists, who rejected symbolism's polysemantics and strove for the precision of the poetic word with a single meaning. It is indicative that Batyushkov was one of Osip Mandelshtam's favorite poets: Mandelshtam spoke of the "grapeflesh" of Batyushkov's verses.

Prince Peter Vyazemsky (1792–1878), Zhukovsky's and Batyushkov's younger contemporary, belonged to the Karamzin entourage: he was the younger brother of Karamzin's second wife, and Karamzin treated him as though he were his own son. Vyazemsky reciprocated with respect and intense love.

Vyazemsky had no great poetic gift, although his best poetry displays the casual quality of good conversation and offers vivid portrayals of Russian life. Such, for example, is the poem "First snow" ("Pervy sneg," 1819), which Pushkin liked immensely and which later engendered numerous echoes in Pushkin's own work.

Vyazemsky made up for his lack of poetic expressiveness with his wit and aggressive temperament. He wrote political poetry in which he fought for the liberation of the serfs and attacked serf-owners, bureaucrats and others: see his "Indignation" ("Negodo-vanie," 1820), "St. Petersburg" (1824), and "The Russian God" ("Russky Bog," 1828). Vyazemsky acquired special renown as a polemicist during the literary conflict which burst out between the Karamzinists and the archaists around 1815. He wrote malicious epigrams against the Shishkovites – including an entire "poetic bouquet" of them against Shakhovskoy – as well as parodies of Count Khvostov's fables and dashing epistles to his friends.

His gift for polemics made Vyazemsky a leading literary critic of the 1820s. Although his critical pieces were not distinguished by either precision or intellectual profundity, he played a major role in formulating the theoretical foundations of Russian romanticism through his articles on Pushkin's poems *The Prisoner of the Caucasus* (1822), *The Fountain of Bakhchisarai* (1824), and *The Gypsies* (1827).

One should also mention Vyazemsky's contributions to the field of literary history: he was the author of a fine monograph on Fonvizin (1848) as well as articles on Ozerov (1817), Dmitriev (1821), Sumarokov (1830) and others.

Denis Davydov (1784–1839) occupies a special niche in the glittering pleiad of early romantics: he was a spectacular soldier, a bully of a hussar, a participant in guerrilla warfare and a hero of 1812. That was the way he depicted himself in his verse and in his autobiography ("Some events from the life of Denis Vasilevich Davydov"); he designed his own life to fit his poetry.

The hero in Davydov's verse occupies the military world of the bivouac. He uses his Hussar sword for a mirror, instead of sofas a bag of oats, instead of marble vases – glasses full of punch. He is always first to the table, first to raise his glass, with his pipe ever gripped between his teeth, but he is also first in bloody battle as well.

Davydov remains a Hussar in his love poetry. He is consumed

by the impatience of passion, insists on immediate answers to his demands from his beloved, does not fear ambiguity and sometimes even a certain frivolity, and cures his disappointments in love by drink. Of course the correspondence between the writer and his poetic image could not have been complete. This was all a literary mask which the poet sought to wear in real life. But he provided an example – unique even for romantic poetry – of the combination of reality and literature.

The appearance on the scene around 1815 of some gifted followers of Karamzin's caused literary debates to become much sharper. They began when Shakhovskoy derided Karamzin and his followers in the narrative poem *Stolen Overcoats* (*Raskhishchennye shuby*, 1811–5). And in 1815 he staged one of his best comedies, *Lipetsk Spa* (*Lipetskie vody*). This play contains an episodic character, the poet Fialkin, who was a maliciously witty caricature of Zhukovsky. Fialkin composes lengthy ballads on topics from medieval and ancient cultures in which contemporary theatergoers easily caught hints at Zhukovsky's ballads "Lyudmila" and "Achilles." That caused a scandal.

Zhukovsky's friends Dmitry Dashkov, Dmitry Bludov and Vyazemsky came to the defense of the offended poet with polemical letters, sketches, epigrams, and even cantatas. Bludov wrote a satire entitled "A Vision at the inn at Arzamas, published by the society of scholars" ("Videnie v arzamasskom traktire, izdannoe obshchestvom uchenykh lyudey"), which depicted a group of modest provincial writers who overhear some delirious ravings from Shakhovskoy, who is asleep on the other side of a partition. This satire led to the founding of a friendly literary society of "Unfamous Arzamas Writers," which has gone down in literary history under the name of Arzamas. The Arzamas members consisted of gifted literary men, Karamzin's supporters and people close to his circle: Zhukovsky, Batyushkov, Davydov, Alexander Voeykov, Dashkov, Filipp Vigel, Andrey Turgenev, Vasily Pushkin, Alexander Pushkin, and others. The Arzamassians emphasized their group's informal character, which they contrasted with that of the primly official Colloquy. They held their meetings in various places: one even occurred in a carriage on the way from St. Petersburg to Tsarskoe Selo. The society's permanent secretary, Zhukovsky, kept humorously solemn minutes of these meetings in hexameter. The members of Arzamas adopted nicknames taken from Zhukovsky's ballads. Zhukovsky himself was called Svetlana, Batyushkov – Achilles, Vyazemsky – Asmodeus, and so on. The main content of the Arzamas group's humorous works consisted of attacks on the Colloquy. The Arzamassians delivered funeral eulogies of their opponents, the "living dead," and made fun of the solemn rituals they observed at their sessions. To be sure, the Arzamassians also read and discussed their own serious works, but that did not constitute the group's center of gravity: they concentrated on pranks and literary polemics.

One of the best polemicists in the circle was Vasily Pushkin (1770–1830), Alexander Pushkin's uncle. He had begun mounting attacks on the archaists and Slavophiles from the Colloquy's very beginnings in 1810–11 (and on his deathbed he inveighed against the critical articles of the most junior archaist, Paul Katenin). In his epistle "To Zhukovsky" ("K Zhukovskomu," 1810) Pushkin attacked the "illiterate Slavs" who were trampling underfoot that true enlightenment which was oriented toward Europe. In his epistle "To Dashkov" ("K D. V. Dashkovu") he defended himself vigorously against Shishkov's attacks and scolded bad writers. But the poem "A dangerous neighbor" ("Opasny sosed," 1811) was Vasily Pushkin's genuine polemical masterpiece. The work is set in a brothel whose inhabitants are ecstatic over the Slavophiles' writings, and especially those of Pushkin's old enemy Shakhovskoy. After he joined Arzamas, where he was received with a great many humorous and complicated ceremonies, Pushkin wrote an epistle to Vyazemsky, an epistle to the Arzamassians and several epigrams, but he could never again attain the level of his polemic verse of 1810–11.

The Arzamas group included writers who were too individualistic and too talented for it ever to become such a serious and established union of literary allies as was the Colloquy. In 1816–17 Arzamas attracted several men who would become Decembrists in the future: Nikolay Turgenev, Mikhail Orlov and Nikita Muravyov. They sought to deflect the group's activity into more serious, primarily political, channels; and they insisted that Arzamas publish a literary and political journal, for which they had already begun to prepare and collect material. These reform efforts led to bitter arguments within the group and to its rapid disintegration by the fall of 1817. The last meeting of Arzamas occurred in April 1818. It did not outlive the Colloquy by much, since its main reason for existence had after all been its polemics with the Colloquy. Thus Arzamas was not so influential in the history of Russian literature as is sometimes thought. The individuals who made it up were much more significant – both in their gifts and in their role in the history of Russian culture – than was an ephemeral and humorous group brought into existence for a short time.

Much as Karamzin was succeeded by a younger generation of early romantics, so the Slavophiles and members of the Colloquy gave way to a younger generation of archaists: Paul Katenin, Wilhelm Küchelbecker, Fyodor Glinka, Alexander Griboedov and a few others. In a paradox of literary history, while the older archaists were conservatives who found themselves in opposition to the government, the majority of the young archaists, though they shared the Shishkovites' Slavophile and anti-western aspirations, were more or less closely connected to the anti-government Decembrist movement, a revolutionary liberal effort.

The most important figure among the young archaists was undoubtedly Alexander Griboedov (1795–1829). Ties of friendship linked him to Küchelbecker and Katenin, as well as to Shakhovskoy from the older generation of the archaists.

Griboedov's life was brief and intense. A person of outstanding ability, he entered Moscow University at the age of eleven; by sixteen he had successfully completed the literary, law, and natural science and mathematical faculties, learned French, German, English and Italian, and was preparing to take his doctorate.

The Napoleonic invasion of 1812 interrupted these peaceful scholarly endeavors, and Griboedov never returned to them. From 1812 to 1816 he was in the military service, although he never had occasion to participate directly in battle. From 1817 on Griboedov worked for the Foreign Ministry.

But then a duel terminated his pleasant St. Petersburg life, with his initial literary successes, drinking bouts with his young friends, and romantic adventures. Anxious to leave St. Petersburg, Griboedov accepted appointment as first secretary of the Russian embassy in Persia, and thus commenced his diplomatic career in

1818. The young diplomat quickly learned Arabic and Persian and acquired remarkable erudition in the area of Middle Eastern cultures.

After the uprising of 14 December 1825 Griboedov came under official suspicion, since he was linked both in personal and literary ways with several of the Decembrists, and his comedy *Woe from Wit* promoted many clearly liberal ideas. Griboedov was arrested, but since his connections with the secret revolutionary societies could not be demonstrated he was released after a few months with a promotion and a monetary reward.

In 1828, under Griboedov's guidance, Russia signed the peace of Turkmanchay with Persia, a quite favorable treaty for Russia. Griboedov received a medal, a monetary award, and the high rank of State Councillor; in addition he was soon appointed the Resident Minister (Ambassador) to Persia. On the way to his assignment he delayed for some time in the Georgian capital of Tiflis (now Tbilisi) to marry the daughter of an old friend of his, the famous Georgian poet and social activist Alexander Chavchavadze. The beautiful young Nina – she had not yet turned sixteen – had been in love for some time with Griboedov, who had tutored her in music and kept close track of her education and upbringing. Griboedov did not take his wife with him to Teheran, for he realized how dangerous his mission was. Being well informed on eastern questions, he knew how much the Persians hated the Russians, since they were burdened with large financial obligations to pay the restitution which the victors had imposed on the defeated country. In accordance with the provisions of the Treaty of Turkmanchay, the Russian ambassador demanded the return of Russian prisoners (including women in harems) as well as military deserters and runaway serfs, many of whom had long since settled down in Persia, converted to Islam, served in the army (often in high ranks), and had not the slightest desire to return to Russia. On 30 January 1829 an enraged mob, urged on by fanatic mullahs and with the tacit encouragement of the government, invaded the Russian embassy and slaughtered all the Russian representatives (only one survived by chance). Griboedov perished in that bloody episode as he bravely and calmly fought to the end. "His death was instantaneous and magnificent," Alexander Pushkin wrote of him.

Since he was constantly absorbed by his official duties, Griboedov managed to write very little in the course of his life. His literary work consisted primarily of dramatic works, a few articles and some poems. From the start of his literary career Griboedov always adhered to the Karamzinists' opponents: in his comedy *The Student* (*Student*, 1817), co-authored with Katenin, he mocked and parodied the poetry of Karamzin, Zhukovsky, Batyushkov, and the two Pushkins.

Griboedov's protector and mentor was Alexander Sha-khovskoy, member of the Colloquy, consistent anti-Karamzinist and critic of sentimentalism. We have already mentioned his comedies *The New Sterne* (1805) and *Lipetsk Spa* (1815). Sha-khovskoy was the creator of the so-called noble, high-society comedy, distinguished by its lively, free language and its light, entertaining plots. The action in such plays usually takes place in the high society salons of Moscow or St. Petersburg, and their heroes, worldly and well educated people, are often notable for their lofty spiritual aspirations.

Another popular author of high society comedies at the time was Nikolay Khmelnitsky (1789–1845), whose plays *The Indecisive Man* (*Nereshitelny*), *The Chatterbox* (*Govorun*), *Castles in the Air* (*Vozdushnye zamki*) and others were invariably successful. The comedy *Your Own Family, or The Married Fiancée* (*Svoya semya, ili zamuzhnyaya nevesta*, 1817) was written collectively by Sha-khovskoy, Khmelnitsky and Griboedov.

From the soil of the high-society comedy of the early nineteenth century sprang a masterpiece of the Russian theater, *Woe from Wit* (*Gore ot uma*, 1822–4). In the Russian mind Griboedov remains the author of this one work: everything else he wrote is of interest only because it came from the pen of the creator of *Woe from Wit*.

The plot of the comedy is briefly as follows. After an absence of three years the young Alexander Chatsky returns to the home of a wealthy Moscow aristocrat, Paul Famusov, where he had spent his childhood and early adolescence, and where he had fallen in love with Famusov's daughter Sofya. The intelligent and exceedingly well educated Chatsky still loves Sofya ardently, just as before, but she has changed: she now loves her father's secretary, the cowardly scoundrel Molchalin, and has come to hate the man she once loved. When Chatsky tries to discover what has happened to her and with whom she is in love, Sofya declares he has gone mad.

Chatsky suffers and tortures himself as his conflict with those around him gradually intensifies. In the last act, in despair upon learning of Sofya's love for the nonentity Molchalin, Chatsky leaves Moscow forever.

A very important trait of Griboedov's comedy is the combination of romantic and social drama within it. Chatsky suffers from unrequited love, and in his impatience and irritation comes into more and more severe conflict with the nonentities who surround him. The women around him think only of clothes, the men of their careers, everyone seeks his own pleasure and no one has any spiritual interests.

In his passionate monologues Chatsky defends science, art and creative work against the attacks of careerists and rogues. He criticizes the system of serfdom, or more precisely, the abuses and cruelties of that system: the selling of serfs separately from their families, serf theaters and so forth. The struggle against Gallomania also occupies an important place in Chatsky's monologues: in this area Griboedov shares the views of the Shishkovites and the young archaists entirely. His Chatsky defends the purity of the Russian language against pollution by French borrowings, he sorely regrets the abandonment of the comfortable traditional Russian dress which has been replaced in high society by ridiculous frock coats and bizarre women's fashions. Only the common people have preserved the dress, morals and customs of their ancestors, and Chatsky's speeches contain comments on the tragic gulf between the simple people and educated aristocrats whom those simple people, "intelligent and energetic," look upon as another nation quite foreign to themselves.

All these ruminations of Chatsky's correspond in considerable degree to the views and ideas of the Decembrists, who were naturally quite enthusiastic about the comedy and spoke of it frequently while they were under police investigation and in their subsequent memoirs. Still, although he mostly shared the social and political ideas of the Decembrists, Griboedov was also a sceptic who looked with a jaundiced eye upon conspiracies, plots, revolutions and the other romantic schemes of his Decembrist friends. Thus in the fourth act of his play he introduces the episodic character of Repetilov, a chatterbox, drunkard and fool who claims to belong to a "most secret union" of "decisive men." This was an obvious caricature on secrecy and conspiracies.

Griboedov's comedy is linked structurally to the traditions of classicism. The classical unities of time, place, and action are strictly observed (one day, the Famusov home, Chatsky's unrequited love). The comedy's precise and aphoristic language remains to this day the finest anthological example of living colloquial Russian. This prevalence of the well-formed aphorism also connects Griboedov's comedy with the finest models of the classical comedy, and primarily with Molière, whose *Misanthrope* undoubtedly influenced Griboedov's conception of Chatsky.

At the same time certain romantic traits are detectible within the main hero's character, in his lyrical monologues, in his solitude, in that juxtaposition of the hero with the banal and worthless world surrounding him that we find in Schiller's plays, for example. The play's central conflict also remains unresolved, in the romantic tradition: the hero departs, but without our knowing why, where he is going, or what he will do in the future. For many decades down to the present day writers such as Dostoevsky, Saltykov and Goncharov, as well as theatrical directors like Konstantin Stanislavsky and Georgy Tovstonogov have sought to interpret, elucidate and elaborate Griboedov's thoughts about Chatsky as a hero of his time and about the channels of Russia's historical development.

4

THE NINETEENTH CENTURY: ROMANTICISM, 1820–40

The decades between 1820 and 1840 witnessed simultaneously the zenith of Russian romanticism and the first stages of Russian literature's greatest period, which extended from approximately 1820 to the time of the First World War. In terms of genres, Russian romanticism began with a strong emphasis on poetry (it is appropriate that *Ruslan and Lyudmila* of 1820 should be a narrative poem), but in the course of its development shifted toward prose. Thus Pushkin, though he never abandoned poetry by any means, turned definitely toward prose in 1830 with the composition of his *Tales of Belkin*, a cycle of works which laid the foundations of the Russian short story yet to come; Gogol began his literary career with a poetic failure but soon found his place as a writer of elaborate prose; and Lermontov, in numerous ways the most characteristic figure of the romantic period, remained not only a fine poet – many think him second only to Pushkin among nineteenth-century poets – but became an excellent prose-writer as well, and it is proper that his novel, or cycle of short stories, *A Hero of Our Time* (1840), should mark the end of Russian romanticism, and rather decisively at that. The transition from *Ruslan and Lyudmila* to *A Hero of Our Time* marks not only a shift from an early romanticism based upon national folklore to a romanticism oriented toward the extraordinary individual, the "superfluous man," in a social context, but also a shift from poetry to prose. And yet both works are plainly romantic in their thrust.

By around 1820, and certainly by 1825, neoclassicism had receded into the past: though Pushkin's literary approach retained many classical elements, few were to be found in Gogol or in Lermontov. The new literature emphasized the individual spirit, generally the extraordinary man who stood in some way above society, who had something peculiarly his own to offer. Ivan Turgenev, who lived through the height of Russian romanticism in the 1830s as a very young man, in 1870 deftly outlined what he called the "Marlinsky type" of that time:

What was lacking in that type? There were Byronism and romanticism; reminiscences of the French revolution and of the Decembrists – and adoration of Napoleon; a belief in fate, in one's lucky star, in one's strength of character; a pose and a phrase – and the anguish of emptiness; the trembling anxieties of a shallow self-love – as well as genuine power and courage; noble aspirations along with ignorance and poor upbringing [. . .]

There was, in short, something admirable about the romantic hero with his exotic dreams, even though he could be comic too. A romantic like the Gogol of the 1830s could overdo things considerably, with his tales of wizards, incestuous fathers, great sinners; Lermontov loved the exotic settings of the Caucasus, although he was considerably more sober than Gogol in his approach. But no doubt the Marlinsky type as Turgenev describes him was most characteristic of the romantic mind.

It was also during the romantic period that the Russian writer began to view himself as normally an adversary of the existing order. This frame of mind came into being especially after the suppression of the Decembrist uprising of 1825 and the execution or exile of many of its participants. Nicholas I, who came to the throne then, found little sympathy from intellectuals and writers, and in turn entrusted them with little authority. Where only a few years before writers like Karamzin and Derzhavin had been influential in high government circles or held lofty official positions, now writers rarely obtained anything more than modest government positions, and certainly had little to do with the formulation of high government policy. The writer thus adopted a posture of hostility to the government, and viewed himself as primarily a critic of his society.

During the romantic period another important change occurred in the writer's status. Earlier authors did not expect to gain a living from their writing, or even to receive much in the way of income from it, but now literature became more commercialized. In order to support himself the writer had to produce things the reading public would accept and therefore pay for, but this meant that he was more than ever dependent upon the tastes of his audience. During the eighteenth century writers had been members of the landowning aristocracy or else supported by the government in some fashion, but as the nineteenth century wore on they became more and more dependent upon the reading public.

In an effort to reach that public the so-called "thick journals" were created. The first important such journal was Osip Senkovsky's *Library for Reading*, founded in 1834; it was followed in short order by Pushkin's *The Contemporary* in 1836 and *Fatherland Notes* in 1839. All of these lasted at least until into the 1860s. Such journals published writing of various sorts: poetry, prose, history, commentary, in a volume the size of a book which appeared monthly and provided general intellectual fare for the reader. Among the writing included in the "thick journals" was literary criticism, which developed quickly now that there was some original literature to write about. Vissarion Belinsky, the most outstanding critic of the century, began his career in the 1830s, and in the subsequent decade would exercise a profound influence upon Russian literature. Before Belinsky Russian criticism was a feeble reed; after him it laid just claim to an important place in the history of Russian culture.

The "thick journals" also had another significant function. With the virtual disappearance of the literary societies which had been so vital at the beginning of the century, they supplied focal points for literary life: now writers might run into one another at the editorial offices of the journals in which they published rather than at evening gatherings at Derzhavin's home, for example. But the journals also reinforced the spirit of faction in literature, for each journal generally espoused a certain approach and gathered to itself writers who agreed with that approach. Thus they sowed division as well as unity among writers.

OUR TENDENCY to think in terms of schools and movements suggests that literature consists of discrete blocs of artistically homogeneous works. Of course, that is not the case, since literature is constantly evolving, and every period, in addition to its exemplary figures, has its epigones from past movements and precursors of things to come. Thus, it is difficult to place even approximate limits on a movement or a school. Given this caveat, we may say that Russian romanticism begins to emerge from sentimentalism around 1815, that it gains the high ground in the 1820s and 1830s, and by the early 1840s is on the verge of displacement by realism, whose harbingers have appeared over the previous decade.

Works in verse formed the centerpiece of Russian romantic literature: so brilliant and rich was the product of that period that by general acceptance it has been termed "The Golden Age" of Russian poetry. The poetry of Baratynsky, Tyutchev, Delvig, Yazykov, along with that of some less well-known talents, would justify that appellation even were one to exclude all of Pushkin's contribution, as unthinkable as that might be.

With some justification literary historians extend the final limit of the Golden Age until the death of Lermontov in 1841. Be that as it may, poetry as the dominant literary form began to be displaced by prose at the end of the 1820s, quite probably because the reading public had simply become sated with an abundance of good verse. By 1830 prose was preeminent, and even poets *par excellence* such as Pushkin increasingly turned to fiction.

Some social considerations must be taken into account in any survey of romanticism, for to a degree they affected prevailing literary themes and their treatment. Almost without exception, the romantic poets belonged to the gentry class. Accordingly, most of them had some formal education, which put them in touch with the more important examples of ancient poetry and of classicism, foreign and domestic. Most knew French at least as well as Russian, and used French in conversation, in correspondence, and sometimes in their compositions. The new generation of romantics devoted considerable effort to Anacreontic and fugitive verse celebrating the pleasures of friendship and the good life. If a change of mood seemed appropriate, the elegy was a favorite form. When protest motivated them, they inveighed against restrictions on personal freedom, rather than seeking equality for the masses. Most of them accepted serfdom: however liberal or democratic their political orientation, they were not vocal proponents of emancipation.

Since personal freedom was at issue, it was natural that Byron enjoyed a vogue in the early 1820s. But the banner of protest which the Englishman had raised and which seemed destined to be grasped by eager Russian hands after his death in 1824 was dropped summarily after the suppression of the Decembrist uprising of 1825. A number of writers were exiled, including Küchelbecker and Alexander Bestuzhev-Marlinsky; the poet Kondraty Ryleev was hanged; and everyone else, including Pushkin, came under suspicion. From then on poets sought to keep away from the gaze of officialdom.

Meanwhile, men of a new social class were entering the literary arena, not only as writers but as journalists, publishers, and critics. Although not exactly from the lower strata of society, they were hardly prepared to join the so-called St. Petersburg "mandarins," for whom literary activity was an endeavor for which remuneration had seldom been expected or provided. This new group of *littérateurs* were professionals who sought – often with pathetic results – to gain a livelihood from their efforts, and that injected a new note of economic necessity into the general literary scene. At this point we begin to see literary criticism, never noted for its gentility, acquiring acrimonious tones and slanderous overtones. Literary piracy became common as publishers and booksellers sought to outsmart and outsell their competition.

With political protest strictly proscribed, and certainly unappealing in view of the fate of the Decembrists, social protest was nonetheless implicit in some of the poetry and prose of the late 1820s. This was particularly true of prose after it began to dominate literature in the early 1830s. This protest was made on behalf of painters, musicians, and other persons of artistic talent, who because of their plebeian, or even serf, origins were scorned or unappreciated by a vacuous society. But again, the protest was most often voiced on behalf of their unrecognized talent, not on behalf of the class from which they had emerged.

The dominant figure of this period was the poet Alexander Pushkin (1799–1837), who even as a student at the lyceum for gentry youth at Tsarskoe Selo had displayed uncommon poetic ability. In fact, when Derzhavin visited the school in 1815 and heard him declaim his own verses, he had announced: "This is he who will replace Derzhavin." His prediction quickly proved correct, for within four years Pushkin's *Ruslan and Lyudmila* (*Ruslan i Lyudmila*) appeared.

Ruslan and Lyudmila is conventionally called a "mock epic," but it has many more prototypes than merely, for example, Voltaire's *La Pucelle*. One may find in it stylistic features of diverse European and Russian origins, such as medieval fabliaux, the *Orlando Furioso*, the Russian *bylina*, or modern efforts to imitate folklore, such as Zhukovsky's "Twelve sleeping maidens." High adventure, magic, spells, and a giant disembodied head which speaks are involved as three champions seek to recover Lyudmila, kidnapped by the hideous dwarf-magician Chernomor. There is considerable erotic suggestiveness in this comedy, which in the end ingeniously unites Lyudmila with her rightful beloved, Ruslan.

Conservatives were (at least publicly) disturbed by the eroticism and other "low" features of *Ruslan and Lyudmila*, and faulted Pushkin for failing to provide a *bona fide* epic, a feat beyond their own powers. Others were perplexed by the eclectic nature of the work and the heterogeneity of its language, which ranged from

Church Slavic to vernacular Russian. Discerning critics saw it as a demonstration of the triumph of innovations begun by Karamzin, and Zhukovsky sent Pushkin a portrait of himself generously inscribed "To the victorious student from his vanquished mentor."

Pushkin had no use for Alexander I, whom he considered a usurper, and upon graduation from the Tsarskoe Selo lyceum he wrote several poems with political implications, including "Liberty" ("Volnost," 1817), an ode calling for the lawful punishment of tyrants, and "To Chaadaev" ("Chaadaevu," 1818), in which he pledges himself to the cause of freedom. These and other poems, as well as an incendiary epigram directed at the tsar's favorite, Count Alexey Arakcheev, came to the attention of the authorities, and Pushkin was exiled to the south of Russia. *En route* he fell ill and was aided by the Raevsky family, with whom he traveled across the Crimea. Alexander Raevsky, somewhat older than Pushkin and a hardened cynic, seems to have influenced the young poet, at least if one interprets "My demon" ("Moy demon," 1823) as alluding to their relationship. Less ambivalent were Pushkin's feelings about Maria Raevskaya, the seventeen-year-old daughter of the family, who seems to have become a muse for Pushkin, or at least the addressee of several lyrics.

Three narrative poems form the so-called southern cycle *The Prisoner of the Caucasus* (*Kavkazsky plennik*), *The Fountain of Bakhchisarai* (*Bakhchisaraysky fontan*), and *The Gypsies* (*Tsygany*) all show Byron's influence in setting, theme, and character types. They exploit the exoticism of the remote Circassian *aul*, the Crimean palace of the Tatar khans, and the gypsy camp; unrequited love and violence are common to all three. The prisoner is a disaffected Russian officer whose devoted Circassian lover frees him from his captors and drowns herself. In *The Fountain of Bakhchisarai* a jealous odalisque slays her rival. By the time Pushkin finished *The Gypsies*, he presumably had overcome the Byronic influence, for the protagonist, Aleko, is depicted as inherently selfish and desirous of freedom only for himself: when his gypsy lover leaves him for another, he murders her. He is then banished by the tribe.

While still in the south, Bessarabia, Pushkin began his most famous work, the "novel in verse" *Eugene Onegin* (*Evgeny Onegin*).

Once again we have a selfish hero, a jaded St. Petersburg youth who pompously rejects the love of a naive provincial girl, Tatyana, only to fall hopelessly in love with her when she has become the unattainable ornament of the St. Petersburg *haut monde*. Pushkin worked at his masterpiece at least seven years, and the final canto of the eight he completed appeared in 1830. As one moves through the story, the effervescent and light-hearted stanzas of the early cantos are replaced by more sober verses, a development we may attribute to the growing maturity of Pushkin's "lyric I."

Eugene Onegin is a conglomerate work, combining the story of Onegin and Tatyana with extensive digressions reflecting Pushkin's *ars poetica*, *ars amatoria*, and autobiography, critical opinions and social commentary. The story is presented in an unusual manner, for while Onegin is represented in ways which later became standard for realist literature, and his portrait is in fact a psychological one, the secondary characters Olga and Lensky are purely satirical. The girl, we are told, is a typical blonde, and the narrator leaves it to the reader to complete her description. Lensky, a parody of the would-be poet imbued with German romantic philosophy, is as foggy as his elegies. When he becomes Onegin's victim in a pointless duel, the narrator forestalls the readers' sympathies by suggesting that Lensky might have ended up rusticating in the country, wearing horns and a quilted dressing gown.

Interestingly enough, the two romantic works which most influenced the development of the Russian novel of psychological realism – *Eugene Onegin* and Lermontov's *A Hero of Our Time* – frustrated any imitation, the former because of its unique form and vast scope (Vissarion Belinsky called it an encyclopedia of Russian life, but it is not) and the latter owing to its unusual combination of genres. Thus, when writers sought to exploit Lermontov's work, they could utilize only facets of Pechorin's complex personality, as, for example, Ivan Turgenev with his indifferent Andrey Kolosov or the vicious duellist Luchkov.

While Pushkin was still in southern exile, or later living at his parental estate of Mikhaylovskoe, an at times bitter and mostly pointless battle raged over the meaning of romanticism and its companion term *narodnost*. The controversy was in part a legacy of the old conflict between the conservative literary camp, which resisted innovation, and liberal writers who opposed constraints. We have seen that *Ruslan and Lyudmila* not only offended but also perplexed some readers, who objected to the inclusion of the vulgar within it and were mystified by its unknown "genre." In his review of that work Alexander Voeykov provided a good example of the prevailing confusion when he said that its mixture of the comic and the epic qualified it as romantic. Pushkin complained to Küchelbecker that even Prince Peter Vyazemsky, who had attempted to defend Pushkin and *The Fountain of Bakhchisarai* in a critical article, was wrong about romanticism. As for him, Pushkin held that the verse forms known to the ancients were "classical," while those new on the scene were "romantic." Simplicity recommends this definition, but it is hardly very useful. *Narodnost*, which may be translated somewhat inadequately as "national identity" or "national culture," also cried out for a definition, and the arguments over it were just as futile as those about romanticism.

Some light was cast on the subject by Orest Somov's three-part essay of 1823 entitled "About romantic poetry" ("O romanticheskoy poezii"), which appeared in *The Emulator* (*Sorevnovatel*), the journal of The Free Society of Lovers of Russian Letters. The first two parts are an acknowledged paraphrase of ideas from Madame de Staël's *De l'Allemagne* (1813); in the third and original section Somov noted the vast potential for an original romanticism to be found in Russian chronicles, history, landscape, ethnic types, and language. Somov's essay was not a definition, but it did isolate the ingredients which might contribute to a romanticism based on *narodnost* and its companion term, *mestnost*, or national locale.

Another term that has caused more trouble than its utility merits is "The Pushkin Pleiad," which by general agreement includes Baratynsky, Delvig, and Yazykov, but conceivably can be extended to include such lesser figures as Vyazemsky, Victor Teplyakov, Vasily Tumansky, Dmitry Struysky, Peter Pletnyov, and Alexey Koltsov. The term "Pleiad" does not, however, define a group who wrote under Pushkin's influence, but rather a group of poets who shared an art-for-art's-sake philosophy and (Koltsov aside) gentry origins. As with Pushkin, their education had introduced them to classical literature, evidence of which may be found in many of their otherwise romantic works.

Baron Anton Delvig (1798–1831) is remembered almost as much for his friendship with Pushkin and his publishing ventures as for his poetry. He attended the Tsarskoe Selo lyceum with Pushkin, where he, along with Küchelbecker, shared that poetic ambiance. After leaving school, Delvig lived in St. Petersburg, for a time sharing an apartment with Baratynsky. His talent and good relations with gentry poets made him one of the "literary mandarins" of St. Petersburg, and in 1824 he had no difficulty in mobilizing his friends to contribute to the almanac *Northern Flowers for 1825* (*Severnye tsvety na 1825 god*). His house became a gathering place for St. Petersburg *literati* and ultimately a center of opposition to the "literary shopkeepers" Nikolay Grech and Faddey Bulgarin.

Delvig's poems are largely of the kind termed "occasional," such as epistles to his poet friends or elegies. Many pieces are entitled simply "A romance," and deal with personal circumstances and intimate thoughts. A number of poems display an original combination of meters, evidence of the experimentation typical of romantics, but Delvig's constant allusions to classical mythology in much of his verse (except the popular songs) reveal an orientation toward the *Greek Anthology* not typical of his contemporaries. His use of hexameters in much of his mature poetry was also unusual.

Delvig's mature poetry includes a number of idylls and sonnets, not ordinary for Russian romantics, and imitations of popular songs, some so "authentic" as to have been accepted as the real thing. Many of these are titled "A Russian song" ("Russkaya pesnya"), and share the features of this folklore genre: an abundance of diminutives, repetition, apostrophe, particles with no meaning inserted for emphasis or the meter, and parallel constructions:

Ach thou, night thou,	Akh ty, noch li,
Nightlet!	Nochenka!
Ach thou, night thou	Akh ty, noch li
Stormy!	Burnaya!

A number of these songs have been set to music, along with many other poems by Delvig, which testifies to their general appeal.

Delvig was not inclined toward politics, and seems to have had no relations with the Decembrists other than those based on personal friendship. There is a story that on 14 December 1825, he blithely crossed Senate Square oblivious of what was going on. In 1826 Delvig enlisted the aid of Orest Somov as managing editor for *Northern Flowers,* and from that point on Somov became a fixture of the almanac's editorial staff. With the support of the finest contemporary writers, in 1830 Delvig launched *The Literary Gazette (Literaturnaya gazeta),* an eight-page newspaper which appeared every five days.

Several of Delvig's idylls have become anthology pieces, among them "The bathing women" ("Kupalnitsy," 1825), which D. S. Mirsky called "the highest achievement in Russian poetry in the more purely sensuous vision of classical antiquity." Also noteworthy are "The end of the golden age" ("Konets zolotogo veka," 1829) and "The retired soldier" ("Otstavnoy soldat," 1829), which employs the idyll as a vehicle for the tale of a wounded veteran of the war with Napoleon.

Eugene Baratynsky (1800–44) is in the good company of poets second only to Pushkin. Although he is indisputably a romantic, his poetry is highly intellectual, and he has been called "the poet of thought."

Baratynsky's life was marred by an incident in his youth which prevented him from enjoying the privileged status to which his gentry descent entitled him. At the age of sixteen he was dismissed from the Corps of Pages for involvement in a prank which aroused the ire of Alexander I. Three years later he was permitted to enroll as a common soldier with private quarters. Then followed four years of not too arduous service in Finland. In 1825 he became an officer, and that December he was in Moscow on extended furlough. Despite his many friends among the Decembrists, he seems not to have had any connection with the conspiracy, nor any deep political convictions.

Baratynsky is known for his narrative poetry and for his lyrics, all permeated by a pervasive pessimism. *Eda* (1825) is the tale of a naive Finnish girl who is abandoned by her Russian officer lover. Except for some excellent descriptions of the Finnish landscape and a touching portrait of the heroine, the work is not unusual, and critics have not unjustly seen it as a Finnish variant of Karamzin's "Poor Liza" or Pushkin's *Prisoner of the Caucasus.* Two later narrative poems – *The Ball* (*Bal*, 1828) and *The Concubine* (*Nalozhnitsa*, 1831) – concern contemporary society and are closer in concept to *Eugene Onegin*: that is, they present psychological portraits of the central characters and satirical depictions of society. In *The Ball* Princess Nina, abandoned by her Byronic lover Arseny, takes poison. In *The Concubine* (in later editions retitled *The Gypsy Woman* [*Tsyganka*]), the title character, a prostitute, finds her lover Eletsky is devoted to another woman. Hoping to regain his affections, she gives him a love potion which turns out to be a fatal poison.

While it would be wrong to ignore Baratynsky's narrative poems, his lyric poetry is much more original and distinctive. His early mastery of the elegy caught the attention of Pushkin, who wrote Vyazemsky in 1822 that "he will outdo both Parny and Batyushkov if he keeps on advancing as he has until now." Pushkin's comment identifies two important influences upon Baratynsky, to whom must be added Millevoye, a number of whose poems he translated.

Pessimism about poetry, the poet's lot, love, culture, and the future is a common denominator of these lyrics. In "A complaint" ("Ropot," 1820) the poet expresses his inability to respond to joy; in "An admission" ("Priznanie," 1823) the lyric "I" declares itself unable to love again. Even the epistles to friends strike a somber note, as "To Delvig" ("Delvigu," 1821), which begins:

> In vain, Delvig, we dream of finding
> Happiness here in this life;
> The gods of heaven will not share it
> With Prometheus' mundane children.

All of Baratynsky's poetry has a forcefulness of expression which elevates it above the usual trite words about jaundiced emotions and premature disillusionment typical of much other occasional verse of the period.

After 1826 Baratynsky left the service, married, and moved to Moscow, where he associated with members of the disbanded Lovers of Wisdom Society. Though he was never a disciple of Schelling, who was, after all, an optimist, Baratynsky's poetry now acquires a philosophical quality which reflects careful thought about art, the poet's role, the fate of civilization. Death becomes an overt theme, as in "The last death" ("Poslednyaya smert," 1827), a vision of a world devoid of life; "The last poet" ("Posledny poet," 1834–5), which casts the poet in the role of a superfluous and ridiculous member of society; and "Autumn" ("Osen," 1837), an ode of 160 lines finished just after Baratynsky learned of Pushkin's death: autumn is the time of harvest, and winter effaces all, but for you [Pushkin] there is no future harvest. The last two of these poems appeared in Baratynsky's final collection, *Twilights* (*Sumerki*), which contained poems written between 1834 and 1841.

Baratynsky parted company with most of his Moscow literary friends at the end of the 1830s, unable to share their Slavophile enthusiasms. In the fall of 1843 he began a tour of Europe during which he met a number of famous French writers. In the spring of 1844 he left Paris for Italy, and died unexpectedly in Naples in June of that year.

Today Baratynsky's reputation is secure, but during his lifetime he did not enjoy the fame he deserved. His poetry of ideas, psychological and philosophical, was too serious for a public accustomed to album verse, and although he enjoyed the respect of his fellow poets he found the critics rather severe. Many viewed the subject matter of his narrative poems as uncouth and even Belinsky, while recognizing Baratynsky's talent, criticized his relentless pessimism (in the 1830s Belinsky was an optimistic disciple of German romantic idealism).

Nikolay Yazykov (1803–46) is the third charter member of the Pushkin Pleiad. While most of the writers of the romantic period improved as they grew older, Yazykov was an exception, for the verses of the first decade of his creative life are generally recognized as superior to those of the final two decades. Commenting upon his move from Dorpat (now Tartu) to Moscow at the end of the 1820s, Yazykov said that he had "gone straight from the tavern to the church": he had also gone from being a university student majoring in revelry and a writer of excellent occasional poetry to a militant Russian-Orthodox-Slavophile and author of excessively tendentious verse.

Yazykov's surname was fully appropriate, since *yazyk* means "tongue" in Russian, and no poet surpassed him in verbal felicity. The inspiration for the poetry of his Dorpat period came mostly from wine, women, and song, which he celebrated enthusiastically and incessantly. In endless epistles and works he called elegies (though their subject matter was atypical of the genre) he lauded friendship, drinking, feasting, and amorous adventures (in explicit language). These verses, many of which could circulate only in hand-written copies, reveal unusual craftsmanship, but their beauty is superficial, for there is nothing conceptually new about them and they display no particular intellectual content. Yazykov is more serious in his verse devoted to freedom, which, of course, he enjoyed fully at Dorpat, far removed from the center of autocracy and the pale of serfdom. At that time the poet was an outspoken enemy of the tsar and his minions, and like contemporary "civic" poets, he turned to Russia's heroic past for examples of patriotic virtue. "Boyan to the Russian warrior during the time of Dimitry Donskoy" ("Bayan k russkomu voinu pri Dimitrii donskom") presumably is the exhortation of a patriotic bard to the troops combatting the Tatars, but it might also be relevant to contemporary circumstances:

> An end to tyrants' reign:
> The Tatar khan was fearsome,
> But the Russian sword killed him!

In poems such as this we find a reflection of the romantic ideal of the poet as seer or prophet, the bearer of truth, the leader of the people.

During the summer months of 1826 Yazykov had the good fortune to stay at Trigorskoe, an estate adjacent to Mikhaylovskoe, where Pushkin resided at the time, and the two poets became fast friends. For Yazykov Pushkin was a "free-thinking poet, an heir to Voltaire's wisdom." The cycle of poems connected with this summer (usually referred to as the Pushkin cycle) represents the best of Yazykov, who was perhaps on his mettle. These verses include epistles to Pushkin and to other friends, and a tribute to Pushkin's nurse, Arina Rodionovna, who provided the young poets with food and drink and entertained them with folk tales. Also among them is "Trigorskoe," one of the most highly regarded of his works, a long reminiscence of his visit to that estate which ranges widely from allusions to the freedom of the past to a vivid description of a summer storm, the latter rather unusual in the work of a poet not noted for his attachment to nature.

Yazykov's association with the Slavophiles was not accompanied by any intellectual maturation on his part. In fact, some of his verses attacking the westernizers Peter Chaadaev and Alexander Herzen were so abusive as to offend even those of his own persuasion. He spent his final years traveling about Europe in the vain hope of finding a cure for his progressively poorer health. After his death he was largely forgotten until rediscovered by the symbolists, who saw in him the ability to express the inexpressible.

The Pushkin Pleiad may be expanded to include many poets of talent and accomplishment. Some must be mentioned, because they were important in their own right and because they contributed to the heritage of the Golden Age. Dmitry Venevitinov (1805–27) during his brief career was recognized by his fellow *literati* as a poet of considerable potential and was a leading figure in the Lovers of Wisdom in the early 1820s. His entire work consists of less than fifty poems. The last ones, dealing with unrequited love and hinting at suicide, strengthened the aura of romantic fatalism which surrounded his untimely death (due, however, to a most unromantic case of pneumonia). Ivan Kozlov (1779–1840) is remembered for his accomplishments as a translator, which rivaled those of Zhukovsky. By the age of forty he was blind and paralyzed, but he learned English and German (he already knew French and Italian) and began translating Scott, Byron, and Moore. His Byronic narrative poem *The Monk* (*Chernets*, 1825) produced a large number of imitations. His original lyrics are marked by a feeling of religious resignation and are notable for their vivid nature descriptions. Alexander Polezhaev (1805–38) achieved notoriety in 1825 for *Sashka*, a parody of the first cantos of *Eugene Onegin*. Tsar Nicholas was outraged by its salacious content and sent Polezhaev to the Caucasus as a common soldier, where he continued writing. He is remembered today for his protest verses and his narrative poems which seek to deromanticize the Caucasus.

Fyodor Tyutchev (1803–73) is often ranked next to Pushkin and sometimes even higher than Lermontov. While Lermontov was clearly a disciple of Pushkin and Byron, Tyutchev was oriented toward Derzhavin, Goethe and Schiller. His early association with the Lovers of Wisdom Society while a student at the University of

Moscow and his reading of Schelling permanently influenced his world view. During the period of romantic dominance he spent most of his time in Germany and Italy as a diplomat, and did not return permanently to Russia until the mid 1840s. While abroad he attended Schelling's lectures in Munich, where he was also close to Heine. Since he remained active as a poet for many decades after the end of romanticism's supremacy, much of his later poetry was out of touch with prevailing tastes.

Tyutchev never took himself seriously as a poet, and because of his own indifference many of his compositions simply disappeared. His typical form is the short poem, a casual effort to assuage boredom, jotted down on whatever was available. The romantic concept of the poet-prophet did not infect him, and, although he was consistently didactic, he apparently was unconcerned about seeing his poems in print. When Pushkin "discovered" him in 1836 and printed several of his poems in *The Contemporary* (*Sovremennik*), they were signed only with his initials.

Tyutchev's thoughtful content, his rhetorical quality, and his somewhat archaic diction make him seem much more formal than any of his romantic contemporaries. But he was typically a romantic in his attraction to nature: the sea, the sky, night, stars, the seasons, brooks and streams, and other natural features are constant elements in his poetry. In Tyutchev nature is always anthropomorphized, living, providing clues to the meaning of a perplexing universe.

The appellation "metaphysical poet" has been applied to Tyutchev because his constant theme is the dilemma of man caught between Cosmos and Chaos, good and evil, day and night, in his personal vision of Manichean dualism. But this philosophical content is not categoric, and his system, if such it be, is susceptible to multiple interpretations. Accordingly, his poems more often provoke questions than answer them.

Perhaps Tyutchev's most quoted line is from "Silentium" (1830), "A thought once spoken is a lie," an idea which appealed to the symbolists, who recast it as: "Only that is true which one heart can say to another in mute greeting." "Silentium" – three stanzas of six lines each – exhorts us to live within ourselves, for in our souls is a whole world of secret magical thoughts. We are advised to attend to their song – and be silent! This poem offers several examples of Tyutchev's innovative metrics, with amphibrachs injected into the iambic patterns. Later editors saw fit to correct these illicit lines and force them into the conventional mold.

An unusual figure on the Russian romantic Parnassus was Alexey Koltsov (1809–1842), often called the Russian Robert Burns, though not by those familiar with both authors. He was the son of a domineering cattle merchant, who frustrated his son's endeavors to acquire an education. Koltsov's discovery by the Stankevich–Belinsky circle in Moscow in the early 1830s led to ten years of recognition by the literary community, though Koltsov did not enjoy happiness in his personal life, which was marred by his father's autocratic control and destruction of the poet's marital intentions.

There is little point in winnowing the wheat from the chaff in Koltsov's occasional verse, and even less in his efforts to poeticize his philosophical musings, which, although earnest, reveal his absence of a formal education. Of importance are his Russian songs, themselves imitations of folk forms, though, owing to his direct contact with peasants as drover and cattle dealer, less artificial than Delvig's. Lyric songs come in many forms: dance, harvest, marriage, love, recruitment and others linked to pagan or Orthodox celebrations. Many of these are laments at a personal loss, such as the death of a lover, the departure of a bride from her father's house, the recruit's farewell. Koltsov's songs are those of individuals who face the reality of their hard lot with fortitude, as, for example, the rejected fiancé in "The betrothed's betrayal" ("Izmena suzhenoy," 1838). Something new in Russian literature at that time was Koltsov's depiction of peasant life as a not unsatisfying combination of toil and fulfillment, and there is quiet optimism in his "Song of the plowman" ("Pesnya pakharya," 1831), in which the peasant cheerfully delivers to his horse a monologue extolling labor and the cooperation of beneficent nature. "The harvest" ("Urozhay", 1835) recounts the labors leading to the harvest and voices the peasants' confidence in God's grace. These poems convey a feeling of the wholeness of a life which submerges the individual identity in an integration of nature, the peasant, and toil.

Koltsov's songs are not strictly canonical, for he uses stanza divisions and sometimes employs a thrice accented unrhymed line rather than the traditional folksong line of two accents. However, they do reproduce the effect of the popular song and provided new perspectives on a world little known to the educated public.

Paul Katenin (1792–1853) was an important figure on the literary scene during the 1810s and 1820s. Of the well-to-do gentry, he took part in the Napoleonic wars and reached the rank of colonel, but in 1822 he was summarily exiled to his family estates. Later he resumed his military career, and ultimately retired with the rank of general.

The critic Yury Tynyanov classifies Katenin, along with Griboedov and Küchelbecker, as a "young archaist," a literary nationalist who inveighed against slavish imitation of foreign models and style and who advocated classical traditions with their roots in Lomonosov and Derzhavin. His first efforts were in the field of drama, with translations from Corneille and Racine, original comedies (he collaborated with Griboedov on *The Student*), and a classical verse tragedy entitled *Andromache* (1828). One of his most popular works was "An old tale" ("Staraya byl," 1828), a ballad set in Kiev during the time of Prince Vladimir. The setting and content reflect contemporary romantic interests, but the language has a sinewy quality absent from the ballads of the Zhukovsky school.

Katenin's *Princess Milusha* (*Knyazhna Milusha*), a verse fairy tale, was finished in 1833. Again set in Vladimir's time, its action prompts comparison with *Ruslan and Lyudmila*. The hero, Vseslav, a knight of martial and erotic prowess, must prove his suitability to marry Vladimir's daughter Milusha by remaining chaste for an entire year. The work describes the traps laid for him by the witch Proveda, Milusha's guardian, who assumes various disguises in her attempt to cause the libidinous Vseslav to fail the test. The tale is withal rather amusing, with its tongue in cheek attitude toward romantic clichés associated with folklore, the good old days of Vladimir, and its well meaning but weak protagonist. The verses are marked by archaic diction and syntax, but Katenin achieved a *tour de force* by incorporating a multitude of Russian proverbs and sayings into his work appropriately and seemingly without effort.

Although many of the poets commonly associated with the Pleiad shared liberal ideals, for the most part they were not directly engaged in what might be called revolutionary activities. Such was not the case, however, with Alexander Bestuzhev, Kondraty Ryleev, Wilhelm Küchelbecker, and Alexander Odoevsky, who used their pens to advance their political ideas overtly and covertly.

Wilhelm Küchelbecker (1797–1846) is remembered today for his literary theory and criticism, a small corpus of poems, and for his attractive eccentricity. From a Russified German family he was educated at the Tsarskoe Selo lyceum along with his close friends Pushkin and Delvig. His unusual name (Küchelbecker means "cupcake baker"), odd appearance, and animated, Quixotic behavior drove his coevals to tease him, but they also admired him for his lofty aspirations, his enthusiasm, and his intelligence. After graduation from the lyceum, he took a post in the Ministry of Foreign Affairs, when he apparently established contact with the future Decembrists. From 1820 to 1822 he served first in Paris and then Tiflis. On his return to Russia, he gravitated towards the Lovers of Wisdom society (*Lyubomudry*), with whom he shared an enthusiasm for the romantic idealism of Schelling; he and Vladimir Odoevsky became co-editors of *Mnemosyne* (*Mnemosyna*), the group's unofficial almanac. There Küchelbecker published "On the direction of our poetry, especially lyrical, in the last decade" ("O napravlenii nashey poezii, osobenno liricheskoy, v poslednee desyatiletie"), in which he criticized his friends Zhukovsky, Baratynsky, and Pushkin for imitativeness and repetitiousness in their poetry, which he felt was typified by indefiniteness, standardized imagery, bogus landscapes, tasteless personification of such abstract concepts as Peace, Joy, Sadness, and Labor, and inevitable *fog*, "fog over the pine copse, fog over the fields, and fog in the writer's head."

Küchelbecker's literary position was idiosyncratic: he called himself "a romantic in classicism." Küchelbecker found his model in Derzhavin: in an age when the elegy had triumphed he called for a revival of the ode, which he considered the loftiest of genres. For him the poet was the bearer of truth, the eloquent citizen-patriot who scorned the crowd, a frivolous mob of pleasure seekers without vital concerns of the spirit, such as a thirst for freedom. Küchelbecker's poetry occasionally suffers from exaggerated emotionalism and declamatory pomposity, although he was no doubt quite sincere in his manner of expression.

The Argives (*Argivyane*), an unfinished dramatic tragedy in verse, was a typical effort in a "civic" vein which encouraged the quest for freedom from tyranny. *Ado*, published in *Mnemosyne* in 1824, is a prose tale of the tribulations of Ado, a pagan Livonian priest who leads a resistance movement against the Teutonic Knights, who are subjugating his people. Ultimately he and his followers are saved by Prince Yaroslav, and Ado becomes a Christian. The characters are puppets, the plot banal, and the ethnographic material largely the author's invention.

Küchelbecker was on the Senate Square on 14 December 1825, where he attacked two high officials. On both occasions his pistol misfired. He escaped to Warsaw, was captured, and spent the final two decades of his life in Siberia. He continued to write, and some of his work done in exile – for example his reminiscences of Griboedov and Ryleev and a poem on Pushkin's death – have an affective power.

Polar Star (*Polyarnaya zvezda*), a literary annual published by Ryleev and Bestuzhev, appeared in 1823, 1824, and 1825. Its contributors represented the best of Russia's writers, including those from the Pleiad and those of an earlier generation such as Zhukovsky, Gnedich, Fyodor Glinka, and Batyushkov. Also included were works by Faddey Bulgarin, Osip Senkovsky (1800–58) and Nikolay Grech (1787–1867), the group which later attained almost monopolistic control over St. Petersburg periodical publications. Since Ryleev and Bestuzhev were both involved in secret political activities, it was natural that their publication should to the greatest possible extent serve their liberal ideals and disseminate their concepts of civic virtue. In this respect their almanac followed the pattern set by *The Emulator*, the monthly publication of the Free Society of Lovers of Russian Letters (1818–25), which sought to inculcate ideals of civic responsibility and self-sacrifice in a gentry largely concerned with self-gratification and status. The success of *Polar Star* led to a proliferation of literary almanacs, of which the most prestigious and the best was Delvig's *Northern Flowers*. It was so successful that the editors of *Polar Star* decided to withdraw and conclude their venture with a final issue, smaller than the previous three and thus to be called *Little Star* (*Zvezdochka*). However, before it could appear the events of 14 December took place, and it never came out.

Kondraty Ryleev (1795–1826) was educated in the Corps of Pages, took part in the final campaign against Napoleon, and accompanied the army occupying Paris. His subsequent service on the Don River engendered a deep affection for the Ukrainian land and its culture within him, and a large part of his mature poetry is patterned on Ukrainian historical songs, or *dumy*. In 1818 he retired from the army and settled in St. Petersburg, serving first in the judiciary and subsequently as a director of the Russian-American Company. In 1820 he published "To the favorite" ("K vremenshchiku"), a denunciation, though not by name, of the tsar's advisor Count Arakcheev so scathing that officialdom was powerless to punish its author, because that would have required acknowledging that Arakcheev was the addressee.

Ryleev worked on his historical songs in 1821–3, completing almost a score of them. From Karamzin's *History of the Russian State* Ryleev chose figures notable for their patriotism, love of freedom, steadfastness in adversity, and courage, such as Oleg, Svyatoslav, Dmitry Donskoy, Ermak, Ivan Susanin, and Bogdan Khmelnitsky. These heroic types speak the language of romantic heroes: his patriot Artemy Volynsky, executed by the Empress Anna at the instigation of Count Biron, goes to his death proclaiming that he has served "sacred truth, and my execution will be my triumph." Those were prophetic words from the pen of one soon to be hanged for his role in the Decembrist conspiracy.

Ryleev's *Voynarovsky* (1824) is a long narrative poem in which the title figure, the nephew of Mazeppa, describes the anguish of his uncle after he has betrayed Peter the Great and joined forces with Charles I of Sweden, only to suffer defeat and bring retribution upon his beloved Ukraine. The work resembles the author's historical songs by its inflated rhetorical style and the adaptation of history to suit its moralistic purposes. Ryleev presents extensive descriptions of the harsh Siberian landscape, the site of Voynarovsky's exile, to intensify the emotional content.

In the early 1820s Ryleev became deeply involved in clandestine political activities, and soon acquired a prominent position in the Decembrist organization. His part in recruiting conspirators, planning the revolt, and inciting the troops to rebel, along with his presence on Senate Square on that fateful 14 December, made it clear he was a central figure in the uprising. For that he was executed.

Northern Flowers was not designed to serve any cause other than that of literature *per se*. In general, the Pushkin–Delvig circle in St. Petersburg was committed to art for art's sake: Pushkin declared that "the aim of poetry is poetry." Orest Somov's annual surveys of Russian literature, which appeared from 1827 to 1831, stressed the importance of developing high literary standards and, most particularly, a literary language purged of foreign borrowings and rude vernacular and adequate for fiction, essays, and technical exposition. He also called for "verisimilitude" in fiction, by which he seems to have meant a concern for description in accordance with reality.

Somov's critical essays reflected the confused circumstances in which prose found itself during the 1820s. While poetry had a long tradition and established (even clichéd) means of expression, prose was still in a developmental state. Many authors, including Pushkin, complained that prose expression was incondite, imprecise, unsuited for the conveyance of ideas. Others noted that there was no tradition for the representation of conversation in Russian, since conversations in society were usually conducted in French. So one of the main tasks of Russian authors in the 1820s and even in the 1830s was the forging of a viable prose language.

The genre pool available to prose writers at the beginning of the 1820s included travel notes, the intensified anecdote of adventure, the military memoir, the historical tale, the "psychological novel," the supernatural tale, and the eastern tale. These categories were not mutually exclusive, and so one finds combinations of them, such as an adventure anecdote interpolated in travel notes. Travel notes, in fact, were a favorite choice, for their flexible format permitted "adaptations" of real experience to exploit suspense or add pathos which bridged autobiography and fiction. Thus *The Inn Stairs (Traktirnaya lestnitsa)* by Nikolay Bestuzhev, the seafaring brother of Alexander, employs travel notes to frame a "psychological" novelette, the fatuous confession of a soul gone astray.

Alexander Bestuzhev (1797–1837) is known also by his pseudonym Marlinsky, a name derived from the village of Marli near

Peterhof, where he served as an officer of Dragoons in 1817. His first prose was a travel sketch, "A Journey to Revel" ("Poezdka v Revel"), which appeared in *The Emulator* in 1821, signed Marlinsky. This long sketch filled with all manner of historical, anthropological, and geographical information about Estonia and Revel also included poetry and anecdotes. Bestuzhev then published a number of historical tales, the longest and most important of which was "Roman and Olga" ("Roman i Olga"), which came out in the first issue of *Polar Star* in 1823. This didactic tale focuses upon the civic virtues and heroism of Roman, a citizen-soldier of old Novgorod, who sacrifices his personal happiness to undertake a dangerous mission on behalf of that city-state when its independence is threatened by Muscovy. Ultimately he leads Novgorod to victory and is reunited with his Olga. This tale displays stylistic qualities widely associated with this author (hyperbole, metaphorical saturation, sentimental rhetoric), features which came to be known as "Marlinisms." At the same time, the author advanced the art of fiction by his obvious employment of (some) dialogue as a means of characterization.

Bestuzhev wrote three historical tales with castles in their titles: "Wenden Castle" ("Zamok Venden," 1823), "Neuhausen Castle" ("Zamok Neygauzen," 1824), and "Eisen Castle" ("Zamok Eyzen," published in 1826 anonymously under the title *Blood for Blood*). These stories of villainy in Baltic climes feature bloody acts worthy of *l'école frénétique*. "The Tournament at Revel" ("Revelsky turnir," 1825) is a comic work attacking the prejudices of the Estonian knights, who stubbornly refuse to adapt to new economic circumstances or to recognize the importance of a developing merchant class. The work features witty dialogue, like much of Bestuzhev's work.

Following his arrest and exile, Bestuzhev did not appear again until 1830, when his society tale "The Test" ("Ispytanie") was published in *The Son of the Fatherland* (*Syn Otechestva*) over the initials "A. M." As a convicted Decembrist then serving as a common soldier in the Caucasus, he could not use his own name, so his works appeared either anonymously or over the Marlinsky pseudonym.

The year 1829 saw the publication of the first Russian historical novel in the manner of Walter Scott. The Scots bard had enjoyed a fantastic popularity in France, and the Russian reading public was well aware of the Waverley series through French translations or the scores of French imitations. Mikhail Zagoskin (1789–1852) was the first to provide his audience with a Russian historical novel, *Yury Miloslavsky, or the Russians in 1612* (*Yury Miloslavsky, ili Russkie v 1612 godu*). This was a lively tale of the Russo-Polish conflict from the Time of Troubles, employing the usual Scottian formula of lovers separated by the fortunes of war against a colorful canvas of past events and historical figures. Yury himself was rather on the lines of Marlinsky's Roman ("Roman and Olga"), but, coming as he did just four years after the Decembrist catastrophe, he must have seemed a welcome paragon of courage, devotion, patriotism, and self-sacrifice. Pushkin congratulated Zagoskin on his triumph, saying: "Everyone is reading it. The ladies are in ecstasies. Zhukovsky spent an entire night with it." At the same time, in a letter to Zhukovsky, Pushkin criticized Zagoskin for his unjust depiction of the poet Trediakovsky as a sycophant and talentless fool. Zagoskin's initial success encouraged him to produce a whole series of historical novels. *Roslavlev, or the Russians in 1812* (*Roslavlev, ili Russkie v 1812 godu*) appeared in 1830, and he was still writing in this genre by the end of the 1840s. Meanwhile *Yury Miloslavsky* had set a pattern for his compatriots, and some quite respectable Russian historical novels shortly appeared.

One of the best story tellers was Ivan Kalashnikov (1797–1863), the scion of a merchant family from Irkutsk. His *The Daughter of the Merchant Zholobov. A Novel Drawn from Irkutsk Legends* (*Doch kuptsa Zholobova. Roman izvlechenny iz irkutskikh predaniy*), published in 1831, had the attraction not only of an exotic Siberian setting but an involved plot with separated lovers. It has no participating historical figures, but boasts all the other ingredients of the novel *à la Scott*. There are also numerous ethnographic details connected with the pagan Buryats, sociological information on the life of the merchant class, and geographical descriptions of the region around Lake Baikal. The characters are flat and simply serve to act out the complicated plot. Kalashnikov's *The Kamchatka Girl* (*Kamchadalka*) came out in 1833. Set in the previous century, it offers an interesting picture of Eskimo life and customs, and again employs the separated-lovers formula.

Probably the best of these works, excluding Pushkin's *The Captain's Daughter*, were the novels of Ivan Lazhechnikov (1792–1869), who styled himself "the grandson of Walter Scott." Known originally for a military memoir of the campaign of 1812, he published his first historical novel, *The Last Novik* (*Posledny Novik*), in 1831–3. It deals with Peter the Great's conflict with Sweden. *The Ice Palace* (*Ledyanoy dom*, 1835) details intrigues at the court of Empress Anna (reigned 1730–40) and features horrors derived from *l'école frénétique*. Lazhechnikov's *The Infidel* (*Basurman*), set in the time of Grand Prince Ivan III, and *The Bodyguard of Ivan the Terrible* (*Oprichnik*) continued the tradition. Bulgarin catered to the fad with *Dmitry the Impostor* (*Dmitry samozvanets*) and *Mazeppa*, in 1830 and 1833 respectively, while Nikolay Polevoy's *The Oath at the Lord's Tomb* (*Klyatva pri grobe gospodnem*) came out in 1832. Other popular authors were Konstantin Masalsky and Rafail Zotov, who each produced several historical novels in the late 1830s.

It is difficult today to explain the extraordinary popularity of Faddey Bulgarin's (1789–1859) *Ivan Vyzhigin*, which in 1829 became Russia's first best-seller, with over 6,000 copies sold. Bulgarin was not unknown to the public as an author, for a number of his military anecdotes, eastern tales, and historical tales had been published in *The Polar Star* and *Northern Flowers*. Parts of *Vyzhigin* began appearing as early as 1825, when the book was titled *Ivan Vyzhigin, or a Russian Gil Blas*, and fanciers of these selections were doubtless moved to purchase the complete work when it appeared in four volumes. The absence of the name of Lesage's hero from the final version of the title is significant, because in his foreword Bulgarin insisted that "*this is the first original Russian novel of its kind. I dare to assert that I imitated no one*, copied no one, and wrote that which was conceived in my mind alone" (italics in the original). This puffery is the more amusing if one knows that Bulgarin had also borrowed significant episodes from Bishop Ignacy Krasicki's *Pan Podstoli*, a picaresque work of 1778.

Vyzhigin is an amorphous work with a vast setting both inside and outside Russia. Bulgarin's stated intention was to reform society through satire (to those who know the man, this was hilarious!), and thus he sought to forestall criticism of his hero, whose transgressions the author graciously pardons because the lad is well-meaning but has a weak spirit. Vyzhigin undergoes all manner of adventures as he moves from childhood as a despised gooseherd to manhood as the scion of an illustrious father. Occasionally his escapades are entertaining. Orest Somov damned the work with faint praise but criticized the author for several scenes which revealed his lack of knowledge of St. Petersburg and Moscow high society. This criticism must have galled Bulgarin, who suffered from an inferiority complex in his relations with the literary mandarins of St. Petersburg.

The literary mandarins were enthusiastic about a novel of manners written by one of their own, Alexey Perovsky (1787–1836), whose pseudonym was Antony Pogorelsky, entitled *The Smolny Institute Graduate* (*Monastyrka* [sometimes translated *The Convent Girl*]). The 17 May 1830 issue of *The Literary Gazette* referred to this work as "probably the first real novel of manners in Russia," doubtless an allusion to Bulgarin's self-serving assessment of his *Vyzhigin* as "the first original Russian novel." Perovsky's novel is set in the provincial Ukraine, to which the heroine, Anyuta, newly graduated from the Smolny convent in St. Petersburg, returns. In a lightly ironic tone the narrator describes her efforts to adjust to the rustic manners of her home area after she has received a refined education. The first volume, which consists of Anyuta's letters to a cousin and the omniscient narration of a relative, a certain Antony Pogorelsky, promises some psychological development in the depiction of the heroine, but the hero, the officer Blistovsky, a model of rectitude, is quite flat and rather tedious. This is not true of the secondary figures, especially Anyuta's outspoken aunt, the girl's sanctimoniously perfidious guardian Klim Dyundik and his terrifying wife, a shrew of epic proportions. (This work is a precursor to Gogol's *Dead Souls*, for Dyundik and his wife are stylized in a Gogolian manner and Dyundik equals Chichikov as a schemer and purveyor of banality.) Unfortunately, the second volume of this work, albeit engaging, focused primarily upon Anyuta's attempts to escape from her guardian, and the delineation of her psychology is scanted.

The Literary Gazette was conceived by the Pushkin–Delvig camp as a means of competing with the influence of Grech and Bulgarin, which they considered deleterious to literature and culture. Earlier efforts to foster rival periodicals, such as Prince Vyazemsky's support of Nikolay Polevoy's bi-weekly *The Moscow Telegraph* (*Moskovsky telegraf*) or Pushkin's collaboration with Mikhail Pogodin's *The Moscow Herald* (*Moskovsky vestnik*), had proved disappointing. Polevoy showed poor judgment in permitting criticism of Karamzin's *History of the Russian State* to appear in his periodical; even worse, his polemical *History of the Russian People* (*Istoriya russkogo naroda*) was seen as an inept insult to Karamzin. *The Moscow Herald*, inaugurated in 1827, fared somewhat better, and it enjoyed contributions from the St. Petersburg literary mandarins. However, its Moscow contributors' interest in German romanticism was not shared by the Pushkin circle, and when the poet Venevitinov and Vladimir Odoevsky, who had been closely involved with it, moved to St. Petersburg, Pogodin's scholarly interests increasingly dominated the periodical. Possibly the unprecedented success in 1829 of *Ivan Vyzhigin* emphasized the urgency of finding ways to curb the expanding influence of Bulgarin and his cohorts.

The Literary Gazette began publication on 1 January 1830. Delvig was editor-in-chief, Orest Somov filled a post analogous to that he held on *Northern Flowers*, and Vladimir Shchastny, a poet of limited range, was secretary. *The Gazette* appeared every five days in eight pages for its eighteen months of publication. Each of the pages was in two columns. The first four pages were devoted to prose, with poetry generally confined to one or two short pieces. The "Bibliography" section announced new works, some of which were reviewed. "Miscellany" occupied the last pages with a hodge-podge of anecdotes and brief notes on literary matters.

Even as word of the venture spread through literary circles, doubts arose as to its feasibility. Vyazemsky wrote to Pushkin that it was unlikely that the paper would succeed: "There is little hope for *The Literary Gazette*. Delvig is lazy and writes nothing, and he relies exclusively *sur sa bête de somme ou de Somoff*." In a letter to Pogodin, Yazykov rephrased Vyazemsky's doubts and also alluded to the competition the paper would face from Grech and Bulgarin: "Delvig is excessively lazy and Somov is enthusiastic but incapable. It is not likely they will succeed against those names who have somehow already entrenched themselves on our Parnassus." Yazykov was correct in anticipating opposition from

Bulgarin's *The Northern Bee* (*Severnaya pchela*), for even before the first issue of *The Gazette* appeared, Bulgarin was attacking it in his paper.

The Gazette opened as scheduled, with prose by Perovsky-Pogorelsky, literary history by Paul Katenin, and contributions by Pushkin and the extended Pleiad. Matters proceeded smoothly until March, when Delvig printed a very negative review of Bulgarin's *Dmitry the Impostor*. The paranoid Bulgarin attributed the review to Pushkin, and in retaliation published a scathing commentary on Canto VII of *Eugene Onegin*. The tone of this review so offended the tsar that he told the chief of his Third Section, Count Benckendorff, to forbid Bulgarin to publish literary criticism, and threatened to prohibit criticism in general.

The 28 October edition of *The Literary Gazette* contained a brief poem by Casimir Delavigne which alluded to the heroes of the July revolution. Benckendorff then threatened Delvig with exile to Siberia along with Pushkin and Vyazemsky, a reprimand so insulting to Delvig that he totally lost interest in all his literary activities, including *Northern Flowers*. He was not allowed to continue as editor of *The Gazette*, but the paper itself was not banned in order not to disappoint the prepaid subscribers. Somov assumed the editorship, and served in that capacity until the periodical closed in the summer of 1831.

Perhaps the most popular form of fiction in the 1830s was the society tale, short novels describing the lives and loves of the *haut monde*. A taste for this type of literature had been created by Balzac's many stories about French provincials and Parisiennes which had appeared in Russia in the original or in excerpts and translations. An early attempt in this genre was Orest Somov's "The Fool in Christ" ("Yurodivy", 1827), which combined a physiological sketch of a typical mendicant holy fool with a plot involving features which were to become standard for the society tale: a ball, arrogant officers, an insult, a challenge, a duel, an innocent victim. Bestuzhev-Marlinsky is usually credited with the first society tale, but his "The Test" ("Ispytanie"), published in 1830, followed not only Somov but also an interesting epistolary society tale entitled "Coquetry and Love" ("Koketstvo i lyubov"), the work of a certain Peter Sumarokov which appeared in *The Moscow Telegraph* in 1829. One of the most prolific practitioners of the genre was Ivan Panaev (1812–62), whose "The Boudoir of a fashionable lady. An episode from the life of a poet in society" ("Spalnya svetskoy zhenshchiny. Epizod iz zhizni poeta v obshchestve," 1824) introduces an element of social protest in the person of the poet scorned by an insensate society.

In general, the society tale in its canonical form satirized high society, exposing its frivolity, false values, and moral vacuity. The typical plot involved an illicit affair between someone from outside the *haut monde* and a countess or princess, unhappily married to an older, stupid, and rich husband. A common variant genre took as its protagonist a young man of unusual sensitivity and ability, often a poet, painter, or musician, always poor. Here the society tale merged with the so-called *Kuenstlernovelle*, which had as its hero an artist or would-be artist scorned by the unfeeling upper classes. A well-known example is "The Name Day Party" ("Imeniny," 1835) of Nikolay Pavlov (1805–64), which chronicles the unhappy love of a serf musician for the daughter of a gentry family. This story is marred by sentimentalism, a mistake not repeated in Pavlov's "Yataghan" ("Yatagan") (both works were collected in the volume *Three Tales* [*Tri povesti*, 1835], a suspenseful and psychologically engaging tale of violent revenge stemming from a false sense of honor and class prejudice.

Several women writers published society tales. The best-known of them was Countess Evdokia Rostopchina, *née* Sushkova (1811–58), who entered the lists in 1838 with two works, "Rank and Money" ("Chiny i dengi") and "The Duel" ("Poedinok"), both of which feature self-sacrificing heroines who are victims of rigid rules of behavior and lack any power to alter their social circumstances. Rostopchina's championing of the rights of women earned for her the title of "the Russian George Sand," with whom she also shared a propensity for hyperbole and prolixity. Elena Gan, *née* Fadeeva (1814–42), also concerned herself with the plight of the intelligent woman in circumstances which stifle her interests and instincts. "The Ideal" ("Ideal") is unusual in its depiction of the oppressive atmosphere and stultifying routine of life in a provincial garrison town from which its heroine seeks to escape, but otherwise the story is improbable and the style sententious. Gan travelled widely, and some of her other works are set in remote regions with plots involving love affairs between Russians and natives, such as Kalmyks and Tatars. She has been called "the female Lermontov," but except for their nearly coincident dates of birth and death, their extensive travels, and their choice of exotic settings, they have little in common.

Nadezhda Durova (1783–1866) is in a class by herself owing to her unusual biography. Outraged at the submissive behavior which her domineering mother and society required of her, she fled her home. She entered the army disguised as a man, and after training as a cavalryman took part in several battles during the campaign of 1807, for which she received a medal from Tsar Alexander. Later she saw action at Borodino, was wounded, and subsequently served as orderly to General Kutuzov. She retired from the cavalry in 1816 with the rank of junior captain and returned to her home in a remote province east of Kazan. Some years later Pushkin became acquainted with her brother, learned of her exceptional experience, and encouraged her to write her memoirs. She brought them to him in St. Petersburg in 1836, and he published excerpts in *The Contemporary* under the title *Notes of a Cavalry Maiden* (*Zapiski kavalerist-devitsy*). They occasioned considerable comment, as did their author, who wore male attire and spoke of herself using masculine forms. However, despite their renown, the *Notes* did not sell well. Durova then turned to fiction, over the next four years producing a number of society tales and a novel, none of them very noteworthy. In 1840 she abruptly ceased publishing.

Soon after its advent the society tale acquired what might be called formulaic characteristics, and it was not long before parodies on it began to appear, Pushkin's "The Queen of Spades" ("Pikovaya dama," 1834) being the most famous. One of the most amusing – and far fetched – is from the pen of the prolific Alexander Veltman (1800–60). His "Erotida" (1835) describes a vain and unfaithful officer, a certain G., who forgets his first love Erotida, seeks an affair with her several years later when she appears at Carlsbad disguised as Emilia, a widow, and then kills her in a duel when she, further disguised as a young man, appears to be G.'s rival for Emilia's affections. Although many a society tale concludes with sentimental effusions, in this case the narrator informs us that G. simply threw his victim's body into the river (there were no seconds at the duel) and returned to town to continue his pursuit of yet another young lady.

One author whom we may categorically label a romantic is Prince Vladimir Odoevsky (1804–69), co-founder of The Lovers of Wisdom Society and one of the principal figures behind its publication, *Mnemosyne*. Odoevsky is often linked to E. T. A. Hoffmann, with whom he shared an almost obsessive curiosity about the supernatural, an affinity for music and musicians, and pessimism as to the artistic spirit's ability to flourish in the philistine atmosphere of modern life. He created his own unique *Kuenstlernovellen* in which, with intentional disregard for biographical accuracy, he mobilized Beethoven, Bach, and the Venetian architect and engraver Piranesi to exemplify his own ideas on creativity, the lonely mission of the artist, the effect of music on the human spirit. Odoevsky's Beethoven is a frenetic, deranged, and decrepit ancient who hammers out his last quartet on a stringless harpsichord, oblivious to the world around him. "Beethoven's Last Quartet" ("Posledny kvartet Betkhovena," 1831) concludes with a scene in which society indifferently notes the musician's death. The story of Piranesi ("Opere del Cavaliere Giambatista Piranesi," 1832) combines the supernatural with the sublime in describing the madness of the Venetian's scheme to build an arch joining Mt. Vesuvius and Mt. Etna and his jealous effort to destroy his rival's work (to topple the tower of Pisa by hanging on to it). The Hoffmannesque combination of genius and insanity is absent from "Sebastian Bach" ("Sebastyan Bakh," 1835), an overtly didactic work which emphasizes the spiritual nature of Bach's creation as opposed to the destructive sensuality of Italian music.

Motley Fairy Tales (*Pestrye skazki*, 1833), a cycle ostensibly presented by the impecunious philosopher Ireney Modestovich Gomozeyko, contains several didactic pieces with engaging titles, such as "The Fairy Tale About the Corpse Which Belonged to Who Knows Whom" ("Skazka o mertvom tele, neizvestno komu prinadlezhashchem") or "The Fairy Tale About Why It Is Dangerous for Young Ladies to Walk in a Crowd Along Nevsky Prospect" ("Skazka o tom, kak opasno devushkam khodit tolpoyu po Nevskomu prospektu"). In the latter a young girl is detained by the evil owner of a dress shop, turned into a fashionable doll, and sold to a young man. Later he discovers that she is alive, but her modish existence has rendered her unfit to be the companion of a thinking individual. "The Sylph" ("Silfida," 1837) suggests that retreat to an ideal world of insanity is preferable to a conventional life. Odoevsky's typical didacticism is represented in less fantastic settings by his two society tales, "Princess Mimi" ("Knyazhna Mimi," 1834) and "Princess Zizi" ("Knyazhna Zizi," 1839). The former chronicles the human suffering caused by the vicious gossip of the spinster Mimi, who dominates her circle by her slander. The work follows the standard pattern of the genre, except that the preface suddenly appears in the middle of the story – so we will pay attention to it, as the author explains.

Russian Nights (*Russkie nochi*, 1844) is a collection of ten tales, nine of which had already been published, arranged within the frame of a dialogue among four friends. Functioning as a chorus, the friends discuss the philosophical content of the stories, with the principal commentator, Faust, serving as the author's *porte parole*. The discussions range far and wide in an effort to find some principles unifying science and art, while at the same time maintaining credence in the world beyond the five senses. The general criticism of western thought and behavior and hints at the superiority of Russian moral nature reflect Odoevsky's Slavophile beliefs, which became more pronounced as he grew older. However, Odoevsky never adopted the chauvinistic postures typical of the more conservative Slavophiles, like Yazykov.

Nikolay Gogol (1809–52) is one of the "big three" of Russian romantic writers. Born into a Ukrainian family of the petty gentry, he began his career inauspiciously with the idyll *Ganz Kuechelgarten* (1829), derived from Voss's *Louise*. A chapter of an unfinished historical novel, *The Hetman* (*Ataman*), an effort combining Scott and *l'école frénétique*, appeared in *Northern Flowers for 1831*. He achieved success with *Evenings on a Farm Near Dikanka* (*Vechera na khutore bliz Dikanki*, 1831–2), a collection of stories introduced by a folksy Ukrainian beekeeper, Rudy Panko. Derived from the puppet theatre and folklore, the eight tales range from somber treatments of demonic entrapment to ribald slapstick. Devils, witches, river spirits, boisterous villagers combine with elements of popular superstition, including huts on hens' legs and fires marking buried treasure, to produce improbable but entertaining tales, narrated in a style ranging from effusive descriptions of nature to uncouth dialogue. One might suppose that these stories reflected Gogol's romantic interest in the folklore of his native region, but more probably he was merely responding to the literary market: Somov had already published several tales derived from Ukrainian folklore.

One of these eight tales, "Ivan Fyodorovich Shponka and His Aunt" ("Ivan Fedorovich Shponka i ego tetushka"), presages the classic Gogol, the unmasker of *poshlost*, a term peculiar to Russian suggesting, among other things, banality, self-satisfied mediocrity, phony sentiment, and vegetative existence. Gogol believed in the devil, and saw his hand behind any human behavior which seemed unworthy of man's high mission, with *poshlost* as his instrument. In "Shponka," *poshlost* manifests itself in Shponka's total passivity, his lack of any passion or drive, his mental vacuity. The method of characterization used here becomes typical for Gogol's later prose: he stylizes all aspects of the hero to conform to an essential quality, in this case the total lack of any significant physical or mental activity. Shponka, a military officer, spends his life lying on his bed, setting mouse traps and polishing his buttons. In like manner the hallmark of the mature Gogol would be the depiction of *life as it should not be*.

Gogol later enlivened the romantic prose scene with another collection, *Mirgorod* (1835). "Viy" is a horror story featuring a folklore monster of Gogol's invention with eyelids falling to its feet. Less fanciful but still imaginative is the pseudo-historical novel *Taras Bulba*, an exotic pageant uniting features of the Scottian novel, the Ukrainian historical song, and *l'école frénétique*. Set in an indeterminate century, the work glorifies the good old days on the Russian frontier when Cossacks from the republic of Sech-Beyond-the-Falls (on the Dnepr River) used to slaughter infidel Jews, Tatars and heretical Poles as much for the sport of it as to punish the enemies of Orthodoxy. Though morally unappealing, the work is colorful and has an exciting plot.

·Mirgorod also included "Old World Landowners" ("Starosvetskie pomeshchiki"), which externally is a nostalgic reminiscence of the quiet pleasures of rural gentry life but in fact attacks the *poshlost* of a spiritless existence devoted to gourmandizing and self-gratification. The same irony pervades "The Tale of How

Ivan Ivanovich Quarreled with Ivan Nikiforovich" ("Povest o tom, kak possorilsya Ivan Ivanovich s Ivanom Nikiforovichem"), which recounts how the two estimable gentlemen of the title ruin themselves through an extended and nonsensical lawsuit. Gogol here depends in part upon Vasily Narezhny's work of 1825, *The Two Ivans* (*Dva Ivana*), a didactic satire on Ukrainians' devotion to self-destructive litigation.

The year 1835 also saw the appearance of *Arabesques* (*Arabeski*), a collection which included, among some thematically related essays, stories forming part of Gogol's St. Petersburg cycle: "Nevsky Prospect" ("Nevsky Prospekt"), "Diary of a Madman" ("Zapiski sumasshedshego"), and "The Portrait" ("Portret"). To this cycle we must add "The Nose" ("Nos"), published in Pushkin's *Contemporary* in 1836, and "The Overcoat" (1842). All of these stories raise problems for the reader, who may find himself deceived should he accept the narrator's implied sentiment or empathize too quickly with the protagonists.

"Nevsky Prospect" chronicles the dire fate of a naive painter, Piskaryov, who believes he has discovered his ideal woman only to learn that she is a vulgar prostitute. Emotionally destroyed, he seeks refuge in opium and ultimately commits suicide. This pathetic version of the *Kuenstlernovelle*, which seems to reflect Hoffmann's philanthropic treatment of the sensitive artist defeated by the mundane world, is contrasted in the same story with an account of the adventures of an officer, Pirogov, whose attempt to seduce the wife of a drunken tinsmith (whose name is Hoffmann and whose cobbler friend is named Schiller) results in his being beaten, vowing revenge, and then forgetting the whole thing by dancing the mazurka at a banal *soirée*. The officer's easy acceptance of a mortal insult at the hands of the drunken artisans contrasts sharply with Piskaryov's essentially pompous idealizations and his suicide.

The plot of "The Nose" involves the snobbish affectations of the eponymous organ after its separation from the face of a Major Kovalyov, a social climber who needs that appendage to find a wife with a large dowry. In this story we find both the *Doppelgänger* theme from Hoffmann and the nose from *Tristram Shandy*'s Slawkenburgius, yet further indications of Gogol's familiarity with western European themes and his readiness to appropriate them for his own purposes.

"The Portrait" caused Gogol difficulties – later to be shared by his commentators – and he considerably altered the initial version of 1835 for publication in 1842. The tale chronicles the disintegration of Chartkov, a poor but promising painter, whose downfall begins when he purchases the forbidding portrait of an Asiatic money-lender and later finds a considerable sum of money hidden in its frame. Now able to dress fashionably, Chartkov becomes an enormously successful society painter, but pandering to his clients erodes his talent, and he becomes incapable of creating anything of value. In jealous despair he buys up works of true artists and slashes them to ribbons, ultimately to die destitute and insane. In the second part of the story the reader learns of the malevolent portrait's origin and how the artist overcame its pernicious effects by retreating to a monastery. Presumably the reader is to understand that talent may be destroyed if an artist seeks easy success, although in fact Chartkov seems to be a victim of some supernatural force associated with the subject of the portrait. The reworked version, considerably longer, places excessive emphasis upon the story's didactic and moralistic content.

In 1836 appeared Gogol's play *The Inspector General* (*Revizor*), usually categorized as a satire upon corrupt officials. The "hero," a brainless young clerk named Khlestakov, is mistaken for a government inspector travelling *incognito* by the worthies of a provincial town, who give him bribes to overlook their many transgressions. The insouciant clerk is initially oblivious to their error and assumes that their toadying is the natural result of his charm and his hyperbolically mendacious account of his position in St. Petersburg. In the end Khlestakov's servant suggests they take French leave while they can. The officials then learn to their chagrin of their self-deception, and the play concludes with the stunning news that a real inspector has arrived.

In *The Inspector General* Gogol seems deliberately to have violated the conventions of classical comedy: his "hero" arrives in Act Two and leaves in Act Four, he proposes almost simultaneously to the mayor's wife and daughter, and the play has no positive characters. Reportedly the tsar himself was amused by the play, which he saw as a satire against corruption; others interpreted it as an indictment of the governmental system. Its real value, however, lies in its grotesque characters, the creative lies of Khlestakov, the incomprehensible "reasoning" which afflicts the townspeople, and the agglomeration of nonsense which motivates their actions.

Despite the tsar's approbation, political conservatives attacked the play, and the hypersensitive author sought refuge abroad. For much of the next twelve years he lived principally in Rome, and it was there he composed his masterpiece, *Dead Souls*, a primary work of the 1840s.

While still in exile at Mikhaylovskoe, Pushkin had expanded his creative horizon to include drama, a move prompted by a growing general interest in Shakespeare. *Boris Godunov*, which Pushkin called "a romantic tragedy," was the fruit of an effort which extended over the better part of 1825. Informed by Karamzin's account of the reign of the "usurper" Boris and inspired by Shakespeare's freedom of composition, Pushkin combined blank verse, prose, lofty rhetoric and vernacular, the somber and the comic, in chronicling the inevitable disaster facing Boris and his family. In Pushkin's treatment of the conflict between Tsar Boris and the pretender to the throne, the false Dmitry, the former proves incapable of mastering his own destiny, while the usurper succeeds almost without effort. Boris's psychological disintegration contrasts sharply with the naive confidence of the pretender and provides the reader – the play is seldom staged – with a depth not found in Karamzin's account. In 1826, when Pushkin favored his literary friends with readings of his drama, they were astonished at its apparent innovations and gave it the highest praise, but after it was published in 1830 the critics and public reacted otherwise: they complained about its violation of the classical unities and preferred the more traditional treatment of historical subjects found in the contemporary novel in the manner of Walter Scott.

Pushkin remained at Mikhaylovskoe following the Decembrist uprising until the following September, when he was summoned to Moscow by Nicholas. The tsar apparently persuaded Pushkin of his good will and proposed to serve as his personal censor. In fact, however, the poet was still regarded with suspicion and remained under police surveillance. Still, his exile was over. He was now famous, free to enjoy the accolades of the public, and able to renew the bachelor pursuits denied him at Mikhaylovskoe. His somewhat irregular life (wine, women, and gambling) did not keep him from writing, but now he moved toward prose. *The Moor of Peter the Great* (*Arap Petra velikogo*), begun in 1828, was a fictionalized account of the youth of the poet's great grandfather, Abraham Hannibal, an Abyssinian who became a favorite of Peter the Great. The effort consisted of seven chapters, the last unfinished, and was only published completely in *The Contemporary* in 1837. In 1829, among other prose efforts, Pushkin tried his hand at an epistolary novel, *A Novel in Letters* (*Roman v pismakh*), now also unfinished but nevertheless a rich source on the author's ideas on the obligations of the gentry, particularly as regards their serfs. It also reveals a strong interest in the psychology of the protagonists, and had it been completed and published it doubtless would have contributed much to the emerging genre of the society tale.

Pushkin's developing interest in history, and in particular in Peter the Great, was further manifested in the long narrative poem *Poltava*, completed in 1828. The work's originality caused difficulties for the critics: it combined features of the Byronic poem, though without a subjective authorial voice, and the epic, though without a central heroic figure, and lacked the traditional intervention by supernatural powers. The poem is in three parts, with the first a family drama in which Maria, daughter of the nobleman Kochubey, declares her love for the aged Mazeppa, Hetman of the Ukraine, who is also her godfather and thus forbidden by church law from marrying her. She flees to him, so angering her father that he reveals to Tsar Peter Mazeppa's plan to betray Russia. In part two, Kochubey has been imprisoned and tortured by Mazeppa, who hides from Maria his intention to execute her father. She learns of his plan and seeks to intercede, but is too late. She flees, and the distraught Mazeppa cannot find her. The historical implications are broadened in the third and final part describing the battle of Poltava (1709), in which Peter defeated the Swedish king Charles XII and his turncoat ally Mazeppa. Charles and the distraught Hetman flee the field of battle, and in a remote village Mazeppa encounters Maria, who has gone insane.

In general the historical details of *Poltava* are correct, although the final encounter between the crazed Maria and her treacherous husband was doubtless poetic license. Oddly, although the hero of the piece is Peter, until the battle itself the poem focuses upon Kochubey, Maria, and in particular upon Mazeppa, depicted as a gloomy and perfidious tyrant prepared to sacrifice his devoted wife and his beloved homeland to avenge a petty insult Peter had inflicted on him years before.

Atmospheric nature descriptions, intriguing dialogues between Maria and Mazeppa, and an effective impressionistic description of the battle of Poltava are highpoints of this work, but the absence of a unifying central character, the shifting of scenes from the domestic to the international, and the range of tones and diction make the work appear episodic rather than organic and bespeak its experimental essence.

In the summer of 1829, following the rejection of his marriage proposal to Natalya Goncharova, Pushkin set off for Persia to view the Russo-Turkish conflict at first hand. He crossed the Caucasus and witnessed combat at Ezerum. His account of this adventure, "A Journey to Ezerum" ("Puteshestvie v Arzrum"), is an excellent example of the literary travelogue, one of those genres popular with aspiring prose writers since the days of Karamzin.

The fall of 1830 found Pushkin, now officially engaged to Natalya Goncharova, quarantined at his paternal estate of Boldino owing to a cholera epidemic. Here he wrote his *Tales of Belkin* (*Povesti Belkina*), five short stories ostensibly recorded by a provincial gentleman who had heard them from various narrators. The pieces are ironical treatments of romantic types, situations, and styles. Efforts to discover some organizing principle uniting the pieces have not proved convincing.

As a student of human behavior, Pushkin was intrigued by what has been termed the "psychological impostor," a person lacking natural leadership qualities who strives to maintain ascendancy by calculated role playing. "The Shot" ("Vystrel"), the most psychological of the Belkin tales, treats the obsession to dominate of a mysterious Byronic type, Sylvio, who finds his preeminence in his regiment challenged by a certain Count, a natural leader who effortlessly arouses the admiration of his fellow officers. Sylvio provokes him to a challenge, relying upon his skill in duelling to kill his adversary. After the Count has fired, he awaits Sylvio's fatal bullet with such insouciance that the frustrated Sylvio decides to postpone his own shot until such time as the Count shall fear death. Five years later, upon learning that the Count has just married, Sylvio appears at his estate and demands his shot. When the Count exhibits agitation and anxiety, Sylvio is satisfied that he has proven his superiority and spares his life, confident that the Count will suffer untold agonies at this "defeat." Of course, the mental anguish with which Sylvio seeks to poison the Count's life is based on a reading of how he, Sylvio, would react in the Count's place, and the Count behaves otherwise. Ironically, the diabolic revenge to which Sylvio devotes years of preparation proves worthless. Pushkin's story, which cleverly combines multiple narrators to exploit suspense and mystery, stands in sharp and deliberate contrast to Alexander Bestuzhev-Marlinsky's anecdote in "An Evening on Bivouac" ("Vecher na bivuake," 1823), which also treats the theme of the postponed shot but is withal an insipidly sentimentalized tale.

"The Stationmaster" ("Stantsionny smotritel") is in part a parody of "Poor Liza" (1792), Karamzin's sentimental tale of the spiritually beautiful flower girl deceived by a morally weak young officer, Erast. Pushkin's narrator, a naive traveller, recalls three visits to a provincial posting station. The first introduces a robust and cheerful stationmaster whose pride and joy is his flirtatious daughter Dunya. The report of the second visit depicts a now demoralized and alcoholic stationmaster, whose "poor Dunya" has run off with a hussar officer and is living with him in St. Petersburg. In his account of the third visit, the narrator ruefully reports the stationmaster's premature death, but also informs us that a beautiful lady had recently visited his grave: Dunya is obviously alive and well in St. Petersburg.

The critic Mikhail Gershenzon was intrigued by the fact that in this otherwise laconic narrative there is a long digression describing four panels in the posting station depicting the story of the prodigal son. He concluded that "The Stationmaster" was not, as many believed, a compassionate tale of a poor father whose daughter had been seduced by an insensate officer, but rather an ironic depiction of a man misled by the biblical parable who needlessly drank himself to death because he believed his daughter would inevitably end up badly. Many of the lamentations of the broken stationmaster recall "Poor Liza," and there is even a scene in Pushkin's work which parallels one in which Erast seeks to "buy off" his deceived mistress.

The remaining three tales are less complex and more obviously ironical in their treatment of romantic clichés. "The Undertaker" ("Grobovshchik") is ostensibly an account of a supernatural visitation by the clientele of an undertaker, who rashly invites his "customers" to a housewarming. It turns out that the visitation is a nightmare caused by overindulgence. "The Squire's Daughter" ("Baryshnya-krestyanka") and "The Blizzard" ("Metel") develop the theme of mistaken identity. In the former, a provincial miss masquerades as a peasant girl to capture a blasé young nobleman. "The Blizzard" plays with the theme of star-crossed lovers: a couple determined to marry without parental permission plan to meet at a remote church, but the young man is delayed by a blizzard and his bride, swooning from anxiety, is mistakenly married to a passing hussar, who lightheartedly accepts the role of groom. Years later the couple meet by chance, fall in love, and then discover that they are already married.

Pushkin returned to the dramatic form that fall of 1830 in Boldino when he composed his so-called "little tragedies," succinct studies of obsessive personalities in unrhymed iambic pentameter. Three of these took their origins from the poet's stay at Mikhaylovskoe, as his notes indicate, and their perfection may be owing to a long period of gestation. "The Covetous Knight" ("Skupoy rytsar") dramatizes the conflict between an impecunious knight, Albert, and his egregiously covetous father, the Baron. The son is desperate for funds to enable him to take part in activities at court, and the father is relentlessly determined to protect his arduously acquired wealth. The pathology of the miser is wonderfully represented in the second scene (there are three), in which the Baron communes with his hoard and recalls the circumstances accompanying the acquisition of each coin. The play concludes melodramatically, as Albert accepts a challenge from his father. The Baron then suffers a fatal seizure and dies calling for the keys to his chests of gold.

"Mozart and Salieri" ("Motsart i Saleri") is based on a rumor that Salieri poisoned the great composer. Here again we have the theme of the individual gifted by nature for whom all things come easily in conflict with the person who must strain every nerve to enjoy only modest success. With no apparent effort Mozart achieves sublime heights of composition, which Salieri cannot remotely approach for all his desire and endless effort. Deeply affronted by Mozart's preeminence, his nonchalance about his talent, and his indifference to his calling, Salieri poisons him. However, his revenge is undermined by Mozart's dictum that genius and villainy are incompatible.

"The Stone Guest" ("Kamenny gost") is a variation of the Don Juan theme. Here the exiled voluptuary returns to Madrid to visit his favorite Laura, only to find her consorting with Don Carlos, the brother of the Commander, whom he had earlier slain. Don Juan kills Don Carlos, and in a defiant mood decides to court Dona Anna, the widow of the Commander. To this end he disguises himself as a monk and waits for her at her husband's grave, which is adorned by his granite statue. Confronting her, he identifies himself as Don Diego, an ardent admirer, and gains an invitation to her house. Don Juan's fearful servant, Leporello, notes that the statue appears angry, but his master remains unperturbed and commands Leporello to invite the Commander to guard the door during his tryst with the widow. The statue nods acceptance. At his meeting with Dona Anna, Don Juan discloses his true identity and overcomes her objections and sense of guilt. A noise is heard, the statue appears, takes Don Juan's hand, and both sink into the earth. Notwithstanding this work's supernatural element and legendary origins, there is a strong element of realism in its dialogue and in the psychological portrait of Don Juan, an egomaniac who views life as a game and others as his playthings. Don Juan's audacious behavior and his readiness to challenge fate make him an engaging villain, whose descendant we shall shortly meet as the protagonist of Lermontov's *A Hero of Our Time*.

"The Feast During the Plague" ("Pir vo vremya chumy") is a translation of a portion of John Wilson's *The City of the Plague*, a scene in which a group of those still surviving the plague are banqueting on the street. The original is significantly altered only by the interpolating of two songs: a touching one in which the plague-stricken Jenny admonishes her lover Edmond to stay away from her to save his own life, and "The hymn in honor of the plague." Like the feast itself, the hymn is a gesture of anguished bravado, a toast to death-dealing pestilence in defiance of sense and religion.

"The Queen of Spades" ("Pikovaya dama") was the product of yet another productive Boldino autumn. Written in 1833, it was published in *The Library for Reading* (*Biblioteka dlya chteniya*) the following year. Like "The Stationmaster," the story has a history of misinterpretation. This is not a tale of the supernatural in which the protagonist falls victim to a ghost, but a parody of both the supernatural tale and the society tale. Here again Pushkin treats the psychological impostor, the individual who rashly seeks to play a role beyond his abilities.

Hermann, a prudent officer of Engineers, seeks to discover the secret of three winning cards, which he is told had saved an old countess from bankruptcy at the gambling tables many years before. Obsessed by the possibility of obtaining instant wealth, Hermann gains access to the old lady's mansion by pretending infatuation with her abused ward Elizabeth. When he confronts the Countess, she denies there is any secret, and then dies of fright. The superstitious Hermann attends her funeral to seek forgiveness, only to faint when she winks at him from her coffin. That night, after drinking more than usual, he is visited by her ghost, which reveals the sequence of the three cards – three, seven, and ace – in exchange for his promise to marry Elizabeth. Hermann then stakes his savings on the three and wins, puts the total on the seven and wins, but in the final round selects the queen of spades instead of the ace. As his mistake is revealed to him, the card assumes the features of the Countess. He loses all, and goes mad. The highly ironic epilogue describes the fates of the various characters, among them Elizabeth, who has acquired affluence through marriage to the son of the Countess's embezzling bailiff, and now has a ward of her own! Hermann is hospitalized, reduced to muttering the winning and losing card sequences.

The story has many levels of interest, including a host of covert references to Masonic symbolism and play with numbers, but its basic contribution is the revelation of the obsessive personality of Hermann, an impecunious and cautious man who, inspired by an anecdote which others dismissed, aspired to instant wealth on the grounds, as he declared to the Countess during their fatal confrontation, that he deserved the fortune to which she held the key. But he is innately weak, and, unstrung by his own audacity, his overwrought nerves, his superstition and anxiety, he breaks down at the critical moment to become his own victim. This story was a seminal one for Dostoevsky's *Crime and Punishment*, whose protagonist, Raskolnikov, is also a would-be superman defeated by his own inadequacies. One must reject a common misinterpretation which sees Hermann as destroyed by the Countess's supernatural intervention, for if this is correct the whole psychological significance of the story is vitiated and Pushkin is deprived of his proper claim to have introduced a significant theme into Russian fiction.

Pushkin's interest in history intensified in 1832 when he was granted permission to work in the historical archives. There he researched the uprising led by the illiterate Cossack Emelyan Pugachov, who, pretending to be Peter III, seriously threatened the rule of Catherine the Great in 1773–4. In the late summer of 1833 Pushkin visited important sites of the conflict, and that fall, once again at Boldino, finished his *History of the Pugachov Rebellion* (*Istoriya pugachevskogo bunta*). Meanwhile, he was working on a historical romance based on the same event, *The Captain's Daughter* (*Kapitanskaya dochka*), published in 1836. This is probably the best of the Russian historical novels in the style of Walter Scott, with whose works it shares certain plot-features, though it differs from them in its lack of sociological and anthropological baggage. Pushkin's story focuses upon character, especially that of Pugachov, whose extraordinary leadership abilities made his rebellion so successful. As with "The Stationmaster" and "The Shot," Pushkin utilizes a naive narrator, in this case a young officer, Grinyov, whose fiancée Marya is abducted by the rebels after they kill her parents, Captain Mironov and his wife. The use of a naive narrator here made it possible for Pushkin to show some of Pugachov's charismatic qualities without falling afoul of the censorship. Grinyov and Marya are somewhat colorless, but Pugachov's portrait is engaging, albeit enigmatic. Particularly attractive are the portraits of Marya's parents, the simple but heroic Captain Mironov and his domineering wife, who abjure allegiance to the pretender and pay for their steadfastness with their lives, and Grinyov's obstinate but faithful servant, Savelich. Mironov became a prototype for Tolstoy's self-effacing Captain Tushin (*War and Peace*), the unsung hero of the battle of Borodino.

History once again is central to what many consider Pushkin's finest verse work, the narrative poem *The Bronze Horseman* (*Medny vsadnik*), yet another fruit of the Boldino harvest of 1833. The setting is essentially contemporary – the disastrous flood of 1824 in St. Petersburg – but the theme is historical, for the poem explores the conflict between the individual, represented by the poor clerk Eugene whose fiancée drowns in the flood, and Peter the Great, the embodiment of *la raison d'état*, who established a city on the marshes of the Neva river with apparent unconcern for the thousands of victims his project claimed. The demented Eugene identifies as his enemy the equestrian statue of Peter which dominates Senate Square, and he dares to threaten it, then flees hopelessly from its merciless pursuit and dies. The work has the unusual quality of simultaneously lauding the vision and will of Peter while treating his victim compassionately: in effect, both are right. This attitude perhaps reflected Pushkin's own frustrations in his relationship to Nicholas I, who for personal and state reasons kept the poet in physical and economic bondage.

As with *Poltava*, this narrative ranges from the individual to the international, from the powerless Eugene and his poor Parasha to Peter and his creation of a city intended to thwart the "haughty neighbor" Sweden and break through a window to Europe. The opening apotheosis to St. Petersburg is also a rebuttal of the Polish poet Adam Mickiewicz's harshly critical vision of the city (and of Russia and Peter as well) in his *Forefathers' Eve Part III*. The polemics between the two poets, who knew and admired each other, arose not because of differing tastes for climate and urban landscapes but over their opposing views on the fate of Poland, long a restless thrall of Russia's. This answer to Mickiewicz represents a "personal" element in *The Bronze Horseman* not found in *Poltava*.

Despite Pushkin's defense of St. Petersburg and his rationalization of its human cost, his poem presages a new assessment of the city, which theretofore had enjoyed poetic adulation as the Venice of the north and the eighth wonder of the world. In the eyes of the crazed Eugene, the city is a sinister and threatening place, a haunted house dominated by a demonic force. This interpretation captured the imagination of Russian authors, and almost immediately this new image of St. Petersburg was developed by other writers, notably Gogol in "Nevsky Prospect," in which the Devil lights the city's street lamps at night to deceive mortals.

The estate at Boldino was particularly congenial for the pro-

178

duction of fairy tales, and Pushkin completed several of them on each of his sojourns in the autumns of 1830 and 1833. It was generally believed that these works originated with Arina Rodionovna, the poet's nurse, who used to entertain him with Russian folk tales during his exile at Mikhaylovskoe, but several of them share common features with tales from western Europe. This does not, however, detract from their apparent Russianness and charming simplicity. The first of them "The fairy tale of the priest and his manservant Balda" ("Skazka o pope i o rabotnike ego Balde," 1830), was prohibited by the censorship during the poet's lifetime and appeared, with alterations, only in 1840. The story is based on the traditional folklore theme of the simpleton getting the best of a deceitful and venal master, and is striking for its uneven lines with rhymed couplets, which impart an atmosphere of crudeness suiting the protagonists and their actions. "The fairy tale about the fisherman and the fish" ("Skazka o rybake i rybke," 1833) exploits the theme of the greedy wife who is never satisfied with the gifts a thaumaturgical fish grants her husband, until ultimately she gets nothing. "The fairy tale about the dead princess and the seven champions" ("Skazka o mertvoy tsarevne i o semi bogatyryakh," 1833) is a variant of the Snow White theme, replete with an evil stepmother who interrogates her mirror seeking flattering responses. "The fairy tale about Tsar Saltan" ("Skazka o tsare Saltane," 1831) and "The fairy tale about the golden cockerel" ("Skazka o zolotom petukhe," 1834) are by common agreement considered the best of this genre. The first, narrated in lilting trochaic tetrameter couplets, recounts the cruel deception of Tsar Saltan by his wife's two envious sisters and an evil matchmaker, who report to the tsar, then on campaign, that the tsarina has given birth to a monster, and then set her adrift in a cask with her newborn son Gvidon. The castaways survive on a foreign island, and thanks to the youth's having saved an endangered swan with magical powers, he can return to his father's kingdom as a mosquito, a fly, and a bee. On each occasion he stings or bites one of the evildoers. Meanwhile, the swan bequeaths to Gvidon such marvels as a squirrel that eats nuts with golden shells and emerald kernels, and a personal guard of thirty-three champions led by Chernomor. The third wonder is a beautiful maiden who turns out to be the swan itself, and Gvidon marries her. Learning of this last marvel from marine traders, Tsar Saltan fulfills his wish to visit the island, where he rediscovers his wife and son, and in his joy forgives the evil sisters and the conniving matchmaker. "The golden cockerel," linked to one of the legends included by Washington Irving in his *Alhambra*, contains certain indications that Tsar Dadon, the foolish and lazy ruler who entrusted the safety of his kingdom to a watchbird, the golden cockerel, refers to Alexander I, but it is difficult to substantiate this on internal evidence. One should simply enjoy the couplets of trochaic tetrameter and take pleasure in the poet's wit.

Although some may hold that Pushkin's narrative poetry, especially *Eugene Onegin* and *The Bronze Horseman*, are his most significant achievements, he possibly made his greatest contribution to Russian literature through his lyrics. Their range is extensive, from casual and flippant epigrams to serious statements of the lyric "I," from album verses of transitory importance to scenes of nature striking in pictorial vividness and mood, from anniversary verses to expressions of friendship and solidarity. Contemporary critics generally agree that Pushkin's verse is more classical than romantic, for it does not display the high passion and unsublimated emotion, the lack of control, or the exuberance one usually associates with romantic poetry. Moreover, if one maintains that poetry is "thinking in metaphors," it is difficult to explain the completely unornamented "I loved you once...," ("Ya vas lyubil...," 1829), which contains only the already dead metaphor of "extinguished love." Pushkin's verse, when compared with some of the colorful and highly ornate vessels of his romantic contemporaries, resembles a crystal goblet, elegant, symmetrical, and transparent, which gives forth a clear and resonant sound when struck. And while we may feel that some of Pushkin's poems bear the mark of pure inspiration, his manuscripts reveal that their ease of expression and apparent effortlessness were the result of careful revision.

A significant part of Pushkin's lyrics have to do with affairs of the heart, displaying the anticipated range of emotions from tender concern and joy to jealousy and despair. Despite the kaleidoscopic nature of his erotic attachments, Pushkin seems to have been deeply affected by them.

Pushkin's lyrics ordinarily express ideas and feelings in an uncomplicated manner, without philosophical overtones. In this respect he is poles apart from his contemporaries Baratynsky and Tyutchev, both "metaphysical" poets. By nature Pushkin was neither a dreamer nor a seer, but rather a pragmatist. A fine example of his Voltairean rationalism is his comment about Richardson's Clarissa Harlowe, who willed her own death after having been dishonored by Lovelace: Pushkin's assessment was: "What a ninny!" Of course he never cared for the abstractions of the Lovers of Wisdom or their flights into romantic Schellingian idealism.

As for his poetic vocation Pushkin could adopt many views. In his "Conversation between a bookseller and a poet" ("Razgovor knigoprodavtsa s poetom," 1824), the poet at first recalls his early days of inspiration, his happy isolation from the crowd, his lofty indifference to fame; but in the end he concedes that without money there is no freedom and starts to negotiate a price for his work. Although Pushkin here expresses a thoroughly unromantic view in treating the poet as an artisan or tradesman, he in fact had a high opinion of his calling. The lengthy poem "André Chénier" (1825) lauds the heroism of the martyred poet-patriot, and in "The prophet" ("Prorok," 1826) a seraphim transforms a mortal into a prophet and admonishes him to "burn the hearts of men with the word." While not indulging in the romantic fantasy of the poet as a kind of divine being who in moments of inspiration might glimpse the *truth*, Pushkin considered the poet superior to the "crowd," which for him consisted of the gentry, sycophants and toadies, the hypocrites and intellectual Yahoos of society. "To the poet" ("Poetu," 1830) admonishes the poet to disdain popularity: "You are a tsar. Live alone." If he had harsh words for the crowd, Pushkin was even more contemptuous toward Alexander I, the man responsible for his six-year exile. In his famous Horatian variation "Exegi monumentum" (1836), the poet proudly claims to have raised a miraculous (*nerukotvorny*, literally "not made by human hands") monument to himself, which is higher than the Alexander Pillar, the monument to the tsar erected in St. Petersburg in 1834.

Pushkin was at his most romantic in his choice of works to translate or imitate, such as the Psalms or the Koran, whose exoticism captivated him. We may also note his translations of Prosper Merimée's *Songs of the Western Slavs*, to which he added his own imitations of south Slavic folk poetry. One of the most romantic of his original works is the poignant "God grant I don't go mad!" ("Ne day mne Bog soyti s uma," 1833), in which the poet longs for the oblivion and freedom of madness, but finally concludes that madness means incarceration, where the song of the nightingale and the rustle of the oaks will be replaced by the cries of inmates, the curses of the guards, and the sound of chains. The pragmatic Pushkin can find no joy in madness.

Pushkin's poems containing nature descriptions are most engaging, perhaps owing to their pictorial effect. They are filled with details of specific landscapes, as, for example, "Once again I visited" ("Vnov ya posetil...," 1835), written upon a return visit to Mikhaylovskoe. Thoughts of his earlier exile there mingle with circumstantial descriptions of the setting, including references to actual trees. "The rainy day has ended..." ("Nenastny den potukh...," 1824) starts with a description of dreary nature at Mikhaylovskoe and the poet's anguish before turning to thoughts of his beloved pining on a distant shore beneath blue skies. Nature has a more ominous quality in "The Upas tree" ("Anchar," 1828), which paints a picture of a solitary tree growing in a pestilential desert, exuding its poisonous resin and shunned by bird and beast. But a tsar sacrifices a servant to get the poison, which he puts on his arrows to kill his neighbors. The poem is powerful and suggestive, as Turgenev demonstrated in his story "A Quiet Spot," where knowledge of these verses catalyzes the heroine's suicide.

Alexander Bestuzhev-Marlinsky resumed publishing in 1830 following his release from prison to serve as a soldier in the Caucasus, and he became one of the most popular authors of the 1830s. Three of his stories have nautical settings, and all are saturated with technical terms connected with ships, a reflection of their author's experiences aboard ship with his naval-officer brothers. "Lieutenant Belozor" ("Leytenant Belozor," 1831) is an adventure love story in which the title figure, stranded in Holland during the continental blockade, wins the daughter of his Dutch protector and escapes the traps of his French adversary. "The Frigate 'Hope" ("Fregat 'Nadezhda,'" 1832) is a society tale of an illicit and ultimately tragic affair between Captain Pravin and Vera, the unhappily married wife of a St. Petersburg magnate. The names of the protagonists and the ship may allude to the

Decembrist catastrophe. However, stripped of its allegorical potential, the work is overly long and filled with Marlinisms. "Nikitin the Sailor" ("Morekhod Nikitin," 1834) is a fictionalized version of an actual adventure in which Russian merchant sailors captured by the English took over a ship and escaped. Marlinsky's most famous work is "Ammalat Bek" (1832), the story of a Tatar warrior befriended by a Russian officer, whom he later kills, mistakenly thinking the Russian has betrayed him. The work was an excellent vehicle for Marlinsky's hyperbolism, overdone metaphors, exaggerated character types, harangues, descriptions of untamed nature, and embellishment with Caucasian languages and ethnography. At the same time the work is highly moralistic, seeking to demonstrate the superiority of Christianity, as exemplified by the cheek-turning Russian, to Islam, represented by the vengeful Ammalat. Despite its occasionally engaging narrative, which is colorful and suspenseful, the characters are quite flat. Vissarion Belinsky correctly noted in a long critical essay of 1834 that all of Marlinsky's heroes somehow resemble one another, be they Novgorodian soldiers or Caucasian tribesmen.

In 1837 Marlinsky disappeared during a Russian landing at Cape Adler on the Black Sea, presumably killed by the mountaineers led by the prophet Shamil. Whether his life reflected his fiction or his fiction reflected his life is difficult to say, but in either case as a person and as an author he epitomized the romantic era.

Much less colorful, but of almost equal importance, was Orest Somov (1793–1833), whose name has already been mentioned in connection with *Polar Star*, *Northern Flowers*, and *The Literary Gazette*. Somov was an innovator, one of the first writers of society tales, the author of numerous tales of the supernatural and variations on legends derived from his native Ukraine, the author of many anecdotal stories presented as tales of a traveler (in the tradition of Washington Irving), and several quite competent novellas of manners. Among the latter are "A Novel in Two Letters" ("Roman v dvukh pismakh," 1832), a lightly facetious treatment of Ukrainian provincial society; "Matchmaking" ("Svatovstvo," 1832), a humble clerk's poignant account of frustrated happiness; and the amusing "Mommy and Sonny" ("Matushka i synok," 1833), a spoof on provincial pretensions. In the last work an ignorant but obdurate proprietress addicted to

Gothic novels seeks to dominate her milksop son, whose reading of sentimental tales has distorted his already limited capacities. Somov should also be remembered for his efforts to improve Russian prose, his broadening of fiction to include plebeian types, his success in using his characters' speech as keys to personality and emotional states, and his faithful service to literature as a critic and journalist.

If one were to seek the author who best fits the stereotype of "the romantic poet," Mikhail Lermontov (1814–41) would win without question. The child of an ill-matched marriage, while still an infant he lost his mother. Through adolescence he was sensitive and alienated, and suffered from the strife between his improvident father and his maternal grandmother, his guardian. At the University of Moscow he was aloof and contemptuous of his fellow students and the faculty. He left, or was dismissed, to enter the School of Cavalry Junkers and Ensigns of the Guard in St. Petersburg. There his denigration of authority led to periods in the guardhouse, but he was commissioned a cornet in the Life Guard Hussars in 1834. His frivolous and dissolute life changed suddenly in January 1837, when Alexander Pushkin was slain by Georges d'Anthès. Overnight Lermontov became the conscience of Russian liberals with his poem "Death of a poet" ("Smert poeta"), an elegy excoriating d'Anthès and blaming the aristocrats of the Imperial court for Pushkin's death. Subsequent exile to the Caucasus, heroism in battle, a duel with the son of the French ambassador, along with a rapidly developing literary reputation, enhanced his position. His somber and disquieting gaze, which everyone noted, his premonitions of an early death and his poem describing its circumstances, all of this reinforced the image of Lermontov's romantic genius, the *poète-maudit*, the rebel, the God-fighter, the judge and the prophet.

Customarily little attention is paid to Lermontov's work before 1837, but only because what followed was so truly outstanding. He produced a number of lyrics (many derived from his unrequited summer romances while a student), some dramas redolent of Lessing and Schiller, and narrative poems patterned on Byron and Pushkin. An unfinished historical novel – customarily titled *Vadim*, from the name of its demonic hunchbacked protagonist – was set against the background of the Pugachov Rebellion and revealed a close acquaintance with Hugo's *Bug-Jargal*, Balzac's *Les Chouans*, and Scott's *The Black Monk*. Less derivative were *The Masquerade* (*Maskarad*, begun 1835), a melodrama satirizing society and exploiting the Othello theme, and the unfinished society tale *Princess Ligovskaya* (*Knyaginya Ligovskaya*), which offered a bold step toward the delineation of individual psychology in the characterization of the protagonist, Grigory Pechorin.

Lermontov's maturation as a poet to some extent paralleled that of Byron. Early narcissistic exaggeration of personal feelings was gradually replaced by condemnation of contemporary society, particularly vitriolic in the poem "Meditation" ("Duma," 1838). "1 January 1840" ("Pervoe yanvarya 1840") concludes with an expression of the poet's desire to "throw an iron verse" into the face of the "motley crowd." But his caustic remarks about society did not prevent the poet from loving the Russian land and its people. In "When billows the yellowing grain" ("Kogda volnuet-sya zhelteyushchaya niva," 1837) contemplation of nature leads the poet to a vision of God, and in "Homeland" ("Rodina," 1841) it is not the glory of Russia which he loves but its land and its people, exemplified by the raucous dancing of drunken peasants. "Borodino" 1837) ascribes the victory of the Russian over the French in 1812 to the courage of the common soldier, a theme later developed by Tolstoy. "The prophet" ("Prorok," 1841) stresses the isolation of the poet-prophet, and the theme of alienation recurs in a number of other pieces, such as "Alone I set forth upon the road" ("Vykhozhu odin ya na dorogu," 1841) or the lyric beginning "I am bored and sad and there's no one to take my hand" ("I skuchno i grustno i nekomu ruku podat," 1840). There are hints of impending death in the 1837 lyric "Do not mock my prophetic anguish" ("Ne smeysya nad moey prorocheskoy toskoyu"), while "The dream" ("Son," 1841), written just before his final exile to the Caucasus, outlines in graphic detail his actual death scene.

Three narrative poems of Lermontov's mature period are of particular significance. *The Song of Tsar Ivan Vasilevich, The Young Oprichnik and the Audacious Merchant Kalashnikov* (*Pesnya pro tsarya Ivana Vasilevicha, molodogo oprichnika i udalogo kuptsa Kalashnikova*, 1837) is a stylization of the Russian historical song, a folk genre with involved metrical features and other unique prosodic requirements. The poem relates how the merchant avenged an insult to his wife by slaying the *oprichnik* (member of the tsar's bodyguard) at a boxing match in the presence of Ivan the Terrible. For this act of *lèse-majesté* the merchant is sentenced to death, though the merciful tsar promises to protect his wife and orphans. Lermontov wrote only one work of this sort, and he composed it while confined to bed with rheumatism immediately after his arrival in Piatigorsk in 1837 during his first exile to the Caucasus. The work is recognized as probably the best "literary" attempt by any Russian poet at imitating the historical song. What many fail to recognize is that it is an allegorical treatment of Pushkin's domestic and court tribulations, as its many overt anachronisms and numerous cryptic allusions suggest. Smarting over his punishment for his poem on Pushkin's death, Lermontov took his secret revenge with this work, which not only told the whole story of Pushkin's frustrations at d'Anthès' attentions to his wife but "corrected" fate by making the bodyguard the victim of the merchant's single blow (each of the antagonists strikes the other once, as in a duel each fires once). Incidentally, the cynical Nicholas I sent the dying Pushkin assurances that he would look after the poet's wife and children, much as Ivan promises Kalashnikov to protect his family.

Lermontov worked on his narrative poem *The Demon* (*Demon*) from 1829 until 1840, producing no fewer than eight redactions of it. The theme of a fallen angel's love for a mortal was not new with Lermontov: Goethe, Moore, Byron, Alfred de Vigny and others had dealt with it. Lermontov's version, originally set in Spain, was moved to the Caucasus, and the mortal, a nun, originally suffered damnation for her effort to rescue the suffering demon with her love. In the final version the nun's guardian angel saves her soul, while the demon is condemned to suffer eternal solitude. Somewhat more original, although perhaps based upon a story Lermontov heard in the Caucasus, is *Mtsyri* (*The Novice*, 1840). Set against the grandiose background of the Caucasus, it depicts the ecstasy and agony experienced by a novice during three days of freedom from his monastery. Presented as a confession or *profession de foi*, a form Lermontov favored, the tale is wonderfully romantic: the beauty of the mountains, the joy of freedom, the majesty of a storm, inchoate feelings of love, a mortal battle with a snow leopard, and the hero's final insistence that his brief escape was worth the price of death – all this captivates the reader.

While working on *The Demon* and *Mtsyri*, Lermontov also

indulged his sense of satire by writing narrative poems set in contemporary Russia. The most notable of these is the humorous and slightly ribald *The Tambov Treasurer's Wife* (*Tambovskaya kaznacheysha*, 1837–8), in which a hussar wins a provincial official's wife at cards. The triviality of society and its abysmal moral values are amusingly depicted. Some other satirical narrative poems – such as *Sashka* (1835–9) and *A Fairy Tale for Children* (*Skazka dlya detey*, 1840), which appears to have a basis in the poet's own biography – remained unfinished, and, to judge by the extant versions, could not have been published in the Russia of Nicholas I.

A Hero of Our Time (*Geroy nashego vremeni*, 1840), Lermontov's prose masterpiece, is unique in that, although it employs the forms and clichés of romantic fiction, the result is the first fully developed novel of psychological realism in Russian literature. Travel notes, the physiological sketch, the adventure story (a variant of the military memoir), the society tale, are combined to present an increasingly intimate portrait of the protagonist, Grigory Pechorin, an intelligent but totally egocentric young officer who affects the role of an innocent fated to destroy the happiness, even lives, of others.

We are introduced to Pechorin through Maxim Maximych, an old Caucasus veteran who picturesquely relates to a chance traveling companion the tale of Pechorin's abduction of a Chechen maiden, unaware that the theme of the tragic love of a *giaour* and a native girl is hardly new. His interlocutor, an author, has an opportunity to meet Pechorin, for whom he provides a "literary" evaluation on the basis of external appearance. Thus armed with a "hearsay" and then a first-hand account of Pechorin, we are finally provided "autobiographical" materials in the form of three selections from Pechorin's Journal, two of which are anecdotes of adventure and the central one a fully developed society tale set in Piatigorsk. As the reader becomes better acquainted with Pechorin, he is both attracted by the man, who is analytical, aloof, and clearly superior to his social milieu, and at the same time repelled by his arrogance, cruelty, and moral ambivalence. When we finish the final tale, we are still faced with an enigma: is Pechorin a victim of hostile fate, or is he a demonic personality determined to dominate others at whatever cost?

Pechorin has a rich ancestry. Domestically, of course, he derives from Eugene Onegin. As usual in Russian literature throughout the nineteenth century, the heroes' names are significant: the Pechora River is wild and turbulent, the Onega River placid and slow. In European literature Pechorin's origins may be found in Richardson's Lovelace, Chateaubriand's René, de Senancour's Obermann, Benjamin Constant's Adolphe, and the protagonist of Alfred de Musset's *La Confession d'un enfant du siècle*. The device of the veteran who relates a tale of tragic love to a traveller duplicates the method in Alfred de Vigny's "Laurette, ou le cachet rouge" from *Servitude et grandeurs militaires*, and there are some situational parallels between the society tale in Lermontov's novel ("Princess Mary") and Charles de Bernard's *Gerfaut* as well as Walter Scott's *Saint Ronan's Well*.

A Hero of Our Time appeared in 1840 and was soon republished with an author's preface in which he denied that Pechorin was a self-portrait or that he approved of his behavior: "Our public is still so young and naive that it fails to understand a fable unless it finds a lesson at its end," he wrote. Pechorin was a composite figure embodying the vices of his generation for which he, Lermontov, had no intention of providing remedies.

While Lermontov's Pechorin was being denounced as a model of immorality, others promenaded on the streets of Piatigorsk claiming to be his prototype. More modest impostors assumed the identity of Grushnitsky, the Byronic *poseur* of "Princess Mary," whom Pechorin unceremoniously dispatches to his death with the epitaph "Finita la commedia!" Several ladies vied for the honor of having inspired either Princess Mary or Vera, both victims of Pechorin's vicious machinations.

Lermontov's death in 1841 marks the end of the Golden Age of Russian poetry, which only someone of his spectacular powers could have extended after Pushkin's death. The 1840s saw the rapid development of the "natural school," a by-product of Gogol's presumed concern for "the little man" and his interest in sordid environments. By the end of the decade Turgenev and Dostoevsky were already on stage, and Tolstoy was in the wings. All of them owed a great debt to their romantic forebears, who had contrived a prose literary language and developed the genres and devices which were to serve them so well.

5

THE NINETEENTH CENTURY: THE NATURAL SCHOOL AND ITS AFTERMATH, 1840–55

The 1840s – that "marvellous decade," in Paul Annenkov's phrase – occupy a special place in the historical memory of the Russian intelligentsia. For most of its length the decade was a time of great philosophical, cultural, and literary beginnings, which then came to an abrupt ending in the so-called "epoch of censorship terror" commencing with the European revolutions of 1848 and continuing through Russia's losing involvement in the Crimean war of 1853–6. The second portion of the years from 1840 to 1855 transformed the entire period from a beginning to something more like a transition, from the great years of romanticism to the time of the Russian realists who would win for Russian literature a worldwide reputation. It was also a period of continuing transition from an age of poetry to an epoch when prose writing dominated the literary arena.

Philosophically, the early 1840s were a time when young Russians eagerly followed and endlessly discussed all the latest theories, emanating especially from Germany. Young people formally enrolled in universities found it much more interesting to spend their hours participating in small "circles" and all-night debates about the good, the true and the beautiful, than attending classes. That frame of mind is epitomized in Turgenev's vignette of an instance when he and Belinsky were summoned to dinner by Belinsky's wife and the critic objected to being interrupted for a meal when the two of them had not yet settled the question of God's existence.

Belinsky was at the philosophical and literary center of the 1840s. At its inception he was a well-established literary critic whose personal charisma and literary acumen endowed him with an authority unparalleled in his generation, and indeed in the entire century. Belinsky decided how literary works were to be viewed: it was he in particular who decreed that the multi-faceted Gogol should be interpreted as a writer whose works were models of social commitment, and that "The Overcoat" of 1842 – the most important literary work of the period – should be regarded as an apotheosis of the "little man."

That interpretation of this story played a major role in the development of the "natural school," a literary tendency which might be termed "prerealism," as a parallel to the "preromanticism" of some three decades earlier. The adepts of the natural school displayed a keen interest in literary sociology, examining the hitherto neglected "little men" of urban society such as clerks and janitors; before long they launched literary investigations of the peasantry as well. If during the romantic period the emphasis was on the genuinely or supposedly extraordinary individual, during the 1840s the focus shifted to the ordinary individual, or even the person who was rather less than ordinarily capable, like Gogol's Akaky Akakievich from "The Overcoat."

Belinsky also provided personal guidance to that superb group of prose writers who first came on the scene between 1840 and 1848. He was nearly the first to read Dostoevsky's maiden work, and sought to direct his early development thereafter, he was a close friend and literary adviser to Turgenev, and he welcomed Goncharov's first important work. He attacked Gogol sharply when the latter's *Selected Passages from Correspondence with Friends* made his political views clear, and he found them unacceptable. Belinsky turned out to be very much at the right spot. He exercised his influence not only directly, as a pre-publication critic, but also through his extensive reviews of published works in the "thick journals" with which he was associated, and which were assuming an ever greater importance at this stage.

Belinsky's response to Gogol's *Selected Passages* in his famous "Letter" points up another aspect of the literary atmosphere of that time: the conviction that the genuine writer must almost invariably reject official government viewpoints. Writers were gradually gaining more and more of their livelihood from writing, and fewer of them from the government (if they were so employed, they tended to subsist at relatively low levels, and bore little policy-making responsibility). The man of letters must necessarily be a critic of his society from the left, Belinsky held in the 1840s, and if he were not in fact, then his work must be interpreted so as to make him so.

At the time of Belinsky's death in 1848, when he was just short of 37, the cultural atmosphere was changing drastically. Herzen had emigrated, Dostoevsky was soon to go into Siberian exile on political grounds, Gogol died in 1852 and Turgenev was punished for publishing an obituary article on him. Many writers experienced severe difficulties with the censorship over those years. But even this could not last forever, and with the death of Nicholas I in 1855 the repressed forces of Russian literature burst forth to create what is no doubt the finest quarter-century of achievement that any modern literature has ever witnessed.

DURING THE 1840s the Russian political climate was dominated by the figure of Tsar Nicholas I; literary life was under the spell of Nikolay Gogol; and the chief arbiter of literary taste was the critic Vissarion Belinsky (1811–48). Thus it is not surprising that Paul Annenkov's famous memoir of the period, *The Remarkable Decade*, has Belinsky as its central figure, and that Nikolay Cherny-shevsky's *Essays on the Gogol Period of Russian Literature* (1855–6) bears a title which is in effect a euphemism, since by 1855 Belinsky, who is again its central figure, could not be mentioned in print.

Literature could not escape the political realities of the times. The official values of the regime, formulated by the Minister of Education, Sergey Uvarov, as "Autocracy, Orthodoxy and Nationality," impinged on cultural life in a direct way. But if the first two elements in this formula could not be questioned, even by implication, the third was a matter of some debate: what was Russian nationality (i.e. *narodnost*, or "folkness")? Was it a quality totally reserved to the *narod*, the folk, the great masses of the illiterate Russian peasantry who were in bondage to their more educated and often Europeanized masters; or was the culture of the French-speaking elite of Russian society also part of the concept? What was Russia's national identity? Was Russia to be inward and backward-looking, or did it belong to Europe? This debate lay at the heart of the controversy between Slavophiles and westernizers in the 1840s, and each view to some extent became associated with a different capital: Moscow with the values of the old Russia; St. Petersburg with those of the new, Europeanized Russia.

The *narodnost* debated by writers and intellectuals was not the nationalism of official Russia, though this was also represented, in St. Petersburg by Faddey Bulgarin and Nikolay Grech's *Northern Bee*, and in Moscow by two professors of the University – Mikhail Pogodin and Stepan Shevyryov. Pogodin's journal *The Muscovite* (*Moskvityanin*) was regarded as a vehicle for "official nationality": in its very first number, in 1841, Shevyryov spoke of the west as "rotting." Issue was joined by another professor of Moscow University, the historian Timofey Granovsky, who began a series of public lectures in the autumn of 1843, in which he spoke energetically of Russia as part of Europe and of her indebtedness to the west. The lectures were rapturously received, and Shevyryov felt called on to reply with his own series of lectures.

The question of Russia and her role in the world was the theme of Nikolay Gogol's last great work, *Dead Souls*. Part I, which gave a very negative picture of Russian reality, appeared in 1842, but subsequent parts of this ambitious work, which were to provide a more positive answer to the question of Russia's national destiny, were unfortunately never completed. Belinsky saw Gogol's writings as an exposé of the existing Russian society and, as an ardent westernizer, he championed the view of Gogol as the scourge of the *status quo*. At the same time Belinsky was looking for *narodnost* in literature in a more positive sense, and refused to see its center of gravity in any one social group. Nevertheless the literature of the period is marked by a growing interest in social categories: humble clerks, the urban poor, beggars and petty tradesmen, the peasants, and later, at the beginning of the 1850s – the merchant class. Such "sociological" writing is humanitarian in treatment, but there is also an attempt to see the individual behind the representative of the group. In fact a chronicler of these times, Vasily Cheshikhin-Vetrinsky, quoting Granovsky's phrase "the individual and a society conforming to its demands," sees the point at which this idea began to enter the general consciousness as the true beginning of our period.

Overlying the sociological and humanitarian concerns – particularly in the case of the peasants – are political drives (the need for emancipation) and ideological issues (the questions of the *narod* and *narodnost*). Later on the "young editors" (including Apollon Grigorev and Alexander Ostrovsky), who gave Pogodin's *The Muscovite* a new lease of life in the 1850s, made an attempt to move the discussion of *narodnost* away from the peasant to another class – that of the traditional Russian merchant. On the other side of the debate, a figure already dealt with in the previous decade, the rootless, westernized nobleman, is also in evidence. The term "superfluous man" will first be used during the 1840s to refer to such figures.

The idea that Europe was "rotting" was dramatically brought home to official Russia in 1848, when all the states of continental Europe apart from Russia herself were wracked by revolutionary turmoil. The reaction of Nicholas I was to clamp down even more harshly on all forms of free expression within his own country. A secret committee under Dmitry Buturlin was set up to supervise the censorship itself. The period from 1848 to the death of Nicholas I in 1855, the so-called "gloomy seven years" (*mrachnoe semiletie*), was a bleak time for Russian literature and Russian culture. In 1849 members of the Petrashevsky circle, a debating group which also had political aims, were arrested. The group included several writers, most prominent among whom was Dostoevsky. By now Belinsky had died, but many of the writers he had championed – Dostoevsky, Saltykov-Shchedrin, Dahl, Turgenev and the newcomer Ostrovsky – all suffered persecution. Paul Annenkov records the words of his namesake on the Buturlin committee, Nikolay Annenkov: "Tell me, why do these people waste time on literature? After all we've decided not to pass anything, so why should they go to the trouble?" To Buturlin himself Annenkov ascribes the view that if the Gospel were not so widespread, it would be necessary to ban it on account of its democratic spirit. Nevertheless, the men of the 1840s saw literature itself as holy writ. Like the Gospel, the more it was suppressed the more vigor the movement behind it acquired: the period 1840–55 is rich in literary and intellectual achievement.

In 1839 Belinsky left Moscow for St. Petersburg to work for Andrey Kraevsky's *Fatherland Notes* (*Otechestvennye zapiski*), and a great change soon took place in his entire attitude. Earlier, in the latter half of the 1830s, he had grappled with the problems of *narodnost* in literature within the framework of Schelling's esthetic system, but the negative aspects of Russian reality appeared to offer scant support for a truly national literature and the truly national within literature. Then after 1838 he had fallen under the spell of Hegel and his formula "the real is rational," which appeared to offer a way out – absurd and brutish as many aspects of Russian life undoubtedly were, Russian life was real; what was real was rational, and must therefore be accepted. Thus, under the influence of Hegel, Belinsky entered a short period of arch-conservatism in which he saw literature as reflecting, even championing, the *status quo*.

However, in 1840 Belinsky began gradually to reject this interpretation of Hegel. There was, after all, a different and left-wing interpretation of Hegel's famous phrase: i.e. only that which is rational can be accepted as "real." It was this interpretation which led Herzen to regard Hegel's philosophy as the "algebra of revolution." Belinsky became interested in the fashionable left-wing Hegelian Ludwig Feuerbach, and moved on from German thought to the French socialists. It led him to endorse "society" and "nationality," but only as concepts which at the same time recognized the existence and the worth of even their most insignificant constituent members. The principle of Russian nationhood, however, did not reside solely in the illiterate peasant masses of the *narod*, nor yet in the educated classes: it embraced everybody within the nation. Thus in his article of 1844 on Pushkin Belinsky championed his novel in verse *Eugene Onegin* for precisely these qualities; it was, in his celebrated phrase, "an encyclopedia of Russian life" and to the highest degree a national (*narodnoe*) work.

The Slavophiles, by contrast, in their desire to limit nationhood to the values of pre-Petrine Russia, folklore and ancient peasant institutions, indulged in a form of romanticism which bore little relationship to Russian reality. Belinsky was skeptical of folk literature and folklore. It was not the same as *narodnost* in literature: an expression of the life of the nation as a whole.

For all Belinsky's apparent enslavement to systems of abstract thought, literature had far more direct influence over him. Thus an important stage in his abandonment of right-wing Hegelian ideas was his reading of Lermontov's *Hero of Our Time*, with its hero Pechorin, whose corrosive rationality did not move him to "real" behavior. At the same time it must be conceded that Belinsky's interpretation of many literary works was actually colored by the philosophical and esthetic position he had already adopted. Thus in a sense Belinsky actually invented Gogol – the realist Gogol, that is, whom he handed down to nineteenth-century and Soviet criticism; for highly as Belinsky regarded Pushkin, he saw in the 1840s the need for a greater social content in art. This was an age for prose rather than poetry, and in his review of literature for 1842 he asserted: "However, we see in Gogol a greater significance for Russian society than in Pushkin, for Gogol is more a social poet, therefore more a poet in the spirit of the times."

Unfortunately, throughout the 1840s Gogol was growing steadily less like "a poet in the spirit of the times." The publication of *Selected Passages from Correspondence with Friends* (1847) revealed a

Gogol who championed the very institutions which Belinsky believed he attacked. That work might have found some favor with the Belinsky of 1838-9, the period of his "reconciliation with reality," but not with the socially orientated critic of the 1840s. Yet Belinsky's famous letter denouncing Gogol's book is not so much an attack on the author as a bitter assault on Russian society and its institutions. In a sense it is also a self-indictment; for Belinsky had been betrayed by a false image of his own making. His only defense is to draw a distinction between the profundity of Gogol as an artist and his shallowness as a thinker.

Nevertheless, in that very same year he could console himself with another of his "inventions," the "natural school," the direct inheritor of a legacy which Gogol himself had renounced. In his review of literature for 1847 Belinsky wrote: "Some say (and quite rightly in this instance) that the natural school was founded by Gogol." There is a degree of wishful thinking in this statement. The term "natural school" had actually been invented by Belinsky's arch-enemy Bulgarin, who the year before had used it in a derogatory sense when reviewing Nekrasov's *St. Petersburg Miscellany*. Belinsky picked up the polemical gauntlet and used the term in a positive way. In this same review of the literature of 1847, Belinsky saw the natural school as without leaders: "its active figures are not talents of the first rank, but at the same time it has its own character, and without help is already going along the real road, which it itself sees."

Once again Belinsky was wrong. There was no natural school as such, and some of the talents he ascribed to it – Goncharov, Turgenev, Dostoevsky – were certainly "talents of the first rank" even though they had not yet proved themselves. As Annenkov comments: "The so-called 'natural school' ripened under the influence of Gogol – Gogol interpreted in the way Belinsky interpreted him. One could well claim that the real father of the natural school was Belinsky."

Belinsky had begun his career in the 1830s with the cry: "We have no literature." He entered the period of the 1840s with a similar, but qualified assertion: "We have no literature in the precise and defined meaning of the word, but we already have the beginning of a literature, and bearing in mind the means and especially time, one cannot but wonder at how much has already been done." That much had been done to lay the foundations of a national literature was in no small measure due to Belinsky himself. Not that he was in any sense an artist: indeed his literary style is verbose, effusive, and at times purposely opaque. Nor did Belinsky provide deep and brilliant analyses of the works he discussed – he was a critic of quite another stamp, and one far more important for his time. Belinsky was the founder of a canon. He decided what Russian literature *was*, and his instinct for the writers of importance was almost unerring. Pushkin, Gogol, Lermontov, Turgenev, Goncharov, Dostoevsky built the high road of Russian literature, and Belinsky was its "civic engineer." To be sure, he was not always right in his judgments; he recognized the talent of both Gogol and Dostoevsky, but did not quite realize the true nature of what he had discovered. Yet it is certain that without Belinsky the course of Russian literature would not have been the same.

Belinsky died of consumption in 1848. Throughout the 1840s he had been associated with St. Petersburg and with westernism. At the end of his short life, in 1847, he had moved to *The Contemporary* under Nikolay Nekrasov and Ivan Panaev, a journal which a decade later would become one of Russia's most radical organs. The two chief critics of that later *Contemporary*, Nikolay Chernyshevsky and Nikolay Dobrolyubov, would both consider themselves bearers of the Belinskian tradition.

The decade of the 1840s was to see the apogee of Gogol's career as a writer with the publication, in 1842, of Part I of *Dead Souls* and the famous short story "The Overcoat" ("Shinel"), but it was also to mark an apparent artistic decline: his failure to complete Part II of *Dead Souls* to his own satisfaction, and a growing sense of his own importance to Russian culture, though less as a writer than as a preacher and moral guide. Gogol's growing religiosity is often dated to an event at the beginning of the decade. In June 1840 Gogol, returning from his first trip back to Russia from abroad, stopped in Vienna, where he experienced something in the nature of a spiritual crisis. More significantly, perhaps, the seeds of Gogol's art really lie in the preceding decade, and even more precisely in that brief period 1835–6 when most of his works were not only planned, but actually begun. It is almost as if the seed-corn of those early years had been consumed by the beginning of the 1840s; what was left was the hollow husk which he strove to fill with a bogus moral authority.

Another factor in Gogol's artistic make-up was the constant need for others to supply him with ideas. He had begun his career by pestering his mother to provide him with details of Ukrainian folk customs and beliefs, and the themes of his two major works, *The Inspector General* and *Dead Souls*, had both been given him by Pushkin, or so he claimed. After Pushkin's death in 1837 there was no one whose artistic authority Gogol could naturally acknowledge, and he felt that Pushkin's mantle had now fallen on him (a view reinforced by Belinsky). Yet henceforward Gogol would seek to assert his own authority more as a prophet and moralist than as the early writer of sadly comic tales with a strong hint of social criticism.

Nevertheless, the most famous of all his stories, "The Overcoat," was published in 1842, and in it the social themes of the earlier Gogol appear to reach their fruition. At the level of plot it is about a poor St. Petersburg clerk with the comic name of Akaky Akakievich Bashmachkin, who scrimps and saves to buy a decent overcoat to keep out the St. Petersburg frosts, but is robbed of it on the very first night he wears it. After vain attempts to enlist the help of the authorities, he receives such a telling off that he dies, but returns as a ghost to rob others of their overcoats, and it is only when he takes the coat of the important person (literally: significant face, or *znachitelnoe litso*) whose stern words had caused his death, that the ghost finally disappears.

This strange story has been remarkably influential in the development of Russian literature. It has been seen as a cornerstone in the building of the Russian realistic tradition, a work of central importance for the development of the natural school: "We have all come out from under Gogol's 'Overcoat,'" Dostoevsky is supposed to have said. To it was also ascribed that moment when the humanitarian line, the concern for the little man, became firmly established in Russian literature. On both these scores the story is far from unambiguous. In the first place, the ghost sequence of the denouement subverts the very concept of realism. Moreover, the "realistic" detail itself is presented with comic distortion, and the reader becomes aware that verbal play, comic names, and the patterning of incidents are leading him away from the surface patina of "realism" and suggesting other, deeper, and more devious semantic complexities.

Nor, in the second place, is Gogol's treatment of the "little man" unequivocally humanitarian. The narrator of "The Overcoat" reduces his hero to a figure of fun, who always manages to pass under a window when rubbish is thrown out, who does not know that he has had enough to eat until he sees that his stomach has swollen. Yet by a sleight of hand Gogol manages to suggest human sympathy for a figure whom he has deliberately and grotesquely dehumanized, an automaton obsessed by writing to the exclusion of all other aspects of life, until writing itself is displaced by another obsession – the overcoat. Nor yet can it be said that Bashmachkin's poverty is treated realistically. His whole way of life and the economies he effects are presented hyperbolically. What is really at issue is less his material indigence than his spiritual poverty: Gogol, as is his wont, uses the external, material world to hint at inner and more psychological matters. The title itself focuses attention, not on a human being, but on a "mantle," and it is Gogol's own sense of artistic crisis as a writer which lies buried at a metaphorical and deep semantic level within the story. The obsessive writer Bashmachkin is in fact merely a copier of external forms; inner meaning escapes him until he discovers it in a "mantle," which, ironically, is again but mere outward form of which he is soon deprived by others, then finally he is deprived of his very life by a "significant face." The story hints at Gogol's secret fears about the nature of his own writing, and its inability to come to terms with content (be it psychological or ideological) except through the filter of the external world.

The problem of revealing meaning through art is paramount in Gogol's consciousness throughout this period. The year 1842 is one of particular activity, when he consolidated the achievement of the 1830s by bringing out his collected works, and it is no accident that two of his stories which were substantially rewritten at this time reflect in their new versions the artistic problems which Gogol faced in the 1840s. "The Portrait," the revised version of which appeared in *The Contemporary* in 1842, is about art itself: its demonic as well as its divine potential. It is significant that the problem of art is posed in terms of surfaces (the canvases of a painter), and yet these are surfaces which must .reveal inner content. The monk who in his youth had been guilty of painting the diabolic portrait of the title now passes on his new and holy wisdom to his son: "Research and study everything you see. Subject everything to your brush, but learn how to find an inner idea in everything, and above all try to comprehend the lofty secret of creation." This was virtually Gogol's own artistic program for the 1840s.

The second story to be substantially reworked for the 1842 collection of Gogol's works was *Taras Bulba*. Here the elements of Ukrainian Cossack national identity of the earlier version were recast in terms of Great Russian nationalism. Thus, if the second version of "The Portrait" suggested Gogol's new artistic aims, the revised emphasis of Taras Bulba indicated their chief focus: the greatness of Russia, the spiritual superiority of Russian Orthodoxy and the Russian nation. The vehicle for this, of course, was to be Gogol's *magnum opus* – *Dead Souls* (*Mertvye dushi*).

Dead Souls had been conceived back in the fruitful period of 1835–6, supposedly on the basis of an idea given Gogol by Pushkin. Part I is the artistic culmination of the Gogol of the 1830s in both method and themes. In it he perfects the art of external description, the art of the portrait. The theme, although it is Russia, is nevertheless her negative aspects – the brilliant projection of a grotesque reality which, at one and the same time, contrives to be both comic and to suggest a motif of social criticism. Part I of *Dead Souls*, for all the grandeur of its conception, is well within the esthetic parameters of the Gogol of the 1830s. Like his earlier stories, the work is conceived less in terms of plot than of Gogolian portraiture. The motivation for the "events" – why Chichikov is actually buying dead souls – is a mystification concealed from the reader until the final chapter, much as earlier (in stories such as "The Old World Landowners" and "The Nose") Gogol presents causality as an enigma at which his readers must guess.

Chichikov, a mysterious new arrival in the town of N., visits a series of local landowners: Manilov, the essence of ineffectual niceness; Korobochka, a suspicious and superstitious "old world landowner"; Nozdryov, a rogue, cheat and bully; Sobakevich, a ponderous, hard-faced kulak; and finally the miser Plyushkin. All these are immediately recognizable as human types: their names have entered into the language and the currency of everyday life. Yet Gogol never attempts to get inside his characters. The traits of their psychology are to be deduced from the bizarre world of objects with which they surround themselves. Nor, with one exception, do these types show any character development; they are presented as ready made with characteristics as inalienable and as static as the qualities of objects themselves. The exception is Plyushkin, the only character, apart from Chichikov himself, to be supplied with a biography, which allows for the process of psychological development. The static solidity with which the other characters are invested is in marked contrast to the vacuous mobility of the "hero," Chichikov, who wishes to appear as all things to all men. Psychological penetration of such a bubble is virtually impossible; his positive features can only be sensed between the self-cancelling extremes of double negatives: he is not too fat and not too thin; not too old and not too young; and his rank is not too high and not too low.

Extended similes are a prominent feature of the first part of *Dead Souls*. These are often said to be Homeric, and yet they too often produce a self-cancelling effect, inasmuch as the amount of detail invoked to expand the point of comparison tends to make that point itself recede further and further from view. Thus in chapter 1 the comparison of black tail coats and pretty women to flies on sugar in reality achieves the effect of extended bathos, and the account of Nozdryov's threatened attack on Chichikov, likened in chapter 4 to the assault of a giddy lieutenant on an impregnable fortress, ends by explicitly subverting the proposition with which it begins.

In its original conception as a novel about a rogue who tours Russia buying up the documents of dead peasants in order to perpetrate a legal swindle *Dead Souls* belongs to the comic world of the Gogol of the 1830s, but superimposed upon the original conception are distinct elements of Gogol's new esthetic outlook of the 1840s: the need for art to reveal an inner truth, to propound a positive message, and thus for the comic vision to yield to one that is serious and didactic. A new tone can be sensed from chapter 6 on. There is much more authorial intrusion into the text, greater examination of authorial intentions and of the problems of art itself. Gogol's undertaking has become far more ambitious. There are to be further parts which will demonstrate progression towards the moral and the positive, and the work now seems to be conceived more on the lines of Dante's *Inferno*, with such characters as Plyushkin and even Chichikov himself undergoing spiritual resurrection. It was to become something like an apotheosis of positive Russian values, and for such a work the designation "novel" was clearly inadequate. Thus Gogol chose the more resounding title *Poema*, which in Russian has the connotation of "epic poem."

Since 1836 Gogol had been living abroad, mostly in Rome. He returned to Moscow in the autumn of 1841 with the manuscript of *Dead Souls*, intent on personally supervising its progress through the various stages of publication. The first hazard was the Moscow Board of Censors, whose chairman, according to Gogol, objected to the title on religious grounds: the soul, he said, was immortal. When it was pointed out that the title referred to "souls" in their legal sense of "peasants," the reaction was hardly more favorable – the system of serfdom was not to be criticized either. The Moscow censors would not pass the manuscript for publication, so Belinsky took it to St. Petersburg, where the censorship was more liberal. Here it was finally passed for publication, provided that the satirical implications of an insert story about Captain Kopeykin be toned down. Yet once more the title came in for criticism: Gogol was allowed to keep *Dead Souls* as a sub-title, but was required to call his work *The Adventures of Chichikov*. With typical deviousness Gogol managed to subvert the intention of the censors and retain the ambiguous impact of his original title, which, as the Moscow censors had realized, suggested both a social and a metaphysical theme. He himself designed the cover, and although *The Adventures of Chichikov* appeared towards the top of his design, it was in much smaller letters than the boldly proclaimed *Dead Souls* of the supposed sub-title. Yet boldest of all was his generic title *Poema*; for it was with the realization of this new definition of his work that he was now above all else concerned.

Gogol had embarked on Part II of his *Poema* before submitting Part I for publication, and he returned to Europe, and to Rome, without even waiting for the first part to come off the presses. Work on Part II, however, proved difficult. His hypochondria increased, and he toured the spas of Europe in search of a cure. By 1845 the second part of *Dead Souls* was completed and apparently ready for publication, but then Gogol suddenly burned it. The version as it stood did not match Gogol's great hopes for his work; it was not enough to portray one or two good people, the path to goodness must be clearly marked. From the ashes of his manuscript Gogol claimed to see a whole new conception of Part II arising like a phoenix, but he did not begin work immediately. Instead he followed his old practice of seeking inspiration from others, pestering friends and contacts with requests for information and facts on Russia and Russian life.

The problem which confronted Gogol was not merely the portrayal of "good people" – though this in itself was no minor matter, since up to now his art had excelled in the projection of negative types. More significantly, he had set himself the task of showing spiritual regeneration, and for this he would need to enter the minds and thoughts of his characters – a technique quite foreign to his external method of psychological presentation.

The year 1842, remarkable in so many ways for Gogol's writing, also saw the publication of another work, which if not distinguished by literary merit, is nevertheless worthy of literary note: it is a fragment entitled "Rome," from a projected novel, *Annunciata*. It evoked Belinsky's censure as much for its anti-French sentiments as for its stilted prose. Nevertheless the work is remarkable in that, for the first time in a sustained manner, Gogol attempts to enter the thought processes of his central character, an Italian prince newly returned home from a trip to France. Gogol would need to develop and perfect this technique if he were ever to achieve his stated aims in *Dead Souls* itself.

A further problem lay, not just in transforming negative characters into exemplars of virtue, but also in the very nature of this virtue – the character of the positive message. An indication of what this might be came in 1847 with the publication of *Selected Passages from Correspondence with Friends* (*Vybrannye mesta iz perepiski s druzyami*). The title suggests the work is an actual correspondence, but in fact it contains much specifically written for the collection. Its themes range from literary criticism (including analyses of Russian poetry and a discussion of his own *Dead Souls*) to the portentous assertion of moral and social precepts. Belinsky was not alone in rejecting such homilies, for they even embarrassed many of Gogol's Slavophile friends. Particularly disturbing was the fact that actions which in the earlier Gogol might have been welcomed as bizarre detail in the comic portrayal of character were here put forward as worthy of emulation: thus landowners were exhorted to burn banknotes in front of their peasants in order to demonstrate their lack of greed.

All this did not augur well for the spiritual message to be proclaimed in *Dead Souls*. After all, Gogol's arch-enemy Bulgarin had written a picaresque novel, *Ivan Vyzhigin*, which also turned out to have a positive message: the defense of the existing social order. Moreover, in 1847 Gogol had begun to correspond with a priest, Father Matvey Konstantinovsky, whom many commentators consider a malign influence upon him, particularly as he denounced Gogol's earlier writing as sinful and wished to make him renounce Pushkin.

Gogol's own spiritual state at the time was anything but healthy. In January 1848 he sought religious inspiration in a trip to the Holy Land, but found only disillusionment and despondency. In April he returned by sea to Odessa, and the rest of his short life he would spend in Russia. Now he was working on his second version of Part II of *Dead Souls*. By the beginning of 1852 it was apparently ready, but with the onset of Lent in February Gogol undertook a rigorous fast, and on 11 February he again burned Part II of *Dead Souls* in its revised version. He claimed it had been a mistake, that the Devil had played a trick on him, and he refused all food, even though many cruel and bizarre methods were used to induce him to eat. On 21 February 1852 he died.

Nevertheless, not all of the second part of *Dead Souls*, in either its first or its second version, was destroyed. What remained was published in 1855, and gives a partial idea of what Gogol had in mind. Although some of the new characters, such as Petukh, reveal all the comic genius of the old Gogol, the positive figures are imbued with that naiveté which characterized *Selected Passages from Correspondence with Friends*. Thus the Christian message is borne by the most suspect of worldly vessels, the millionaire tax farmer Murazov, while the claim of the "positive" landowner, Kostanzhoglo, that every bit of rubbish can yield a profit seems merely to echo the philosophy of Plyushkin in a more practical vein. Yet it does more; for the central swindle of Part I – the buying up of "worthless" documents to make a fortune – is merely the negative face of Kostanzhoglo's principle. Thus the central theme of Part I has been refurbished, rather unconvincingly, to provide a positive message for Part II.

Despite the nature of Gogol's own artistic problems during the 1840s, writers who followed where they thought he was leading for the most part seemed "to come out from under" the master's "Overcoat." The figure of the poor civil servant was dominant throughout the period: as many as one hundred and fifty depictions of this figure have been counted during a mere two or three years of periodical publication. There was a new and more realistic attitude to the theme of poverty, exemplified by writers such as Yakov Butkov (ca. 1820–56), who in 1844–5 published a series of sketches and stories under the title *St. Petersburg Summits* (*Peterburgskie vershiny*). These summits were, in fact, the attics inhabited by the poor of the capital, "heights" which in social terms were "depths." The poor clerks of Gogol's St. Petersburg were depicted in a manner shortly to be identified as that of the natural school. In Butkov's sketches sociological and humanitarian considerations were very much to the fore. Belinsky likened them to daguerrotypes, and viewed their relationship to the larger forms of the novel and the novella (*povest*) as that of "statistics to history, or reality to poetry." A sober appraisal of the salient features of the natural school was given by Yury Samarin (1819–76), from the opposing standpoint of the Slavophiles: "The characters are divided into two groups: those who beat and swear, and those who are beaten and sworn at. The nature of the furniture, the stains on the wall, tears in the wallpaper, all must be enumerated as in a model inventory. The titles they take are the simplest and as general as possible, for example: 'The Landowners,' 'The Mistress,' 'The Village,' 'Relatives,' etc."

In 1845 Nikolay Nekrasov brought out an almanac published in two parts, *The Physiology of St. Petersburg* (*Fiziologiya Peterburga*), which resembled a manifesto for the new literary trend. Behind the project could be sensed the guiding spirit of Belinsky. He wrote the introduction and made three other contributions to the collection. The very title seemed to suggest an objective, scientific study of the capital city, the deployment of a dispassionate realism. The term "physiology," which as a literary concept derived from Balzac, was borrowed from the French (a number of works with titles including the word *physiologie* had already been published by writers like Paul de Kock). However, many contributors were obviously looking back to Gogol and his St. Petersburg stories, even though the reality he depicted bordered on the fantastic and his vision of St. Petersburg was grotesque. *The Physiology of St. Petersburg* was an attempt to deepen Gogol's realism, to show the grim face of existence in St. Petersburg for various groups of its inhabitants, to substitute a more sober sociological approach for the pseudo-sociological method of Gogol's "Nevsky Prospect."

Vladimir Dahl (1801–72) was already an established writer, whose contribution to *The Physiology of St. Petersburg*, "The Yardman" ("Dvornik"), had actually been published the previous year. It is a typical piece of naturalism emphasizing the squalor in which the yardman Grigory lives: his bed full of vermin, his unwillingness to wash his cooking utensils, his idiosyncratic view of morality. Yet Dahl's knowledgeable discussion of thieves' jargon reveals his own strong ethnographic and lexicographic interests. There is, indeed, a certain irony in the fact that Dahl, who was of direct Danish descent, was one of the figures in the nineteenth century most actively interested in the concept of Russianness. He explored this as ethnographer and folklorist, collecting Russian proverbs, folk superstitions and customs, but his most significant work in this field is undoubtedly his dictionary (*Tolkovy slovar zhivogo velikorusskogo yazyka*) which came out between 1863 and 1867, and remains to this day a mine of linguistic information on non-literary variants of the Russian language.

As a writer Dahl adopted the pseudonym "Cossack of Lugan" (from the little town where he was born), and sometimes also called himself V. I. Lugansky. Dahl made the physiological sketch his own, but although he contributed to such anthologies as *The Physiology of St. Petersburg* and *Our People Painted from Nature* (*Nashi spisannye s natury*), his interest in national types was not linked to the reforming spirit often associated with the natural school. Indeed his writings appealed to Bulgarin as well as to the Slavophiles, and he contributed to Pogodin's *The Muscovite*. In 1839 the Slavophile Konstantin Aksakov saw one of Dahl's stories, "Night at the Crossroads" ("Noch na rasputi") as opening a new epoch in Russian literature.

Dahl had been a close friend of Pushkin's, and had been present when he died. His literary career had begun in the 1830s, but attained its high point in the 1840s. In 1846 a four-volume collection of his short novels, stories and fairy tales was published, to be reviewed by Turgenev the following year in exceedingly favorable terms. Typically, Belinsky saw him as continuing the legacy of Gogol, and there is much in Dahl's writing which is reminiscent of Gogol at his best. Both Gogol and Belinsky spoke of Dahl's sketches as "living statistics," obviously having in mind such works as "The Ural Cossack" (Uralsky kazak, 1842); "The Yardman" of 1844; "The Russian" ("Rusak") and "Finns in St. Petersburg" ("Chukhontsy v Pitere"). Belinsky, however, was less generous, claiming that a story with action and a denouement was not within Dahl's abilities, and that all his attempts in this genre were remarkable merely in part, but not as a whole.

Dahl himself may have suggested this criticism, in a short introduction to "Vakkh Sidorov Chaykin" (1842) where he warns his readers not to expect a novel but rather what he terms the "genre of living pictures." Nevertheless, the criticism is not entirely well founded: Dahl can handle a plot. In "Intoxication, Dream and Reality" ("Khmel, son i yav," 1843) a murder is the inception of the action (*zavyazka*): it forces the hero Stepan to confess to a murder he has not committed, and then leads to a resultant denouement (*razvyazka*). Gogol was kinder, arguing that Dahl had no need of *zavyazka* and *razvyazka* in order to construct an absolutely enthralling story. Perhaps he sensed in Dahl a talent close to his own, and certainly Dahl has a gift for painting vivid, idiosyncratic figures with very little brushwork, characters such as Gonobobel and Rotmister Shilokhvostov in the short novel *Pavel Alexeevich Igrivy* (1847) or the pigeon-fancier known as "Three Ivans" in "Vakkh Sidorov Chaykin." In this latter work there occurs the Gogolian swindle of buying up dead souls and mortgaging them as a viable estate, but what constitutes Gogol's central plot is here merely an episodic detail of characterization.

Like Gogol, Dahl has a good ear for the language of his characters, and is particularly fond of linguistic jokes. Gogolian, too, is his comic emphasis on clothes. Thus Ivan Yakovlevich Sheloumov in "Vakkh Sidorov Chaykin" wears different clothes according to his various psychological moods; in the same work the Kalyuzhin daughters are required to share communal clothing, which is so inadequate that not all can have underwear. Nevertheless, in *Pavel Alexeevich Igrivy*, Dahl appears to be polemicizing with Gogol's "external" method of characterization: the novel sets out to prove that it is impossible to tell a man's character merely from outward appearances.

As with Gogol, there is a strong element of social criticism in some of Dahl's writing, though Dahl's strength is more as an observer of life than as a social critic. Still, in the fateful year of 1848 Dahl found himself in trouble with the Buturlin secret committee over his story "The Fortune Teller" ("Vorozheyka"), about a peasant woman deceived by a gipsy, in which there occurred the sentence: "The authorities, as always, did nothing." The author, who also worked as a civil servant in St. Petersburg, was summoned before the Minister of Internal Affairs, reprimanded, and told that he had to choose between writing and civil service employment. In a moment often repeated in the history of Russian literature, Dahl burned many of his papers, and decided to reserve his stories for a future time when publication might once again be possible. When this time arrived, after the death of Nicholas I, Dahl brought out a collection entitled *Pictures of Russian Life* (*Kartiny russkogo byta*, 1856). Unfortunately, in the radical atmosphere of the post–Crimean war period his stories seemed rather old-fashioned. They were attacked by the rising radical star, Chernyshevsky, and Dahl's reputation as a writer took a long time to recover.

Unlike Dahl, the literary career of Dmitry Grigorovich (1822–99) really begins with his work for *The Physiology of St. Petersburg*: "St. Petersburg Organ-Grinders" ("Peterburgskie sharmanshchiki"). In the spring of 1846 he left the capital for his mother's estate in the country, intending to find a new subject, and he found it, not only for himself, but also for Russian literature. He had taken with him the works of the folk poet Koltsov and Dickens' *Oliver Twist*; what emerged was a short novel about a Russian Oliver Twist, though his orphan was not a town boy but a country girl, Akulina. Emphasis on the peasant heroine had been established in the late eighteenth century by Karamzin in "Poor Liza"; it would be continued later by Nekrasov in *Red-Nosed Frost* and other poems. Although Karamzin's tale had been a landmark in a shift of attitude by the upper classes towards the peasant, it is a mannered, sentimentalist tale which gives no idea of the realities of peasant life.

Grigorovich, however, approached the subject from the viewpoint of an artist of the natural school, and with an eye for realistic detail. It is consistent with the new approach that his story bears, not the name of his heroine, but rather a "sociological" title suggesting a way of life – *The Village* (*Derevnya*). Although the central thread of Grigorovich's tale is the life of Akulina, one senses in his compositional methods the sketch writer rather than an author with an interest in plot as such. Accordingly he places emphasis on peasant *mores*, folklore, and vernacular expressions.

Akulina, an orphan, is brought up by the cowherd Domna. It is a hard life; her "education" consists principally of beatings, but she also learns the village folklore, and encounters holy wanderers. Akulina is not coarsened by this life; she has sensitivity and finer feelings. Once, when she comes across the grave of her mother, she is emotionally overwhelmed, and we realize that peasants are human beings with human emotions (Turgenev will develop this theme, first adumbrated by Karamzin, with more realistic artistry in his *Sportsman's Sketches*). The master on a rare visit to the village sees Akulina, and decides to marry her to the smith's son Grigory, but his values are so western he does not realize that it is an insult for the smith's son to marry an orphan raised by a cattle woman. Unfortunately, life for Akulina in her new household is full of misery. She is beaten by her drunken husband who, it is suggested, is not a real peasant but a man corrupted by the idle life of the village factory. Akulina's one consolation is her daughter Dunka, but her husband's family, surprised that she has not died in child-birth, do their best to remedy the situation by subjecting her to harsh conditions which can only weaken her health. Although she has a protector in the wife of the village manager, she is nevertheless sent out to work whilst still ill and in conditions which can only bring about her death. The funeral scene, some of the best writing in the story, depicts Grigory driving off through a fierce snowstorm to bury his wife's body as his distraught daughter Dunka runs behind through the snow drifts trying to keep up with him.

Grigorovich's next work on the peasant theme, *Anton the*

Unfortunate (*Anton Goremyka*, 1847), places greater emphasis on plot, and is generally regarded as Grigorovich's best work. It is the tale of a poor peasant Anton, who is behind with his taxes and is ordered by a hostile bailiff to sell his horse to meet his debts. He goes to a fair in the local town, but his horse is stolen when he spends the night in a thieves' tavern, and he is even forced to leave his coat behind in payment of his board. Braving the cold, he wanders off in search of his horse and ends up in the company of a robber band, who are all arrested and sent off to Siberia. In Grigorovich's original conception, the story ended with a peasant uprising against the tyrannical bailiff. Such an outcome could not be sanctioned, so the censor, Alexander Nikitenko, wrote what is now the present ending himself. Nevertheless a strong element of social commentary remains, as in the "bourgeois" values of the bailiff and his wife (the discarded mistress of the landowner), which are contrasted to the stark lot of Anton himself. There are also fine descriptions of a provincial fair, a country highway and the Russian countryside.

In the short story "The Loner" ("Bobyl," 1847) a dying stranger is driven out of a village, both by the mistress of the manor and by the peasants themselves, because they are frightened of the legal consequences which would inevitably arise if the body of an unknown man were discovered on their land. This lack of charity is pointed up by the fact that the mistress is deeply interested in folk medicine, and her peasants are in the middle of an autumn feast at the time.

If Grigorovich was successful in shifting the focus of the natural school, which had tended to concentrate on the city, it was nevertheless Turgenev who first came to real prominence through his treatment of the village. Ivan Turgenev (1818–83) was born in Orel province, a countryside which features prominently in much of his early writing. His mother was a rich but embittered woman, at odds with her husband and tyrannical in her relations with her peasants and with her son.

Turgenev went to the Universities of Moscow (1833) and St. Petersburg (1834–7) (where he had the strange experience of hearing Gogol lecture); then he continued his education for three years at the University of Berlin (1838–41). This background gave him an obvious western orientation, yet made him conscious of the intellectual currents of Moscow University in the 1830s. He never married, but the great love of his life was the opera singer Pauline Viardot. His attachment to her and her family (which included a husband) was constant, and its exact nature has been the subject of much speculation. It was over Mme. Viardot that Turgenev quarrelled with his mother in 1845, and left Russia in 1847 to be with the Viardots, only returning in 1850 on the news of his mother's serious illness. After her death Turgenev was relatively rich and able to indulge his taste for travel in Europe, usually in the company of Pauline and her family.

Turgenev began his literary career as a poet, a fact of significance for his later prose writing, which is marked by a sense of good Russian style, a search for elegant simplicity: the sort of discipline that a poet following in the footsteps of Pushkin had to learn. Turgenev's prose works are "poetic" too in their evocation of nature. More than any other prose writer of the period Turgenev loved the Russian countryside, and natural description always had a prominent place in his works. The poem for which the early Turgenev was best known is the long poem *Parasha* (1843). Its verses are polished and urbane; in style and conception it is clearly Pushkinian. It is in fact a rewriting of *Eugene Onegin*, not in Pushkin's fourteen line stanza, but in a reasonably close thirteen line imitation. Perhaps Turgenev had nothing new to say in verse, but it was a good school for the future prose writer, and his first efforts in this field owe a great deal to the prose of another poet.

Lermontov had an undoubted influence on Turgenev's early stories. There is, for instance, his fascination with strong, demonic, Pechorinesque figures such as Andrey Kolosov in the story of the same name (1844) or Vasily Luchinov in "Three Portraits" (1846). It is the romanticism of the preceding generation, and a significant feature of these stories is the duel as a climactic element (it will also figure in the mature Turgenev). Thus the very title of a story of 1847, "The Dueller" ("Breter"), has a distinct Lermontovian ring, and its chief character, Luchkov, the dueller of the title, is an unpoetic, unsophisticated version of Pechorin. The Lermontovian debt even extends to direct quotation. When – using his sword, symbolically – Luchkov procures for Masha the water lily she admires, he repeats the unheroic statement of Pechorin in "Taman": "I cannot swim"; and Turgenev's description of the young Jewish girl in "The Jew" ("Zhid," 1847) as a wild creature and a snake is obviously influenced by Lermontov's "Ondine" from the same story.

Yet, alongside this early fascination with the "strong man," there is also the theme of self-sacrifice, particularly in matters of love. This is most marked in the figure of the narrator in "Andrey Kolosov," and in Kister in "The Dueller." Here again, this is a romantic theme, typical too of the "dreamer" heroes of the early Dostoevsky, but it is also related to Turgenev's concept of the Quixotic principle in literature, which will be prominent in his later writing and even in his life, especially in his relations with Pauline Viardot.

The other undoubted influence on Turgenev's early writing is, of course, Gogol. The fact that this is particularly noticeable from 1848 on has been linked by critics to the publication of *Selected Passages from Correspondence with Friends*, and the need suddenly felt among Belinsky's followers to save Gogol's legacy from Gogol himself. Yet this legacy had already itself suffered revision: Dostoevsky in *Poor Folk*, *The Double*, and other stories had shown how its wealth could be minted anew.

Turgenev's "Petushkov" of 1848 is certainly Gogolian, particularly in its portrayal of a servant, Onisim, who is quite close in conception to Osip from *The Inspector General*. Nevertheless, as Victor Vinogradov has pointed out, the speech patterns and general presentation of Petushkov himself owe much to the early Dostoevsky. The year 1848 initiated a difficult period for literature in the mold of Gogol, as a report by a contemporary made clear: "In elevating Gogol alone, the writers of the natural school are prey to extreme immoderation; they praise only those works which describe drunks, debauchees, sinful and revolting people, and they themselves write in this manner." Turgenev's story also depicts drunkenness and low life, and in addition is not very flattering to authority, represented by Petushkov's superior, a major: thus it is not surprising that "Petushkov" suffered greatly at the hands of the censor, and Turgenev could remedy the many cuts and distortions only in 1856. Turgenev was now clearly identified with the natural school even though he had been considered an adherent of the tendency in 1846 when he contributed to *The St. Petersburg Miscellany*.

The influence of Gogol, seen in the new Dostoevskian focus, is even more striking in two stories of 1849 and 1850. "The Hamlet of the Shchigrov Province" ("Gamlet Shchigrovskogo uezda"), which was included in *Sportsman's Sketches*, is in two parts. The first, which describes an evening gathering at a country house, not only provides a "gallery of portraits" of highly idiosyncratic local landowners, but also uses some of Gogol's other devices: descriptive names, characterization through speech habits, extended similes, and the pretense of refusing to describe what is actually being described. If all this is typically Gogolian, the second part of the story, the "confession" of the "Hamlet" himself, with his acute self-consciousness, his readiness to take offence, and his irrationally contradictory behavior, is almost pure Dostoevsky.

The second story, "The Diary of a Superfluous Man" ("Dnevnik lishnego cheloveka," 1850), shows a similar Gogolian influence with a Dostoevskian overlay. It owes an obvious debt to "The Diary of a Madman," although the literal title of Gogol's story is "Notes" (Zapiski), and unlike the garbled dates given by Poprishchin, Turgenev's hero Chulkaturin enters a day by day account, with one exception: 28 March. However, the entry of the following day excuses the omission with a reference to Gogol's hero: "Yesterday I hadn't the energy to continue my diary. Like Poprishchin, for the most part I lay on my bed and chatted with Terenteva." (Also, in both works there is a dog called Trésor). Although Chulkaturin's diary has none of Gogol's comic mystification with dates, it is significant that the final date is given as 1 April, and that this is immediately followed by an illiterate comment from a supposed reader with the comically Gogolian name of Peter Zudoteshin (Peter Itchcomforter).

"The Diary of a Madman" was also a starting point for the psychologically realistic reworking of Gogol undertaken by Dostoevsky. Gogol's story deals with the psychological problems of an insignificant little man with an inferiority complex, who is in love with an unattainable woman and envious of a socially more acceptable rival. Dostoevsky, like Gogol before him, develops this theme in *The Double* through the unbalanced consciousness of his central character, but Turgenev's Chulkaturin preserves his sanity, and, like Lermontov's Pechorin, carefully analyzes his own actions and emotions. The pleasure he apparently finds in his own suffering might seem Dostoevskian, but Chulkaturin thinks of Lermontov when he speaks of "the pleasure which Lermontov had in mind – 'It is joyful and painful to disturb the ulcers of old wounds.'"

Despite its comic overtones, the tale is serious, with a distinct autobiographical resonance. It is the story of a man of Turgenev's own age (30), the son of a well-off landowner, brought up by a strong mother whom he cannot love, yet attracted to a weak and dissolute father with no authority in the household. As a result, in adulthood he finds it difficult to establish a proper relationship with a woman, and feels superfluous in life. In a strange way Turgenev's story anticipates Dostoevsky's *Notes from Underground*, published in 1864. The central figures are not dissimilar in their sense of alienation and love of self–abasement. In both works there is a similar mixture of present and past; there is a continual sparring with a servant; and the central female figure in both cases is called Liza. Moreover, there are strong "underground" notes present in "The Hamlet of the Shchigrov Province" as well, so that Turgenev was not only influenced by the young Dostoevsky via Lermontov but also anticipated important themes in Dostoevsky's mature writing. This link between the clear, classical Turgenev and the darker side of Dostoevsky may on the face of it seem unexpected, but it will recur in "First Love" (1860), where again Turgenev touches on a personal theme and the peculiarities of his own upbringing.

It is typical of the orientation which literature, and more particularly literary criticism, was taking that these two psychological portraits – of the "superfluous man" and the "Hamlet" – became part of the armament, not of the psychological, but of the social critics of literature. The term "superfluous man," used here for the first time by Turgenev, took on a completely different sense and was employed to describe such figures as Onegin and Oblomov, or such heroes of Turgenev's own later works as Rudin. They were the "fifth horse" or the "fifth wheel," superfluous to the power that drove the state and pulled the carriage of society; they were seen as "Hamlets" less for personal reasons than for social ones.

In 1852 Turgenev found himself under arrest for publishing an obituary of Gogol (just three years before, Dostoevsky had been arrested for reading Belinsky's letter to Gogol). Whilst he was in custody Turgenev wrote his tearfully sentimental tale "Mumu," the story of a deaf and dumb peasant forced to drown his pet dog. However, when Turgenev next returned to a Gogolian theme, it seemed completely purged of the influence of his forgotten rival Dostoevsky. "Two Friends" ("Dva priyatelya," 1854), like Gogol's story of the two Ivans, is concerned with two completely dissimilar friends. Yet in contrast to Gogol's characters a quarrel (in this case between their peasants) does not set them at odds, but unites them. Another Gogolian theme – one friend's attempt to marry off the other (as in Gogol's *Marriage*) – leads them to visit a "gallery" of local landowners, much as in *Dead Souls* (one of these, an "emancipated" widow, even anticipates the portrait of Kukshina in *Fathers and Sons*). Yet for all its Gogolian characters with their typical Gogolian names, the story exhibits a basic weakness. It revolves around a series of portraits rather than a well-constructed plot, and the death of the central figure is contrived: initially he was to have been drowned at sea, then Turgenev substituted the stock device of the duel.

Even looser in structure are "A Quiet Spot" ("Zatishe," 1854) and "Yakov Pasynkov" (1855), notable chiefly for its portrait of the young Belinsky. Turgenev had already used similar biographical material in his first story, "Andrey Kolosov," supposedly based on members of the Stankevich circle. On the other hand "The Inn" ("Postoyaly dvor," 1852) shows good plot structure and is even more remarkable for the portrait of its hero, the peasant inn-keeper Akim, who accepts the great injustices done to him and becomes a holy wanderer, a figure more in keeping with the writing of Dostoevsky or Tolstoy. Like "Mumu," "The Inn" is a story on a peasant theme which Turgenev did not include in *A Sportsman's Sketches*. Also excluded are two stories with a hunting motif, "Three Portraits" ("Tri portreta," 1846) and "Three Meetings" ("Tri vstrechi," 1852). "Three Meetings" with its romantic atmosphere and its semi-fantastic coincidences looks forward to another strand in Turgenev's writing: the supernatural elements in certain stories written towards the end of his life. Quite improbably, "Three Meetings" caused the young radical critic Nikolay Dobrolyubov to cry.

In January 1847 Turgenev's short story "Khor and Kalinych" appeared in *The Contemporary*, with the sub-title "From A Sportsman's Sketches." This was the start of Turgenev's most influential work of his early period, for the success of "Khor and Kalinych" was so great that the author was encouraged to publish more in the same vein. Between 1847 and 1851 twenty-two stories of the collection appeared in *The Contemporary*, ending with "Kasyan from the Beautiful Lands." The first separate edition of *A Sportsman's Sketches (Zapiski okhotnika)* came out in 1852 with a rearranged sequence and an additional story, "Two Landowners" ("Dva pomeshchika"). Much later three other stories were added: "The End of Chertopkhanov" ("Konets Chertopkhanova," 1872); "Rattling Wheels" ("Stuchit"), and "Living Relics" ("Zhivye moshchi," 1874).

In *A Sportsman's Sketches* Turgenev portrayed the peasant as a human being with finer feelings and even with artistic sensitivity (see "The Singers" ["Pevtsy"]). By contrast, their masters often appeared as inhuman, insensitive and cruel. Although the stories are loosely linked by the theme of hunting (a device Anton Chekhov would later borrow for a trilogy of his stories), the title is, perhaps deliberately, deceptive, for hunting is hardly the author's chief concern. It is first and foremost the peasant and his lot. This is made clear in the reasons which Turgenev gave in 1868 for his absence from Russia while he wrote these stories: "It was absolutely necessary for me to remove myself from my enemy, in order to attack it all the more strongly from this distance of mine. In my eyes this enemy had a definite form, it bore a well known name: this enemy was serfdom."

Around this time Harriet Beecher Stowe's *Uncle Tom's Cabin* also appeared, in 1858, and Russian readers could draw a parallel between the enslaved Negroes of America and their own indigenous "people," the Russian peasants. It is claimed that after reading *A Sportsman's Sketches* the future Tsar Alexander II vowed that he would emancipate the serfs when he came to power.

Turgenev's title is itself ambiguous. Besides "hunter" or "sportsman" the word *okhotnik* can also mean "a person who has a liking for something," and the penchant which emerges is less for game than for peasants and their way of life. For the most part, the stories are portraits, and although anecdotal material is included it plays, on the whole, a subordinate role to sociological and psychological description. The first story, "Khor and Kalinych," is based on a contrast of character: the practical and hard-headed Khor (the name means "polecat") is opposed to the gentler and more artistic Kalinych: Khor "was a positive, practical person, with a head for administration, a rationalist. Kalinych, on the other hand, belonged to the category of idealists, romantics, enthusiasts and dreamers". The author is surprised when Kalinych calls on his friend and brings with him a present of wild strawberries: "I confess, I did not expect such 'niceties' from a peasant." Nevertheless, Turgenev avoids sentimentality in his portraits of the peasants. They are shown with some of the grim detail associated with the natural school. Thus Khor's treatment of women is harsh and cynical; animals, too, are often treated cruelly, as the dog in this story, or, at the least, with little compassion, as Ermolay's dog in the story "Ermolay and the Miller's Wife" ("Ermolay i melnichikha").

The fact that Turgenev showed the independence of Khor, and that he could get on without his master (his dwelling is actually called *usadba*, or a "nobleman's estate"); that he is described as having interests and capabilities beyond his station ("Khor was concerned with administrative and state questions") – all this was seen officially as dangerous exaggeration. Moreover, the nobleman Polutykin in this sketch is presented critically, and it is made plain that Khor can see through him.

If in these works Turgenev is attacking the self-interested official view of the peasant, he is also criticizing another and more "ideological" view, that of the Slavophiles, who saw the peasants as the real Russian people, to whom the reforms of Peter I were entirely foreign. These ideas are explicitly rejected by Turgenev. His conversations with Khor convince him that "Peter the Great was above all a Russian, and Russian in his very reforms." In another story, "Ovsyanikov the Freeholder" ("Odnodvorets Ovsyanikov"), Turgenev draws a polemical portrait of the Slavophile Konstantin Aksakov under the satirical name of Lyubozvonov (i.e. "Lover of sound"). Lyubozvonov affects "Russian" dress and claims to understand his peasants, but he fails to recognize their exploitation by his peasant bailiff, and for all Lyubozvonov's fine talk the lot of his peasants does not change. Such masters who claim to know their peasants, be they fashionable Slavophiles or landowners of the old school like the reactionary Zverkov (*zver* means "wild beast") in "Ermolay and the Miller's Wife," reveal by their behavior a failure to treat their serfs as full human beings. The same is true for that other type of master, the sort who vaunts his western education. Penochkin, in "The Steward" ("Burmistr"), punishes his peasant servant because the wine is not served at the right temperature, and when his cook is run over by a cart his only concern is that his hands should not be injured. Penochkin's peasants are in a pitiable state, yet less because of his own activities than his inability to see that both they and he are being exploited by his peasant bailiff.

The peasants in Turgenev's stories have no monopoly on virtue. They, too, exploit one another, both economically – as in "The Steward" and "The Office" ("Kontora") – and emotionally. In "The Meeting" ("Svidanie") the author is the unseen witness of the rejection of a peasant sweetheart by a westernized lackey, a situation which foreshadows the relationship between Yasha and Dunyasha in Chekhov's play *The Cherry Orchard*. On the other hand the peasant can also show pity for his own kind. In "The Lone Wolf" ("Biryuk") a fierce peasant forester who has caught a poor peasant stealing timber finally lets him go.

"The Steward" bears the date July 1847 and the place Salzbrunn, a hint that this indictment of pre-reform Russia is linked to Belinsky's famous letter denouncing Gogol. In his attack on the "enemy" Turgenev does not even spare his own relations. The refusal to let a maid get married in "Ermolay and the Miller's Wife" is based on an incident involving Turgenev's own mother, and in "Ovsyanikov the Freeholder" the homesteader reveals that it was the author's own grandfather who deprived him of land that belonged to him by right. When he complained, Turgenev's grandfather had him flogged under the windows of the patriarchal home, watched by the author's grandmother.

As a homesteader, Ovsyanikov is in an anomalous position. He is free and able to own a small holding, but is still a peasant. Even though his son has obtained some education, he cannot find employment suited to his skills; he and his family will always remain despised peasants. His situation is given ironic point by the anecdote which ends the tale: a young French drummer boy, Lejeune, fleeing with Napoleon's routed army in 1812, is saved from summary drowning at the hands of peasants because the landowner suddenly gets the idea that he may be able to teach his daughters to play the piano. Lejeune has no knowledge of the piano, but the landowner is quite satisfied with his drumming on it. Despite Lejeune's lowly position and the fact that he is a former "enemy," he is after all French, and so prospers in Russia. Eventually he becomes a landowner and enjoys a status denied to the native Russian "freeman" Ovsyanikov.

Nevertheless, Turgenev's depiction of the landowners is not entirely one-sided. For all their blindness they can often exhibit quixotic characteristics with an obvious appeal for the author. In the stories "Chertopkhanov and Nedopyuskin" and "The End of Chertopkhanov," we see the eccentric but tragic figure of Chertopkhanov, a poor yet proud landowner with a strong sense of human dignity, who protects the unfortunate Nedopyuskin and ends up losing both his gipsy mistress and his highly prized horse.

The stories of *A Sportsman's Sketches* are permeated with a love for the Russian countryside and with poetic descriptions of nature. In "Bezhin Meadow" ("Bezhin lug") Turgenev evokes the magic of a summer night spent in the open and the conversation of village lads sent out to guard the horses. In an enchanted setting they recount folklore and discuss their superstitions. In another story, "Kasyan from the Beautiful Lands," we learn of a peasant's own love for nature. Kasyan, a strange, dwarf-like figure with a pantheistic attitude to life (he is probably a member of the Russian sect of "wanderers") rebukes the sportsman for killing God's creatures. Yet the author himself is a great lover of the natural world, and it is fitting that he chooses to end the collection with "Forest and Steppe" ("Les i step"), a poetic evocation of the many moods of the Russian countryside.

Fyodor Dostoevsky (1821–81) was born the second son of a doctor at a paupers' hospital in Moscow. He was educated as a military engineer in St. Petersburg, but left the service in 1844 to devote himself to literature, after receiving a small inheritance on the death of his father. At this time Dostoevsky was sharing an apartment in St. Petersburg with Grigorovich, and his first work, *Poor Folk* (*Bednye lyudi*), launched him, almost literally, into overnight success. Grigorovich took the manuscript of *Poor Folk* to Nekrasov. They read it all night, and in a state of excitement returned in the early hours to Dostoevsky's apartment to proclaim him a genius. Nekrasov then took the manuscript to Belinsky with the declaration that a new Gogol had appeared. Belinsky's initial skepticism disappeared once he had read the manuscript, and Dostoevsky was suddenly proclaimed a genius to the literary world of St. Petersburg before a word of his masterpiece had been published.

Belinsky and his contemporaries saw *Poor Folk* as continuing the theme of the "little man," and it must obviously be viewed in relation to Gogol's "The Overcoat." Yet what socially oriented critics wished to see in Gogol's work was actually realized in *Poor Folk*. The very title calls attention to poverty, and unlike the central hero of "The Overcoat," Makar Devushkin's poverty is not only presented realistically but also in a relative context, set against the utter destitution of such figures as Gorshkov and the poor of the St. Petersburg streets. In such details Dostoevsky is much nearer to the themes of the natural school than Gogol was himself. Moreover, Dostoevsky humanizes Gogol's tale. Akaky Akakievich's relationship had been with a coat, described with clear sexual overtones; the relationship of Makar Devushkin is with a young girl, Varvara; and whereas the name of Gogol's Bashmachkin is itself derived from an article of clothing (*bashmak* = "shoe") – a fact to which the narrator calls comic attention – the name of Dostoevsky's Devushkin suggests *devushka* ("maiden"), which not only implies a more human relationship but also hints at the hero's psychological attitude to a central issue: as he tells Varvara, the question of his poverty is a matter of acute sensitivity comparable to her own maidenly modesty.

Dostoevsky not only humanizes the Gogolian theme, he also "psychologizes" it. Bashmachkin has no inner world: at a crucial point in the story the narrator refuses to enter the mind of his hero, claiming that such an intrusion is impossible. Bashmachkin is so inarticulate that we can only guess at his inner world through the outer world which surrounds him. Dostoevsky reverses this process. Clothing, claims Devushkin, is not for oneself, it is for other people. Thus in Dostoevsky's work clothing is a mark of his hero's psychological sensitivity and of his acute awareness of himself in the outer world, whereas in Gogol clothing manifests his hero's inner deadness: it is the psychologized wrapping of a solipsistic vacuum. Bashmachkin loves a coat, Devushkin a girl. In

Dostoevsky the psychological implications of clothing have a humanizing effect on other characters too. The loss of a button from Devushkin's threadbare uniform evokes pity as well as financial help from his superior, whereas the loss of Bashmachkin's coat provokes a dressing down from an important person and leads directly to his death. Yet there is an ironical twist at the end of Dostoevsky's novel. Devushkin loses Varvara (much as Bashmachkin loses his coat) when she departs to marry her would-be seducer, Bykov, and now the motif of clothing becomes so paramount as to usurp the former human relationship. Devushkin discovers that Varvara had used their only means of communication, his letters, to card threads, and she now sends him on errands to buy items for her trousseau. From the moving words on frippery which end Devushkin's correspondence, we see that once more clothing has been substituted for life.

The question of communication is fundamental to both works. The inarticulate Bashmachkin is obsessed by writing, but this is not actual communication, it is merely copying. Devushkin also expresses his personal life in writing, but it is through his letters that he reveals himself. Moreover, in Dostoevsky there is no semi-competent narrator with a comically distorting viewpoint, as there is in Gogol's story: the two central characters, Devushkin and Varvara, tell their own stories. The issue of "writing" has other overtones as well, for there is more than a hint in Gogol's story of the author's own artistic difficulties with form and content. Dostoevsky seems to pick this up. Devushkin is very responsive to literature and even thinks of himself as an author. The polemical point is reinforced when Devushkin reads "The Overcoat" and reacts strongly against it, taking the portrait of Bashmachkin almost as a personal insult.

Dostoevsky polemicizes with Gogol on a broad front: he seeks to revise his "realism," his "humanism," and his methods of psychological portrayal. In order to enter the psychological worlds of his characters directly Dostoevsky reverts to the earlier eighteenth century form of the novel in letters, associated with Rousseau and sentimentalism. It is almost as though he wanted to jump over Gogol and return to the roots of Russian humanism, which lay in sentimentalism. Indeed some of the more maudlin aspects of this earlier manner emerge in Varvara's descriptions of the poor student Pokrovsky and of his father, particularly in the scene of the son's funeral.

Poor Folk is not a work in the modern taste, but it reveals much about the future novelist: the uncompromising emphasis on human psychology; the interest in figures defeated by life; the attraction of an older man for a young girl (present not merely in the Devushkin/Varvara relationship, but also in the shadowy and typically Dostoevskian figure of Varvara's seducer Bykov). It also shows Dostoevsky's fascination with Gogol and the way in which he would reinterpret the Gogolian legacy.

Dostoevsky's next published work, *The Double* (*Dvoynik*, 1846), marks a clear step forward in artistic maturity, but unfortunately Belinsky did not see it as such. Dostoevsky is again apparently looking back. The double was a favorite theme of German romantic writers, principally Hoffmann and such Russian imitators of theirs as Pogorelsky. Yet its significance with them is chiefly philosophical, whereas Dostoevsky's treatment is uncompromisingly psychological. Nevertheless, he is once again merely developing and making explicit certain themes implicit in Gogol. The subtitle Dostoevsky later gives his work – "A St. Petersburg Poem" – is in itself suggestive, with its overtones both of *Dead Souls* and the St. Petersburg stories. It is from two of these latter, "The Nose" and "The Diary of a Madman," that Dostoevsky's story springs. The text contains clear references to both, as well as more general echoes of Gogol's comic manner. The hero Golyadkin, like Gogol's Kovalyov ("The Nose"), wakes up in the morning and then consults a mirror to see whether a pimple or some other misfortune has not been added to his face, much as Kovalyov had done. Kovalyov, however, finds his nose missing entirely, and in Gogol's story it will become his double, though of higher rank. Golyadkin sees in the mirror the very face that will haunt him as his own more competent double, both in his private life and his civil service career. Just as in Gogol's story, mirrors play an important but ambiguous role throughout *The Double*.

Dostoevsky's story is presented through a narrator, but his function is not to provide an objective sense of reality against which Golyadkin's actions can be judged. One senses at times a fluidity of boundary between narrator and protagonist which allows the narrator to describe events in the hero's own voice. This device reflects an issue central to the story itself – the confusion between "I" and "he." Golyadkin's behavior at the beginning of the novel is extremely enigmatic, yet the clue to it lies in the revelations he makes when, on a sudden impulse, he consults his doctor. The doctor is referred to as a "confessor" (*dukhovnik*), and Golyadkin's visit indeed amounts to a confession, which begins in the third person, as though Golyadkin were talking about someone else, but keeps breaking into a first-person narrative. From it we discover that Golyadkin has insulted a colleague and his fiancée, because he has learned that the colleague, Vladimir Semyonovich, has been promoted to the rank of Collegiate Assessor through what Golyadkin suspects is nepotism (the boss Andrey Filippovich is his uncle). Vladimir Semyonovich is also engaged to Klara Olsufevna, with whom Golyadkin himself is in love. Golyadkin's mental problems, therefore, center round those which appear to unhinge Poprishchin in "The Diary of a Madman": defeat in both career expectations and love.

As the novel opens we witness Golyadkin's attempts at self-assertion. He has hired a carriage with a coat of arms and, instead of going to the office, is riding round St. Petersburg in his best uniform, accompanied by his servant in a livery and wearing a sword. Unfortunately he meets Andrey Filippovich, his head of department, in the street, and his immediate response is to pretend that he is someone else – "It is not I, Andrey Filippovich, not I." Apparently this conflict between a third and first person identity compels him to make his unexpected visit to the doctor. Somewhat reassured by his consultation, he continues his drive and pretends to buy a great number of expensive items, including furniture and ladies' attire. He asserts victory in amorous defeat by creating the illusion that he is preparing for marriage. Because of his earlier behavior, as may be deduced from his confession to the doctor, he has not been invited to Klara Olsufevna's birthday party: he gatecrashes it and is thrown out. Once again he is faced with personal defeat, and it is as he is returning home late at night through the streets of St. Petersburg that he first becomes aware of his double, who not only looks like him but actually bears the same name and patronymic. This third person "I" (Golyadkin junior) is more intelligent than Golyadkin senior, and in a series of incidents, both at home and in the office – where the double also appears to work – Golyadkin senior is made to feel inferior to his own third person projection. He is finally taken away to a mental institution, but not before he obtains a momentary glimpse of normality, during which he experiences love for his supposed enemies and realizes that the figure he perceives as his double is not really his double at all.

The Double is full of allusions to Gogol's works, and displays that Gogolian mixture of humor and pathos known as "laughter through tears." It is nevertheless a penetrating and serious account of a mental breakdown, much too far ahead of its time for Dostoevsky's contemporaries, who scarcely understood it. As a work of art its chief faults were prolixity and lack of clarity. The second flowed from the nature of the subject, but the first could be remedied, and for the 1865–6 collection of his works Dostoevsky shortened it, cutting out amongst other things the ponderously humorous "Gogolian" chapter headings of the original version.

Dostoevsky returned to the theme of the little man in his story "Mr. Prokharchin" (1846). This time his impoverished civil servant is a miser who lives in overcrowded accommodation, where he is teased by the other occupants. When he dies from fear, he is discovered to have a small fortune in his mattress. The story is full of bizarre and naturalistic detail, and may be read as a further commentary on the supposed "poverty" of Gogol's Bashmachkin.

For all his overwhelming enthusiasm for *Poor Folk*, Belinsky had reservations about *The Double*, and for "The Landlady" ("Khozyayka"), published in 1847, he had nothing but censure. It is indeed a strange work. The boundary between the hero's subjective world and the objective world of the tale's narrator is eroded to such an extent as to obfuscate the action of the narrative itself.

A young man, Ordynov – the first of Dostoevsky's dreamer types – is strangely attracted to a fey young woman, Katerina – the landlady of the title – who is under the protection of a sinister, wizard-like older man named Murin. Their relationship is not clear; Murin could be either or both her father and her husband. Ordynov lodges with them but falls ill, so that real events and the delusions of delirium become difficult to disentangle. At one point he is about to be shot by Murin, but is saved when Murin suffers an epileptic fit; on another occasion he himself appears ready to attack Murin with a knife. The situation is further complicated by another figure – Alyosha (now dead probably at Murin's hands) – with whom Katerina seems to identify Ordynov.

Yet behind this strange story one can again sense Gogol's presence, and especially his poetic tale of magic, legend and incest, "The Terrible Vengeance" ("Strashnaya mest," 1832). Gogol's heroine is also called Katerina; she too is under the spell of a wizard who is her father; and she too speaks in the poetic language of Russian folklore. The fact that Ordynov intends to write a book on the history of the church and that Murin appears to read sectarian literature, has led certain scholars to interpret the story as religious allegory. However this may be, it is certainly the most impenetrable of Dostoevsky's works, though not without interest in the light of his later writing. The fusion of reality and delirium will be brought to perfection in *Crime and Punishment*, and Katerina is a forerunner of Marya Lebyadkina in *The Possessed*. The linking between epilepsy and murder looks forward to *The Idiot*, even perhaps to *The Brothers Karamazov*. The young woman enslaved to the will of an older man will appear again in "A Gentle Creature" (1876). Most striking of all, Murin's words on freedom foreshadow a celebrated passage in "The Legend of the Grand Inquisitor."

Murin refers to Katerina as a "faint heart," and this is the title of another of Dostoevsky's early stories about a dreamer ("Slaboe serdtse," 1848). Vasya Shumkov is a sentimental young copy clerk, whose heart is too weak to withstand the combination of being betrothed and coping with the work given to him by his benefactor. Another story, "White Nights" ("Belye nochi," 1848), continues the sentimental theme of the dreamer, and actually bears the sub-title: "A Sentimental Novel – from the Reminiscences of a Dreamer" (its epigraph is from a poem by Turgenev). Against the dream-like setting of the white nights of St. Petersburg an idealistic young man meets a young woman, Nastenka, who undertakes to continue their relationship provided he does not fall in love with her, as she is in love with another. The narration is in the first person, and the narrator introduces himself as the "type" of the dreamer. The meetings continue for four nights, but the morning of the fifth day sees a return to reality, when the dreamer receives a letter from Nastenka informing him that her lover has returned and she will marry him next week. The theme of the dreamer in early Dostoevsky is closely associated with idealistic, unconsummated love, though not without its hint of sexual titillation. When they recur in the later novels, such relationships will substitute allegory for sentimentality, as in the case of Myshkin and Nastasya Filippovna in *The Idiot*.

Amongst Dostoevsky's early work are obvious "potboilers" such as the "Novel in Nine Letters" ("Roman v devyati pismakh," 1847), a correspondence between cardsharpers written in one night for the money, and only interesting in that it shows Dostoevsky continuing to use the epistolary form immediately after *Poor Folk*. There is also a crude imitation of Paul de Kock's farcical love intrigues, "Another Man's Wife and a Husband under the Bed" ("Chuzhaya zhena i muzh pod krovatyu," 1848), originally published as two separate stories ("Another Man's Wife" and "A Jealous Husband").

"Polzunkov" (1848) is a tale of trickery and deceit among civil servants, with a weak denouement hinging on an April-Fools-day joke. It is principally remarkable for its portrait of the "crawler," Polzunkov, the first depiction of a particularly Dostoevskian type, the clownish hanger-on. "The Honest Thief" ("Chestny vor," 1848) deals with another Dostoevskian theme, the power of conscience. A reprobate drunkard steals from his humble benefactor, but returns when at the point of death to confess his crime. "A Christmas Tree and a Wedding" ("Elka i svadba," 1848), depicts the unpleasant spectacle of an older man making up to a child in whom he sees a rich prospective bride. This attraction of an older man to a little girl is another theme which will resurface in the mature Dostoevsky.

Dostoevsky's most ambitious work of his pre-Siberian period is *Netochka Nezvanova*. It was to have been a full length novel, but only three parts were published before his arrest: "Childhood," "A New Life," and "A Secret." In preparing this work for the 1861 edition of his writings, Dostoevsky abandoned these section headings in favor of numbered chapters, and at the same time excluded the story of Larya, a young male parallel to Netochka herself. Nevertheless the plot does not cohere, but falls obviously into three distinct episodes. The first deals with the stock romantic theme of the musician who has sold his soul. This figure is Efimov, a former serf musician who becomes Netochka's stepfather. A central motif here is adolescent eroticism: Netochka at ten conceives a passion for Efimov (whom she considers to be her father) and a hatred for her mother. After their death she is taken into an aristocratic household ("A New Life") and forms an explicitly erotic relationship with a young princess, Katya. In the third section she is sent to another household, that of Katya's half-sister, who is tyrannized by a cold, unforgiving husband, a relationship into which Netochka herself is drawn when she finds a letter in a book. This final section is weaker than the preceding ones, but the work as a whole is remarkable for its concern with children, a constant theme in Dostoevsky's writing, and for its treatment of behavior on the very edge of the acceptable.

The theme of a child's awakening sexuality is also dealt with in "The Little Hero" ("Malenky geroy"), a story Dostoevsky wrote in the Peter and Paul Fortress in 1849 whilst under arrest, though it was not published until 1857. The little hero, like Netochka Nezvanova, is plunged into a world of adult eroticism, yet he is also a little knight who dares to ride a wild stallion in response to a lady's challenge and save a lady he admires by returning lost letters. There is a Dostoevskian kernel in this story, but the flavor of the "flesh" is undoubtedly French.

Mikhail Saltykov (1826–89) began writing in the 1840s. Like Dostoevsky, he was attracted to the Petrashevsky circle and its utopian socialism. He too was seen as a writer of the natural school, and his first short novel, Contradictions (Protivorechiya), published in 1847 under the pseudonym of N. Nepanov, depicts its hero Nagibin as a man caught between his own ideals and the reality of life as it is – a romantic theme, but one also capable of political interpretation. In his next short novel A Muddled Affair (Zaputannoe delo), published in 1848 under the initials M.S., the political nature of Saltykov's "naturalism" became more explicit. Michulin, the hero, is that well-known figure the poor clerk, but he has a dream in which he sees society as a pyramid, with the poor at its base weighed down by the privileged at the top. In 1848 such an image did not go unnoticed. Saltykov was arrested and sent off to Vyatka, where Herzen had been exiled before him. He returned to the literary scene in 1856, and from that point on became one of Russia's leading satirists under the pseudonym of N. Shchedrin.

Ivan Goncharov (1812–91) was born into a merchant family of

Simbirsk. His father died when he was seven and he was brought up by his mother and a family friend. He was a student at Moscow University at the same time as both Lermontov and Belinsky, but he mixed with neither of them. In 1835 he became a civil servant in St. Petersburg, and also developed a close relationship with the Maykov family, acting as tutor to the two eldest boys: Apollon (the future poet) and Valerian (the literary critic). Goncharov met most of the literary figures of the time at the Maykov salon and contributed poems and stories to the family's handwritten almanacs.

Goncharov's first published work was the novel *A Common Story* (*Obyknovennaya istoriya*), which came out in 1847. Belinsky hailed it as an event of the year, a sign of the growing strength of the natural school, and an attack on outdated romanticism. Certainly the novel appears to deal with the education of an incorrigible romantic, Alexander Aduev, who comes to St. Petersburg from the depths of the countryside to be taken under the wing of his uncle, Peter Aduev, a cold and rational man of affairs. Yet the matter is not so simple: we are presented with two contrasting attitudes to life, and ultimately two views of Russia, but the author does not come down on either side.

The poetic younger Aduev is romantic in another sense: his heart is only too vulnerable to the fair sex. Yet in reality he runs away from all the women with whom he falls in love. Indeed, at the point of his greatest defeat he runs away literally, to his mother in the country. Inability to take the initiative in love is a major characteristic of the so-called "superfluous men," and the author comments at the beginning of part II: "All such natures as his love to surrender their will to the control of another – for them a nurse is a necessity." Alexander appears to find this nurse-figure in his aunt, who is more like a sister to him. She sees the difference between her husband and her nephew as that of "two terrible extremes," and it is from one of these extremes – her husband's cold rationality – that she herself suffers. Her problems as a married woman anticipate those of Olga Ilinskaya in Goncharov's masterpiece, *Oblomov* (1859). Indeed, in certain respects *A Common Story* reads like a rehearsal for that novel. In both, a romantic, artistic nature is confronted by a practical man of affairs, and the sparring between master and servant (Oblomov and

Zakhar) is anticipated in the relationship between Alexander Aduev and Evsey. Like Oblomov, Aduev exhibits a vulnerable, romantic ego; he too is critical of the people he meets. At one point he even appears to lapse into "Oblomovism" itself.

The novel is far from that strain of sociological writing associated with the natural school, but it is linked to this tendency by the apparent assertion of the St. Petersburg principle. Thus, when the nephew upbraids his uncle with the words: "You forget that man is happy through his errors, his dreams, his hopes. Reality does not make him happy," his uncle cuts him short: "What nonsense you are talking. You have brought this opinion from the Asiatic border: in Europe they have long ago ceased believing in that." If Belinsky adhered to such sentiments, we can see why the critic grew increasingly more disillusioned with Dostoevsky and his depiction of the "dreamer" as a product of St. Petersburg itself.

The central antithesis of *A Common Story* is not just that of practical man and dreamer; it is also that of the western values of the capital opposed to those of backward, semi-Asiatic Russia. However, Goncharov is not entirely successful in keeping the antithesis alive in the reader's mind: the country has no palpable existence when Aduev is away from it, and only comes to life on his return. Belinsky identified a similar weakness in Goncharov's portrayal of character. Speaking in the author's presence about the most important and most successful of his female characters, Nadenka, he remarked: "As long as he needs her, he takes trouble with her, and then he flings her aside."

In 1848 Goncharov published a story "Ivan Savich Podzhabrin," which he had written in 1841. It is set in the civil service milieu of St. Petersburg, and its subtitle – *ocherki* (essays) – links it with the natural school. The central figure, Podzhabrin, owes something to Gogol's Khlestakov, and his manservant Avdey to Gogol's Osip.

The following year, 1849, saw the publication of "Oblomov's Dream" ("Son Oblomova"), which for ten years stood on its own as an independent work until it was incorporated into *Oblomov*. This description of an old fashioned patriarchal way of life, hovering between nostalgic endorsement and whimsically critical appraisal, recalls Gogol's "Old World Landowners," with one important difference: Goncharov's ambivalent idyll is seen through the eyes of a child. With acute psychological insight

Goncharov suggests how such a world forms the future adult. At the same time, it was a dream "brought from the Asiatic border," and therefore appealed to the Slavophiles. The antithesis between two ways of life, between two Russias, would subsist unresolved in his later writing, and Goncharov would later claim that *A Common Story* was the first novel in a thematic trilogy which included *Oblomov* and *The Precipice* (1869).

Alexander Herzen (1812–70) was the illegitimate son of a wealthy nobleman and the daughter of a German civil servant. As a child of love who could not be given his father's name, he was called "Herzen" ("love-child"). He studied at Moscow University but in 1834 was arrested for alleged complicity in a student plot and was exiled to Vyatka for four years. In 1840 he was again exiled for a year to Novgorod for speaking disparagingly of the police in his letters. In 1846 his father died, leaving him a considerable fortune, and the following year he left for Europe quite disillusioned with Russia. He would never return.

Herzen's two most important publicistic writings of this period are *Dilettantism in Science* (*Dilletantizm v nauke*, 1843) and *Letters on the Study of Nature* (*Pisma ob izuchenii prirody*, 1845–6). Both these works, published in *Fatherland Notes*, are concerned with philosophy. In fact the latter amounts almost to a history of philosophy.

Herzen's fiction of this period, published under the pseudonym of Iskander, shows a concern with social issues. "The Thieving Magpie" ("Soroka vorovka," 1848), deals with the humanitarian theme of the evil of serfdom, through the anomaly of the peasant theaters which noblemen often kept for their amusement. It depicts the plight of an educated serf actress viewed as a concubine by a new master who buys the troupe. "Dr. Krupov," published in *The Contemporary* in 1847, presents the idea of madness as purely relative and suggests the presence of epidemic madness in society itself and the whole course of human history. The Voltairean sarcasm of this story was only too apparent to the contemporary reader.

The novel *Who is to Blame?* (*Kto vinovat?*, 1847), was one of the first Russian problem novels, posing a question its very title. Part I, first published in 1845, introduces a *déclassé* intellectual, Krutsifersky (the very name hints at crucifixion and idealistic sacrifice), who is a private tutor in the house of a retired general, Negrov. Lyubonka, Negrov's illegitimate daughter by a female serf, also lives there, and a bond of sympathy grows up between them in response to Negrov's bullying, patriarchal ways. When Krutsifersky receives an assignation, he assumes it is to meet Lyubonka, and not the portly wife of Negrov, whom Herzen unkindly likens to a baobab tree. The letter addressed to Lyubonka, which Krutsifersky in confusion leaves behind, makes it clear where his true affections lie, and when this comes to Negrov's attention he is only too glad to marry off his illegitimate daughter to the penniless tutor. Thus plot devices of the French society novel are used to highlight a matter of personal concern to Herzen: the issue of moral, social and intellectual legitimacy within a framework of despotism.

In Part II we are introduced to Beltov, the son of a nobleman, who has been brought up on Rousseau and is quite unfitted to Russian life. This is another portrait of the superfluous man, who like Onegin falls in love with another man's wife (Lyubonka). She gives him the moral reply which Tatyana gave to Onegin.

Herzen's enthusiasm for Europe quickly cooled when he encountered it in reality. In 1847 he wrote the *Letters from Avenue Marigny*, criticizing Paris for that very philistinism he thought he had left behind in Russia. The crushing of the 1848 revolution was the final blow. The bourgeoisie was now triumphant, along with that liberalism which he regarded as their religion – the religion of mediocrity. The intellectual crisis of these years is reflected in a collection of essays written from 1847 to 1850, entitled *From the Other Shore* (*S togo berega*), and first published in German in 1850. Many of these pieces take the form of a dialogue, and stylistically represent some of Herzen's best writing. They display a certain bitterness, often a mood of nihilism, but there is also a sense of aristocratic dignity: the impulse to withdraw from a corrupt world, to stand aloof and preserve one's own truth. This was Herzen in a Voltairean mood: his attack on Rousseau's concept of primal freedom looks forward to Dostoevsky's Grand Inquisitor.

From now on Herzen began to invert his former values: no longer did Russia need Europe, but rather Europe itself would be saved by Russia. He saw in the Russian peasant commune, or *mir*, a form of cooperation and land-sharing which constituted a simple agrarian socialism capable of saving Europe from its bourgeoisie. In a strange way Herzen found himself developing the debate he had conducted with the Slavophiles in the 1840s, but now he had himself appropriated one of the Slavophiles' most cherished concepts, that of the peasant *mir*, and decked it out in purely socialist ideological clothing rather than patriarchal and religious garb. Such "fiction" may, on the face of it, have little to do with literature as such, but Herzen's new-found allegiances are symptomatic of the growing importance the peasant was assuming both in literature and in political thought. Indeed Turgenev, who had himself played no small part in bringing the peasant to the forefront of Russian consciousness, accused Herzen of bowing down to the peasant's sheepskin coat. However, the real literary apotheosis of the peasant had to wait upon Leo Tolstoy's later years.

The Slavophiles were a philosophical and cultural group of great importance. Centered in Moscow, they were the ideological opponents of the westernizers, whose base was St. Petersburg. The group is usually considered to consist of Alexey Khomyakov (1804–60), Ivan Kircevsky (1806–56), and Konstantin Aksakov (1817–61). This is the group's core, but others may be added to it, principally Yury Samarin (1819–76), Peter Kireevsky (1808–56), Ivan's brother and a collector of folk songs, and Ivan Aksakov (1823–86), the brother of Konstantin and a figure influential in the later development of Slavophile ideas.

The Slavophiles believed Russia's ills had originated with Peter I and his forcible attempt to westernize Russia. They strove to return to the real Russian roots of pre-Petrine society, and thus had an important role to play in the "search for nationality." They were the first group of intellectuals to place a positive emphasis on the Russian peasant, whom they saw as little affected by Peter's reforms; the peasant had retained his ancient customs and institutions, principally the peasant commune (*mir*), which was self-regulating and took unanimous decisions. The Slavophiles themselves were landowners and their wealth depended on serf-owning, but some of them took to growing beards and wearing peasant dress. In the revolutionary year of 1848 Konstantin Aksakov was officially required by the police to shave.

Yet for all the Slavophiles' championship of indigenous culture, their intellectual roots lay in the teachings of Schelling and Herder.

They were themselves the product of western European culture, and in fact the first journal Kireevsky established was called *The European* (*Evropeets*). One of the group's chief meeting places was the salon of the Kireevskys' mother, Mme. Avdotya Elagina, where they encountered such opponents as Herzen, Granovsky and Belinsky. In fact, before the two factions finally separated after the departure of Belinsky for St. Petersburg in 1839, there was much friendly contact between them and a strong degree of mutual respect. The chief gladiators of each side were more often than not Khomyakov and Herzen, whose intellects and debating skills were closely matched. The main points at issue were the influence of the Orthodox Church, the role of Peter I, and the vexed question of whether Russia's future lay with the west or with an indigenous culture now in danger of being lost through Peter's reforms.

The Slavophiles were not prolific writers; they seemed to suffer from a kind of "Oblomovism." Khomyakov wrote poems, and articles on Orthodoxy, but his major work, *Notes on World History*, remained in the form of draft notes. Nor had the Slavophiles a journal of their own. In 1845 Kireevsky became co-editor of *The Muscovite*, but he was not allowed to continue because his appointment had not received official approval. In 1852 the group tried to bring out a series of *Moscow Miscellanies* (*Moskovsky sbornik*), but this venture was halted after the first issue. For all their nationalism, the authorities regarded the Slavophiles with suspicion because of their criticism of the modern Petrine state – after all, Nicholas I himself looked back with pride to his ancestor Peter the Great – and it is important to distinguish them from such truly right-wing figures of official nationalism as Shevyryov and Pogodin, even though Kireevsky agreed to edit *The Muscovite*.

Slavophilism was a form of right-wing radical romanticism, which emphasized organic wholeness and rejected the analytic rationalism of the west. The Slavophiles' chief doctrine was a religious one, the concept of *sobornost*, or a mystical sense of oneness which was the spirit of the true church. Their arguments on the relationship between church and state in the east and in the west influenced the ideas advanced in Dostoevsky's novel *The Brothers Karamazov*. Gogol, too, felt their influence; he was close to the Aksakov family. The Slavophiles, especially the Aksakov

232

family, felt Gogol was their writer, just as Belinsky claimed Gogol for his cause. After the publication of *Dead Souls* a famous tussle developed between Konstantin Aksakov and Belinsky over the nature of Gogol's masterpiece. In 1842 Konstantin Aksakov wrote a brochure on that subject to which Belinsky felt obliged to respond. Another point at issue was the literary tendency represented by the natural school, which Belinsky championed as following Gogol's lead. Samarin emerged as one of the natural school's strongest critics with a series of three articles in *The Muscovite* for 1847. It was not Konstantin, however, but his father Sergey Aksakov who ultimately produced work of real literary merit. Urged on by Gogol, in 1840 he began writing *A Family Chronicle*, and although it was not fully published until 1856, substantial extracts from it appeared in a Slavophile miscellany in 1846.

Slavophile ideas also permeate *The Tarantas*, by Count Vladimir Sollogub (1813–82). Extracts first appeared in 1840, and the complete work came out in 1845. The work, whose title refers to an old-fashioned type of Russian coach, is the literary record of a journey undertaken by Ivan Vasilevich and Vasily Ivanovich. These inverted names are not merely a Gogolian comic device: they hint at the various arguments between the two friends of which the piece is largely composed. *The Tarantas* is a kind of ideological *Dead Souls*, in which the heroes set out in their coach to see Russia, its antiquities, its people, and above all to discover the quality of its nationhood – its *narodnost*. They meet peasants, merchants and landowners; they also discuss fundamental problems: Russia and Europe; Russia versus both east and west. Some of the ideas are presented with a degree of irony, so that critics (Belinsky among them) have regarded Ivan Vasilevich as a parodying portrait of Ivan Kireevsky, who bore the same Christian name and patronymic. Undoubtedly many Slavophile ideas are advanced in the work, but the ironical note is not always present. Indeed *The Tarantas* is based on an actual journey undertaken by the author and Prince G. G. Gagarin, who would later become a vice president of the Academy of Arts. The work caused a stir in the 1840s principally because in its dialogues it raised many questions of the times: *narodnost*, Russia's position in the world, Slavophilism, the nature of the Russian peasant.

Alexey Pisemsky (1821–81) began his writing career during this period. His short novel *The Simpleton* (*Tyufyak*) appeared in *The Muscovite* in 1850 and aroused critical interest. Its milieu is that of the provincial gentry, its theme – an unsuitable marriage. The denouement is pessimistic in tone and technically weak. The novel itself, close to western models of society literature, was equally distant from the tenets of the natural school and from any programmatic sense of *narodnost* associated with the journal in which it appeared.

In his short stories, however, Pisemsky turned his attention to the peasant. "The Petersburger" ("Pitershchik") of 1852 gives a portrait of a peasant working as a painter in the capital and succumbing to its blandishments, though solid rural values win through in the end. "The Wood Demon" ("Leshy," 1853) also deals with the corrupting effect of city life on the village. A manager sent from the city to oversee his master's estates abuses his position to gain the sexual favors of peasant women, but is unmasked before the village commune by the local police officer. "The Carpenters' Guild" ("Plotnichya artel," 1855) is about the *artel*, another peasant institution which appealed to the Slavophiles, but this time corruption comes from within in the form of a peasant contractor, Puzich, who exploits his guild of workmen. The plot line, which ends with the death of Puzich is simple, but the story is filled out with ethnographic detail. These three stories, which had appeared in different journals, were brought together in 1856 and published under the title *Sketches from Peasant Life* (*Ocherki iz krestyanskogo byta*). They evoked comparison with Turgenev, though not always in Pisemsky's favor.

Alongside the emphasis on the grimmer aspects of life so typical of the natural school, there is another, apparently quite different strain of romantic idealism also characteristic of the 1840s. This is most in evidence in the treatment of friendship and, more particularly, love between the sexes. In many of the stories, poems and novels of the period which deal with the relationships between men and women, the dominant theme is one of self-sacrifice. We see it in Nekrasov's poetry, in Dostoevsky's stories, in Dahl's *Pavel Alexeevich Igrivy*, in Herzen's *Who is to Blame?*, but perhaps most of all in the short novel *Polinka Saks* (1847) by Alexander Druzhinin (1824–64). The novel is partly epistolary, but unlike

234

Dostoevsky's *Poor Folk*, it is set in a society milieu. Polinka, the heroine, has married an up-and-coming civil servant, Konstantin Saks, in order to please her father, but her real affection is directed toward a "superfluous man," Prince Galitsky. When Saks learns of their relationship he magnanimously yields to Galitsky, but on the understanding that he must make her happy. Polinka dies realizing that her self-sacrificing husband is the better man, and it is he she really loves. In its sentiment, as well as perhaps in plot, the story owes a debt to George Sand, and its appeal to the contemporary reader can, perhaps, be explained only in the light of the vogue she enjoyed in Russia during the 1840s. In the sympathetic portrait of the heroine and her central role, we nevertheless also see a strength typical of the Russian novel in general. There is more than a suggestion that society is to blame for its attitude toward women: it treats them as children or "angels" rather than human beings. The idealistic theme of self-sacrifice in love and the down-to-earth realism of the natural school are perhaps not so far apart as they may at first seem. They are but different aspects of the struggle for a humanizing role for literature which Belinsky advocated; but whereas the focus of the natural school is on social groups and society at large, works such as *Polinka Saks* sought to advance the new humanism at the level of individual relationships.

Another novel dealing with the position of women in society is Karolina Pavlova's (1807–93) "Twofold" ("Dvoynaya zhizn"), published the following year and taking its title from Byron. It too is set in high society. The heroine Cecily von Lindenborn is maneuvered into marrying the "wrong man" by her friend's mother so that she will not pose a threat to her own daughter's chances with the highly eligible Prince Victor. Irony is more in evidence than sentiment, but as with *Polinka Saks* the work is a mixed genre, not in this case narrative and epistolary, but prose and verse. Poetry is used to reveal the inner world of the heroine. Of German origin, Karolina Pavlova was also a poet, who moved in high society. During the early 1840s her salon was frequented by westernizers and Slavophiles. Though her poetry was not taken seriously by her contemporaries, it was rediscovered at the turn of the century by the symbolists.

Although the 1840s are regarded as a period when prose was paramount, there is equal, if not greater, literary merit in much of its poetry. A major figure is Afanasy Fet (1820–92), the son of a Russian landowner, Afanasy Shenshin, who had carried off the wife of a German official. As the future poet was born before their marriage took place, he could not bear his real father's name and was officially classed as a foreigner. This lack of status affected him profoundly, and his hopes of gaining gentry status through service in the army were dashed when the rules were arbitrarily changed. Bitterly disappointed, he left the service to become a landowner. In 1876 he finally gained the coveted title of "noble."

A second profound sadness in his life was his love for a Polish girl, Maria Lazich, whom he met while serving in Poland. As both were poor they decided to part, and she died afterwards by fire, in what might have been suicide. Although Fet married Maria Botkina in 1857, his love for Maria Lazich was a recurring theme in his poetry. Fet always suffered from bouts of depression (indeed Apollon Grigorev, who was at Moscow University with him, regarded Fet as suicidal), but little of this darker side of his nature emerged in his verse.

Fet's first book of poems, *The Lyrical Pantheon* (*Lirichesky panteon*), came out in 1840, but when he published his collected verse, in 1850, he included only four poems from this early series. Fet was a meticulous craftsman; during this earlier period we find him experimenting with different styles and themes, but the essential Fet is very much in evidence. His basic themes are nature, love and art, and he is at his best as a "lyrical miniaturist" in short, simple poems remarkable for their clearly observed detail, telling juxtaposition of images, and musicality. At times his art recalls Chinese poetry. During this period, by contrast, he experimented with very long lines of verse, which on the whole were less successful. There are also poems on classical themes, the most famous on the goddess Diana. Yet in general Fet's poetry eschews the cold impersonalism of classicism. The author is very much present in his poetry. A number of his poems actually begin with "I," though this is not the self-indulgent romanticism of an earlier period. There is objectivity in Fet's descriptions of the natural world, and yet at the same time his language and imagery convey emotion. Although his gift for observation and presentation of detail might suggest a static, contemplative quality in his poetry, it in fact contains a great deal of movement. He even manages to create an illusion of movement in his description of a statue of Diana ("Diana," 1847), through her reflection in water stirred by a breeze. In other poems movement is suggested by linguistic means (exclamations and imperatives), or by the fact that the observing "I" is himself in movement, as in "I came to you" ("Ya prishel k tebe," 1843), "The old park" ("Stary park," 1853), "Ah, youth is no joke!" ("Ekh, shutka molodost!," 1847).

Fet is an innovative poet. His technique of creating poetry out of the juxtaposition of auditory and visual images is seen at its starkest in "Whisper, timid breathing" ("Shepot, robkoe dykhane," 1850), which evokes a lovers' meeting at night without using a single verb. On the other hand a poem such as "On the Dnepr in flood" ("Na Dnepre v polovode," 1853) is remarkable for its fresh and challenging use of adjectives, and another poem with the opening line "Bad weather, autumn, you smoke" ("Nepogoda, osen, kurish") uses a colloquial style in an almost modern idiom. Such aspects of Fet's poetry look forward to the twentieth century, to poets like Pasternak and Zabolotsky.

Unfortunately Fet was not fully appreciated in his own time, and particularly in the 1860s, though his reputation reestablished itself in the 1880s. Fet was not a poet who addressed social issues. A poem of 1854 with a title recalling the subject matter of the natural school, "The hurdy-gurdy man" ("Sharmanshchik"), immediately deceives such expectations: it is concerned with private feelings and personal memories, and at the end it dismisses the hurdy-gurdy player as a grey-haired clown with an importunate hurdy-gurdy.

The early poetry of Yakov Polonsky (1819–98) is considered to be his best. He has a clear lyrical voice and a flowing mellifluous style, so it is not surprising that many of his early poems are better known as songs. Polonsky was born in Ryazan, the son of a civil servant. He studied law at Moscow University and became friendly there with Apollon Grigorev and Fet. Although less original than Fet (his poetry clearly derives from Pushkin and Lermontov), Polonsky still has an impressive lyrical gift and a voice of his own.

His first published poem, "The holy peal solemnly sounds" ("Svyashchenny blagovest torzhestvenno zvuchit"), appeared in *Fatherland Notes* in 1840; and two years later several of his verses were published in a student collection. In that same year of 1842 Polonsky sent his poem "Shadows of night arrived" ("Prishli i stali teni nochi") to Belinsky, who printed it in *Fatherland Notes*, and the poem caught Gogol's attention (he copied it into one of his notebooks). Polonsky's first book of poems, *Gammy* (*Scales*), came out in 1844.

In the same year Polonsky moved to Odessa, where a second, and less successful, collection appeared. In June 1846 he was appointed to a post in the office of the viceroy of the Caucasus, and his move to Tiflis occasioned a whole series of inspired poems on Caucasian themes. From there he published in 1849 a collection entitled *Sazandar* (a Caucasian word for "bard"), followed by *Several Poems* (*Neskolko stikhotvoreniy*) in 1851. Polonsky's Caucasian poetry is imbued with a feeling for the folklore and customs of the Caucasus, and he has an obvious predecessor in Lermontov. Nevertheless, Polonsky manages to make the theme of the Caucasus very much his own, and upon leaving the Caucasus even casts an ironical eye on Lermontov's legacy. In "On the way back from the Caucasus" ("Na puti iz-za Kavkaza"), the poet hears the croak of a raven and makes out the body of a horse (a hint at the collapse of Pechorin's horse in *Hero of Our Time*), but exclaims: "Drive on, drive on! The shade of Pechorin pursues my tracks." Later, in "The Finnish coast" ("Finsky bereg"), he writes a parody on Lermontov's "Taman" in a Finnish setting.

In keeping with the growing prose tradition of the natural school, Polonsky's Caucasian poetry shows a greater sense of "realistic" detail than Lermontov's. Thus in "The mountain road in Georgia" ("Gornaya doroga v Gruzii," 1847), the poet is concerned less with the beauty of the scenery than with the perils of the road: indeed the scenery is part of his boredom. A remarkable example of Polonsky's eye for realistic detail is the long poem of 1846 "A stroll through Tiflis" ("Progulka po Tiflisu"), written in the form of a verse letter to Pushkin's brother Leo. It describes Tiflis life, the street scenes and the views, with a vivid directness which makes it a masterpiece of its kind. The natural school's preoccupation with the social theme may also account for Polonsky's interest in beggars. A poem of 1847, "The beggar" ("Nishchy"), depicts a beggar who collects money for those less fortunate than himself, and another poem, of 1851, describes the attempt by the beggars of Tiflis to choose a head of their guild.

Night is a subject which Polonsky often treats with success. It was one of his very first themes, and he returns to it in "Georgian night" ("Gruzinskaya noch") and in "Night" ("Noch"), written in the Crimea in 1850, where he asks why he loves the night, even though it can bring no alleviation of his suffering. Some of Polonsky's best effects are achieved through a dream state evoked by the real world. In "Tossed in a storm" ("Kachka v buryu") of 1850, a boat's rocking in a storm keeps sending the poet to sleep, to dream of childhood in his cradle or of sitting on a swing with his beloved. Perhaps Polonsky's most famous poem is "Sleigh bell" ("Kolokolchik," 1854) in which the sound of a sleigh bell evokes a dream state and images of lost love.

In 1855 another collection of Polonsky's verse came out in St. Petersburg, and he published regularly until his death, avoiding the opprobrium suffered by Fet in the 1860s by developing the social themes already latent in some of his earlier poetry. But the poems which have remained favourites with the Russian reading public are those from the 1840s and early 1850s: "Sun and moon" ("Solntse i mesyats"), "Winter journey" ("Zimny put"), "The prisoner" ("Zatvornitsa"), "Night," "Gipsy song" ("Pesnya tsyganki"), and "Sleigh bell."

The poet most closely associated with the natural school is Nikolay Nekrasov (1821–78). He was born in 1821 (or possibly 1822) into a noble family which claimed to go back some two hundred years, but whose members in more recent times had shown a penchant for dissolute living. Nekrasov's father was a gambler, drunkard, lecher and tyrant, whose victims, apart from his peasants, were his own wife and daughters. One of Nekrasov's most heart-felt and best early poems is "Homeland" ("Rodina") of 1846, in which he gives a picture of his home life and the sufferings of his mother. This background, perhaps above all else, determined the choice of themes for his poetry: his loud protest against tyranny and violence; his compassion for the lot of women; his championship of the oppressed. The village of Greshnevo, where he grew up, was on the Vladimir High Road, the route by which convicts were taken to Siberia. He had ample opportunity to witness their plight, as well as the hard lot of his father's serfs. He also hunted and, like Turgenev, got to know another side of peasant life through his contacts with peasant huntsmen.

As a student in St. Petersburg Nekrasov experienced extreme poverty, real hunger, and was even reduced to begging. Yet there was another side to him, one inherited from his ancestors: he was a remarkably skilful gambler and a hard-headed business man. As an entrepreneur in literature he had few equals. He brought out the famous *St. Petersburg Miscellany* in which Dostoevsky published his first work; in 1847 he and Panaev took over the ailing *Contemporary* and made it the foremost literary journal of its time, with some help from his casino winnings when times were hard.

Nekrasov was undoubtedly a complex man, one driven by feelings of guilt and anger. He exhibited sensitivity, tenderness and compassion, but these qualities were often subverted by the cruder and more unscrupulous aspects of his character. The discrepancy is visible in his writing, in which the lyrical and truly poetic are found alongside uninspired but business-like verse.

Nekrasov's first collection, *Dreams and Sounds* (*Mechty i zvuki*, 1840), was very romantic and derivative. It was strongly criticized by Belinsky, who later arrived at quite a different view of the poet. Nekrasov is chiefly known for the civic theme in his poetry, verse which complements the natural school in prose, as can be seen from one of his contributions to *The Physiology of St. Petersburg*, the poem "The civil servant" ("Chinovnik"). There are many similar "physiological" portraits in his early verse. "In the street" ("Na ulitse," 1850) gives four street scenes and portraits of St. Petersburg types. "The cabby" ("Izvozchik," 1855) portrays both a cabby and a merchant but at the same time also has a strong narrative element. Nekrasov's best poems in this genre, however, are set in the country, where his ear for the rhythms of folk speech and poetry is his strongest asset. In a poem of 1854, "In the village" ("V derevne"), the rhythmic complaints of an old widow who has just lost her son are set against the apparent indifference of the huntsman-author and the hostility of nature, symbolized by the gathering of crows. "The forgotten village" ("Zabytaya derevnya," 1855) raises, through folk speech and authorial irony, the problem of the absentee landlord, whilst "Vlas" (1855) offers a fine portrait of a wandering holy man, a repentant sinner.

In an eight-line poem of 1848, Nekrasov describes the beating of a young peasant woman on the Haymarket Square of St. Petersburg, and concludes: "and I said to my muse – Look, here is your blood sister." This is a telling statement. Throughout Nekrasov's work the lot of women is a constant concern. We see it in "When from the gloom of erring ways" ("Kogda iz mraka zabluzhdeniya," 1845), "The troyka" (1846), "If I drive by night" ("Edu li nochyu," 1847), "In the village," "A heavy cross" ("Tyazhely krest," 1855). In his mature work this concern will produce such masterpieces as *Red-Nosed Frost* of 1863.

Nekrasov's treatment of social themes is not without a suspicion of sentimentality, yet irony here can be a saving grace. Irony is certainly prominent in his parody of Lermontov's "Cradle song" (1845) and in the bitterly satirical "A moral man" ("Nravstvenny chelovek," 1847).

Some of Nekrasov's poems touch a personal theme. Apart from the truly remarkable "Homeland," there is another poem of 1846 written "in imitation of Lermontov" in which the poet links the formative experiences of his childhood and youth to his present behavior, and hopes to be saved by love. This other, darker side, of Nekrasov is frankly expressed in "The reason why I deeply despise myself" ("Ya za to gluboko prezirayu sebya," 1845) and in "I am today in such a gloomy mood" ("Ya segodnya tak grustno nastroen," 1855).

Of the longer poems of this period, "Hunting with hounds" ("Psovaya okhota," 1847) tells of hounds killing a peasant's sheep, and of a huntsman striking a peasant with a whip, as Nekrasov returns to the brutal behavior of his own father. The long poem *Sasha* (1855), written in rhymed couplets, is on the theme of the superfluous man, though the poet places his hope not on him, but on the young girl Sasha who has fallen under his influence. The poem begins with the "homeland" theme – the poet's return to his home and the dark memories it evokes – but some of its best passages are those describing the freedom of a young girl in the Russian countryside. Along with "Homeland" *Sasha* is undoubtedly the peak of Nekrasov's poetic achievement during his early years.

The early poetry of Apollon Maykov (1821–97) is imbued with a classicism derived from Greek and Latin masters. Such poetry –

also written at the time by Fet and Nikolay Shcherbina (1821–69) – is often called "anthological" verse, and represents a conscious attempt to reject the romantically introspective poetry of the previous generation. For all its classicism there is little which has endured in such poetry, although two longer poems of Maykov's earlier period have real merit: *Savonarola* (1851), a poem about the reformer of fifteenth-century Florence which earned Gogol's praise, and the delightful "Fishing" ("Rybnaya lovlya," 1855), with its almost Wordsworthian evocation of nature and man's relationship to it.

The early poetry of Apollon Grigorev (1822–64) treats principally the theme of love and suffering. Like many writers of his generation, Grigorev was influenced by George Sand, although some of his more philosophical poems oppose Freemasonry to egoism. The Petrashevsky circle also had its minor poets: Alexey Pleshcheev (1823–93), Alexander Palm (1822–85), Sergey Durov (1816–69), who apart from lyrical verse also wrote political poetry treating the theme of the heroic struggle in the name of the future happiness of humanity. Herzen's friend Nikolay Ogaryov (1813–77) also wrote poetry in the 1840s and 1850s. Though principally a lyric poet, he also had a strong interest in political themes.

There is a notable hiatus in the theater between the early 1840s and the early 1850s, a fact no doubt connected with its status: although publishing might be in private hands, management of the theaters was a monopoly of the crown. There was a tendency to treat theaters either as pulpits for officially approved views or as purveyors of light entertainments known as vaudevilles.

The gap is between the theater of Gogol and that of Alexander Ostrovsky. In 1836 Gogol had set new standards for the Russian stage with *The Inspector General* and his demand for a more realistic style of acting. The year 1841 saw the publication of a lesser theatrical piece on which he had been working for some time, *Marriage (Zhenitba)*, staged in St. Petersburg in December 1842. Gogol's play deals fairly light-heartedly with a theme prominent at the beginning of his career: the reluctant suitor's fear of marriage. But this work is set in a social milieu new for Gogol, that of the merchant class, and it inaugurated certain motifs which would be developed in the 1850s in Ostrovsky's writing: marriage as a business deal; relationships between wealthy merchants and the impoverished nobility; and a stylistic focus on merchant vocabulary and pithy folk expressions.

Alexander Ostrovsky (1823–86) was born in Zamoskvoreche, the merchant quarter of Moscow. His father worked as an advocate in a court specializing in merchant affairs, and his son left his law studies at Moscow University prematurely to take up a minor post in a Moscow court which dealt with wills and inheritances, later moving to the Moscow Commercial Court. He thus had direct knowledge of legal swindles and merchant practices both from his own experience and that of his father.

Ostrovsky's early prose work *Notes of an Inhabitant of Zamoskvoreche* (*Zapiski zamoskvoretskogo zhitelya*, 1847) is in the manner of the natural school, but he would come into his own in the theater. In 1847 an excerpt from a play later to be called *It's a Family Affair, We'll Settle it Ourselves* (*Svoi lyudi, sochtemsya*) was printed in the *Moscow Flysheet* (*Moskovsky listok*) along with the one act *Scenes of Family Happiness* (*Stseny semeynogo schastya*). Ostrovsky also gave readings of his first full length play, entitled at this stage *The Bankrupt*, to private audiences, where it was well received, and it finally appeared in *The Muscovite* in 1850 under its present title.

The plot obviously derives from Ostrovsky's own professional experience. A merchant, Samson Bolshoy, devises a swindle: he will make his money over to his clerk Podkhalyuzin, who is to marry his daughter and then declare himself bankrupt, but his daughter and his new son-in-law outwit him by keeping the money. In spite of the fact that the play came out in *The Muscovite*, a journal with strong Slavophile leanings, it was viewed as a contribution to the natural school in its uncovering of social abuse. The government reacted strongly to it, placing Ostrovsky under police surveillance and forbidding its staging and all mention of it in the press. When it was allowed to be reprinted in the more relaxed atmosphere of the post-Crimean war period (1859), it was rewritten with a more positive ending.

The play obviously owes much to Gogol. There are no positive characters, and the denouement, like that of *The Inspector General*, derives from the defeat of one set of negative values and characters by another set equally as negative. One of the play's strengths lies in its comic characterization, especially that of the hack legal operator Rispolozhensky, with his permanent inability to refuse vodka. Alcoholism as a motif runs through all the early plays of Ostrovsky, and the use of repetitive catch phrases (e.g. in the case of Rispolozhensky: "I will drink a little glass") is a typical feature of Ostrovsky's comic presentation of character, developed most highly, perhaps, in the figure of Anna Petrovna Nezabudkina in *The Poor Bride*.

There was something of a paradox in the fact that a contributor to a journal identified with "official nationality" had been placed under police surveillance, and on the face of it the negative "natural school" tendency of *It's a Family Affair* did not seem to fit the journal's policy. In 1850 *The Muscovite* was taken over by the so-called "young editors": Apollon Grigorev, Eugene Edelson, Alexey Pisemsky, Boris Almazov, Leo Mey, who eagerly promoted what they saw as the positive aspects of Ostrovsky's writing. They had found a new solution to the problem of *narod-nost*: for them the real bearers of national culture were not so much the peasants as the merchant class, among whom the values of old Russia still subsisted, but in a much richer (literally so) environment. This was a revision of traditional Slavophilism, and the new ideologues found their writer in Ostrovsky. Indeed, in his next full length play to be published in *The Muscovite*, *The Poor Bride* (*Bednaya nevesta*, 1852 – first staged August 1853), critics detected a movement away from the natural school in the direction of the conservative values associated with Pogodin's journal. The play is long by Ostrovsky's standards, with five acts and a great number of characters. The chief asset of Marya Andreevna, the poor bride, is her beauty. She has many suitors, but in the end bows to pressure from her mother to marry an older man, Benevolensky, who has obtained his wealth by dubious means. Though there is a suggestion in the final act that she will reform him, such a conversion seems hardly likely, although it is lent authorial weight in the selection of the name Benevolensky ("Well-wisher"). Meaningful names in the eighteenth-century tradition are typical devices of characterization in Ostrovsky's early plays. Thus Marya Andre-evna's mother, the embodiment of forgetfulness, bears the ironic surname Nezabudkina (Forget-me-not).

The moral ending of the play – the "reconciliation with reality" of Marya Andreevna's self-abnegation and compliance with her mother's will – led radical critics to believe Ostrovsky was abandoning the tenets of the natural school. The period 1852–5 is regarded as that of Ostrovsky's flirtation with the "Slavophile" tendencies of *The Muscovite*. Indeed, in a letter to Pogodin of 1853 Ostrovsky seems to regret his entirely negative portrayal of Russian life in *It's a Family Affair* and hopes the Russian would in future be pleased to see himself portrayed on stage.

A tendency towards more positive folk-characters is observable in Ostrovsky's next play *Don't Sit in Another Man's Sledge (Ne v svoi sani ne sadis)*, produced on stage in January 1853 before it appeared in print. The merchant Rusakov (*rusak* = "Russian") is set against a scheming nobleman, a retired cavalry officer named Vikhorev, who wishes to marry the merchant's daughter for her money. Rusakov outwits the nobleman and, even though his daughter had been temporarily abducted, all is well when the other positive character, the young merchant Borodkin, offers to marry her and saves her reputation. Rusakov's magnanimity is further shown by his gesture of paying Vikhorev's bill at the local inn. A further positive folk element is introduced into the play through the use of songs.

This new lyrical element quite dominates Ostrovsky's next play, the three-act *Poverty is No Crime (Bednost ne porok)*, first produced in January 1854 and published the same year. Folk culture and native entertainment are also quite prominent in it. Apart from songs sung to a guitar, there are: an accordion, a performing bear, a goat, and mummers. Excerpts from a folk tale are recited on stage as well as verses of the folk poet Koltsov; there is a folk game involving rings, references to Slavonic wedding symbolism (a hawk and swans), and a spirited defense of old Russian tradition from the play's central matriarch, Pelageya Egorovna. The plot, however, is much the sort we have seen before. The nubile daughter of a rich merchant is threatened with marriage to an unsuitable older man, Afrikan Savich Korshunov (*korshun* is a bird of prey, a kite), who, however, is not a merchant but a factory owner, and represents new ways. He looks down on local society, and his views influence the bride's father, Gordey Tortsov (the young editors of *The Muscovite*, especially Edelson, saw a clash between old values and false civilisation in the play). The eyes of Gordey Karpych are opened in the final act through a scandal caused by his reprobate brother, Lyubim Tortsov, a very Dostoevskian figure, and the daughter's hand is offered instead to the worthy but indigent Mitya, whom she really loves.

The folk element persists in Ostrovsky's next play, *You Can't Live Just as You Please (Ne tak zhivi kak khochetsya)*, first staged in December 1854 and published the following year. It bears the sub-title "A folk drama in four acts," and we are told that the action takes place at the end of the eighteenth century, and that the play's content is "taken from folk accounts." Again we have the lyrical element of folk song, but the plot is entirely unconvincing. A merchant who is almost permanently drunk is unfaithful to Dasha, his devoted and long suffering wife, but he experiences a sudden change of heart in the final act. His plans to seduce Dunya, the daughter of an innkeeper, have been thwarted by a most unlikely combination of circumstances: his wife, upon running away to her parents, meets them by chance at the very inn where Dunya lives, and Dunya, overhearing their conversation, realizes that her lover is a married man. The moral position of Dasha's parents is clear: a wife cannot leave her husband and her problems are anyway her punishment for eloping in the first place.

All this shows that plot is not of much interest in Ostrovsky, and his denouement is often weak and unconvincing. The sudden conversion of Peter in *You Can't Live Just as You Please* is completely unprepared psychologically; the scandal scene which precipitates the change of heart in *Poverty is No Crime* seems a kind of *deus ex machina* device; and in *The Poor Bride* Ostrovsky seems to be toying with the idea of such a scandal to save his heroine when he suddenly introduces Benevolensky's discarded mistress in the final act, but then he discards the opportunity and sacrifices his heroine to the principle of parental obedience.

Ostrovsky's strength lies in his portrayal of character, his ear for colloquial speech, and his insights into the way of life of a social group. In all this he is close to the natural school, but the new elements of lyricism and folklore which he introduced into his plays in the early 1850s became part of his mature style, and are very much in evidence in his masterpiece *The Storm* (1859). Ostrovsky's comedies are much looser in construction than Gogol's, and in this, as well as in the inclusion of snatches of song, the tuning of guitars, the pauses (Ostrovsky uses the word "silence" rather than "pause"), the theater of Ostrovsky looks forward to that of Chekhov. In addition, Ostrovsky was not only a playwright, he was very much a man of the theater. He took an active part in the production of his own plays, and under his guidance a whole tradition of acting formed at the Maly theater in Moscow, and to some extent also in St. Petersburg: "a school of natural and expressive acting," as he himself called it.

Alexey Pisemsky, also associated with *The Muscovite*, wrote three plays in this period. The best known of them, *The Hypochondriac (Ipokhondrik)*, was published in 1852 but not staged until 1855. Like Ostrovsky, Pisemsky is little interested in plot, and his play is perhaps too long. Its theme is typical of the classical comedy of Molière, but Gogol is the more important influence.

Turgenev's most famous play, *A Month in the Country (Mesyats v derevne)*, written in 1850, for reasons of censorship did not appear in print until 1855 and was not staged until 1872. The work owes a debt to Balzac's *La Marâtre*, but it is based on an emotional triangle which reflects, through Rakitin, something of Turgenev's own position in the Viardot household. The portrait of the young tutor Belyaev is based on Belinsky. Among Turgenev's other short pieces for the stage, the best known is the one-act *Provincial Lady (Provintsialka)*, which was premiered at a benefit performance for the actor Mikhail Shchepkin at the Maly theater in January 1851.

The period 1840–55 is important in Russian life and literature more for what it initiated than for what it achieved. It is a period of paradoxes: a time when ideas were officially discouraged, but one which nevertheless produced the great debates of the Slavophiles and westernizers, as well as the peasant socialism of that cosmopolitan aristocrat Herzen; a period of national self-examination which laid the firm foundations of a national literature; an era of high ideals, yet one obsessed by the baser aspects of Russian life; a time when the legacy of its major writer, Gogol, had to be rescued from Gogol himself; a period of significant works by minor writers and of minor works by major writers; an epoch when prose is supposedly paramount but poetry is no less vigorous, and the Russian theater finds its champion in Ostrovsky. Above all it is a period in which critics and ideas shape literature and point the way to the creation of a great literary tradition.

6

THE NINETEENTH CENTURY: THE AGE OF REALISM, 1855–80

The zenith of Russian realistic prose is treated here as beginning in 1855, a date of political significance, the year in which Nicholas I passed from the scene, but also of literary importance, as the year which saw the publication of Chernyshevsky's *Esthetic Relations of Art to Reality*. That essay formulated the principles upon which literary critics, by then quite numerous, would judge and interpret the literary masterpieces shortly to be produced. Chernyshevsky's was a straightforwardly materialist esthetic, based on the central propositions that "the beautiful is life" and that art is in every meaningful sense inferior to a reality subject to rational comprehension. His critical followers elaborated upon his ideas with such enthusiasm that by 1865 his doctrine had become the dominant critical view. Even those numerous critics and even more numerous writers who rejected Chernyshevsky's approach had to take it into serious account, and in this sense his ideas defined the course of the literary discussion in large measure until about 1870.

The years from 1855 to 1880 were the time when the Russian realists flourished. A mere listing of names is sufficient to make the point: Dostoevsky, Tolstoy, Turgenev, Goncharov, Saltykov-Shchedrin, Pisemsky, Ostrovsky, Leskov – the literary careers of all these reached their peak during this quarter-century. It was also a stimulating period for criticism, with critics of sufficient stature at least to compare with the writers they interpreted: Chernyshevsky, Dobrolyubov and Pisarev among the radicals, Grigorev among their opponents.

The radical critics set forth their own definition of realism as the straightforward, almost scientific description of the underside of existing social reality, an extreme extension of the principles upon which the natural school had operated. They interpreted many of the works of the outstanding realists along such lines, and encouraged the work of radical writers done for the primary purpose of negating existing reality and pointing toward a better future. Among the leading realists Saltykov-Shchedrin was closest to them: Russian reality as he depicts it has only a this-worldly dimension and is meaningless, sordid and utterly depressing. Pisemsky's view of reality was similar to Salty-kov's, although not so extreme: he encountered political difficulties with the radicals of the 1860s when he cast his jaundiced eye not only upon established society but upon the burgeoning revolutionary movement as well. Turgenev took a more balanced, objective approach which retained elements of romanticism in his exquisite feeling for the natural beauties of the world but which has provided us with some of the finest descriptions we have of the society in which he lived: indeed his depiction of the radical personality in *Fathers and Sons* (1862) determined the parameters for the discussion of the radical generation of the 1860s even down to the present day. Like Turgenev, Goncharov was something of a lyrical realist with a sense of the world's beauty and absurdity and a tendency to excuse human weakness, but also an unsurpassed ability to render the very texture of human existence. Tolstoy achieved to a remarkable degree a realism which depicted both the good and evil in human life but which worked to remove the author from the scene entirely: in his earlier works readers often feel that they are perceiving reality unmediatedly, experiencing his characters' emotions without any barriers. Dostoevsky considered himself a "fantastic realist," one who dealt with the crucial moments of human experience and strange personalities, who, he contended, were none the less genuine for being unusual: did not journalism offer us reports of that which was extraordinary but still real? Leskov dealt with similar events – crimes, catastrophes – but primarily as a brilliant narrator and master of an inimitable style, without the psychological or philosophical depth of his contemporaries. In short, in this age of realists, realism had many mansions.

Russian society of the 1860s raised crucial questions for the realists to deal with. Indeed the 1860s brought to the fore nearly all the problems with which modern man has grappled ever since, and it is no accident that of Dostoevsky's four great novels two were both published and set in the 1860s, and the other two set then. The final date for this period, 1880, is the year in which Dostoevsky completed the publication of *The Brothers Karamazov*, a belated novel of the 1860s which many consider his greatest work. The central issue of the 1860s as Dostoevsky saw it was that of belief in God: the radicals rejected religious faith and preached a monistic materialism which led to the negation of the existing order and at least implied advocacy of a future socialist social structure based on economic cooperatives. Their doctrines included a critique of the family and promotion of what we would now call feminism. They propounded not only their critique of the existing society but also their ideas about the future through literature, and especially Chernyshevsky's novel *What is to be Done?* (1863). Radical doctrines were subjected to extensive criticism by Turgenev, Leskov, Goncharov and especially Dostoevsky during the 1860s. Indeed esthetics itself became the focus of intense controversy at this time, since the radicals perceived that the notion that art occupied a sphere superior to reality supported doctrines of philosophical dualism which they thoroughly rejected.

The realist period was also the time of the greatest influence of the "thick journals," as various political and literary camps fought for control of the best of them. The radical camp was grounded primarily in *The Contemporary* and *Russian Word*, and later in *Fatherland Notes*. Most of the leading realists published in the politically conservative *Russian Herald* and in between these two camps there were such centrist publications as the *Library for Reading*. Literary contacts tended to focus on journals, and literary relationships were, unhappily, often distorted by political conviction, in a foreshadowing of the twentieth-century situation.

The 1860s formed the heart of the quarter-century of Russian realism, and its energies – including its dedication to radical politics, its emphasis upon prose, and its denigration of lyric poetry – affected the development of Russian literature for many years after it ended. The 1870s witnessed a diminution of cultural vigor, although several masterpieces – including Tolstoy's *Anna Karenina*, Saltykov's *The Golovlyov Family*, and Dostoevsky's *Brothers Karamazov* – were written during that time. But by 1880 the realist period was drawing to an end. Chernyshevsky, Dobrolyubov and Pisarev had passed from the scene long before; Nekrasov died in 1878, Dostoevsky and Pisemsky in early 1881, Turgenev in 1883. Goncharov had ceased to publish, Saltykov's best work was behind him, and Tolstoy was undergoing a spiritual crisis which led him to condemn all his own earlier work. The year 1881 also witnessed a traumatic political event in the violent assassination of Tsar Alexander II in the middle of his own capital. By 1880 the finest attainments of the greatest period of nineteenth-century Russian literature were almost entirely things of the past.

THE AGE OF REALISM coincided with the reign of Emperor Alexander II and a period of far-reaching reforms. Ascending the throne at the height of the Crimean war, Alexander himself took steps in the immediate post-war period to introduce the most important of these reforms, the emancipation of the serfs. It was generally conceded that serfdom had been a principal reason for Russia's backwardness and a contributory factor in the military defeat of the Crimean war. More aptly, it was recognized that serfdom impeded the growth of modern socio-economic relations. Although the vested interests of the serf-owning nobility led to procrastination and serious delays in the framing of the Emancipation Act, when it was promulgated in 1861 it proved to be a landmark in nineteenth-century Russian history. Despite the imposition of harsh redemption payments, the peasantry were guaranteed certain "rights" and "freedoms," though the Emancipation Act by itself was hardly sufficient to generate a process of modernization.

Since it was feared that change of any kind might unleash revolutionary forces, caution dictated that what had been conceded on the one hand should be clawed back on the other. In place of the power previously exercised over them by the landowning nobility, the peasantry were now made subject to the authority of their communes and assemblies, which in some ways proved more restrictive than that of their former masters. Similarly, to fill the power vacuum, new organs of local government were created, the so called *zemstva* or local councils, which were empowered to see to hospitals, roads and other amenities. The reform process extended to the judiciary (the most enlightened reformative legislation of the period), finances, the universities and the armed forces. In the midst of these changes, which came to be known as the Epoch of Great Reforms (approximately 1856–66) the autocratic principle of central government remained unaltered. The paradox of autocracy in central government while an elective principle (admittedly on a limited franchise excluding the peasantry) was permitted in local government merely highlighted the fundamental injustice of Russian society. No amount of reform could stem the growing demand for political changes to ensure that the mass of the people, meaning chiefly the peasantry, became directly involved in the governmental process.

If the people, the *narod*, had no effective political voice, there was no shortage of intelligentsia voices ready to speak on their behalf. Not that the intelligentsia itself could claim to exercise any real power. In terms of that vague but influential weapon known as public opinion, the different wings of the intelligentsia exercised varying degrees of authority, usually in the teeth of government hostility and always to its annoyance. By far the most influential of the voices heard in Russian public life in the period immediately succeeding the Crimean war was that of a younger generation known as the *raznochintsy*. They received that title because they were the offspring of minor public servants (*raznochintsy* meaning "of various ranks") and of the clergy. They were by and large self-educated, at least so far as their principal ideas were concerned. Disciples of Nikolay Chernyshevsky (1828–89), who, from 1855 onwards, was the dominant member of the editorial board of *The Contemporary*, the leading radical journal of the day, they were initiated into a program of new ideas and attitudes designed to produce a radical change in their thinking. Although political by implication, the change could never be represented as political due to government censorship. Chernyshevsky, therefore, and his younger associate Nikolay Dobrolyubov (1836–61) became skilled in promoting their program by oblique, "Aesopian" means.

Their program aimed to create a generation of young Russians who would reject all received opinion, all the establishment ideas of the older generation, and acknowledge instead only those ideas and concepts consistent with the laws of the natural sciences. In place of God and the established church they revered science and "humanity"; in place of man as body and spirit they took the anthropological view that man and his needs should be understood only in material terms; in the ethical sphere they thought man, as a rational creature, was guided only by self-interest and rational egoism. On the basis of such materialism and utilitarianism they constructed a justification for a "new man" in Russian society, someone motivated to change society in the name of "progress," equality and, above all, socialism. This last aim led to ready acceptance of the idea that such "new men" were to be regarded as "nihilists" prepared to deny all past values, wipe the slate clean and bring about a revolutionary overthrow of the status quo.

Opposed to such "radicals" or "revolutionary democrats" (as they have come to be known in Soviet terminology) was the "liberal" wing of the intelligentsia, those, broadly speaking, of an older generation who looked to the west for inspiration. Theirs was to prove a difficult, middle-ground position. Although Herzen with his fortnightly journal *The Bell (Kolokol)*, published in London and clandestinely distributed in Russia, had assumed the role of their spokesman, many liberals did not share his quasi-socialist, increasingly pro-peasant views. They supported gradual change and were ready to cooperate in the reforms, but they could neither abandon their oppositional role nor commit themselves wholeheartedly to radical change for fear that revolution might endanger their privileged status as landowners. To the far right of such liberalism were the Slavophiles, who abhorred revolution and western influence and fervently advocated that the Russian intelligentsia should return to religious bases of Russian life. Their extreme patriotism exercised great appeal after the Crimean war, though their advocacy of freedom of speeech, not to mention their fondness for wearing outlandish peasant-style costumes, aroused official mistrust and persecution.

Of all the groupings within the intelligentsia who claimed to speak for "the people" – and all, even the ultra-conservatives, made such a claim – none were more actively committed to the task than the nihilists. The revolutionary manifestoes of 1862 and the acts of arson in St. Petersburg were all attributed to them. But the silencing of their main spokesmen – by the death of Dobrolyubov in 1861 and the arrest (in 1862) and exiling (in 1864) of Chernyshevsky – curtailed nihilist influence and even assisted an antinihilist backlash that gained widespread popular support when, in 1866, a young nobleman, Karakozov, attempted to assassinate the tsar. His action, attributable, so he claimed, to the influence of *The Contemporary*, brought the swift suppression of that journal and marked the end of the Epoch of Great Reforms. Meanwhile, as the internal mood of the country changed, so did Russia's role in European affairs. The occasion was the Franco-Prussian war of 1870–1.

For the Russian government that conflict provided a pretext for renouncing those clauses of the Crimean war peace treaty which denied Russia the right to station naval vessels in the Black Sea. This reassertion of a Russian role in the eastern Mediterranean was accompanied by the emergence of a messianic dream of uniting all Orthodox Slavs under a Russian aegis. Panslavism, as the dream was called, came to dominate Russian foreign policy in the 1870s and naturally led to conflict with Turkey. On the other hand, the spectacle of capitalist Europe engaged in the internecine strife of the Franco-Prussian war seemed to confirm the Russian intelligentsia in its growing conviction that Russia should seek a noncapitalist path of development. The intelligentsia became seized by a belief in a morally rejuvenated, agrarian socialist society. This movement, known historically as populism (*narodnichestvo*), was based on a general readiness to see in the liberated Russian peasantry the only means of challenging the tsar's power and achieving the changes which the intelligentsia envisaged. There was no homogeneity of purpose, strictly speaking, in populism. It united many strands of thinking, including anarchism, ideas of moral self-perfection and extreme Jacobinism, but it did assume in certain respects the features of a movement. This manifested itself for the first time on a wide scale in 1874 when several thousand young populists, mostly university students, left the cities and undertook what was known as "a going to the people" (*khozhdenie v narod*). Such a pilgrimage into the countryside, generally apolitical in character, aimed to instil in the peasant masses an awareness of their role in promoting agrarian socialism. That the young populist intellectuals were largely ignorant of peasant obtuseness was hardly surprising; more certain is that they did not anticipate how readily a conservative peasantry would reject their overtures and even cooperate in turning them over to the authorities. Large numbers were arrested and held in detention until the mass trials of 1877. The failure of this phase of populism made sections of the intelligentsia aware that autocracy could only be defeated by political means reinforced by violence.

Until 1876 there had been no organized political party in Russia. In December of that year, at a rally at the Kazan Cathedral in St. Petersburg, the "Land and Freedom" (*Zemlya i volya*) party was formed. Largely clandestine, its aim was initially propagandist, but it sought above all to achieve social justice for the mass of the peasantry. Soon, though, domestic issues were overtaken by the Russian declaration of war against Turkey in April 1877. This so-called "war of liberation" was a direct result of a Panslavist drive to free the Orthodox Slavs in the Balkans from Turkish domination. Russian society gave wide approval to the tsarist government in its new military adventure, but the losses sustained during the prolonged siege of Plevna caused such dismay that the government hoped to distract public opinion by bringing to justice, in large show trials of 50 and 197, the many populists who had been held in jail since the "goings to the people." The result was generally the reverse of what the government had intended. Many of the defendants were acquitted or received light sentences. More seriously, at the conclusion of the second trial, in January 1878, a young noblewoman named Vera Zasulich walked into the office of the Governor-General of St. Petersburg and wounded him with a pistol shot at point-blank range. This violent act, though undertaken with the best of intentions in retribution for the alleged maltreatment of a prisoner, in fact marked the beginning of a new phase in the relations between the oppositional intelligentsia and the government.

Just as the dream of Panslavism ended in the carnage and bloodshed of the Russo-Turkish war, so the dream of a morally rejuvenated society which had so excited the intelligentsia deteriorated into terrorism. Populism has come to be equated in historical terms with the activities of a small, tightly-knit organization of conspiratorial revolutionaries which sprang up within the "Land and Freedom" party and then broke away from it in 1879. Known as "The People's Will" (*Narodnaya volya*), this organization pursued a policy of terrorism aimed at undermining the government and, eventually, destroying the very center of governmental power, the tsar himself. The Executive Committee of "The People's Will" hoped by this means to incite the peasant masses into revolt against tsarism. For a time, during 1880, it appeared that the policy was meeting with some success. The government seemed ready to make concessions, even to the extent of acknowledging the need for a constitution, but on 1 March 1881 the terrorism of "The People's Will" achieved its final bloody triumph when the second of two bomb-throwers inflicted mortal wounds on the tsar after he had stopped to investigate the effects of the first bomb thrown at his carriage on the Catherine Quay in St. Petersburg. The death of Alexander II provoked an instantaneous popular reaction against the terrorists, who were quickly rounded up and eliminated. It ended an era of intelligentsia hopes of changing Russian society by what were known as "great endeavors"; it reinforced the most reactionary and obscurantist elements in Russian society and government; and it so reduced intelligentsia influence by and large that for the next decade and a half the intelligentsia had to be content with working within the framework of existing institutions, particularly the *zemstva*, during an epoch of so-called "small endeavors" (*epokha malykh del*) which received its most sensitive literary depiction in the works of Chekhov.

From national defeat to assassination of the sovereign, from high hopes of reform to the desperation of terrorism, from renunciation of the past in the name of science to anarchic use of the bomb in the name of justice, the reign of Alexander II, the "age of realism," exhibits a fearful symmetry. It can be fairly easily comprehended as a whole, despite its complexities and contradictions. But what features of the history can be said to have contributed to that "realistic" view of life and the human condition which characterized the literature of the age?

In cultural terms it was an age dominated by ideas. Ideas were not only accepted, enthused over and endlessly discussed, they were *lived*. It was in the living enactment of ideas that the Russian intelligentsia discovered its purpose and achieved its greatest influence. In this process literature had a high and noble role, for it served to reflect the ideas, illuminate them and transmit them while also molding them and transforming them – to the extent, it may be argued, of molding the age to its own image. There is more than jest or deliberate irreverence in Oscar Wilde's assertion that "literature always anticipates life. It does not copy it, but molds it to its purpose. The nineteenth century, as we know it, is largely an invention of Balzac." The reign of Alexander II in Russia, as we know it now, is largely an invention of the major novelists, of Turgenev and Tolstoy and Dostoevsky. For want of any official institutions within which public debate of pressing issues could be conducted, the printed word – chiefly in the form of literature and principally in the genre of the novel – served as the only real means of conveying the buzz of implication so essential to the formation of public opinion and a national awareness of problems and purposes.

The "national" issue was of course paramount. Russian literature of the period was a self-examining, self-defining literature, concerned to explore the roots of national experience. Nowhere is this more evident than in the concern for "the people," the interests of the *narod* or peasantry. It is arguable that the emancipation of the serfs was the enactment in life of the hopes for freedom and a new society which had first been engendered in literature, whether in the work of Radishchev at the end of the eighteenth century or in the literature of the 1840s. Apart from the political and socio-economic significance of the event, it presupposed the liberation of new and multitudinous human forces that brought new and altogether larger dimensions to the backdrop against which the literature was to be understood. Consequently, there is in the "realism" an assumption of multiplicity, of spaciousness and depth, to be seen in the sheer plenitude of words or the sheer multitude of persons, lives, relationships and places which the foreground of the fiction subsumes. Hierarchies, or even class differences, seem blurred or diminished to the point of caricature through the literature's profound concern to enfranchise all conditions of humanity, from the highest to the humblest. Freedom, equality and brotherhood may not have existed in the reality of Russian life, but in the "realism" of Russian literature they were the motive forces which determined the veracity of the realism.

Justice in human relations, in determining the degree of guilt between generations, between nations, between the criminal and the law, became an overriding theme in the realistic literature of the age. If justice in social terms was reflected in the literature in a whole variety of ways, justice for the individual, so pronounced an issue in the literature of the earlier decades, became of even greater importance. The individual hero or heroine may no longer have been predominantly of noble birth, just as the authorship and the readership became socially more diversified, but the concern of the greatest works for the inherent value of the individual was the very source of the literature's greatness and its universal appeal. Reinforcement and enhancement of this concern came with growing awareness of the scientific approach to the study of personality, not only through the anthropological principles which guided Chernyshevsky and his followers, but also through a gradually widening acceptance of the complexity and pathology of human psychology. Simplistically it might be supposed that repressive government and consequent social tensions contributed to the emphasis, so marked in the literature, on abnormal psychological states. To many readers Russian "realism" can easily seem a literature populated by abnormal and outlandish figures. Seen in closer relationship to the historical circumstances, the literature may be regarded more justly as concerned with the realities of individual human experience in a spirit of protest, even outrage. It was literature's duty, in pursuit of reality, to enfranchise the

257

eccentric as well as the highest, the murderer as well as the
humblest, the social outcast as well as the positive hero.

In an age so preoccupied with ideas and their enactment in
reality, it was natural that the literature should reflect nihilism and
explore the ultimate meaning of that freedom to which nihilism
laid claim. The literature illustrated the social reality, showed the
transitional condition of life as a semi-feudal society yielded
rapidly to bourgeois capitalist pressures and therefore provided a
"realistic" setting for that revolutionary break with the past which
expressed itself as nihilism. But the literature asserted its own right
as literature to expose the false premises of nihilist thought. Just as
the growing urbanization of human experience, consequent
largely upon the emancipation of the serfs and spread of railways
and industry, became a feature of literary portrayals, so the literature expanded and diversified the frame of reference by increasingly showing the differences between urban and rural in a social-
psychological sense as part of that on-going conflict between new
and old which pervaded the whole character of the age. Much of
the special vitality which attaches to the "realism" of the literature
was due to the conflicting elements that it sought to body forth –
the conflicts, that is, between ideas and generations as well as
between rich and poor, between the sexes as much as between
classes or, in a private and most personal sense, the conflict
between the individual's awareness of self and the realities of the
surrounding world.

In the end Russian literature in the age of realism was most
notable for its special and novel vision of man emancipated
morally and intellectually from his former condition. Whether in
the emancipation of women, nihilistic emancipation through
suicide, the liberation attained through scientific or political conviction, whether in an image of humanity morally renewed
through the re-organization of society or transformed spiritually
through a new awareness of divine purpose, the literature posed
the issue of man freed from the past always in terms of the realities
of choice available to him in an ever-changing age. The "modernity" of Russian nineteenth-century realism must be partly attributable to its vision of humanity as unstable and unsure of itself in
ways which seem especially appropriate to twentieth-century
experience. But the realism was anticipatory in other senses as

well: intended as a blueprint, it served as a warning; celebrating emancipation, it illuminated in sharp relief the image of mankind imprisoned by its own ideologies. Finally, in being related supposedly so closely to the realities of the period, the realism of the literature could hardly avoid penetrating to the limits of what is verifiably real in human experience. The reality often shaded off into fantasy, the conscious into the unconscious, thus heightening the issue of choice facing humanity in its constant will to be, to improve and to outlive.

The polemic about the nature and purpose of literature, its "realism," began with the publication of Chernyshevsky's master's essay *The Esthetic Relations of Art to Reality* (*Esteticheskie otnosheniya iskusstva k deystvitelnosti*) in 1855. Nothing as programmatic or doctrinal as this had appeared in Russian literary theory since Belinsky's "Annual review of literature for 1847," which had determined the policy to be followed by *The Contemporary* under the editorship of Nekrasov. In the years of government repression between 1848 and 1855 the journal had been "liberal" in its orientation, but with the arrival of Chernyshevsky in the mid 1850s and, more particularly, his co-option on to the editorial board of his young protégé Dobrolyubov in 1856, its orientation became markedly more radical and belligerent. Chernyshevsky's dissertation, Feuerbachian and materialist in its approach, asserted that art could never be superior to life, that the true criterion of beauty is life itself, that a beautiful object or work of art serves only to remind man of the beautiful in life as he understands it. Apart from its accent on representationalism in art, Chernyshevsky's theory stressed the democratic, utilitarian purposes which he believed art should serve. More explicitly, he insisted that art should have a didactic role as "a textbook on life" (*uchebnik zhizni*).

Chernyshevsky's disparagement of artistic values *per se* immediately antagonized those of an older generation, particularly Ivan Turgenev and his close friend Paul Annenkov, who cherished Pushkin as the epitome of poetic excellence. In a strictly literary context it was over the legacy of Pushkin that the esthetic polemic became most heated. To Chernyshevsky Gogol was more important than Pushkin because he signified the priority of subject-matter over style in literature. But for Annenkov, Vasily Botkin and Alexander Druzhinin, the leading exponents of what was, broadly speaking, an art-oriented view of literary values, literature should be free from class conflict and topical concerns, and instead embody, as did Pushkin's work, the most elevated Olympian ideals. The freedom of literature was their fundamental concern, even though it might have seemed ultra-conservative. They themselves, driven from the pages of *The Contemporary*, were obliged to curb their ideas to suit such moderate or conservative journals as Mikhail Katkov's *Russian Herald* (*Russky vestnik*) and Andrey Kraevsky's *Fatherland Notes*. But there is no doubt that they saw in Chernyshevsky's programmatic views a serious challenge to artistic values as well as to artistic freedom. Their critical stance and generally their critical writings suffered from vagueness and long-windedness, though this was also true of the most original literary critic of the period, Apollon Grigorev, the advocate of an "organic" criticism which endeavored to pursue a middle way between the topical emphases of the radicals and the pure-art bias of the liberals.

Grigorev believed that criticism should respect literature as an organic growth that reflected essential national traits and aspirations, while also serving to anticipate and guide them. A moral link with the soil and the people, as epitomized by Lavretsky in Turgenev's novel *Home of the Gentry*, was for Grigorev an important element in the organic growth of Russian literature. In contrast to the liberal tendency to interpret Pushkin as Olympian, Grigorev saw him as principally an embodiment of the Russian national spirit. His critical approach, if woolly in its generalities, displayed flashes of originality in its particular treatments of Pushkin's work (his positive appraisal, for example, of Pushkin's prose). He offered valuable assessments of such contemporaries as Ostrovsky, Pisemsky, Goncharov, Turgenev, Nekrasov and Leo Tolstoy. His fondness for "the soil" as a critical concept drew him at the end of his career towards the native soil conservatism (*pochvennichestvo*) of Dostoevsky, in whose journals *Time* (*Vremya*) and *Epoch* (*Epokha*) he published some of his best later criticism, as well as his reminiscences. Indeed, Dostoevsky was to prove to be the most articulate – and certainly the most important – of all the opponents of radicalism, and joined battle especially with Dobrolyubov over the question of realism in literature.

Dostoevsky's publicistic article of 1861 "Mr. -bov and the question of art" ("G. -bov i vopros ob iskusstve") was a concise and well-argued presentation of the issues which divided the radical and liberal parties in the esthetic polemic. For his part, as a writer, he was critical of the radical tendency, epitomized by Dobrolyu-bov, to demand that literature should be concerned only with matters of civic or, by implication, political relevance. It was of the first importance, he insisted,

> not to hedge in art with various aims, not to prescribe laws for it [. . .] The more freely it grows, the more normally it'll develop and the quicker it'll find a real and *useful* way forward [. . .] It has always been true to reality and has always gone hand in hand with the progress and development of man. The ideal of beauty and normality cannot perish in a healthy society [. . .] Beauty is useful because it is beauty, because in humanity there has always been a demand for beauty and its higher ideal. If the ideal of beauty and the need for it are preserved within a people, so is the need for health and normality, and by that means there is a guarantee of that people's higher development.

If such an argument seems unexceptional in its highmindedness and common sense, it was in its time regarded as basically con-servative and therefore dangerous after its fashion; and it attracted scarcely more attention than would a small-scale counter-attack in the face of what amounted to a full-scale invasion. For, though Dostoevsky used all the standard terms in their correct relationship – freedom:usefulness; reality:development; beauty:people – he did not accompany them with the militant trumpet-calls of radical criticism.

There is no doubt that the publicistic activity of Chernyshevsky and Dobrolyubov exercised more influence than any other in the years 1856–61. It was militant in its determination to illuminate the class basis of literature and to prescribe ways in which literature should best serve the interests of the people. Chernyshevsky's review of Turgenev's short story "Asya," for example, entitled "The Russian at the Rendez-vous" ("Russky chelovek na Rendez-vous," 1858), was an attack on the nobility as superfluous in the changed circumstances in Russia after the Crimean war; and an argument that in their place an active type of social leader was needed – the *raznochintsy*, in short. Under the guise of literary criticism Dobrolyubov carried the attack home more vigorously with his brilliant analysis of Goncharov's *Oblomov* in his article "What is Oblomovism?" ("Chto takoe oblomovshchina?," 1859).

This demonstrated that the landowning nobility and the enserfed peasantry were, each in their respective ways, caught in the thralls of a moral compromise and that it was consequently not to the nobility intelligentsia, or the liberal wing of the intelligentsia, that Russian society should look for guidance, but rather to the "new men," the *raznochintsy*. Implicit in such militant literary criticism was a revolutionary intent that stressed the utilitarian importance of subject-matter over form, of the needs of the people over the requirements of art. To be realistic literature had to be close to reality, in the sense of being close to society, and it had to serve the needs of society as the radicals understood them. Dobrolyubov's vigorous and persuasive reviews tended to be tendentious, but not to the exclusion of critical sense. He recognized the tragedy of the heroine's suicide in Ostrovsky's play *The Storm* ("A ray of light in the Kingdom of Darkness" ["Luch sveta v Temnom tsarstve," 1860] or the helplessness of the socially "humiliated and insulted" ("Beaten people" ["Zabitye lyudi," 1861, a review of Dostoevsky's first novel]). All Dobrolyubov's criticism was imbued with a passionate moral protest against social injustice, an impatience with the slowness of change and an urgency about the people's cause heightened by his own failing health that brought about his death at twenty-five.

Chernyshevsky's contribution to the controversy over "realism" was made rather as a novelist than as a critic. Arrested in 1862 and imprisoned in the notorious Peter and Paul fortress in St. Petersburg, he wrote a novel which was then smuggled out of prison, accidentally mislaid, advertised for – of all places – in the *St. Petersburg Police Gazette* and finally published, through a muddle between censors, in *The Contemporary*. Immediately afterwards it was banned for almost half a century, but the deed had been done: the most explicit programmatic statement of "realism" as a life-style had been legally published under a title which could hardly fail to provoke attention – *What is to be Done?* (*Chto delat?*, 1863). Although much of the behavior and talk of the characters seems fatuously earnest nowadays, as a blueprint for social and political change the novel exerted widespread influence and, through its effect on Lenin, contributed directly to changing the world. The themes of female emancipation and cooperative socialist labor principles coalesce in the heroine Vera Pavlovna's role as an *emancipée* and an organizer of sewing workshops, just as her lifestyle is governed by theories of "rational egoism" which prompt her to follow her "real desires" and reject one husband in favor of another. But the "realistic" purposes of the work were best served, firstly, by the heroine's dreams, especially her final dream of an all-aluminum socialist future; and, secondly, by the creation of an epitome of the "new man," the revolutionary hero of the future, Rakhmetov, who devotes himself wholeheartedly to a rigorous program of self-discipline and self-improvement ("rigorism") designed to convert him into "the flower of the best people, the movers of the movers, the salt of the salt of the earth." Under the leadership of such supermen, so Chernyshevsky's message goes, the dream of the socialist future will become reality.

The appeal of such "realism," for all its covert romanticism and utopianism, was far-reaching. In the decade and a half after the publication of *What is to be Done?* in 1863, Russian literature contrived both to emulate the novel's effect, if not consciously then by implication, in its pursuit of the ideal of a positive hero, and to counteract the novel's influence, its assertion of a scientific and rational basis to human conduct, by attacking it as a philosophy and denouncing it as socially and politically opportunist. The practical message of the novel as a utilitarian tract received its most ardent support from Dmitry Pisarev (1840–68), the most obviously "nihilistic" of the critics of the 1860s. He turned the journal *Russian Word* (*Russkoe slovo*) into a democratic organ and, even though arrested in 1862, continued to write for it over the four years of his imprisonment. Although eloquent in his advocacy of such practical social types as Bazarov, the hero of Turgenev's *Fathers and Sons*, whom he celebrated as "realists" – i.e. intelligentsia activists with a scientific understanding of society's needs who would play the role of a "thinking proletariat" – Pisarev was not an advocate of political revolution. He believed society, and above all the mass of the people, could be transformed through socio-economic change, but he denounced whatever stood in the way of such change more outspokenly than had any of his predecessors, and his call to hit out right and left at whatever seemed socially useless *sounded* more revolutionary than it actually was. His most notorious hatchet job was performed on Pushkin's reputation and Belinsky's support of it, and then he carried his more general, nihilistic attack on esthetics to an ultimate extreme by demanding their total destruction in "The destruction of esthetics" ("Razrushenie estetiki," 1865). By contrast with all this blood and thunder, his critical manner, like his dress and deportment (he was of nobility origin), was often elegant, and redeemed by a nicely honed cutting edge of humor and sarcasm.

With Pisarev's death in 1868 the polemic over esthetics virtually ended. "Realism" had become so firmly entrenched as the literary manner of the age that, with the increasing politicization of the intelligentsia and the spread of ideas in society at large, the issues with which the literature dealt tended naturally to reflect – usually objectively, sometimes critically – the main topical concerns of the day. For example, the *Historical Letters* (*Istoricheskie pisma*) of Peter Lavrov (1823–1900), which appeared in 1868–9, held out to the younger generation of the intelligentsia the ideal of the "critically thinking personality." This ideal presupposed chiefly that the intelligentsia as a whole, though in particular the nobility intelligentsia, had incurred a moral debt to the people which could only be repaid by actively assisting the people to free themselves from economic oppression and ignorance. The theory advanced by Nikolay Mikhaylovsky (1842–1904) in his article of 1869 "What is progress?" ("Chto takoe progress?") assisted the process by promoting a "subjective sociology," meaning a view of social progress which emphasized the individual. In combination, Lavrov's and Mikhaylovsky's views provided a theoretical basis for the intelligentsia's repudiation of capitalism and division of labor, a justification of their almost religious belief in the peasant commune and their need to "repent" before the peasantry (hence the title "repentant noblemen"), and a pretext, if not an actual program, for their "going to the people." These – the basic moral assumptions of populism – informed and influenced the literature. Along with them, however, there was also a violent streak, best represented by the anarchist Mikhail Bakunin (1814–76), who argued a strong and attractive case for regarding the Russian peasantry as innately revolutionary and communistic; or by Peter Tkachov (1844–85), who asserted that revolution could not be left to the peasantry but had to be implemented by a dedicated elite in a Blanquist takeover of political power. In the popular mind, and for literary purposes, such incendiarism was epitomized by Sergey Nechaev (1847–72), the young protégé of Bakunin and author of the most radical document of the age, "The Catechism of a Revolutionary." His extreme revolutionism – or the illusion of such commitment which he contrived to convey – illustrated the apocalyptic aspects of populism satirized so bitterly by Dostoevsky in *The Possessed*.

The connection between literature and revolution found its clearest expression in the life and literary activity of Sergey Kravchinsky (1851–95), known popularly as "Stepniak." Although his literary reputation was created later, it was in 1878 that he stabbed to death the St. Petersburg Chief of Police in broad daylight and thus became notorious as a revolutionary terrorist. He was acting, he claimed, not against the government as such but against its interference in the rightful struggle of the people against the hated bourgeoisie. After escaping abroad, he lived mostly in London, where he acquired an honorable reputation as a chronicler of the Russian revolutionary movement (*Underground Russia*, 1882) and the author of the first Russian revolutionary novel (*The Career of a Nihilist*, 1889).

But the increased politicizing of values also gave rise to a gradual, if less intense, reaction to such pressures. Although the influence of Konstantin Leontev (1831–91) was not felt strongly until later, in 1871–2 he published his manifesto "Byzantinism and Slavdom" ("Vizantizm i slavyanstvo") and began to acquire a reputation as a fiercely eloquent advocate of the esthetic and sensuous in art allied to religious feeling, or in bitter conflict with it. Leontev's challenge to the simplistic, prescriptive character of "realism" showed up its inadequacies and yet highlighted the reality of spiritual experience. This was also to be the role of the leading philosopher of the period, Vladimir Solovyov (1853–1900).

"I will speak," wrote Solovyov in the opening of his famous "Lectures on Godmanhood" (1878), "about the truths of positive religion [. . .]" In doing so he was greatly enlarging the meaning of "realism" in ways which appealed particularly to the greatest novelist of the period, Dostoevsky, and which were to inspire the intelligentsia when it was confronted at the turn of the century with the dialectical and historical materialism of Marx. Solovyov's theosophical idealism, although channelled for a considerable part of his career into a lively concern for the establishment of a free theocracy, which failed ultimately and degenerated into a pessimistic vision of the Antichrist, was an inspired and visionary teaching about the spiritual potential of humanity. In some of its fundamental tenets it drew upon the views of the early Slavophiles. In certain of its more esoteric principles it verged on mysticism. Its potency as a doctrine relevant to the realities of its time was largely attributable to its messianic vision of the role Russia should play in rebutting western influence and synthesizing east and west. But Solovyov's boldness in defying materialism involved a reassertion of the spiritual values in life that exercised a growing appeal for an intelligentsia disillusioned by the facile scientism of the 1860s and the terrorism of the 1870s. Central to Solovyov's thought was the idea that religion should be "the link connecting man and the world with an absolute principle and the focal point of all that exists." His philosophy aimed to achieve a unity of man and the world based on an identification not between man–become–God (in the Feuerbachian sense) but between God and man in a human–divine unity: hence his emphasis on God-manhood.

The principle of unity enshrined in Solovyov's thinking reflected a tendency apparent in the literature as well: a sense that reconciliation and unification, not rift and revolution, were the prime needs of Russian society and therefore essential for a realistic view of life. Such reconciliation of necessity implied an awareness of religious values, and the incorporation of religious values into the realistic view proved to be a major enhancement of the literature as a whole. It contributed to that vision of a liberated humanity which can be regarded as the supreme achievement of Russian literature in the nineteenth century.

The esthetic polemic between "realism" and the values of pure art was nowhere more violent than in poetry. Here there existed a relatively clear line between those poets who upheld the ideals of pure art and those who believed that poetry, like all literature, should serve a civic purpose. On the whole, though, Russian poetry in this period was mediocre. There were several minor talents of some interest, and one poet of real stature, Nekrasov, but the general mood of the age was not conducive to poetic endeavor and tended to distort such poetic strains as strove to emerge.

The "art for art's sake" school of poetry was represented by Afanasy Fet (Shenshin), Fyodor Tyutchev, Alexey Konstantinovich Tolstoy, Yakov Polonsky, and Apollon Maykov.

Fet, a close friend of Leo Tolstoy and Ivan Turgenev, was a lyric and nature poet of considerable distinction, even though his range rarely extended beyond the short poem couched in emotional terms. His belief in poetry and the poet as a means of transmitting a sense of transcendental beauty and thereby giving expression to ideal values was reinforced by the sheer melodiousness of his own lyrical gift. This naturally led to many of his poems being set to music – by Tchaikovsky and Rimsky-Korsakov among others. But the poet was also a seer in a literal sense: Fet maintained that the poet was one "who sees in an object something that without him another will not see." And Fet literally "saw into" nature with remarkable sensitivity, expressing in unforgettable poems the atmosphere of springtime, evening, thunder or the sea, and always there was a sense, for all the absence of an actual addressee, that he was writing a love poem. Though not experimental, he sometimes showed an authoritative boldness in technique, as can be seen from a three-stanza poem of 1858 in which each stanza concludes with a one-word line. The first verse runs:

We went through the wood by the only way
  At darkling eventide.
I saw how the western sky quivered and the day
  Died.

[Lesom my shli po tropinke edinstvennoy
  V pozdny i sumrachny chas.
Ya posmotrel: zapad s drozhyie tainstvennoy
  Gas.]

Here the impact of the single-syllable "gas" is only partly conveyed by the English "died," and yet it suffices to suggest the miniaturist power of Fet's achievement. That achievement received widespread recognition with the publication of a collection of Fet's poems in 1856, but in the following quarter of a century his reputation became less secure both because his output diminished and because he remained a steadfast advocate of the beautiful, rather than the civic, as the sole ideal to which poetry should aspire. That advocacy naturally brought him into conflict with the radical critics, whose unfair mockery of his lyrical manner caused his original work to decrease to no more than a trickle of lyrical poems from the late 1860s to the end of the 1870s.

Even so, some of Fet's loveliest pieces date from this period. The impressionistic evocation of the power of music is striking in his beautiful poem "The singer" ("Pevitse," 1857), in which he asks that a singer's voice should carry off his heart into a resonant distance, where sorrow smiles shyly as love, and he will ever ascend along a silvery path, light as the fugitive shadow of a bird's wing. For Fet, his poetic muse rose above the mundane and everyday. Almost defiantly he proclaimed himself, not a citizen in a civic sense, but "an eternal citizen of a youthful world" ("The quail's cry..." ["Krichat perepela...," 1859]) in which the twin poles of nature – the sea and stars – become a balm for all human ills ("Sea and stars" ["More i zvezdy," 1859]).

The influence of Schelling's thought may be felt in some of Fet's work, but more conspicuous at this period is the impact of Arthur Schopenhauer, several of whose works, particularly *The World as Will and Idea*, Fet would translate into Russian. The consequence for his poetry was ever greater emphasis on the dreamlike ephemerality of life. In a notable two-part poem of 1864, "Tormented by life..." ("Izmuchen zhiznyu..."), which bears an epigraph from Schopenhauer, Fet celebrated the dream of life as beatified by a sense of eternity, and described himself as looking out of time into the eternal. Increasingly he became, not a celebrant of the momentarily experienced beauty of life, but the seer of an eternal beauty beyond life's limits.

Equally as small-scale as Fet's, but possessing in precision and detailed implication something of the appeal of a Fabergé ornament, was the poetry of Tyutchev's last years. In the post-Crimean-war period his reputation as a poet began to reach a wider public, but it still remained limited and specialized. Some of his finest nature lyrics belong to this period, among them the beautiful celebration of early autumn (dated 22 August 1857) which begins with the verse:

There is at autumn's opening
A short but wondrous time –

The days are still as crystal
And the evenings full of light . . .

The intimation of the ephemeral in that "short but wondrous
time" of early autumn had a personal meaning for Tyutchev in his
poetry of this period. Although the brief cycle of poems devoted to
his "last love" date from the beginning of the 1850s, when he first
met Elena Deniseva, they culminate in the most profoundly
poignant of them devoted to her death in 1864. The first and last
stanzas of that poem illustrate the nearly unbearable heartbreak
which accompanied her passing:

All day she lay unconscious,
And all of her was drowned in darkness.
Warm summer rain poured down – its streams
    Pattering happily among the leaves.
[. . . . . .]
You loved, and to love as you did
No one's ever yet succeeded!
O God! . . . To outlive this
And not have one's heart in pieces . . .

If the counterpoint of the "happily" pattering rain accompanying
her death beautifully suggests the bittersweet sadness of the
moment, the words addressed to her in the last stanza refer not
only to the depth of her love but also to the tragic irony of the
poet's survival. Loneliness, impermanency, an autumnal sense of
the approach of death naturally become the private themes of
Tyutchev's last poems. Though he also composed political verse,
of generally inferior quality, the anguished irony of his address to a
Russia of wretched settlements and impoverished nature, "the
homeland of longsuffering" (from "These poor settlements" ["Eti
bednye selenya," 1855]) is matched towards the end of his life by
the bitter notion that nature is a Sphinx destroying man all the
more surely because there never was any ultimate riddle to be
discovered ("Nature is a Sphinx" ["Priroda – sfinks," 1869]). Yet
the harshness of nature could also seem illusory for Tyutchev, as in
a beautiful poem of 1865 which speaks of a singing in the sea's
waves, a harmony within the strife of nature, whereas only in
man's supposed freedom is discord discernible. Tyutchev's love

poetry and his philosophical nature lyrics, often as multifaceted as diamonds, remain his supreme legacy and the enduring source of his very special appeal.

The work of Alexey Konstantinovich Tolstoy (1817–75) (a distant cousin of the more famous Leo Tolstoy) has not lasted as well. A dramatic trilogy – *The Death of Ivan The Terrible* (*Smert Ivana groznogo*, 1866), *Tsar Fyodor* (1868), and *Tsar Boris* (1870) – formed the core of his reputation, but what now survives is his fame as a folksy balladeer, sometimes enlivened by a rumbustious humor (he contributed to the creation of Kozma Prutkov, an invented satirical poet). His nature lyrics have an old-fashioned charm. Polonsky was a poet of genuine gifts, particularly successful in the expression of deep feeling in his more personal poetry, but he acceded to the demand for ideological substance and consequently wrote poems of dubious worth on topical issues, such as a poem of 1878 on an imprisoned girl ("Uznitsa") which obviously refers to Vera Zasulich or other young female populists imprisoned at the time. Maykov's work was by contrast more consistent, although in its elevated lyrical pantheism it contrived to reflect the divide between east and west. His major work, a tragedy entitled *Two Worlds* (*Dva mira*, 1872), exemplifies this divide. As with all those so far mentioned, Maykov attained his greatest success when he aspired to achieve least. Pretentiousness marked these poets' grandest endeavours, but their occasional pieces composed in response to nature or the most honest of feelings have survived.

Of nobility background, usually wealthy, such dwellers on the slopes of Parnassus were naturally defensive when confronted by the vigorous poetry of Nikolay Nekrasov. Throughout his career Nekrasov was at the center of Russian literary life, first as the editor of *The Contemporary* from 1847 to 1866, when it was closed after Karakozov's attempt to assassinate the tsar, and secondly as the editor of *Fatherland Notes* from 1868. Having a shrewd eye for new talent, he published the early work of all his most illustrious contemporaries, but after the Crimean war he associated himself deliberately with the radicals and turned his poetry into a crusading weapon on their behalf. He declared himself a "Poet-citizen" (as the Citizen tells the Poet in the poetic dialogue "Poet and Citizen" ["Poet i grazhdanin"] of 1856: "You need not be a poet, but it's your duty to be a citizen"), and he therefore consciously repudiated Parnassus in order to make his poetry serve civic needs.

Immediately after the Crimean war Nekrasov sought to express the anguish of the peasantry. In a series of poems, long and short, he portrayed the misery accompanying the injustice of serfdom and the iniquity of the bureaucracy that exercised wanton power over the people. His extraordinary facility for meter and rhyme can often give the impression that his poetry resembles verse, and the unpretentious, unpoetic diction, designed so clearly for recitation, can produce an effect of rollicking which undermines and even parodies the poetry's avowed seriousness of intention. This effect can be felt even in his most intimate poems, especially his introspective and self-pitying love poems. As a result there is some justice in the judgement of the pre-revolutionary critic Vladimir Kranikhfeld that Nekrasov's poetry "affects the reader like a strong narcotic: in small doses it excites and arouses, but taken in large doses it is tiring." By contrast with other contemporary poets he lacked a sense of proportion. But it was precisely such Russian breadth of spirit in the service of large themes that redeemed the prosaic feel of his poetry and endowed it with genuine grandeur. Apart from the theme of peasant suffering and the peasant's lament for his lot, his topics included the intelligentsia, his lifelong love for his mother (always contrasted with the boorish insensitivity of his father), touching portrayals of the exiled Decembrist wives, and his own partly uprooted social condition as a son of the nobility who had deliberately renounced his birthright. He exhibited a bitter satirical manner on occasion. This picture of his life would not be complete without mention of the fact that he was hugely fond of gambling, good food and women.

Nekrasov's place in Russian poetry must rest largely on his major achievements in the last two decades of his life: his masterpiece *Red Nosed Frost* (*Moroz krasny-nos*, 1863) and his long unfinished poem on the state of Russia after the emancipation of the serfs, *Who Can Be Happy and Free in Russia?* (*Komu na Rusi zhit khorosho?*). The former is a remarkably powerful and well-sustained work in two parts describing the life and sorrows of a peasant woman, Darya. In part one she recalls the happiness of her life, her marriage, the death of her husband and the ensuing hardship. In the second part, while collecting wood in the depths of the freezing forest she encounters the King Frost of peasant legend and freezes to death in her dream of peasant happiness, caught monumentally in the poem's final statement:

> And Darya stood and froze
> In her enchanted dream . . .

A master of bouncy ternary metres, Nekrasov here succeeded in conveying through his metrical jauntiness the poignancy of Darya's life and death. A similar jauntiness informed the confident Prologue and Part I of his long unfinished poem about seven peasants searching for a happy man in Russia. As the work progressed Nekrasov proved unable to sustain either his manner or the theme, and it lost coherence. Parts, such as the section entitled "The feast for the whole world," have vigor and excitement; others are flat. Such unevenness characterized Nekrasov's achievement as a whole, and yet at his funeral, after an orator compared him to Pushkin and Lermontov, voices from the crowd shouted "Higher! Higher!" That his greatness does not match that of his famous predecessors must now be recognized. His poetry had a crude, cumulative power through its sheer stridency, and in its pursuit of civic themes at the expense of poetic sensibility it legitimized in Russian literature the priority of matter over form which has since been largely endorsed by the public posturing of Vladimir Mayakovsky's "loudspeaker" manner and so much of the officially approved poetry of socialist realism.

Disciples of Nekrasov as much as of Koltsov were the so-called "self-taught" peasant poets first given public prominence by Ivan Surikov (1841–80) in 1872. Their poetry, of amateur standard, was mostly devoted to melancholy themes of peasant heartache and despair; when it did not strive too earnestly to be literary, it possessed a moving simplicity. The poetry associated with the revolutionary populism of the 1870s has by contrast a generally highflown rhetorical manner which merely exposes its inherent mediocrity.

If mediocrity tended to be the dominant state of Russian poetry in this period, then in the drama there was a rising tide of realism which promised – even if it did not entirely achieve – the establishment of a vigorous and outstanding tradition of Russian realistic theater. One reason for the drama's relative failure was repressive governmental control and censorship. Although works of considerable dramatic power were written, often they remained unpublished or – more seriously – unproduced for long periods, so that the laboratory experience of reformulation so essential to the development of a lively theater was denied to the majority of playwrights. The theaters were for the most part dominated by actor-managers or stars and the plays often had to suit their tastes, but in the case of the actor-manager Mikhail Shchepkin (1788–1863), who became responsible for the Maly theater in Moscow, realistic drama was venerated almost religiously, and accorded the highest standards of acting and production. Even so, Russian realistic drama of the mid nineteenth century has not travelled well. Although works from this period remain extremely popular in the repertoires of Soviet theaters, they have not enjoyed the same popularity in the west. They seem indeed to illustrate one of the principal differences between east and west: whereas Russian audiences have an insatiable appetite for the strong meat of realistic drama, in the west such fare can be box-office poison.

The close association between drama and prose literature is demonstrated by the fact that two dramatists who qualify for mention in this period were better known as novelists. Mikhail Saltykov-Shchedrin composed his satirical comedy *The Death of Pazukhin* (*Smert Pazukhina*) in 1857, and it has remained popular ever since. Certain features of death-bed farce, concerning the last will and testament of a dying millionaire, combine with caricatured portrayals of such stock types as a grasping son, dim daughter and an avaricious official to suggest not only the evils of human greed but also, and more specifically, the anti-social cynicism of an ultimately triumphant merchant class. The farcical elements make the message palatable, but the bitterness of Saltykov's censure cannot be concealed. Of equally keen social relevance was the drama of 1859 *A Bitter Fate* (*Gorkaya sudbina*) by Alexey Pisemsky. A realistic work about a peasant who returns to his village from St. Petersburg to discover that his wife has had a child by the local landowner, it explores in social and psychological terms the complexities, as well as the inevitabilities, of the moral and class divisions created by serfdom. The peasant murders the child but finally repents of his crime. The fact that the wife genuinely loves the landowner for his tenderness, and that the peasant's portrait is given moral and psychological depth, endows the play with unusual subtlety. In the history of realistic Russian drama this is the only major play except Leo Tolstoy's *The Power of Darkness* (1886) to deal with a peasant theme, and this must partly account for its enduring place in Soviet theatrical repertoires.

The most unusual playwright to achieve prominence in this period was Alexander Sukhovo-Kobylin (1817–1903). Born to wealth and privilege, he came face to face with the seamier aspects of Russian bureaucratic practice when he was accused of murdering his mistress and spent seven years endeavoring to exonerate himself. The cynicism engendered by the experience expressed itself in a trilogy of plays – *Krechinsky's Wedding* (*Svadba Krechinskogo*, 1854), *The Case* (*Delo*, 1861) and *The Death of Tarelkin* (*Smert Tarelkina*, 1869) – all loosely linked together, although only the first enjoyed the success of immediate stage production in Moscow (1855) and St. Petersburg (1856). The second play achieved only a partial production in 1882 and did not become fully known until after 1917; the third, and most difficult, has never been a popular success. But Sukhovo-Kobylin had a remarkable and original dramatic talent that might have proved more durable had he been allowed to cultivate his craft in workshop circumstances. As it was, he remained aloof from theatrical life and spent his last years in total obscurity.

Based on French comedy conventions, *Krechinsky's Wedding* was written while the playwright was in prison. It tells of Krechinsky's attempt by unscrupulous means to regain social status through marriage to the daughter of a wealthy landowner. The craving for money governs all his actions, as it does those of his associate Rasplyuev. The latter proves a tenuous but characteristic link between the parts of the trilogy. If the second play depicts a venal bureaucracy cooking up a "case" against the landowner, then in the third part any distinction between good and bad disappears in a black farce in which Rasplyuev, the epitome of cynical careerism, achieves a grotesquely shabby victory.

Alexey Potekhin (1829–1908) was another minor novelist who became popular as a playwright, and Nikolay Leskov (1831–95) may also be included in such a list for his play *The Spendthrift* (*Rastochitel*, 1867). However, the dominant figure of the period was Alexander Ostrovsky. Virtually singlehanded, as the author of forty-seven original plays in the space of forty years, he created a Russian realistic theater, so that such international reputation as attaches to Russian drama of the age of realism is largely due to him.

Although his first works earned him popularity in the preceding decade, it was only in 1855 with his comedy *Your Drink – My Hangover* (*V chuzhom piru pokhmele*) that he first introduced the *samodur* type in the figure of the merchant Bruskov. *Samodurstvo*, or the self-arrogated right of the newly rich merchant class to tyrannize over others, became the hallmark of the "dark kingdom" (Dobrolyubov's phrase) of Russian merchant life, against which, in terms of Ostrovsky's drama, the only protest was the assertion of other, more intelligent and more sensitive norms of behavior which did not depend on money to be effective. The petty tyrannies of merchant coarseness, money, bureaucratic dishonesty and careerism (as in the play *A Profitable Post* [*Dokhodnoe mesto*, 1858]), so clearly representative of the larger political tyranny of tsarism, were opposed by the moral rebellion of the educated but dispossessed, the honest but impoverished. Ostrovsky's picture of Russian life in the period before the emancipation of the serfs does not suggest that conditions could be genuinely alleviated by official means. But when his approach transcended such essentially national, though important, concerns and introduced a tragic element into the picture, he achieved his masterpiece, *The Storm* (*Groza*, 1859).

Set on the banks of the Volga in a small town of unchanging patriarchal habits, *The Storm* offers an explosive confrontation between the twin extremes of old-fashioned, ritualistic conformity to tradition and a naively trusting and creative faith in an ideal of human dignity and freedom. The extremes are exemplified by Kabanikha, an archetypical mother-in-law figure of such domineering and small-minded self-righteousness that she borders on caricature, and Katerina, her daughter-in-law, a dreamy, attractive girl consumed by religious inspiration and visions of future happiness. The girl's challenge to the ritualized life of her mother-in-law's house takes the form of a desire to rise above it, to escape in flight, but the solace of dreams proves ineffective and eventually, in desperation, her flight becomes more literal as she flees to the banks of the Volga and drowns herself. Though this may be the core of the play, in dramatic terms the confrontation is heightened by an ensemble of secondary characters who mirror or like a chorus interpret the larger meanings of the work, emphasizing the contrasts between rationalism and spontaneity, dogma and emotional ardor, the minor tragedy of Katerina's individual revolt and the broader inferred tragedy of the national condition. Such contrasts are augmented by the movement of scene from stuffy domestic setting to the panorama of the Volga, just as particular national issues develop into the universality of Katerina's tragedy as a symbol of the eternal revolt of youth against age, spontaneity against conformity.

Ostrovsky never achieved a greater success than *The Storm*, although in the ensuing quarter century he wrote such fine plays as *The Forest* (*Les*, 1871) about provincial actors, and the verse drama *Snegurochka* (1873) (*The Snow Maiden*, used by Rimsky-Korsakov as the basis of his opera of the same title) on utopian themes. Historical dramas and comedies came almost annually from his pen. He showed a mastery of language unequalled among his contemporaries, and he did much to ensure that the Russian theater became enriched by generations of actors devoted to the realistic playing of the manifold roles he created.

The Soviet critic Lydia Lotman has said that "Ostrovsky served as a kind of go-between between Russia's great realistic literature and its mass public." There is a twofold truth here. Not only did Ostrovsky provide a mass auditorium for the major themes of the realistic, social-psychological literature, but his realistic drama also served as a model for the prose literature in the emphasis given not so much to narrative as to social setting, not to plot, strictly speaking, so much as to psychological portraiture, not to the free flow of the chronicle so much as to the sudden revelation of the dramatic moment, not to exclusive enhancement of hero or heroine so much as to the meticulous representation of ensemble worlds. The conventions of the realistic theater, in short, were discernible, though masked by the freedoms of a novelist's prerogative, in the disciplines governing the form of the Russian realistic novel.

The period 1855–69, broadly speaking known as "the sixties," saw the realistic novel emerge as the dominant literary genre. All the major examples were published initially in the so-called "fat journals" – chiefly *The Contemporary* (until its suppression in 1866), *Fatherland Notes*, *The Russian Herald* and *The Russian Word* (also suppressed in 1866) – each of which enjoyed a circulation of a few thousands at most. Separate editions usually followed, which naturally increased the readership; but it has to be stressed that in a population numbered in tens of millions the readership for the literature could be numbered in tens of thousands and was confined largely to the two capitals and the major urban centers. Although the 1860s were notable for the democratization of the literature, it was a process best measured in quality and kind rather than scale. The radical intelligentsia, represented by the *razno-chintsy*, made their first mark in the literature at this time, as did peasant writers, though in a limited way. Still, their work usually took the form of the sketch or short, often fragmentary, prose piece, and when it aspired to larger scale it grew formless and sometimes turgid. The most notable of these minor writers were Nikolay Pomyalovsky (1835–63), Vasily Sleptsov (1836–78), Gleb Uspensky (1843–1902), Fyodor Reshetnikov (1841–71) and Alexander Levitov (1835–77). Their achievement on the fringes of the major literature showed the democratic process at work, but its slightness also highlighted the true greatness of the dominant genre, the realistic novel.

Pomyalovsky's was a somber, introspective talent, embittered by a seminary upbringing and finally destroyed by depression and alcohol. His most famous work, *Seminary Sketches* (*Ocherki bursy*, 1862–3), is a harrowing account of the cruel and inhuman education meted out to boys in training for the priesthood. Less powerful, and no doubt less truthful, were the two novella-type works, *Bourgeois Happiness* (*Meshchanskoe schaste*, 1861) and its sequel of the same year, *Molotov*. The influence of Turgenev can be detected in both works, but Pomyalovsky's depiction of a young *raznochinets* confronted by the blandishments of bourgeois life has a sentimental, apologetic air and the censure of contemporary reality provided by the "nihilist" Cherevanin, with his "graveyard philosophy," is incredible in its pessimism.

Sleptsov's reputation rests chiefly on his short novel *Hard Times* (*Trudnoe vremya*, 1865), which also owes something to Turgenev in that it depicts a radical nihilist similar to Turgenev's Bazarov, although Sleptsov's Ryazanov, portrayed as unduly stern in his censoriousness, discovers that it is indeed hard to stimulate interest in radical ideas in post-emancipation Russia. Sleptsov himself, actively associated with the organization of revolutionary communes, was arrested after the Karakozov affair of 1866, and the conditions of his imprisonment seriously impaired his health. *Hard Times* may be regarded as one of the minor works that contributed to the development of the revolutionary novel in Russian literature in the wake of Chernyshevsky's *What is to be Done?*

The work by which Gleb Uspensky is now best remembered is his collection of sketches entitled *Manners of Rasteryaeva Street* (*Nravy Rasteryaevoy ulitsy*, 1866), based on the town of Tula and describing with particular sensibility the plight of the urban poor. Craftsmen, poor officials and petit-bourgeois tradespeople were the focus of Uspensky's attention, though towards the end of the 1860s, in his cycle of stories *Ruin* (*Razorenie*, 1869–71), he began depicting the working class and the peasantry. His realism was documentary and unremitting in its exposure of social evils. His older namesake Nikolay Uspensky (1837–89), a cousin of his, was a protégé of Chernyshevsky's and received radical applause for his compassionate and unadorned stories depicting peasant poverty and vulnerability to exploitation. Reshetnikov gained a reputation for portraying in harsh but concrete terms the condition of the peasantry in the Perm region with the publication in 1864 of his *Podlipovtsy*. Later in his career he depicted working conditions and industrial unrest among miners in the Urals. A somber writer, he won the approval of the left-wing intelligentsia, but that approval was usually granted all documentary-style writers. Among these the most popular was Levitov. His stories of urban and rural poverty have an unembellished realism notable for an expert use of lower-class language. He led an itinerant, poverty-stricken life reflected in his work in a formlessness bordering on improvization.

Such concentration on *byt*, the seamy side of social conditions, was characteristic of a prose literature given over principally to realistic exposure of social injustice. The political implications of such realism, however covert for censorship reasons, were food and drink to the disaffected younger intelligentsia of the *raznochintsy*. They sought to act, to *do*, on the pattern suggested by *What is to be Done?* If that novel was obviously revolutionary and invited literature to play a revolutionary role in changing society, then in fact its most immediate literary consequence was – politically – the exact opposite: a string of reactionary novels, of dubious quality, attacking nihilism. The antinihilist novels of the 1860s were basically pamphlet works hastily cobbled together with poorly developed and often far-fetched plot-lines designed to do no more than expose the nihilists as unscrupulous, uncaring and unpatriotic. Among the most prominent examples of these were Pisemsky's *Troubled Seas* (*Vzbalamuchennoe more*, 1863), Leskov's *No Way Out* (*Nekuda*, 1864) and *At Daggers Drawn* (*Na nozhakh*, 1870–1), Victor Klyushnikov's *Mirage* (*Marevo*, 1864), Vsevolod Krestovsky's *Panurge's Herd* (*Panurgovo stado*, 1869) and Ivan Goncharov's *The Precipice* (*Obryv*, 1869). They comprised the most obvious and topical contributions in literature to the polemic between old and new, between generations and attitudes, which inspired and permeated the 1860s as a whole, but almost all the major works mirrored the polemic as well – and were indeed the product of it – in one form or another. The greatest novels, of course, transcended the topical and gave the polemic a realistic perspective in historical, ideological and, by implication, political terms.

No single body of writing contributed more to this process than the remarkable memoirs composed by Alexander Herzen in his emigration in London and Switzerland between 1852 and 1868. Entitled *My Past and Thoughts* (*Byloe i dumy*), they are among the most sparkling and perceptive political memoirs written in nineteenth-century Europe. Their picture of the early years of the Russian intelligentsia, the 1830s and the 1840s, conveys with love and insight the enthusiasm of the handful of intelligent individuals who made up "the men of the 1840s." Masterly in his power of evoking character in lively thumbnail sketches, Herzen combined the merits of a superb diarist with the metaphorical eloquence of a very acute, if disillusioned, political commentator. Inclined to slip up over details, often sardonic, forgivably subjective in the treatment of personal matters, he contributed both to Russian literature itself and to its source material as a chronicle of the Russian intelligentsia by evoking the intellectual spirit of the 1840s when he, a committed westernizer, broke with the Slavophiles and became isolated even from many of his friends through his decision to emigrate. He was not an exile by nature, but his exile allowed him to preserve his "free voice" as a publicist even if he could not exercise such a direct influence on opinion in Russia as did the censored literature. Herzen in large part supplied the record of the real political experience of the intelligentsia which the realistic novels endeavored to depict in generalizing, typical forms through fictional heroes and heroines.

Ivan Turgenev reached the height of his fame in Russia between 1855 and 1862, by expanding the form of the sketch and short story into the form of the short novel. Exile to his estate between 1852 and 1856, combined with the fact of the defeat of Nicholas I's Russia in the Crimean war, led him not only to rethink his own attitude to his literary work but also made him realize the extent to which the experience and the role of his own generation of the 1840s had been overtaken by events. It was more by accident than intention that he became renowned as a chronicler of the Russian intelligentsia, just as in some ways his reputation as champion of the peasantry was accidental. The main difference between the two roles was that, in the case of the peasantry, he was hardly ever more than an observer, whereas in chronicling the development of the intelligentsia from the 1840s to the 1860s, he was inevitably engaged in a process akin to writing autobiography, with an attendant need to objectify his personal preferences and dislikes. The genre of the short novel as it evolved at his hands proved to be an admirable vehicle for portraying successive types of representative heroes and heroines. The simplicity of its construction may nowadays make it seem unsophisticated and dated, but it was always elaborate enough as a form to suggest the atmosphere of the times, the summer climate of the settings and the tragi-comic poignancy of love denied and hopes forsaken.

A certain formulaic pattern is discernible in the Turgenevan novel. Each of his novels is "placed," whether it be in a country house in the Russian provinces, a number of closely-knit provincial locales or a provincial resort (such as Baden-Baden in *Smoke*); and each of his novels, in terms of fictional chronology, is usually "a month in the country" or at least fairly limited in time-scale: the experience of his only major play seems to have influenced him in the construction of his novels. They are all concerned with the effect of a character from outside upon the characters in the "place" of the fiction; and the reader, informed about the secondary characters by biographical excerpts, witnesses the events occurring in the "place" as if he were watching a stage performance. The developing relationship between the hero from outside and the heroine of the "place" involves a love anticipated and then abandoned, but the resultant scrutiny of both sets in relief in particular the personality and ideas of the stranger-hero, his typical features, his message and his inherent worth.

Rudin, Turgenev's first novel, written just after the end of the Crimean war and first published in *The Contemporary* in 1856, tells the story of the unexpected arrival of Dmitry Rudin at a country house in the Russian provinces where his eloquence and the novelty of his ideas immediately capture the attention of the assembled guests. He is lionized and persuaded to stay for a time. Soon the heroine Natalya, daughter of the lady of the house, falls in love with him. When their relationship becomes known, Rudin fails to live up to her youthful convictions and can say only that they must "submit to fate," meaning that he must leave. That he does, ignominiously, and the rest of his story is a saga of failures until, in a final epilogue (added in 1860), he redeems himself – and becomes the first revolutionary hero in Russian fiction – by laying down his life on the Paris barricades of 1848. Rudin's portrait can thus be seen as a study in failure which, though illustrated by a conventional love story, tragically demonstrates the inability of "the men of the 1840s" to rise above eloquence and act upon their ideas. But the total effect of the portrayal is more memorable than this. It is a subtle, multifaceted examination of the plight of the "superfluous man" intellectual, a man genuinely committed to ideas but genuinely incapable of implementing them, who is confronted by the still more devastating truth that the divide between his head and his heart makes him ineffectual in love, inept in relationships and superfluous in his own time.

Some of Turgenev's friends thought the portrait, bearing so close a resemblance to Bakunin's, too harsh. In any case, permitted once more to go abroad and renew his attachment to Pauline Viardot, Turgenev turned to themes of love in such characteristic stories as "Faust" (1856), "Asya" (1858) and his finest, "First Love" ("Pervaya lyubov," 1860), a brilliantly evocative study in nostalgia. It was his novels, though, that represented the true landmarks in his achievement. Of these his second, *Home of the*

Gentry (*Dvoryanskoe gnezdo*, 1859), proved to be the most characteristic, least controversial and most popular.

The hero Lavretsky's return to his "nest," his gentry home, symbolizes the anguished reassessment of their view of Russia undertaken by Turgenev's generation after the Crimean war. His disorienting, western-style education, designed by his father to force his Russian spirit into the straitjacket of a supposed Anglomane ideal, makes Lavretsky as rootless and "cosmopolitan" as Rudin, but through his love for the heroine, Liza, he senses his deep, even religious, need for reconciliation with his birthright. Though ultimately heartbroken, he accepts in the end that his destiny is to do no more than "plow the land" in humble service to his country and his people. Turgenev, always by conviction a westernizer, here demonstrates his objectivity as a writer by his sympathetic portrayal of the religious, Slavophile traits in his heroine. Liza has a nun-like innocence and calm which can seem unbearably mawkish, especially in the love-scenes with Lavretsky, but her purity merges with the soft, evocative atmosphere of the novel as a kind of music. Music is a clue to the novel's meaning. The ecstatic music of the elderly German music teacher Lemm suggests the spell exerted by Liza's religious presence, whereas the showy Parisian music favored by Lavretsky's wife, who is thought to be dead but suddenly returns to destroy his happiness, is as meretricious as the superficial westernism of the socialite Panshin, Lavretsky's rival. The hero's story has a valedictory character, for in it Turgenev was bidding farewell to his own generation, and the elegiac tone of the whole novel marks the end of a phase in his evolution as a novelist.

Turgenev's next two novels were devoted to portrayal of the new, post-Crimean war generation of the intelligentsia. Conscious of his role as a social chronicler, Turgenev could hardly fail to notice the clamor for positive heroes which arose from the radical publicists, but he was by inclination opposed to it, and when he sought to define this new phenomenon he resorted to a universalizing contrast between the twin poles of human personality and experience, those of Hamlet and Don Quixote. In a lecture of 1860, "Hamlet and Don Quixote," he suggested that human beings seemed to be divisible into those who, like Hamlet, were introspective but incapable of action and therefore tragic in their egoism, and those like Don Quixote who were extrovert but little given to reflection and therefore predominantly comic in their altruism. If he had previously been inclined to concentrate on Hamlet types, to which his somewhat reflective character naturally inclined him, he now deliberately set himself the task of portraying the Quixotic traits in the younger generation of the intelligentsia. His strong-minded young heroines, who had always posed a challenge to the moral fiber of his heroes, now acquired a political purposefulness which translated itself into defiant action in the case of Elena of his third novel, *On the Eve* (*Nakanune*, 1860).

The "eve" referred to here obviously meant the eve of the emancipation of the serfs, although in the fiction itself it had to do with the beginnings of the Crimean war. In fact this novel, though more loosely constructed and therefore less satisfactory than any other Turgenevan novel, is important as a watershed in Turgenev's development because it is not a chronicle of the past so much as an attempt to grapple with issues of topical relevance to Russian society. The emphasis on youthful rejection of received opinion is seen in Elena's case to mean not only the rejection of her parents' standards but also the rejection of the moral standards of Russian society as a whole. Her decision to accompany the Bulgarian revolutionary Insarov on his fruitless exploit of national liberation demonstrated her generation's readiness to employ revolutionary means in achieving their ends. Their love story, though, must seem one-sided and contrived. Insarov is shallow and improbable as a piece of characterization, despite the attempt to give him some sort of verisimilitude as a type of *raznochinets*, and even if Elena herself is the most fully-drawn of all Turgenev's heroines to date, she is devoid of interest as an ideological figure. Ideas find fuller expression in the contrast between the aspiring professor, Bersenev, and the dilettante artist Shubin (a fairly simplistic illustration of the contrast between Quixotic altruism and Hamletic egoism), who can be regarded as the type of choices which face Elena in Russian society. She rejects them, chooses her Bulgarian revolutionary and, in anticipating happiness, falls victim to what can only be defined as a growing philosophical pessimism in Turgenev's world-view. Insarov dies in Venice – by no means the last such literary death – and Elena disappears after setting out for Bulgaria, determined to pursue his cause of national liberation.

In so identifying the new, optimistic, youthful forces at work in Russian society, Turgenev seemingly could not avoid balancing the picture by suggesting that all such attempts to change the world were doomed, that personal happiness was impossible and that, in any truly realistic appraisal of the world, death ultimately awaited all heroism.

On the Eve aroused bitter reproaches from Dobrolyubov for the author's failure to paint a more positive picture of the younger generation. Turgenev was understandably aggrieved by such a reception of his work. In August 1860, while staying for three weeks in Ventnor on the Isle of Wight, where he was ostensibly engaged in discussing the future of Russia on the eve of the emancipation of the serfs, he planned a novel that would portray a new type of hero, a "nihilist," as he called him, one truly representative in his view of the younger, scientific generation. He appears to have conceived of his hero initially as "a dying man," but allied to this were two more positive traits: his apostolic, educative role and his possible function as "a pendant to Pugachov," meaning as a revolutionary. What in fact eventually emerged from the three wet and stormy weeks of his stay in Ventnor was the greatest of his literary creations, the figure of Bazarov, hero of his greatest novel *Fathers and Sons* (*Ottsy i deti*, 1862).

The novel is set in 1859 in three different locales – the run-down Kirsanov estate of Marino, the wealthy estate of Nikolskoe belonging to the widow Odintsova, and the modest homestead of Bazarov's elderly parents. The three locales can be seen as stages in the evolving portrayal of the one figure in the fiction who, strictly speaking, belongs to none of them – Bazarov himself. He arrives unannounced and unanticipated in this country setting in the company of Arkady Kirsanov. Both are on vacation from university, but if Arkady is at least at home at Marino, Bazarov is portrayed as the stranger who eccentrically addresses the servants on familiar terms, sports unusual clothes and occasionally absents himself on little expeditions to collect frogs for dissection. Training to become a doctor, in the Marino setting Bazarov is chiefly novel as an apostle of nihilism, or one of the "new men" who reject all authority save that justified by the laws of the natural sciences. He engages in a bitter controversy with Arkady's uncle,

Paul Kirsanov, over such questions as idealization of the peasantry, esthetics, parliamentarianism, the "isms" of highminded liberal conviction and the purpose of science. Bazarov's position is one of denial. He is not concerned with principles and ideals so much as with practical economics and social welfare, but the nub of the controversy is civilization itself, for his spirit of nihilistic denial was likely to lead to the use of force and thus cause irreparable damage to all the civilized values which Turgenev and his generation cherished.

In the confrontation at Marino between the generations of the intelligentsia, between the older generation of the "fathers" represented by Paul Kirsanov and the younger generation of "children" represented by Bazarov, ideological victory clearly goes to the latter. Quixotic, anti-romantic, hard-headed, practical, Bazarov is victorious mainly as a representative of the *raznochintsy*, as one of non-noble background. If his heroism at this stage is defined principally in social and ideological terms, the shift to Nikolskoe after his meeting with the attractive young widow Odintsova highlights his all-too-human frailty as a man in love and forced to acknowledge the romanticism in his nature. Idolized though he may be by Arkady and by his own father, a retired army doctor, Bazarov recognizes only too clearly when he finally reaches his parental home how insignificant he is in relation to nature and eternity, and the moral of his musings reflects both the philosophy of Pascal and Turgenev's own pessimistic assumption that man is but the creature of a single day. Bazarov's significance – and his portrait – is fully sketched during the return visits which he makes to each locale: at Marino, where he finally triumphs over his opponent Paul Kirsanov in a farcical duel; at Nikolskoe, where it is acknowledged that he and Odintsova do not need each other and it is not his destiny to find happiness in love; and at his parental home where, recognizing that his is to be a lonely destiny of service to the peasantry, he assists his father in his medical practice, contracts typhus during an autopsy and dies.

The death of Bazarov is a masterpiece of Turgenev's art. Though obviously a final pessimistic verdict on such a strong hero, it also endows his portrait with the dimension of tragedy. Bazarov's is a tragic death not only in its accidental futility, in the extinguishing of a life so full of hope, but also in its suggestion of

Bazarov's superfluity, as if in his arrogance he had stolen forbidden fire and suffered the punishment of all mortals. Yet Bazarov's significance is manifold. As an apotheosis of scientific respect for truth, as an epitome of human self-sufficiency and independence, as a threat of technocratic Jacobinism, as a vision of human perfectibility, Bazarov was supremely a new figure, typical of his age yet possessing finely drawn individual characteristics of brashness, egoism, evenhandedness and honesty. In terms of his objectivity as a chronicler of his time Turgenev never achieved anything finer.

Of all Bazarov's traits Turgenev claimed that he abhorred only his anti-estheticism, yet it was precisely this quality, allied to his practical, utilitarian realism, which endeared him as a type to the radical critic Pisarev. In general, though, the reception given Bazarov by both left- and right-wing opinion was so unfavorable and misguided that Turgenev decided to abandon Russia and make his home in Germany, in Baden-Baden, where he could be close to Pauline Viardot. For the rest of his life he chose for himself a state of "absenteeism," as he was later to call it. This meant that from 1862 until the end of the decade his work embodied much overt criticism of his own country, accompanied by an increasingly pessimistic, Schopenhauerian view of the human condition. Moreover, he became increasingly isolated. It is arguable that he, of all the leading members of his generation, remained true to his westernist convictions in the sense that his belief in the need for Russia to learn from Europe never altered substantially, whereas Herzen, the acknowledged spokesman of liberal westernism, compromised his westernist ideals by dismissing Europe as bourgeois and by emphasizing the socialist and revolutionary potential of the Russian peasantry. Shortly after the publication of *Fathers and Sons* Turgenev and Herzen quarrelled more or less publicly over this very issue. To Turgenev the only real possibility of beneficial change in Russia lay with the educated classes; to Herzen it lay with the peasantry. But Turgenev viewed the Russian peasantry as fundamentally conservative, and he could never see them as a progressive social force. Symptomatic of his general pessimism at this time were his short prose pieces "Phantoms" ("Prizraki," 1863) and "Enough!" ("Dovolno!," 1864), which represented a sad contrast in their slightness with the achievement of his novels. However, his own position, both as a writer and as a leader of intelligentsia opinion, became clear in his fifth novel *Smoke* (*Dym*, 1867).

Smoke is the only one of Turgenev's novels not to have a Russian setting. It is set in Baden-Baden in the summer of 1862 and tells of a couple of weeks which the hero, Litvinov, spends there, during which time he meets Russians of both left-wing and right-wing persuasion while also encountering a former love of his, Irina. This "second love" forces him into a betrayal of his fiancée. Finally he returns to Russia heartbroken and embittered: "suddenly everything seemed to him to resemble smoke – everything, his own life, Russian life, everything human, especially everything Russian." Indeed, if on the emotional level Litvinov's involvements seem shallow – for as a hero he is deliberately made to appear ordinary and intermediary in his role – then on the level of ideological polemic *Smoke* is the most caustic and pessimistic of all Turgenev's works, and as a condemnation of all things Russian it is one of the most explicit such statements in Russian literature, comparable to Peter Chaadaev's first "Philosophical Letter." Turgenev uses his novel in many respects as a pamphlet with the object of attacking the extremes of left-wing and right-wing opinion and expressing his own views through the figure of Potugin. Left-wing opinion, with its idolatrous attitude toward the peasant commune as a nucleus of socialism, and right-wing pleas for as little change as possible are both dismissed as dotty, while Potugin's analysis of the Russian need to be led and Russia's love-hate relationship with the west arouses Turgenev's evident approval. His political gradualism expressed itself through Potugin's insistence on the need to respect European *civilization* and ensure that whatever was done in Russia should have an educative, European character.

Largely due to the weakness of its central figure, *Smoke* has neither the strength nor cohesion of *Fathers and Sons*, but in its evocation of the small-town world of Baden-Baden, its venomously satirical character-vignettes and, above all, its depiction of the passion of "second love" as dark and soul-destroying it illustrates very fully the somber aspect of Turgenev's talent. Angered, frustrated and isolated, he chose – as Dostoevsky taunted during a bitter quarrel of 1867 between them – to look at Russia through his telescope. Turgenev's vision was acute in its perception of the self-deluding tendencies at work among the intelligentsia. His readiness, though, to criticize Russia from afar was offensive not only to Dostoevsky, it smacked of sour grapes to the public at large. In any case, advocacy of European superiority was hardly calculated to bring him widespread popularity at a time when educated Russian opinion was becoming attracted to essentially native, populist solutions to the national problem. Turgenev, so clearsighted in his realism as fictional chronicler of the evolving intelligentsia scene, had neither the stomach nor the gift for polemic, save in short needle-sharp thrusts, and polemic had become the very climate in which Russian literature existed by the end of the 1860s.

Ivan Goncharov has achieved international renown as the author of *Oblomov* (1859), the archetypal Russian realistic novel containing the portrait of the archetypal Russian landowner of the nineteenth century, the epitome of slothfulness. No Russian writer did more than Goncharov to achieve the cumulative, brick-by-brick effect of realistic grandeur that now attaches to the reputation of the nineteenth-century Russian realistic novel. He did it not consciously, let alone with any intention of creating a universal image for his times, but intuitively, partly out of his own experience, partly out of an awareness of the transitional period through which Russian society was passing. Yet the abiding impression of his achievement is one of an inevitable accumulation of detail, of *Kleinmalerei* artfully used to suggest the whole genesis of a way of life as well as its present state, and in the unhurried exposition of all the *realia* of his fiction a moral coloring enters the picture that hints at, but never underscores, the intent of the realism. Stillness appears to be the greatest achievement of his literary art, and that in itself is remarkable enough, but the stillness can soon be understood to conceal the vital susurration and abundant ticking of a life ready to emerge from some chrysalis state; or perhaps that distant subterranean sound is the faintest echo of tremors in the body politic that may eventually be recorded on a Richter scale of social unrest. Goncharov did not know; he simply transmitted them unobtrusively through his art.

Goncharov took a larger view of his art as a novelist than any Russian writer before him, including Turgenev. To him Turgenev pencilled in or sketched his novels, no more, whereas Goncharov liked to claim that he *painted*, he used brushwork. It was a sign of a literature's maturity, in his view, that it should explain life to its readers through the genre of the novel, "within whose frame are encompassed large episodes in life, sometimes an entire life, in which, as in a large picture, any reader will find something close and familiar to him." He therefore painted his novels on a large canvas, and the visual criteria which dominated his art served also to explain the transitional process that he sought to depict in his triptych of novels, *An Ordinary Story*, *Oblomov* and *The Precipice*, books he later described as *galleries* which showed the passage of Russian social consciousness from romanticism to realism. The central "gallery" was *Oblomov*, which depicted "The Sleep" of Russian life, while the third "gallery" and novel depicted "The Awakening." Although there may have been a certain amount of objective truth in this claim, this particular transition was as much a part of Goncharov's autobiography as it was a part of Russian life.

Goncharov experienced the trauma of transition as literal physical transference from the placid provincial world of his Simbirsk birthplace to the St. Petersburg where, due to his unprivileged status as a member of the merchant class, he was forced to make a career for himself. For some thirty years he was a civil servant, and for part of that time a government censor. His was on the surface a life without major events, with no marriage, no children, a life of contented, well-upholstered bachelorhood. It is therefore surprising to realize that Goncharov probably saw more of the world at large than any of his illustrious contemporaries on the literary scene. For in 1852 he joined the voyage of a Russian ship, the frigate *Pallas*, to the Far East and spent about three years in circumnavigating the globe. From this came one of the most brilliant examples of literary travelogue in Russian literature, *The Frigate Pallas* (*Fregat Pallada*, 1858). Shrewd and yet always sympathetically observant, Goncharov looked at the world with the eye of a provincial Russian hoping to discover the exotic, only to be constantly confounded by the uniformly mundane, western-influenced and pedestrian character of foreign reality. The English presence, in the shape of the black-coated, umbrella-ed English colonialist, dispelled all illusions of romance in faraway places, no matter how greatly Goncharov admired the Japanese or painted his picture of assorted ports of call with rich pigments. If the experience of government service in the Russian capital had first set the steel of realism in his soul, his trip round the world sealed it there. But it did not extinguish within him a nostalgia for some remote, romantic, provincial paradise of his own devising.

The publication in 1849 of "Oblomov's Dream" provided the nucleus of this nostalgia. Within the novel as a whole "Oblomov's Dream" is the culmination of the first part, a detailed set scene which "places" Oblomov in the setting of his St. Petersburg apartment and establishes once and for all his essentially static image of slothfulness and indecision. The novel, though, is more than this. Between the creation of "Oblomov's Dream," first published in 1849, and his completion of the novel ten years later, Goncharov not only went round the world, but also spent seven weeks in Marienbad in 1857 when he wrote the last three parts almost at one sitting. The consequence was that the novel as a whole divides into two appreciably different segments, the first being theatrical in form, with Oblomov presented to us scenically in the squalor of his St. Petersburg apartment leading a "dressing-gown existence." The second is a more conventional novel form of the love-story type which tells of the hero's relations with Olga, their eventual parting and Oblomov's return to his former state of near-hibernation in the company of the peasant woman Pshenit-syna who becomes his wife. In the course of this twofold presentation of his hero Goncharov succeeded in establishing new norms of literary portraiture in the Russian realistic novel. Oblomov is depicted for us virtually from boyhood to death, in almost a whole life-cycle. But even though the scale of the portraiture may be greatly enlarged by this means, the status of the hero as socially superfluous receives greater depth of meaning through Goncharov's emphasis on the enduring significance of that romantic nucleus which Oblomov epitomizes, which is both his fatal flaw and his glowing memorial. Partly through this Oblomov acquires his universal appeal; partly through this, censure of the hero becomes justification, and his humanity outlives the socio-political meaning attaching to his name.

Oblomov's portrayal in the first part of the novel consists of a slow, multifaceted description of the hero through a succession of encounters between him and his serf Zakhar, his visitors "from the cold" (who tend to represent the typical attitudes of urban society), and finally his friend Stolz, the "positive hero," who terms the malaise from which Oblomov is suffering "Oblomovism." This manner of static portraiture naturally highlights the image of Oblomov as slothful. Reinforced by his clumsily adoring manservant Zakhar in his belief that he is not like the rest of mankind, Oblomov may well seem to be the product of a semifeudal society in the last stages of decay. But the comicality of this self-deluding state is offset by the latent sense that Oblomov, in opting out of such supposedly purposeful activities as those engaged in by his visitors, is asserting a basic human right to be himself, to pursue that dream of innocent pleasure devoid of adult responsibility which Stolz categorizes as "Oblomovism." That the very cossetings of Oblomovka, his home, may have made him an eternally dependent being must be seen as one aspect of his problem. But the ethos of Oblomovka lends his life a cyclical pattern, a roundness, perhaps even a completeness. At the heart of his Oblomovism is a dream of paradise. Though it makes him impractical and irrelevant where reality is concerned, this dream transcends time and history, and ultimately proves redemptive.

Andrey Stolz, Oblomov's half-German friend, may represent the virtues of hard work and commercial good sense which Oblomov manifestly lacks, but even if he, like Olga, whom he eventually marries, can be said to typify the future awaiting an awakened Russia, the focus of the novel is always on Oblomov. His is always the more interesting of the portrayals even during his protracted and finally unsuccessful courtship of Olga. Indeed, tedium enters the narrative at this point, just as Oblomov yawns despite himself while in Olga's company. When they part, it is as if he had deliberately chosen to return to his hibernation. His life spirals suddenly downwards into the vegetative idyll of his final years; and when he dies it was as if he had been a clock that someone had forgotten to wind up. He moves literally to the other side of the tracks in a social sense in his marriage to Pshenitsyna, but Stolz's final verdict on his friend places things in perspective: Oblomov's "is a crystal, pellucid soul," he says. "There are few people like that; they are rare; they are pearls among the crowd!" Oblomov's sheer niceness, which beguiled even his creator, one feels, infuses his whole image with a childlike honesty, making all other human types and aspirations seem shabby by comparison, even though the pathology of his ingrown laziness can never be denied.

Goncharov's own pathology as a writer expressed itself not only in his hero, but also in his ill-founded accusations of plagiarism brought against Turgenev in the late 1850s. His final novel, a very poor work by comparison with *Oblomov*, may have aimed to challenge Turgenev's mastery as a socio-political chronicler, but in fact grew into a protracted, dialogue-dominated saga which uneasily mixed art, love, seduction and politics. *The Precipice* can claim a reader's attention for the character of Raysky, an artist and dilettante who seeks out his own provincial paradise (his name has "paradise" at its root), only to find that Vera, the object of his attentions, is beset in her paradise by two other suitors, Tushin, the good landowner, and Mark Volokhov, the nihilist, by whom she is eventually seduced. Her "fall" is the only crisis in the novel. The introduction of an imitation of Bazarov in the figure of Volokhov is incongruously accompanied by a fairly phallic symbolism of gun-toting and other sexually suggestive parallels, such as the taboo associated with the "ravine" or "precipice" of the novel's title, where Vera, the "faith" of Old Russia (*vera* means faith), succumbs, if only momentarily, to the physical blandishments of the new morality. The "old morality" epitomized by the presiding matriarch, the grandmother or *babushka*, Tatyana Markovna, is not strong enough to protect Vera from such temptations, though in the end she is forgiven and Tushin, the conventionally "good" figure in this unsubtle allegory, comes to her rescue. The whole narrative has a generally flowing effect and is often felicitious in the imperfective languorousness of its prose manner, but it is also tedious and at moments of emotional intensity sadly melodramatic.

Goncharov's reputation is secure as the author of his masterpiece *Oblomov*, but his third novel reveals the dangers to which realism was heir. Though it is much more than an antinihilist novel, its courting of politics to the detriment of art illustrated how the chronicle form demanded of the novelist all the arts associated with fiction as well as the ability to understand history. Goncharov's gifts lay rather in the transmutation of subjective experience into a brilliant static image, the universality of which has become imperishably his legacy.

The understanding of history depended naturally on many factors, but of these the evocation of the past in the form of realistic reconstruction of past times and issues was among the most significant. Sergey Aksakov (1791–1859), the father of the leading Slavophiles Konstantin and Ivan Aksakov, was an outstanding example of an autobiographer and memoirist who transcended the subjective limitations of such genres and in his obvious masterpieces *A Family Chronicle* (*Semeynaya khronika*, 1856) and *Years of Childhood* (*Detskie gody Bagrova-vnuka*, 1858) succeeded in achieving remarkable recreations of the past. *A Family Chronicle* was based on Aksakov family lore, but evoked with astonishing immediacy and understanding the life of the serf-owning nobility in eighteenth-century Russia. No rural idyll – it depicted the suffering of the peasantry due to the enforced transfer of the Bagrov estate from Simbirsk province to Ufa as well as the harshness of the more unscrupulous landowners – Aksakov's chronicle combined magnificently a seemingly truthful account of past times with a Slavophile-inspired approval of the patriarchalism and social solidarity that marked serf-owning Russia in its heyday. The portraits of Aksakov's mother and father were lovingly drawn, beautifully observed studies of figures from a patriarchal past, whereas the detailed self-portraiture of *Years of Childhood* depicted, with lucid charm, the true world of Oblomovka as Aksakov experienced it. It also contributed to that concern for the portrayal of evolving character which had become a significant feature of the realism of the period.

The chronicle form accompanied evolving portrayal of character in the novel that first brought literary recognition to Alexey Pisemsky. His long novel of 1858 *A Thousand Souls* (*Tysyacha dush*) concentrated on the rise and fall of an ambitious young man from the provinces, Kalinovich, who contracts an unhappy marriage to a wealthy woman with the aim of gaining a toehold on the bureaucratic ladder. Though he eventually rises to governor, his reformative plans are blunted by a venal local nobility and he is finally brought low. Kalinovich's story is on the whole more interesting than his character. He certainly gains in stature as the novel progresses, but his central role is often subordinated to the portrayal of other figures who illustrate the greed, ambition and corruption in Russian society. As a novel designed to expose such ills, *A Thousand Souls* achieved considerable popularity in its time. However, when Pisemsky went on to attack nihilism in his avowedly pamphlet-style novel *Troubled Seas* of 1863, his popularity waned almost to zero, which in the case of this novel was not without justice, but it meant that a serious injustice was later done to his talent through the neglect of his interesting novel *Men of the 1840s* (*Lyudi sorokovykh godov*, 1869) and his work of the 1870s.

A similar fate befell the reputation of Nikolay Leskov. Scarcely had he begun his literary career than, in 1862, he stung the radical press into unremitting hostility by seeming to suggest that the disturbances of that year were due to nihilist agitation. Though many editorial doors closed upon him, he steadily attracted popularity through vigorous, racily written *skaz*-type stories, in which the personality and social origin of the narrator or "teller" (hence the term *skaz*) colored the narrative manner. Such stories of 1863 as "The Musk-ox" ("Ovtsebyk") and "The Life of a Peasant-woman" ("Zhitie odnoy baby"), whether dealing with the unhappy character of a religious dissident or the miserable life of a peasant girl forced into the martyrdom of a cruel marriage, showed the unusual range of subject-matter and the realistic compassion of which Leskov was capable. Never successful as a novelist, he contributed to the polemics of the period with his *No Way Out* (1864), a flawed but outspoken political novel attacking radicalism and liberalism. When he was less ambitious in scope, as in the extended short-story form, he created masterpieces. The most famous of his stories is "Lady Macbeth of the Mtsensk District" ("Ledi Makbet Mtsenskogo uezda," 1865), the basis for Dmitry Shostakovich's opera. A fast moving story of passion and murder, it eschews all politics or even social comment, but succeeds in creating memorable, sharply sketched characters and episodes drawn from merchant life. Leskov's knowledge of the less familiar sides of Russian life, including the milieu of Old Believers and the clergy, suited his eccentric narrative skills.

But for all the acuteness of his vision, Leskov was no satirist; that was the province of Mikhail Saltykov-Shchedrin. Exiled to Vyatka in 1848, he served as a bureaucrat in the provincial administration and based his first major published work, *Provincial Sketches* (*Gubernskie ocherki*, 1856–7), on his experiences. His satire of the bureaucracy was merciless but always laced with humor.

During most of the 1860s he alternated journalism with government service, and paradoxically managed to satirize while serving for some years. Finally he was forced to resign, and by the late 1860s, after the closure of *The Contemporary*, he became the leading editor of the new citadel of radical journalism, *Fatherland Notes*. It was in this journal that he published his finest work.

For the ten years 1855–65 Leo Tolstoy (1828–1910) was groping his way towards the masterpiece of historical fiction with which his name is now chiefly associated, *War and Peace* (*Voyna i mir*, completed 1869). Without that masterpiece his reputation in 'the 1860s' would be minor. A few outstanding short studies, mostly autobiographical, and one or two longer works of exceptional power comprise his achievement in these years, but it is only with the aid of hindsight that one may ascribe to them any real importance, let alone greatness. They show the way forward but without giving more than a hint of what was to come.

At the end of the Crimean war, which the young Count Tolstoy knew at first hand as an artillery officer, he went to St. Petersburg, was lionized, taken up by Turgenev and recognized as a new star in the literary firmament of the capital. His brilliant *Childhood* (*Detstvo*, 1852) had already earned him popularity and his remarkable first-hand reportage from Sevastopol, the *Sevastopol Stories*, was winning him new admirers. But his St. Petersburg hosts soon found him exceptionally prickly. Unimpressed by the capital and its literary scene, and on the whole out of harmony with the growing radicalism of *The Contemporary*, he soon returned to his estate of Yasnaya Polyana. Already nearly thirty, he naturally had thoughts of marriage, and so embarked upon a somewhat lukewarm courtship of an eligible local girl. In his solemnly moralistic way he eventually turned the relationship into the substance of his short novel *Family Happiness* (*Semeynoe schaste*, 1858–9).

This work demonstrated to Tolstoy's satisfaction that relationships between the sexes which do not have marriage and family as their real aim should be regarded as morally questionable. Not that his own conduct was above reproach, as he honestly admitted in his diaries. But the moral quest was paramount. His dislike of serfdom was morally based and showed itself in such a striking quasi-autobiographical work as "A Landowner's Morning" ("Utro pomeshchika," 1856), which highlighted the gulf, as much moral as socio-economic, between landowner and peasant and the peasant's profound human desire for freedom. Finally released from army service, he went abroad for the first time in 1857. The European tour in his case involved much sight-seeing in France, Switzerland and Italy, but he was shaken by a public guillotining in Paris and equally shocked by the callous attitude of tourists in Lucerne to the talents of an itinerant street-singer. The latter provided him with material for the story "Lucerne," based upon the experiences of his literary *persona* Prince Nekhlyudov. Similarly, "Albert," the study of a drunken violinist, was designed to emphasize the eternal, moral bases of art in opposition to the prevailing radical criteria of artistic value.

In all Tolstoy's published work, diaries and letters of this period the salient feature is an honesty of viewpoint and purpose which made it seem that he alone knew the truth. He claimed that the hero of his most perceptive study of the Crimean campaign, "Sevastopol in May," was "truth" – "whom I love with all the strength of my spirit, whom I have striven to depict in all his beauty . . ." The arrogance of such a claim startled his contemporaries, but technically it had a certain justification. Tolstoy's authorial viewpoint presupposed his own disappearance. The camera-eye of his narrative manner, always so visual in its directness and pictorially representational in its result, resembles the cinematic in its liveliness. His ability to conjure up an impression of movement literally animated his fiction, so that the reader has a sense of being admitted to an enormous range of locales and circumstances. But, more significantly, from the beginning of his career as a writer he showed a readiness to psychologize, to enter into the consciousness of his characters, to animate them as if he were not only offering a stream of consciousness but also recording their reactions to life in the most intimate and immediate of diary entries. This was accompanied by a seemingly simplistic, but in fact very artful, technique of "defamiliarization" or "making strange" (*ostranenie*) which depended on the illusion that the world was being viewed either by an observer-narrator who did not understand what he was seeing, or by some childlike camera-eye which described pictorially without any awareness of motivation. Viewpoint was therefore an essential element in Tolstoy's realism. Linked to that kinetic or cinematic function of narrative which is so conspicuous in his work, it tended simultaneously to involve what Chernyshevsky called "a dialectic of the spirit" (*dialektika dushi*) as a principal feature in the process of Tolstoyan characterization. This meant that, in apprehending surrounding reality, the character related to it, reacted to it and underwent a dialectic of spiritual and moral growth in gradually understanding it. In fact, Tolstoyan characterization, although dependent on this process, is shown in evolution usually through moral crises and illustrates certain fairly rigid moral precepts which can be said to govern the conduct of human beings in their social and moral relations. Such governance is as absolute a factor in determining a Tolstoyan view of the world as is the pictorial criterion governing the presentation of his fiction and suggests that, in the final analysis, his world-view, like his picture of the world, is constrained by certain limits.

Such limits can be easily seen in the aristocratism of his own attitude to life, his rationalism with its eighteenth-century leanings, his rural utopianism fuelled by the virtual self-sufficiency of his life at Yasnaya Polyana where he spent approximately 70 of his 82 years, and his seer-like awareness of the sheer physicality of existence. No other Russian writer suggested as fully as Tolstoy the physical richness of life. Even so, life was limited, and its inevitable ending in death seemed to offer Tolstoy a lifelong challenge. He answered the challenge by seeking moral answers in his own conduct and then through the search for God projected in the experience of his major heroes. Finally he sought an answer in his own religious philosophy, his "Tolstoyanism." But if all such issues indicate the extent to which Tolstoy recognized limits, what endures of his reputation and continually renews it is the ennobling sense that human beings in his world live and grow and change and have a potential for self-improvement. His realism is so related to his own age that it can seem dated in its verisimilitude, and yet this is also his realism's strength. It is a realism related to history, redolent of a world governed by minutes and hours and days in the easily ticking movement of its prose and suffused with a sense of the breathed moment, the solidity of fixed norms, the density of immediate reality. Though related to history and seemingly excerpted from it, Tolstoy's realism is essentially and invincibly of the present time.

Tolstoy chose bold themes. His treatment of war in his *Sevasto-pol Stories* does not shy from actually describing the mental and physical process of violent death, just as it points up the vainglorious character of martial heroism. Suspicious of novelty, he contrasted the decency of past norms of conduct with the hypocrisy and materialism of present trends in his short story "Two Hussars" ("Dva gusara," 1856). More boldly, he examined the meaning of death in the three examples of an old woman's, a peasant's and a tree's demise in his "Three Deaths" ("Tri smerti," 1859). Meantime, a further feature of his personality and his times gained ascendancy. He became seized with the idea of educating the peasant children on his estate, as his natural didacticism united with the demand for social action so characteristic of the 1860s. Never content with half measures, he decided to visit Europe and study the latest educational methods, setting out in the summer of 1860. What turned out to be his second and final trip abroad was marked by an event which caused him lasting anguish, the death of his eldest brother. Even so, he met such educationalists as Julius Froebel and possibly had contact with Matthew Arnold in London. What is certain is that a meeting with Herzen led to a meeting with Pierre-Joseph Proudhon, and discussions of history and the meaning of war and peace became intermingled with the didactic purposes of his educational interests. Although he established his Yasnaya Polyana school for peasant children and issued twelve numbers of an educational journal based on his experience, his yearning for marriage and family life, along with a renewal of his literary interests, caused him to abandon the project. In 1862 he married Sonya Bers, sixteen years his junior, and settled down to a life of family contentment.

Two works of 1863 proved to be among the most important works Tolstoy had so far written. "Polikushka," the story of a wretched peasant horse-doctor who hangs himself when he realizes that he has inadvertently lost his mistress's money, is a study of the pervasive evil of money in a peasant society. It shows Tolstoy's mastery in suggesting the intricacies of relationships which govern societies, even the most primitive. *The Cossacks* (*Kazaki*), his longest work to date, carries the investigation decisively further. Deriving from his experiences in the Caucasus ten years previously, it offers Tolstoy's version of the "superfluous man" problem, but translated in this case into the circumstances of his hero Olenin's encounter with the world of Cossack frontiersmen. Olenin seeks to emulate the ways of such "noble savages" in a Rousseauistic spirit but finds himself in the end as decisively rejected as was Tolstoy by his own peasants (as he fictionalized the matter in "A Landowner's Morning" ["Utro pomeshchika"]). The Tolstoyan hero's preoccupation with "living for others" emphasizes the moral purpose of his life, but Cossack society neglects such niceties, preferring instead the full-blooded, normal passions of a closely-knit society battling for survival. Where Tolstoy excels, despite the travelogue manner and didactic interludes accompanying *The Cossacks*, is in describing the richly human relationships of the Cossack world.

Certain features of Tolstoy's realism were thus well developed long before he began writing *War and Peace*, the epic work on the Napoleonic invasion of 1812 which occupied the next seven years and brought him lasting international fame. But if his technique was manifestly realistic, the scale of his work had so far been small. The precise reasons for his decision to write a historical work on such a scale as *War and Peace* are hard to adduce, but were related in certain ways to the 1860s. It was patriotic; it celebrated above all the valor and constancy of Tolstoy's class of the nobility; it emphasized family values; it presupposed that war should be fought to ensure the survival of a patriarchal *status quo* in time of peace; it also implied that, in the end, justice and a just social system, with all the latent political meaning attaching to it, should be the aim of the "active virtue" animating the best men in Russian society. In short, it is not hard to see the polemical element even in a literary work of this stature which was ostensibly unrelated to the period of writing. These issues apart, Tolstoy's epic work remains the greatest historical novel of nineteenth-century Russian literature, and for most readers that is precisely because it evokes the historical scene so successfully and blends the historical and the fictional into a single monolithic whole.

Early readers soon realized that a historical fatalism governed the development of events in *War and Peace*. History was the motivation, naturally, but Tolstoy appears to have begun the novel as much with a political motive in mind as a historical one: he went back to the Decembrist revolt of 1825. Gradually, in seeking a source for that revolt of the nobility against their tsar, Tolstoy regressed historically to the Napoleonic invasion of 1812, and that involved him in a further regression, to the first confrontation between Russia and Napoleon in the nineteenth century, at the battle of Austerlitz in 1805. The figure of Napoleon, for all the deliberately parodic manner in which Tolstoy describes him, took the role of a catalyst for the fiction, as he had in some ways for the history as well. But there were other forces at work in the Tolstoyan picture of the period. Of these the dominant, if not most immediately conspicuous, was a fatalism which dictated both the course of history and the destinies of the Tolstoyan heroes and heroines. At work within the process was a moral mechanism that indicated the right and wrong paths of social conduct.

The novel grew like Topsy, and did not even receive its present title until 1865. It exists now in four volumes with two epilogues. The first volume covers approximately the six months from June to late November 1805; the second volume as many years, from 1806 to 1811. The final two volumes deal with the climactic events of 1812, culminating in the battle of Borodino, the burning of Moscow and the French retreat. The first epilogue carries the story forward to approximately 1820 and ties certain knots; the second epilogue develops Tolstoy's theory of history, based largely on the preceding fiction. Time, therefore, passes and all people and things change in the process, or so it might seem. But Tolstoy sought to illustrate the permanencies. He expressed them mainly in two ways: through his heroes Andrey Bolkonsky and Pierre Bezukhov, and through the Rostov and Bolkonsky families.

War and Peace opens with an encounter between his two heroes in the artificial ambience of a St. Petersburg high-society salon. The talk turns naturally to the question of Napoleon and his role in Europe. Andrey Bolkonsky – princely, detached, militaristic – begins by expressing admiration for the heroic dimension of Napoleon's achievement, but he ends the first volume by rejecting any such heroic ideal as vainglorious when he lies wounded on the battlefield of Austerlitz. Such reversal of attitude, such *peripeteia*, offers a foretaste of the principal ideological movement of the novel, for Pierre will similarly change his views radically; it is also characteristic of the way Tolstoy organizes the scene-by-scene movement of his first volume. Indeed, throughout the first volume, in a series of dramatic episodes each character undergoes a moment of crisis that alters fundamentally the course of his or her life. Andrey suddenly sees the endless blue sky above him as he lies wounded and receives a vision of the divine, and Pierre finds his role in life totally reversed. From dubious legitimacy and financial dependence he rises, through Count Bezukhov's death, to legitimate nobility and wealth and, ironically, to uneasy status and happiness in his marriage to the cold beauty Helene Kuragina. Nikolay Rostov receives his baptism of fire at the Enns bridge and suddenly realizes when wounded that he is no longer a little boy protected by the love and loyalty of his family. Natasha Rostova spontaneously declares her love for Boris Drubetskoy and realizes that she is no longer a little girl. Cumulatively, through kaleidoscopic glimpses, the world of the Rostov family in its Moscow setting and the Bolkonskys on their estate of Bald Hills emerges as normative, opposed to the fashionable sphere of St. Petersburg society; and within that chrysalis world of family life the psychologizing process of characterization depends on each member's personal fantasy, on a privately intuited magic, so that to us as readers, although we know the Rostovs individually, it is the corporateness of family experience that seems to dominate all else. Such corporateness of experience gradually assumes a deeper significance and extends beyond family limits to define not only the loyalty of the Russians to their country and their tsar but also to that national epic ideal which Tolstoy's whole novel sought to project as a positive contrast to the evil of Napoleonic vanity.

War always sets in sharp relief the pretensions and frailties of human ambition, and Tolstoy reinforces this impression by giving a panoramic description of the background, whether at Enns or Austerlitz, against which fragmentary instances of battle occur and men die and no guiding hand, let alone any providence, seems capable of bringing order out of chaos. Tolstoy's is of course an officers' war predominantly, but its effect on those of his characters who experience it intimately – Andrey, Nikolay and, later, Pierre – is morally transforming. Such transformation does not strictly speaking occur deliberately. It occurs through the explosive effect of external events upon the psyche so that man is changed, as Andrey is changed after Austerlitz. He is altered much less by his subsequent love for Natasha, and although Pierre seeks to effect changes in himself and in his world through charitable acts, Freemasonry and numerology, the search for a personal God requires the catalyst of war to bring it close to resolution. Meanwhile, the flow of public and private occasions, upon which the narrative floats slowly, sometimes tediously by, in volume two, concludes with the magical evocation of family understanding among the Rostovs during the night sleigh ride to Melyukovka and, finally, with Natasha's elopement and disgrace. Pierre steps in to banish the captivating Anatole Kuragin from the scene, but Andrey cannot forgive Natasha's disloyalty. Love for him has become as elevated and remote an experience as the sky. The only real tragic hero in the novel, he appears consumed by a death-wish on the eve of Borodino, and when a shell mortally wounds him he accepts the total abnegation of egoism that fatalism entails and recognizes his love for Natasha as transcendent and not personal: "Love is God, and to die means for me, a particle of love, to return to a universal and eternal source." The same fatalistic principle is apparent in Kutuzov's battle strategy, but it seems inseparable from the larger Tolstoyan ideal of corporate unity which embraces all conditions of men and is demonstrated most obviously – even if simplistically and naively – in the only true peasant portrait in the entire fiction, that homespun philosopher from the common people, Platon Karataev.

Pierre's encounter with Platon Karataev as a French prisoner during the retreat from Moscow is the catalyst for his own search for God. Platon embodies roundness, wholeness and total acceptance of life's goodness. His intuitive identification of life with the divine acts upon Pierre to make him realize that "Life is all. Life is God. All is change and movement, and this movement is God [. . .] To love life is to love God." In its slogan-like simplicity such vitalism can seem too declarative; in Pierre's case, it affirms a vision of life's potential which not only affords him an intuitive sense of unity with "the people," but also inspires him, we have to assume, to put into effect the "active virtue" that should govern all social relations and will eventually turn him into a Decembrist. Before that happens, the youngest Rostov son, Petya, dies in a youthful exploit with the partisans. The swarm life of war has consumed so much, though the threat posed to the patriarchal rule of the nobility at Bald Hills after old Prince Bolkonsky's death is averted by the timely arrival of Nikolay Rostov and the ensuing romance between him and Princess Mary. With the end of hostilities there is a reassertion of patriarchal standards, as the first epilogue shows. Nikolay Rostov and Princess Mary are married, Pierre and Natasha are married, and with the exception of Sonya, whom Tolstoy appears to have forgotten, the living are involved in the on-going permanence of life as Tolstoy understood it. As a family chronicle based largely on his own and his wife's family, *War and Peace* ends at this point.

As an investigation of the supposed mainsprings of history, and as a historical novel, however, it ends with the second epilogue. Here the fatalism which seems to govern so much of the historical fiction is given an extended theoretical justification which owes something to Herzen, Schopenhauer, de Maistre and others but, in all its essentials, is Tolstoyan. The main target of the theory is the idea of historical leadership, to which Tolstoy opposes the notion of history as a movement of peoples generated "not by power, not by mental activity, not even by a combination of one and the other, as historians have thought, but by the activity of *all* people taking part in the action and combining always so that those who take the greatest direct part in an event take upon themselves the least responsibility; and vice-versa." In fact, for all the apparatus of philosophical argument which Tolstoy brings to bear, his theory of history no more reconciles the concepts of freedom and necessity, of individual and swarm life, which comprise the experience of his fictional heroes and heroines, than it satisfactorily explains exactly why the Napoleonic invasion occurred and why in the end the *status quo* was restored. It does emphasize the didactic purpose behind Tolstoy's intention, an element that would dominate his work in the final three decades of his life and has obscured for many the greatness of his achievement as a writer.

The greatness of *War and Peace* lies in the very multiplicity of its many locales, characters and viewpoints, in its boldness as a fiction that makes experience of the past more realistic than any historical record, and in its power totally to absorb the reader in a range of emotions and ideas without parallel in earlier historical novels. The true merit of its achievement is that it has become a benchmark of greatness for historical fiction in any language since its time.

In a famous letter to the wife of an exiled Decembrist which he sent after his own release from penal servitude in 1854, Dostoevsky admitted that "I am a child of the age, a child of disbelief and doubt up to this time and even (I know this) to the end of my life." His awareness of such doubt proved to be the future novelist's most fruitful single source of inspiration. It meant that out of his own doubts were born the manifold ideological figures who express so powerfully the dialectical conflicts of his major fiction. None, though, expressed such a commitment to belief as did Dostoevsky himself in this same letter, when he went on to assert that God sometimes sent him moments of perfect peace, and from such moments he composed for himself a very simple credo:

> To believe that there is nothing more beautiful, more profound, more loving, more wise, more courageous and more perfect than Christ, and not only is there not, but I tell myself with jealous love that there cannot be. What is more, if someone proved to me that Christ was outside the truth, and it was *really true* that the truth was outside Christ, then I would still prefer to remain with Christ than with the truth.

The defiant note is more an epigraph to Dostoevsky's whole life than to the four years spent in penal servitude. He was to defy materialism, socialism and all visions of a golden age by asserting the truth of Christ, and the epileptic's momentary glimpse of heavenly peace was to reinforce him in his conviction, but the long agony of penal servitude, followed by the protracted half-freedom of his years of administrative exile in Siberia, was to temper the defiance into something unbending that turned his life, no matter how chaotic it may have been at times, into a magnificent nineteenth-century Calvary leading to the very gates of Paradise.

With the help of books sent to him in Siberian exile by his brother Mikhail, Dostoevsky reacquainted himself with current European thinking, but he was far removed from the intellectual centers of Russian life, so that the two literary works he wrote in this period owed much to the literary atmosphere of the 1840s. "The Uncle's Dream" ("Dyadyushkin son," 1859) and "The Village of Stepanchikovo and its Inhabitants" ("Selo Stepanchikovo i ego obitateli," 1859) have in common a farce-like, rumbustious manner reminiscent of Gogol's lighter stage pieces. Conceived, it seems, for the stage, the first of them is basically an elaborate *skandal*-scene, involving a kind of operatic ensemble of characters which leads to some scandalous exposure. In this case, the central figure is a comic prince, scarcely more than a marionette, whose role as suitor is shown to be manifestly improbable. The caricature of authority implicit in such a creation matched the caricature treatment accorded to provincialism in this intentionally comic picture of the Russian squirearchy. In the second, more extended, work of the Siberian period Dostoevsky for the first time integrated ideological polemic into his fiction in the Tartuffe-like figure of Foma Opiskin. This loquacious phrase-monger, spouting grandiose Gogolian sentiments mixed with covert pleas for justice and magnanimity, may have belonged to the westernizer–Slavophile polemics of the 1840s, but he also anticipated Dostoevsky's future creation of idea-carrying heroes. Although the works of the period were of little inherent significance, they contained important pointers to the later evolution of Dostoevsky's art as a novelist.

Dostoevsky's personal circumstances in Siberia were lightened by his courtship of Maria Isaeva, a consumptive widow who offered him no grand passion but at least provided companionship, even though theirs was not a marriage of minds and caused him much later anguish. Only in 1859 did he finally receive permission to return to European Russia. His immediate intention was to re-establish his reputation in the literary world, for which purpose he joined with his brother Mikhail in launching a journal, *Time* (1861–63). Journalism always nourished his art, for he throve on the topical and polemical. His literary reputation, though, depended on his ability to meet the demand for size and realistic relevance which the spirit of the 1860s demanded. In short, he had to become a novelist, and *The Insulted and Injured* (*Unizhennye i oskorblennye*, 1861) was his first successful essay in the genre.

Dickensian in its plotting, its concern with complexities of litigation and the ant-heap world of urban life, *The Insulted and Injured* was both the reminiscence of a melancholy narrator, which related the work in some respects to Dostoevsky's experience of the 1840s, and a remarkably acute diagnosis of a new phenomenon, the power of metropolitan capitalism to exert arbitrary authority over "the insulted and injured" of a modern city. Such power is embodied in the sinister figure of Prince Valkovsky. He epitomizes rampant sensuality and free will, corrupt plutocracy and a salaciously articulate immorality. His victims, by contrast, almost need him to justify the masochistic egoism of their own suffering; and no character exemplifies this need more powerfully than the girl Nelly who turns out to be his daughter. Nelly is to all appearances a Dickensian heroine, but Dostoevsky has achieved in her portrayal what Dickens would never have dared attempt; a depiction of the dawning of adolescent female sexuality. The novel is otherwise derivative, and Dostoevsky was never really happy with it.

If he had not until this moment in his career created what could be regarded as a masterpiece, Dostoevsky then drew on his own experience to rectify the omission. In 1860–2 he published the work that was to be a lasting monument, his account of his imprisonment in Omsk, *The House of the Dead (Zapiski iz mertvogo doma)*. In certain respects, because it was written at a remove of some years from the actual experience, Dostoevsky's picture of peasant criminality is softened by his idealistic philosophy of the soil. *Pochvennichestvo*, the principal ideological platform of his journalism in the early 1860s, derived from a conservative belief in the morally regenerative power of the Russian peasantry and the need for the intelligentsia to respect the "soil" (*pochva*). In such famous scenes as the one in the bath-house, Dante-esque in its picture of naked souls in torment, or the joyous picture of general pleasure at a theatrical entertainment, Dostoevsky indicated the extent to which closer knowledge of the peasantry enabled class barriers to be overcome, but in essence his description of the criminal world emphasized the unspeakable depravity of the peasantry, the vileness of the punishments inflicted on them and the general squalor of a penal servitude that reflected in miniature, but in grotesquely exaggerated form, the squalor of serfdom itself. Those fellow convicts with whom he established some form of personal intimacy seem not to have been Russian in origin. From the experience he acquired a knowledge of the criminal mind that was to prove invaluable to him in creating his greatest novels.

The House of the Dead describes the gaping wound at the center of Dostoevsky's life. There were other traumas to come, however, in the years immediately following its publication. In 1863 *Time* was closed down because of an article on the Polish rebellion of that same year. Meanwhile, in 1862, he had been abroad for the first time, and in his impressions of the capitalist west he stressed the awfulness of urban poverty as well as that vision of the ideal socialist future epitomized by the Crystal Palace on Sydenham Hill (see his *Winter Notes on Summer Impressions* [*Zimnie zametki o letnikh vpechatleniyakh*, 1863]). After the closure of his journal he attempted to reduce his increasing indebtedness by gambling in European casinos while simultaneously pursuing his infatuation for Polina Suslova, an intelligent, hypochondriac *femme fatale*; but neither course brought satisfaction. Then, in 1864, came what Dostoevsky called his "terrible year": his wife died in April, his beloved brother Mikhail in July, and he found himself saddled with still more debts. Desperately he strove to make a success of a second journal, *Epoch*, but it was to fail in the following year. Meanwhile, if the year had seemed to bring him nothing but disaster, it also brought him to a watershed in his literary career with the publication of his *Notes from Underground* (*Zapiski iz podpolya*, 1864).

The "underground man," the ostensible author of *Notes from Underground*, is a hypersensitive paradoxicalist, angrily cynical about the supposed inherent virtue of humanity. Denying the pre-eminence of human reason and hugely skeptical about rational self-interest as a motivation of human conduct, the "underground man" sees humans as divided into bulls and mice, dominant and dominated, who will always reject the rationally advantageous in favor of self-indulgent caprice, always prefer the "elevated sufferings" associated with individual free choice to the "cheap happiness" promised by the social utopians. A brilliant blend of publicistic rhetoric and comic hyperbole, confession and illustrative anecdote, the *Notes* diagnosed the dilemma of choice facing mankind at the dawn of a supposed scientific era and attacked the arrogant assumptions of nihilism. It marked the beginning of a process that would reach full polemical strength in Dostoevsky's great novels.

Deeper in debt than ever, Dostoevsky went abroad in the summer of 1865 in the hope of recouping his losses at the gaming tables but became stranded in Wiesbaden. Penniless and faced with starvation, he wrote to Mikhail Katkov, editor of *The Russian Herald*, offering him the plan of a psychological novel about a crime committed by a young university drop-out. The idea was sufficiently intriguing to prompt the arrival of desperately needed funds; the resulting book laid the foundation of his international fame as a novelist.

Crime and Punishment (*Prestuplenie i nakazanie*, 1866) tells the story of Raskolnikov, an impoverished student drop-out who murders a moneylender and is eventually persuaded by a young prostitute, Sonya, to confess his crime. He does so and is sentenced to Siberian exile. The work's romantic, even melodramatic, antecedents are revealed by these bare bones. But Dostoevsky's great novel is supremely a realistic work in the best nineteenth-century tradition and contains many elements now commonly termed "Dostoevskian." Of these possibly the most contentious is the notion of the "polyphonic" Dostoevskian novel.

The term was coined by Mikhail Bakhtin in his milestone critical study *Problems of Dostoevsky's Poetics* (1929). He argued that Dostoevsky's art as a novelist is distinguished from all others by its polyphonic character, that is, by its propensity for suggesting that the authorial voice is never omniscient but in some sense equal to the voices of the fictional characters. That there is no obvious "feel" of an author or omniscient narrator in *Crime and Punishment* is one significant feature of its realism. The reality of the fiction is frequently apprehended by the reader as it is filtered through Raskolnikov's supposed consciousness (and it is worth noting that the work was originally conceived as a first-person confession). The passage of time, changing locales, manifold smells, colors, the *realia*, in short, of the torrid July St. Petersburg through which Raskolnikov moves exist for us chiefly as he is conscious of them; and when he experiences nightmares and delirium, the "sickness" associated with his crime, they assume as detailed a presence as the supposed real world. "Polyphony" is arguably one way of defining the originality of Dostoevsky's achievement, since it is often hard to distinguish between one voice and another in Dostoevsky's cluttered fiction. It is equally important not to be hoodwinked into imagining that Dostoevsky, in placing Raskolnikov in such a realistic setting, was doing anything more than method-acting himself into a role, employing psychological means similar to those used by Tolstoy and other contemporary realists, if more profoundly and with greater ideological emphasis. His dramatic use of time, which concentrated greater interest on problems of motivation, was also a daring innovation in the novel-form. That *Crime and Punishment* is structured like an Attic tragedy, governed by the three unities of time, place and action, and by a process of *peripeteia* (reversal) and *catharsis* (purging of emotion), is also conceivable, as Vyacheslav Ivanov has argued. That it combines detective fiction with the novel of ideas, or has symbolic meaning as a mystery play in which good and evil vie for the soul of nineteenth-century man, are also possible interpretations. There is no denying, though, that it is one of the great realistic novels of urban life, and depicts the squalid circumstances of that life, as well as the warped psychological and emotional states associated with it, in unforgettable images.

Raskolnikov, rehearsing and then committing his planned murder in Part one of the novel, conceals only his "idea," his motivation. When the homicide involves the moneylender's sister as well, the brutality of the deed cannot fail to shock. His later delirium, the supposition that his mother, sister Dunya and friends and acquaintances simply do not suspect the blackness within him and his own success, or luck, in avoiding suspicion contribute to the growth of tension, but the novel's main interest lies not in *who* did it, but *what* did it. The criminality of Raskolnikov gradually reveals itself in ideological terms through the twofold pressures from Porfiry Petrovich, the examining magistrate, and Raskolnikov's conscience. Broadly speaking, his motives combine a supposed altruistic desire to rid the world of an evil by murdering the moneylender and a megalomaniac, or Napoleonic, concern to prove nihilistically that he is above the law and can commit murder with impunity. The two motives impinge upon his consciousness in the forms of his relationship with Sonya Marmeladova, the young prostitute who believes in God and seeks to bring him to repentance, and with Svidrigaylov, Dunya's suitor, who represents in seedily beguiling form the notion that man is conscience-less, concerned only with his own free will, and derives pleasure in life only from extreme, often perverse, sensuality. Thus, if Sonya offers him the possibility of moral rehabilitation through humility and the grace of an all-forgiving God, Svidrigaylov, by committing suicide at the conclusion of a magnificently nightmarish scene, demonstrates to him the choice awaiting all those who arrogantly seek to usurp God's place in the moral universe. Whether or not

Raskolnikov abandons such arrogance even in his Siberian imprisonment must remain in doubt.

Raskolnikov, then, does not murder for money; he murders to prove himself, or so he likes to imagine, though he might just as well have been "possessed" by some rational microbe. During the writing of *Crime and Punishment*, in October 1866, Dostoevsky decided to hire the services of a stenographer to meet a deadline for a novel for an unscrupulous publisher. The resultant work was the short novel *The Gambler* (*Igrok*), which deals with "possession" by gambling and money-fever. Dostoevsky, though, was struck by another fever: he fell in love with the young stenographer, Anna Snitkina, and early the following year they married. Despite the quarter of a century in age separating them, their marriage proved successful, providing Dostoevsky with increasing family security in the last decade of his life. But in the immediate wake of marriage the newlyweds were forced to go abroad to escape from Dostoevsky's creditors. The four years of his second, self-imposed exile, 1867–71, were spent in Europe, mostly in Dresden. They witnessed the gestation of his second great novel, *The Idiot* (*Idiot*, 1868).

There is little doubt that Dostoevsky originally intended to develop the "satanic" aspects of Raskolnikov in his second novel, but then was seized by another vision, that of "the positively beautiful man," the nineteenth-century Christ. In the figure of the epileptic Prince Myshkin he offered a daring portrait of a new kind of savior intended to redeem a Russia caught in the toils of nihilism and capitalism. Dostoevsky was on the whole not very successful in blending ideology and fiction here. The novel smacks too obviously of a pamphlet in sections of Parts three and four; sub-plots and loquacious secondary characters clog the story to the detriment of the central portrayals. But in Part one and in the novel's finale Dostoevsky was writing at his superb best.

At the opening of the novel the child-like former "idiot," Prince Myshkin, is returning by train to St. Petersburg. On the way he encounters Rogozhin, a figure who epitomizes the darkest and most libidinous aspects of Russian life. Both men vie for the hand of the beautiful Nastasya Filippovna. She, in her vulnerable arrogance, seeks to avoid falling victim to the mercenary world of wealthy generals and merchants and in a magnificent *skandal* scene at the end of Part one hurls Rogozhin's packet of 100,000 roubles into the fire to test her supposed fiancé's strength of purpose. Myshkin's message in the face of the tumultuous Epanchin and Ivolgin households, the wheelings and dealings of this capitalist vortex and the nihilists' denial of all moral values seems hardly adequate: it is that beauty will redeem the world. But can he save the beautiful Nastasya Filippovna? His ultimate answer to the most devastating of nihilist statements, the "Necessary Explanation" of the consumptive student Ippolit, which can threaten a man's faith in much the same way as Holbein's painting of "Christ in the Tomb," was to proclaim the idea of the Russian Christ, to attack atheism and Roman catholicism and to announce his own role as savior. Yet this did not save Nastasya, whom he intended to marry, from falling victim to Rogozhin's murderous jealousy. The novel concludes with the nightlong vigil of Rogozhin and Myshkin at her deathbed and the savior's return to a state of idiocy.

As a statement of Dostoevsky's view of Russia from his European exile, *The Idiot* was pessimistic despite its vision of a Russian Christ and its messianic hope that Russia would become the moral savior of the west. As his exile continued his project for a species of latterday hagiography entitled *The Life of a Great Sinner* brought him ever closer to the view that Russia was "possessed" by some great sinfulness.

The dominance of the novel as the principal means of realistic expression in literature was beyond dispute by the beginning of the 1870s. Moreover, with the emergence of strong populist feeling the polemical spirit that had so invigorated literature in the previous decade now began to undergo a subtle seachange, to demand of literature positive answers to pressing social questions. Strictly speaking, none of this was a stimulus to literary experiment. What it stimulated was a serious literature. The most serious of the issues raised was that of the "positive" hero, the hero-exemplar, though of almost equal importance was the "woman question," having to do with female emancipation, divorce and the social role of women generally. The conspicuous part played by women in populist revolutionary activities added to this interest. The "woman question" also involved another important theme, that of the role of the family in Russian social life. To these should be added a more universal preoccupation, the topic of capitalism in post-Emancipation Russia and the evils associated with money. But broadly in harmony with the ideals of populism were many concerns in literature which stressed not so much class divisions and political antagonisms (marked though these were in the history of the period) as the need for social reconciliation and social justice, love rather than hatred, a readiness to seek religious rather than revolutionary answers. The Russian realistic novel of the 1870s confronted these issues in a spirit of assurance and hope, as culminating moments in the novelists' search for belief after a decade of doubts.

The anti-revolutionism of the literature is seen at its most marked in the major work of Nikolay Leskov. His formless anti-revolutionary novel *At Daggers Drawn* (1871) was followed in 1872 by one of his most famous works, *Cathedral Folk* (*Soboryane*), which celebrated the lives of the Russian priesthood. The priest Tuberozov and his deacon Akhilla are memorable creations, especially the former, with his evident resemblance to Archpriest Avvakum and his defiant, old-fashioned defense of Orthodoxy. Far removed from the world of Trollope though Leskov's picture of the clergy may be, it suggested, in compassionate but realistic terms, the positive role of the clergy in Russian society. Leskov's fondness for the original and unconventional was also demonstrated in two remarkable short stories of 1873, "The Sealed Angel" ("Zapechatlenny angel") and "The Enchanted Wanderer" ("Ocharovanny strannik"). The first of these describes in attractively racey terms the devotion shown by a group of religious schismatics to a special sealed icon, while the second has some features of a mini-epic in its account of the life of a serf, Ivan Flyagin, who experiences extraordinary and often horrifying adventures. Never a celebrant of institutions or institutionalized attitudes, and always a critic of the bureaucracy, in his story "At the Edge of the World" ("Na krayu sveta," 1875) Leskov portrays the dilemma facing an ambitious Orthodox bishop when, in a Siberian snowstorm, he discovers that his heathen guide has more truly Christian impulses than supposedly firm adherents of the Christian church.

As a counterpoint to Leskov's unobtrusively subversive manner, the arch-critic of the *status quo*, Saltykov-Shchedrin, was quite open about his oppositional role as a satirist. His *History of a Town* (*Istoriya odnogo goroda*, 1869–70) is a history of Russian rulers disguised as a history of a small provincial town, Glupov (literally Stupidville), written by a clerkish archivist in naively hyperbolic terms that cannot fail to elicit howls of laughter from the most indifferent of readers. The implications of such satire clearly enough impugn the political immaturity of the Russian attitude towards government as well as the apparently craven submission of the populace to the farcical whims of authority. The most egregiously awful of the rulers is Ugryum-Burcheev, modelled on Alexander I's loyal minister Alexey Arakcheev, whose capacity for devising outlandishly oppressive schemes and draconian regulations was to be matched in later history only by Joseph Stalin. A clever combination of realistic exposition and outrageous hyperbole, nowadays reminiscent of a grotesque expressionism and therefore seemingly overdone, formed the basic style of Saltykov's satirical manner in this work. In his masterpiece *The Golovlyov Family* (*Gospoda Golovlevy*, 1875–80), on the other hand, the dominant stylistic note was realistic, but of such unrelenting gloom that the hyperbole present in the grotesque characterization of the leading figure seems wholly appropriate.

It is only on the strength of this loosely constructed novel that Saltykov-Shchedrin can claim an international reputation. Written over a number of years and published in separate episodes, the novel's narrative thread suffers from the occasional chronological inconsistency and prolixity. The basic theme of the decline of a serf-owning family in the aftermath of the Emancipation and its eventual total disintegration is not seriously impaired by such inconsistency, for the emphasis is always placed on the central characters, first on the matriarch of the family, Arina Petrovna, and then on her son and heir, Porfiry, or "Iudushka," as he is more familiarly known. A virulent and abiding hatred, discernible in the very steeliness of his writing, appears to have informed Saltykov's attitude toward family relationships. Painful autobiographical experience lay at the root of it. In his merciless portrayal of the hard-hearted, censorious skinflint of a mother, Arina Petrovna, the reader can hardly fail to perceive a settling of old scores. And yet the portrait has grace notes. Although money-grubbing, Arina Petrovna is exceptionally vigorous and enterprising, and if she creates monsters out of those closest to her by her insatiable acquisitiveness she can also experience compassion for her victims. Precisely such compassion is missing in Iudushka Golovlyov. Iudushka disguises his skinflint attributes with a hypocritical phrasemongering and a sententiousness that embellishes as it beggars. His is so splendidly grotesque a portrayal that the very awfulness of his character suggests pathology rather than evil. Indeed, in the festering world of the Russian landowning family as Saltykov conceived it, Iudushka Golovlyov represents the ultimate stage of such corruption much as Oblomov suggested the ultimate stage of superfluity. There is, however, such depth and atmospheric richness to the novel's realism in its depiction of the soulless isolation of the Golovlyovs' world that it sometimes reads, hardly surprisingly, like a Victorian tract against the evils of drink: most of the characters are brought low by alcoholism. As satire, the novel is so deeply scathing that it calls in question the likelihood of any amelioration in such a reprobate humanity, despite the pangs of conscience that affect Iudushka near the end.

During the 1870s Saltykov also published a number of works containing satirical sketches of new types of capitalist entrepreneurs, corrupt bureaucrats and assorted contemporary miscreants (*Pompadours and Pompadouresses* [*Pompadury i pompadurshi*, 1863–74]; *The Diary of a Provincial in St. Petersburg* [*Dnevnik provintsiala v Peterburge*, 1872–3]; *Gentlemen of Tashkent* [*Gospoda Tashkentsy*, 1869–72]). At the end of the decade he published the most outstanding of such satirical compilations, *The Sanctuary of Mon Repos* (*Ubezhishche Monrepo*, 1878–9).

Critically realistic treatments of the growing bourgeois influence in Russian society were also to be found in Alexey Pisemsky's writing of the period. His novel of 1871 *In the Whirlpool* (*V vodovorote*) demonstrated how noble passions can be lost in the whirlpool of mundane bourgeois life. If his plays dealt mostly with the social evils of a burgeoning capitalism, their stagecraft was generally sadly wanting and the rancorous tone of Pisemsky's writing made them into little more than theatrical tracts for the times. His two final novels reflect his generally right-wing approach to the changes occurring in Russian society. *The Bourgeois* (*Meshchane*, 1877) attempts largely declaratively to resuscitate true "knightly" idealism in the struggle against bourgeois standards; and *The Masons* (*Masony*, 1880), a historical novel, unsuccessfully turns to Freemasonry to suggest a possible antidote to the prevailing mercantilism. Of rather more interest as an assertion of right-wing values, although derivative in manner, was the work of Boleslav Markevich (1822–84). His novel *Marina from Red Horn* (*Marina iz Alogo Roga*, 1873) melodramatically depicts a heroine who abandons her nihilism and marries into the aristocracy. In 1878, with the publication of *A Quarter of a Century Ago* (*Chetvert veka nazad*), Markevich embarked on a trilogy of novels about the pre- and post-Emancipation period, of which this one dealt principally with the generational conflict in the higher reaches of the nobility.

In general terms, the literature of populism was left-wing, critical of capitalism and orientated towards the notion of "serving the people," both peasant and proletariat. Innokenty Omulevsky (1836–83) in his novel *Step by Step* (*Shag za shagom*, 1870) used autobiographical experience to describe the politically propagandist aims of gradualist populism, but it was a poor work despite the interest of its Siberian setting; while Ivan Kushchevsky (1847–76), with his *Nikolay Negorev; or, The Successful Russian* (*Nikola Negorev, ili blagopoluchny rossiyanin*, 1872) produced a minor classic of semi-autobiographical fiction on the theme of education. By contrast, the many novels by Alexander Sheller-Mikhaylov (1838–1900) provided a generally shallow and stereotyped view of the spirit of the 1860s (*Rotten Marshes* [*Gnilye bolota*, 1864], for example) and tended to idealize the progressive forces in society pitted against a backward establishment, as in *The Obnoskov Family* (*Gospoda Obnoskovy*, 1868) and *Old Nests* (*Starye gnezda*, 1875). Although best known for his studies of naval life, Konstantin Stanyukovich (1843–1903) made a significant contribution to the literature of populism with his novels *Without Issue* (*Bez iskhoda*, 1873) and *Two Brothers* (*Dva brata*, 1880) about the propagandist activities of the populists.

The "woman question" received a full airing in the work of Nadezhda Khvoshchinskaya-Zayonchkovskaya (1825–89), who published mostly under the pseudonym V. Krestovsky. Her early short stories and novels of the 1850s painted a somber picture of oppressed Russian womanhood, but in her work of the following two decades, more especially in the 1870s, she concentrated on the positive aspects of populist self-sacrifice in the people's cause, as in the novel *Ursa Major* (*Bolshaya medveditsa*, 1872) and in *The Schoolmistress* (*Uchitelnitsa*, 1880). The most conscientiously "documentary" of the realist-writers associated with populism was Nikolay Zlatovratsky (1845-1911), whose short study "Peasant Jurors" ("Krestyane-prisyazhnye," 1874–5) exposed the unthinking cruelty of the judiciary towards the peasantry. A more successful example of the same kind of treatment, and of considerably greater literary merit, was Gleb Uspensky's collection of studies and observations devoted to peasant life entitled *From a Country Diary* (*Iz derevenskogo dnevnika*, 1877–80).

Among the most original talents to reach maturity in the 1870s was that of Paul Melnikov-Pechersky (1818–83). A career bureaucrat in the area of Nizhny Novgorod (now Gorky), he put his training as an ethnographer and historian to good use in studying the communities of religious schismatics, or Old Believers, which proliferated along the banks of the Volga. Many of his short studies were published from the 1850s onwards, but his reputation rests chiefly on the novel *In the Woods* (*V lesakh*, 1875) and its sequel *In the Hills* (*V gorakh*, 1875–81). The first of these describes in abundant detail the vigorous, devout, resourceful lives of Old Believers on the wooded left bank of the Volga, describing Russian peasant ways that had hitherto been unknown to the reading public. The second, lacking the poetic atmosphere of the first, concentrated more on the emergence of a moneyed class and the consequent exploitation of the peasantry living on the Volga's hilly left bank. The author's knowledge joined with his powers of observation and description to produce masterpieces of regional literature in these works.

In short, the prose literature of the 1870s was copious, serious in intent and uneven in quality, but it always strove to enlarge its horizons through the elaboration of the novel-form. The culmination of this process, and its greatest achievements, occurred in the work of Tolstoy and Dostoevsky, and in the work of their major predecessor Turgenev.

During the 1870s, resident as he was mostly in Paris, Turgenev grew ever more conscious of his absentee status as a Russian writer. Henry James, who became a close friend during this period, thought it no indignity to include him in his *French Poets and Novelists* (1878), but Turgenev knew that his reputation depended on regaining favor with the younger generation of the Russian intelligentsia. To this end he made serious efforts to overcome the pessimistic philosophy and the nostalgic bias characteristic of his writings after *Fathers and Sons*. His *Literary Memoirs* (*Literaturnye i zhiteyskie vospominaniya*, 1868) emphasized his closeness to Belinsky, his commitment to the west and his unique experience of revolution. The theme of betrayal which permeated his "King Lear of the Steppes" ("Stepnoy korol Lir," 1870) implied his own disillusionment with the fickleness of popular tastes. His novella-length work "Spring Torrents" ("Veshnie vody," 1872) was the last major love story he wrote, typically "Turgenevan" in its emphasis on first love but also cynically realistic in its study of such love betrayed. The vagaries of love were further explored in such stories as "The End of Chertopkhanov" (1872) and "Punin and Baburin" (1874), though in the latter the interest of the portraiture stems to a large degree from the political significance of the two main figures in their opposition to serfdom. They point the way to the representatives of "nameless Russia" who Turgenev thought would be the true source of social and political change in Russian life, if we judge by his last novel, *Virgin Soil* (Nov, 1877).

Virgin Soil dominates all Turgenev's work of the 1870s. The longest of his novels, it is also the least successful in its characterization and ideas. Basically a political novel, its central figure, Nezhdanov, is "a romantic of realism," as he was called, but he is too shallow a character to sustain the reader's interest. Hamletically aspiring to be a Don Quixote, he is an unheroic hero with poetic ambitions who attempts to become a practical revolutionary, fails in this as well as in his love for the heroine Marianna, and ends in suicide. Marianna then marries the book's "positive hero", Solomin, who, if only sketchily, is depicted as the true practical man "on the American pattern" (as Turgenev's notes for the novel described him). Representative of proletarian virtues and industrial ideals, Solomin is by way of foreshadowing the future socialist realist hero of Soviet literature, though obviously without the political motivation of such a type. If in this respect Turgenev showed remarkable prescience, in his treatment of populist political ideas he was lukewarm while sincerely admiring the dedication of the young populists themselves.

The novel's best parts are those at which Turgenev was always most successful: his description of the provincial, country-house world of the Russian nobility. He lends his picture of the Sipyagins, landowners with bureaucratic ambitions, an acerbic edge of irony which neatly highlights their pretensions and their self-importance without descending to caricature. Caricature, though, and tedium take their toll in the portrayal of the populists and their activities, with the result that, as an anatomy of incipient political revolt in the Russian countryside the novel fails to be convincing and, as a political novel designed to show that only a deep plowing of the virgin soil of the Russian peasantry can really rouse them to action, it reads more as a warning against fundamental change than as an endorsement of the revolutionaries' views. The novel failed to rehabilitate Turgenev's reputation with the younger generation, but it did not seriously inhibit the warm welcome which he received in his native country during a visit in 1879. In that year he received the further honor of being the first Russian writer to be awarded a doctorate of Civil Law by Oxford University; and it was also in 1879 that he renewed his friendship with Tolstoy following a seventeen-year rift in their relations.

After the enormous effort of writing *War and Peace* it is hardly surprising that Tolstoy should have suffered a mental and physical breakdown. His marriage, though providing general domestic contentment, had been marred by quarrels and bitter recriminations. Then in 1869, during a night spent in Arzamas, he seems to have experienced a bout of madness that involved a horrifying vision of death. His urge to find religious answers led him to take up Greek so that he could study the Gospels at first hand; and there was the added inducement of classical Greek literature. He abandoned an earlier plan to write a novel on the period of Peter the Great. Under the weight of marital problems and these new interests, his health suffered, and he sought relief by taking a cure in the Samara region. When he returned he felt sufficiently restored to renew his previous educational interests and plunged immediately into composing a four-part *ABC Book* (*Azbuka*), or elementary guide to literacy for peasant children. This led to disagreements with the educational establishment and claims by Tolstoy that he understood the educational needs of the peasantry better than others. In practical terms, this was Tolstoy's direct contribution to the vexed populist issue of how the privileged classes could best serve the needs of the peasantry. No matter how socially responsible such educational efforts were, they served the needs of literature only obliquely; and by 1873 Tolstoy had become consumed by a new literary passion: to write a work (so he had rather grandiosely described it to his wife two years earlier) as pure and elegant and refined as the whole of ancient Greek literature and art. This work took the form of his novel *Anna Karenina* (1873–7).

There is a purity, elegance and refinement about *Anna Karenina* which the sprawling *War and Peace* cannot match. It deals with such contemporary themes as the "woman question," the peasant question, the role of the family, marriage as the basic social contract, the relationship between the nobility and peasantry, between city and country, between old patriarchal ways and the industrial nineteenth century. The didactic Tolstoy may not be obtrusive, though he is everywhere discernible, and he makes of Konstantin Levin the most opinionated hero in Russian literature. But such didacticism is dissolved in the brilliantly kinetic manner of the novel and the sense of a reality governed by social norms, by routines, times of day, manners of speaking and habits of behavior. The dominant animating element in the whole fiction is movement. Tolstoy summons into being a whole society as he moves the reader effortlessly from scene to scene, from one social milieu to another, evoking innumerable shades of emotion, intellectual attitude, familial and social relationship with supreme mastery. *Anna Karenina* is the most truly adult and mature of Tolstoy's novels, and its central attraction, giving it unmatched power and poignancy, is the figure of Anna herself, the heroine of this Tolstoyan version of Greek tragedy.

Perhaps in its ultimate message the novel is not tragic, but in his conception of his heroine there is no doubt that Tolstoy intended to point a moral lesson. The famous epigraph – "Vengeance is Mine and I will repay" – clearly suggests as much. Tolstoy's was no doubt a harsh morality so far as his heroine is concerned, but it is equally true that in the very portrayal of Anna the moralizing yields to a growing sense of the tragic dimension of her life. Tolstoy denies his heroine the pre-history of childhood and youth that might have explained her conduct, as he also denies her the possibility of choice in any real sense once her destiny is pointed towards tragedy. The consolations of religion, as of divorce or spinsterhood, are denied to her in Tolstoy's rigid concept of women's social role. Anna appears to be pursued by fateful Eumenides who constrain her life and her choices as rigidly as the parallel lines of railway track on which she enters the fiction and on which she kills herself. Leaving her son Seryozha for the first time to travel to Moscow to patch up her brother's, Stiva Oblonsky's, shaky marriage, she is fatefully seated in the train next to Vronsky's mother and so can hardly fail to meet him on her arrival. At first glance Vronsky sees her suppressed vitality and the light in her eyes which she strives to extinguish but which still glows in her smile. This is no romantic heroine but a vital woman of her time who seeks the happiness which her husband cannot give her and, in pursuing that happiness with Vronsky, slowly becomes a social pariah. Tolstoyan morality rigidly enforces the notion that violation of the marriage bond is a form of apostasy and brings in its train the tragic loss of all that is most dear, imperilling in the end all life and happiness.

Anna Karenina falls into two parts in two ways. Until the conclusion of Part four (which, like Part eight, is shorter than the other parts), Anna's story is that of a wife who has sinned by falling in love with Vronsky and having his child. From the beginning of Part five onwards she is depicted as a woman who has violated her marriage, abandoned her husband and become an outcast. Her choices are fined down to the ultimate need to remain sexually attractive to her lover; when such attraction ceases her sole recourse is to jealous vindictiveness. She kills herself partly at least in order to hurt Vronsky for his disloyalty. But in deliberate mitigation of this tragedy there is the counterbalancing story of Konstantin Levin, who seeks through marriage to Kitty Shcherbatskaya to achieve a philosophical and emotional equilibrium he has not achieved before. The axial point is the opening of Part five, with Levin's wedding, which leads by uneven but inevitable stages, through marital disagreements, his brother's death (which bears the only chapter heading in the novel), Kitty's pregnancy and the gradual creation of an assured family life, to Levin's eventual discovery of a meaning to life, or as the concluding lines of the novel put it in conveying his thoughts: ". . . but my life, my whole life now, no matter what may happen to me, every minute of it is not only not meaningless as it was before, but has the undoubted meaning of goodness which I have the power to put into it."

The two stories of Anna Karenina and Konstantin Levin are almost separate narratives, but they illustrate a similar morality. Tolstoyan morality, concerned in this novel so obviously with marriage as the basic social contract, insists that violation of that contract brings tragedy in its wake, while observance brings the possibility of an ultimately meaningful life. All those caught in Anna's tragedy lose what they most sought: Anna her son Seryozha, Karenin advancement in his bureaucratic career, Vronsky the chance of legitimizing his children and ensuring his family name. Yet if Anna's was intended to be the portrait of a passionate woman caught up in a sexual infatuation, Tolstoy succeeds only in making her sexuality appear reprehensible and sinful and he permits her to wrestle with her sinful conscience only by rational means. So she becomes divided against herself, incapable of escaping from the logical dead-end of her thinking and therefore with no choice but suicide. Levin does not escape such a fate himself. By a similar logical process he is also driven to thoughts of suicide. But his observance of the morality of marriage permits him to discover a religious, and not a rational, answer, so that by realizing that good and bad are outside the chain of cause and effect he is enabled to understand the law of right and wrong known intuitively to the peasantry and to count himself one of them. In this way, however facile the Tolstoyan solution may seem, he can live "for his soul."

When Tolstoyan morality withdraws its cobwebby skeins from the fiction, what shines through is the poignant vitality of Anna herself. That society world of St. Petersburg upon which the moral Tolstoy frowned so fiercely has an inherent iridescence and suavity. She moves through it elegantly, with an effortless sophistication that contrives to show up the creaking, vindictive mechanism of that *comme il faut* for what it is. Few guess the true anguish within her. Even Levin, when he meets her for the first and only time shortly before her death (Part seven, chs. ix–xi), can see her intelligence, elegance, beauty and honesty, but he barely discerns the mental torment that poisons her life and eventually makes it unbearable. Though feminist opinion may deny Tolstoy's achievement in creating Anna Karenina, natural justice must allow that, for all its faults, the portrait has a vital likeness, an appeal and vulnerability that make Anna's death seem as wanton as any sad suicide at the end of love. Despite himself, Tolstoy breathed life into her, and her death has outlasted his morality.

As a novel on social themes, *Anna Karenina* is concerned not only with the problem of marriage in an illiberal society but also with the issue of social reconciliation and the religious commitment that such reconciliation demands. Archaic and peasant-orientated though Tolstoy's view of the world may have been, through the example of Konstantin Levin he attempted to show how Russian society could liberate itself from the antagonisms between peasantry and nobility. Simultaneously Levin could emancipate himself from the constraining evils of his former life through his new-found religious convictions. Tolstoy's attempt to demonstrate such spiritual liberation continued for the next thirty years of his religious conversion and devotion to Tolstoyanism, but it is doubtful whether it was ever expressed with greater hope of fulfillment than in Levin's final thoughts at the end of *Anna Karenina*.

In 1869, writing to the critic Nikolay Strakhov, Dostoevsky claimed: "I have my own special view of reality [in art], and what the majority call almost fantastic and exceptional for me sometimes comprises the very essence of the real. The ordinariness of phenomena and a conventional view of them are not to me realism but rather the opposite." Defending, as he was, his novel *The Idiot* from the charge of being unreal, he knew the daily press offered increasing evidence of the political and moral unreality spreading through Russian society. In his exile he was of course out of touch. Though he might make admiring visits to Geneva, Vevey, Milan and Florence, he was growing increasingly homesick for Russia. The black comedy to which he turned his hand in the meantime – "The Eternal Husband" ("Vechny muzh," 1870) – showed how expert he was in that genre, and when he learned in late 1869 of the murder of a student named Ivanov on the orders of Nechaev he found the blackness of his mood as well as his literary method drew him away from his projected hagiography *The Life of a Great Sinner* towards a more sinister political topic. The result was the most somber of his novels, *The Possessed* or *The Devils* (*Besy*, 1871–2).

The Possessed revolves about the murder of a young intellectual, Shatov, whose repudiation of socialism supposedly poses a threat to the revolutionary cell of which he is a member. On the orders of the book's Nechaev-figure, Peter Verkhovensky, the other members of the cell become accomplices in Shatov's murder. What possessed such supposed revolutionaries to kill one of their number, what devils made them do it?

The Possessed is Dostoevsky's anatomy of the state of the Russian intelligentsia at the beginning of the 1870s. The first generation of the intelligentsia is represented by Stepan Verkhovensky, a typical "man of the 1840s," European in orientation and vaguely liberal in his high-minded concern with ideals. Ineffectual, sprinkling his talk with French phrases, he had the role of tutor to the brilliant son of the wealthiest family in the district, Nikolay Stavrogin. Stavrogin, though, has disciples of his own, Kirillov and Shatov, into whom his ideas have entered, as it were, much as the devils entered into the herd of swine and ran violently down a steep place in the story of Christ and the man possessed by devils (which forms one of the epigraphs [Luke 8:32–6] to the novel). Kirillov is possessed by the idea that by killing himself he can liberate humanity forever from the fear of death and turn all men into men-gods; Shatov is equally possessed by the idea that the Russian people are God-bearing, even though he is still shaky about his personal belief in God (as his name Shatov, from *shatky* or "shaky," implies). Such devils may have gone out of Stavrogin, but others have been spawned by the first generation of the intelligentsia in the shape of Stepan Trofimovich's son, Peter Verkhovensky, and his plans to turn Stavrogin into a godhead of revolution. Peter is the ultimate petty nihilist revolutionary. With his bogus claims of international revolutionary connections, he spreads mayhem not only among local factory workers but also among his sheep-like revolutionary associates and the equally gullible provincial governor and his wife. The line between black farce and high tragedy dissolves in the fierce mill-race of the novel's narrative. Some of the most outrageously funny *skandal* scenes accompany some of the bitterest characterizations, notably the acid caricature of Turgenev as the famous writer Karmazinov. The novel also contains some of the most somber moments in Dostoevsky's fiction, among them the nightmarish scene of

Kirillov's suicide and the horrifying description of Stavrogin's violation of a little girl who then hangs herself from shame (from an unpublished chapter "At Tikhon's" which contains Stavrogin's "Confession").

At the heart of *The Possessed* is a darkness, epitomized by the impotence and ideological emptiness of Stavrogin, from whom the devils have gone out. His "great sin," as depicted in his "Confession," amounts to no more than squalid abuse of a defenseless child; his marriage to a crippled madwoman may seem merely a symptom of the grotesque nihilism that finally reduces him, the supposed leader of a future Russian revolution, to death by hanging on a strong silk cord. His greatness is emptied of meaning, but it is left to Stepan Verkhovensky, after embarking on his own "going to the people," to proclaim as he dies the only positive message of the novel:

> The entire law of human existence is that each man should always be able to bow down before what is infinitely great. If people are deprived of what is infinitely great, then they'll give up living and die in despair. The infinite and eternal are just as essential to man as this little planet on which he dwells [...] My friends, everyone, everyone: Long live the Great Idea! The eternal, infinite Idea!

The Great Idea, though not present in this novel save in such declarative terms, is the idea of Christ the Savior to which Dostoevsky pledged his lifelong allegiance immediately on release from penal servitude.

For some Dostoevsky never wrote anything better than *The Possessed*. However, in the ten years of life remaining to him after his return to Russia in 1871 he enhanced his reputation with two further novels, his topical journalism in *Diary of a Writer* (*Dnevnik pisatelya*, 1873–4, 1876–7, 1880–1), his editorship of Prince Vladimir Meshchersky's journal *The Citizen* (*Grazhdanin*, 1873), his public readings of his works and the ultimate triumph of his speech at the unveiling of the Pushkin memorial in Moscow in 1880. Contented family life, as well as his wife's skillful management of his financial and publishing affairs, provided a secure background for his writing. Staraya Russa in Novgorod province became the Dostoevsky family retreat from the pressures of life in the capital. Save for trips to Bad Ems to be treated for what was diagnosed as emphysema, and despite regular epileptic attacks ·(probably every three weeks), Dostoevsky was not, strictly speaking, in poor health, as the vigor of his work attests. His manner became on the whole less caustic as his interests underwent a gradual reorientation from the political to the social and religious.

The social and religious meaning of the family is the dominant concern of *The Raw Youth* (*Podrostok*, 1875), the least successful novel of Dostoevsky's maturity. Concerned with the twenty-year-old hero's search for his true father, it is encumbered with sub-plots and side issues. In its melodramatic treatment of relationships, it diminishes the problem of "the accidental family," described as the novel's central concern; but in the rhetoric of Versilov, the hero's natural father, the vision of a golden age of humanity raises the novel's intellectual level to embrace a new concept of justice. The problem of justice, seen in relation both to the family and the idea of a just world, inspired Dostoevsky's last great novel *The Brothers Karamazov* (*Bratya Karamazovy*, 1878–80), but at its heart lay the natural criminality of man. It was this criminality which Dostoevsky examined in two remarkable short works, "A Gentle Creature" ("Krotkaya," 1876) and "The Dream of a Ridiculous Man" ("Son smeshnogo cheloveka," 1877), which he published in *Diary of a Writer* before embarking on his last novel.

The inspiration for *The Brothers Karamazov* was principally the trial of Vera Zasulich at the end of March 1878. Dostoevsky attended it, studied the court procedure (on the advice of a leading St. Petersburg jurist) and based the climax of his novel on a similar scene in which not only the Karamazov family, but the whole of Russian society was tried before the eyes of the world. This profound novel was designed as the first part of a two-part work, so that the extant novel has both an anticipatory and a pseudo-historical character contained within the form of a detective fiction. The events leading to the murder of Fyodor Karamazov and the subsequent trial occur ostensibly thirteen years before the time of writing – therefore presumably in the late 1860s – but Dostoevsky tends occasionally to "forget" this time difference. A poetics of memory has therefore an appreciable role to play in the motivation of the work, which incidentally includes more autobiographical references than any other major Dostoevskian fiction. On the other hand, the novel is essentially concerned with a miscarriage of justice. The most dramatic of Dostoevsky's novels in terms of its construction, the first three parts are designed to explore the events of the three days leading up to the murder and, in so doing, to reveal the real motives of the Karamazov brothers, which were not fully divulged or understood at the trial and resulted in the conviction of an innocent man. Dostoevsky knew of the case of a fellow convict from his days of penal servitude who had been wrongly convicted of parricide and apparently used this case for his novel.

Considered as detective fiction, *The Brothers Karamazov* is about money and sex. The rivalry between the eldest Karamazov brother, Dmitry, and his father, Fyodor, over money and their mutual infatuation for Grushenka, a highly attractive woman of shady background, can be regarded as the volatile factors leading to parricide. But as a philosophical novel about the choices facing Russia and mankind, the roles of the two other Karamazov brothers by their father's second marriage, Ivan and Alyosha, have supreme importance. They epitomize the two choices ranged on Dmitry's either hand: that of the western-orientated, nihilistic Ivan, who argues that "all is permitted" in the moral sphere; and that of the spiritually committed, neophyte monk Alyosha, who proclaims in a Christian spirit the mutual responsibility of all men for all other men's sins. A fourth Karamazov brother, the illegitimate Smerdyakov, becomes the instrument of Ivan's philosophy, is responsible for Fyodor's murder and ends by committing suicide.

If *The Brothers Karamazov* is a novel about the murder of a father, it is also a novel about fatherhood and its denial. The image of fatherhood is twofold. On the one hand, there is the lustful, satyr-like image of the biological father Fyodor Karamazov, a masterly portrayal in its own right, and, on the other, the fainter image of the elder Zosima, Alyosha's spiritual father, whose view of the world is governed by principles of forgiveness and love. Ivan's aim, though, is to liberate humanity from the authority of fatherhood, whether that take the form of the idea of God or the biological priority which the fact of human fatherhood entails. He seeks to negate the idea of an all-merciful God by demonstrating that, in his Euclidian view, God's world is fundamentally unjust since the unassuaged and unavenged suffering of innocent children exists within it. His answer to Alyosha's protest that he had forgotten Christ's legacy to mankind is to assert (in the famous chapter "The Grand Inquisitor") that humanity was too weak to accept the freedom of choice in the knowledge of good and evil offered by Christ, and that it has become the duty of "the elect" – meaning the church as epitomized by the Grand Inquisitor – to take upon themselves the fatherly responsibility of proclaiming immortality as the reward for a virtuous life. In this way human conscience has allowed itself to be suborned in the name of mystery, miracle and authority, the three temptations offered to Christ in the wilderness. But what Ivan left out of account in his denial of divine fatherhood was the more insidious temptation of trying to deny the role of the devil in his own life.

Ivan Karamazov's "respectable" devil may seem to be no more than a figment of his imagination. On the principle that his own theory of total permissiveness in the moral sphere found its mocking embodiment in the character of Smerdyakov, so his insistence on a Euclidian view of reality is mocked, as the whole amoral edifice of his argument is mocked, by the supposed reality of his talkative devil. The fact that his devil challenges him to perform an act of virtue and testify on his brother's behalf at his trial is one significant aspect of the devil's ironic meaning; equally ironic is the devil's challenge to the very idea of realism and the notion that the real and the unreal, the conscious reality and the reality of dream, are necessarily and always distinguishable. Because Ivan finds himself unable to distinguish between them, he cannot testify accurately at the trial, any more than Alyosha can distinguish, as a "realist-believer," between the real and the miraculous. Thus when Zosima dies and revisits him in spectral form (in the beautiful chapter "Cana of Galilee") Alyosha experiences a unique moment of epiphany as he runs out into the starlit monastery garden and falls on the ground. Conscious of contact with other worlds, the narrator tells us, he fell on the ground "a weak boy, but he rose up a strong and lifelong fighter and knew and recognized this suddenly, at that instant of his ecstasy. And Alyosha could never, never again forget that moment throughout his life. 'Someone visited my soul at that hour,' he used to say afterwards with firm belief in his own words [...]" No doubt from this point forward he is destined to become the leader of the

327

boy disciples to whom he promises the miracle of immortality in the novel's concluding words.

Dostoevsky's realism in *The Brothers Karamazov* has the power to penetrate reality and encompass the miracle of religious ecstasy or the nightmare of demonic visitation with as great a veracity as it exhibits in suggesting the seediness of the small provincial town of Skotoprigonevsk (based on Staraya Russa) where the events occur. Grounded as Dostoevsky's realism always was in mundane *realia*, it made no attempt to ennoble or idealize. It was a realistic literature that grew increasingly accessible to a wider and more international readership because, in its readiness to make no assertive moral distinction between normal and abnormal, it implied a universality of experience that matched Dostoevsky's insistence in his journalism on the remarkable Russian capacity for universal feeling. He discovered such universality particularly in Pushkin (as his famous speech of 1880 testified), and the highflown rhetoric of his sentiments elicited an ovation. But Dostoevsky's honestly held convictions about Russian universality and messianism involved varying degrees of anti-western, anti-Semitic and anti-Catholic jingoism which can nowadays seem bigoted and politically reactionary.

They are a reminder that Dostoevsky was inherently a devotee of paradox with an essentially deviant view of life. His own experience of poverty, initial literary triumph, arrest, imprisonment, penal servitude, epilepsy, addiction to gambling and eventual, hard-won security and success can explain to some extent his predilection for the paradoxical in his writing, but it is to his own mysterious genius that one must look for that sense of a reality which was never strictly speaking static or normative but always definable only through a continual dialectic of pro and contra. The inherent dynamism which informed his realism has contributed directly to its universality and its universal appeal. It was a realism in which there was "a higher sense," as he himself described it, and this meant that, in Dostoevsky's version of the real, the idea occupied as conspicuous a place in human consciousness as *realia* and was the avenue through which he penetrated to the archetypal forms which shape the human spirit. These are represented in Dostoevsky as always in conflict, striving, seeking redemption from sin, trying to discover in the sick conscience of mankind the way to a discovery of God's truth. Like all truth it has to be validated by doubt. Dostoevsky validated it in his own life by his Christian commitment, but he knew the effort of faith required for human beings to pass through their own crucibles of doubt and make their own commitment. This compassion lends his realism unique spiritual depth and unique awareness of the love which each human being should bring to the act of living. Dostoevsky's witness to life's spiritual meaning has secured for his work lasting popularity and a renown far surpassing that of any other Russian writer.

The age of realism in Russian nineteenth-century literature was the age of the realistic novel. No greater examples of the genre are to be found than those created by Tolstoy and Dostoevsky in the 1860s and the 1870s, especially *Anna Karenina* and *The Brothers Karamazov*. As exemplary realistic novels they create a sense of multifaceted and multidimensional reality based on detailed description, character-enhancing dialogue, a multiplication of locales and the use of such locales as settings for portraiture. As socially orientated fictions they mirrored the reality of their day, but despite such specific topicality their realism has a universal appeal because it emphasizes the particular psychological and emotional experience of heroes and heroines who dominate the foreground, though not to the exclusion of the figures dwelling in the receding perspectives of the picture. The multiplicity that is a first principle of the Russian realistic novel, whether it be polyphonic or kaleidoscopic, ensures that in its finest examples there is no single hero or heroine, no single viewpoint that may be said to be authorial, just as there is no single intrigue or motivation or plot-line. The impression of a manifold, evolving, kinetically fluid reality burgeoning into fiction and seeking expression through the frail means of language is matched in the realistic content of the novels by the process of revelation through which, as readers, we experience a gradual initiation into the privacies of lives and discover, as though privileged, an ever deepening awareness of what is supposedly the most precious ingredient in each character's life. For it is the vitality that matters; there would be no urge to read otherwise.

The vitality of such realism in its greatest examples was undoubtedly due to two factors: the conviction felt by both

Tolstoy and Dostoevsky that there were religious grounds for humanity's redemption and the general expectation in Russia during the 1870s, particularly among the intelligentsia, that society should be morally rejuvenated after centuries of serfdom. The realism presupposed a teleological impulse. It portrayed a reality in which moral improvement was latent if not actual, and that in so literal a sense that it seemed to offer a philosophical challenge to the materialist view. Although Chernyshevsky had wanted literature to serve as a blueprint for social and political change, in Tolstoy and Dostoevsky the impulse to change suggested a blueprint of right conduct which based itself on complex choices. They did not shirk confrontation with the most paradoxical issues of the day, nor were the answers they offered so simplistic that they have since lost their vital relevance. They were illustrated in the contradictions which drove Anna Karenina to suicide and made Konstantin Levin gradually aware of the meaning of goodness that he had the power to put into his life; or in the paradoxes of justice which made Ivan Karamazov repudiate the idea of a just world and simultaneously reinforced in Alyosha the idea that justice and universal responsibility for sin were inseparable. There is no longer any need to adopt the blinkered view that such problems were simply a product of capitalism at one stage in its development. They remain as universally comprehensible in moral terms and as relevant to the human spirit as the dilemmas of choice facing Hamlet or Faust; and they are of that order of greatness.

The age of realism gave rise ultimately to a literature that was orientated towards the future while remaining firmly rooted in the realistic issues of the present. In this respect it answered the problems of its time by projecting images of "positive heroes," exemplary figures such as Konstantin Levin and Alyosha Karamazov who could be regarded as having undergone fundamentally liberating transformations in their lives. Though their view of life may have been revolutionized through such changes, they were in no sense political revolutionaries. They projected instead a vision of a liberated humanity committed to moral improvement of the world as they knew it. To this end they stressed the need for reconciliation between all men and all classes. Doubtless the high moral seriousness of such an aim must seem pretentious by normal human standards. But such positive heroes of Russian realism were not cast in the molds of gods. They were all-too-human, all-too-real in their mortal semblance. They appear to have fictional vitality because they have not outgrown their freshness of response to such ideas as freedom, responsibility, spiritual renewal, moral choice and belief in God.

To a similar extent the literature of the age of realism established enduring traditions of excellence both in the formal range of the novel and in the genre's capacious content. The Russian realistic novel as it evolved in this period was a surrogate parliament, second government, open university, academy of sciences, forum of public opinion and national conscience. As the formal characteristics of the genre expanded, so its function extended beyond the purely literary and embraced publicistic issues, economic and political as well as social, in a fashion so authoritative that it spoke more directly to national hopes and anxieties than any other manifestation of national life. Moreover, at this period it was predominantly a literature not only of large forms and large issues but also a literature of the central areas of Russian life, of the two capitals and the central Muscovite heritage. Despite censorship and a limited readership, it assumed the right to speak without constraint on every injustice observable in Russian society in a generally more candid spirit than prevailed in the major contemporary European literatures. The high seriousness, devotion to ideas and concern for spiritual values, as well as an unequalled power of psychological characterization, contributed to the most significant achievements of Russian literature in the age of realism. This was the dominant place it achieved in European prose writing. If in the immediate post-Crimean-war period Russian literature was little-known in the west, a quarter of a century later it had won widespread attention in Europe and North America and the foundation was laid for its fame as one of the greatest of world literatures.

The appeal of Russian realism, its power to dominate the mind and possess the emotions, must be attributed to a supposition that reality can be "penetrated," as Dostoevsky phrased it. Such "penetration of reality" implied a revolutionizing of normal perceptions, a process of defamiliarization in Tolstoy or of visionary, epileptic glimpses of an ultimate truth in Dostoevsky. It also implied a criticism of all supposed orthodoxies, whether religious, social, political or literary. An important feature of the success enjoyed by the Russian realistic novel in Europe and North America was precisely its critique of nineteenth-century bourgeois norms and its warning against materialistic, capitalist values. But in its very range and depth it far outreached the norms of the conventional bourgeois novel of the time and seemed indeed to invite comparison rather with the major achievements of European antiquity, the Homeric epic and Attic tragedy. Critical interpretations have pointed not only to its socio-politial, sociological and psychological meanings, but also to its symbolical, mythic, Freudian and other characteristics. Although to many readers it may seem on first acquaintance to be long-winded and tedious, full of talkative characters and improbable situations, and ultimately depressing in its somber view of the human condition, once its portals have been entered it can become so uplifting a place in which to dwell that all other literary experiences seem small-scale by comparison. What is certain is that the Russian realistic novel of the age of realism remains the most precious and influential cultural heritage of nineteenth-century Russian literature. No other body of writing or period in Russian literature since that time has been able to match it, no matter how determined have been the attempts to overcome its influence or outshine its luster.

7

THE NINETEENTH CENTURY: BETWEEN REALISM AND MODERNISM, 1880–95

After the powerful impetus given Russian literature by the flowering of realism from 1855 to 1880, the period from 1880 – the year when Dostoevsky completed publication of his last novel, and Tolstoy underwent his spiritual conversion – to 1895 was perhaps inevitably a time of lesser cultural energies, although any epoch which contained writers of the stature of a Chekhov is still a remarkable one. In 1894 Alexander III had died after reigning for almost this entire period and taking very little interest in literary matters, unlike most of his predecessors. In literary terms 1895 is the year which saw the creation of Chekhov's *The Seagull* – the first of his four outstanding plays which followed upon a period dedicated for the most part to the short story – a major work which incorporated modernist and even symbolist elements, foreshadowing the cultural revival to come.

This transitional period was dominated ideologically by the late Tolstoy, who after his spiritual crisis of 1879–80 turned to moral didacticism in literature, developed a viewpoint which came to be known as Tolstoyanism (advocating primarily non-violent resistance to evil), and gathered disciples about him. In his short story "The Death of Ivan Ilyich" he argued that the most ordinary life is the most terrible life; and in "The Kreutzer Sonata" he suggested that since sexual passion was the root of all evil, human beings might abstain from sexual relations even if this meant the end of the human race. Tolstoy's ideas were very extreme, but power of his literary talent obtained a respectful hearing for them even if his readers ultimately rejected them.

But Tolstoy had been a literary presence for some time, and the new approach in these years was that of Anton Chekhov, the "voice of twilight Russia," as he has been called, the chronicler of the landowning class which was becoming ever less economically viable after the liberation of the serfs in 1861, the observer of the intelligentsia which had somehow lost its spiritual moorings, a physician who could diagnose his society's ailments brilliantly, but who – like Lermontov in

A Hero of Our Time – had no prescription for a cure. He chronicled the cultural and spiritual malaise of his day, but, as the outwardly success-ful doctor-narrator of "A Boring Story" says of himself, he lacked any "guiding idea" in his life, unlike Tolstoy. Chekhov was the historian of the age of "small deeds" which had succeeded the era of great dreams of the 1860s, but he was by no means certain that these "small deeds" would ever amount to anything.

Another typical figure of the 1880s was Vsevolod Garshin, who dealt with psychological and social pathologies as well as with outright insanity, as in his most famous short story "The Red Flower," which describes a madman convinced that all the evil of the world is con-tained in a few flowers which he must destroy. Garshin himself suffered from mental instability and ended his life by suicide at a very young age.

Although poetry had remained under a shadow since the esthetic controversies of the 1860s, it began to recover during the 1880s, when certain poets became very popular because they accurately expressed the contemporary cultural mood. Perhaps the best known of them at the time – though he is little remembered now – was Semyon Nadson, who died prematurely of consumption, as Chekhov would later. Years afterwards Ivan Bunin in a fictionalized autobiography would recall his reaction to Nadson in a passage which evokes the cultural atmosphere of the 1880s:

> What enthusiasm [Nadson's] name then aroused, in even the remotest parts of the country! I had already read some Nadson, and, try as I might, could not make myself respond. "Let the poison of pitiless doubts expire in the tormented breast" seemed to me mere rhetoric in bad taste [. . .] But never mind – Nadson was a poet who died untimely, a young man with a beautiful and sad look in his eyes, of whom people wrote that he "expired amid roses and cypresses on the shores of the azure southern sea" [. . .] When, during the winter, I read of his death and his metal coffin, "all drowned in flowers," being sent for solemn funeral to "frosty and foggy St. Petersburg," I came down to dinner so pale and excited that even my father looked anxiously at me [. . .]

Political passions were by no means dead, of course. The most power-ful of them in the 1880s was populism, preached by Gleb Uspensky and some of his colleagues, which emphasized the political and cultural potential of the peasantry. But there was always an ambivalence in the mind of the Russian intelligentsia toward the peasantry and rural life: while some, like Tolstoy, saw them as the source of all good, others with equal conviction dismissed rural backwardness as a hindrance to cultural progress. Thus, while there was always a peasant-oriented current in Russian literature, one which reached its apogee in the 1880s, it never gathered sufficient force to dominate the cultural scene, although in the 1980s it is still with us in the work of the so-called "village writers."

Still, despite its positive cultural contributions, in the long view of history the period 1880–95 was primarily a transition from the era of Russian realistic prose to the years dominated by modernism and symbolism, the "silver age" of Russian culture stretching from the turn of the century down to the outbreak of the First World War.

THE YEARS from 1880 to 1895 stand out as a transitional period in Russian literature, a period characterized by decisive conclusions and tentative beginnings. Many of the major founders of nineteenth-century realism – Dostoevsky, Turgenev, Pisemsky – died within a few years after 1880, and other established writers, such as Ostrovsky and Saltykov-Shchedrin, died later in the decade. Another major literary figure, Leo Tolstoy, underwent at the beginning of the decade a profound spiritual crisis that led to his temporary withdrawal from literature; when he eventually returned to writing, his work was markedly different from his earlier fiction. In the socio-political sphere as well, one observes significant demarcations and changes. The reformist Tsar Alexander II was assassinated in 1881, and his successor, Alexander III, ushered in a reign of severe repression. This repression, coupled with the recent collapse of the "going to the people" movement in the mid-1870s, led to a palpable sense of disillusionment and depression among a large segment of the intelligentsia in the early 1880s. Anton Chekhov wrote with dismay about his entire generation in a letter of 1892: "We truly lack a certain something: if you lift up the skirts of our muse, all you see is a flat area. [...] We have neither immediate nor remote goals, and there is an emptiness in our souls."

Over the course of this fifteen-year period, however, the air of exhaustion evident at the outset gradually yielded to signs of renewal. New voices in prose, especially Vsevolod Garshin, Vladimir Korolenko, and Chekhov himself, were matched by the reappearance in poetry of such writers as Afanasy Fet and Konstantin Sluchevsky. Although a fundamental departure from patterns of the past would not be accomplished until the turn of the century, writers in the period from 1880 to 1895 were already beginning to search for new modes of expression. During this time many of them avoided the longer narrative forms which had dominated literature in the preceding decades and instead turned to the smaller forms such as the sketch, the short story, or the fable. Often these short works were grouped together in cycles, which served as a kind of intermediary genre before writers returned to the novel at the end of the century. Within the works themselves, many writers not only sought to portray contemporary scenes in the naturalistic traditions of nineteenth-century realism, they also began to utilize allegorical narrative techniques more extensively than in the past, in part to avoid constraints imposed by the censor, but also to suggest the vague and intangible impressions of their souls. This shift toward the allegorical and allusive would eventually become the prevailing artistic method in the late 1890s.

In the early part of this period, however, the literary arena was still dominated by writers who had established their reputation much earlier. One of the most important of these was Ivan Turgenev, whose health had worsened in recent years. His small literary output at the end of his career displays an unremitting concern with death and the impersonal processes of nature, a concern shaped in part by his longstanding interest in Schopenhauer. Representative of this concern are his *Poems in Prose* (*Stikhotvoreniya v proze*), a series of eighty-three short compositions to which Turgenev himself gave the name *Senilia*. Turgenev wrote them in two clusters – sixty eight from 1877 to 1879, and fifteen more in 1881 and 1882 – but only fifty were published during his lifetime in the journal *Herald of Europe* (*Vestnik Evropy*).

Lyrical in style and intimate in tone, these concise vignettes, some no more than four or five lines long, have reminded some readers of Charles Baudelaire's *Petits poèmes en prose* (published 1869) and Novalis' *Hymnen an die Nacht* (1800), both in their form and in their broad philosophical content. Through them Turgenev touches upon a wide range of subjects. Graceful portraits of Russia's landscapes and people alternate with hymns to feminine beauty, panegyrics to the proud spirit of those who risk much in pursuit of political reform, and personal observations on the prevalence of cruelty in the world. Dominating the whole is Turgenev's ever-present consciousness of mortality, which finds direct reflection in "The Old Woman" ("Starukha"), "The End of the World" ("Konets sveta"), and "'What Will I Be Thinking?'"

("'Chto ya budu dumat?'"). Many sketches resemble fables or allegories, and the writer may express his preoccupation with death in a vision in which he faces his destiny in symbolic form: in "The Old Woman" he is pursued by a predatory crone who declares that he "will not escape." The works are uneven in quality, frequently marred by excessive sentimentality or exaggerated emotion. Only in the very best of them does Turgenev balance his somber perceptions with an undercurrent of animating irony or wit. Nevertheless, these lyrical metaphysical musings won praise from several of the Russian symbolists later on.

Turgenev's concern with the unfathomable processes ruling human existence also surfaces in his two major short stories of the 1880s – "The Song of Triumphant Love" ("Pesn torzhestvuyushchey lyubvi," 1881) and "Clara Milich (After Death)" ("Klara Milich [Posle smerti]," 1882, published 1883). The former work is particularly distinctive. Ostensibly translated from an Italian manuscript, it is heavily stylized to evoke the atmosphere of the Italian Renaissance. In it Turgenev illustrates the power of irrational passion to disrupt the placid existence of ordinary individuals. His story centers on the fate of three people: two friends named Fabius and Mucius who are both in love with the beautiful Valeria. After Valeria's mother chooses Fabius to marry her daughter, Mucius leaves Ferrara to seek oblivion in the east. When he returns five years later, he has undergone an ominous change: accompanied by a mute Malay servant, he seems to possess strange powers of enchantment. After he plays a stirringly sensuous melody he calls "The song of triumphant love" on his violin, Valeria is plagued with erotic dreams about him. On successive nights she is hypnotically drawn to Mucius, who himself seems to be in an uncanny trance. The jealous Fabius stabs Mucius one night but is stunned to find that the Malay has the power to reanimate the lifeless body. After the Malay and the catatonic Mucius leave the household, the nightmare of their presence seems to yield to tranquility. One day, however, as Valeria is playing the organ, her fingers spontaneously pick out Mucius's "Song of triumphant love," and at that very instant she feels within her womb the stirrings of new life. Although its conclusion carries a certain impact, the tale itself seldom rises above the ornate trappings by means of which Turgenev tries to create an exotic atmosphere. His characters tend to be one-dimensional, and thus the author is only intermittently successful at forging emotional empathy between reader and character.

Somewhat more accomplished is "Clara Milich." Based in part on an actual incident, the story depicts the fatal effect produced by the suicide of a singer, Clara Milich, on a sensitive young man named Yakov Aratov. Clara Milich and Aratov meet only once, at the outset of the story, and he reacts coolly to her attempts to establish a closer friendship. When he subsequently learns that she has committed suicide, perhaps because of unrequited love, he becomes obsessed with her memory. His dreams of the dead woman become increasingly more tangible, until at last he obtains a passionate kiss from her, after which he collapses in a faint. The very next night he faints again, and this time never regains consciousness. On his face is an uncannily beautiful smile, and in his clenched fist – a strand of a woman's hair. Turgenev's method of shading psychological abnormality with tinges of the super-natural recalls the work of Edgar Allan Poe, and Turgenev himself mentioned Poe when writing about the event on which his story is based. In contrast to "The Song of Triumphant Love," however, Turgenev grounds "Clara Milich" in the *realia* of nineteenth-century Russia, and his portrait of Aratov's solicitous aunt adds a humorous touch to his tale of the uncanny. Although readers can find a rational explanation for all that occurs in the story, Turgenev utilizes his psychological portrait of the possessed Aratov to articu-late the premise that "love is stronger than death," an idea that appears repeatedly in his late work. As he approached his own death Turgenev seemed to seek reassurance that some positive element in the human spirit transcends the grave, and his late tales show a shift away from the realist tendencies of his most famous earlier works. The writer's inquiry into the forces lying beneath the visible surface of human experience anticipates developments that reached fruition among the subsequent generation of Russian writers – the symbolists.

While Turgenev's literary career came to an end in the early 1880s, Leo Tolstoy's career was setting out in an entirely new direction. Tolstoy had always been intensely absorbed by the question of how one should live. Readers of his early fiction have noted an apparent dichotomy between those characters who continually probe their beliefs about life and those who live freely and spontaneously, without excessive self-analysis. During this period Tolstoy experienced a spiritual crisis that had a major impact on his writing, and which he recorded in a remarkable work entitled *A Confession* (*Ispoved*, written 1879–1882, published 1884), a forceful piece of self-examination and sustained rhetoric.

Building his discourse out of long chains of questions and arguments, Tolstoy recapitulates the desperate search for meaning in life which obsessed him in the late 1870s. He recalls how he had attempted to live his life according to the conventions of his social circle, and how he found societal approval even for those activities which he now regards as depraved. His placid sense of self-satisfaction began to erode, however, when he asked himself the simple question: "What is it all for?" The more avidly he sought a rational answer – in science and in philosophy – the more he realized that no rational answer existed, and the more empty he came to feel, so that his thoughts turned to suicide. Yet at the same time, he knew that millions of people were living lives of peace and fulfillment, and he began to probe the source of their happiness. Gradually he realized that it was erroneous to seek the meaning of life through reason, that only irrational knowledge – faith – could give meaning to life. Then he turned to religion for possible guidance. Once more, his intellect discovered much hypocrisy in the dictates of organized religion, but he perceived in the Gospel itself a foundation upon which to build a life of true faith. His *Confession* concludes with an admission of the limits of his intellect and a pledge to seek religious truth.

Tolstoy's religious conversion had several consequences for his literary productivity. He initially rejected his previous mode of writing as immoral, and although he did return to artistic literature in the mid-1880s, he first composed a series of theological studies in which he criticized the established church and formulated his own conception of Christianity. Tolstoy promoted the conscience and the basic teachings of Christ as guides toward achieving a life of goodness, simplicity, and non-violence. In addition to this series of works, which includes *A Study of Dogmatic Theology* (*Issledovanie dogmaticheskogo bogosloviya*), *A Union and Translation of the Four Gospels* (*Soedinenie i perevod chetyrekh evangeliy*), and *What I Believe* (*V chem moya vera?*), Tolstoy also wrote a number of short

339

instructional works derived from popular legends and early Christian stories. Wishing to reach a wide audience with his tales, the writer utilized a simple style based on colloquial Russian. Frequently ending with aphoristic sayings or scripture quotations such as "Unless you become like children, you will not enter the kingdom of Heaven" ("Little Girls Are More Clever Than Old Men" ["Devchonki umnee starikov," 1885]), these works illustrate basic Tolstoyan truths. In "What Men Live By" ("Chem lyudi zhivy," 1881), for example, a rebellious angel sent to earth is taken in by a poor shoemaker and his wife, and there he learns that people live "not by concern for themselves, but by love alone." A similarly anti-materialistic message concludes "How Much Land Does a Man Need" ("Mnogo li cheloveku zemli nuzhno," 1886). Lured by the promise of obtaining as much land as he can encircle in a day's walk, an avaricious peasant strides around a huge tract, only to collapse in mortal exhaustion before reaching his departure point. Instead of a large domain, the man now needs only six feet of earth, just enough for his burial. To facilitate the dissemination of these moral tales Tolstoy and Vladimir Chertkov founded a publishing house called the Intermediary (Posrednik) in 1884. The Intermediary later became a major publisher of mass-edition works, listing among its contributors such writers as Vsevolod Garshin, Vladimir Korolenko, and Maxim Gorky.

Tolstoy later distilled his convictions on the merits of an esthetic which promoted moral truths through simple forms into a theoretical treatise entitled *What is Art?* (*Chto takoe iskusstvo?*), published in 1897–8 (the first complete, uncensored version appeared in English translation in 1898). He begins by challenging those theories which invoke the nebulous concept of "beauty" in evaluating and defining works of art. Tolstoy concentrates on the relationship between the artist and the receiver of his work, declaring that the aim of art is to transmit feelings from artist to audience. Genuine art is successful in "infecting" its audience: "The stronger the infection, the better is the art as art." In Tolstoy's view, art with a universal appeal is superior to art that speaks only to the elite, as does French symbolism. Having acknowledged that genuine art has the power to infect its audience, Tolstoy further comments on the types of feelings which art may evoke in its audience. Genuine art can arouse negative emotions such as rage or desire as well as positive ones, but the best art is that which transmits the highest feelings of its time. Such feelings are primarily religious. Thus Tolstoy categorizes art on the basis of the kinds of feelings it evokes. In the highest category is "Christian" art – art transmitting feelings flowing from a religious perception of our filial relationship to God and our fraternal relationship to our fellow humans. Works in this category include Dickens' "A Christmas Carol" and *A Tale of Two Cities*, Stowe's *Uncle Tom's Cabin*, and several of Dostoevsky's works. The next category contains works which convey the simplest feelings of common life: *Don Quixote, David Copperfield*, and the tales of Gogol and Pushkin belong here.

In his own work as well, Tolstoy moved beyond the simple tales he had written for a popular audience in the early 1880s. Later in the decade he again began to write fiction for a more sophisticated audience, setting forth in carefully crafted works the lessons he had derived from his recent spiritual turmoil.

Perhaps the finest of these is "The Death of Ivan Ilyich" ("Smert Ivana Ilicha," 1886), a sobering study of very basic questions of life and death. From the outset Tolstoy demonstrates an unerring mastery of narrative structure and technique. Opening his tale with an ironic exposé of the egocentric responses of Ivan Ilyich's colleagues and family to his death, Tolstoy gradually narrows his focus from a detached account of how Ivan had lived to an intimate exploration of the psychology of the man as he lay dying.

At each stage in this process Tolstoy peels back the layers of hypocrisy and convention within which society cloaks itself. Thus he notes that even though Ivan Ilyich's colleagues liked him, their first thoughts upon learning of his death had to do with their new opportunities for promotion. Likewise, the supposedly grief-stricken widow seems more concerned with obtaining a pension than with the loss of her spouse. By launching his narrative with a depiction of shallow people's selfish responses to Ivan's death, Tolstoy creates a model of societal behavior against which the conventionality of his hero's life and the unconventionality of his ultimate conversion may be measured.

When he turns to a description of Ivan's career, Tolstoy reveals his predilection for making authoritative pronouncements about life. The narrative voice declares: "The past history of Ivan Ilyich's

life was most simple and ordinary, and therefore most terrible."
Tracing his hero's pursuit of material possessions, Tolstoy embellishes his chronicle with symbolic detail, and it becomes clear that
Ivan's preoccupation with worldly goods was not a sign of health
but a presage of death. Indeed, it is while hanging curtains in his
new house that Ivan suffers the injury that results in his death.

Tolstoy's handling of the dying man's thoughts provides a fine
example of what the Russian critic Konstantin Leontev called
"psychological eavesdropping." The reader closely follows every
turn in Ivan's emotions – from anger and denial to fear, hope, and
finally, reconciliation. Tolstoy indicates that as long as Ivan clings
to the belief that he has lived his life well, he will suffer terribly
from the prospect of death. Only at the end, when Ivan acknowledges that his life of external propriety has been a lie and that there
is a more selfless way to live, does he realize that there is no death,
but rather joyous light. This narrative reflects Tolstoy's own
experiences as recorded in *A Confession*, but here the writer has
dropped the complex philosophical arguments of the earlier work
to fashion instead a simpler document of lasting artistic merit.

Similar to "The Death of Ivan Ilyich" with its focus on a moral
epiphany at the moment of death is a tale that Tolstoy wrote a
decade later – "Master and Man" ("Khozyain i rabotnik," 1895).
This story depicts the internal metamorphosis of a self-centered
merchant named Brekhunov after he is trapped with his servant in
a raging blizzard. When faced with death, Brekhunov finally
sacrifices his own life to save his workman from dying. Like Ivan
Ilyich, Brekhunov discovers that when one ceases to cling selfishly
to life, one finds not "death," but liberation. Unlike the earlier
tale, though, the hero's conversion here has a tangible effect on the
living: while it is not at all clear that Ivan Ilyich's understanding is
communicated to his family, Brekhunov's revelation leads to the
preservation of another's life.

One of Tolstoy's admirers, the writer Ivan Bunin, claimed that
Tolstoy's preoccupation with death stemmed from his fervid
appreciation of life and its physical pleasures. Yet in Tolstoy's late
fiction one notes a nagging distrust of physical urges, particularly
sexual desire. Two stories of 1889, "The Kreutzer Sonata"
("Kreytserova sonata") and "The Devil" ("Dyavol"), portray this
force in the darkest colors. The former work presents the story of a

man named Pozdnyshev who has killed his wife in a jealous rage over her relationship with a musician. As in "The Death of Ivan Ilyich" Tolstoy begins the story with an introductory scene in which conventional societal views of love and marriage are aired, only to be rebutted by the main protagonist on the basis of his experiences. After listening to a group of train passengers discussing the sanctity of love in marriage, Pozdnyshev delivers an impassioned diatribe in which he declares that the educated class's view that marriage must be based on love is pure delusion. The true motive behind marriage, he asserts, is primitive, animal lust. Pozdnyshev argues that the sexual drive is a pernicious force, that it would be better for the human race to practice celibacy than to continue the manipulative practices of modern society. His speech has more the character of a didactic lecture than a dramatic illustration of human weakness, and its monochromatic quality undermines the artistic value of the piece. Nevertheless, the work contains several fine scenes, as when Pozdnyshev recalls revelling in his anger at his wife and when he describes his rising fury in the moments before he murders her. The publication of the story in 1896 provoked a strong reaction among the reading public. Russian literature had remained remarkably chaste during most of the nineteenth century, but Tolstoy's work paved the way for increasingly frank treatments of sexuality in literature.

The second work Tolstoy devoted to the problem of human sexuality – "The Devil" – is more conventional, and yet it too contains some impressive moments. The story outlines the emotional struggle of a decent young landowner named Irtenev who is overcome by uncontrollable desire for a peasant woman who lives on his estate and with whom he had had a sexual liaison before his marriage. Deriving elements of this plot from personal experience, Tolstoy once more exposes the basic failings of a society which condones sexual activity so long as it is kept within the proper boundaries of discretion. Irtenev is dismayed as his irresistible desire destroys his peace of mind and his harmonious relationship with his family, but he obtains no guidance from others. In the tale's original conclusion Irtenev shoots himself to end his suffering, but Tolstoy was dissatisfied with that resolution and rewrote the ending so that Irtenev shoots his former lover instead. The two endings reflect differing conceptions of evil in human life: in the first case evil emanates from within, and thus can be eradicated only by killing oneself; in the second case evil comes from without, and must be eradicated by destroying the external source. In either case, though, Tolstoy's point remains: lust can destroy a human life.

The pernicious consequences of human desire emerge vividly from two other works Tolstoy wrote in the 1890s: "Father Sergius" ("Otets Sergiy") and *Resurrection* (*Voskresenie*). Composed between 1890 and 1898 and published posthumously in 1911, "Father Sergius" opens with a portrait of Stepan Kasatsky, a gifted young nobleman ready to embark upon a brilliant career in high social circles. However, when Kasatsky discovers that his fiancée has been the Tsar's mistress, he abruptly abandons her and society itself to become a monk. The central portion of the tale delineates the hero's ever more rigorous attempts to purge himself of his emotional and psychological vices, particularly pride and carnal desire. Faced with sexual temptation in his hermit's cell, he resorts to the kind of drastic measures adopted by medieval Russian saints: he chops off one of his fingers to resist the provocations of an impulsive divorcee. The gesture so stuns her that within a year she too joins a convent. Yet beneath Kasatsky's zeal lies a corrosive force: it is vanity which impels him to excel as much in his religious pursuits as he had in his secular activities. Even as his apparent piety shines more brightly to the outside world, he finds the inner light of true religion steadily diminishing. After succumbing to the seduction of a merchant's daughter, Kasatsky abandons the monastic world in despair, and finds peace only when he visits a simple woman whose life of unconscious submission to others points the way for Kasatsky to attain an authentic state of humility. Tolstoy informs this tale of human failure and regeneration with an effective spirit of stern solemnity.

Tolstoy provides another view of a young social lion who turns his back on the conventions of his milieu in *Resurrection*, which he worked on for some ten years and hastily published in 1898 to raise funds to support the emigration of the persecuted religious sect of Dukhobors to Canada. Like Kasatsky, Dmitry Nekhlyudov enjoys high society life until he is abruptly confronted with the consequences of his unthinking orientation toward selfish pleasure. In an episode that Tolstoy drew from real life, Nekhlyudov is called to serve on a jury at the trial of a prostitute named Maslova who has been charged with murder, and he recognizes in the accused a woman whom he had seduced and abandoned years earlier. Feeling responsible for her plight, he offers to marry her even as she is found guilty and sentenced to hard labor in Siberia through a careless judicial error. The major part of the novel depicts Nekhlyudov's experience of the corruption and abuse widespread in every segment of Russian society and his growing conviction of men's need to observe a simple moral law.

The novel offers certain rewards to the reader. Tolstoy's detailed descriptions of varied social types, from passionate political prisoners to bathetic evangelical preachers, are swiftly sketched with a characteristic penchant for exposing covert hypocrisy and inflated egotism, and they are charged with vibrant verisimilitude. Similarly, his concentrated vignettes of the brutalities of the Russian penal system retain their impact. It is interesting to note the way Tolstoy's favorite devices reappear in this last novel of his. The technique of "making things strange," partly humorous when utilized to depict such events as a visit to the opera in *War and Peace*, takes on a ferocious sharpness when applied to a description of an Orthodox religious service, with its ritual consumption of the flesh and the blood of Jesus. On the whole, however, *Resurrection* is marred by lengthy passages of unincorporated didacticism and moral preaching. After the initial period of turmoil Nekhlyudov experiences upon encountering Maslova, he ceases to evince any real vitality, becoming merely a vehicle for the author to vent his indignation over social injustice. His discovery of the basic Christian precepts of forgiveness and love seems arid and cerebral.

More effective as a work of art is the long tale entitled "Hadji Murat," written from 1896 to 1904 and published posthumously. In spirit the work recalls the pantheistic celebration of natural life found in *War and Peace* and "The Cossacks." Based on historical characters, the work focuses on a valiant warrior of the Caucasus, Hadji Murat, a noble, elemental soul who briefly joins the ranks of the Russians but then is killed by them as he tries to escape to rescue his family from the clutches of his enemy, the native leader Shamil. Tolstoy's portrayal of Hadji Murat is deft and sure. The character's simplicity, purity, and innate grace contrast with the venality infecting Russian and native leaders alike. The author's bitterness over the destructiveness and vanity of "civilized" man is as evident here as in *Resurrection*, but he conveys this not so much in passages of summary exposition as through the behavior of the characters themselves. Especially memorable is the portrait of the egocentric and lascivious Tsar Nicholas, a portrait which influenced Solzhenitsyn's handling of Stalin in *The First Circle*. Tolstoy underscores the natural beauty and resilience of Hadji Murat himself by comparing him to a wild thistle which valiantly resists the wanton destructiveness of human society. Nevertheless, even this strong character is no match for the rapacity of the mighty of this world.

Along with his prose fiction Tolstoy also experimented with playwriting in the 1880s. After trying his hand at stage adaptations of his own prose compositions, he wrote two notable plays which convey his moral indignation over contemporary social mores: *The Power of Darkness* (*Vlast tmy*, 1886) and *The Fruits of Enlightenment* (*Plody prosveshcheniya*, 1889–90). The first of these was written in response to a request from the director of the Moscow National Theater to help establish a repertoire for a popular theater; its title recalls Gleb Uspensky's novella *The Power of the Soil* (*Vlast zemli*, see below). Inspired by testimony at a recent trial, *The Power of Darkness* dramatizes a spiraling sequence of misdeeds in a peasant household. Tolstoy subtitled his play "If One Claw is Caught, the Whole Bird is Lost," and in the course of his five-act drama he shows how one crime inevitably entails another, until they eventually crush the protagonist under a mounting burden of guilt. The central figure of the play is a peasant laborer named Nikita who enters into an adulterous relationship with his ailing master's wife Aksinya. Renouncing another woman whom he had once seduced, he marries Aksinya after poisoning her husband. He then takes up with her daughter Akulina, impregnates her, and kills the illegitimate baby upon its birth. In the climactic scene, ravaged by the weight of his accumulated sins, Nikita confesses his guilt before the entire peasant commune gathered at Akulina's arranged wedding. The tightly-constructed play makes effective use of colloquial speech, and Tolstoy couches his warnings about the evils of greed and sexual desire in pithy folk sayings. Although the play encountered problems with the censorship and was not produced before a broad rural audience, it enjoyed great success when first performed in Moscow in 1895.

More light-hearted in tone is *The Fruits of Enlightenment*, a farcical satire contrasting the foolish egocentricity of the Moscow aristocracy with the cunning and energy of the peasant class. The plot involves an attempt by a group of peasants to purchase some much-needed land from a nobleman in Moscow. The latter initially refuses to sell, but he is taken with the current vogue of spiritualism, and a clever servant girl tricks him into signing the sales agreement at a comical seance. Tolstoy's use of pungent vernacular adds a rich element of humor to the play. Although his achievements as a playwright were much less substantial than his accomplishments in prose, the two plays Tolstoy wrote in the 1880s have earned a place in the repertory of classic Russian theater. Also retaining its popularity is Tolstoy's last major play, *The Live Corpse* (*Zhivoy trup*, written 1900, published posthumously in 1911), a broad drama depicting the futile struggle of a pathetically dissolute man to release his wife from his own unreliability. After first faking suicide to set his wife free, he is driven to kill himself in actuality when he realizes that his wife, now remarried, will be convicted of bigamy. Tolstoy here softens his customary concern for moral fiber with a compassionate treatment of the hero's desire not to ruin other lives as he has ruined his own.

As Tolstoy's life drew to a close, he became increasingly controversial. Excommunicated for his teachings by the Orthodox Church in 1901, he was encouraged by Chertkov and others to devote more time to his publicistic work and to eschew the type of artistic activity represented by "Hadji Murat." Consequently, Tolstoy's artistic output diminished after the turn of the century, and although he did produce such engaging works as "After the Ball" ("Posle bala," 1903), "The False Coupon" ("Falshivy kupon," finished 1904 and published posthumously in 1911), and "Alyosha the Pot" ("Alesha Gorshok," written 1905, published 1911), he also wrote numerous religious and political tracts, such as "I Cannot Be Silent" ("Ne mogu molchat," 1908), a denunciation of the reprisals taken against political activists following the civil unrest of 1905–6. Debilitated by ill health and by the conflicting demands of his followers and his family, Tolstoy felt increasingly dispirited. Finally, at the end of October 1910, he left home to die a few days later on 7 November at the small railway station of Astapovo, leaving behind an enormous literary legacy whose impact continues to be felt a century later.

While Tolstoy embarked upon a brief career as a playwright in the 1880s, Alexander Ostrovsky concluded his dramatic career during that decade. The elderly playwright wrote several works that continued the concerns of his earlier work, concentrating on domestic conflicts among middle-class or merchant families – *Slaves* (*Nevolnitsy*, written 1880, published 1881), *Not Of This World* (*Ne ot mira sego*, written 1884, published 1885), and *The Handsome Man* (*Krasavets-muzhchina*, written 1882, published 1883), which aroused controversy by its treatment of a wastrel's plan to divorce his wife and marry a rich woman. Ostrovsky also wrote two plays that shed light upon the lifestyle of provincial actors: *Career Woman* (*Talanty i poklonniki*, literally – *Talents and Admirers*, written 1881, published 1882) and *Guilty without Guilt* (*Bez viny vinovatye*, written 1883, published 1884). The first of these two is of particular interest for its treatment of the pressures faced by an actress struggling to make a life for herself in the theater. Victimized by the intrigues of a rich theater patron, the actress Negina must decide whether she will marry a poor but loving student or abandon the student for a rich landowner who can help her in her career. Ostrovsky's handling of dialogue here anticipates Chekhov as he manipulates sense and nonsense, dialogue and monologue. *Guilty without Guilt* also probes the character and psychology of an actress, but in this case the dramatic conflict centers on the tearful reunion of the actress with her illegitimate son, whom she had long believed dead. The play's melodramatic tendencies are counteracted by the strength and nobility of the central character.

Like Ostrovsky, Nikolay Leskov entered the 1880s with a reputation already firmly established, and the work he produced in the 1880s and 1890s indicates that his creative talents had not diminished. As in such earlier pieces as "The Enchanted Wanderer" and "The Sealed Angel," Leskov displayed in his later work an impressive capacity for constructing fast-paced narratives whose rapid succession of stirring episodes is carried in a densely expressive verbal idiom. One of his most widely admired tales is "The Lefthanded Craftsman" ("Levsha," 1881), a story built upon an anecdote about one-upmanship on a grand scale. Impressed by a marvelous piece of British craftsmanship – a small steel flea that dances when wound with a minute key – Tsar Nicholas I orders the famed craftsmen of Tula to create something even finer. After much labor they come up with tiny shoes for the flea which they mount with minuscule nails. Nicholas sends the flea and one of its makers to England to impress the British, but the stalwart Russian finds British women pretentious, the tea sweet, and the alcohol suspect. He insists on going home, but on the return voyage he participates in a drinking match and after much abuse by his own countrymen dies in a charity hospital. Leskov counters his warmly humorous portrait of the simple craftsmen with pointed sketches of the callous selfishness of the Russian bureaucracy, but the real glory of the story is the narrative style itself. Written in a colorful *skaz* mode, the tale contains several examples of ingeniously corrupted borrowings from western languages, such as *melkoskop* (from the Russian root *melk-*, "shallow, petty") for "microscope."

Leskov's penchant for suspenseful narration stands out in other tales such as "The Robbery" ("Grabezh," 1887) and "Tupeyny khudozhnik" ("The Toupée Artist," 1883). The latter offers a dark first-person account of a despotic landowner's mistreatment of his serfs and consists of swiftly alternating scenes of imminent danger and sudden rescue: just as the heroine and her beloved escape one hazard, they are confronted with another. The story concludes on a somber note, with a final glimpse of the heroine, now an elderly nanny, drinking furtively at night to numb the gnawing memories of her ruined life. Also engaging is the pseudo-supernatural story "The White Eagle" ("Bely orel," 1880), one of several Christmas stories that Leskov wrote in the 1880s. Ostensibly a narrative about the persecution of a government official by a ghost, the tale in fact offers a veiled indictment of official malfeasance so subtle that many readers have missed its point altogether.

Leskov's sympathy for the neglected good inspired a series of works focusing on the lives of *pravedniki* (righteous people). These stories – which include "The Bogey-Man" ("Pugalo," 1885), "Figura" (1889), and "The Sentry" ("Chelovek na chasakh," 1887) – disclose Leskov's admiration for the innate decency of the ordinary individual. The last work, for example, describes how government officials may sacrifice their subordinates for the sake of their own careers. Based on a real incident, the story traces the tribulations of a palace sentry who leaves his post to save a drowning man. While another man takes credit for the feat and receives an award from the tsar, the poor private is thrown into solitary confinement and flogged for deserting his post. Yet the gentle soul bears no malice against his superiors; he is merely relieved that his punishment was not more severe.

Leskov found support for his humanitarian impulses in Tolstoy's ethical writings of the 1880s: he admired his colleague deeply. His own imagination, however, produced more exotic and ornate tales about Christian life than did Tolstoy, and his personal vision of morality was less austere than Tolstoy's. During the 1880s he produced a set of colorful works based in part on the Russian *Prolog*, a medieval compendium of saints' lives and religious matter. While some of these stories, such as "Conscience-Stricken Danila" ("Sovestny Danila," 1888), are flawed by an uneven attempt to merge didacticism with entertainment, others such as "Beautiful Aza" ("Prekrasnaya Aza," 1888) and "Pamfalon the Clown" ("Skomorokh Pamfalon," 1887) achieve considerable success. The former work highlights the inherent nobility of a struggling prostitute, while the latter tale contrasts the search to attain salvation through barren asceticism with the higher goal of service to one's fellow human beings.

In the last years of his life Leskov wrote a cycle of satiric works lampooning the narrow-minded philistinism of contemporary Russian society. Of this cycle, which includes "Night Owls" ("Polunoshchniki," published 1891), "The Cattle-pen" ("Zagon," 1893), "A Winter Day" ("Zimny den," 1894), and the unfinished novel *The Devil's Dolls* (*Chertovy kukly*, 1890), perhaps the most entertaining is "The Rabbit Warren" ("Zayachy remiz"), written in 1894. This is the first-person account of one Onopry Peregud, a simple-minded fellow who becomes obsessed with the notion that in order to earn an official decoration he must seek out and capture people bent on "shaking the foundations" of society, i.e. nihilists. Led astray by his own enthusiasm, the poor soul ends up by aiding a political agitator and arresting a police agent, and is subsequently confined in an insane asylum. Although Leskov set the story in the Ukraine and embellished it with many farcical elements, no journal would publish it because of its caustic view of official paranoia, and it did not appear in print until 1917. Political convictions of various sorts diminished the contemporary appreciation of Leskov's talent, but his innovative approach to language and narrative style exerted a major influence on such twentieth-century artists as Alexey Remizov, Eugene Zamyatin, and Boris Pilnyak.

Even more than in Leskov's work, political satire played a leading role in Mikhail Saltykov's prose of the 1880s. Saltykov had long been a prominent representative of the radical intelligentsia, and he continued to direct his critical eye on the major socio-political developments of his day, despite the 1884 closing of his major editorial outlet, the progressive journal *Fatherland Notes*. The satirical thrust of Saltykov's prose is evident in such cycles as *Abroad* (*Za rubezhom*, 1880–1), a caustic survey of the prevailing social order in France and Germany; *Letters to Auntie* (*Pisma k tetenke*, 1881–2), a series of epistolary exhortations to resist deceit and depression in Russia; *A Contemporary Idyll* (*Sovremennaya idilliya*, 1877–83), a parodic vision of Russian society as represented in the activities around a St. Petersburg police station; and numerous *skazki* (fairy tales) written from 1880 to 1886. Saltykov was a master of "Aesopian language" – a method of circumventing the censorship by couching one's observations in complex, allegoric images decipherable only by a sophisticated reader. As a result, much of his satiric work has become nearly inaccessible to a modern reader because of its topicality and allusiveness. Some of Saltykov's *skazki*, however, retain their impact because of their expressive language and broad human relevance.

A prime target of Saltykov's fairy tales is a simplistic view of society and its problems. While defending the necessity of social change, the writer is dismayed over the pace at which such change occurs. Thus in "The Liberal" ("Liberal," 1885) he depicts a liberal dreamer who agrees to ever-greater compromises to influence those around him and eventually ends with nothing but "rubbish." Some of these stories create unrelievedly dark impressions. Even the Easter tale "Christ's Night" ("Khristova noch," 1886), in which Saltykov illuminates the compassion of the resurrected Christ for the downtrodden poor, concludes with a picture of a resurrected Judas condemned by Christ to wander the world "sowing discord, treachery, and dissension" down to the present day. Saltykov's language merits notice. He blends folk-tale

formulas with colloquial slang, the language of abstract philosophy, and foreign terms to fashion an unusual conglomerate that
highlights the folly or wisdom of his characters.

Very different in tone are Saltykov's two prose cycles dealing
more openly with Russian social issues – *Trifles of Life* (*Melochi
zhizni*, 1886–7), and *Old Days in Poshekhone* (*Poshekhonskaya
starina*, 1887–9). Written after the suppression of *Fatherland Notes*,
Trifles of Life is one of the darkest works Saltykov ever created. He
himself admitted in 1887 that his "humor had entirely disappeared,
and it had always been [his] main strength." In this cycle Saltykov
surveys the sociological and psychological make-up of numerous
segments of Russian society, from priests and peasants to lawyers,
journalists, and readers. No matter where he looks, he finds no
indication that life has improved materially since the reforms of the
1860s. In the concluding sketch, "So and So" ("Imyarek"), the
ailing writer's despair as he gazes upon the failed aspirations of the
past attains a chilling depth. He concludes: "behind him trailed a
heap of crumbs and trifles, while ahead lay nothing but solitude
and neglect."

Saltykov followed this somber evaluation of the recent past with
an equally gloomy depiction of relationships between land-owners
and peasants of the pre-Reform era in *Old Days in Poshekhone*.
Although ostensibly the family chronicle of a first-person narrator
named Nikanor Zatrapezny (whose surname means "ordinary,
average"), the narrative incorporates certain autobiographical
elements as well. Through Zatrapezny's panoramic yet detailed
account of gentry life the reader is immersed in a turbid stream of
domestic tyranny, child abuse, and mistreatment of servants and
peasants. As the narrator recounts his life story he comments on its
larger significance, and in this way charges a personal document
with broad social relevance. One is reminded of *The Golovlyov
Family*, but this late work is devoid even of the infrequent rays of
joy found in the earlier novel. From *The Golovlyov Family* to *Old
Days in Poshekhone* Mikhail Saltykov fashioned a striking
indictment of social and personal injustice that has earned him a
unique place in nineteenth-century Russian literature.

Saltykov was not alone in his exploration of the grim conditions
prevailing in the Russian countryside. The present status and
future outlook of the village drew the attention of numerous

writers loosely linked to the populist movement. The 1880s proved to be a difficult time for the populists. After the failure of the "going to the people" movement and the political repression that followed the assassination of Tsar Alexander II by members of the People's Will party, the populists found scant reason for optimism about the prospects for radical change in society. However, one influential spokesman for the populists – Nikolay K. Mikhaylovsky – continued trying to rally the spirits of the progressive movement. Mikhaylovsky had already established himself as a major theoretician of populism with such tracts as "What is progress?" (1869) and *Struggle for Individuality* (*Borba za individualnost*, 1875–6), where he outlined his ideal of an ethical social order in which a spirit of individualism would flourish in a collective society founded upon principles of cooperation, harmony and creative labor. In the 1880s he criticized the contemporary trend toward "small deeds" and warned against a retreat into the passivity of Tolstoyanism or seduction by apolitical estheticism in art. Mikhaylovsky discussed all the major writers of the 1880s – Saltykov-Shchedrin, Garshin, Chekhov, Uspensky – but one of his essays in particular – "A cruel talent" ("Zhestoky talant," 1882) – stands out for its novel focus on the prominence of suffering in Dostoevsky's art.

While mindful of Mikhaylovsky's call for sustained social activism, most populist writers of the 1880s centered their work on two major topics: a detailed depiction of conditions in the Russian village in the post-Emancipation period, and an examination of the fate of the progressive intelligentsia. A writer noted for his contribution to the second trend was Andrey Osipovich Novodvorsky (who used the name A. Osipovich, 1853–82). Osipovich-Novodvorsky probed the mentality of those who sought to join the revolutionary struggle, and he highlighted the internal and external difficulties that hampered its advance. Among his major works are *The Aunt* (*Tetushka*, 1880) and *Dreamers* (*Mechtateli*, 1881).

Writers who focused more on the village than on the intelligentsia include: Paul Zasodimsky (1843–1912), who achieved renown for his novel *The Chronicle of the Village of Smurin* (*Khronika sela Smurina*, 1874) and who later authored such novels as *Secrets of the Steppe* (*Stepnye tayny*, 1880) and *Through Cities and*

Hamlets (*Po gradam i vesyam*, 1885), as well as children's stories; Filipp Nefyodov (1835–1902), who began writing in the late 1850s, was arrested in 1881, and published numerous works about the life of the peasant, worker, and intelligentsia with an idealized attitude toward the peasant commune (cf. "Ionych," 1888); Nikolay Naumov (1831–1901), who first achieved popularity in the 1870s and went on to produce striking sketches about the Siberian populace and the plight of the workers there (especially in the cycle *The Spider Web* [*Pautina*], 1880); and S. Karonin (pen name of Nikolay Petropavlovsky, 1853–92), who depicted the darker side of village life by pinpointing the economic inequalities emerging in the post-Reform era, as in "Two Desyatins" ("Dve desyatiny," 1882).

The most distinctive of this group was Nikolay Zlatovratsky. His major contribution to populist literature was the novel *Foundations* (*Ustoi*), which appeared as a series of sketches in *Fatherland Notes* from 1878 to 1883, and which is remarkable for its breadth of scope. Outlining the history and social structures of a Russian village, Zlatovratsky delineates the class differentiation that emerged in the post-Reform period and examines the conflict between the poorest stratum and the *miroedy* ("commune devourers"), the rich kulaks. In affirming the viability of the commune as the appropriate vehicle for promoting social equality, the author waxes lyrical about the potential harmony of peasant life, and certain of his descriptions have a markedly romantic coloring. As the 1880s wore on, however, the thrust of Zlatovratsky's work shifted, and he began examining the status of the populist intelligentsia in such works as "The Wanderer" ("Skitalets," 1881–4), and "The Karavaevs" ("Karavaevy," 1885). He himself was drawn to the ideals of Tolstoyanism, which he treated in "My Visions" ("Moi videniya," 1885). Eventually Zlatovratsky was made an honorary member of the Imperial Academy.

Standing somewhat apart from the populists mentioned above, but very much in the thick of the debate over the future of the Russian village, was Gleb Uspensky, whose work went beyond facile idealization of the peasant and offered a careful analysis of the benefits and drawbacks of village life. His major contribution in the 1880s was the cycle *The Power of the Soil* (1882). In this and related works Uspensky provides an unvarnished assessment of the peasant's world view. Noting that the peasant's dependence on the soil shapes his entire life, Uspensky declares that if one were to uproot the peasant from the land, there would be no people (*narod*). Everything in the peasant's life – his family relationships, his livestock, his household – is adapted to earning a livelihood from the land: this is the true "power of the soil." Yet this very dependence lends a certain lightness to the peasant's life: because all that he does stems from the demands of nature, he is relieved of any personal responsibility for his actions. Even if he were to drive his wife into the grave, he would be blameless if his wife had been lazy and had hindered his productivity. Uspensky finds such a moral code unacceptable: in opposition to this primitive world view he urges the intelligentsia to introduce a more humane truth into the commune.

Uspensky's reflections on the power of the soil occasioned much contemporary comment. In subsequent years he delved further into the changes within Russian society. Along with the power of the soil he detected a growing "power of capital," which he depicted in such sketches as "Living Numbers" ("Zhivye tsifry," 1888). Uspensky seemed to respond personally as well as professionally to the stresses of a society in transition: in the early 1890s he fell prey to a mental illness that led to his institutionalization. His work still had a substantial impact on his peers, especially Gorky.

A number of other writers who attempted to chart the changing terrain of Russian society underwent populist influence but departed from that movement in certain respects. One such writer was Alexander Ertel (1855–1908), the self-educated son of an estate manager who entered literature as a disciple of Koltsov and Nekrasov, later tried his hand at playwriting (with *Women's Revolt* [*Baby bunt*, 1884]), and ultimately achieved distinction as a prose-writer. His first collection of stories, *Notes of a Steppe-dweller* (*Zapiski stepnyaka*, 1880–1), shed light on the wholesale transformation of societal relationships in the countryside and its concomitant effects on the consciousness of the intelligentsia; as the title suggests, the influence of Turgenev was present. In 1884 Ertel was arrested for his links to the radical movement, and after his release from SS. Peter and Paul Prison was exiled to Tver for four years. Although initially drawn to the populist program, Ertel did not share its perspective fully. Instead of radical activism he became interested in the development of internal spiritual values, and he acknowledged the appeal of Tolstoy's teachings in the mid 1880s. Tolstoy's impact is evident in such works of Ertel's as "A Greedy Peasant" ("Zhadny muzhik," [originally entitled "Povest o zhadnom muzhike Ermile"]), published by The Intermediary in 1886, and "Two Pairs" ("Dve pary," 1887). The end of the decade saw Ertel's major contribution to the literature of his day, a two-volume novel *The Gardenins* (*Gardeniny*, 1889). A panoramic portrait of rural life, *The Gardenins* manifests Ertel's desire to apprehend Russian society during a period of profound mutability. The novel is distinguished both for its vivid character sketches and for its individualized, expressive language. In a preface to the novel Tolstoy declared that one who wishes to know the language of the Russian people must study Ertel's prose. Ertel continued his exploration of social evolution in his later novel *Change* (*Smena*, 1891), a depiction of the gentry's and intelligentsia's search for new codes of conduct in contemporary Russia, and in his last major work "Strukov's Career" ("Karera Strukova," published 1895–6).

Another writer who began his literary career under the influence of populism but later turned away from it was Nikolay G. Mikhaylovsky (who wrote under the name N. Garin, 1852–1906). Although an engineer by training (and a contributor to the construction of Siberian railroads), Mikhaylovsky was interested in populist ideas and experimented with progressive estate management policies, recording the disheartening results of his experiment in *Several Years in the Countryside* (*Neskolko let v derevne*, 1892). Later in the 1890s he wrote a series of stories which underscored the hardships of peasant life (cf. "In Motion" ["Na khodu," 1893] and "Village Panoramas" ["Derevenskie panoramy," 1894]). More distinctive was his tetralogy – *Tyoma's Childhood* (*Detstvo Temy*, 1892), *High-School Students* (*Gimnazisty*, 1893), *Students* (*Studenty*, 1895), and *Engineers* (*Inzhenery*, published posthumously in 1907) – which outlines the emotional development of a youth sensitive to the societal pressures shaping the lives of the intelligentsia. Garin subsequently aligned himself with the Marxists, and joined the Knowledge (Znanie) group in the 1900s.

Among the other minor novelists who gained popularity with the reading public in the 1880s and early 1890s, 'two widely divergent writers deserve mention: Dmitry Mamin (who used the pen name Mamin-Sibiryak, 1852–1912) and Peter Boborykin (1836–1921). The son of a peasant in the Urals, Mamin-Sibiryak received his early education in religious schools, and then went to St. Petersburg where he became interested in radical politics. Returning to the Urals in 1877 (where he remained until 1891), he wrote a series of works chronicling the deleterious effects of expanding capitalism in Siberia. The most notable of these include *Privalov's Millions* (*Privalovskie milliony*, 1884), an exposé of the insatiable greed of financial schemers; *A Mountain Nest* (*Gornoe gnezdo*, 1884), an examination of the unbridgeable gulf between the mighty and the weak in the Urals; *Wild Happiness* (*Dikoe schaste*, 1884) and *Stormy Torrent* (*Burny potok*, 1886), both of which cast a critical eye on the self-interest of bourgeois morality; and *Gold* (*Zoloto*, 1892), which refutes the populist belief in the salutary benefits of collective artels. For all their local color, however, Mamin-Sibiryak's novels are poorly structured and marred by schematic plots and dense descriptive passages. The writer also tried his hand at other genres; of particular interest are such children's stories and fables as *Alyonushka's Fairy Tales* (*Alenushkiny skazki*, 1894–6) and the semi-autobiographical novel *Features from Pepko's Life* (*Cherty iz zhizni Pepko*, 1894).

Even more prolific than Mamin-Sibiryak was Boborykin, a liberal nobleman whose literary career began in 1860 and continued into the 1900s. He was the author of more than one hundred novels, tales, and plays documenting the sociological changes affecting Russia, and particularly its middle class. His very prolixity, and his tendency to pad his novels with superfluous scenes and details, led to the coining of a pejorative verb derived from his name. Of the popular works Boborykin wrote in the 1880s and 1890s, including *On the Wane* (*Na ushcherbe*, 1890), *The Pass* (*Pereval*, 1894), and *Draft* (*Tyaga*, 1898), two stand out: *Chinatown* (*Kitay-gorod* [a section of Moscow], 1882), which contrasts the decline of the gentry class with the rising activism of the enlightened merchant class in Moscow and is often considered Boborykin's best work; and *Vasily Tyorkin* (1892), which delineates the world-view of a peasant who has become a merchant.

A final writer whose works bear the mark of populist influence was Vladimir Korolenko (1853–1921). Born in the Ukraine, Korolenko was educated in St. Petersburg and Moscow, where he became inspired by populist ideas and took part in local protests. After several confrontations with the authorities Korolenko was arrested in 1879 and exiled, eventually landing in Siberia. His early literary works grew out of his prison experience: he wrote the story "The Strange Girl" ("Chudnaya," 1880) in a transit prison. It contains a nuanced treatment of the relationship between a proud political prisoner and a sympathetic guard accompanying her to her place of exile. Although one admires the prisoner's strength of will, her cold refusal to respond to the guard's kind overtures makes her seem remote; by the same token, the frank colloquial manner adopted by the guard (who narrates the tale) underscores his simple good will and accentuates the gap between him and his charge.

Korolenko's stay in Siberia also inspired a series of sketches on the life of the simple folk who roam the region (e.g. "Sokolinets," 1885 and "Cherkes," 1888). Many of his works describe the land's rugged beauty in lyric passages reminiscent of Turgenev (e.g. "The Forest Rustles" ["Les shumit," 1886] and "The River Plays" ["Reka igraet"]). A more substantial piece of writing is "Makar's Dream" ("Son Makara," published 1885), the first of Korolenko's works to bring him major notice. This story deals with the difficult life of a primitive Siberian peasant who becomes drunk on cheap vodka and dreams that he has frozen to death in the taiga. Rich in descriptive detail, the story concludes with Makar's experiences after death, when he travels to meet the great Toyon ("master" in Yakut), who will pass judgement on his life. The tale displays Korolenko's characteristic blend of light humor and compassion for human travail. Sentenced to punishment as a cart horse, Makar delivers an emotional speech about the hardships he has suffered in life, and his plea softens the great master's heart.

A similar sympathy informs "The Blind Musician" ("Slepoy muzykant," 1886), a tale in which a blind youth overcomes his absorption with his own condition to become a sensitive performer whose music takes on universal resonance. Less sentimental and more humorous are such works as "Without Language" ("Bez yazyka," 1895), which was inspired by Korolenko's trip to America in 1893 and which depicts the struggle of a Ukrainian trying to get along in America without a knowledge of English.

Although Korolenko's works concentrate upon the emotional and spiritual dimensions of life, he did not believe that one should stand idly by in the face of injustice. Thus he composed a historical story about the revolt of the Jews against the Romans – "A Tale about Florus, Agrippa, and Menachem, the Son of Jehudah" ("Skazanie o Flore, Agrippe i Menakheme, syne Iegudy," 1886) – as a rebuttal to Tolstoy's doctrine of non-violent resistance to evil. He also took issue with anti-Semitism in works such as "The Day of Atonement" ("Sudny den," first entitled "Iom-Kipur," 1890) and later in "House Number 13" ("Dom No. 13," 1905). Korolenko felt that literature should play a leading role in advancing human progress, for which purpose he intentionally set out to create works that would unite realism and romanticism in a new organic synthesis. In his best work, he meets that goal, and his lessons about life are conveyed through an engaging verbal medium. After 1896, when he moved to St. Petersburg, his work became more journalistic. Modern readers may prefer the benevolent spirit of the earlier fiction.

A very different response to the hardships of life is manifest in the work of Vsevolod Garshin (1855–88). Garshin's was one of the most promising voices in Russian literature of the 1880s, but he eventually felt overwhelmed by the pressures of life and threw himself down a stairwell in 1888. At his death, however, he left a small literary legacy which, albeit tainted by melodramatic tendencies, reveals signs of genuine talent.

The son of a military officer, Garshin was educated at the Mining Institute in St. Petersburg. When war broke out with the Turks in 1877 he volunteered, served as an enlisted man, and was wounded in combat. This experience inspired his first important literary work, "Four Days" ("Chetyre dnya," 1877). A first-person narrative, the story recounts the impressions of a volunteer named Ivanov who is wounded in battle and compelled to remain immobilized for four days next to the decaying corpse of a Turkish soldier he himself has killed. In its stark portrayal of Ivanov's physical suffering and his psychological torment, the story makes a jarring statement about the senselessness of war. Confronted with the body of his victim, Ivanov bitterly contemplates the injustice involved in uprooting innocent people from their homes and sending them out to do violence. He sees the Turk as a blameless pawn, and comprehends the disparity between one's romantic ideals of patriotic battle and the reality of mutilation and death. Garshin neatly interweaves snatches of Ivanov's thoughts with graphic descriptions of the setting, and especially of the Turk's decomposing body. Wrenched from the normal routines of life, Ivanov perceives the world in a new light, and Garshin's narrative provides a remarkable model of the device known as *ostranenie* ("making things strange"). In this charged narrative the putrefying corpse assumes symbolic overtones: as the Turk's flesh falls away, a deeper reality surfaces before Ivanov's eyes and he recognizes in the Turk's horrible skull the face of war itself. Garshin's compressed narrative, with its episodic structure and terse yet vivid phrasing, established the young writer's reputation.

Garshin's subsequent work included other military tales, such as "The Coward" ("Trus," 1879) and "The Orderly and the Officer" ("Denshchik i ofitser," 1880), allegorical fables, and several stories depicting the emotional troubles of sensitive young intellectuals. Two of these – "An Incident" ("Proisshestvie," 1878) and "Nadezhda Nikolaevna" (1885) – feature St. Petersburg prostitutes as protagonists, and the reader finds traces of Dostoevsky in Garshin's portraits of people who feel the baseness of their condition acutely but take morbid pride in their wretchedness. But Garshin's characterizations lack the depth or complexity of Dostoevsky's, and these works illustrate his tendency to lapse into melodrama or bathos. At the end of "An Incident" a young civil servant who has fallen in love with a proudly embittered prostitute, Nadezhda Nikolaevna, cannot bear her rejection of his efforts to save her, and shoots himself. In "Nadezhda Nikolaevna" Garshin recasts the central characters somewhat and adds additional plot entanglements (creating a series of love triangles that recalls Dostoevsky's *The Idiot*), but the ending is even more violent. Bessonov, one of the rivals for Nadezhda's affections, kills her with a gun and is in turn killed by the other rival, Lopatin. Lopatin, however, is mortally wounded in the fray, and he concludes his diary account of the incident by expressing the hope that he will meet the other two in a realm "where our passions and sufferings will seem insignificant to us and will drown in the light of eternal love."

Garshin's most effective treatment of psychological excesses occurs in the story "The Red Flower" ("Krasny tsvetok," 1883), which he dedicated to the recently deceased Turgenev. In this story he describes a mental patient's attempt to eradicate what he believes is the embodiment of all evil in the world – three red poppies growing in the asylum's garden. Garshin himself had spent time in a mental hospital after a breakdown in 1880, and he provides haunting descriptions of the gloomy institution and the patient's incredible nervous energy as he fluctuates between lucidity and madness. The reader intimately feels the intensity of the man's belief that the world is locked in a mortal struggle between good and evil, and that he himself occupies a pivotal position as potential savior. As the story rises to a climax, the patient succeeds in tearing out the last poppy blossom. His is a Pyrrhic victory, however, for the battle has drained his strength. Returning to his bed, he dies with an expression of "proud happiness" on his face, convinced that he has vanquished the roots of evil in his world. This conclusion aptly reflects Garshin's complicated view of life. While wanting to believe in the value of sacrificial struggle and the possibility of achieving meaningful change in life, he remained painfully aware of the limitations of individual initiative.

Such a fusion of ideas informs Garshin's allegorical works too. "*Attalea princeps*" (1880) depicts the rebellion of a tropical plant growing in a conservatory in a northern city. Stifled by her hothouse captivity, she shrugs off the skepticism of the other plants and makes a concentrated effort to break through the dirty panes of greenhouse glass. She is successful in her struggle, but as she lifts her head high in freedom, she sees around her nothing but a grim autumn landscape over which the wind drives sleet and snow. As the story ends, the philistine conservatory director orders the greenhouse workers to destroy the proud tree. Garshin's contemporaries saw the story as an allegorical commentary on Russia's socio-political situation with specific application to the revolutionary movement, but the work contains a wider message about the merits and problems inherent in individual aspiration.

In the loaded atmosphere of Garshin's day political lessons were often drawn from a writer's work, and stories such as "The Signal" ("Signal," 1887) still stimulate debate over their ultimate implications. Some readers see an endorsement of Tolstoyanism in the story's portrait of the humble railway worker Semyon, who slashed his arm, drenched a white rag in his own blood, and used the rag as a red flag to warn a train of impending derailment. Yet while Garshin generally admired Tolstoy, he did not agree entirely with his ideas, and thus other readers may conclude that Semyon is less heroic than Vasily, the angry peasant who initially tore up the rails to protest bureaucratic injustice and then took up the bloody signal from the exhausted Semyon and succeeded in stopping the train. Whether or not they fully understood Garshin, however, the writer's contemporaries found his works deeply moving, and they were captivated by the image of the man they perceived behind the prose – a man who agonized over suffering in life and who sought to express and counter it through his art. Even modern readers recognize that Garshin's intuitive understanding of psychology merged with a new appreciation of the power of symbolic imagery and verbal economy to create a body of work that sets him apart from the majority of his peers.

While Garshin's career came to an abrupt end in the late 1880s, the career of the greatest new talent to emerge during that decade – Anton Chekhov (1860–1904) – was just beginning. Both as a short-story writer and as a playwright, Chekhov was unquestionably the finest Russian writer of his time. Yet despite his significance in Russian literature, his work has remained difficult for literary critics to analyze. Unlike Dostoevsky or Tolstoy, Chekhov avoided sermonizing in his fiction. He preferred subtle understatement to bold generalizations, and he resisted attempts to pigeonhole his art. He claimed that his "holy of holies" was a simple creed: "the human body, health, intelligence, talent, inspiration, love and the most absolute freedom imaginable, freedom from violence and lies, no matter what form the latter two take."

Proclaiming that the aim of art is unconditional truth, Chekhov exposed hypocrisy and deception wherever he found it, and his world contains a wide range of Russian types, from peasants to priests. Because his critical eye touched so many kinds of people, some of his contemporaries regarded him as an outright pessimist. Thus the philosopher Leo Shestov called Chekhov a "poet of helplessness," who stubbornly for twenty years "did one thing only: [. . .] he killed human hopes." Shestov's view is too simplistic. Although Chekhov populates his work with characters living lives of delusion and futility, his handling of those lives suggests that something better is possible. Moreover, he is not callous in his treatment of his characters' imperfections. While he may offer little hope of redemption for some of his heroes, he portrays their travail with compassionate understanding. Only the arrogant and insensitive are deprived of this ameliorating warmth.

Trained as a doctor, Chekhov once declared that a writer must possess the objectivity of a chemist, but denied that such objectivity implied an indifference to good and evil or the absence of ideals and ideas. While agreeing that "it would be nice to combine art with sermonizing," he claimed that for him personally it would be almost impossible: to inject his own viewpoint into his narrative would be to dilute his images and destroy the compactness of his tale. He concludes: "When I write, I rely fully on the reader, presuming that he himself will add the subjective elements missing in my story."

This observation defines a basic principle of Chekhov's art. By declining to mold his reader's viewpoint through traditional methods of authorial omniscience, he demands that the reader invest individual effort to derive meaning from a work. In structure, Chekhov eliminates much of the expository material that earlier writers used to establish a background for their characters and plots. Paring descriptions to a minimum, he relies on select detail to evoke a mood or feeling. In many tales he sets up expectations that he eventually overturns. His plots have been compared to gradual curves that begin in one direction but gently arc to end in an unexpected place. Instead of a dramatic denouement that releases the tension built up over the course of the story, the writer often provides no denouement at all. Such "zero" endings have since become a common element in the modern short story. The writer's predilection for understatement especially manifests itself in his use of language and imagery. Tolstoy was among the first to call Chekhov's manner "impressionist": instead of trying to reproduce a scene in all its naturalistic detail, Chekhov suggested the emotional atmosphere of a moment, melding a small number of meaningful details with subtle touches of color, allusive sounds and rhythms. To highlight the subjective essence of his characters' perceptions, he frequently used passive and impersonal constructions such as "it seemed" or "it appeared."

Chekhov did not develop this impressionistic style, however, at the very outset of his career; his work underwent extensive evolution. The son of a grocer and the grandson of a serf, Chekhov moved in 1879 from Taganrog to Moscow, where he enrolled in medical school. While still in school (he received his degree in 1884), he made his literary debut with contributions to popular humor magazines such as *Dragonfly* (*Strekoza*) and *Fragments* (*Oskolki*). Although his early short pieces are quite different from his more famous later works, he would retain and refine certain elements within them, such as an emphasis on concision. Chekhov's early subject matter often reflected seasonal topics or current events. He proved quite prolific at this time: from 1883 to 1885 he published some two hundred short pieces, most of which he did not consider worthy of later republication in his collected writings.

A distinctive feature of this early work is Chekhov's language. Parodies of legal jargon, ecclesiastical terminology, and street vernacular fill his sketches, and he mixes different stylistic layers to humorous effect. He also parodied popular literary genres, including the horror tale (e.g. "The Crooked Mirror" ["Krivoe zerkalo," 1883], detective stories (e.g. "The Safety Match" ["Shvedskaya spichka," 1883]), and the romantic tale after Victor Hugo (e.g. "A Thousand and One Passions, or A Terrible Night" ["Tysyacha odna strast, ili Strashnaya noch," 1880]). Another genre had important antecedents in earlier Russian literature: tales about the lives of petty officials. In the Gogolian tradition, Chekhov wrote a number of stories emphasizing the insecurity and rank consciousness that plagued the lowly bureaucrat. "Fat and Thin" ("Tolsty i tonky," 1883) describes an amiable meeting of two former schoolmates which declines into a humiliating ritual of self-abnegation when one realizes that the other is of higher rank. Another official dies from horror when his attempts to apologize for sneezing on a high-ranking official are not taken seriously by the latter ("The Death of a Government Clerk" ["Smert chinovnika," 1883]). These sketches evince a definite evolution in the writer's narrative stance. In his earliest work Chekhov's narrator is intrusive, addressing the reader with direct commentary. Later he moves away from this subjective mode to a more neutral position, until he finally arrives at the impressionistic manner described above, in which the characters' perceptions become the prevailing perspective.

Interspersed among Chekhov's humorous tales are a few works more serious in tone (e.g. "The Lady" ["Barynya," 1882] and "Late-Blooming Flowers" ["Tsvety zapozdalye," 1882]), but it was not until 1885–6 that Chekhov began to write stories indicative of his future course. One such work is "The Huntsman" ("Eger," 1885), a brief narrative depicting a meeting between a lonely peasant woman and a huntsman whom she married twelve years ago but who does not love her or live with her. Chekhov's evocative use of select detail and his understated handling of his characters' emotions testify to his growing talent.

A pivotal work in Chekhov's career is "The Steppe" ("Step," 1888), a long, almost plotless piece that consists of a series of descriptive vignettes tracing the journey of a boy named Egor from his native village to the town where he will attend school. Much of the work focuses on the journey itself, conveying predominantly through Egor's eyes the events he witnesses on his trip. Egor's passage through the steppe suggests an initiation into the mysteries of existence. The natural world seems alive, a strange realm marked by recurring images of random violence and death. Against such a background the human world appears trivial. Despite its lyricism, "The Steppe" is not a perfect work of art: Chekhov's attempt to tie the tale together through Egor's character and through a series of interweaving motifs does not overcome its looseness. Nevertheless, it marks a turning point for Chekhov: he now leaves the humorous sketches of his early years and concentrates on the problems of existence itself.

The first of Chekhov's major "existential" works after "The Steppe" bears the ironic title "A Boring Story" ("Skuchnaya istoriya," 1889). A first-person narrative, it presents the thoughts of an aging professor who realizes he will soon die. His narrative exposes a state of profound emotional paralysis and spiritual emptiness: he takes no comfort in his work, feels alienated from his family, and cannot escape from his own self-consciousness. Probing the source of his distress, he surmises that his life lacks a central focus. In all his thoughts, he says, one cannot find anything that might be called "a general idea or the god of the living man." Some readers have seized upon this statement as the key to understanding the professor's plight, and they have not hesitated to offer him that missing "idea." Dmitry Merezhkovsky declared that the professor suffered from a lack of spiritual values, while Soviet critics identify his problem as a failure to participate in progressive social movements. Such solutions are too ingenuous. The professor in fact retains one overarching belief: even now he affirms that science is the most beautiful and necessary thing in human life. Yet this belief brings him no comfort, and so one must look beyond the lack of a "general idea" to explain his malaise. The professor's description of his family relationships offers a telling clue: he feels estranged from his wife, and he does not know how to console his daughter when she is emotionally distraught. This alienation emerges even more sharply in the professor's relationship with a woman named Katya, the one person he truly loves. Although in the final scene Katya comes to him in tears and begs him to help shape her life, he has nothing to say to her, and can think only of his own inevitable death. It is not merely the lack of a general idea that plagues this man; he is emotionally crippled, unable to communicate or feel empathy with others.

This distressing portrait of human isolation reveals Chekhov's growing technical mastery. The narrative begins in the third person, with a detached description of a man who has become an iconostasis to the world at large. Only at the end of the paragraph does the professor reveal that he is describing himself, and it is not until several paragraphs later that he moves behind his external image to delve into his own personality. Such a device encapsulates the professor's essential problem: he manifests to the world an impressive exterior, but the man within is trapped and cannot break through the hardened shell. Even the specter of death, which triggered such dramatic revelations for Tolstoy's hero in "The Death of Ivan Ilyich," cannot draw him out of his self-imposed isolation. Indeed, Tolstoy's story provides a significant backdrop against which the professor's emotional paralysis stands out in sharp relief.

Chekhov would return to this character type in later years, but in 1889–90 his exploration of the human condition took on broader dimensions. In 1890 he visited the penal colony on Sakhalin island, and his discovery of the barbarous conditions prevalent there intensified his awareness of the cruelty inherent in life. The experience stripped him of some of the idealist leanings of his youth. Formerly a great admirer of Tolstoy and his ideas of moral improvement through hard work and non-violent resistance to evil, Chekhov could no longer accept Tolstoy's remedies for the problems of evil in the world.

One of the first works to reflect Chekhov's experiences on Sakhalin is "Gusev" (1890), a short piece depicting two men dying on a ship returning from the Far East. One, an intellectual named Pavel Ivanych, has an unpleasant, almost Dostoevskian personality. Calling himself "protest personified," he rails against social injustice and denounces people like the peasant Gusev for being too acquiescent. Although his concern with justice is commendable, the virulence of his diatribe undermines its effectiveness. Yet Gusev's stolidity has scarcely more appeal. While he accepts adversity without complaint, there is something animalistic in this impassivity. Staring at a Chinese man, he thinks: "It would be good to bash that fat fellow in the neck."

Significantly, both personages meet the same end: they die and are buried at sea. Chekhov's depiction of Gusev's canvas-wrapped body attacked by a passing shark indicates that the cosmos is a realm of blind, indifferent power, and the author offers no easy solutions to life's travails. Instead, he ends the tale with a description of the seascape. Noting the beautiful play of light at sunset, he concludes: "Looking at this magnificent, enchanting sky, the ocean at first frowns, but soon it also takes on tender, joyful, and passionate colors difficult even to name in human words." The scene carries a symbolic resonance. Like the ocean, the human world – the world "below" – is dark and disordered. Neither vehement protest nor apathetic resignation can provide fulfillment. Rather, one must observe and absorb the mute lessons of nature. Only through a kind of wordless communion with the natural world can one transcend the limitations of the self and attain a measure of tranquility.

Chekhov's expository method here is noteworthy. If he adopts a monological approach in "A Boring Story," here the writer's philosophical explorations take the form of a confrontation between two contrasting points of view. He himself does not choose sides, but allows the reader to judge the merits and flaws of each approach. Above everything stands the world of nature, in a silent commentary on the limited vision of the ordinary mortal. Chekhov repeats the strategy of juxtaposing two contradictory viewpoints in a single work in several other stories written at this time, most notably in "The Duel" ("Duel," 1891) and "Ward Six" ("Palata No. 6," 1892).

The latter is one of Chekhov's most famous works. It contains a confrontation between Ivan Gromov, an inmate at a provincial mental asylum, and Dr. Andrey Ragin, the man in charge of the institution. Gromov is an intelligent young man who recalls Pavel Ivanych in his critical attitude toward the ignorance of the town in which he lives. Distressed at the thought of potential injustice in life, he falls prey to paranoid fears of false arrest and becomes incapable of functioning in the outside world. Dr. Ragin is also an intellectual, but he takes a different approach to life's harsh realities. Rather than worry about injustice, he blocks it from his mind. Although physically strong, he is emotionally weak, and while he is aware of the backwardness of his medical facility, he does not try to correct it. Instead, he hides behind easy rationalizations such as "why hinder people from dying if death is the normal and legitimate end of us all?"

The clash between the two men forms the ideological core of the story. To Ragin's claim that one can enjoy peace of mind anywhere, even in prison, Gromov counters that men are made of flesh and blood, and that to ignore the pains of the flesh is to reject life itself. Accusing Ragin of laziness, Gromov finds in the doctor's words an empty philosophy of expedience. This perception is borne out when Ragin himself is institutionalized for his erratic behavior. Now Ragin undergoes a chilling epiphany. As he stares out the asylum window he sees the blank walls of a prison and the dark flames of a bone-mill, and realizes: "There is reality!" Panicked, he tries to leave the ward, but is beaten by the warder. The next day he dies of a stroke. Of the two men, Gromov is the more sympathetic. His cry "I desperately want to live!" rings with conviction. Yet he, like Ragin, finds it easier to talk about life than to live it. Neither man has the strength to play an active role in the world.

Chekhov's setting for the tale is a felicitous one. Not only does he follow Garshin's "The Red Flower" in exposing the ignorance that hinders treatment of the emotionally disturbed, he endows the asylum itself with symbolic import. Gromov complains that scores of madmen walk about free outside the asylum, while people like himself are imprisoned. Ragin agrees, commenting that such things are all a matter of chance. These comments, taken together with the character sketches of the people that Ragin encounters in his town and on a trip to Moscow and St. Petersburg, enable one to exclaim, with Leskov, that Ward Six is Russia itself. Chekhov's perception of the world as mental asylum made a significant impression on later writers, such as Fyodor Sologub and Leonid Andreev.

Chekhov himself created a very different image of mental illness in "The Black Monk" ("Cherny monakh," 1894), an intriguing study of the solace found by a man visited by a spectral monk who tells him he is one of the world's elect. The discovery of fleeting moments of happiness amidst sorrow also figures in the lyrical sketch "The Student" ("Student," 1894), a minor gem of evocative lyrical narration. A theology student's despondency over the endless miseries of life turns into joy when he perceives that human compassion is timeless as well.

While the short stories that Chekhov wrote in the early and middle 1890s demonstrate that he had found his mature voice as a prose writer, his forays into playwriting up to this point were less polished. He began writing dramas while still in school in Taganrog, though much of this material has been lost. As a young writer he experimented both with full-length dramas and with shorter pieces; the public initially proved more receptive to the latter. Chekhov's first brief dramatic work was "On the Highway" ("Na bolshoy doroge," 1884). Based on a story of his – "In Autumn" ("Osenyu") – the play depicts the misery of a nobleman driven to drink by the infidelity of his bride. The adaptation was overly sentimental, and Chekhov abandoned this style in favor of more light-hearted sketches. From 1888 to 1891 he wrote several comic plays reminiscent of his early prose works, and indeed some were adaptations: "The Wedding" ("Svadba," 1889) sprang from the 1884 stories "A Wedding with a General" ("Svadba s generalom") and "Marrying for Money" ("Brak po raschetu"); "A Tragic Role" ("Tragik ponevole," 1889) was adapted from "One of Many" ("Odin iz mnogikh," 1887); and "The Jubilee" ("Yubiley," 1891) derived from "A Defenseless Creature" ("Bezzashchitnoe sushchestvo," 1887).

In a letter of 1887 Chekhov delineated the elements he considered essential in staging his short plays, which he often termed "farces" (*shutki*). Among them were "complete confusion," individualized characters, "an absence of long speeches, unbroken action." His two most popular "farces" – "The Bear" ("Medved," 1888) and "The Proposal" ("Predlozhenie," 1888) – embody these principles, as well as another essential trait of his early work: the characters are so completely self-absorbed that their dialogues become exercises in miscommunication. In "The Proposal" a timid landowner comes to propose to a neighbor's daughter, but before he can do so the two become embroiled in a dispute over property. After the suitor leaves in a huff, the maiden discovers he had meant to propose, and so calls him back, only to plunge into a new round of insults. As the play ends the bride's father declares the quarrelsome couple engaged even though they continue to bicker.

A chronic inability to communicate with others became a recurring theme in Chekhov's mature plays, but the writer was not immediately successful in his attempts to portray human foibles in a serious manner on stage. His earliest extant dramatic work, conventionally entitled *Platonov* after its main character, was apparently written around 1880–1 but underwent extensive revision. A long and unwieldy piece, *Platonov* concentrates on the activities of a kind of superfluous man who finds no constructive outlet for his energy and thus spends his time dallying with provincial women equally dissatisfied with their lives; in the end he is shot by a jilted paramour. Although the play is of some interest for its treatment of elements which later become significant in Chekhov, it contains evident flaws in structure and focus. Platonov himself is unconvincing as a character: while Chekhov indicates that Platonov takes his own apathy seriously, the playwright fails to create genuine empathy between him and the audience.

Somewhat more satisfying is *Ivanov*, originally written in 1887 but revised over the next few years. This play again provides a character study of a prematurely exhausted man who at the age of thirty-five has succumbed to failed ideals. Like Platonov, the married Ivanov is swept up in a liaison with a younger and more idealistic woman who wishes to save him from his own disillusionment. In contrast to the earlier play, however, Chekhov reduces the number of characters and plot complications so that Ivanov's numbing emptiness looms more starkly before the audience. The writer intended his play to sum up and end all writing about this type of person, but the play's original ending, in which Ivanov dies of a heart attack because of the abuse he suffers from his neighbors, led to misinterpretations from audiences. To emphasize Ivanov's own inner weakness, Chekhov reworked the conclusion so that Ivanov dies not from a heart attack but by his own hand. Despite these revisions, some flaws remain. Although Chekhov was beginning to show how trivial activities mask tragic relationships, many of his secondary characters are one-dimensional, and the play suffers from an overly schematic plot. Chekhov's true genius as a playwright did not emerge until later in the 1890s.

While Chekhov's career was reaching its zenith in the mid 1890s, the careers of two writers who would subsequently attain prominent places in the literary pantheon – Maxim Gorky and Alexander Kuprin – were just getting underway. Born in Nizhny Novgorod on the Volga river, Gorky (pseudonym of Alexey Peshkov, 1869–1936) was raised by his grandparents in an atmosphere of avarice and abuse. Forced to earn his keep at an early age, Gorky held numerous jobs, from picking rags to working as a baker in Kazan. Eventually his life of material hardship and his perception of poverty as inescapable took its toll, and he made an unsuccessful attempt at suicide in 1887. His first literary success came with the publication of "Makar Chudra" in 1892. A short narrative about the fatal passion felt by a gypsy bandit named Loyko Zobar for a dazzling beauty, Radda, the story exhibits Gorky's early fascination with a romantic spirit of independence and bold gestures. Though deeply in love with each other, both Loyko and Radda value their freedom more highly than their love. To escape these straits Loyko stabs Radda, and is stabbed by her father in turn. The story is related by Makar Chudra, an old gypsy who begins the tale by discussing a prominent theme of Gorky's early fiction – the disparity between the masses of people who live lives of dreary toil and the proud few who cherish their independence.

Gorky returned to this theme in "Chelkash" (written 1894, published 1895), in which he draws a sharp contrast between the freedom-loving title character – a vagabond thief – and a slavish peasant named Gavrila whom Chelkash recruits for a smuggling operation. Gorky underscores the contrast between the two through such devices as comparing their attitudes towards the sea. While Chelkash feels an elemental kinship with the "boundless, free, and powerful" sea, Gavrila cowers before its force. Gorky paints a nuanced portrait of Chelkash, who understands Gavrila's attachment to village life because he nostalgically recalls the security of his own peasant childhood. Yet though he is now a rootless criminal, he proves more noble than Gavrila. After the latter tries to kill him to steal the money they have made smuggling, Chelkash gives him the money anyway, feeling nothing but contempt for the depths to which greed reduces humanity. Gorky's dismay over the degradation of the human spirit wrought by relentless toil informs the opening pages of "Chelkash," with their description of bustling commercial activity on the docks. In such descriptions Gorky tends towards the hyperbolic, and is much less subtle and graceful than Chekhov. Nevertheless, the raw energy of Gorky's style impressed later writers, and early Soviet literature owes much to his charged narrative manner.

During the mid 1890s Gorky wrote feuilletons, reviews, and stories for papers in Samara and Nizhny Novgorod. Among the better-known works of this period are "Old Izergil" ("Starukha Izergil," 1895), "On the Rafts" ("Na plotakh," 1895), and "The Song of the Falcon" ("Pesnya o sokole," 1895). Several of his works draw on folklore traditions to create striking allegorical images, such as that of the heroic Danko, who tears out his heart and uses it as a beacon to guide his people out of a dark forest ("Old Izergil"), or the wounded falcon which strives to return to the sky at the cost of its life. Gorky's vibrant portraits of the bold *bosyaki* (tramps) who scorn the restraints of ordinary life appealed to a public tired of a literary diet of impoverished landowners, downtrodden peasants, and unhappy intellectuals. When a two-volume edition of his work appeared in 1898, it sold 100,000 copies, a figure rivalled only by Tolstoy's sales. Gorky became something of a cult figure, and his work grew increasingly critical of injustice, which he perceived as a social problem, not an existential one. His writing both documented the specific features of human injustice and conveyed a message of hope for eventual improvement. This combination of graphic analysis and lyrical emotion became his hallmark.

Alexander Kuprin's career followed a different path from Gorky's. Born in southern Russia, Kuprin (1870–1938) grew up in Moscow, where he attended a military high school and the Alexander Military Academy. While still in school he wrote poetry and published his first story, "The Last Debut" ("Posledny debyut," 1889). For two years he served in garrisons in the Ukraine, and his experience there inspired several short stories and his most famous novel, *The Duel* (*Poedinok*, 1905). After leaving the army in 1894 he held a number of jobs, from journalist to carpenter; this familiarity with various occupations is made manifest in his fiction, with its colorful portraits of various character types. His early work reveals a fascination with unusual psychological states, but the stories dealing with this theme (such as "Psyche" ["Psikheya," 1892] and "In Darkness" ["Vpot-makh," 1893]) are often marred by a melodramatic quality. More accomplished is "The Inquiry" ("Doznanie," 1894), a tale of a sensitive young officer's disillusionment with the harshness of army life; it anticipates *The Duel*. A series of sketches written in the mid 1890s under the general title *Kievan Types* (*Kievskie tipy*) reveals Kuprin's penchant for depicting the lifestyles of various social groups, from thieves to choir singers. This facility also surfaces in his collection *Miniatures* (*Miniatyury*, 1897), which contains some twenty-five short stories. Among the better known is "Allez!," about a young circus performer's lack of control over her own life. Built on the repetition of the command "Allez!," the story follows the girl as she is ordered about by adults – first to perform circus stunts, and then into and out of an affair with a callous clown. The story ends with her rejection by her lover and her suicide leap from a window as she is urged on by an inner voice commanding "Allez!" Kuprin also wrote a series of sketches in industrial settings culminating in his long tale *Moloch* (*Molokh*, 1896), an indictment of capitalist exploitation. Over the next two decades, Kuprin steadily honed his talent, and in his mature work developed a distinctive manner in which broad emotions are cast in colorful and engaging plots.

As the period from 1880 to 1895 witnessed a transition in prose fiction from the major founders of nineteenth-century Russian realism to a set of younger writers with different interests, so one may observe similar signs of evolution and new growth in poetry. For two decades critical opinion in Russia had been dominated by those who looked to a civic message as the main criterion of value in a literary work. Such an atmosphere was not conducive to the development of lyric poetry. In the 1880s, however, signs of change were evident. The reading public had no doubt become disenchanted with the endlessly recurrent studies of social problems, and now wanted something more intimate. A number of poets responded to this mood. A prime representative of the changing climate for poetic creation was Afanasy Fet, whose work had been condemned by the radical critics of the 1860s. In 1883 Fet published his first collection of original verse in nearly twenty years – *Evening Lights* (*Vechernie ogni*) – and followed this up with three more collections bearing that name (published in 1885, 1888, 1891).

Throughout his long career Fet had remained a champion of what he called "pure" art, by which he meant "free art, free first of all from any worldly aims, interests, desires, practical concerns, or use." His imagery is often unusual and subjective; he himself declared: "For an artist, the impression which has called forth a work is more valuable than the very thing which evoked the impression." Not surprisingly, Fet's method has been called impressionistic, and it has affinities with the descriptive methods of Chekhov's work. Also, because of his attempts to trigger emotional responses in his reader through allusive imagery and the musicality of his verse, Fet was hailed by the symbolists as a precursor of their movement, and they further appreciated the philosophical dimension that emerged in his late work.

During the 1860s Fet had become interested in Schopenhauer. He was particularly intrigued by Schopenhauer's dualistic view of reality: as a counter to the stark reality of the world as "will," a realm dominated by struggle, suffering, and death, the philosopher held out the possibility of relief through esthetic contemplation. Fet incorporates this concept into several poems of the 1870s and 1880s. In the programmatic piece "The muse" ("Muza," 1887) he declares that the soul of the lyre brings to earth "not a passionate storm, not summons to battle, / But the healing of torment." In numerous other poems he contrasts the physical world of transience and death to an ideal realm of stability and timeless joy, and suggests that the other realm may be reached through poetry or moments of irrational insight (cf. "To poets" ["Poetam," 1890]).

While several of Fet's poems directly echo Schopenhauer's teachings (e.g. "Death" ["Smert," 1878], and "Good and evil" ["Dobro i zlo," 1884]), a more impressive portion of his late work is devoted to love. The poet imbues these short lyrics with an effective complex of intense emotions: elements of deep passion and sensual intoxication fuse with a haunting recognition of the inevitability of loss. Yet while the poet signals his awareness of impending loss, he does not yield to despair. On the contrary, he repeatedly asserts his faith in ultimate reunion and joy. Above all, one notes Fet's faith in the power of the poetic word to make eternal the transient experiences of life and love.

While the thematics of Fet's work changed somewhat in the course of his career, his reliance on allusive imagery remained constant. Several of his favorite images developed complex sets of associations: the rose, for example, was often linked with inspiration or the muse, and songbirds, especially nightingales, were connected with the figure of the poet. His late verse, however, resists allegorical decoding. Because Fet concentrates on the inner experiences of the poet's persona, the addressee of many of his poems remains an abstract or generalized figure; the female whom the poet addresses as "ty" (thou) could be a specific woman, the muse, or some blend of the two. The ambiguity of these poems along with their attendant intensity had a measurable impact on the poetic practices of succeeding poets, especially Alexander Blok. Also impressive were Fet's experiments with meter, rhyme, and stanzaic structures, and his predilection for repetition in the form of anaphora or analepsis. Technically as well as thematically Fet towered above his contemporaries in poetic innovation.

Even though not up to Fet's standard, several other poets who had begun their careers much earlier found a newly responsive audience for their work in the 1880s. While some of these, such as Apollon Maykov, added relatively little to their established *œuvre* in the 1880s, others – Yakov Polonsky, Alexey Apukhtin, and Konstantin Sluchevsky – experienced a fresh creative impetus. Polonsky, whose first collection of verse had appeared in 1844, released a new volume of verse in 1881 – *At Sunset* (*Na zakate*) – and followed this with another collection in 1890: *Evening Bell* (*Vecherny zvon*). Two separate editions of his collected works also were published in the 1880s and 1890s. As the titles of his late collections suggest, Polonsky's verse exhibits an elegiac, meditative character. Mindful of passing time and the loss of close friends, Polonsky reflects on the vicissitudes of life in brief lyrics that are models of poetic elegance. Testifying to his gift for penning mellifluous verse (often with folk accents) is the fact that several of his poems were later accepted as folk songs. Along with his short lyrics Polonsky wrote in other genres, including stories in verse (e.g. "Phantom" ["Prizrak"]), dialogues ("A Conversation" ["Razgovor"]), *poemy* and ballads. In "Prometheus" ("Prometey") he reworks a common romantic theme into a vigorous affirmation of the supremacy of love over violence, and in "Cassandra" ("Kassandra") he paints a nuanced portrait of the joy and torment arising out of his heroine's encounter with Apollo.

A second writer whose reputation revived in the 1880s was Konstantin Sluchevsky. The son of a prominent senator, Sluchevsky was educated in military schools and served briefly in the military before leaving the service in 1860 to study abroad. He took his doctorate in Heidelberg and returned to Russia in 1866, when he embarked upon a career in government. Though he had begun publishing poetry as early as 1857, he did not find a responsive audience at that time. While critics such as Apollon Grigorev applauded his work, radical critics like Nikolay Dobrolyubov sharply criticized his verse and parodied his predilection for unusual, "unpoetic" imagery. As a consequence Sluchevsky withdrew from the literary arena for many years; only in the mid 1870s did he resume printing his poetry under his own name. His career finally flourished in the 1880s: during that decade he published four volumes entitled *Stikhotvoreniya* (*Poems*) as well as several prose works (including *Virtuosos* [*Virtuozy*, 1882] and *Thirty Three Stories* [*Tridtsat tri rasskaza*, 1887]) and geographical sketches. A six-volume edition of his writings appeared in 1898.

The unusual imagery which caught the attention of Sluchevsky's first detractors was a hallmark of his early verse, and although he moderated his predilection for the unusual in later years, this feature continued to set him apart from his contemporaries. Sluchevsky's poetry offers a unique perspective on the world. A sensitive observer, the poet highlights the contradictions and tensions of human existence in striking images. A particular concern of his was the disparity between human ideals and the inescapable reality of human injustice. Sluchevsky's absorption with this disparity reminds one of Dostoevsky, on whom the poet published an essay in 1889. His renowned poem "After an execution in Geneva" ("Posle kazni v Zheneve") paints a haunting picture of the effect produced on the lyric hero by an execution he witnessed: in a strange dream the poet feels himself becoming a taut string plucked by a sick nun who plaintively sings "How glorious is our Lord." Reflections on suffering, suicide, and insanity appear frequently in Sluchevsky's work, and even his nature poetry discloses hidden or unnoticed aspects of the environment. Though not especially innovative in metrics or prosody, Sluchevsky liked to mix stylistic levels in his work, combining elevated rhetoric with unexpected prosaisms. Along with his numerous short lyrics Sluchevsky also wrote narrative poems, often featuring people caught in moral quandaries, torn between the constraints of society and the impulses of their hearts (cf. *Without a Name* [*Bez imeni*] and *Elisey the Priest* [*Pop Elisey*]).

Less dramatic than Sluchevsky, but very popular in the 1880s, was Alexey Apukhtin (1840–93), who first appeared in print in 1854. The scion of an old noble family, Apukhtin attended the St. Petersburg Institute of Jurisprudence, where he became friends with the future composer Peter Ilyich Tchaikovsky. After an initial period of publishing in progressive journals Apukhtin retired from the literary marketplace, although he continued to write poems, a number of which were set to music by Tchaikovsky (later on Rachmaninov, Prokofiev, and others wrote music for Apukhtin's lyrics). When he finally published the first collection of his verse in 1886, the volume sold out rapidly. The upper-class reading public to which Apukhtin's verse appealed was taken with his pensive ruminations over shattered love, frustrated dreams, and the senselessness of a life devoid of responsive companionship. Many of these works are short lyrics treating one dominant mood or experience, but the poet also wrote longer works, such as the narrative poem *A Year in a Monastery* (*God v monastyre*), which describes a disillusioned man's futile attempt to flee a world of hypocrisy and romantic betrayal, and such dramatic monologues as "Before the operation" ("Pered operatsiey") and "The madman" ("Sumasshedshy"). Apukhtin also experimented in prose genres with such works as "The Diary of Paul Dolsky" ("Dnevnik Pavlika Dolskogo," 1891) and the epistolary tale "The Archive of Countess D," ("Arkhiv grafini D."), but these works appeared posthumously.

Along with those writers whose established careers underwent a revival in the 1880s, there emerged a host of new figures who sought to give voice to the mood of the era; one observer noted at the time that young poets were cropping up like mushrooms. A few continued the tradition of politically oriented verse dominant in the 1860s and 1870s: Vera Figner (1852–1942), G. A. Lopatin (1845–1918), and Peter Yakubovich (1860–1911). Many more poets, however, turned inward for inspiration. Of this group, the writer who garnered the most astonishing (if fleeting) success was Semyon Nadson (1862–87). Nadson's childhood had been marked by loss: his father died when he was two; his stepfather committed suicide; and his mother died while he was still a child. The youth attended a military institute in Pavlovsk and served as an officer from 1882 to 1885. He published his first poem in 1878, but achieved true fame with the appearance of his only collection of verse in 1885; this volume would undergo five editions during the poet's brief life, before he died of consumption at twenty-four.

Nadson's immense popularity stems from the fact that his verse crystallized the dispirited atmosphere of his time. His poetry is filled with expressions of impatient longing and melancholy. While the poet declares his fervid desire to contribute to the struggle for universal happiness and justice, he also acknowledges a gnawing awareness of his own impotence. Typical is the poem "The word" ("Slovo," 1879), which the poet begins by expressing the wish that the Muse might have endowed him with "a fiery word" which would amaze the world; he concludes, however, that such a word has not been given him: "My weak voice is powerless, / ... / And my heart is oppressed by the consciousness, / That I – I am a slave, and not a prophet!" In his very impotence Nadson sees himself as the voice of his land ("In response" ["V otvet," 1886]) and the son of his day – "A son of contemplation, anxiety, and doubts" ("Don't reproach me, my friend..." ["Ne vin menya, drug moy…," 1883]). He admires those who are warriors, and looks with envy at "their crown of thorns" ("As a convict drags his chain behind him…" ["Kak katorzhnik vlachit okovy za soboy…," 1884]). At times he yearns for a realm of peace and all-forgiving love, but has no hope of attaining that goal either. Although his poems are smoothly constructed, they are so devoid of genuine energy or originality that they quickly become repetitious and monotonous. Structurally, they are transparently simple. Much influenced by Lermontov, Nadson exhibits a penchant for antithesis and contrast, and often employs rhetorical intonations and aphoristic conclusions.

While Nadson was the most popular of the new poets of the 1880s, numerous other writers found responses for their work. The contemporary reading public apparently was in accord with the well-known formulations of Edgar Allan Poe that Sergey Andreevsky (1847–1919) took as the epigraph for his first collection of poetry, *Poems 1878–1885* (*Stikhotvoreniya 1878–1885*), published in 1886: "Beauty is the sole legitimate province of poetry" and "melancholy is the most legitimate of all the poetical tones." Representative of the many writers whose work echoes the tonality and imagery of Fet, Maykov, and Polonsky, and who treated broad themes of regret over lost happiness and anxiety over future destiny were: Arseny Golenishchev-Kutuzov (1848–1913), whose early lyrics were set to music by Modest Musorgsky; Dmitry Tsertelev (1852–1911), whose scholarly study of Schopenhauer's philosophy informed his poetry too (particularly the series of poems he wrote on Buddhist and eastern themes); and K.R. (the pseudonym of Grand Prince Konstantin Romanov, 1858–1917), who received a Pushkin Prize from the Imperial Academy for his melodious, spiritual poems, several of which were set to music by Tchaikovsky. Lesser figures include Apollon Korinsky (1868–1937) and Peter Buturlin (1859–95).

Standing above the growing crowd of lyric poets at this time were two writers whose work gave indications of moving in new directions – Nikolay Minsky and Konstantin Fofanov. Nikolay Minsky (the pseudonym for Nikolay Maximovich Vilenkin, 1855–1937) entered literature in 1876, and his early work displays evident links to Nekrasov and the civic poets (his *poema*, *The Last Confession* [*Poslednyaya ispoved*], which touches upon the execution of a political prisoner, could only be printed illegally). In 1884, however, Minsky published an article entitled "An ancient argument" ("Starinny spor") in a Kiev newspaper. Here he rejected the use of poetry for journalistic purposes and called for an independent art which would serve only the eternal and the pure. This article, together with a companion piece by Ieronim Vilenkin (1850–1931), was one of the first signs of a critical offensive against literature with a political orientation, an offensive that would reach its culmination at the turn of the century with the triumph of the symbolist movement in Russia. Minsky himself went on to write poetry of a reflective nature, declaring in one poem that "he is most immortal who can descry through the dust of the earth some kind of new world – non-material and eternal – in the distance" ("As a dream, the deeds and inventions of people pass away . . ." ["Kak son, proydut dela i pomysli lyudey . . ."]). He developed an eclectic philosophy of idealism which he called "meonism" (from the Greek *me' on* – "being not yet in existence"), and which blends ideas drawn from Kant, Nietzsche, and eastern philosophy. His philosophical tracts, such as *By the Light of Conscience* (*Pri svete sovesti*), are dense and turgid, but he gradually moved away from his abstract orientation. In 1905 he collaborated in Bolshevik publications and wrote a "Worker's Hymn" that begins with the famous words: "Workers of the world, unite."

Less erratic in his literary career was Konstantin Fofanov (1862–1911). The son of a shopkeeper, Fofanov tried his hand at civic verse but soon revealed a preference for intimate poetry. Even more than Minsky, Fofanov articulated his impulse to withdraw from everyday life and its contradictions. One poem begins: "Wandering in a world of falsehood and prose, / I love the secrets of divinity: / Harmonious reveries, / And musical words" (1887). The poetry he wrote in the 1880s and published in the collections *Poems* (*Stikhotvoreniya*, 1887 and 1889) and *Shadows and Secrets* (*Teni i tayny*, 1892) displays a markedly harmonious character. Concentrating on the world of nature, and also on the world of his own enchanting dreams (his last collection was entitled *Illusions* [*Illyuzii*, 1900]), Fofanov left a body of work that is uneven in quality, but distinctive in its fluid musicality; his work was well liked by the symbolists who followed him.

Both Fofanov and Minsky (along with such prose writers as

Garshin and Chekhov) were cited by the poet and critic Dmitry Merezhkovsky (1865–1941) as harbingers of a new and long-awaited spirit in Russian literature. Merezhkovsky made his analysis in a seminal article of 1893 entitled *On the reasons for the decline and on the new currents in contemporary Russian literature (O prichinakh upadka i o novykh techeniyakh sovremennoy russkoy literatury)*. In this essay – which many scholars regard as one of the opening sallies of the nascent symbolist movement in Russia – Merezhkovsky set out to delineate the reasons behind the perceived sterility of Russian literature. Among the factors he identifies are: the deterioration of the literary language, the rise of the profit motive in literature, and the failure of the utilitarian critics to promote a favorable climate for literary development. He maintains that there are two opposing impulses in Russian literature of the day: extreme materialism and passionate, "idealistic" outbursts of the spirit. Down to the present, the prevailing taste of the "crowd" has been for realism and materialism. Now, however, Merezhkovsky sees an important reaction forming. He declares that the three main elements of the new art are "mystical content, symbols, and the broadening of artistic impressionability." He concludes his essay with the optimistic observation that the modern generation has felt "the first quivering of a new life, the first breath of a great future."

Merezhkovsky's essay is of value less for its specific evaluations of individual writers than for its identification of a new mood among the reading public. Indeed, many readers were tired of tenebrous accounts of the wretched conditions of rural life; they thirsted for literature that would speak to their emotions and dreams. The symbolist movement, which would come to the fore in the late 1890s, seemed to answer that need. Merezhkovsky himself was a forerunner of this movement. Raised and educated in St. Petersburg, he was originally inspired by populist theoreticians, especially Mikhaylovsky, and his early poetry urges poets to "get to know and love the simple, dark populace" ("To the poet" ["Poetu," 1883]). This early work, published in his first collection entitled *Poems (Stikhotvoreniya,* 1888), bears certain affinities with Nadson's: the poet wants to contribute to social justice, but feels enervating doubts and internal weakness. Late in the 1880s, however, Merezhkovsky shifted away from the civic trend and became more interested in the impulses of the soul. His second volume of verse – Symbols (*Simvoly*, 1892) – reveals a palpable debt to Baudelaire and Poe, and his poem "Children of the night" ("Deti nochi," 1894) might be considered a programmatic expression of the decadent world view as defined by the symbolist writer Vyacheslav Ivanov. In Ivanov's opinion, decadence was characterized by a consciousness, "both oppressive and proud," of being the final representatives of an entire cultural lineage. The speaker in Merezhkovsky's lyric states that as "too early forerunners of a [too] belated spring," he and his kind are condemned to death: "Children of the night, we await the sun: / We shall see the light – and, like shadows, / We shall die in its rays." Merezhkovsky's intellectual explorations subsequently assumed an increasingly religious character, and he would articulate his religious beliefs in numerous critical essays and prose works during the late 1890s and the first decades of the twentieth century.

As Merezhkovsky pointed out, a resurgent interest in philosophical speculation could be discerned in Russia in the concluding years of the nineteenth century. Numerous philosophers would eventually contribute to this trend. Among the most notable of them were Nikolay Berdyaev (1874–1948), Leo Shestov, and Vasily Rozanov. By the 1890s, however, one man had already developed into a distinguished thinker and writer – Vladimir Solovyov. As the son of an eminent historian at Moscow University, Solovyov grew up in an atmosphere of intellectual stimulation, and pursued an academic career at Moscow University with an emphasis first on science, then on philosophy. After a year at the Moscow Theological Academy Solovyov in 1874 defended his Master's thesis, "The Crisis of Western Philosophy" ("Krizis zapadnoy filosofii"), which provided a critique of western positivism. This was followed by his doctoral dissertation, *A Critique of Abstract Principles* (*Kritika otvlechennykh nachal*), in 1880. Solovyov's promising career as an academic was cut short by the negative reaction to his impromptu public appeal to the government to have mercy on the assassins of Tsar Alexander II. Shortly after this speech Solovyov was compelled to resign his academic post in St. Petersburg, and thus turned to philosophical inquiry and to literature. Among his most significant historical and philosophical works are *The Spiritual Foundations of Life* (*Dukhovnye osnovy zhizni*, 1884), *The History and Future of Theocracy* (*Istoriya i budush-chnost teokratii*, 1887), *La Russie et l'église universelle* (1889; Russian translation 1911), *The Meaning of Love* (*Smysl lyubvi*, 1892–4), and *Three Conversations* (1900), with its appendix, "A Short Tale about the Antichrist" ("Kratkaya povest ob antikhriste"). His numerous essays on literature and esthetics include the general studies *The General Meaning of Art* (*Obshchy smysl iskusstva*, 1890) and *Beauty in Nature* (*Krasota v prirode*, 1889), the more specialized works *Three Talks in Memory of Dostoevsky* (*Tri rechi v pamyat Dostoevskogo*, 1881–3), "Pushkin's fate" ("Sudba Pushkina," 1897), and a series of essays on the poetry of such writers as Pushkin, Lermontov, Fet, Tyutchev, and Polonsky.

Solovyov's philosophy underwent a complex evolution. An early admirer of Büchner, Pisarev, Darwin, and Feuerbach, Solovyov gradually turned to the idealist doctrines of Kant and Schopenhauer, immersed himself in Schelling and Hegel, and finally abandoned the atheistic materialism of his adolescence for a philosophical program with deep religious roots. A basic concern of his work was humanity's potential for the attainment of moral and spiritual perfection. Pointing to Christ as the inspirational model of God made human, Solovyov envisioned an ultimate fusion of the human with the divine in which the division between the corporeal and the spiritual, the earthly and the ideal, would be eliminated. Believing that a theocratic social order would best facilitate this process, Solovyov examined the existing Christian churches and, after an early preference for Rome, affirmed that a union of the three main branches of Christianity – Roman Catholic, Orthodox, and Protestant – would best serve the interests of humanity. Late in life Solovyov became increasingly absorbed with eschatology. A firm believer in the objective existence of God and the ultimate victory of the forces of good, he foresaw a cataclysm in which the forces of the Antichrist would threaten human civilization from the east.

Solovyov's apocalyptic vision, along with many other of his religious convictions, was vividly reflected in his poetry, a small body of work marked by an interesting blend of emotional intensity and delicate lyricism. Preoccupied with the duality of the spiritual and the material, Solovyov constructed his verse upon blocks of antithesis and opposition in which elements from the natural environment such as day and night are charged with a pronounced symbolic content. Many of these poems depict the poet moving through a world of darkness or confusion but bearing the expectation of a "new eternal day" (e.g. "In an earthly dream we are shadows, shadows..." ["V sne zemnom my teni, teni...," 1875]). A key character in Solovyov's work is a generalized female figure whom the poet identified with Sophia – an incarnation of the eternal feminine whose nature combines the elements of love and goodness and whose advent will facilitate humanity's future happiness. This female figure is the subject of numerous individual poems (e.g. "My empress has a high palace..." ["U tsaritsy moey est vysoky dvorets...," 1875–6]), and even in those love lyrics occasioned by Solovyov's relationships with actual women (for example, in his poems of 1892–4 connected with S. M. Martynova), the presence of this more abstract female figure adds resonance to the poet's evocations of feminine beauty. This blend of the erotic and the spiritual had a considerable influence on Alexander Blok, as is evident from the latter's cycle of poems dedicated to the "Beautiful Lady."

It is interesting to note, though, that in Solovyov's longest work about the divine Sophia – "Three Meetings" ("Tri svidaniya," 1898) – the poet's serious treatment of his three visionary encounters with an ethereal woman (first at the age of nine, then in the British Museum, and finally in the sands of Egypt) is interlaced with unexpected notes of ironic self-deprecation and humor. These humorous notes accentuate the disparity between the imperfect, often foolish world of ordinary life and the radiant world of spiritual perfection. Solovyov's comic streak inspired a series of poems and plays (especially noteworthy is *The White Lily* [*Belaya liliya*], a semi-parodic treatment of the mystic quest written in 1878–80). The writer's penchant for parody may have been enhanced by his close contact with the family of Alexey Konstantinovich Tolstoy, one of the creators of the Kozma Prutkov poems.

As Solovyov's poems on Sophia proved influential for Blok, so too did his poems on apocalyptic questions make a tangible impression on the succeeding generation of Russian poets. In poems such as "*Ex oriente lux*" (1890) and "Panmongolism" (1894) he touched upon Russia's national destiny and the future of humanity at large. While the former poem suggests that Russia could play a messianic role on the world stage if it chose to follow the teachings of Christ, the latter seems to crush that hope: having forgotten the "behest of love," the third Rome (Russia) "lies in the dust, / And there will be no fourth one." Such a vision later triggered responses in the poetry of Valery Bryusov ("The coming Huns" ["Gryadushchie gunny," 1905]) and Alexander Blok (*The Scythians* [*Skify*, 1918]), and in the prose of Andrey Bely (cf. his *Petersburg*). Blok, Bely, and their fellow symbolist Vyacheslav Ivanov also drew inspiration from Solovyov's view of the poet's mission. In Solovyov's view, the poet's role must have something of a theurgic character. It is not enough for the artist to emulate Pygmalion and to give life to esthetic dream; rather the artist must follow Orpheus, and through his art lead Eurydice from the prisonhouse of death to the realm of light (cf. "Three exploits" ["Tri podviga," 1882]).

Although the legacy of Solovyov's work had a considerable influence on the second generation of Russian symbolists, the writer himself viewed with some skepticism the early efforts of the first generation of writers who introduced a bold new esthetic program and who called themselves symbolists. Ironically, the parodies of symbolist poetry that he wrote in 1895 had the effect not of crushing the incipient movement, but rather of drawing attention to it. The object of Solovyov's parodies was a series of three collections which appeared in 1894 and 1895 and bore the title *The Russian Symbolists*. As it turned out, these three volumes announced that a fresh new direction in Russian literature was at hand.

Whereas this period had begun with a generation of writers trying to accept the disappointments of an ongoing socio-political struggle, the new period seemed to have other and very different concerns. The brash experiments of Konstantin Balmont, whose first collection *Mountain Heights* (*Gornye vershiny*) appeared in 1894, and of Valery Bryusov, the prime contributor to *The Russian Symbolists*, whose own first collection came out in 1895, drew inspiration less from the classic masters of Russian literature than from the innovative work of such writers as Charles Baudelaire, Paul Verlaine, and Stéphane Mallarmé. The reading public could not doubt that an entirely new spirit was at work when they caught sight of Bryusov's notorious one-line poem in *The Russian Symbolists* of 1894: "Oh, cover thy pale legs." The emerging Russian decadents and symbolists were convinced that the artistic structures and intellectual world views of the era of mid-nineteenth-century Russian realism had come to an end, and they were eager to usher in a new epoch in which a more personal, allusive, and visionary esthetic would reign supreme. The period from 1880 to 1895 was indeed a period of transition. By 1895 the end of that process was in sight.

8

TURN OF A CENTURY: MODERNISM, 1895–1925

The period from 1895 to 1925, arguably the most complex in the entire history of Russian literature, may be characterized as the era of modernism in its various manifestations: decadence, symbolism, avant-gardism, futurism, acmeism, formalism, and a number of other doctrines, all of which were formulated by writers acutely conscious of culture as an entity created by human minds. The beginnings of Russian modernism are generally traced to an important critical piece of 1893 by Dmitry Merezhkovsky entitled *On the reasons for the decline and on the new currents in contemporary Russian literature*, an article which defined the new mood of the Russian intelligentsia, now prepared for a quite different sort of literature than it had welcomed theretofore. When modernism in its various forms did prevail, it held the stage for some time, even past the political cataclysms of the First World War and the October revolution: the literature of the early 1920s which dealt with these events still remained modernist in its approach until about 1925.

The year 1925 functions as a dividing point in literary terms for several reasons, of which two may be noted here. First, in that year the Central Committee of the Communist Party of the Soviet Union passed a resolution enunciating a comprehensive position on questions of literature and art. Although it did not actually exert its control at that stage over such matters, it asserted its right to do so in the future, and eventually did so. Second, this was the year in which many literary émigrés realized that their exile would be lengthy and began seriously to create a branch of Russian culture in emigration. Symbolic of this is the fact that Vladislav Khodasevich, a leading creator of émigré Russian culture, settled in Paris in 1925 and helped make it the leading center of émigré literature until the Second World War.

The epoch of modernism began as a clear rebellion against the materialist legacy of the 1860s. Where the older generation had preached monism, the new generation turned to philosophical dualism, which found obvious expression in symbolism, with its orientation toward other worlds. Where the older generation had rejected supernatural religion, the new intellectuals took a keen interest not only in Russian Orthodoxy but in religions of all sorts. Where the older generation had denigrated poetry, writers of the newer generation often began as poets and continued to produce poetry even when they turned to prose as well.

The modernist era likewise promoted a strong consciousness of literature as process; the reader was asked to fill in much of a text which was often fragmented, distorted, and difficult to understand. Writers took a renewed interest in questions of the literary language, although now they were primarily concerned with questions of language as a general human phenomenon, so much so that they sought to create neologisms and even an entire "language" (*zaum*, or "transsense" language) using newly recognized phonetic possibilities. The formalist school of the 1920s gave critical structure to the modernist understanding of literature as a linguistic artifact.

The number of writers at this period was still sufficiently small to allow personal contact. The "thick journals" of the nineteenth century had either disappeared or no longer served as such important focal points for literary discourse as they had before. Instead writers formed shifting groupings, some with a political base but most founded on literary theories. Among the most famous of these gatherings were those in The Tower, the apartment of the symbolist leader and theoretician Vyacheslav Ivanov, and the Knowledge group, led by Maxim Gorky, which maintained its loyalties to the old realist traditions. Although the symbolists were culturally dominant from about the turn of the century until roughly the First World War, their hegemony was sharply challenged in the final years before the outbreak of the First World War by such groups as the futurists and the acmeists, and after the revolution most of the prominent symbolists either soon died (Blok), went into emigration (Ivanov), or became supporters of the new order (Bryusov). In short, the symbolist variant of modernism did not long survive the October revolution and the civil war, though other forms of modernism continued to exist for some years.

Although the year 1917 is not a very important demarcation line in literary theoretical terms – and so this chapter does not end with that year – it was of importance to writers in practical terms, for it brought about the first mass cultural emigration in Russian history. There had been scattered instances of emigration in Russian literature before, going back at least to Andrey Kurbsky, who fled the wrath of Ivan the Terrible in the sixteenth century. In the nineteenth century Alexander Herzen and his colleague Nikolay Ogaryov had been total political and literary exiles in western Europe, and such writers as Gogol, Turgenev, and even Dostoevsky had lived and worked for extended periods on occasion outside Russia. But writers had never before left their homeland in such numbers as they did during the years following the October revolution. In the early 1920s those living abroad thought the political situation might change sufficiently soon that they could return, or else believed they could maintain a dialogue with those they had left behind through the written word. By about 1925, however, most of those in the "first wave" of the emigration realized that neither of these possibilities was realistic, and decided to do what lay within their power to preserve the traditional values of Russian culture abroad. Soviet writers and critics, especially after the Stalinization of Soviet culture, dismissed the émigrés as political renegades and sought to isolate Russian literature within the Soviet Union as thoroughly as possible from Russian literary development outside the country. Russian emigre writers felt their isolation keenly – especially since western specialists also tended to ignore their achievements – but valued the intellectual freedom they enjoyed in the west more highly than their roots in native soil. And so, tragically, Russian literature in the early 1920s was divided into two important but unequal segments.

IN THE EARLY YEARS of the twentieth century the European literary world was split between two opposing movements, realism and symbolism, neither of which was powerful enough to prevail over the other. The realists took some of their interests, as well as the core of their esthetic doctrine, from the school that had been dominant in the mid nineteenth century. Some – H. G. Wells, for example – still believed in the possibility of progress and wrote works calculated to lead to social change. Such views found a reflection in the writing of Maxim Gorky, who was much concerned with contemporary life, frequently in its practical aspects, and also displayed a typically Russian compassion for his characters, who were often economically deprived. Other western realists, such as Joseph Conrad, were skeptical of social institutions and portrayed the existential struggles of the individual, and some-times quite lonely, human spirit. Chekhov and Bunin worked in that tradition: the types they created were universal, and the fact that they were representatives of a declining gentry class was of only secondary importance.

Symbolism and decadence, on the other hand, sprang from what had once been an undercurrent in the nineteenth century. The neo-romantic movement flourished in the century's early years in France, which experienced what one might term a "symbolist era" dominated by Marcel Proust and Paul Valéry. Russian symbolism enjoyed a similar but briefer period of popularity just after the revolution of 1905, when Alexander Blok came on the scene. The Russian symbolist school was more religious than the French in its orientation, and absorbed more from German romantic thought. And whereas the experimental avant-garde which followed symbolism in France and Italy tended to be quite radical – even notoriously so – the Russian avant-garde would produce more durable voices, such as that of Boris Pasternak.

Anton Chekhov in his work pointed toward certain possibilities for literary renewal within the realist tradition. He was among those new realists who undermined any belief in inevitable progress. Those characters in his plays and short stories who look toward a better future make their hope appear the airiest of daydreams: "Let's say in a thousand years – the time doesn't matter – a new, happy life will dawn," remarks Vershinin (*The Three Sisters*). The social changes which Chekhov envisions are on the whole melancholy, for he shows the kulaks and merchants who are replacing the declining gentry class as greedy and unscrupulous: the merchant Lopakhin (*The Cherry Orchard*) has little feeling for the beautiful though unproductive trees which he orders to be destroyed. In its sum total Chekhov's work disheartens the reader; and his world is not in fact reality, but a private vision.

Chekhov's four major plays – written and staged from 1896 to 1904, the work of a relatively young man who knew he had not long to live – were a new departure not only for Russian drama but for the European theater as a whole. He built upon the foundation left him by Alexander Ostrovsky, whose plays exposed the weaknesses of the merchant class (monetary greed, craftiness, personal despotism), taking from Ostrovsky the approach of working through types. Chekhov also admired Ibsen, whose plays illuminate the rigidities of society by confronting it with strong, unique characters, and learned from him the use of symbols and leitmotifs as well as the techniques of mirroring society and revealing the inner psychological motivations of individuals. But he chose to portray the foibles of the gentry, particularly their fetishes about artistic and cultural trends, their stuffiness, their baseless idealism, and their inability to change, and to picture these things in his own very personal way.

The Seagull (*Chayka*, 1896), designated as a "comedy," describes two generations of artists caught in a period of rapid cultural change: in the dramatic conflict between Arkadina, an actress specializing in classical plays, and her son Treplyov, author of an innovative, decadent play, the audience comes to sympathize with the younger generation. The fame of established artists is shown to be tainted by self-love, coldness and stinginess. Thus Arkadina begrudges her family money, and the established novelist Trigorin destroys the young actress Nina. The play reminds us that the immaturity of the young is not a moral, or serious, flaw, though it may be fatal.

The play's overarching symbol is the seagull. In Act I Nina chooses it as the symbol of her desires; in Act II Treplyov accuses her of coldness when he has shot a seagull – and in the end Treplyov shoots himself. Though it is ambiguous, the death of the seagull seems to signify the death of desire, or the destruction of youth and innovative energy. The play may be perceived as an intimate drama within a single person, a conflict between fresh, pure impulses and the power of routine.

Like other works of Chekhov's, *The Seagull* displays resonances in its parallels. The steward's daughter, an underling, chooses to marry an unimaginative, conventional schoolteacher even though she loves the vital if disturbed Treplyov. Like others of Chekhov's servants, she shares the aristocracy's vague malaises: "I am in mourning for my life," she says as the play opens. The leitmotifs of the minor characters are humorous but always sad. The dry stick of a schoolteacher talks constantly of salaries and wages, while the steward will never supply horses for the carriage, sending them to work in the fields instead.

Chekhov confounded his critics from the start by terming *The Seagull* a comedy. Perhaps by that he meant simply that the concepts of classical tragedy cannot be applied to it: the fates do not exist, and we are to blame for our own situations.

Uncle Vanya (*Dyadya Vanya*, 1899), though the second play to appear, was in fact conceived before the others, in a variant entitled *The Wood Demon* (*Leshy*). It describes an eminent professor Serebryakov, who has exploited his first wife's family – and especially her brother Vanya – for twenty-five years, a fact to which Vanya has suddenly awakened just before the play begins. Serebryakov has taken a second and much younger wife, an idle and provocative beauty named Elena (Helen), who drives Vanya and the local doctor, Astrov, to distraction. Astrov upholds the one pure motivation in the play: his dedication to the planting of trees in the service of ecology. The other positive character, Serebryakov's daughter Sonya, suffers from Elena's allure by contrast, as her devotion to mere work comes to seem sterile. Consequently, the work's message remains cloudy. Moreover, this play is less resonant than the others: it has neither secondary characters with parallel stories nor strikingly suggestive symbols.

The dramatic contrast in *The Three Sisters* (*Tri sestry*, 1901) is between the lively and well-educated sisters and the stifling provincial society in which they must live even as they long to return to Moscow as a token of their desire for spontaneity, fulfilment, and achievement. They and their ally, Baron Tuzenbakh, are devoted to the ideal of work, which, however, seems born of desperation and so smacks of futility.

The frustrations of these still vital people are suggested by the absence of any happy love in *The Three Sisters*. Of the three sisters, Masha is married to a pedantic schoolteacher but loves Vershinin, who is tied down to a woman of suicidal inclinations; Olga is a matron without a family; and Irina is a dreamer incapable of responding to Tuzenbakh's devotion. The sisters' one brother, Andrey, is soon also disillusioned in his marriage to Natasha. The forces of stagnation are represented by Natasha and also by an army lieutenant, Solyony, Tuzenbakh's rival for Irina's affections. In the end they both display an aggressive viciousness growing out of what had initially seemed to be mere trivial vulgarity. Thus Natasha begins by wearing a tasteless green belt, and ends by acquiring all the family assets. Solyony begins as a man lacking in the social and conversational graces, and ends by killing Tuzenbakh in a duel.

Like *The Seagull*, *The Cherry Orchard* (*Vishnevy sad*, 1904) is outwardly about changing times, in this case the displacement of a declining aristocracy by crass *parvenu* merchants; in this instance the symbol of the cherry orchard points not only to the economic transition from which the landowners are suffering, but also to their highly developed sense of their cultural heritage and love of beauty. However, unlike *The Seagull*, in *The Cherry Orchard* the viewer's sympathies are with the old order, headed by Madame Ranevskaya, which is passing from the scene, for the new world, embodied in the merchant Lopakhin, displays a faceless, menacing energy already previewed in Natasha.

This is not to say that the old order does not exhibit substantial weaknesses: for example, the selfish silliness of Ranevskaya's brother Gaev is plain for all to see as the family tries to think of a way to save the estate, including the orchard, from auction in payment of debts. The extent to which this aristocratic family allows its basic cultural snobbishness to destroy it is the chief unexpected development in the play. Another is Ranevskaya's denunciation as sterile and inhuman of her child's former tutor's dedication to work and progress. She defends her own disastrous behavior as gratifying, although irrational. She will return to Paris to succor a womanizing parasite with whom she is in love, deserting her family and servants and making off with eighteen thousand rubles sent by a distant great aunt to save the estate. The play is thus easily seen as an arena for opposing humors in which there is no way out.

In the formal sense *The Cherry Orchard* is exquisitely structured. First on stage are servants of the household: Dunyasha, the maid with a lady's nerves; Epikhodov the clerk, persecuted by fate; the butler Yasha, who is quite a dandy; and the companion Charlotta, who is quite unsure who she is. Ranevskaya's squeamishness about commercial enterprises is contrasted to the eagerness of her neighbor, Pishchik, to allow exploitation of clay deposits discovered on his land. Ranevskaya's two daughters are complete opposites: one is all housekeeper, the other all pointless inspiration. In Act III, when Ranevskaya has arranged an inappropriate ball, the various characters jostle one another in disorder, each repeating his own leitmotif. At the conclusion the aging servant Firs is inadvertently left behind in the house.

Each of Chekhov's plays may be melancholy in its inspiration, but all are worked out with great energy. Moreover, there is an order in their sequence. *The Seagull* is a remembrance of youth; *Uncle Vanya* describes the appearance of middle-aged resentment; *The Three Sisters* explores the state of having no directions in life; and in *The Cherry Orchard* there is a discovery of the ignoble self.

Each play is great in and of itself. Alone or together they may be seen as works of "lyrical realism" in the sense that they express a private vision stemming from a deep underlying inspiration.

The Russian realists viewed their approach as the traditional one in Russian culture, and themselves as heirs of a legacy which had never been seriously questioned in its fundamentals. And yet they were very different from the realists of the nineteenth century. Writers like Gorky displayed a new political radicalism, turning to social concerns with even greater emphasis than before, and a didactic edge. Naturalism in the style of Émile Zola never found much footing in Russia, although it occasionally enjoyed temporary success in the works of Alexander Kuprin, Leonid Andreev, and Mikhail Artsybashev. Gorky typified the work of most Russians in that his philosophical premises always remained optimistic; but he and others painted quite depressing scenes of the homeless, overworked and browbeaten, of drunkenness and physical violence, of depravity and criminality. Another kind of realism, sometimes called "lyrical," which derived from elements to be found earlier in Turgenev and Chekhov, came to special fruition in the writings of Ivan Bunin. An essential element of this style was the impressionistic narration, seemingly spun out by a consciousness subject only to its own emotions and processes of association. Its themes included nature and the natural or biological aspects of human behavior, especially if they were associated with sex or death. The works of Andreev and Artsybashev sometimes exhibited a sensationalized cynicism derived from a materialist philosophy.

Maxim Gorky's writings served as models of politically engaged, or even outright Marxist, literature. After beginning to publish in 1892, he gained some fame in the later 1890s with depictions of downtrodden figures who are captives of the capitalist economic order, of which the story "Creatures That Once Were Men" ("Byvshie lyudi," 1897) may serve as a prototype. In "Twenty Six Men and a Girl" ("Dvadtsat shest i odna," 1899) he depicted a basement sweatshop in which a group of baker-prisoners embody their ideal of better things in the purity of one young girl who visits them, only to be disillusioned by her fall. Gorky was also esteemed for two revolutionary "poems" (although they were in fact lyrical prose pieces): "The Song of the

Falcon" ("Pesnya o sokole," 1895) and "The Song of the Stormy Petrel" ("Pesnya o burevestnike," 1901), in which he offered an allegorical depiction of the bravery of an ideal radical hero.

As a result of his socially oriented writings, Gorky soon became rather a celebrity and an activist. In 1900 he began exerting influence with the Knowledge (Znanie) publishing house, and attracted his fellow realist authors to it. In 1902 he was elected to the Russian Academy but then denied entrance because of his political sympathies. In 1905 he joined the Bolshevik party and became a friend of Lenin's. In the following year he visited the United States to raise money for the revolutionary cause but was embittered by the social ostracism which he encountered there. His precarious health as well as his political difficulties led him to live in Capri until 1913. Following the revolution of 1917 he was instrumental in founding writers' organizations which fostered proletarian literature and saved established writers, including some former enemies, from perishing under the harsh conditions of civil war. Gorky did not find the Soviet system entirely to his liking, however, and lived abroad for some time in the 1920s before he was induced to return to the Soviet Union in the early 1930s.

Gorky's greatest early success was the play *The Lower Depths* (*Na dne*, 1902), whose characters are the inhabitants of a flophouse. Some of them are captivated by the "beautiful lies" of Luka, a wandering preacher who speaks of hope and who is opposed by a character who defends truth, human dignity and independence. A combination of these two tendencies would lie at the core of the later doctrine of socialist realism as Gorky would formulate it when the Writers Union was established in 1932.

An early novel of Gorky's was *Foma Gordeev* (1899), in which the author pictured a segment of the population to which he had been close in his childhood: that of a grubby rising commercial class which was warped by its peasant origins but still destined to supplant the Russian gentry.

In 1907 Gorky published the novel for which he is best known in the west (and which in fact he wrote during his visit to the United States in 1906): *Mother* (*Mat*), a work destined to be the founding document of socialist realism. The book is a rather primitively constructed chronicle of daily life without much of a plot; it is written in a journalistic style, and the portrayal of character is largely limited to physical description and depiction of simple emotions. The opening section describes the miserable lives of factory workers in a provincial town: the men have no other entertainment but drinking, fighting, and beating their wives. This is the background against which the lives of the exemplary young people who are secret Social Democrats are lived. Led by the mother's son, Paul, they print and distribute political pamphlets, existing in constant danger of night searches, arrests, and the gratuitous brutality of the police.

The narrative has two intersecting lines. One involves the mother, Pelagea Nilovna, who soon comes to admire the young people who gather to read, plan and argue at her house. She realizes that these young people continually sacrifice their private lives to the necessities of political strategy, and that they support their colleagues in difficulties with affection. Although first attracted to them by maternal feeling, in time she learns to be a political activist in her own right: when her son is arrested, she takes on the task of smuggling leaflets. Paul refuses a chance to escape from prison in order to stand trial to gain a public platform for the movement. The two lines of the narration come together in the final scene, when the mother, about to be arrested herself, impulsively makes public distribution of clandestinely produced copies of her son's speech at his trial. Thus she too becomes a martyr to the cause.

Gorky's later novels were ambitious, conventional, and not particularly influential. The best known of them are *The Artamonov Business* (*Delo Artamonovykh*, 1925), about the generations of a *parvenu* commercial family before the revolution, and the unfinished epic novel *Life of Klim Samgin* (*Zhizn Klima Samgina*, begun in 1925), which traces the experience of an intellectual through the revolutions of 1905 and 1917.

Gorky's most durable works, however, are his memoirs: *Childhood* (*Detstvo*, 1913); *In the World* (*V lyudyakh*, 1916); and *My Universities* (*Moi universitety*, 1922). They depict a child reared by its grandparents in a roistering, sometimes violent, but close-knit provincial family, the multitude of characters (including underground radical organizers) the narrator meets in his years of wandering and doing odd jobs, and the narrator's own growing attraction to the promises of political doctrine. The trilogy is more arresting for its local color than for any depth of insight or intro-spection. Gorky also left some very memorable reminiscences of other authors, particularly Tolstoy and Chekhov.

Alexander Kuprin was a versatile and competent realist whose short stories and novels reveal a vigorous but rather conventional mind. He was schooled in military academies in Moscow and served as an army officer before resigning his commission in 1894 and eventually ending up in St. Petersburg, associated with Gorky and the Knowledge publishing house. After the revolution of 1917 he emigrated to France.

In his short stories Kuprin displayed a considerable narrative gift, though his early stories had at their core a cynical, knowing attitude toward life and remained essentially shallow. He relied more on wit and irony than on psychological depiction: his char-acters are types, sometimes with one exaggerated trait, or humor. In his later stories Kuprin betrays more compassion for his char-acters, as, for example, he does for the hero of "The Bracelet of Garnets" ("Granatovy braslet," 1911), a sentimental tale of ideal love. The hero is an ordinary man who loves a society lioness from afar. She senses after his suicide that in the midst of her hollow concerns something of an undefined significance has touched her life. The yearning for happiness which this story displays is rare in Kuprin's works.

Kuprin's novels and novelettes have a more social thrust. *Moloch* (*Molokh*, 1896) depicts a factory and its capacity to drain the very vitality of its workers; and *The Pit* (*Yama*, 1915) portrays the world of prostitutes as though it were the most ordinary existence, and any other were scarcely imaginable. But Kuprin's most famous single novel was *The Duel* (*Poedinok*, 1905), which an enthusiastic public saw as a just indictment of the Russian armed forces in the wake of their defeat in the Russo-Japanese war of 1904–5. *The Duel* is in fact not a blatant exposé (it is even rather conventional), but it is permeated with Kuprin's usual cynicism. The book is a por-trayal of life among young married couples in the military who lack ideals or worthy goals and stoop to petty betrayals motivated by selfishness. The work is Chekhovian in its absence of suspense and uplift.

Ivan Bunin (1870–1953), who began simultaneously with poetry and prose, produced several of the finest Russian stories and novels of the twentieth century, but his fame has been limited because he went into emigration after 1917 – although he was the first Russian to receive the Nobel Prize for literature (in 1933).

Bunin belonged to an impoverished aristocratic family of central Russia. Instead of seeking a higher education he launched out upon a writing career, and in the early 1900s attached himself to the Knowledge group. He later traveled extensively in Europe, the Near East, India and Ceylon, and thus a number of his stories and lyrics are set in exotic locales.

Bunin's poetry is often overlooked, probably because it was old-fashioned even in its own time, but he himself at first saw his poetry as intertwined with his prose, and published poetic and prose works together in a single volume. His lyrics are brief and extraordinarily dispassionate. His early poems tend to depict the Russian landscape, while his later ones picture exotic scenes, particularly from the Near East. His earlier poems were at first almost entirely graphic, but his later ones contain numerous allusions to myths, world literature, and history. He can evoke the spirit of a place very well, but his verse's impersonal quality suggests that he wrote under some sort of enigmatic discipline, as if he were very much within the classical tradition.

Bunin has been called the novelist of the declining gentry. More accurately, his works might be described as philosophical in that they deal with love and death, but then one can derive no consistent world-view from them. His fiction is impressionistic and open-ended. His pieces range from a few pages to book-length, as Bunin tended to make no distinction between short stories and novels. Two of his most ambitious works were two relatively early novels, both provincial in setting but opposite in their tone and effect. *The Village* (*Derevnya*, 1910) reflects the revulsion that the violence of the 1905 uprisings aroused in Bunin, normally an apolitical man, as he describes the appalling circumstances that planted the seeds of political conflict. In form it is a biography of two brothers descended from serfs who now own a business. One is a sadistic, greedy tyrant, the other a poetic and longsuffering martyr. The book depicts provincial life in general as primitive and ruthless; the very landscape is spoiled and forbidding.

Sukhodol (*Dry Valley* [the name of an estate], 1912) is set on a nineteenth-century gentry estate. Much of the narration is done by a woman, a former serf, who has suffered many injustices: despite its depiction of dramatic acts of cruelty and violence which have set the stage for modern times, the work has a nostalgic tone. At the end the once thriving estate has become a desolate hideout for three decrepit and impoverished women, one of whom is insane. The past is superseded and any indignation is pointless.

The fiction stemming from Bunin's travel years demonstrates that his interests were not confined to Russian soil: his real concern was with the human condition generally. In his single work best known abroad, "The Gentleman from San Francisco" ("Gospodin iz San-Frantsisko," 1915), the sudden death of a rich American on vacation in Capri exposes the emptiness of his self-important, avaricious and relentlessly busy life. The American is first shown in the dubiously tawdry glamor of a luxury ship crossing the Atlantic to Europe. When he dies of a heart attack at his hotel in Capri he is returned as a corpse in the hold of that same ship, after his wife is made to feel that her presence is an embarrassment to the tourist trade in Capri. In "Dreams of Chang" ("Sny Changa," 1916) death is transcended in the limited intelligence of a former ship's captain's dog. The animal, Chang, recalls the life and death of his master, and senses, in a new haven, the existence of a "third truth," suggestive of an afterlife, or heaven.

When Bunin emigrated to France, the nature of his literary approach remained unchanged. In his best pieces there is an awareness that life is an incomparable gift; tragedies and disillusionment are not isolated, but rather are inseparably connected with life itself, with its vibrancy and rewards. All this is particularly evident in Bunin's later works. For example, in "Mitya's Love" ("Mitina lyubov," 1924) love and pain are so intertwined that the hero's sudden suicide at the end almost comes as a relief to the reader. In "Sunstroke" ("Solnechny udar," 1925) a riverboat passenger abruptly realizes that he has fallen in love with a fellow passenger who has left and whose name he never knew.

Bunin's fiction has the unfettered structure of inner monologue, of fantasies in which the narrator's perceptions are altered and the ending is always unforeseen. This is one reason why life and the world seem to be fresh, close and precious in his rendering of them. His nature descriptions are evocative, often with original observations. One's perceptions of the scene he recreates are the important thing, and his details are compelling.

Another member of the Knowledge group associated with Gorky whose work was extraordinarily popular in its time and obviously spoke to a contemporary taste for change was Leonid Andreev (1871–1919). After graduating in law from Moscow University, Andreev worked for a time as a law reporter before turning to fiction which in its early stages dealt with such themes as alcoholism, sex and death and realistically treated shocking subjects such as drunks, prostitutes and suicides. Thus his story of 1902 "In the Fog" ("V tumane") describes a young man attending to his father's naive warnings about sex when he, the son, is already infected with syphilis. In such works as these Andreev seemed to evoke horror for its own sake, and sometimes erred in treating the tragic as commonplace. This latter fault, however, is not found in Andreev's stories springing from the Russo-Japanese war of 1904–5 and the revolution of 1905. In "The Red Laugh" ("Krasny-smekh," 1905) he describes the madness induced by participation in the violence of war, objectifying in the "red laugh" the horrors of military conflict as perceived through the mind of a deranged man. One of his finest works is "The Governor" ("Gubernator," 1906), depicting a public official who has ordered the violent suppression of some revolutionaries and who now awaits what he knows is certain assassination at the hands of their associates. Andreev's fame rested most of all on the long short story "Seven Who Were Hanged" ("Rasskaz o semi poveshennykh," 1908), which dealt with terrorism and offered a compelling psychological description of five political terrorists and two common criminals as the time of their execution approaches. Andreev clearly sympathized with the terrorists as human beings, if not with their cause.

In the years between 1905 and the outbreak of the First World War Andreev turned to a cosmic sort of pessimism. He wrote plays more than short stories, and between 1907 and 1909 was associated with the Sweetbriar (Shipovnik) Publishing House, which brought out many works of the symbolist school. Consequently, though he was an atheist, Andreev was influenced by the metaphysical vision of the symbolists, and also used an allegorical setting for many of his works. Thus in *Lazarus* (1906) the resurrected hero simply sits in a vast, empty space where nothing happens. *The Life of Man* (*Zhizn cheloveka*, 1906 and 1908) is a symbolic play in which Fate reads the uneventful biography of an Everyman. Andreev made the same point in a later and more realistic play, *Professor Storitsyn* (1912), in which he portrayed a set of intellectuals as pointlessly concerned with mere money and romantic realignments. Andreev's best play was published in 1915 under the title *He Who Gets Slapped* (*Tot, kto poluchaet poshchechinu*). The central figure is a circus clown who has been a melancholy snob and dandy in real life but who has decided to subject himself to humiliations in his performances. He poisons a bareback rider whom he loves to prevent her from making a marriage which her father has arranged for her purely for money. The play engenders in the spectator an ambivalent admiration for the human spirit because men are capable of conceiving of honor and idealism in a world devoid of metaphysical meaning.

Andreev was one of the few Russian writers to lend avid support to Russia's participation in the First World War. The events of 1917 caught him at his home in Finland, where he remained until his death in 1919. His renown faded quickly thereafter, but his great popularity in his own time speaks of the age's eagerness for wider horizons and fewer restrictions. Though his works were mannered, they were linked to the work of the avant-garde.

Mikhail Artsybashev (1878–1927) is remembered primarily as the author of a single sensational novel, *Sanin* (the name of its hero, 1907). He had begun publishing fiction in 1901, stories which dealt with such themes as suicide, rape, and executions in the aftermath of the revolution of 1905. In *Sanin*, the second of a series of novels, he describes young people who speak freely of their sexual desires and espouse the principle of free love. Through his narration Artsybashev seeks to create in his reader a feeling of sexual awareness, and his nature descriptions provide an aura of vital warmth which seems to be an implicit sign of his approval for such a philosophical approach. Popular critics in Russia soon came to regard such amoral evocation of sexual desire as the chief feature of contemporary "naturalism." In *At the Brink* (*U posledney cherty*, 1912) he scandalized the public by depicting an epidemic of suicides among the politically engaged. In 1923 Artsybashev was expelled from the Soviet Union and became a journalist abroad.

Among the most respected of the new thinkers was Dmitry

Merezhkovsky, who displayed in his writing not only the influence of Vladimir Solovyov, but also – after a trip to Greece which stimulated his interest in the ancient cult of Aphrodite – that of Nietzsche, and especially his *The Birth of Tragedy from the Spirit of Music*, with its criticism of Christianity and its theory that western literature took its origin in the rituals of the cult of Dionysus. Consequently he embarked upon a trilogy of historical novels under the overall title of *Christ and Antichrist* (*Khristos i antikhrist*), dedicated to the continuing historical conflict between "spirit" and "flesh," and to the proposition that this clash would be overcome at the millennium. Its individual parts are: *The Death of the Gods. Julian the Apostate* (*Smert bogov. Yulian otstupnik*, 1896); *The Resurrection of the Gods. Leonardo da Vinci* (*Voskresshie bogi. Leonardo da Vinchi*, 1901); and *Antichrist. Peter and Alexis* (*Antikhrist. Petr i Aleksey*, 1905).

Like other symbolists, Merezhkovsky used his literary criticism as a vehicle for the propagation of his ideas. Thus in his book *Tolstoy and Dostoevsky* (1902) he presented Dostoevsky as a "seer" of the spirit and Tolstoy as a "seer" of the flesh, while in *Gogol and the Devil* (*Gogol i chort*, 1906) he viewed Gogol as one who exorcized the demon of shallow vulgarity, or the absence of ideals.

Merezhkovsky sympathized with the revolutionary movement of 1905 because he interpreted it as an apocalyptic religious event. In 1906 he and his wife Hippius emigrated temporarily to France, where they published an anti-monarchist tract. Upon their return to Russia they never regained their former influence, even though Merezhkovsky published several historical novels and plays before the outbreak of the First World War.

Two cultural essayists who occasionally dealt with literary problems challenged the efficacy of rationalism as a guide to the conduct of human affairs: Vasily Rozanov and Leo Shestov. Rozanov (1815–1919) was trained as an historian at Moscow University and taught in secondary schools before he achieved renown as a writer. His essay of 1894, *The Legend of the Grand Inquisitor by F. M. Dostoevsky* (*Legenda o velikom inkvizitore F. M. Dostoevskogo*), inaugurated the era in which Dostoevsky was seen as a philosophical author. Rozanov held that Dostoevsky agreed with his Underground Man in asserting that the individual values his own free will above the dictates of reason. Rozanov also held that, despite the received critical tradition, Gogol had never been a realist, and that his characters are humors.

Rozanov was married for a time to one of Dostoevsky's former mistresses, and when the Orthodox Church would not permit him to divorce her, he became an opponent of its ascetic tendencies, denouncing the church's opposition to joy, in particular sexual joy, and what he considered its undue reverence for sorrow and abstinence. He advocated a return to Old Testament mores. He put forth ideas of this sort in his best known work, a series of causeries entitled *Fallen Leaves* (*Opavshie listya*, 1915).

The opposition of Leo Shestov (real name: Shvartsman, 1866–1938) to rationalism was even more directly self-conscious than Rozanov's. Originally a wealthy Kievan businessman who lived in Italy and Switzerland from 1895 to 1914, he made his intellectual reputation with two works of 1903 and 1907 on Tolstoy, Dostoevsky, and Nietzsche. In the first of these – *Dostoevsky and Nietzsche* (*The Philosophy of Tragedy*) (*Dostoevsky i Nitsshe* [*Filosofiya tragedii*]) – he also maintained that Dostoevsky had opted for freedom and opposed the arrogance of science. In the second, *The Idea of the Good in Tolstoy and Nietzsche. Philosophy and Preaching* (*Dobro v uchenii gr. Tolstogo i F. Nitsshe* [*Filosofiya i propoved*]), his expressed preference for Nietzsche over Tolstoy was a signal of his opposition to any systematized morality. In subsequent books he grounded his defense of the individual against dogma firmly on philosophical foundations.

In 1919 Shestov emigrated to France, where he taught at the Sorbonne and continued to write, with the most celebrated of his later books being *In Job's Balances* (*Na vesakh Iova*, 1929). Although Shestov may appear to have foreshadowed existentialism in his capacity to view the world through the individual consciousness, he also believed in the rewards of a life of faith.

The realist writers grouped about Gorky and the Knowledge publishing house competed against a powerful current of decadence and symbolism which arose in reaction to the domination of the realist esthetic in the final decades of the nineteenth century in Russia and also in response to the rise of symbolism in France (Russian translations of the work of Baudelaire, Verlaine and Mallarmé, as well as studies of their writing, began to appear in the early 1890s), but with a considerable infusion of German idealist thought. These movements were sufficiently influential that they gave rise to a "silver age" of Russian culture generally. There was moreover in Russian symbolism a sense of religious mission not characteristic of symbolism in its western variants. Indeed the term "symbolist" was pre-empted in Russia by a group of writers who subscribed to some form of neo-Platonism. This group included some seven well-known poets, among them Valery Bryusov and Alexander Blok. A few writers of mystical or decadent inclination – Innokenty Annensky, for example – remained outside the "school": though they were clearly symbolists in the European sense, they were denied that title by their Russian contemporaries.

The Russian symbolists, who began publishing in the middle 1890s, wrote both poetry and prose, and dealt with many of the moral and religious questions which Dostoevsky had raised before them. Members of the so-called "first wave" of the symbolist school, whom hostile critics called decadents, an appellation which they accepted for themselves, dealt with topics displaying a religious malaise and a self-indulgent preoccupation with melancholia and unwholesome tendencies. One of the most typical representatives of the "decadents" of this period was the poet Konstantin Balmont. The movement as a whole found an outlet in the luxury journal *World of Art* (*Mir iskusstva*), founded in 1898 by Sergei Diaghilev and other connoisseurs of art, which continued to appear until 1904.

By the beginning of the century, however, a new literary self-confidence had replaced the passive melancholia of the first wave of symbolists, as several new poets who adhered to the movement at that time and constituted its second wave brought with them a psychology which might be referred to as a "dawn" mentality. The sanguine cultural expectations of this period were linked to a rising tide of political hopes, hopes which vanished with the suppression of the revolution of 1905. There ensued a new era of pessimism which engulfed a broad segment of the intelligentsia as the symbolists reverted to decadent themes. Their principal literary journal of the time was *The Scales* (*Vesy*, 1904–9). Still, it was during this period of doubt that many of their greatest works were written, and Alexander Blok even became a celebrity. But it was also at this time that several "symbolists" who had not previously been members of the inner group gained prominence, including the outstanding prose-writer Alexey Remizov.

By 1910 the symbolists had easily become the literary establishment, the establishment against which avant-garde writers now rebelled as they founded new literary movements. After the revolution of 1917 about half the Russian symbolists went into emigration.

As we have already noted, in its early stages the prolific but very uneven poet Konstantin Balmont (1867–1942) won notoriety for the new "decadent" current, and he remained the most celebrated Russian symbolist until about 1906. He originally studied at the Moscow University Law faculty until a nervous breakdown forced him to leave in 1887 and he became a poet and translator. A stay in England enabled him to become acquainted with the new literary currents as exemplified in the writings of Oscar Wilde and his entourage.

Upon his return to Russia Balmont first achieved literary success with *Under Northern Skies* (*Pod severnym nebom*, 1894): the atmosphere of the book is compounded primarily of a mysterious sadness and a spiritual nostalgia. In his subsequent publications – *Beyond All Limits* (*V bezbrezhnosti*, 1895) and *Silence* (*Tishina*, 1898) – he elaborated a coherent philosophy steeped in Schopenhauerian pessimism: the poet longs for communion with a world soul or ideal, as do all mankind and nature in all its phenomena, but all are doomed to frustration. Art is the only way in which such frustration can be overcome.

Since Balmont was something of a cultural barometer, he quickly signalled the general shift to a mood of optimism at the very turn of the century. In *Buildings on Fire* (*Goryashchie zdaniya*, 1900) and *Let Us Be Like the Sun* (*Budem kak solntse*, 1903) he expressed the new poles of his experience as the ecstasy of attainment and the spite born of a will denied. He was a pantheist who sought to share in the might and delicate beauty of the universe. The cosmos as he interpreted it was amoral, and his aim became the experience of passion and esthetic delight in themselves. This vision of life as an esthetic whole suggests the influence of Nietzsche, as do elements of a superman credo to be found in his writing.

In addition to poetry Balmont wrote fiction, plays and travel impressions, which have never been properly assessed. He was a great world traveler and pictured exotic tropical places, especially Mexico and the Mayan culture as well as Africa and the Pacific, in his travel sketches. Among foreign cultures Balmont was always closest to English: he translated Shelley, Poe, Whitman, Wilde and others.

At the time of the revolution of 1905 Balmont joined the Social Democratic party, but then left Russia in disillusionment in 1906. In 1907 he published a seditious volume of lyrics, *Songs of an Avenger* (*Pesni mstitelya*), in Paris, where he resided until 1911, during which time he lost the esteem of the Russian reading public. In the meantime he turned to Russian and Slavic folk culture, among other things, for inspiration. Thus he collected verse tales written for his daughter in *Fairy Tales* (*Feynye rasskazy*, 1905), and paraphrased popular curses in verse in *Evil Spells* (*Zlye chary*, 1906). In *The Firebird* (*Zhar-ptitsa*, 1907) he praised the achievements of medieval Slavic cultures, and especially those of ancient Kiev. The best of his "popular" books was *The Green Garden* (*Zeleny vertograd*, 1909), in which he recast the passionate religious songs of flagellant sectarians.

In 1918 Balmont emigrated to France permanently, and in exile his poetry became less and less convincing. He ultimately died in a mental institution. Though he had once been very popular for his audacity, time showed that his amoral tendencies were not just a literary device but a genuine fault. He authored a number of outstanding poems, but seldom wrote at his best.

Fyodor Sologub (real name: Fyodor Teternikov, 1863–1927), remembered as the chief decadent among the symbolists, was the author of one of the two best novels to come out of the symbolist movement. He spent almost a decade in the provinces as a schoolteacher before returning to his native St. Petersburg in the early 1890s, and soon he joined the symbolist milieu. He thought of himself largely as a poet, but he also wrote plays, short stories and novels. Indeed he first attracted public attention with prose fiction depicting mental aberration. His first novel, *Bad Dreams* (*Tyazhelye sny*, 1896), describes a provincial schoolteacher who shares the interests of the European decadent movement, suffers from nightmares, and commits murder while in a state of hallucination. The short stories he wrote before 1905 have to do with children almost exclusively as they pose the metaphysical problems of decadence: these young people are usually depicted as victims of an unjust fate, and although they may appear to be sweetly innocent, in fact some are already tainted by the evil impulses characteristic of the adult psychology.

The four collections of lyric poetry which Sologub published between 1896 and 1904 constitute in effect his spiritual auto-biography. His earliest poems were dedicated to melancholia and also to nature, which he obviously loved because he never tired of landscape descriptions in his verse. Later these subjects were fol-lowed by escapist fantasies and confessions of his "sins." In the late 1890s he spoke of nostalgia for an ideal which he symbolized by stars, in the best romantic tradition. Afterwards came visions of a cruel universe ruled by a tyrannical spirit which evolves forever but aimlessly: Sologub's conception of the universe no doubt owed a great deal to Schopenhauer. Sologub often used the source of all earthly life, the sun, to symbolize the tyrant. His world view was thus never stable in its particulars, but he displayed a per-vasively Manichean tendency to speak in terms of polar oppo-sitions between the forces of light and of darkness.

In the years between 1905 and the First World War Sologub traversed a great change in general mood, from anger to recon-ciliation. At the beginning of that era he expressed his support for radical causes through political verse published in clandestine magazines in 1904 and 1905. His most outstanding work, the novel *The Petty Demon* (*Melky bes*, 1907), was composed in the accusatory period before 1905 and describes a provincial society both malicious and ridiculous in its triviality and governed by a senselessly rigid bureaucracy. His schoolteacher hero, who repre-sents the worst of this society, murders his only friend in a fit of paranoid rage. The author designed the book as an allegory of earthly life, but it came through as an indictment of provincial stagnation. In any case it brought Sologub fame, and enabled him to retire from teaching to dedicate himself to literature.

Sologub sought to summarize his poetic thematics with a volume of 1908 entitled *Flaming Circle* (*Plamenny krug*). It opens with poems depicting the poet in his supposed former lives begin-ning with Adam, and ends with works in which the poet regards death both with horror and as "the last consolation." His inclination to view the universe with spiritual optimism gained impetus, however, in the lyric plays he wrote following his younger sister's death of tuberculosis in 1907. In them, and especially in *The Victory of Death* (*Pobeda smerti*, 1908), the love of earthbound humans is seen as transcending, or "conquering," death. At the same time Sologub explored the notion that reality may be confronted or ameliorated through art. In an article entitled "The demons of poets" ("Demony poetov," 1907) he argued that the lyric artist rejects reality for fantasy while the realist works with irony. In the poetry of his late period Sologub succeeded in blending a new joy in life with a continuing love of fantasy.

Among Sologub's most extensive prose works was a trilogy of novels entitled *The Created Legend* (*Tvorimaya legenda*, 1914), in which he sought to demonstrate that human intuitive abilities can alter or transform reality. His schoolteacher is now a magus who has ties with the living dead; he and his love are translated from the chaotic and dangerous circumstances of the 1905 revolution to a state called the United Isles in the Mediterranean, where she is Queen Ortruda. These novels, however, are of value primarily as entertainment: they lack the power of their angry predecessor *The Petty Demon*.

In 1920 Sologub was denied permission to go abroad, and in 1921 his wife of thirteen years committed suicide. He was unable to publish any original works after 1923, and so turned to translations, especially from the French, to support himself before he died in 1927.

Valery Bryusov (1873–1924) was the leader of the Russian symbolist movement, a position which he achieved not so much by his poetic attainments, which were considerable, as through his organizational ability: he was a talented editor who founded and managed the principal organs of the school, the Scorpion Publishing House (1900–16) and *The Scales* (1904–9). He proved to be a dedicated and even-handed editor whose policies shaped the entire development of the Russian symbolists: he so balanced the needs of rival factions within the group that the symbolist school emerged as a larger and stronger force than the sum of its individual parts.

Bryusov came originally from the merchant class, a group once known for its cultural isolation which nevertheless produced some wealthy art patrons at the turn of the century. While still a student at Moscow University Bryusov brought out three issues of a miscellany entitled *The Russian Symbolists* (*Russkie simvolisty*, 1894–5), which contained poems written in imitation of the French symbolists, mostly authored by himself.

Bryusov began bringing out his own original verse with *Chefs d'œuvre* of 1895. Although the popular press printed mocking parodies of his work, he did establish in this first volume his partiality for exotic settings (including the Easter Islands and other primitive areas), erotic themes, and scenes of physical torture. The collection *Me eum esse* (1897) includes poems on these themes as well as others displaying a nostalgia for ideals of purity and spiritual elevation, although this latter stance seemed much more characteristic of some other symbolists than it ever did of him.

Bryusov gained the respect of both readers and critics with the poems of his collection *Tertia vigilia* of 1900. Here, though he abandoned none of his earlier themes, he added new perspectives to them. He reenacted moments from history and from the myths of antiquity and described rulers and heroes whom he obviously admired and among whom his favorite was in later books to be the bard and warrior Orpheus. Bryusov also portrayed models of pagan honor and eroticism. In this he followed the tradition of the French Parnassians, rivals of the symbolists, led by Leconte de Lisle, who wrote almost exclusively about the myths and legends of Greece, Rome and northern Europe. Bryusov also moved to new and further horizons in poems about artists, about children and about philosophy as his work became less egocentric and more reflective on the subject of human nature and its potentialities. In subsequent books of poetry such as *Urbi et orbi* (1903) and *Stephanos* (1906) he continued to develop along the same lines. He was famed for introducing the urban theme – the city perceived as the locale of passion, squalor and violence – in *Urbi et orbi*. And *Stephanos* included his famous poem "The pale horse" ("Kon bled"), an apocalyptic view of the revolutionary movement.

Bryusov also continued his organizational activities in support of the symbolist movement. When *The Scales* first appeared in 1904, the lead article of the first issue was one of his very few articles on esthetics, "The keys of mysteries" ("Klyuchi tayn"), in which he argued that art is revelation. Under his editorship *The Scales* published literary and art news from western Europe, translations of works by foreign writers, critical articles by Russian symbolists, original poetry and prose, and plates by Russian *art nouveau* artists, chief among them Alexander Benois.

Bryusov's own prose fiction tended to be fantastic and a bit sensational. His first collection of short stories, *The Earth's Axis* (*Zemnaya os*), appeared in 1907. His stories are at some times about psychotic individuals, at others about cities or civilizations in the throes of some ghastly cataclysm. The best known of them is "The Republic of the Southern Cross" ("Respublika yuzhnogo kresta"), which describes the disintegration of a utopian city built by commercial concerns for mining at the South Pole. His stories suggest that civilization is an insufficient constraint upon a human psyche which is fundamentally bestial.

In addition to short stories, Bryusov also wrote two historical novels. *The Fiery Angel* (*Ognenny angel*, 1909), set in sixteenth-century Germany, concerns a contest between the church and would-be wielders of satanic or pagan power. The work is also a *roman à clef* based upon the private lives of certain Russian symbolists. *Altar of Victory* (*Altar pobedy*, 1911–12) is set in Rome of the fourth century and describes the struggle of that time between pagan and Christian cultures.

Bryusov welcomed the revolution of 1917, becoming a functionary of the Commissariat of Education and joining the communist party in 1920. He also continued to publish poetry, but now with little success. In his lifetime some labeled him an opportunist, but his service to literature was genuine, sincerely offered and truly beneficial.

Zinaida Hippius (1869–1945) has come to be regarded as one of Russia's finest religious poets, whose verse reflects her belief, derived from Vladimir Solovyov, in a principle of love governing the universe. She came from a provincial gentry family, married Dmitry Merezhkovsky in 1889, and thereafter presided over a Sunday salon in St. Petersburg which became an early center of Russian symbolism. She and Merezhkovsky shared many convictions as well as a sense of cultural mission, and undertook all their projects as joint endeavors.

Hippius's first collection of short stories, *New People* (*Novye lyudi*), appeared in 1896, and her first novel, *The Victors* (*Pobediteli*), in 1898. All her prose deals in one way or another with the operation of the principle of divine love in the universe and its hindrance by individual pride and social convention. Her characters and plots are seemingly ordinary: she writes about love, marriage, friendship, family and servants in both rural and urban settings. But in fact her fiction is quite didactic: her prose works are slow-paced and predictable in their outcomes. By 1906 Hippius had published an additional three volumes of short stories.

Although Hippius and Merezhkovsky contributed prose and poetry to the *World of Art*, in time they reacted against the pure estheticism of that grouping in favor of religiously oriented cultural activity. In 1901 they founded the Religious Philosophical Society and in 1903 the journal which served as its organ, *New Path* (*Novy put*). Hippius also turned to poetry (her first collection of verse appeared in 1904), which was always greater than her prose. In her poetry she speaks as though for herself, and her best poems exhibit the self-laceration of a clever, proud intelligence. Their tone is never patronizing. The sin from which she suffers most is spiritual pride, that "sin of angels." Her spiritual states include thirst for fulfilment, dejection, terror at the thought of ostracism, guilt, temptation, and cowardice. She speaks of death, of earthly love, of nature, and of the depravity of society. Among poets she has been known as an influential innovator in prosody: she helped to popularize the *dolnik*, an "impaired" rhythm reminiscent of trisyllabic feet.

The events of 1905 interrupted the literary careers of Hippius and Merezhkovsky, but Hippius in time returned to fiction, publishing two volumes of short stories which included anti-militaristic themes, and two novels. The novels – *The Devil's Doll* (*Chertova kukla*, 1911) and *Roman Tsarevich* (1913) – assess the forces working against the revolution. She faulted society for its bourgeois tendencies, which stemmed in her view from greed and reliance on an empty rationalism. The only longer work of hers which acquired public renown was a play entitled *The Green Ring* (*Zelenoe koltso*, 1916), which describes a cultural club for young people in an avant-garde era and takes up the topics of morality in marriage and family life.

Hippius and Merezhkovsky were convinced opponents of the

revolution of 1917. In 1918 she published a volume of poetry which contained both radical and anti-Soviet sentiments. In 1919 she and her husband emigrated, first to Poland and then to France, where they spent most of the remainder of their lives as a center of religious and anti-communist organizations. The emigration did not support a very extensive cultural life, but she did what she could to encourage it. Her memoirs, *Living Faces* (*Zhivye litsa*), published in Prague in 1925, will endure, however. The book describes her encounters with leading writers of her day, mostly symbolists.

The turn of the century saw the temporary popularity of several poets of an "idealist" bent who have since been largely forgotten. One of them was Alexander Dobrolyubov (1876–?1944), a minor religious poet whose work anticipated that of the later avant-garde. Though he had only brief contact with the Russian symbol-ists, he had lived in France and gained a good knowledge of French symbolism. His major collections were *Natura naturans. Natura naturata* (1895) and *Collected Verse* (*Sobranie stikhov*, 1900). His lyrics are slight but full of nature imagery, syntactically primitive and yet erudite. In rapt tones the poet expresses his religious awe in the face of the universe, life and death. Dobrolyubov uses tropes that are brief and strange, makes mannered allusions to foreign poets and employs musical notations, such as "allegro." Some of his works are fragments, and some are wholly or partially in prose. In the late 1890s Dobrolyubov took up the life of a religious wanderer and eventually founded his own religious sect in the south of the country.

The writers comprising the second wave of Russian symbolism which dated from the early years of the twentieth century tended to write of otherworldly nostalgias and mystical ecstasies. Their ideas and some of their imagery had medieval origins as well as roots in nineteenth-century philosophical idealism: they were impatient with mundane limitations and anticipated the millen-nium. Adopting a tack not typical of European symbolism in general, they nourished rash metaphysical hopes and implausible political expectations of great social changes in Russia, which, however, did not survive the collapse of the 1905 revolution. They also devoted painstaking effort to the achievement of technical excellence and the resurrection and refinement of older European literary forms such as the wreath of sonnets. At the same time their hubris was very modern in some ways, and they conducted literary experiments which served as an impetus for the later development of the avant-garde. Thus the greatest of the Russian symbolists, Alexander Blok, was both a traditionalist and an innovator.

Andrey Bely (real name: Boris Bugaev, 1880–1934) is remembered as the author of the finest experimental novel of the symbolist period: *Petersburg* (1916). Bely's father was a professor of mathematics at Moscow University with ties to the family of Vladimir Solovyov, who exerted a strong early influence on his outlook. His initial works were experimental prose "symphonies" intended to synthesize all the arts and displaying an obvious Wagnerian influence, of which he published four between 1902 and 1908. Three of them are long fairy tales about kings, queens, knights and other medieval figures, in four movements, with leitmotifs and containing a philosophical objective: the discovery and adoration of the Divine Wisdom, St. Sophia. The third, entitled *The Return* (*Vozvrat*, 1905), is the most arresting of them. It has only three movements, and its central episode describes the reality of a graduate student at Moscow University who is losing his mind.

Bely had acquired some public notoriety earlier with the rather immature but whimsical lyrics of *Gold in Azure* (*Zoloto v lazuri*, 1904). The collection opens with skyscapes depicting sunsets which, the poet hints, mask a mystical passage to new times. The volume includes childish fantasies about giants and centaurs deriving from nineteenth-century German poetry as well as notes of a gentle spiritual nostalgia. Bely contributed most explicitly to the general "dawn" psychology of the time through essays written in ecstatic tones and employing colorful images as he looked forward to the coming of the "woman clothed in the sun" and the end of world history, a millennium which he believed would result from the alteration of human consciousness. Also, Bely regarded his friendship with Blok at the time as a mystical bond, and both men viewed Blok's wife Lyubov as the earthly embodiment of Holy Wisdom.

The failure of the revolution of 1905, however, led to the destruction of Bely's millennarian hopes and to deep disillusionment on his part. A love triangle developed between Bely, Blok and Lyubov which Lyubov resolved by going off with a third man. Bely himself left Russia in 1906 for an extended sojourn in Germany and France and later brought out two volumes of poetry in 1909: *Ashes* (*Pepel*) and *The Urn* (*Urna*). The first contained pessimistic depictions of Russia as a cruel and backward rural country but also pictures of the miseries of any philistine urban society, including those found in Russia. Other poems in the collection point to his own personal crisis, with descriptions of a bout with insanity and visions of clowns and doubles. The poems of the second collection are more philosophical, dealing with such themes as the loss of love, the emptiness of doctrine, and the approach of death.

Bely was also a prominent theoretician of the symbolist movement and an active participant in the doctrinal controversies which led to a so-called "crisis of symbolism" around 1910. The disputes in question revolved about the role of religion and even epistemology in what should have been a purely literary movement.

In 1910 Bely published *The Silver Dove* (*Serebryany golub*), the first of two novels setting forth his pessimistic vision of Russia's destiny. Here he shows the nation as fatally split between its civilized western character and its chaotic eastern nature. Its religious sectarianism threatens to engulf and annihilate its enlightened segment, embodied in the person of a graduate student on vacation in the provinces.

Eventually Bely again departed for the west, this time with a companion, Asya Turgeneva; the two of them came under the influence of Rudolph Steiner's anthroposophical theories and spent four years at the group's Swiss headquarters. Upon his return to Russia Bely published *Petersburg*, in 1916. A Prologue describing the situation of St. Petersburg on the map suggests that the book's subject is really the nation of which St. Petersburg is the capital, a nation displaying eastern and western components which Bely now perceives as inextricably intertwined and equally destructive. The two central protagonists are father and son. The father is a senator, Apollon Apollonovich Ableukhov, a man with a Tatar surname but a western given name, who serves the government. He is united to his son Nikolay, a graduate student in philosophy, through the Dostoevskian theme of patricide: Nikolay has agreed, though very reluctantly, to assassinate his father using a bomb in a sardine tin. He is preoccupied with Kant, which suggests his western roots, but at the same time his chaotic habits are allegedly asiatic.

A major presence in *Petersburg* is that of Pushkin, whose narrative poem *The Bronze Horseman* is among other things an assessment of the place of revolution in Russian history. In that poem the "bronze horseman," the equestrian statue of Peter the Great, who founded the capital to be a "window on the west," pursues an angry citizen through the city streets. In Bely's work the same statue pays a nocturnal visit to the revolutionary who must oversee the senator's assassination. Pushkin had long before foreseen the threat of tyranny from two sources: one the autocracy, the other the people.

Petersburg is also a satire, attacking both the millennarian and the revolutionary hopes of 1905. The millennarian predictions made by Bely's friends are satirized in the story of Nikolay's love for the wife of an army officer, Sophia Petrovna, an empty-headed flirt described as a "Japanese doll" who takes an interest in political meetings. The triangle recalls that between Bely and the Bloks. In his anguish Nikolay wears a red domino, a clown suit familiar from the poems included in *Ashes*.

The book's denouement commences when Senator Ableukhov's estranged wife returns to him after having lived with another man in Spain. When the bomb explodes, it harms no one physically, but severs the tenuous tie between father and son. Nikolay leaves for north Africa, where he devotes himself to esoteric cultural studies, communicating with his family only through letters.

In its narration *Petersburg* is elusive and fragmentary, but evokes the inner states of many of its characters, although the epilogue describing the north African period is cast in straightforward language. All in all, the work is one of the greatest achievements of Russian avant-garde prose.

Bely's long poem "Christ is risen" ("Khristos voskrese," 1918) welcomed the revolution as an apocalyptic event, while "The fiirst meeting" ("Pervoe svidanie") celebrates the beginnings of Bely's own career and Vladimir Solovyov's influence upon it. In the 1920s Bely wrote a number of autobiographical novels and memoirs. Bely's post-revolutionary fictional works are little known, partially because they bear such a powerful imprint of Steiner's anthroposophical ideas. Thus *Kotik Letaev* (1922) depicts the developing consciousness within the soul of an infant and child, and had a sequel in *The Baptized Chinaman* (*Kreshchenny kitaets*, 1922). This was followed by a trilogy of experimental novels set in Moscow. Bely's *Recollections of A. A. Blok* (*Vospominaniya ob A. A. Bloke*, 1922) was followed by another trilogy of personal memoirs dealing with the period of the turn of the century but published in the 1930s. Bely's memoirs are both subjective and unreliable, but they are nevertheless indispensable to the historian simply because Bely's works and theories were so seminal in the development of the Russian avant-garde.

Alexander Blok (1880–1921) was not only the greatest poet of his time, he best exemplified the mysticism which lay at the core of the school of Russian symbolism. Blok's grandfather was rector of St. Petersburg University, and his mother was close to the family of Vladimir Solovyov, whose Sophian philosophy was the chief subject of Blok's early verse. In 1903 Blok married Lyubov Mendeleeva, daughter of the famous chemist Dmitry Mendeleev, seeing in her an earthly vessel of the Divine Wisdom. His collection entitled *Verses on the Beautiful Lady* (*Stikhi o prekrasnoy dame*, 1905) was in effect a poetic diary of his longing for mystical communion with St. Sophia and became the most perfect expression of the religious strivings of Russian symbolism. Blok pictures himself in a suburbia of dawns and sunsets, thriving or not according to the progress of his chivalric dedication. In time, however, ominous presentiments engender doubts, romantic ironies, and fears of a malicious double, a Harlequin to his Pierrot. And in fact his marriage did founder on a romantic triangle with Andrey Bely.

Blok matured as a poet only after the disillusionments of the failure of the revolution of 1905 and of his marriage. As early as 1904 he had begun to reflect erotic temptations outside his marriage, and subsequently he pictured himself in very debased conditions and his ideal of the Divine Wisdom in warped, degraded and earthly guises. In his famous lyric drama *The Puppet Show* (*Balaganchik*, 1906) he is the familiar Pierrot, but his Columbine, stolen anew from him by Harlequin, is in any case "only a cardboard bride." Many of his lyric poems of this period are set in taverns where the poet indulges in debauchery. In "The stranger" ("Neznakomka," 1906), the finest lyric of this "tavern" period, he discerns his former ideal in a lone and enigmatic woman of the night in a tavern. In his drama *The Stranger* (*Neznakomka*, 1906) the poet is a bohemian who fails to recognize his mystic love in a woman called Maria, who is apparently a fallen star. In January 1907 Blok wrote a remarkable cycle of poems, "The Snow Mask" ("Snezhnaya maska"), inspired by his infatuation with an actress. Her blandishments are sinister corruptions of the attributes of the Beautiful Lady: the blue train of her gown, her blue eyes, her luminosity. But she poses a cosmic danger – the damnation of a soul. The setting is replete with blizzards and skyscapes. Blok's lyric drama *The Song of Fate* (*Pesnya sudby*, 1908) was written under the impact of the same infatuation and pictures the lure of an earthbound vibrancy. In sum, this body of work demonstrates that although Blok was disappointed in Solovyov's millennarian expectations, he retained his belief in divine principle.

Blok reached the height of his powers between 1908 and 1918. He continued to intertwine philosophical and personal themes, and his erotic focus still wavered between the earthly and the otherworldly, but his love of country became significantly more important than it had been before. If in his early poetry he had expressed his dedication to a land lacerated by historical adversity, by 1908 his nation had become an object of mystical reverence to him. His cycle "On Kulikovo Field" ("Na pole kulikovom," the name of the battlefield on which Dmitry Donskoy won his first great victory over the Tatars in 1381) contains the most memorable poems setting forth this tendency. In them Blok views Russia both as a metaphysical entity and as a "wife." He takes a more analytical view in such articles as "The people and the intelligentsia" ("Narod i intelligentsiya," 1908), in which he discerns an impassable barrier between the two groups mentioned in the title. Dismissing the gentry intelligentsia as a mere imitation of the west, he views the lower classes as the only true Russia, the bearer of the mystical soul of the nation. In such pieces he was also influenced by Nietzsche's notion that vital peoples are animated by a "spirit of music."

At the same time Blok continued in his poetry to develop philosophical and erotic themes along lines established earlier. In 1909 he wrote a magnificent cycle of *Italian Poems* (*Italyanskie stikhi*) after taking a tour of Italy with his wife, who had returned to him to bear a child he had not fathered. For Blok Italy was the ancient setting for mankind's most complex spiritual problems and the homeland of his predecessor Dante, and in his cycle he dealt with the eternal dilemma of any neo-Platonist: his desire for the fulness of earthly experience contrasted with his wish to attain the highest rungs of the spiritual life. Thus Blok's most ambitious play, *The Rose and the Cross* (*Roza i krest*, 1913), is a story of ideal and profane love: the foolish wife of a medieval count thinks she loves a distant troubadour while ignoring a perfect love right at hand, that of a self-sacrificing old knight who guards the castle. In the cycle *Carmen* (1914), occasioned by an affair with an opera singer, Blok set forth his sorest dilemma: he sees art as an irresistible but unalterably earthly endeavor whose objective, beauty, is amoral. Beauty is not the divine, as Solovyov had once taught. In his narrative poem of 1915, *The Nightingale Garden* (*Soloviny sad*), Blok makes quite the opposite point, that art may be such an obsession as to devastate one's life.

Blok's final longer works were inspired by love of country at a time of great crisis. He worked over *Retribution* (*Vozmezdie*) from 1909 until after the revolution of 1917. The poem, which seems to have links to the family of Blok's mother, describes three generations of an intelligentsia family as it prepares for the revolution which will destroy its class. But Blok's masterpiece is generally considered to be *The Twelve* (*Dvenadtsat*, 1918), a depiction of revolutionary soldiers patrolling the streets of Petrograd in 1918.

The action of *The Twelve* is set during a blizzard, which is in Blok's work a sign of the metaphysical importance of what he is describing: later he said that while writing the poem he "heard" the sound of the old world "crumbling." As the work opens, the derelict remnants of the past consist of a lonely bourgeois, a fat priest and a mangy dog, but the point of view is that of the Red Guardsmen, whose shallow attitudes and racy vocabulary Blok adopts. The main occurrence of the piece is the accidental shooting of a prostitute by a Red Guardsman, her former lover Petya, as she rides by with an officer. The fallen woman in the snow recalls the "cardboard bride" of *The Puppet Show*; she is, despite all the calumny heaped upon her, transparently a symbol of the Beautiful Lady. The other soldiers enjoin Petya not to mourn her, in ridicule which suggests that Blok felt there was a gap between a private spiritual quest and a sense of solidarity with the nation.

The Twelve contains a striking religious element. The guardsmen number twelve, and thus are inescapably associated with the group of Christ's disciples; and the work is divided into twelve parts. At the poem's enigmatic conclusion, Christ appears before the Red Guards almost as their leader, but they, blinded by the snow, shoot at Him. This conclusion has been the subject of much scholarly dispute: some critics argue that Christ leads the men, while others hold that the men reject Him. In any case, the figure reminds the reader of Christ's mission as savior and redeemer.

The Twelve was formally innovative, and obviously influenced in its rhythms by the urban factory song, or *chastushka*, and by hawkers' rhymes. Blok maintained a harshly strident tone throughout nearly all the work as he gave an aggressive and lacerating performance, though at the point of Christ's appearance he suddenly spoke in the gently sophisticated voice of Blok the symbolist poet.

Blok himself suffered from the material deprivations of the revolution and the ensuing civil war, and died in 1921 of illness stemming from those deprivations.

Vyacheslav Ivanov (1866–1949) was an extraordinarily erudite and elegant poet who usually wrote on religious and philosophical subjects, deriving his beliefs from German philosophy, the ecumenical Christianity of Vladimir Solovyov, and the myths of pagan antiquity (he was a classical scholar who specialized in the cult of Dionysus). His first book of verse, *Lodestars* (*Kormchie zvezdy*, 1902), came out while he was still studying for a Master's degree at the University of Berlin. In these poems Ivanov showed that he regarded both ancient and modern myths as emanations of common human spiritual impulses, and all religious perceptions as equally valid: indeed he tended to identify Christ with Pan or Dionysus. Nietzsche's *The Birth of Tragedy from the Spirit of Music* influenced Ivanov in his esteem for ancient cults and for art as a spiritual medium. He regarded the natural world – both in its grandiose mountain ranges and oceans and in its intimate nooks – as an incorporation of the divine. In *Transparency* (*Prozrachnost*, 1904) he allotted more attention to Christianity than to pagan cults, but without ever ceasing to reverse the cycle of death and

resurrection and to view both eros and death as paths of transfiguration. So grandiloquent was his style that his contemporaries soon
dubbed him "Vyacheslav the Magnificent."

After the events of 1905 Ivanov returned to Russia, where he
espoused an idealistic populism termed "mystical anarchism"
which touched a responsive chord in many people. He proclaimed
that the poet is the voice of his people's racial memory and argued
that the artist can create new religious myths. Since he denigrated
individualism and promoted all forms of communality as democratic, he aroused a certain amount of hostility among some other
symbolists, but he nevertheless assumed a position of doctrinal
leadership within the school. His St. Petersburg apartment, called
"The Tower," became a major intellectual center of the capital
between 1905 and 1907. He later published his articles on esthetics
in *By the Stars* (*Po zvezdam*, 1909) and *Furrows and Boundaries*
(*Borozdy i mezhi*, 1916).

Ivanov's influence on Russian literature declined sharply after
1907 when his wife died and he began a liaison with his step-
daughter, living abroad between 1910 and 1913. But he did win
considerable esteem for his collection of lyrics entitled *Cor ardens*
(*Burning Heart*, 1911). His most mystical and symbolic book, it
contains a number of cycles (some of them wreaths of sonnets)
dedicated to certain images. The most impressive of them is the
cycle dedicated to the rose, whose meanings Ivanov shows to have
included both Venus and the Virgin Mary. The collection also
includes some religious reflections or laments in response to his
wife's death.

Many of Ivanov's finest works were written after the revolution
and in emigration. His most deeply moving cycle is *Winter Sonnets*
(*Zimnie sonnety*), written in 1919–20 during the cruel winter of the
civil war. In this cycle winter is primarily the winter of the soul, a
metaphor for spiritual doubt. In the summer of 1920 he was living
at a rest home in Moscow in the same room with the cultural
essayist Mikhail Gershenzon, and the two of them exchanged
letters published a year later as *A Correspondence Between Two
Corners* (*Perepiska iz dvukh uglov*). In this exchange Ivanov
defended the idea of traditional culture while Gershenzon argued
for a break with the past. In 1921 Ivanov accepted a professorship
at Baku University but subsequently emigrated to Italy with his

children in 1924. He remained in emigration there for the rest of his life.

Innokenty Annensky (1856–1909) was a scholar of classical antiquity, a critic and a poet in the French decadent tradition of Baudelaire and Verlaine. Educated at St. Petersburg University, he supported himself as a secondary-school teacher of classical languages and Russian literature. As a classicist he did a complete translation of Euripides which appeared between 1907 and 1921; in addition he composed four classical tragedies on mythical subjects, presenting heroes and heroines in unequal contests with fate, which have never entered the repertory of any theater. He began writing literary criticism in the 1880s, and his critical essays – published in two volumes entitled *Book of Reflections* (*Kniga otrazheniy*, 1906 and 1909) – reveal his antipathy to any form of mysticism and his belief that art, though exalted, was nevertheless a quite natural psychological phenomenon.

As a poet Annensky was very unprolific, and moreover came to poetry rather late. His entire poetic *œuvre* amounts to only some 160 poems published in two collections: *Quiet Songs* (*Tikhie pesni*) of 1904 and *The Cypress Chest* (*Kiparisovy larets*), which came out posthumously in 1910. Many of the poems in the final collection are descriptions of landscapes, seen especially at a seasonal peak; Annensky was very effective at juxtaposing a showy opulence in nature with signs of cold decay. His tone is one of decadent ennui as he deals with the idle passage of time, particularly as seen in nature. But other poems are more directly existential and philosophical. Constantly lamenting a spiritual emptiness within himself which he calls "anguish," he recognizes in quite a modern way what seems to be an inevitable alienation of the heart. And yet he yields to art and longs for love, whose moments are to him brief and unrepeatable. Finally, he often refers to music – to a violin, for example, an old barrel organ or a splendid concert.

Annensky's poetic range in *The Cypress Chest* was wider than in *Quiet Songs*. He speaks of the inadvertent hindrances of the passions, of insomnia and nightmares, and of the painful trivia of life. He finds signs of passion and whimsy, of life and aging, more readily in plants, the winds, clocks or instruments than he does in human beings. His style, which combines the complexities of internal monologue with a pervasive discipline, is also so elliptical as to make considerable demands on the reader, particularly since Annensky is so erudite and imaginative: his work recalls the compressions of a Mallarmé. In any case, Annensky was a poet's poet, a literary mentor, especially to the rising acmeists such as Nikolay Gumilyov and Anna Akhmatova. He attracted them in their reaction against symbolism because his work was grounded in the psychology of real life and eschewed all attempts to comprehend the unknowable.

One of the great masters of twentieth-century Russian prose, Alexey Remizov (1877–1957) was reared in a merchant ghetto area of Moscow. While a student at Moscow University he was arrested for political activity and spent eight years in prison and in eastern exile, during which time he became interested in folklore and married a paleographer. The Remizovs settled in St. Petersburg in 1905, where they joined symbolist literary circles and Remizov began his career by publishing folk tales in his own renditions. The most successful of these collections was *Sunward* (*Posolon*, 1907), and the most renowned *The Parables of St. Nicholas* (*Nikoliny pritchi*, 1918), in which the religious figure was a folk hero.

Remizov won his early literary reputation also with naturalistic prose works depicting the urban poor as he knew them, works of such uncanny psychological perfection that they went beyond the specific social context to universal meaning. Among the best of his novels is *The Clock* (*Chasy*, 1908), whose hero is a hunchbacked, retarded boy through whose eyes we see his deprived and morally tainted family. The two volumes (1908 and 1910) of Remizov's *Devil's Lair* (*Chortov log*) contain relatively conventional stories, such as "The Musician" ("Muzykant"), which sometimes depicts the gentry class as victim of its own sort of pain and ostracism: the hero is a socially inept young man obsessed by the notion that he has a genuine musical gift. Others of Remizov's short stories are set in prison and seem almost to cry out not only against the injustices of a social system but against heaven itself; they also anticipate the avant-garde in their use of apparently unstructured lyrical effusions. One tale, "The Sacrifice" ("Zhertva"), is a rousing Gothic horror story based on folklore traditions: the ghostly double of a father comes to kill his innocent daughter in the mistaken belief that she is a chicken.

One of Remizov's great subjects was Russia, seen as a very bleak but still spiritually quite meaningful entity (in his works the cosmos itself appears meaningless, though animated by mysterious and sometimes ominous forces). Though negative, Remizov's portrayals of Russian life were essentially Slavophilic, albeit the genres in which he worked were uncommon. He began with two blatantly fantastic satirical novels. The first, which appeared in 1910, was entitled *The Indefatigable Cymbal* (*Neuemny buben*) and had as its hero an eccentric religious sectarian in a backward provincial area in which grotesque superstititions were rife. *The Fifth Pestilence* (*Pyataya yazva*, 1912) is set in the same sort of place. Its protagonist is a prosecuting attorney who admires the west, but the author sees Russia, despite all her grotesqueries (one character grows donkey's ears and is healed by a local veterinarian), as possessing much deeper spiritual values than the west. The novel parodies both the *Primary Chronicle* and Gogol's *The Inspector General*. Remizov's affection for the Russian past also led him to produce a paraphrase of an anonymous popular seventeenth-century play, *Tsar Maximilian* (1920).

Remizov was also partial to folklore demons and to practical jokes. He became an expert calligrapher using medieval Russian script, and founded a so-called House of Apes in order to present friends with ornately lettered certificates of membership. He was also an artist, and illustrated his writings with avant-garde paintings.

The revolution of 1917 led Remizov to produce equally original but now more tragic works. One was his "Lay of the Ruin of the Russian Land" ("Slovo o pogibeli zemli russkoy," 1917), an imitation of a fragmentary old Russian work lamenting the fall of Russia to the Tatar yoke. *Sounds of the City* (*Shumy goroda*, 1921) is an impressionistic record of the suffering of citizens in war-torn Petrograd. After Remizov and his wife emigrated to Paris in 1921, he published *Rusalia*, a scenario for an ancient pagan Slavic ritual for the dead, as well as reminiscences and reflections on his native land under the title *Whirlwind Russia* (*Vzvikhrennaya Rus*, 1927).

Mikhail Kuzmin (1875–1936), reared in Saratov and educated at St. Petersburg University, travelled to Egypt, Italy and the sectarian centers of northern Russia before settling in St. Petersburg, where he began contributing first to *The World of Art* and then to symbolist periodicals. He shared with the symbolists their veneration of art above reality, but he lacked their mystical convictions and any strong political sympathies. Eventually, indeed, he moved away from the symbolists, publishing in 1910 an article "On beautiful clarity" ("O prekrasnoy yasnosti") which was taken as a polemic against symbolism and a manifesto of the budding acmeist school. Kuzmin also contributed to *Apollon*, the periodical most closely connected with the acmeist movement.

Kuzmin's fundamental objective was to take epicurean delight in beauty. He set many of his works to music and was closely associated with little theaters and a famous literary cabaret of the day in St. Petersburg called the Stray Dog. His principal subject was love, and he did not conceal his own homosexuality. In fact he early raised a controversy with an erotic novel, *Wings* (*Krylya*, 1907), set in St. Petersburg and Italy, which features a group of young hedonists and discussions of the place of homosexuality in the history of European culture. In 1908 he published a volume of poetry containing the well-known cycle "Alexandrian Songs" ("Aleksandriyskie pesni"), presented as though they were written by a homosexual who lived in the ancient city of Alexandria.

Kuzmin was a prolific writer. He published four volumes of stories in all, including one with war stories, as well as two novels. One of the latter – *Travelers by Sea and Land* (*Plavayushchie-puteshestvuyushchie*, 1915) – describes the erotic entanglements of the bohemian world of St. Petersburg. He wrote several plays, all comedies. And he was a poet: before the revolution he published three volumes of verse, of which one (*The Carillon of Love* [*Kuranty lyubvi*, 1910]) was completely set to music. After the revolution his lyrics tended to deal with more metaphysical and esthetic topics. His masterpiece was a poetic cycle "The Trout Breaks the Ice" ("Forel razbivaet led," 1929) about the return of a homosexual lover after an affair with a woman. Kuzmin was a polished craftsman whose work, however, sometimes suffered from a certain airiness which he purposely cultivated. He is also sometimes unjustly seen as a mere stylizer, an imitator of ancient, eighteenth-century and oriental styles, a reputation reinforced by his achievements as a translator. His purpose was not in these artifices, however: his works are quite expressive of his own experience even though his range of concerns was limited.

424

The minor poet Maximilian Voloshin (real name: Kirienko-Voloshin, 1877–1932) grew up in the Crimea and was later expelled from Moscow University for political activity. After spending several months in Siberia he went to Paris to continue his education, and there fell under the influence of José-Maria de Heredia for his own work. After travelling extensively in Mediterranean countries, he published a collection of poetry in Russia in 1910. Though his poems are often responses to such particular geographical locations as Paris, the Mediterranean, or the Crimea, they are characteristically intimate reflections on broad cultural themes, incorporating frequent allusions to myths, history, and biblical events. He could create memorable scenes of the bleak coastal heights of the Crimea, and he knew the value of small but telling details. His overall philosophy was pessimistic from the start, however.

After experiencing the First World War, the revolution of 1917 and the ensuing civil war, Voloshin wrote anti-militaristic works of which the most popular was *Deaf-Mute Demons* (*Demony glukho-nemye*, 1919), which dealt with the violence and atrocities then afflicting contemporary Russia. He moved permanently to the Crimea, to Koktebel, where his house became a refuge for friends of all political and literary stripes and his poetry was infused with Christian mysticism and a new sense of mission. After 1923, however, he could no longer publish.

On the eve of the First World War symbolism rather abruptly ceased to be a truly vital literary force throughout Europe, although its influence on literature of the new era remained strong in France, where Paul Valéry and Marcel Proust wrote of inner worlds in polished forms which made substantial demands on the reader. In England, on the other hand, the reaction against symbolism and decadence brought realism into favor once more, as John Masefield emerged as a leading poet; and in Italy there arose a vociferous avant-garde in the form of "futurism," a literary counterpart of cubism in painting, led chiefly by Filippo Marinetti.

In Russia, the post-symbolist currents were divided rather evenly in prestige, if not in numbers, between those who accepted the symbolist heritage and called themselves acmeists, and those who rejected that heritage to dedicate themselves to futurism. Both new schools still regarded art as an elevated enterprise embodying the highest aspirations of mankind, both retained symbolism's heightened consciousness of style and craft, and both rejected any mystical, otherworldly goals as inappropriate for literature. It should also be noted that most of the new writers were poets, while prose remained in the hands of the older generation, whether the realists like Gorky and Bunin or the symbolists like Remizov.

The acmeists, who have been called neo-realists, advocated a return to the real world, although they had their own inner view of reality. They have also been termed neo-classicists because of their admiration for clarity and their dependence upon imagery. In many of their best works they displayed an existential weariness and a tendency toward resignation. Though the *maître d'école* was Gumilyov, their best poet was Osip Mandelshtam, who best expressed the movement's sense of existential isolation: *Tristia*, the title of his most mature collection of lyrics, points both to his frame of mind and to his classical roots. There was also a consistent current of sadness in the work of Anna Akhmatova, stemming superficially from her almost exclusive preoccupation with love but more profoundly from her dedication to courage in human life.

The key events which led to the creation of the acmeist movement were relatively few. It began to acquire public recognition with the founding of a highly influential journal of literature and art, *Apollon* (1909–17), which took the place of the defunct symbolist organ *The Scales*. Started by Nikolay Gumilyov and the art historian Sergey Makovsky, *Apollon* carried lead articles by Annensky signalling the demise of symbolism and also printed the acmeist manifestos. In 1911 Gumilyov founded the Poets' Guild (*Tsekh poetov*) as a forum for active acmeists, and the movement existed more or less formally down to Gumilyov's execution in 1921. But Mandelshtam and Akhmatova always took acmeism as their personal credo, considering all who genuinely accepted the label as honorable people.

Nikolay Gumilyov (1886–1921) was not only a leader of the acmeist school but also a poet who through his own work injected a sense of honor and an element of masculine robustness into Russian poetry, very welcome things after the feelings of melancholy and impotence which had long pervaded symbolist poetry, although his vigor when viewed in a European context seems to partake of the bohemianism of late decadence. The son of a naval officer, Gumilyov was reared in St. Petersburg, where he was literally a student of Annensky's at the lyceum. In 1905 he published his first collection of verse, *The Path of the Conquistadors* (*Put konkvistadorov*), in which he displayed his taste for heroic feats and taking risks and a tendency to see life in terms of tests of will and confrontations with rivals in love. But his imagery of kings, queens and knights was taken from the world of fairy tales. After spending a year studying at the Sorbonne he brought out *Romantic Flowers* (*Romanticheskie tsvety*, 1908), in which he displayed a wider erudition in taking more of his imagery from the mythical tradition but also introduced exotic images (leopards, flamingos) designed to startle his readers. The African theme thus entered his verse. Its role in his work as a primitive and cruel setting would expand in subsequent years.

The period of Gumilyov's maturity began after he returned to Russia and founded *Apollon*, in which he regularly published literary criticism. His collection of 1910 entitled *Pearls* (*Zhemchuga*) revealed his new approach to life, one derived from Leconte de Lisle and other French Parnassians as well as from Bryusov, for he uses images drawn from the entire history of European literature and culture, alluding to Dante and Beatrice, Don Juan, Odysseus, and the Greek myths. He pictures himself as an old conquistador; his *personae* contend now with fate, and end defeated. In some poems, to be sure, he does display an Orthodox Christian approach, including in particular an admiration for humility.

In 1910 Gumilyov married his fellow poet Anna Akhmatova, then in 1911 departed for Abyssinia to collect folk songs. He returned to Russia long enough to help bring the acmeist school into being before departing for Africa once more, this time to Somaliland as a member of a group sent in 1913 by the Museum of Anthropology and Ethnology. In 1914 he volunteered for military service and saw active duty during the war.

All these experiences bore poetic fruit in the collection entitled *The Quiver* (*Kolchan*) of 1916. Here he spoke as a modern man who has rejected myths and fantasies as obvious deceits, mere ways of thinking about the contemporary world and man's place in it. He speaks a great deal of Italy, its landscapes, its cityscapes and its

history, both in pagan and in Christian times. He also introduces
the theme of war, which merges with religion in his spiritual
experience since its dangers elicit man's capacities for devotion and
for moral fortitude.

After the revolution Gumilyov's thought developed along
different philosophical channels. In *The Bonfire* (*Koster*, 1918) he
presented painful and abiding religious problems and also pictured
nature and the primitive, sometimes in Russia itself, sometimes in
the Scandinavian countries. In *The Tent* (*Shater*, 1921), comprised
entirely of poems written in response to the poet's African experiences of 1918, Gumilyov seems almost overwhelmed by the existence of evil, cruelty and violence. But the major collection of this
period was *The Pillar of Fire* (*Ognenny stolp*, 1921), where he
ponders the philosophical relationship between the body and the
soul, and is still appalled by the existence of violence in the world.
Two poems from this collection are particularly well-known. In
"Sixth sense" ("Shestoe chuvstvo") he asks whether mankind
might someday produce, however painfully, a new organ for new
spiritual perceptions. And in "The runaway streetcar" ("Zablu-
divshiysya tramvay") he offers an avant-garde set of perceptions
that frighten him, including the sight of his own severed, bloody
head for sale among others arranged like cabbages. In that same
year he was charged with participation in an anti-Soviet conspiracy, and shot.

Perhaps the acmeist goal of clear words about real matters was
best achieved in the work of Anna Akhmatova (real name
Gorenko, 1889–1966), who left a small body of deceptively simple
poems largely about love, sometimes about love of country. Born
near Odessa, she was brought up in Tsarskoe Selo, not far from
St. Petersburg, and studied in Kiev. After marrying Gumilyov in
1910 she lived for a short time in Paris, where she got to know
Modigliani, and gave birth to a son, Leo, in 1912. That same year
saw the publication of her first volume of verse, *Evening* (*Vecher*),
which deals exclusively with love, especially its losses and pains.
Critics have described her as presenting a woman's viewpoint in
such matters, but in fact the hopes and disappointments she
records are universal experiences not peculiar to one gender or to
any culture. Akhmatova's poems are modern in the sense that they
do not idealize love: each love is unique in its character and brings

pain when it ends, but it is never the only love or the last one. Her love lyrics are lessons in courage. Some of her other poems evoke her beloved city of St. Petersburg with its beautiful architecture and illustrious past, a city which defines her identity. A less frequent but still very important theme is that of the muse, a stern disciplinarian who deprives the poet of personal happiness for the sake of a greater reward. Each of Akhmatova's poems is a separate and complete entity. Although their subject matter is apparently quite intimate, her *œuvre* as a whole is impersonal.

Akhmatova's next collection, *Rosary* (*Chetki*, 1914), confirmed the directions in which she was already moving. To be sure, her love poems are now somewhat complicated by a new sense of sin and guilt (she speaks of churches and insomnia). A greater narrative tendency is observable, and many of her poems resemble moments from long and unhappy fictions. She is deliberately unemotional, and emphasizes material details – a glove, a tulip, popular orchestral music – which remind the reader of prose works. Her settings include suburbs, restaurants, gardens and interiors as she creates scenes with a simple palette – mostly black and white, with an occasional stark red or yellow. She is clever in catching herself in self-deceptions, or allowing the reader to do this. She speaks of growing in wisdom, or becoming indifferent, when it is obvious to the reader that she is not.

The theme of Russia gains importance in Akhmatova's subsequent work. *The White Flock* (*Belaya staya*, 1917) is permeated by thoughts of war and expressions of devotion to country. Her viewpoint is Slavophilic but she recasts it with a freshness which makes the reader forget that such ideas had appeared many times earlier in the work of Nekrasov and other poets. Though she describes her country as bleak, unpropitious, and even sinful, she displays a fierce loyalty to it, and is ready to face the deaths of her men, a lover, a son. In the last of her major collections, *Anno domini MCMXXI* (1922), her poems on personal subjects are even more complicated, more effective, and more arid than before. Now she expressed her love of country in the form of a refusal to emigrate to the peaceful west. And so she remained in the Soviet Union for the remainder of her life even though during much of that time she was unable to publish her poetry.

Osip Mandelshtam (1891–1938), Akhmatova's acmeist col-

league and one of the finest Russian poets of this century, left only
two collections of poems in addition to a few unpublished works
and some autobiographical prose. Reared in a merchant family in
St. Petersburg, he lived and studied briefly in Paris and Heidelberg
before entering St. Petersburg University in 1911. In 1911 he
joined the Poets' Guild, the nucleus of the acmeist movement, on
the way to the publication of his first collection, *Stone* (*Kamen*,
1913), which established him in the public mind as an exceptional
author. He also contributed to the definition of the acmeist
outlook with some theoretical articles, of which the best known
was "The morning of acmeism" ("Utro akmeizma," 1913), where
he spoke of the word (*Logos*) as the medium of literature.

The poems of *Stone*, while usually traditional in form, are
pictorial in substance. Mandelshtam's chief theme was then, and
would always remain, the awareness of his own identity. His
earliest poems are discoveries of self in a world of objects. Later he
wrote about a nameless nostalgia. He was also very aware of the
centuries of European cultural and artistic achievements, those
miracles of the spirit, which had preceded him. He paid homage to
such figures as Homer, Bach and Beethoven; to great architectural
monuments such as the Cathedral of Notre Dame in Paris and
Hagia Sofia in Constantinople; and to magnificent cities, including
especially Rome (cityscapes were rather common in his poetry).
And yet these things were not so important in themselves as were
his perceptions of them: he combined their grandeur with the
intimacy of his voice, and their depictions are colored by his
feeling that mankind inhabits a bleak world under an indifferent
overarching sky.

In his second collection of verse, *Tristia* (1922), Mandelshtam
still writes of contemporary mankind, but now he is much more
concerned with the manner in which the past flows into the
present, the way in which the complex mentality of modern man
has been foreshadowed in the past. The stupendous historical
events, and especially the revolution, which Mandelshtam had
lived through since the publication of his first collection created
within him a sense of cultural crisis, of apprehension over his
country's course. But he also shifted his attention somewhat away
from the major European cultural tradition and toward southern
cultures (after the revolution he had lived and worked in the

Crimea and Georgia) and classical myths and settings. Thus the title poem of the collection, "Tristia," is set in an ancient city with night watchmen, oxen, domestic spinning, and an acropolis, but at the same time it deals with the timeless subject of a man's reluctance to leave to go to war. In other, more abstract, poems death and dying are common themes, and Prosperpine is a memorable figure, though Mandelshtam could also write on more current topics, such as the death of St. Petersburg and the mundane vicissitudes of his life at the time. Although his poems were not overtly political, the poet's general cultural anxiety was plain, and Mandelshtam encountered difficulties in his poetic career from the early 1920s on.

Mandelshtam's prose belongs to a period stretching from the middle 1920s to the early 1930s. His prose collection *The Egyptian Stamp* (*Egipetskaya marka*, 1928) includes a well-known earlier study "The noise of time" ("Shum vremeni"), ostensibly the elliptical and elusive autobiography of a young poet named Parnok, and "Theodosia," which contains Mandelshtam's impressions of the sunny but agitated life of the Crimea. Another piece of work which was outwardly travel writing was his *Journey to Armenia* (*Poezdka v Armeniyu*, 1931–2), written after a fairly lengthy sojourn in that part of the world.

In addition to its leaders Gumilyov, Akhmatova, and Mandelshtam, acmeism attracted a small group of lesser poets; and then there were also a certain number of writers who had never been particularly affected by symbolism and retained a traditional core to their writing. Among the former was Sergey Gorodetsky (1884–1967), who in 1911 helped Gumilyov in founding the Poets' Guild and contributed to *Apollon* programmatic anti-symbolist statements in which he came out particularly vehemently against any mystical aims of literature. The son of a minor official and ethnographer, he was reared and educated in the capital. He brought out *Spring Sap* (*Yar*) in 1907, the first of more than a dozen books of verse he would publish in his lifetime, not to mention several collections of short stories and tales. The work in *Spring Sap*, however, was very much in the contemporary tradition of symbolist pantheist and cosmic poetry. In each poem the poet expresses his intuitive sense of being a cosmic or mythic force, or a simple laborer. He dedicates poems to the sun, the moon, earth, to

431

kinship ties, to the ancient Slavic thunder god Perun as well as to other nature deities he made up himself. He writes of the human pain of love and separation. Finally, he speaks for everyday people such as a laundress or a convict, always employing a primitive style, sometimes with very short lines and occasionally with a song-like lilt.

In his subsequent books, however, Gorodetsky abandoned cosmic imagery to offer simple evocations of the countryside and ordinary people in collections with such characteristic titles as *The Willow* (*Iva*, 1912). In 1915 he broke with acmeism to join a group of "peasant" poets who exploited the style of the semi-educated folk, and after the 1917 revolution he became a communist. At that point he began extolling peasant labor as a form of civic heroism, as may be seen in the collection *The Sickle* (*Serp*, 1921). In short, Gorodetsky always moved with the literary fashions, but from the beginning his verse suffered from a tendency toward whimsy and posing.

Vladislav Khodasevich (1886–1939) used the lyric forms of the nineteenth century to write poetry in an era of avant-garde experimentation. He was always a little out of place in his times, for he loved the heritage of the past and disliked the chaos of the present. To be sure, when his first two volumes of verse appeared in 1908 and 1914 he was counted among the symbolists: although he employed neoclassical genres in stylized form and chose subjects which had been quite conventional in the nineteenth century (love, domestic life, nature, art), still his work displayed notes of decadence, of tawdriness and fatigue.

After spending his earlier years in Moscow, where his father was an artist, in 1920 Khodasevich moved to Petrograd, where he became a principal channel of the "Petersburg influence" on subsequent Russian verse. Some of his best collections appeared in these years: *Grain's Way* (*Putem zerna*) in 1920 and *A Heavy Lyre* (*Tyazhelaya lira*) in 1922. In the former collection he found his own genuine poetic voice, a strong, literary and intimate one. His former tawdriness now yields to a real sadness, he employs a notably pictorial style, and his subjects expand to include the city. In *A Heavy Lyre* he developed the philosophical stance for which he is now best remembered, as he writes of his love for his ethereal soul in its imperfect body and expresses his admiration of the material world generally, despite all its inevitable ugliness.

In 1922 Khodasevich went into emigration, living for a time in Czechoslovakia, Germany and Italy (where he was a friend of Gorky's) before settling in Paris in 1925. There, writing for the conservative paper *Renaissance* (*Vozrozhdenie*), he became an active leader of the cultural emigration, primarily through his literary scholarship and literary criticism, to a lesser extent through his continuing poetic production.

Even as symbolism was at the height of its influence in Russia, a reaction in the form of an avant-garde movement centered in Paris, Berlin, Vienna and Italy began to take shape, with the graphic arts leading the way. Cubism, for example, arose in France before 1910, while the origins of the dadaist movement were contemporaneous with the First World War. The pioneer in the field of literary avant-gardism was Filippo Marinetti, who began publishing futurist manifestos in Italy in 1909 in which he rejected the heritage of the past in favor of modern machines and energy. In Russia avant-garde literature was dominated by groups which called themselves futurist, though they had only very indirect links to Italian futurism.

In Russia the cubo-futurists, who included Vladimir Maya-kovsky, were the most vociferous, most extreme and most pro-ductive of the futurist groups. Their name reflected the fact that they were heavily influenced by certain artists who were in turn familiar with contemporary western currents. The cubo-futurists published their principal manifesto, "A slap in the face of public taste" ("Poshchechina obshchestvennomu vkusu"), in 1912: in it they rejected the culture of the past and praised the word as an artistic medium. However, with the exception of Mayakovsky, the cubo-futurists did not follow the Italian dedication to tech-nology or speed but rather developed a pastoral primitivism especially obvious in the work of Velemir Khlebnikov. The cubo-futurists were also great verbal experimenters, who not only created new individual words but a characteristic medium they termed "transsense" language (*zaum*), made up of senseless word fragments and pure sounds.

There were, however, other sub-groupings among the futurists.

One group called the centrifuge, to which Boris Pasternak belonged, did not reject the cultural heritage of the past. There were also ego-futurists, who adopted an esthetic derived from the decadent movement. One of the great avant-garde poets of the era, Marina Tsvetaeva, wrote much like a cubo-futurist and yet clearly revered the achievements of the past. Moreover there were "peasant" poets as well, writers who exploited a semi-educated style who included Gorodetsky and also Sergey Esenin, who had avant-garde links and became a popular idol in the 1920s. Entirely outside the poetic sphere there were avant-garde prose writers like Eugene Zamyatin who belonged to no school and would not come into prominence until after the revolution.

The cubo-futurists acknowledged Velemir Khlebnikov (real given name Victor, 1885–1922) as their master despite his retiring nature and eccentric ways. He was born in an eastern province, where his father was an ornithologist. He attended the university in both Kazan and St. Petersburg, but, feeling unappreciated by the symbolists who met at Vyacheslav Ivanov's "Tower," he attached himself to avant-garde circles dominated by painters rather than poets, and there fell under the influence of such primitivist artists as Mikhail Larionov. He signed the futurist manifestos, including "A slap in the face of public taste," and his fellow poets acknowledged him as the most deeply creative among them, but he was not a *maître* in the sense of one who shepherded his followers. He felt he had only friends, and in addition he travelled a great deal and led an irregular life, which made it difficult for him to guide any sort of movement.

Khlebnikov won the admiration of the public and critics with a small body of relatively conventional lyrics, some experimental lyric and narrative poems which are arresting and occasionally breathtaking, and a number of virtuoso longer poems which are quite refreshing. His viewpoint was that of a utopianist with no feeling for order and a naive faith in love. His vast subjects – the development of cultures, natural forces, human nature, an awareness of the cosmos – must be deduced from simple pictorial images and elliptical statements. His ostensible subjects may be animals, pagan gods, or anonymous and symbolic human beings. He may use myths as the basis for his approach but sometimes makes them up himself: thus in "The shaman and Venus"

("Shaman i Venera") he has the Greek goddess of beauty retiring to Siberia. He often employs pastoral settings, sometimes removed also in time to the stone age or medieval days: in "I and E" ("I i E") he portrays lovers in a primitive society, in an example of what may be termed his arcadian approach to reality.

In the philosophical and religious sense Khlebnikov's poetry suggests that he was a deist, and in "I can see Cancer, Aries" ("Mne vidny – Rak, Oven") he calls himself a younger brother to the stars. His metaphysical awareness emerges in his masterful contrasts between huge expanses of time or space on the one hand, and graphic and sometimes quite unexpected details on the other. He respected religion as a manifestation of human aspirations. In "Sayan" a Siberian elk examines ancient runes left by man, and in "The single book" ("Edinaya kniga") the religious texts of the world are consumed in a Siberian bonfire to clear the way for a universal faith in nature.

Khlebnikov detested every form of violence, and wrote many effective anti-war poems. He had a Dostoevskian sensitivity to others' pain, and unhesitatingly described cruelties inflicted by gods, men, predatory animals, and also machines – which he hated and considered rapacious – but he had the unusual ability to depict scenes of suffering without sentimentality. Khlebnikov was also a fighter in unlikely causes: for instance in his "Frogs' revolt" ("Bunt zhab") he has a horde of amphibians attack a train which crushes them as they cross its path. He was socially engaged as well, and sympathized with the revolution of 1917 as it approached. Afterwards, however, he wrote "The night search" ("Nochnoy obysk"), in which women avenge a wanton shooting by setting fire to their own apartment as an icon of Christ looks on.

Khlebnikov's non-literary projects also stemmed from his utopianism. He conducted linguistic experiments aimed at discovering a proto-language, or universal elements common to all languages. In his verse he experimented with neologisms and transsense language: his famous "Incantation by laughter" ("Zaklyatie smekhom") is made up mostly of words formed on the root for "laugh" with various prefixes and suffixes. He would also attribute meanings to particular sounds and try to work out such theories in his poems. On a more political level, he attempted to predict the future through a mathematical theory of history, and he proposed the formation of a society of good men, or "presidents of the globe," to determine the future of mankind. Such peculiar theories combined with his vagrant ways made him suspect both to Reds and Whites during the Civil War, and he was arrested at one time or another by both of them. He enjoyed a short but happy period as an administrator of army affairs in Persia before he died prematurely in 1922 of an acute attack of an undiagnosed disease. His collected works, published posthumously, include a volume of short stories which have been very little investigated.

Vladimir Mayakovsky (1893–1930) was the single individual who did most to generate public acceptance of avant-garde art and a spirit of cultural nonconformity in general. His father, after working for a time as a park ranger in Georgia, brought his family with him to Moscow in 1906, and two years later the young Vladimir joined the Bolshevik party. He was arrested several times for subversive activity. In 1911 he enrolled in an art school where he met a number of avant-garde artists, and in particular David Burliuk, who had already organized the first futurist group in Russia. It was under his influence that Mayakovsky became a poet, and also signed the famous manifesto of 1912 "A slap in the face of public taste." His first significant publication was a play, *Vladimir Mayakovsky: A Tragedy* (*Vladimir Mayakovsky: Tragediya*), staged in 1913 along with Alexey Kruchonykh's *Victory over the Sun* (*Poebeda solntsa*). It was permeated by a vociferous egotism and a craving for love and approval. Mayakovsky depicts the poet in his play as a martyr who carries away the tears of the misshapen citizens of his community.

In that same year of 1913 Mayakovsky participated in a futurist reading tour intended to scandalize the provincial bourgeoisie. In 1915 he moved to St. Petersburg, where he fell under the influence of an erudite theoretician of modernist literature, Osip Brik, whose wife Lili became the great love of the poet's life. In 1915 Mayakovsky began to publish the anguished love poems which many consider the most attractive portion of his *œuvre*. That year saw the appearance of *A Cloud in Trousers* (*Oblako v shtanakh*) and *The Backbone Flute* (*Fleyta-pozvonochnik*), both of which include cameo autobiographies of their creator. In other long poems written before the revolution, however, he deals with more social themes. Thus in *War and the World* (*Voyna i mir*, 1916) he accepts the guilt of the First World War and promises humankind a utopian future. In *Man* (*Chelovek*, 1917) he suffers death and resurrection in order to redeem mankind, but in the end is most concerned with his own unrequited love. At any rate, through his early longer poems Mayakovsky established a new and very individual style. In a self-assured tone he used racy vocabulary with an array of imaginative metaphors, some quite extended, and lines printed step-like in syntactic units across the page, although his metrics remained fairly traditional. His rhymes were frequently strident off-rhymes. When he was on the road reading he would deliver his poems at the top of his voice, in a shout.

After the revolution Mayakovsky was such an enthusiastic supporter of the new regime that he eventually became its uncrowned poet-laureate. He first attracted the attention of party officials with a short lyric entitled "Our march" ("Nash marsh") written in 1917, which was followed by many lyric poems on public issues ranging from mild criticism of excessive bureaucracy to simple versified statements of the current party line on a number of domestic and foreign questions. He also produced several longer works with the appropriate political slant. In 1918 he came out with another play, *Mystery-Bouffe* (*Misteriya-Buf*), in which the proletariat not only conquers the earth but storms heaven as well. That was followed in 1921 by *150,000,000*, in which he portrays the Russian people as a *bogatyr*, or folk hero, who wades the Atlantic Ocean to defeat the capitalist champion Woodrow Wilson in personal combat. And when Lenin died in 1924, Mayakovsky commemorated his achievements in *Vladimir Ilich Lenin* (1924).

Although such works were clearly propagandistic in their intent, they were not sufficient for Mayakovsky, who after 1919 – when he had moved back to the new capital of Moscow – devoted a great amount of time to the creation of propaganda posters for the windows of the Russian Telegraph Agency (ROSTA) for which he composed four-line jingles; and from 1923 to 1925 he wrote rhymed advertising copy for state consumer goods stores. It was also during that period that Mayakovsky and his futurist colleagues sought to bring their literary philosophy into line with revolutionary goals. Energized by Osip Brik's advocacy of the "social command" for literature and "literature of fact" (a preference for documentary writing over fiction), Mayakovsky helped to found the Left Front of Art organization (*Lef*), which flourished from 1922 to 1928.

Despite his theoretical and practical commitment to political art, Mayakovsky continued to write very personal poetry as well. Indeed two of his greatest love poems, inspired by his passion for Lili Brik, date from this period: "I love" ("Lyublyu," 1922) and *About That* (*Pro eto*, 1923). The former is autobiographical, while the latter describes both his painful search for love and his resistance to the pressures of philistinism. He embodies his emotions in memorable images: a bear on an ice floe, the wide river of his own tears on which he floats. His path takes him to outer space and the distant future; he hopes to meet his love when both have been resurrected and have gone to the zoo, for "she loved animals." In addition, some of Mayakovsky's most effective shorter lyrics date from this period. They include "A good attitude toward horses" ("Khoroshee otnoshenie k loshadyam," 1918), in which he urges compassion for all creatures, and "An extraordinary adventure which befell Vladimir Mayakovsky in a summer cottage" ("Neobychaynoe priklyuchenie, byvshee s Vladimirom Mayakovskim letom na dache," 1920), in which the sun descends from the sky to accept Mayakovsky's invitation to tea.

In 1924 Mayakovsky made his first trip to Paris, which he would visit nearly every year until his death in 1930; and in 1925 a tour of Mexico, Cuba and the United States resulted in a prose work, *My Discovery of America* (*Moe otkrytie Ameriki*, 1926), as well as a cycle of poems which included many anti-American pieces but also the unabashedly eulogistic "Brooklyn Bridge" ("Bruklinsky most," 1925). Parisian themes also appeared in his verse over these years, and descriptions of a new love for a Russian émigré woman in Paris. The last five years of his life also saw the publication of his two most famous plays. The first of them, a comic satire entitled *The Bedbug* (*Klop*, 1929), mounts two attacks, the first against the bourgeois "relics" of the period of the New Economic Policy (NEP) of the early 1920s, and the second against the rigidities of a dystopia scheduled to come into being only fifty years afterwards. The protagonist is a snobbish proletarian who receives his tragic come-uppance when he is resurrected in the future but caged in a

zoo along with a bedbug found on him because he displays inclinations which are still all too human for the scientific society of the
future. His second play of this period, *The Bathhouse* (*Banya*,
1930), is a schematic work in which a "phosphorous" woman
from the future brings to the present a machine which will trans-
port worthy citizens into a future utopia.

It may be said that Mayakovsky's work was the product of a
very divided mind. On the one hand, he hated the bourgeoisie and
its way of life, but he believed that personal love was a valuable
part of that existence. And on the other, he longed for a perfect
social order while at the same time he understood the potential
boredom of a utopian system and the dangers of political tyranny.
His long poems on "civic" topics dating from this period are
frequently mentioned by scholars but not held in great affection by
readers. One of them is "Very good" ("Khorosho," 1927), written
to commemorate the tenth anniversary of the revolution. "At the
top of my voice" ("Vo ves golos," 1930) is more revealing of his
personal conflicts, for in it he comments that he "stepped on the
throat of my own song" in order to describe the life of the streets
and serve the cause of the proletariat. And indeed, by 1930 Mayakovsky was feeling the pressures for conformity, coming to
believe that the revolution he had supported so heartily had been
usurped by the philistines. *Lef* was censured, and Mayakovsky was
compelled to join a party-sponsored writers group, the Russian
Association of Proletarian Writers. Although in 1925 he had censured Sergey Esenin in a powerful and well-known poem for
taking his own life, in 1930 Mayakovsky did the same thing. He
was working on a love poem when he shot himself on the night of
14 April.

Another prominent adherent of the avant-garde, Boris Pasternak (1890–1960), was born in St. Petersburg, the son of a well-
known painter and a pianist, and it is natural that he should have
considered careers in music or philosophy before going into literature: he studied music with Scriabin from 1903 to 1909 and philosophy at Moscow University from 1909 to 1913. But in 1914 he
joined the moderate futurist grouping known as the centrifuge,
and thus his course was set for literature even though it was
interrupted when he was conscripted and sent to the Urals to do
clerical work during the First World War. He returned, though,

and in 1917 brought out the collection which would make his poetic name: *Over the Barriers* (*Poverkh barerov*).

The lyrics of *Over the Barriers* demonstrated Pasternak's sensitivity to nature and his capacity to capture its essence at moments of extremity such as in storm or cold, or in brilliant beauty. As a poet he always preferred surprise to sentimentality. This first collection also displays Pasternak's characteristic style, which abounds in proliferating figures of speech and leaves the impression of great, indeed almost untrammeled, creative energy. But his collections of a few years later – *My Sister Life* (*Sestra moya – zhizn*, 1922) and *Themes and Variations* (*Temy i variatsii*, 1923) – contained greater poems. In them Pasternak continued his tendency to write very little about himself and a great deal about the objects of the world about him, as he dealt with such subjects as nature, love, art, history, and philosophy. *My Sister Life* supports a connected reading as the fragmented and oblique record of a disappointing love encounter in the summer of 1917: Pasternak expressed the pains of various separations through his disjointed responses to provincial train stations and domestic objects. On the other hand, at moments of elation Pasternak is at one with the universe, incapable of distinguishing between himself and, say, the Milky Way seen from the steppes. His apparently impersonal method has its philosophical underpinning in his belief in the equivalence of the many phenomena of the universe.

Though it opens with tributes to Goethe and Pushkin, Pasternak's *Themes and Variations* is essentially a sequel to *My Sister Life*. He speaks once more of love and of poetry, insisting on the ordinariness of poetry's subjects and viewing art as an elemental force which the poet may utilize but never himself possess. Poetry draws on apparently random subjects linked by the consciousness that perceives them. It was at this time that Pasternak's work began to take shape as an alternation between admiration and ennui, the representation of his intuitive response to the world.

In addition to poetry, Pasternak also wrote a certain amount of prose. In the years from 1918 to 1924 he published four prose pieces, including especially *The Childhood of Luvers* (*Detstvo Luvers*, 1922). The work is in the avant-garde, modernist tradition as it replicates the confused vision of a young girl who is its heroine, her perceptions of a trip to the Urals, nature, and the beginnings of her sexual awakening. In the ensuing decades Pasternak would acquire a remarkable reputation as a poet and prose-writer which would culminate in his receipt of the Nobel Prize for literature in 1959 and the controversy surrounding it which would lead him to refuse the award.

Since she wrote most of her finest poetry in emigration, Marina Tsvetaeva (1892–1941) has not yet received the renown she deserves. With a professor of graphic arts as a father and a pianist as a mother, she was reared in Moscow, married early herself, and had a daughter in 1912, at the age of twenty. In the meantime, however, she had made her entrance into literature with her verse collections *Evening Album* (*Vecherny albom*, 1910) and *The Magic Lantern* (*Volshebny fonar*, 1912), which had been welcomed by eminent representatives of several poetic schools. These collections, drawn from the experience of her own childhood and youth, are filled with the romantic clichés that crowd a young person's fantasies and deal with family members (especially "mama"), family friends and domestic events, often framed as daydreams grander than life. Although hers was a particularly bookish imagination, a number of her poems are dedicated to the subject of young men and love. In *The Magic Lantern* the poet expresses her regret at emerging from childhood and her pain at discovering real sources of anxiety and loss.

Tsvetaeva's next collection appeared in difficult times, during the period when her husband, Sergey Efron, was fighting with the White armies in the Crimea. Her new works were linked by the poet's sense of Russianness reinforced by a deep historical awareness. *Mileposts* (*Versty*, 1921) includes poems written between 1917 and 1920 which recreate a popular consciousness molded by Biblical anecdotes and a primitive view of Russian history. The works in *Mileposts I* (*Versty, vypusk I*, 1922) include poems resembling excerpts from adventure ballads or popular seventeenth-century songs on historical topics, such as the False Dmitry and his Polish fiancée Marina Mniszek. Some poems amount to patriotic declarations stimulated by the First World War; in others she wrote on religious topics such as the Holy Family on its journey with a king who is also a child. She used irregular, strident rhythms to create a style clearly imitative of Russian folk songs, rural and urban and of all historical periods.

Tsvetaeva's *The Swan Demesne* (*Lebediny stan*, not published until 1957) contained poetic tributes to the White army that could not be printed in the 1920s. But it also offers echoes of Russia's medieval epics dealing with Russia's conflict with the Tatars, such as the *Igor Tale* and the *Zadonshchina*, and is erudite and factual, with references to André Chénier and Alexander Blok. In several collections of 1922–3 (*Poems to Blok* [*Stikhi k Bloku*, 1923]; *Separation* [*Razluka*, 1922]; *Psyche* [*Psikheya*, 1923]) she brought out poems rather similar to those of the *Milepost* volumes, but less specialized. She may write of her own family, comparing it to the Holy Family, or include in her ballad-like poems allusions to figures of high culture, such as Don Juan or Paganini. At this period as well Tsvetaeva began publishing longer poems, of which the best known all draw upon folk tradition. *The Tsar-Maiden* (*Tsar-devitsa*, 1922) is a retelling of an internationally known folk tale whose subject – the amorous desire of an evil stepmother for her grown stepson – recalls the Phaedra theme so prominent in her lyrics. *On a Red Steed* (*Na krasnom kone*, 1922) is a literary piece in which the horse, a motif drawn from folklore, turns out to be the inspiration which the poet calls her "Genius."

Tsvetaeva's art deepened and matured after she emigrated from Russia in 1922 to join her husband, then a student at Prague University: at that point her interests became not only broader but subtler and more powerful, and a notable element of irony entered her work which had not been there before. Such a shift is immediately evident in *Craft* (*Remeslo*, 1923), even though most of the poems included in it were composed in 1921–2. Her new poems are about states of mind, about qualities of character such as steadfastness, about learning, motherhood, exultation, loss of country. Although some poems are supposed to be about the soul, Tsvetaeva feels at her core that life is forbidding and the thought of eternity little comfort. She often takes as her immediate topics great myths of western civilization such as that of St. George and the dragon (also a symbol of monarchist Russia). She reformulates the tales of Biblical sorrows and Greek tragedies, or speaks of her admiration for such poets as Blok and Akhmatova, or summons up her memories of Russian landscapes and religious holidays: her long poem "Sidestreets" ("Pereulochki") is a lament for her country composed in childish language.

Between 1922 and 1925 Tsvetaeva lived and wrote in Berlin, Prague and Paris, producing a group of poems published in the collection *After Russia* (*Posle Rossii*) in 1928. In 1923 she evidently passed through a dark night of the soul which led her to write of the obsessions of madmen, but at other times she exults; she expresses her anguish in confronting life and gratitude for its rewards as she responds to her surroundings, from the Alps to the filth of factories. Her verse is still very erudite: she alludes to Hamlet, Phaedra, Orpheus, Ariadne, and Biblical figures. She speaks of contests and rivalries, loves, nature, poetry, history, Russia, fears, losses and insomnias. At the same time she seeks to affect a primitive air in emphasizing parts of the body such as the hand and the head. Her style has ceased to be based upon folk traditions and has become quite personal, employing headlong syntax often without verbs, non-literary vocabulary, and high-pitched rhetoric. Her longer poems of the time included *The Groom* (*Molodets*, 1924), a succession of poems based on the folk-songs accompanying the ritual of a peasant wedding.

Most of Tsvetaeva's prose dates from the 1930s, although one of her most famous pieces, "The shimmering rain" ("Svetovoy liven"), written in praise of Pasternak's *My Sister Life*, appeared in 1922. Later she would publish autobiographical and critical prose, some of the best of the latter being dedicated to Pushkin.

In general only the cubo-futurists displayed the characteristics of a true avant-garde. Surely one of the most radical avant-garde theoreticians in all European literature at the time must have been the cubo-futurist Alexey Kruchonykh (1886–?1969). Reared in a peasant family of Kherson province, he attended art school in Odessa and by 1907 had joined forces with David Burliuk in promoting cubism and, as might have been expected, was among the signers of "A slap in the face of public taste." In 1913 he published the long poem *The Hermit Man* (*Pustynnik*), in which he encapsulated the predatory mentality of the stone-age male, who lived by the chase and killing other animals.

The reader might not always have been able to tell when Kruchonykh was entirely serious in his literary works, but he was clearly a fanatic supporter of the futurist cause and the most dedicated creator of transsense works. In his numerous articles, including especially "The word as such" ("Slovo kak takovoe,"

1913), he argued that the poet must constantly reinvent language because usage continually deadens its impact. Later on he experimented with the graphic aspects of poetry as well.

A close friend of Khlebnikov's and a tireless organizer, Kruchonykh kept futurism alive in Georgia in the early years of the Soviet regime, but ultimately joined Mayakovsky in the ranks of *Lef* when it became necessary for him to adapt.

The idea of renewing society through the revitalization of individual freedoms and pastoral virtues runs through the work of Elena Guro (real name: Eleonora von Notenberg, 1877–1913). Reared in St. Petersburg, she studied art with such symbolist artists as Bakst, joined forces with the cubo-futurist David Burliuk, and married an artist and composer, Mikhail Matyushin. She illustrated her own literary works, which blend verse and lyric prose. Guro is best remembered for two books: *The Hurdy Gurdy* (*Sharmanka*, 1909) and the posthumous *Little Camels in the Sky* (*Nebesnye verblyuzhata*, 1914), which both contain poetry and prose, and plays as well in the case of the former. The poet opens *The Hurdy Gurdy* with views of the city seen as a place of constriction and corruption before shifting to a northern setting as she withdraws to a family dacha in Finland: she viewed nature as alive in a spiritual sense. Another contrast in her work is that between oppressive adults on the one hand and victimized children and teenagers on the other, although she was constantly seeking genuine, trusting relationships among friends and family. In much of her work, and especially in *Little Camels in the Sky*, she expressed premonitions of her early death from tuberculosis.

Vasily Kamensky (1884–1961) resembled Guro in his advocacy of the pastoral life and personal freedom. The son of an inspector of mines brought up in the far north near Perm, he began writing poetry very early, became the editor of a minor St. Petersburg periodical, and was another of David Burliuk's associates. His most outstanding work was a novel in lyric prose entitled *The Mud Hut* (*Zemlyanka*, 1910), whose hero obtains a divorce from a society wife to marry a peasant woman, a common theme hinted at in sentimentalist literature of roughly a century earlier. Written in the form of an inner monologue, the novel displays the author's love for nature and feeling of comradeship with animals. In addition to this work, Kamensky also wrote lyric poems, longer

444

poems, and memoirs. In his lyrics he evokes the simple, hard-working inhabitants of picturesque areas of the empire such as the Urals, the Crimea or the Caucasus, and likens the new Soviet order to an eternal spring. In the long poem *Stenka Razin* (1916) he depicts the legendary life of the Cossack rebel, who was quite a favorite with futurist authors. And in 1918 he published his auto-biography, which was factual though nostalgic in tone.

The centrifugists and the ego-futurists in both theory and practice remained much closer to literary tradition. The lesser poets of the centrifuge group – Sergey Bobrov (1889–1971) and Nikolay Aseev (1889–1963) – may be best described as eclectic: though they admired the cultural heritage of civilization, at the same time they sought to renew it constantly as they continued it. Bobrov was the group's founder and theoretician. He worked as a teacher of mathematics and sought to devise a system of prosodic analysis for poetry. In his own verse he effected a return to French decadence, writing of melancholia, mysteries and ecstasies in exotic settings including suggestive nature scenes. In later writings he offered pictures of violent destruction and notes of anger and spleen. After the revolution he produced utopian novels which have remained all but unknown, and literary translations.

Nikolay Aseev was both more intellectual and more experimen-tal than Bobrov, and sometimes composed in transsense language. Like Bobrov's, Aseev's early verse also harked back to *fin de siècle* themes, but he afterwards flirted with cubo-futurism and came under Mayakovsky's influence, especially after returning from a sojourn in the Far East (1916–21) to join Mayakovsky and *Lef* in 1922. He was thereafter a prolific producer of poetry down to 1950 in which he joined the romantic imagery of the stars and open spaces with the propagandistic extolling of labor.

Igor Severyanin (real name Lotaryov, 1887–1941) was among the most popular of the futurists at the time of their ascendancy, although he has faded very considerably by now. Born in St. Petersburg and educated as an engineer, he loved music and dedicated himself to poetry and to the ego-futurist esthetic, which preached the notion of a metaphysical goal beyond the individual's intuitive perceptions. His most noted book remains his first, *The Thunderseething Goblet* (*Gromokipyashchy kubok*, 1913), in which he took his basic inspiration from *fin de siècle* decadence but added to that approach a taste for modern luxury and sensual satiety, which had never been characteristic of that movement in its Russian version. He expressed the attitudes of an idle elite dedicated to trivial and selfish pleasures; many of his poems are dialogues about love encounters. His own vision was not at all obviously superior to the laissez-faire morality and hedonism that he portrayed in his verse.

In 1919 there occurred a revolt against futurism staged by a small group of poets who called themselves "imagists" (*imazhinisty*), led by Vadim Shershenevich (1893–1942) and including the peasant poet Sergey Esenin and the avant-gardist Anatoly Mariengof (1897–1962), who deliberately presented himself as a bohemian and clown. The imagists – so called because they asserted that poetry is based on the flow of images arising from each word in succession – established little magazines, a publishing house, and several cabarets for the promotion of their ideas, and remained active until 1927 in the face of adverse government pressure in response to imagist publications obviously intended to scandalize the reading public.

Shershenevich was born in Kazan, the son of a professor, but was active in Moscow in producing both futurist and imagist works including lyric poems, longer poems and verse dramas as well as theoretical pronouncements. His writings express a fundamentally avant-gardistic rebellion: he is alienated, bitter, aggressively hostile, but at the same time witty, ironic and humorous. After the demise of the imagist movement Shershenevich worked as a translator and screenwriter.

Although Sergey Esenin was associated with the imagists too, he is now remembered in the history of Russian literature as a "peasant poet" rather than an imagist. The peasant poets appeared in the avant-garde era as an outgrowth of the populist sentiments of the time, appealing to a general interest in the primitive, natural and unconventional. There had been similar movements during the nineteenth century, from the time of romantic domination and into the realist period.

Nikolay Klyuev (1887–1937) is generally regarded as the leader of the twentieth-century peasant movement in literature. A peasant himself, born in the Lake Onega region, he travelled throughout Russia in the company of religious sectarians, for whom he wrote songs. But he also wrote poems which won him the support of the literary community through Blok, whom he first approached in 1907. His pre-revolutionary collections exhibit the influence of the folk mentality and folk styles in varying degrees. His first collection was the most literary: *The Ringing of Pines* (*Sosen perezvon*, 1912). In it he speaks of the traditional subjects of peasant poetry (love, death, separation) and employs nature imagery, but with a melancholy philosophical undercurrent. *Fraternal Songs* (*Bratskie pesni*, 1912) was his most sectarian collection: in it he speaks of religious exaltation and the second coming. For all his peasant roots, for the most part Klyuev employed classical meters in his work, although he sometimes wrote without regular rhymes: only the poems of a cycle called "Songs from the Onega Region" ("Pesni iz Onezhya") display the forms of genuine folk poetry.

Klyuev's attitude toward the revolution of 1917 was unsettled. Initially he attached millennarian hopes for the good of the peasantry to that political change, but afterwards he expressed his bitter disillusion in sarcastic laments. The first attitude was expressed most clearly in a cycle entitled "Lenin" and dating from 1918–19, but by 1922 his unhappiness with the regime had become quite apparent, and emerged regularly in his longer poems which appeared thereafter. For example, he complained about the fate of his fellow peasant poet Esenin in "The fourth Rome" ("Chetverty Rim") and "Lament for Esenin" ("Plach o Esenine"). Subsequently he was arrested for giving a reading of one of his works and exiled to Siberia. He died in 1937, on his way back to Moscow.

Sergey Esenin (1895–1925), one of the most popular of twentieth-century Russian poets, became the legendary peasant who succumbed to the temptations of urban bohemia. He was born to a peasant family near Ryazan but moved to Moscow in 1912 and joined several minor literary groups there. In 1915 he moved to Petrograd, where he got to know Blok and fell under Klyuev's influence. The following year he published a collection of lyric poems entitled *Radunitsa* (the name of a pagan Slavic funeral feast), which brought him some visibility, although his subsequent fame rested primarily on the publication of individual poems and on public appearances.

Esenin's poetry between 1910 and 1920 was essentially that of a typical peasant poet, for he used rural imagery and unpretentious language to give voice to unabashedly sentimental tendencies. He wrote often of nature, closely observed as a reflection of human life. He depicted the beauties of the sunset, stars, forests, fields, snow and ice, but he also noticed the signs of hardship and the sources of protection and love needed to overcome it; he was drawn to animals, especially birds, dogs, cats, and horses. Another of his favorite subjects was romantic love, presented in the stylized folk tradition: his lovers are usually separated by some force and doomed to suffer unhappy marriages, retirement to a monastery, or death. Esenin also reflects the peasant's dual loyalty to country and to religious faith, the latter perceived in terms of Christian humility and self-sacrifice, the former in terms of its space and open roads as well as its nurturing agriculture. Although at the beginning of his career Esenin took a rather impersonal approach to his subjects, about 1915 a change is observable, when an un-motivated nostalgia enters his descriptions of the country's vast-ness; later on his moods become more personal as he is visited by presentiments of loss and death. He became increasingly aware of the gulf opening up between himself (the "last village poet," as he called himself) and his peasant home, where he came to seem more and more a mere visitor.

In the last five years of his life Esenin's poetry was more autobiographical as it traced his downward path, picturing his bohemian life in Moscow as a sterile attachment to tavern stupors and risky fights, for example in his poem "Hooligan" ("Khuli-gan") of 1920. But his lyric poetry is silent about some salient parts of his biography, such as his marriage in 1923 to the American dancer Isadora Duncan, their travels in Germany, France, Italy and the United States, and his divorce in 1924 leading to his return to Russia and his renunciation of imagism.

During these last five years Esenin wrote several longer works, including one on the eighteenth-century Cossack rebel, *Pugachov* (1922). During his travels with Isadora Duncan he also began a poem about an ominous double (*Cherny chelovek* [*The Black Man*]) which reminds one of the legends associated with Mozart's Requiem. But his greatest achievements were in the sphere of lyric poetry between 1923 and 1925. His poems of that final period

448

included many anguished memories of home: his mother is old and given to worrying about him, his house is dilapidated, his dog already dead. The poet himself is often bored and empty, resigned to death, and sees the countryside as progressively disappearing. His final lyric, indeed, was a suicide poem, "Goodby, my friend, goodby," written just before he hanged himself in a Leningrad hotel.

Although the October revolution and the ensuing civil war caused enormous dislocations in all areas of the national life, including literature, literary trends were not immediately altered. To be sure, a shortage of printing facilities and of paper reinforced the popularity of cabaret art, which flourished in western Europe as well at the time. There were popular poetry readings of acmeists and futurists at cafes and nightclubs, of which the St. Petersburg cafe called The Stray Dog was the best known, and has been recalled in numerous memoirs. Many of the older writers, whether symbolists or realists, fell silent or went into emigration in the first few years after 1917. The difficulties of the times led to the voluntary formation of writers' unions for the primary purpose of providing material assistance, and not promoting any particular literary tendency. The newly influential Gorky helped establish artists' houses or clubs where older authors could assist in training younger proletarian writers; in addition he organized translation programs which were especially helpful for those writers who could not publish their own works at the time. Poetry was very popular in the initial years of the Soviet era, but before long began to yield to prose.

At this point, moreover, a coherent school of criticism, formalism, for the first time in the twentieth century took an active role in shaping literary development. In a sense formalism sprang from futurism: there were personal ties between the avant-garde poets and the formalists, and formalist theories were influenced by futurist viewpoints. The formalists held that "artifice," or the artistic process itself, was the most essential element of literature, and that word stratagems were its building blocks in the same sense that line and color were for the graphic arts. In theory the formalists did not reject the "message" or moral impact of a literary work, but in practice they paid less attention to it than to such things as verbal repetitions, variations and contrasts.

449

Among the formalist theoreticians there was also an author of arresting historical, or autobiographical, records written in whimsical, elliptical prose: Victor Shklovsky (1893–1984). Among other things Shklovsky lectured at the Petrograd House of Arts to the so-called Serapion Brothers, a group of young literary figures from whose ranks several major writers would come. In his own works – for example *Zoo. Letters Not About Love* (*Zoo. Pisma ne o lyubvi*, 1923) – he described his love for Lili Brik's sister, Elsa Triolet, in thinly disguised fictional form, and pictured the catastrophic eastward migration of a native population during the civil war (*Sentimental Journey* [*Sentimentalnoe puteshestvie*, 1923]). Although he has been accused of capitulating to the regime's cultural demands and his works did become more conventional in the 1930s, he continued to publish his semidocumentary writings into the 1960s, and his contributions to the formation of avant-garde prose cannot be denied.

Critics and literary historians classify the writers of modernistic Russian prose of the early 1920s as "ornamentalists," although they themselves never formed a school, adopted a common platform, or even employed that designation. Experimental prose established itself during the years of the First World War, particularly through the efforts of Boris Pilnyak and Eugene Zamyatin. There was a grouping of sorts called the Serapion Brotherhood, named after E. T. A. Hoffman's hermit Serapion, formed in 1921 as a loose organization of beginning authors and critics who required mutual support in their search for independence: they stipulated their concern for the uniqueness of each of their members. They were students of Zamyatin's, but were also influenced not only by Shklovsky but by Gorky, who exerted a realistic impact indirectly because he was the patron of beneficent literary organizations. The Serapion Brotherhood numbered about a dozen, and included Mikhail Zoshchenko, a promising satirist, and an impressive novelist named Konstantin Fedin.

One very influential experimental prose writer who began to publish before the formation of the Serapion Brotherhood was Boris Pilnyak (real name Vogau, 1894–?1937), a master of "ornamentalism." Pilnyak stemmed from a family of Volga Germans, began publishing in 1915, and achieved fame in 1921 with an antinovel entitled *The Naked Year* (*Goly god*). *The Naked Year* depicts in fragmentary prose the tribulations of the population during the famine winter of 1919–20. Pilnyak's vision of humanity was romantic in the sense that he insisted on the primacy of the irrational, and especially the sexual instinct, in life, but he also demonstrated the ability of some to rise to heroism while others sank to the petty, sordid, or even criminal.

In his stories and novels of the early 1920s Pilnyak promoted two leading themes: first he celebrated humanity's various biological roles, such as mating, motherhood, and the guardianship of territory; and second, he advanced intellectual views of a Slavophile nature, revelling in the depths of Russian history and relishing the rightness of Russian ways for Russians. He continuously depicted the revolution in two versions: the true peasant revolution at odds with a rigidly vicious variant based on western Marxism. To be sure, in one of his most engaging works, *Machines and Wolves* (*Mashiny i volki*, 1924), he sought to extol the urban worker on an equal footing with the peasant. That novel pointed to an ominous split within Pilnyak himself, who desired to win the approval of the social mainstream at the same time as he defiantly defended the primitive. In any case, his rebellious spirit and unique vision in the late 1920s caused him to run afoul of Stalinist cultural policy.

Eugene Zamyatin (1884–1937), the author of novels, short stories, dramatic works and literary criticism, was the most polished and most intellectually stimulating of the Russian prose modernists. Born the son of a priest in central Russia, he was trained in St. Petersburg as an engineer and pursued a dual career as a practical scientist and as a writer. He was also twice exiled, in 1905 and 1911, for his political activities. During his second exile he had the opportunity to produce a novella, *A Provincial Tale* (*Uezdnoe*), which established his literary reputation when it appeared in 1913. He spent the years of the First World War in England supervising the construction of Russian icebreakers, and afterwards published two works based on his experiences there: "The Islanders" ("Ostrovityane," 1918) and "Fisher of Men" ("Lovets chelovekov," 1922). Since the conforming mind was one of the most enduring targets of Zamyatin's displeasure, it is not surprising that these satires depict the English as cunningly hypocritical in defending their petty bourgeois lack of individuality.

451

Zamyatin reached a new level of complexity and maturity in the works he wrote after returning to his homeland in 1917. He published several essays setting forth his general point of view, of which the most important is "On literature, revolution, entropy, and other matters" ("O literature, revolyutsii, entropii i prochem," 1924). In it he argued that revolution was just such a universal force as gravity, one which animated the universe with necessary changes, while entropy was the death of every developing process, a danger to the spiritual and political life of individuals and societies alike. He praised heretics, challengers of all conformities, as the only antidote to dissolution and death.

In the 1920s Zamyatin wrote a small body of diverse short stories. It is not clear that they all celebrate the uniqueness of the individual, although some do. Among them is "The Cave" ("Peshchera," 1922), a small masterpiece describing a cultured middle-aged couple's struggle for physical survival during the famine winter of 1919–20 and written in a style which magnificently combines irony and extended metaphor. Although the story takes place in a Soviet setting, the author's approach is philosophical rather than political. In fact, overall Zamyatin takes the view in his stories that life is painful not only because of social constraints but because of the conflict between the primitive and the altruistic within the self. He sees the human being as a selfish and clumsy creature who suffers from loneliness and searches for love, in that very search causing conflict and inflicting pain. The living of life demands a continuing revolution, although in any case it will eventually end in entropy, or death. Zamyatin was thus not entirely cynical, though neither was he uplifting in any facile way.

Zamyatin regarded sexuality as important as a link between the mere sustaining of biological life in a barren universe and the joys of the individual. He often celebrated sexuality, treating it sometimes with lyrical reverence, then with Biblical solemnity, and again with lighthearted irony. In the memorable and disturbing story "The Flood" ("Navodnenie," 1929) sexuality is both the motivation behind an ax murder and an instrument of redemption.

In general Zamyatin's short stories were the product of an astonishing literary craftsmanship. Though his immediate aims in writing particular stories might vary, he displayed a stylistic elegance and intellectual prowess which set him apart from all others. He was also quite an audacious individual. When he came under heavy press attack in 1929, he published an open letter to Stalin demanding the right to emigrate, and was permitted to do so. He departed in 1931 for Paris, where he died in 1937 while at work on a novel entitled *The Scourge of God* (*Bich bozhy*).

The novel for which Zamyatin is justly famous, however, is *We* (*My*, written in 1920), a direct precursor of Aldous Huxley's *Brave New World* and George Orwell's *1984*, and a successor to such English dystopias as Samuel Butler's *Erewhon* (1872), Edward Bellamy's *Looking Backward* (1888), and H. G. Wells's *The Time Machine* (1895) and *A Modern Utopia* (1905). *We* describes events supposed to be taking place in a United State of the future, and is cast in the form of the diary of an engineer in charge of constructing the first manned spacecraft intended to bring the message of social perfection to non-terrestrial creatures. However, outside the United State, which is surrounded by a Green Wall, there still live retrograde human beings subject to motivations of sexual love and ideals of personal freedom.

The engineer, D-503 (citizens bear only numbers, not names), begins to become disillusioned with the United State when he discovers within himself the ability to love passionately and the existence of an individual "soul." His lover, I-330, an aggressive woman with a facial expression resembling an X, for the mathematical unknown, is sexually alluring, an adept at a museum for the preservation of the ancient culture, and a secret leader of the hordes beyond the Green Wall. Other characters also suggest that loyalty to the United State is not at all complete. These include a poet who writes official odes and a secret agent, or "guardian," who watches D-503: it turns out that both are well known on the other side of the Green Wall.

The suspense of *We* arises partly from D-503's gradual awakening to his genuine situation, the pain his growing sense of individuality causes him, and partly from the fact that the United State is threatened by the plans of the people beyond the wall to gain control of the spacecraft (they are called MEPHI, an abbreviated form of Mephistopheles). Since nearly all the citizens of the United State wish to pursue some form of private life, its leadership decrees that all must undergo a compulsory operation for the elimination of the imagination. D-503 makes the final entry in his diary after undergoing this operation. In it he describes, without emotion or distress, the execution of his lover I-330.

As a piece of prose *We* is brisk, clear-headed, and flawlessly sustained. It has never been published in the Soviet Union, but it circulated there in manuscript and was in time published abroad in several translations.

One writer who worked almost exclusively in the short story form, which he brought to a high level of perfection, was Isaac Babel (1894–1941). Born in Odessa, Babel moved to Petrograd in 1915, where he published some rather sensational stories. In 1918 he worked briefly for the Commissariat of Education and for the Cheka, or secret police organization, and two years later, in 1920, he rode as a war correspondent with General Semyon Budyonny's cavalry in Poland. The result of these experiences was a group of war stories published separately in the early years of the 1920s and then collected in a volume entitled *Red Cavalry* (*Konarmiya*) in 1926. United by the common thread of the narrator, a be-spectacled, intellectual Jew attached to a unit of savage, poorly educated Cossacks whose interests extend no further than combat, horses and women, the stories each stand as separate works, although the true subject of most of them is the narrator's silent astonishment at and occasionally articulated envy of the men he describes. The civil war has divided families quite cruelly: in "The Letter" ("Pismo"), for example, a young Cossack in a letter to his mother describes how their father killed one of his brothers, only to be killed in turn by another brother. The rules by which people have lived previously have broken down, and in several stories the lower classes are shown as hating the gentry more passionately than the Poles whom they are supposed to be fighting. In some stories the norms of decency seem reversed: in "Salt" ("Sol") soldiers shoot a woman when they realize she has tricked them out of a rape they regard as their due.

On the other hand, Babel does occasionally offer what appear to be ways out of the violent situations he describes. In "Pan Apolek" the way out might be through art: the narrator envies a local religious painter who elevates the tainted population around him by using them as models for paintings on Biblical subjects. In "Gedali" (the name of an old Jew) the narrator, Lyutov, observes a man who has faced the double loss of his one ideal of universal love, as the rituals of his Jewish faith seem to be receding into the past while the utopian goals of communism are lost in brutal bloodshed. Lessons in morality do not remain mere abstractions: in "My First Goose" ("Moy pervy gus") Lyutov is confronted by both pride and guilt after he has killed an animal. Such stories as these – and particularly "Gedali" – suggest that the narrator misses the spiritual dimension which he has derived from his Jewish background, but the final story in the collection makes it appear that he has succumbed to the ethic of brutality, for his name, Lyutov, does mean "fierce," and he is proud of having learned to ride a horse.

At one point Budyonny himself objected in print to Babel's depictions of his men, in a demurrer which would not have been necessary had not Babel's stories been cast in a seductive mold of apparent realism. In fact, however, his figures are larger than life, and his subject is not the immediate war at hand but rather larger questions having to do with rules, change, order and instinct. His style is mannered as he juxtaposes grotesque crudities with lyrical details. The reader must assess the narrator's character in part by the imaginative metaphors he uses, while the blunt speech of certain other characters bears its own meaning. Babel's roots in literary tradition go back to Flaubert and Maupassant more than to his Russian predecessors.

The early 1920s saw the initial steps – often experimental ones – in the careers of several authors who would later achieve prominence, and whose early works revealed a capacity for relativism and speculation which would disappear later on. Thus Konstantin Fedin (1892–1977) earned a place among innovative fiction writers with a large first novel entitled *Cities and Years* (*Goroda i gody*, 1924) about two young men at the time of the revolution: one is a weak, self-indulgent Russian intellectual, the other a German artist who becomes a disciplined Soviet communist. The links connecting these two characters are begun in Germany, where the Russian, Andrey Startsov, is caught by the First World War, much as Fedin himself was. Fedin also made audacious use of chronology in his book, beginning it in effect at the end, with the street execution in 1922 of Andrey by his former friend, the German Kurt Wahn, for the crime of permitting the escape of a German prisoner, the

Margraf von Schönau, who had fomented anti-Soviet unrest among the Mordvin. The remainder of the chronology is then fitted in.

Fedin also seeks to paint a broad social canvas, portraying whole populations in their reactions to the First World War and to the civil war in Russia. He depicts the Germans as patriotic but still sympathetic to the socialist movement in their country. He also describes the hardships wrought upon Russian cities by the civil war and the difficulties caused by foreign intervention and native rebellions in the provinces.

Fedin's juxtaposition of cities, populations, and characters in *Cities and Years* suggests that he was probing both the western and the Russian characters as well as the personalities of the revolutionary and the representative of the old order. Andrey certainly has a flawed personality: in the course of the long novel it is explained that he was once engaged to the Margraf's former fiancée but betrayed her for another in the Russian city of Semidol. On the other hand, the author inserts a jarring lyrical digression near the end in which he defends Andrey on the ground that he "never destroyed a single flower." Moreover, the German revolutionary Kurt Wahn, though an artist, displays unfeeling, mechanical traits of the sort the Slavophiles always attributed to westerners. Fedin's ambivalence toward the west may be seen from the fact that the best and the worst of his characters – the villain von Schönau and his former fiancée Marie – are both Germans.

The probing of the Soviet system to determine the extent to which it would tolerate individual weakness was a feature of *Cities and Years*, and also quite a common characteristic of what was termed "fellow traveller" literature at the time. Thus, for example, the first novel published by Leonid Leonov, *Barsuki* (*The Badgers*, 1924), deals with two brothers who are split over the question of the collectivization of agriculture.

A dedicated opponent of convention who would persist in his protests throughout all his life was Mikhail Bulgakov (1891–1941). His first outstanding work was the thoroughly realistic novel *White Guard* (*Belaya gvardiya*, completed in 1924), which, however, portrayed the opponents of Soviet power rather sympathetically. Bulgakov also had a gift for grotesque satire. *The Diaboliad* (*Dyavoliada*, 1925) included three short stories depicting

Soviet bureaucrats and managers as both corrupt and criminally stupid, and the unpublishable – in the eyes of the Soviet literary authorities – "Heart of a Dog" ("Sobache serdtse," written in 1925) describes a dubious experiment in the engineering of the human soul through medicine. All these works reveal the future author of *The Master and Margarita* (*Master i Margarita*), begun in 1928, a novel which could be published in its entirety only some forty years later, and then in the west. Works such as these revealed that his interests were at bottom philosophical, for he was, after all, the son of an eminent theologian.

In general, after 1925 modernist and experimentalist tendencies in literature were on the wane as the pressure mounted for literature which would serve the purpose of the state through the "social command," pressures which would culminate in the formation of the Union of Soviet Writers in 1932.

9

THE TWENTIETH CENTURY: THE ERA OF SOCIALIST REALISM, 1925–53

If the year which begins this period – 1925 – has both literary and political significance, as the year when the newly established communist regime asserted its authority over literature and culture, the ending date is primarily of political significance: it is the year of Joseph Stalin's death. A political date is quite appropriate to close this era of Russian literature, during which literature and politics were more intimately interconnected than at any other time during the entire span of Russian literary history.

The political pressures of the early Soviet era brought about the division of Russian literature into two major if unequal parts: the principal one of Russian literature within the Soviet Union, and the lesser one of the "first wave" of the emigration which began to assume definite form around 1925. When the first wave later subsided – as some writers returned to the Soviet Union during the 1930s or after the Second World War, others died natural deaths or perished during that conflict, and the major centers of émigré culture between the wars were disrupted by that historical cataclysm – it was suddenly reinforced by the so-called "second wave" of the emigration resulting from the dislocations of that very conflict. The "second wave" contained few established writers, but it did provide a much larger audience than before for émigré literature, and boasted a number of talented people who managed to establish themselves as writers later on. The second wave of the emigration was more or less at its height at the time of Stalin's death.

Meanwhile Russian literature within the Soviet Union was traversing a path in its way no less thorny than that trod by Russian literature in emigration. Many gifted writers suffered from the regime's tightening of the cultural reins during the later 1920s: Zamyatin was eventually forced into exile, Pilnyak was compelled to alter his literary approach, Olesha was effectively silenced, Bulgakov turned to writing works for the drawer which would not see publication for many years. Even a man like Mayakovsky, seemingly quite

458

in tune with the epoch, found the party's literary discipline too much to accept, and ended his own life in 1930.

The regime's ultimate objective in disciplining writers in the later 1920s was the hitherto untried one of establishing a single literary approach for an entire national literature by political fiat. That single approach came to be known as "socialist realism," and it has dominated the field of Soviet culture ever since its introduction in the early 1930s. A good official definition of it reads as follows:

> Socialist realism, the fundamental method of Soviet artistic literature and literary criticism, demands of the artist a truthful and historically specific depiction of reality in its revolutionary development. At the same time this truthfulness and historical specificity in the depiction of reality must be linked to the task of ideologically remolding and educating the workers in the spirit of socialism.

Socialist realism had definite historical roots. Its literary approach was theoretically that of the "realist" era of Russian literature between 1855 and 1880, but at the same time, as Andrey Sinyavsky has pointed out, it suddenly acquired a political purpose which it had never possessed before: it became a "teleological" literature. It was called upon to depict the new socialist man as hero of Soviet industrialization as he overcame the obstacles placed in his way by the remnants of the past and even by an intractable reality. The great exemplar of this approach in pre-revolutionary literature was Gorky's *Mother*; the tradition was further elaborated through such works as Fyodor Gladkov's *Cement*, Valentin Kataev's *Time, Forward!*, and Nikolay Ostrovsky's *How the Steel Was Tempered*. When the method of socialist realism reached the height of its influence, in the period between the conclusion of the Second World War and Stalin's death, literature was even encouraged to become "conflictless" as Soviet society supposedly moved toward the elimination of all class distinctions. The apogee of socialist realism was also the period which saw the publication of scarcely a single work that has retained any value in the history of Russian literature.

The state's primary instrument for the enforcement of socialist realism was the Union of Soviet Writers, formed in 1932, which held its first congress in 1934. By that time the lively literary life of the 1920s had been suppressed and all literary groupings dissolved, to be replaced by a mammoth organization to which all who claimed to be writers were to belong: union members enjoyed distinct privileges, and expulsion from the union was ordinarily tantamount to literary annihilation. The formation of the Writers Union codified the general Soviet attitude that literature is so important to the life of the state that it must be strictly regulated: erring writers must be punished, and conforming writers rewarded.

Authors, however, were by no means exempt from the difficulties which beset the ordinary Soviet citizen during the great purges of the 1930s. Many of them perished at the height of their powers. In numerous cases we do not know with certainty the dates of death and places of burial for writers who vanished during the purges.

To be sure, the establishment of the Union of Soviet Writers did provide opportunities for a certain corporate fellowship among writers and fostered a sense of common literary enterprise; but as in every other area at the time, organizational initiatives had to come from the top political leadership, which meant that Soviet Russian cultural life had an inescapably artificial quality. Everything from literary works themselves to the personal relationships among writers was subordinated to the political objectives of the state during the period of high Stalinism. Only with Stalin's death would this situation begin to change.

By 1925 it was clear that the status quo in the Soviet Union would last indefinitely and that Russians abroad would have to reconcile themselves to exile. In the early 1920s there still had been considerable traffic to and from the Soviet Union. Now the only Soviet writers who received passports to visit the west were reliable supporters of the regime, such as Vladimir Mayakovsky or Ilya Erenburg. The permission granted Eugene Zamyatin in 1931 to leave Russia was a rare exception. A very few writers returned to the Soviet Union: Dmitry Svyatopolk-Mirsky in 1932, Alexander Kuprin in 1937, Marina Tsvetaeva in 1939. But by 1925 most writers in exile had established a more or less permanent residence. Only a few could make a living entirely from their literary activities, and those who did (Bunin, Khodasevich, Remizov, Merezhkovsky and his wife Zinaida Hippius) often lived in poverty. A robust literary life nevertheless continued at numerous locations all over the world, until it was interrupted by political events: the invasion of Manchuria by the Japanese in 1932, the ascendancy of Hitler's regime in Germany in 1933, and World War II. The principal foci of émigré literary activity after 1925 were Paris, Berlin, Prague, Belgrade, Warsaw, Riga, and Harbin in the Old World, and New York and San Francisco in the New World. But journals, almanacs, and books appeared, and literary groups were active in many other places as well, such as Tallinn, Helsinki, Brussels, or Buenos Aires.

Paris became the center of émigré literary life. Two major

Russian newspapers appeared here: *Late News* (*Poslednie novosti*), whose literary critic was Georgy Adamovich; and *Renaissance* (*Vozrozhdenie*), whose literary critic after 1927 was the poet Vladislav Khodasevich. Among the many journals that appeared in Paris were *Contemporary Notes* (*Sovremennye zapiski* 1920–40, the only old fashioned thick journal), *New House* (*Novy dom*, 1926–7), *Milestones* (*Versty*, 1926–8), *Theater* (*Teatr*, 1928–34), *New City* (*Novy grad*, 1931–9), *Satirikon* (1931, one of several ephemeral satirical journals), *Numbers* (*Chisla*, 1930–4), and *Encounters* (*Vstrechi*, 1934).

While Berlin was no longer the hub of Russian intellectual life it had been in the early 1920s, many Russian émigrés were still living there. It was the site of several Russian publishing houses, such as Epoch and Petropolis. Among its periodicals were *Firebird* (*Zharptitsa*, 1921–6), *Chronicle* (*Letopis*, 1937–41, devoted to Russian Orthodox thought and culture), *Circle* (*Krug*, 1936–8), and *Socialist Herald* (*Sotsialistichesky vestnik*, 1921–41, continued in New York, 1941–68), which featured reviews and essays by the eminent critic Vera Alexandrova (1895–1966).

Prague, the site of the Russian National University, was also a focus of literary activity. *Russia's Will* (*Volya Rossii*), started in 1920 as a newspaper, appeared here as a monthly "thick journal" from 1925 to 1932.

In Belgrade, the Yugoslav Academy of Sciences published a Russian Library, a series in which new works by Bunin, Kuprin, Merezhkovsky, Shmelyov, Remizov, Hippius, Balmont, Amfiteatrov, Teffi, Chirikov, Severyanin, and others appeared over the years. Belgrade was also the site of the only congress of Russian writers in exile, held in 1928. Warsaw had a literary weekly, *Sword* (*Mech*), which appeared from 1934 to 1939. Riga, the capital of Latvia, which had a strong Russian minority population, had an excellent daily newspaper, *Today* (*Segodnya*), and was the site of several literary ventures, such as two weeklies devoted to art and literature, *Our Flame* (*Nash ogonek*, 1923–8), and *Chimes* (*Perezvony*, 1925–8), whose literary editor was Boris Zaitsev, and a similar monthly, *Garret* (*Mansarda*), six issues of which appeared in 1930. Among several periodicals and almanacs which came out in the Far East, *Ray of Asia* (*Luch Azii*, 1932–45) deserves mention. It is quite typical that one of the leading émigré journals, *Russian Thought* (*Russkaya mysl*, 1921–7), edited by Peter Struve, appeared in succession in Sofia, Prague, Berlin, and Paris.

In all of these, as well as in a number of other cities, organized literary groups existed. In Paris The Green Lamp (Zelenaya lampa) began in 1927 to gather both established and beginning writers at the Merezhkovsky residence. The Encampment group, (Kocheve), founded by Marc Slonim in 1928, united young writers who met regularly for readings and debate, and were joined on occasion by established writers. A similar group, called Crossroads (Perekrestok), was headed by Khodasevich. Studio franco-russe (1919–31), organized by Vsevolod Fokht, was the only major effort to establish regular contact between émigré writers and their French colleagues. Several French writers, such as Paul Valéry, André Malraux, and François Mauriac, contributed to the Studio's work in one way or another, and most leading émigré writers participated in it.

In Prague, a literary society called the "Poets' retreat" (Skit poetov), was active under the leadership of the eminent Dostoevsky scholar Alfred Bem. Berlin had its "Poets' circle" (Kruzhok poetov). Informal literary societies existed in Belgrade, Warsaw, Riga, Tallinn, Helsinki, Harbin, and elsewhere. These groups arranged public readings of literary works and guest appearances of leading émigré writers, and occasionally published almanacs and collections of verse.

With the proliferation of literary societies and journals there went a remarkable pluralism of philosophic, political, and esthetic views. Writers of strong religious convictions gathered around the Paris Theological Institute (Bogoslovsky institut) and the journal *Path* (*Put*, 1925–40), edited by the philosopher Nikolay Berdyaev.

While hopes for a restoration of the monarchy were now rapidly declining, a great deal of retrospective literature of conservative coloration continued to appear, for example, Alexander Kuprin's autobiographic novel *The Cadets* (*Yunkera*, 1933). Hopes for a reconciliation with the Soviets had been dashed by the sad fate of the "Change of landmarks" (Smena vekh, 1921) group, which had advocated a truce with the Bolsheviks; and the Eurasianism and Scythianism of the early 1920s, which urged Russians to recognize the Asian aspects of their civilization, was quickly exposed for what it was: a fanciful conceit lacking any grounding in reality.

Still, the consolidation of Soviet power and Stalin's spectacular industrialization program impressed some émigrés, and even without that there was a leftist element within the émigré community (Mensheviks, Socialist Revolutionaries, National Bolsheviks, etc.). The journal *Positions* (*Utverzhdeniya*, 1931–2), which proposed to unite the various warring factions of émigré intellectuals, was rather leftist on social questions. Likewise, the journal *New City*, while following a strong religious line, voiced utopian ideas which might be called "Christian-Socialist."

Besides a broad spectrum of social, political, and religious views, émigré literature after 1925 began to display a steadily widening rift between the old and the new generation of writers. The groups gathered around the journals *Numbers* and *Circle*, in particular, consisted largely of writers who had begun their careers in emigration. A distinctive trait of the younger generation of writers was their susceptibility to the influence of recent western literature: French surrealism, Kafka, Joyce, Céline.

Several of the major figures of Russian symbolism continued their careers in emigration. Konstantin Balmont, who arrived in France in 1920, remained as prolific as ever almost until his death in 1942. He continued to write rather in the manner of his earlier years, but the virtuosity and musicality of his verse were also intact, and his volume *Northern Lights* (*Severnoe siyanie*, 1931) has some poems "of an unexpected simplicity quite uncharacteristic of him otherwise" (Gleb Struve). Balmont has recently undergone a modest renaissance through the efforts of western critics such as Vladimir Markov and Aleksis Rannit.

Zinaida Hippius wrote little poetry in her Parisian exile, but did publish two volumes of memoirs, *Living Faces* (*Zhivye litsa*, 1925), which Khodasevich found "as fascinating as a novel," and was active as a critic and journalist. Her husband, Dmitry Merezhkovsky, who during the first years of his life in exile had published several historical novels, now abandoned fiction in favor of publicistic writings largely devoted to the struggle against Bolshevism, historical essays continuing his series *Eternal Companions* (*Vechnye sputniki*), and meditations on the philosophy of history, religion, and culture. Merezhkovsky's influence among exile intellectuals continued to be strong in spite of his differences with every major group, including even the Russian Orthodox church. The best known living Russian writer in western Europe, he was especially popular among intellectuals of a religious–mystical orientation.

Vyacheslav Ivanov emigrated only in 1924 and settled in Italy, isolated from other émigré writers. An eminent literary scholar, he published many essays and articles in German and Italian. But he also continued to write poetry. His *Roman Sonnets*, written upon his arrival in Rome in 1924 though published in *Contemporary Notes* as late as 1936, are among his most brilliant. Here Ivanov's formal virtuosity is coupled with a classical elegance and serenity in poetry simpler and more transparent than his earlier verse. But Ivanov's only longer poem published in emigration, *Man* (*Chelovek*, 1939), is esoteric in its religious symbolism and structurally intricate.

Igor Severyanin, at one time the leader of ego–futurism, lived in Estonia after the revolution. He abandoned his earlier extravagant mannerisms to write simple gnomic and nature poetry. He also translated a great deal, particularly from Estonian.

Marina Tsvetaeva moved to Paris from Prague in 1925. Her personal and literary life there was a constant and ever more hopeless struggle which ended in her return to Russia in 1939, where she committed suicide in 1941. Her Paris years were prolific ones, however, and may have witnessed her best work. The stream of Tsvetaeva's lyric poetry continued unabated: it was richly varied thematically, idiosyncratic in its inventive, unpredictable, and punning stream of consciousness, occasionally approaching surrealism, and vigorously dynamic rhythmically. It is remarkable for its idiomatic language, frequent echoes of folk poetry, and yet also for the continuing presence in it of themes of world literature. Tsvetaeva's most important *poema*, *The Ratcatcher* (*Krysolov*), appeared in 1925–6. It uses the story of the piper of Hamlin as an allegory of the poet's encounter with society. The piper (poetry) frees the town from rats (the cares of day-to-day living), but the mayor (philistinism) breaks his promise to give him the hand of his daughter (the soul). The piper takes his revenge. Its satire on small–town philistinism is only one aspect of this intriguing work, whose blend of dreamy lyricism and sharp whimsy recalls the spirit of German romanticism, to which Tsvetaeva, a solitary figure in Russian poetry, is perhaps closest. Classical themes often appear in Tsvetaeva's poetry, and two of her verse dramas, *Theseus–Ariadne* (*Tezey–Ariadna*, 1927) and *Phaedra* (*Fedra*, 1928), the first two parts of a planned trilogy to be called *Aphrodite's Wrath* (*Gnev Afrodity*), continue the tradition of Annensky's and Vyacheslav Ivanov's Greek tragedies. In the 1930s Tsvetaeva wrote a series of brilliant essays on Russian literature and autobiographical prose pieces.

Georgy Ivanov (1894–1958) had launched his career as a member of the acmeist Poets' guild, but developed into a major poet only in his Parisian exile, shared with his wife, the poetess and novelist Irina Odoevtseva. His collections *Roses* (*Rozy*, 1931) and *Sailing to the Island of Cytherea* (*Otplytie na ostrov Tsiteru*, 1937) put him in the forefront of émigré poetry. Here Ivanov created a world "beautiful in its senselessness and fatedness, 'icy and blue,' 'sad and beautiful'" (Gleb Struve), in musical, though formally conventional verses reminiscent of Blok and Kuzmin. At times, though, this work anticipated the utter desolation of the poetry of his last years.

Vladislav Khodasevich settled in Paris in 1925, as editor and chief critic of the literary section of the newspaper *Renaissance*. He was plagued until his death by ill health and poverty. After the appearance in 1927 of his *Collected Verse* (*Sobranie stikhov*) he was generally considered the leading Russian poet in exile. He wrote little poetry thereafter, but his few late poems are of high quality, as, for instance, the brilliant "To the memory of Murr the cat" ("Pamyati kota Murra," 1934). Khodasevich was, however, very active as a literary critic and historian, publishing several excellent monographs (*Derzhavin*, 1931; *On Pushkin* [*O Pushkine*], 1937, etc.) and many fine essays. Khodasevich belonged to none of the schools of twentieth-century poetry. As a poet he faces life squarely, with an unshakable faith in the values of culture yet with a bleak and sometimes bilious sense of the futility and banality of all non-spiritual and non-artistic endeavor. Khodasevich's polished verses are pointedly unmusical. He favors the minor and especially the gnomic forms of verse, though he also wrote some ballads, for example "John Bottom" ("Dzhon Bottom," 1926), an ironic conceit on the theme of the tomb of the unknown soldier.

The younger generation of poets found a mentor in Georgy Adamovich (1884–1972), a minor poet but a major critic. He was mainly responsible for the introduction of the "Parisian note" in émigré literature. It reflected the mood of many poets of the younger generation, rejecting the sibylline rhetoric of symbolism, the "constructivism" of futurism, and even acmeism's cult of world culture. It demanded simplicity, seriousness, and a personal concern with "the most important things": evil and suffering, mortality, and God. The "Parisian note" found its purest expression in the poetry of Anatoly Shteiger, Lydia Chervinskaya, Anna Prismanova, and Igor Chinnov, as well as in the prose of Yury Felzen.

Anatoly Shteiger (1907–44), a Swiss citizen born in Russia, spent his most creative years in Paris and died of tuberculosis in a Swiss sanatorium. His restrained, precisely worded, and formally unpretentious poetry is the purest embodiment of the "Parisian note." Diary-like and personal, it conveys the life experience of a lonely human being, "impotent, dishonest, and inept," with a detachment that turns the personal into the universal.

The poetry of Lydia Chervinskaya (1907–) resembles Shteiger's. Her mood is one of loss, perplexity, and silence. Her imagery is urban – sometimes specifically Parisian – her style discreet, fragmented, never pointed or showy. It is always in impeccable good taste, and the poet's control over her material is never in question.

Among the young poets without the "Parisian note," Boris Poplavsky (1903–35) is the most talented and the most original. He was well read in modern French poetry, and his work is at times reminiscent of Rimbaud, Laforgue, Apollinaire, and the surrealists. He published but one volume in his lifetime, *Flags* (*Flagi*, 1931), and most of his work appeared posthumously. Poplavsky's poetry is vivid and picturesque, and at the same time hallucinatory, nightmarish, and grotesque. Formally, it is unpolished, sometimes simply ragged, but there is much music in it nevertheless.

Antonin Ladinsky (1896–1961) lived mostly in Paris, but returned to Russia after World War II. Ladinsky was one of very few émigré poets to write in a major key. His vision recalls that of Osip Mandelshtam in its vivid historical sense and love of European culture. It is, like Mandelshtam's, also tragic, but the tragic element is tempered by the serenity of the poet's view of the world. Ladinsky also wrote historical novels, two of them in emigration.

Dovid Knut (pen-name of David Fiksman, 1900–55) was one of the few Russian poets of Jewish ancestry to devote his poetry to Jewish themes, to sustain a persistent awareness of the Old Testament, and to cultivate an explicitly Jewish consciousness. He can be eloquent in his meditations on man's alienation from God and the approaching European catastrophe.

Like certain poets of the older generation, some prose writers who had established themselves before the revolution produced their best work in emigration. This is true of Ivan Bunin, the first Russian to win a Nobel prize in literature (1933). His fictionalized autobiography *The Life of Arsenev* (*Zhizn Arseneva*, 1930–9), in English: *The Well of Days*) has been called "a symphonic picture of Russia" (Fyodor Stepun), and its lyric character is clear. It certainly is a masterpiece of Russian prose. But Bunin was at his best in the short story. His stories of these years, such as "Mitya's Love" ("Mitina lyubov," 1925) and "Sunstroke" ("Solnechny udar," 1927), are among his finest. Bunin was one of only few Russian writers who could deal with erotic passion and with death in a detached, purely esthetic way. Despite a Tolstoyan strain, Bunin's was essentially a pagan sensibility which celebrated life and love, and for that very reason had a keenly immediate sense of death.

Ivan Shmelyov (1873–1950) emigrated in 1922 and settled in Paris in 1925. He had witnessed the horrors of the civil war in the Crimea and described them in several works, beginning with *Sun of the Dead* (*Solntse mertvykh*, 1926), a series of impressions, sketches, and stories tied together by the observer's persona, and followed by the collections of short-stories, *On One Old Woman* (*Pro odnu starukhu*, 1927) and *The Light of Reason* (*Svet razuma*, 1928), in which he effectively uses *skaz* technique to describe the travails of Russians from all walks of life during the years of revolution and civil war. Later Shmelyov turned to themes of émigré life, as in *Entering Paris: Tales of Émigré Russia* (*Vezd v Parizh: Rasskazy o Rossii zarubezhnoy*, 1929).

While Alexander Kuprin had done his best work before the revolution and his stories written in emigration were mostly nostalgic recollections of life in prerevolutionary Russia, Boris Zaitsev (1881–1972) wrote some of his most interesting works in his Parisian exile. His first major work written in exile, the novel *The Golden Design* (*Zolotoy uzor*, 1926), is set in prerevolutionary

Russia, but leads up to the catastrophe of war and revolution. Subsequently Zaitsev concentrated on his memoirs, religious works such as *Mount Athos: Travel Notes* (*Afon: putevye zapiski*, 1928), and literary biography (*Turgenev*, 1932; *Zhukovsky*, 1951; *Chekhov*, 1954). Zaitsev's narrative style is graceful and often lyrical. He is a master of stylized speech in the manner of folklore or sacred literature.

Mark Aldanov (pen-name of M. A. Landau, 1886–1957), a research chemist and literary critic before his emigration in 1919, became a major fiction writer in exile. He lived in Paris after 1924 and moved to New York in 1940, where he became the co-founder of the *New Review* (*Novy zhurnal*) in 1942. Aldanov soon gained international recognition. He wrote primarily historical novels, only some of which are set in Russia. Covering the period from 1762 to 1948, each represents an attempt to grasp the meaning of history by juxtaposing the fate of an "ordinary" individual to the drift of events of which he is a part, or by contrasting a great man, such as Beethoven in *The Tenth Symphony* (*Desyataya simfoniya*, 1931), as he appeared to his contemporaries, to his image in history. Aldanov's plots are carefully structured, his style is vigorous, and he has an authoritative command of historical detail which lends credibility to his narrative. He is a rationalist, a skeptic, and a humanist in the best tradition of Russian westernism.

Other prose writers of the older generation active into the 1930s who deserve mention were Eugene Chirikov, Vladimir Krymov, Sergey Mintslov, Mikhail Osorgin, and Nadezhda Teffi (pen-name of Nadezhda Buchinskaya, 1872–1952). Teffi, an immensely popular satirist even before the revolution, became the émigré Zoshchenko. Her humorous sketches, feuilletons, and short stories, published mostly in the daily press, reflected the bewilderment of the émigré who found himself thrust into a puzzling new environment.

The crop of prose writers who established themselves in exile was less impressive than that of poets. It included, however, Vladimir Sirin (Nabokov), one of the most interesting and innovative Russian writers of the twentieth century. He and several other writers of his generation gave Russian literature a solid body of fiction set entirely in the west. Nabokov (1899–1977) emigrated in 1919 and attended Cambridge University. He lived in Berlin from 1922 to 1937, then in France until 1940, when he went to America where he abandoned Russian for English as his literary medium and established himself as a scholarly authority on Russian literature.

Nabokov's Russian *œuvre* consists of nine novels (all on the short side), a number of short stories, poetry, two plays, essays, reviews, and memoirs. His fiction is based on the experience of émigré life: Russia appears only in the background. The writer's personal life (his years in Cambridge, his interest in chess, tennis, and lepidoptera, his idiosyncratic view of Russian literature) often influences his fiction. Nabokov seems to owe little to any Russian writer, but critics have detected resemblances to Kafka, especially in the novel *Invitation to a Beheading* (*Priglashenie na kazn*, 1938), Proust (the pervasive theme of memory), and Céline (a cold rage at the baseness of bourgeois society). The best among Nabokov's novels are: *The Spy* (*Soglyadatay*, 1930), a brilliant treatment of the split consciousness syndrome, employed to create an intricate, baffling, and yet logical plot; *Luzhin's Defense* (*Zashchita Luzhina*, 1930), whose clever plot is based on the isomorphism of a chess game and the hero's fate (Luzhin is a chess grandmaster); *Despair* (*Otchayanie*, 1936), a crime thriller whose implausible plot is generated by the narrator's (he is also the murderer) deranged mind; *The Gift* (*Dar*, 1937–8); and *Invitation to a Beheading*. The latter is an allegory permitting various interpretations. Its hero, Cincinnatus, is awaiting execution for the crime of being different from the other citizens of a mythical totalitarian state. While in his prison cell, he keeps a diary in which he records his intuitions of an ideal world, his true home. As the executioner's axe falls, the stage prop world of the novel disintegrates and Cincinnatus sets out to the world of his intuitions. *The Gift* combines an account of the growth of a poet with a story of young love and a satire on the émigré literary scene. Woven into the text are provocative opinions on Russian history, culture, and literature. A full quarter of the novel is devoted to the hero's biography of Nikolay Chernyshevsky, which deflates his image as a hero and martyr mercilessly.

Nabokov's short stories share the characteristics of his novels: they have ingenious plots, often with unexpected endings. Nabokov's great forté in all his work – including even his not very remarkable poetry – is precision. He unerringly finds *le mot juste*. His descriptive detail is invariably accurate. His psychology, too, is never vague. The insights he formulates are convincing and palpable. Most important of all, Nabokov has a way of eliciting the moral meaning of an act or a thought without so much as a semblance of moralizing.

None of the other prose writers of the younger generation – among whom Nina Berberova (1901–), Yury Felzen, Gaito Gazdanov, Sergey Sharshun (1888–1975), and Vasily Yanovsky (1906–) were the most remarkable – reached the level of Nabokov's art. Among those mentioned, Gaito (Georgy) Gazdanov (1903–71) was hailed as a major talent on the strength of his first novel, *An Evening with Claire (Vecher u Kler*, 1930), and some early short stories. Proust's influence on him was also immediately noted. Gazdanov's narrative manner is episodic. He is good at creating a vivid setting for a scene, he sometimes catches fascinating glimpses of "landscapes of the soul," and he succeeds in drawing some memorable characters. But he is not very good at developing a sustained narrative, and his longer works – for example, his second novel, *The Story of a Journey (Istoriya odnogo puteshestviya*, 1938) – are not only lacking in structure, but also have some weak chapters. Gazdanov came fully into his own only after the war.

Yury Felzen (pen-name of Nikolay Freidenshtein, 1895–1943), who perished in a German concentration camp, began his career as a novelist with *Deception (Obman*, 1930). His remaining two novels, *Happiness (Schaste*, 1932) and *Letters about Lermontov (Pisma o Lermontove*, 1936), are extensions of it. Felzen is clearly influenced by James Joyce and Virginia Woolf. His novels are written in the form of a diary, or rather "inner monologue," which often turns into outright stream of consciousness, all addressed to the same heroine. Their *raison d'être* seems to be an attempt to express with all possible sincerity the movements of the persona's soul.

A Resolution of the Central Committee of the Communist Party, dated 1 July 1925 and published in all Soviet newspapers, established the position of the Soviet authorities with regard to literature. While stressing that "in a class society there is and can be no neutral art," it also made it clear that art and literature should be allowed to approach Soviet reality from different viewpoints. It refused to grant proletarian writers any institutional "hegemony," but promised them the Party's wholehearted moral and material support in earning the right to such hegemony. Peasant writers also were to be supported and their peculiarities respected. "Fellow travellers," insofar as they were willing to march along with the proletariat, were to be treated as skilled specialists who provided valuable services and whose full acceptance of communist ideology should be encouraged. This entire position was essentially that of the critics of the "Divide" (Pereval) group: Alexander Voronsky (1888–1943) and A. Lezhnev (pen-name of Abram Gorelik, 1893–1938) and the journal *Red Virgin Soil* (*Krasnaya nov*), which Voronsky edited from 1921 to 1927. Voronsky and many other members of the "Divide" group, such as Andrey Platonov, Ivan Kataev, and Anna Karavaeva, were Bolsheviks with solid credentials. They believed that "consciously or unconsciously, a scholar or artist carries out orders which he has received from his social class" (Voronsky), but also that a true artist will inevitably see and express the truth of life. The "organic realism" of the "Divide" meant in critical practice that an honest realism was the only proper and natural style of a young, vigorous, and victorious class. The "Divide" engaged in almost incessant polemic exchanges with rival groups, Lef (Left Front of Art) and RAPP (Russian Association of Proletarian Writers) in particular.

Lef, the journal of the avant-garde, had ceased publication in 1925, but was revived as *New Lef* (*Novy Lef*) in 1927. It vigorously promoted a utilitarian and formalist esthetic and a "literature of fact" (topical sketches, documentaries, biography, travel notes, "newsreels," etc.), whose main function was to raise the consciousness of the citizenry of the proletarian state. The theorists and practitioners of "left art" viewed their art as "production" and themselves as skilled professionals. Among the members of the *Lef* group were the poets Vladimir Mayakovsky, Nikolay Aseev, and Vasily Kamensky, the playwright Sergey Tretyakov, the literary theorists Boris Arvatov, Osip Brik, and Victor Shklovsky, the director Vsevolod Meyerhold, and the film-makers Sergei Eisenstein and Dziga Vertov. They all shared the notion that art should be an eloquent statement about life rather than a mere imitation of it. This brought them in conflict with those groups that embraced a mimetic esthetic. *Lef* rejected the psychological realism advocated and practiced by the "Divide" and RAPP, in favor of an art

471

that would explain or hypostatize progressive ideas vigorously. Accordingly, the writers of *Lef* were active in the most modern media: film, radio, and poster art.

The Literary Center of Constructivists (Literaturny tsentr konstruktivistov), founded in 1924, advocated ideas close to those of *Lef*. Kornely Zelinsky (1896–1970), the group's theoretician, developed the idea that the ever greater complexity of the modern world demanded to be reduced to simple formulae if it were to be comprehensible to the masses, and that art had the task of presenting these formulae in an intelligible and challenging way. As a corollary of this functional theory of art, constructivism also demanded a maximal integration of every level of composition, sound, rhythm, imagery, lexicon, and syntax with the intended meaning. The constructivists, like *Lef* and the "Divide" group, had among them a number of talented poets and writers, such as Eduard Bagritsky, Vera Inber, and Ilya Selvinsky, who also eagerly pledged their support to the Soviet regime.

The Resolution of 1 July 1925 chided the groups of "proletarian" writers gathered around the journals *October* (*Oktyabr*) and *On Guard* (*Na postu*) for "communist arrogance" (*komchvanstvo*) and self-serving factionalism. As a result, the "Onguardists" split; and in 1926 the majority faction founded a new journal, *On Literary Guard* (*Na literaturnom postu*), which became the organ of the All-Union Association of Proletarian Writers (VAPP) and later (in 1928) of RAPP. While politically aggressive, VAPP/RAPP developed a conservative philosophy of art. Its theorists and critics – Leopold Averbakh (1903–39), G. Lelevich (pen-name of Labori Kalmanson, 1901–45), and Yury Libedinsky (1898–1959) – vehemently attacked Voronsky and his associates for their tolerance of fellow travellers, but favored a critical realism of the nineteenth-century Tolstoyan type, which they tended to equate with "materialism," and psychological analysis, which they called "the dialectic of the individual psyche." A good deal of creditable work came out of the RAPP ambience also.

While peasant writers were not nearly as well organized as the proletarians, there existed an "All-Union Association of Peasant Writers" whose membership was second only to that of RAPP, and a "peasant literature" continued to exist well into the 1930s. The "peasant writers" published several journals, of which *Land of* the Soviets (*Zemlya sovetskaya*, 1929–32) was the last. Some prominent writers and poets, such as Nikolay Klyuev, Sergey Klychkov, Alexey Chapygin, and Fyodor Panfyorov, were considered to belong to this movement.

There were some less visible and smaller groups also. OBERIU (*Obedinenie realnogo iskusstva*, or the Association of the Art of Reality), a radical avant-garde group, existed between 1927 and 1930. It promoted formal experimentation and continued certain cubo-futurist practices (primitivism, dissolution or segmentation of the depicted object, removing verbal units from their normal context). Through a deliberate alogism, the *oberiuty* sought to uncover a deeper reality. They were the only literary group in Russia which was close to surrealism. The *oberiuty*, led by Daniil Kharms and Alexander Vvedensky, published but little outside literature for children, where several avant-garde writers and artists found a refuge, and the whole movement was so completely forgotten that it had to be literally rediscovered in the 1960s.

Even more obscure were some outright dissident groups, such as "Resurrection" ("Vozrozhdenie," 1917–28), a religious and philosophical circle most of whose members were arrested in 1928 and 1929. The great literary theorist Mikhail Bakhtin was close to this circle.

Many of the most prominent writers and poets belonged to none of the above groups and are most conveniently lumped under the catchall category "fellow travellers." (Of course any writer who wished to appear in print was, even during the NEP period, at least theoretically a supporter of the Soviet regime.) It may also be noted that the eventual survival rate of "fellow travellers" in the purges of the 1930s was, if anything, higher than that of those writers who belonged to organized groups.

In the 1920s and early 1930s rival groups also continued to exist in the field of literary and esthetic theory. The "sociological school" of Paul Sakulin, Valerian Pereverzev, and Vladimir Friche had developed a theory according to which the history of literature was the record of a continuous struggle between warring styles representing opposing social classes. In 1930 the Communist Academy condemned the sociological school's method as "vulgar sociologism," thus putting an end to any free investigation of the relations between art and society.

By the late 1920s the formalist school had retreated from its most radical positions and was placing more emphasis on the "dialectics of form and socio-historical content." Victor Shklovsky, in fact, publicly renounced his formalist theories in 1930. Nevertheless, some of the most important works of the formalist school appeared in the late 1920s. Vladimir Propp's *Morphology of the Folktale (Morfologiya skazki*, 1928) received little attention then, but proved to be of seminal importance when translated into English in 1958. Yury Tynyanov's *Archaists and Innovators (Arkhaisty i novatory*, 1929) established a model of literary evolution based on structural principles. The first volume of Boris Eikhenbaum's monumental study *Leo Tolstoy*, in which he sought to demonstrate that Tolstoy's philosophic and religious crises and quests were conditioned by the novelist's search for new artistic forms, appeared in 1928. The following year saw the appearance of Mikhail Bakhtin's study *Problems of Dostoevsky's Art (Problemy tvorchestva Dostoevskogo*, 1929). Although Bakhtin was not himself a formalist, his work was seminal not only for an interpretation of the structure of Dostoevsky's novels, but for the theory of fiction in general. It thus complemented the pioneer work done by the formalists.

Altogether, the period between 1925 and 1932 was – despite very serious shake-ups in the Academy of Sciences and the universities – a period of considerable scholarly and critical achievement, highlighted by the launching of Academy editions of the collected works of Tolstoy (1928–58), Dostoevsky (1926–30), Chekhov (1930–3), and other classics of Russian literature.

Each of the literary groups mentioned above produced some significant fiction, more or less in accordance with its general ideological drift. Among the prose writers of the "Divide" group, Anna Karavaeva, Ivan Kataev, Andrey Platonov, and Artyom Vesyoly stand out. Anna Karavaeva (1893–1979) wrote about the life of Ural peasants and artisans, past and present. Her novel *The Sawmill (Lesozavod*, 1928) was among the first to depict the coming of mechanization to the Soviet countryside. Karavaeva was editor of *Young Guard (Molodaya gvardiya*), organ of the Komsomol, from 1931 to 1938 and became one of the stalwarts of socialist realism in the years of Stalin's rule.

Ivan Kataev (1902–39) also dealt with life in the Soviet village.

His short novel *Milk* (*Moloko*, 1930) was savagely attacked for its sympathetic depiction of an efficient and successful dairy farmer. Kataev may have foreseen his own fate in a story, "The Poet" ("Poet"), in which he tells of the short and tragic life of a poet of the proletarian culture movement, one of a "doomed generation." Kataev perished in the purges of the 1930s, as did Vesyoly (pen-name of Nikolay Kochkurov, 1899–1939), a writer of working class background and Bolshevik activist. Vesyoly's stories, such as "My Native Land" ("Strana rodnaya," 1926), resemble Boris Pilnyak's in their "ornamentalist" manner and in their emphasis on the chaotic, elemental nature of the revolution. Vesyoly's main works are *Russia Drenched in Blood* (*Rossiya, krovyu umytaya*, 1929–32), a novel about the revolution and civil war, and *Have a Spree, Volga* (*Gulyay, Volga*, 1932), a historical novel about the conquest of Siberia by the Cossack Ermak.

Andrey Platonov (originally Klimentov, 1899–1951) emerged as a major figure of twentieth-century literature only after Stalin's death. Of working class background and self-educated, Platonov worked as an electrical and land reclamation engineer and was only an amateur writer and poet until 1927, when his collection of stories *The Sluices of Epiphany* (*Epifanskie shlyuzy*, entitled after the lead story) attracted favorable attention. "The Sluices of Epiphany" tells the story of a Scottish engineer called to Russia by Peter the Great to work on a grandiose waterway project. As he gradually realizes that the project is not feasible, he knows he is doomed: he will perish and never see his homeland again. The story combines a wealth of graphic detail and skillful treatment of suspense with great symbolic power. In this and many other stories, Platonov develops the theme of a tragic clash between human dreams, or human hubris, and Nature's inertia and the complexity of life. Platonov's two most profound works, the novels *Chevengur* and *The Foundation Pit* (*Kotlovan*), both written in the late 1920s, were never published in the Soviet Union and appeared in the west in 1972 and 1973 respectively. *Chevengur* is an allegory of a quixotic quest for brotherhood and happiness in the land of victorious socialism in 1921, a quest which ends in frustration and tragedy. The Soviet Don Quixote's damsel is Rosa Luxemburg, the communist leader murdered in Berlin in 1919, the decay of whose corpse he hopes will be reversed by the victory of the proletariat. Death itself becomes a positive force as it clears the way for a generation better fit to realize the communist millennium. But there is no indication that the glorious resurrection of which the Chevengur communists dream is anything but a chimera.

The Foundation Pit is equally pessimistic. A team of workers has gathered to erect a huge edifice which will one day house the entire proletariat of the region in brotherly harmony. But all they do is dig an ever deepening hole which will be their grave. The pathos of this allegory derives from the cruel contrast between the trustful expectations of these simple people and the utter hopelessness of their dream. *The Foundation Pit* also treats the collectivization of agriculture, presented as not just cruel but absurdly stupid as well.

Platonov brilliantly mirrors the deformation which the Russian language underwent after the revolution, when the people's traditional consciousness was destroyed and replaced by a new one both artificial and absurd. Platonov had difficulties with his censors and publishers until the end of his life, though a number of somewhat tamer stories, also excellent, were allowed to appear.

The esthetic of *Lef* and the avant-garde was favorable to a peculiar kind of prose, a fusion of the imaginative and documentary modes. Mayakovsky's American travelogue, *My Discovery of America* (*Moe otkrytie Ameriki*, 1926), is one example, the poet Boris Pasternak's *Safe Conduct* (*Okhrannaya gramota*, 1931), an imaginative autobiography, is another. Victor Shklovsky's essays on literature, such as *On the Theory of Prose* (*O teorii prozy*, 1925), and his many books on various historical and literary figures, such as *Matvey Komarov, Resident of the City of Moscow* (*Matvey Komarov, zhitel goroda Moskvy*, 1929), *Chulkov and Levshin* (1933), *Marco Polo* (1936), *On Mayakovsky* (*O Mayakovskom*, 1940), are vivid, witty, and evocative. They feature flashes of insight into moods and thoughts, wry worldly wisdom, and frequent asides and digressions. Shklovsky developed an idiosyncratic, aphoristic style, with poignant phrases, frequent changes of subject, double-takes, and "defamiliarization" achieved by assuming a "naive" point of view. The historical novels of the formalist scholar Yury Tynyanov – *Kyukhlya* (1925), about the poet Wilhelm Küchelbecker, and *The Death of Vizier-Mukhtar* (*Smert Vazir-Mukhtara*, 1927–8), about the playwright Alexander Griboedov, killed in Teheran while on a diplomatic mission – are a successful combination of imagination and scholarship.

The great short-story writer Isaac Babel, a contributor to *Lef*, was close to it in certain other ways as well. His *Odessa Tales* (*Odesskie rasskazy*), published individually in the early 1920s, but in book form as late as 1927, border on the newspaper feuilleton. Babel's stories are an example of a "low" form raised to the level of "high" art. Their modernism is of an expressionist mold, the prose equivalent of Chagall's paintings, whose subject matter it also shares, or of Prokofiev's ballet music, with its rich colors, jagged contours, and jarring dissonances. Babel's great forté is a successful fusion of dreamy lyricism and brutal naturalism: as Shklovsky once put it, Babel contrived to speak in the same voice about heroism and about gonorrhea. The central theme in virtually all of Babel's works is the clash between physical man, who lives by his instincts, and intellectual man, who lives by ideas, with the Cossack horsemen of *Red Cavalry* providing most of the former and Babel's Jewish characters most of the latter, though there are significant exceptions to this pattern on both sides. Jewish themes, which are dominant in Babel's *œuvre*, are concentrated in the idea of a synthesis of Jewishness and a free and vigorous communism. Babel seems to have believed in this ideal to the end, and expressed it even in some stories of the 1930s. Babel, a meticulous craftsman who rewrote his stories interminably, published only little in the 1930s, but the quality of his last works is high and there is no doubt that he perished, a victim of Stalin's purges, at the height of his creative powers.

The *On Guard*/RAPP writers published more conventional prose. Fyodor Gladkov (1883–1958), a protégé of Maxim Gorky's, scored a phenomenal success with *Cement* (*Tsement*, 1925), which became the prototype of the socialist realist "production novel." It describes the heroic and successful struggle of a communist worker and Red Army veteran to start production at a cement factory put out of commission during the war. Critics of the *Lef* group found an unresolved contradiction between the hero's "Herculean" stature and the author's attempts to provide him with a "psychology," but most critics, including Gorky, thought the novel a timely move in the right direction. Gladkov's later works did not enjoy the success of *Cement*. Alexander Fadeev (1901–56) scored an almost equally spectacular success with *The Rout* (*Razgrom*, 1927), a novel about a Red guerrilla detachment fighting in the Far East during the civil war. The influence of Leo Tolstoy is apparent in this work, as it was also in other works of the RAPP school. Fadeev not only presents his characters as individuals, he also probes into their minds, infusing his narrative with a pointedly new sense of values and a new, "Bolshevik" morality. Fadeev went on to a great career, but more as an administrator than as a writer: he headed RAPP and later the Union of Soviet Writers.

Fadeev's younger colleague, Mikhail Sholokhov (1905–84), scored the greatest success of his life at an even earlier age. Coming from the Don region, though not himself a Cossack, Sholokhov had gained only casual attention with his *Tales of the Don* (*Donskie rasskazy*, 1926). His novel *The Quiet Don* (*Tikhy Don*, vol. 1 – 1928, vol. 2 – 1931, vol. 3 – 1933, vol. 4 – 1940) made him the leading Soviet writer, a position he strengthened with *Virgin Soil Upturned* (*Podnyataya tselina*, vol. 1 – 1932, vol. 2 – 1960). *The Quiet Don* covers life in a Don Cossack settlement from 1912 to 1921. Patterned after Tolstoy's *War and Peace* (a number of historical personages and documented historical events appear in the text), it paints a panoramic picture of Cossack life in peace, in wartime, and in the years of revolutionary turmoil. It contains many vividly portrayed characters, of whom some of the most memorable are women. There is little communist bias. The Cossacks, archenemies of the revolution, are shown as coarse and violent, but also as hardworking farmers and brave soldiers. The attractive hero, Grigory Melekhov, whose family owns a good farm, chooses the wrong side in the civil war and ends up as the leader of a counter-revolutionary guerrilla band fighting in a lost cause.

The Quiet Don is one of the few novels in Russian literature which describe the inner life of uneducated men and women convincingly and without condescension. The plot line, dictated by the course of history, intertwines with the tragic love story of Melekhov and Aksinya Astakhova, the wife of his neighbor, an affair complicated by the fact that Melekhov's wife loves him dearly and Astakhov cannot get over the loss of Aksinya. The love story is told believably, unsentimentally, and with tragic power.

Another great forté of Sholokhov's are his magnificent nature descriptions, which blend harmoniously into the narrative. *The Quiet Don* is a masterpiece and justly brought Sholokhov the 1965 Nobel prize in literature.

OBERIU produced two major prose writers, Daniil Kharms (pen-name of Yuvachev, 1905–42) and Konstantin Vaginov (pen-name of Vagingeim, 1899–1934). In Kharms's short and very short stories, a clash between closely observed detail and intruding grotesque creates a world of surrealist wonder. During his lifetime Kharms could publish only his poems and stories for children, in which he could indulge his absurdist sense of humor. His works for adults were rediscovered in the 1960s and published in the west. Vaginov's novels *The Goat Song* (*Kozlinaya pesn*, 1928), *The Works and Days of Svistunov* (*Trudy i dni Svistunova*, 1929), and *Bambochade* (*Bambachada*, 1931) feature grotesque, travesty, puns, verbal collage, and an ever present literary subtext, as even the titles of the novels indicate: *The Goat Song* is a pun on the etymology of Greek *tragoidia*. The novel itself draws a nightmarish picture of Leningrad as a cultural necropolis, populated by ex-intellectuals, with the city's great heritage relegated to the novel's subtext.

Most of the interesting fiction of this period was still produced by "fellow travelers," writers who for various reasons failed to join any organized group. The Serapion Brotherhood of the early 1920s had disbanded and each of its members made his own career, remarkably successful in almost every case. Veniamin Kaverin (1902–) developed into a leading Soviet novelist without sacrificing his integrity as an artist. His novels are interesting structurally, tend to have a literary subtext, and are intellectually challenging. *The Troublemaker* (*Skandalist*, 1928) is a fictionalized putdown of conventional esthetic theory and a thinly disguised chronicle of the downfall of the formalist school. In each of his following novels Kaverin develops his plot in terms of the parallel fate of intellectually and psychologically juxtaposed characters: an engineer and a painter in *Artist Unknown* (*Khudozhnik neizvesten*, 1931); a philologist and a biologist in *Wish-Fulfillment* (*Ispolnenie zhelaniy*, 1934–5); a pre-revolutionary explorer and a young Soviet flyer in *Two Captains* (*Dva kapitana*, 1934–44).

Vsevolod Ivanov (1895–1963) abandoned his ornamentalist and

expressionist manner and tried to join the conformist mainstream of Soviet literature, but never matched the excellence of his early work except perhaps in his autobiographical novel *Adventures of a Fakir* (*Pokhozhdeniya fakira*, 1934–5). Konstantin Fedin followed the same pattern, but with some delay. His long short story "Transvaal" (1926) was attacked for its apparent implication that the crafty and unscrupulous western entrepreneur was the only force that could get the Soviet economy going; his second novel, *Brothers* (*Bratya*, 1928) was a paler version of *Cities and Years*. Fedin's first socialist realist novel was *The Rape of Europe* [or *Europa*] (*Pokhishchenie Evropy*, 1934–5), an attempt to contrast depression-ridden Europe to the bustling Soviet Union under Stalin's Five Year Plan. By far the most successful of the Serapions was Mikhail Zoshchenko, who will be discussed in a different context.

Among the other "fellow travelers," Yury Olesha (1899–1960), who owes his fame largely to a single short novel, *Envy* (*Zavist*, 1927), was the most interesting. *Envy* deals with the conflict between new Soviet men, dedicated yet practical, and ineffectual dreamers who have preserved vestiges of an outmoded bourgeois mentality. Each side is represented by two generations, the fortyish and the young. The conflict is staged with masterful ambiguity. While "Soviet man" is obviously winning, his success is viewed through the eyes of the envious losers, with whom the reader may very well identify, and his positive image is undercut by cleverly planted subliminal detail. Even today *Envy* remains the most "modernist" of all Russian novels. Olesha, a film-maker as well as writer, uses cinematic devices (stills, accelerated motion, zoom lens, isolated and angled shots), blatantly Freudian symbolism, and surrealist plot development throughout a text which is lively and entertaining even on a surface level. Olesha's few short stories, such as "The Cherry Pit" ("Vishnevaya kostochka"), "Love" ("Lyubov"), and "Liompa," are also brilliant, but his total output of serious fiction is small, as he fell almost silent during the Stalin years.

Boris Pilnyak, another "modernist," who had been easily the most visible Soviet prose writer of the early 1920s, now experienced some difficulties which eventually led to his arrest and execution in 1937. His story "Tale of the Unextinguished Moon"

("Povest nepogashennoy luny," 1926) was perceived as a barely disguised provocation, accusing Stalin of the murder of Mikhail Frunze, a popular Red Army commander, and was immediately suppressed. In 1929 Pilnyak's story *Mahogany* (*Krasnoe derevo* was brought out by an émigré publishing house in Berlin. It contained passages which could be interpreted as sympathetic to the defeated Trotskyite faction of the Party and to *kulaks*, who were then being "liquidated." In spite of this, Pilnyak was allowed to travel abroad (to the Near and Far East, and to the United States). His travels led to a number of stories set abroad as well as his impressions of American life, *O. K.: An American Novel* (*Okey: Amerikansky roman*, 1932). Pilnyak's later works, no less than his earlier ones, are enigmatic allegories. His seemingly plotless and chaotic texts still convey an indistinct yet perceptible view of "the pattern in the rug" of Russian life, as well as of human life at large. Pilnyak's prose is as much a part of European "modernism" as the works of his contemporaries Virginia Woolf and James Joyce.

Leonid Leonov (1899–), who earlier wrote in much the same "ornamentalist" manner as Pilnyak, developed a somewhat different style in the first of his many long novels, *The Thief* (*Vor*, 1927). It was, as Leonov himself pointed out, that of Dostoevsky. The "thief" is Mitka Vekshin, a Bolshevik war hero, whose guilt over the gratuitous killing of a White officer and disappointment at the prose of Soviet life under the New Economic Policy (NEP) have caused him to become the leader of a gang of thieves. The novel has an intricate plot, whose main axis is the hero's moral regeneration, and many characters – several of whom are recognizable variants on Dostoevskian ones. An extra twist is given the plot by the presence of Firsov, a writer and the author's alter ego, who is working on a novel about Vekshin and the other characters who populate the text. In spite of some good descriptive detail and plausible psychology in the minor characters, *The Thief* never reaches Dostoevsky's intensity, and at times comes uncomfortably close to an unintentional bathetic travesty of Dostoevsky's imagination.

During the period before 1934 genuine satire was still possible in the Soviet Union, and several writers excelled at it. Mikhail Zoshchenko (1895–1958), one of the Serapion Brothers, was for many years the most popular Russian writer in the Soviet Union, and among émigré readers too. His vignettes of everyday Soviet life, emphasizing its inequities, inconveniences, and absurdities, are told in the language of a Soviet *poluintelligent* (literally: "semi-intellectual"), i.e., a semiliterate philistine who has adjusted to the Soviet order. That philistine is usually the subject of the story also. Zoshchenko's language, a form of *skaz*, creates a humorous effect of absurd incongruity between the fact and the rhetoric used to report it. It also shields the author from the charge that he is lampooning the Soviet order: it is rather the "semi-intellectual's" unregenerate, petit-bourgeois view of it that he mocks, he would respond to his critics. The Soviet reader appreciated Zoshchenko's bathos as welcome relief from the pervasively heroic or militant tone of Soviet literature and public life, while the émigré or dissident saw in it an exposure of the Soviet system as a sham.

The team of Ilya Ilf and Eugene Petrov (pen-names of Ilya Fainzilberg, 1897–1937, and Eugene Petrovich Kataev, 1903–42) scored a huge success with their first joint effort, *Twelve Chairs* (*Dvenadtsat stulev*, 1928). Its plot – the chase for a treasure hidden in one of twelve chairs, each of which was sold to a different party – gave the authors a chance to create satirical scenes of Soviet life under the NEP. The hero, a crafty rogue named Ostap Bender, deals with a world of gullible plodders, dull bureaucrats, and greedy philistines with ironic nonchalance. In *The Golden Calf* (*Zolotoy telenok*, 1931), Bender decides that the simplest way to become a millionaire is to find a Soviet multi-millionaire and relieve him of one of his millions. He finds his man soon enough. The satire on Stalin's Russia under the first Five Year Plan in *The Golden Calf* is even sharper than the lampoon of Russia under the NEP in *Twelve Chairs*. *The Golden Calf* was received coldly by official Soviet criticism, but Ilf and Petrov remained popular. In 1935–6 they undertook a six-month automobile trip across the United States, described in *One-story America* (*Odnoetazhnaya Amerika*, 1936), a perceptive and entertaining travelogue. After Ilf's death of tuberculosis, Petrov wrote nothing of significance. He died in a plane crash as a war correspondent.

Other remarkable satirists of the NEP and Five Year Plan period were Valentin Kataev (1897–), whose novel *The Embezzlers* (*Rastratchiki*, 1927) describes the adventures of two employees of a Moscow state firm who go on a spree with embezzled money, and

Panteleymon Romanov (1885–1938), whose several novels, such as *Comrade Kislyakov* (*Tovarishch Kislyakov*, 1930; in English: *Three Pairs of Silk Stockings*, 1931), and short stories deal with aspects of the seamy side of the new society, such as the ignorance and boorishness of the new "proletarian" bureaucrats and the cynicism of their "fellow traveler" aides, or the appalling coarseness of sexual mores in the new society.

In an ambience where open discussion of contemporary reality was becoming progressively more difficult, historical fiction was bound to draw the attention of some serious writers. Alexey Nikolaevich Tolstoy (1883–1945), a "Change of landmarks" returnee to the Soviet Union in 1923, developed into a fine epic novelist, second perhaps only to Sholokhov. Of his two bulky prose epics, *The Way Through Hell* (*Khozhdenie po mukam*, 1921–40, in English: *The Road to Calvary*, 1923–45) depicts the fate of the Russian intelligentsia on the eve and during the years of the revolution, while the incomplete *Peter I* (*Petr I*, 1929–45) paints a panoramic picture of the great tsar's reign. Tolstoy follows the practice of his namesake in spreading the narrator's attention from the Olympian heights of the tsar and his entourage all the way down the social scale to a wretched convict driving piles into the swampy banks of the Neva river. Like Leo Tolstoy, too, he is a great "painter of the flesh," always ready with *le mot juste* to describe a sense impression or physical reaction. Thanks to his solid historical research, *Peter I* is remarkably rich in concrete detail. Altogether, Tolstoy succeeded in combining a realistic narrative with a noble and awe-inspiring image of Peter the Great – perhaps in conscious violation of historical veracity. It appears that Stalin admired Peter the Great, and also Ivan the Terrible, of whom Tolstoy also created a positive image in a play of that title (1943). *Peter I* was a great success and was made into a monumental film. It stimulated a flood of historical novels and films which marked the tendency toward a conservative, nationalist and militarist ideology on the eve of World War II.

Other historical novels of the period which deserve mention are *Tsushima* (1932–5) by Alexey Novikov-Priboy (1877–1944), a fictionalized documentary of the Russo-Japanese war of 1904–5; *The Ordeal of Sevastopol* (*Sevastopolskaya strada*, 1937–9) by Sergey Sergeev-Tsensky (1875–1958); and a series of novels dealing with high points of Russian literature by Olga Forsh (1873–1961), such as her Radishchev trilogy, *Jacobin Ferment* (*Yakobinsky zakvas*, 1932), *A Landed Lady of Kazan* (*Kazanskaya pomeshchitsa*, 1934), and *A Fateful Book* (*Pagubnaya kniga*, 1939).

The period of the first Five Year Plan (1928–32) saw the development of the canon of the "production novel," which was to become the flagship of socialist realism. Two radically new phenomena combined to create this canon. The first was the initiative of RAPP (which in this case was following ideas developed earlier by *Lef* and the constructivists) in sending teams of writers to building and production sites to acquire actual experience of labor and technical knowhow in the field, apply this knowledge in their fiction, and contribute to the nation's economic progress by giving proper credit to achievement and criticizing shortcomings. Soviet novels from this time on deal more with people at work than with their private lives. The other new development was the emergence of what Katerina Clark has called the "master plot" of the socialist realist novel. The plot is generated by the progress of work at an industrial plant, transportation facility, collective farm, research institute, etc. The actants are the positive hero(es) and/or heroine(s) who overcome all obstacles and lead the work at hand to a successful conclusion; the Party, which backs them and keeps a watchful eye on their progress; and various human as well as non-human actants, e.g. saboteurs and natural disasters, that place obstacles in their way. The role of an individual in the plot is determined by his/her social class. The hero(ine) is of proletarian (the rule) or peasant (the exception) background. Villains belong to a hostile social class: *kulaks*, whiteguardists, capitalists, or priests masquerading as honest Soviet citizens. Peasants and members of the intelligentsia are ideologically and morally labile. The better ones among them eventually follow the hero(ine)'s leadership. The more memorable "production novels" of the earlier years were actually quite interesting reading at the time because of their novelty, and may indeed have served as a catalyst in developing the consciousness of "Soviet man."

Marietta Shaginyan (1888–1982), a highly cultured, versatile, and inventive author who had previously written in various genres, including even the detective story, came up with *Hydro-*

central (*Gidrotsentral*, 1931), a carefully researched novel about a huge construction project. Fyodor Gladkov's *Energy* (*Energiya*, 1932–8) describes a similar project, as does Valentin Kataev's *Time Forward* (*Vremya vpered*, 1932). Kataev's novel, the story of a single action-packed day on a construction detail of a giant metallurgical plant in the Urals during which a team of concrete-casters breaks the world record for units finished in one shift, conveys the excitement of the first Five Year Plan without concealing the harsh conditions under which Soviet workers performed their feats of strength and endurance. *Time Forward* is populated by a host of credible characters, including even an American engineer who makes his contribution to the common effort (he also learns that his life's savings have been lost in a Chicago bank failure).

Mikhail Sholokhov's novel *Virgin Soil Upturned* deals with the forced collectivization of agriculture in the Don region. It follows the "master plot" of a socialist realist novel, but is honest in its approach and presents communists as well as their enemies as credible human beings. However, *Virgin Soil Upturned* lacks the beauty and pathos of Sholokhov's first novel. Perhaps this has to do with its subject matter: the revolution, bloody though it was, seemed to have some meaning and hence was the proper stuff for high tragedy; whereas the "liquidation of the *kulaks* as a class," just as cruel and bloody, was meaningless from the beginning, and so its chronicle could be at best an "ugly tragedy."

Leonid Leonov produced a series of novels which follow the "master plot," though the setting is different in each instance. In *Sot* (a place name, 1930), it is the construction site of a paper factory in the woods of the north; in *Skutarevsky* (1932) it is a scientific research institute; and in *Road to the Ocean* (*Doroga na okean*, 1935) it is a busy railroad depot. Leonov's novels are not so precise in their technical details as some of the better researched "production novels" of the period, but they have other virtues. With interesting plots and some credible psychology, they present the dilemma of the old intelligentsia under the Soviets with a certain honesty. If read from the viewpoint of Leonov's villains, his novels convey a sense of despair with a genuine ring.

Astonishingly, the period of the NEP and the first Five Year Plan produced some of the finest lyric poetry of the century. Even the activism of RAPP found expression in verse, as in the poetry of

Alexander Bezymensky (1898–1973), Mikhail Svetlov (1903–64), Vasily Kazin (1898–), and others. The poets of *Lef* were, if anything, even more directly inspired by "social commissions" (read: the latest *Pravda* editorial). Vladimir Mayakovsky and his able lieutenants Nikolay Aseev and Semyon Kirsanov (1906–72) produced versified journalism, propaganda, and public service messages, some of it technically first rate (ingenious rhymes, clever puns, whimsical conceits, catchy phrases, and driving rhythms). But they also made occasional forays into non-utilitarian poetry, sometimes with interesting results, as, for instance, when Mayakovsky explored the question of "the poet's place in the work force" (in "Conversation with a tax collector on poetry" ["Razgovor s fininspektorom o poezii"], 1927). Some other poems by Mayakovsky ask the same question and give the same answer: that the poet should serve society, but also that he should be accorded the respect due a skilled professional. This seemingly trite theme is treated with brilliance and verve in poems such as "Homeward bound" ("Domoy!," 1925), "To Sergey Esenin" ("Sergeyu Eseninu," 1926), and Mayakovsky's *Exegi monumentum*, "At the top of my voice" ("Vo ves golos," 1930). Kirsanov's versified utopian and science fiction is often ingenious and thought-provoking, for instance, "A last contemporary" ("Posledny sovremennik," 1930), "The golden age" ("Zolotoy vek," 1933), and "Poem about a robot" ("Poema o robote," 1934).

Among the constructivists, there were at least two major poets: Eduard Bagritsky (pen-name of Eduard Dzyubin, 1897–1934) and Ilya Selvinsky (real given name: Karl, 1899–1968), who practiced a pointedly functional approach to poetic composition, seeking to integrate every level of their text – sound, rhythm, imagery, lexicon, syntax – with its intended meaning. Both Bagritsky and Selvinsky used slang, argot, regionalisms, local color, the rhythms of folk poetry whenever a poem's theme demanded it. Bagritsky's "local color" was that of Odessa and the Ukrainian countryside. His *Lay of Opanas* (*Duma ob Opanase*, 1926), loosely patterned after the Ukrainian folk ballad (*duma*), tells the story of the peasant Opanas, who chose the wrong side in the civil war and paid for it with his life. When Bagritsky moved on from themes of the revolution to topics of the Five Year Plan, his poetry retained an air of genuine revolutionary romanticism.

486

Ilya Selvinsky travelled widely, pursued several different professions, participated in a polar expedition, and projected his varied experiences into his work. He was one of the first Soviet writers to do serious research toward his literary projects and to view composing poetry as a goal-directed, rational activity. Like Bagritsky, he adapted his language to the subject at hand, using technical jargon, thieves' cant, Odessa Yiddish, gypsy, and whatever other idiom was required. Selvinsky's best poetic work is the verse epic *The Ulyalaev Uprising* (*Ulyalaevshchina*, written in 1924, published in 1927), which describes the rout of a counter-revolutionary uprising by Communist forces.

OBERIU, too, produced two remarkable poets, Alexander Vvedensky (1904–41) and Nikolay Zabolotsky (1903–58). Vvedensky's absurdist verse, which deals with life, death, and time in a baffling, Dadaist manner, was never printed in his lifetime. It began to be published, in the west, in the 1970s. Like other modernist poets, including Zabolotsky, Vvedensky supported himself by writing for children. Zabolotsky scored a *succès d'estime* among connoisseurs of poetry with his first collection, *Columns* (*Stolbtsy*, 1929), though it displeased the literary establishment. His long allegoric poem *A Celebration of Agriculture* (*Torzhestvo zemledeliya*, 1933) was severely attacked as a lampoon upon collective farming (which it was not, at least not primarily), so that his *Second Book* (*Vtoraya kniga*, 1937), while still remarkable, contained mostly conventional and rather neo-classical nature poetry. Zabolotsky at his early best is at times a surrealist who will express the strangest kind of consciousness in an utterly straightforward and matter-of-fact tone. At times he is an expressionist who presents the hideous horror of the Soviet city in a pointedly unaffected, even brazen manner. In other poems Zabolotsky presents himself as a consummate parodic satirist, who initiates his audience into the world of Zoshchenko's Soviet philistine in sonorous Pushkinian iambs. And then there is Zabolotsky the metaphysical poet, who speaks of immortality, destiny, man and nature directly, concretely, and personally. His *Celebration of Agriculture* is, among other things, a condemnation of man's exploitation of nature and an expression of his longing to be a brother to all creatures. Zabolotsky is one of the major poets of the twentieth century whose greatness the Soviet literary establishment has still failed to recognize.

Of the many poets who belonged to no group, most gradually adjusted to the political climate and in the process ceased being poets. Such was the fate of one of the most talented Serapion Brothers, Nikolay Tikhonov, whose acmeist verse of the early 1920s had been fresh and vigorous. In the late 1920s Tikhonov turned to verse and prose reportage on the progress of "building socialism" in central Asia and other exotic places. Later he developed into a panegyrist of Stalin and became an important functionary in the literary establishment.

Boris Pasternak made some not entirely satisfactory attempts at narrative poetry on revolutionary subjects including *The Year 1905* (*Devyatsot pyaty god*, 1926) and *Lieutenant Schmidt* (*Leytenant Shmidt*, 1927). In his novel in verse *Spektorsky* (1931), which describes episodes of a poet's life before and after the revolution, Pasternak projected some of his own traits, attitudes and idiosyncrasies upon his hero. In 1932, stimulated by a new marriage and a journey to the Caucasus, Pasternak produced a new volume of verse, *Second Birth* (*Vtoroe rozhdenie*), which has some of the vigor and freshness of *My Sister, Life*, but very much less of the latter's provocative estrangement. After 1932 Pasternak no longer risked publishing his own verses, but preferred to work as a prolific translator of English, German, French, and Georgian poetry.

Anna Akhmatova was unable to publish any original poetry after 1922. She functioned as a translator, though, and did some valuable scholarly work on Pushkin. Her friend and fellow acmeist Osip Mandelshtam fared somewhat better. He published a collection, *Poems* (*Stikhotvoreniya*, 1928), which contained some new poems. Subsequently he brought out occasional poems in various periodicals until 1933. He also published a volume of essays, *On Poetry* (*O poezii*, 1928), and a collection of prose pieces entitled *The Egyptian Stamp* (*Egipetskaya marka*, 1928), after its lead story (the remaining pieces, sketches of Mandelshtam's childhood and adolescence, had appeared in 1925 under the title *The Noise of Time* (*Shum vremeni*). After 1933 Mandelshtam could not publish anything at all, and his late work had to wait until the 1960s for posthumous publication in the west.

Even Mandelshtam's published poetry of the period after *Tristia* (1922) shows that his poetic vision was expanding and changing.

While the old "nostalgia for world culture" remained a powerful stimulus, the poet's personal fate in a world that was becoming colder, more alien, and more menacing every day now moved to the foreground. The Parnassian clarity of the earlier period yielded to an enigmatic and cryptic manner. There is some indication that in Mandelshtam's late poetry *logos* (conscious rational meaning) is sometimes replaced by a futurist "word as such" which controls the poet's imagination.

Russian theater had experienced a stormy period of avant-garde activity in the early 1920s. The reaction against this movement ("Back to Ostrovsky!") was initiated as early as 1923 by the People's Commissar of Education, Anatoly Lunacharsky. However, theatrical life continued to be lively, even though the output of good new plays was so modest that the Soviet stage had to depend to a considerable extent on adaptations of successful novels, old as well as new, such as Eugene Zamyatin's hugely popular *The Flea* (*Blokha*, 1926), a dramatized version of Nikolay Leskov's story "The Lefthanded Craftsman," or Yury Olesha's *The Conspiracy of Feelings* (*Zagovor chuvstv*, 1929), a stage version of *Envy*.

The Moscow Art Theater under Konstantin Stanislavsky and Vladimir Nemirovich-Danchenko continued to cultivate its realist style, with some slight concessions to "social commission." The first Soviet plays added to its repertoire were Mikhail Bulgakov's *The Days of the Turbins* (*Dni Turbinykh*, 1926), a stage version of his novel *The White Guard* (*Belaya gvardiya*, 1924), and Vsevolod Ivanov's *Armored Train 14–69* (*Bronepoezd No. 14–69*, 1927), a stage version of his story of the same title (1922). In the 1930s the Moscow Art Theater had to stage a number of socialist realist propaganda pieces.

Until 1938 Vsevolod Meyerhold had his own theater, where he staged innovative performances in his expressionist manner of overstatement, distortion, and stylization, of classics such as Gogol's *The Inspector General* in 1926 and Griboedov's *Woe from Wit* in 1928, as well as of avant-garde Soviet plays by Mayakovsky, Olesha, Tretyakov, and Erdman. Meanwhile Alexander Tairov's "Chamber theater" cultivated a romantic style of "pure theater," pointedly opposed to Stanislavsky's "psychologism."

489

There were several other directors, in Moscow and in Leningrad, who also developed their own distinctive styles: Alexey Popov, Nikolay Okhlopkov, Nikolay Akimov, and others.

Soviet film was also creative until the early 1930s. Directors Leo Kuleshov, Sergei Eisenstein, Dziga Vertov, and Vsevolod Pudovkin, who pioneered various cinematographic devices, were closely allied with the avant-garde stage of Meyerhold and the literary avant-garde of *Lef*. Avant-garde writers such as Mayakovsky, Erdman, Aseev, Olesha, and Tretyakov, wrote film scenarios. In many instances, they employed film techniques in their fiction and plays. In the 1930s Soviet film and theater retreated, with only occasional exceptions, to the officially prescribed mediocrity of socialist realism.

Soviet drama lagged behind other literary genres, so much so that ambitious directors such as Meyerhold actively solicited plays from Soviet writers. The most interesting plays by far came from the avant-garde. Mayakovsky's satirical comedies *The Bedbug* (*Klop*) and *The Bathhouse* (*Banya*), staged by Meyerhold in 1929 and 1930 respectively, were savage attacks on emerging Soviet philistinism, met with official disapproval, and came into their own only after Stalin's death. They resemble Aristophanean political comedy in their inventiveness and verve, their penchant for the grotesque and absurd, their racy dialogue – and their absence of any real plot.

Mayakovsky's friend Sergey Tretyakov (1892–1939) was a consistent exponent of constructivism on the stage and screen. His play *Roar, China!* (*Rychi, Kitay!*, 1926) is the best example of what may be called "poster art." Another member of the *Lef* group, Nikolay Erdman (1902–70), scored a huge success with his riotous satire of life under the NEP, *The Mandate* (*Mandat*), staged by Meyerhold in 1925. His black comedy *The Suicide* (*Samouibiytsa*) went into rehearsal at both the Moscow Art and Meyerhold's theaters, but was then banned by the authorities.

Bulgakov's somewhat tamer comedies – *Zoyka's Apartment* (*Zoykina kvartira*, staged at the Vakhtangov theater, 1926–9) and *Crimson Island* (*Bagrovy ostrov*, staged at the Chamber theater, 1928–9) – still had enough satirical bite to be banned in 1929. In the 1930s only Bulgakov's dramatized version of Gogol's *Dead Souls* (first staged in 1932) and his phenomenally successful *The Days of the Turbins*, dealing with the dilemma of the educated Russian faced with the victory of Bolshevism, were seen on stage. A drama, *A Cabal of Hypocrites* (*Kabala svyatosh*) or *Molière* (*Moler*), which too obviously projected the Soviet playwright's own problems, was banned after only seven performances in 1936. A large portion of Bulgakov's work saw the light of day only in the 1960s.

Valentin Kataev's comedy *Squaring the Circle* (*Kvadratura kruga*, 1928) dealt with marital problems caused by the catastrophic housing shortage of the 1920s in a rather lighthearted manner. It enjoyed long runs all over the Soviet Union for many years.

The first Five Year Plan produced a crop of plays analogous to the "production novel." Nikolay Pogodin's first play in this manner, *Tempo* (*Temp*, 1929), deals with the construction of the gigantic Stalingrad tractor plant. Vladimir Kirshon (1902–38) wrote plays both about industrialization (*Humming Rails* [*Relsy gudeli*, 1927]), and the collectivization of agriculture (*Bread* [*Khleb*, 1930]). Alexander Afinogenov (1904–41) contributed *Eccentric* (*Chudak*, 1929), set in a paper factory, and *Fear* (*Strakh*, 1931), in which wreckers masquerading as honest Soviet scientists promote a theory that humans are motivated primarily by fear, but are fortunately unmasked and removed. In the context of the 1930s the play had a topicality which the author, a true communist, may not even have intended to give it.

Vsevolod Vishnevsky (1900–51) combined roles as a party activist and watchdog of political orthodoxy with that of a playwright. His rhetorical plays and film scenarios were unabashedly propagandistic, a typical example of "revolutionary romanticism." Vishnevsky's play *First Cavalry* (*Pervaya konnaya*, 1929) was a pointed response to and correction of Babel's negative image of Budyonny's Cossacks in *Red Cavalry*. *An Optimistic Tragedy* (*Optimisticheskaya tragediya*, 1933), a "classic" of the Soviet stage for many years, shows how a heroic woman commissar transforms a ragged band of marines into a communist fighting force which perishes for the cause of the revolution. *An Optimistic Tragedy* is formally akin to Bertolt Brecht's "epic theater," which influenced some other Soviet playwrights as well – Alexey Arbuzov, for example.

A resolution of the Central Committee of the Communist Party, "On the restructuring of literary and artistic organizations"

("O perestroyke literaturno-khudozhestvennykh organizatsiy"), dated 23 April 1932, reversed what had seemed to be an unstoppable trend toward the "hegemony" of RAPP. More and more members of the "Divide" group had defected to RAPP since 1929, and although it brought out two more miscellanies – *Contemporaries* (*Rovesniki*, 1930 and 1932) – and an anthology, the group's days were clearly numbered. *New Lef* had ceased publication in 1930 and Mayakovsky himself, after having abandoned it for a futile attempt to form a new organization, *Ref* ("Revolutionary front"), had applied for membership in RAPP in February of 1930, two months before his suicide.

Veniamin Kaverin's "Speech not delivered at the eighth anniversary of the order of the Serapion Brotherhood" of February 1929 merely sealed the *de facto* disintegration of that group. OBERIU had ceased to exist after the appearance of an article in April 1930 branding the *Oberiuty* as "class enemies." The Literary Center of Constructivists disbanded at about the same time. Only *Land of the Soviets*, organ of the "peasant writers," continued publication into 1932.

The resolution of 23 April ordered the dissolution of all existing literary organizations and the creation of a single Union of Soviet Writers (*Soyuz pisateley SSSR*). This meant, among other things, that there was no longer any distinction between "proletarians" and "fellow travelers."

The official reason for the party's decision was that the second Five Year Plan provided for the establishment of a classless society in the Soviet Union. Actually, the fact that some of the leaders of RAPP – and in particular their ideologues G. Lelevich and Leopold Averbakh – had connections with Leon Trotsky may have been more important. In any case, the party ideologues now proceeded to work out an esthetic theory and artistic method for the unified arts and letters of the Soviet Union. This task fell to a five-man commission, one of whose members was Stalin himself. The commission quickly agreed on the principles of socialist realism (*sotsialistichesky realizm*), a term first used by Ivan Gronsky, editor of *Izvestiya* (*News*), organ of the Soviet government, and chairman of the Organizing Committee of the Union of Soviet Writers, who wrote in May 1932: "The basic method of Soviet literature is the method of socialist realism." Subsequently Stalin himself pointed out that socialist realism meant "the truthful description of that which leads life toward socialism." The task of determining what precisely "leads life toward socialism" was left to the party, certainly for all practical purposes. In theory the old idea – formulated by Belinsky and later by Plekhanov and Lunacharsky – that a true artist would unfailingly side with truth and that truth could not possibly be on the side of reaction, was allowed to stand. It permitted one to embrace such writers of the past as Pushkin or Turgenev, who had belonged to the upper classes, for after all they had been, in their own day and age, "on the side of progress."

As for the present, socialist realism was based on the principles of "typicality," "historicism," "ideological commitment," and, first and foremost, "partymindedness" (*partiynost*). "Typicality" meant the exclusion from literature (and from art at large) of the fortuitous or exceptional, a theoretical principle certainly compatible with traditional realist esthetics. In practice, it meant that whatever the Party decreed to be "atypical" of Soviet reality was to be excluded from literature. "Historicism" suggested that reality should be perceived in its revolutionary development, which meant that Soviet reality was to be presented as moving vigorously toward socialism, regardless of the actual facts. "Ideological commitment" required that a work of literature approach life seriously and armed with the right ideology (to be determined by the party). Finally, "partymindedness," officially derived from Lenin's article "Party organization and party literature" (1905), demanded that the writer's position coincide with the party's. Obviously, if it differed, the party would offer him guidance. The rationale behind "partymindedness" was that the party, being the vanguard of the proletariat, the most progressive class, had to be in sole possession of the truth of history.

The principles of socialist realism were enunciated at the first plenary session of the Organizing Committee of the Union of Soviet Writers (29 October–3 November 1932) and conveyed to the assembled writers of the Soviet Union at the first all-USSR Congress of Writers in August 1934. The keynote address was given by Andrey Zhdanov, Stalin's right hand man in cultural affairs, who told his audience that Comrade Stalin had described them as "engineers of human minds" and urged them to depict life not merely in terms of "objective reality," but rather "in its revolutionary development." The Congress heard a great deal of genuine debate, honest if cautiously worded opinions by several prominent writers such as Olesha, Shklovsky, and Vsevolod Ivanov, and controversial statements by Nikolay Bukharin and Karl Radek, leading party functionaries who were soon to be purged by Stalin. Nevertheless, the Congress made it quite clear that "modernism," Russian or foreign, was henceforth prohibited, that contemporary writers should learn from the classics of nineteenth-century realism and not from innovative western writers such as Joyce or Kafka, and that the party would henceforth watch literature very closely. Signs of a turn toward Russian patriotism and militarism were also apparent.

In the same year Stalin's great purges began; they continued until 1938. Hundreds of writers either perished or spent years in prison or labor camps. All too many biographies in the Soviet *Concise Literary Encyclopedia* of 1962–75 (*Kratkaya literaturnaya entsiklopediya*) end with the formula "illegally repressed, posthumously rehabilitated." Among the victims of the Great Terror were many loyal communists. Members of the Proletarian Culture movement perished, as did the ideologues of RAPP, Lelevich and Averbakh, and of the "Divide," Lezhnev and Voronsky. Among the "peasant writers" purged were Nikolay Klyuev, Sergey Klychkov, and Paul Vasilev. The avant-garde lost the great director Meyerhold and the playwright Tretyakov. The toll was heavy among the OBERIU group: Vvedensky, Kharms and Zabolotsky (the latter survived years in various labor camps to return a sick and broken man). Other prominent victims were Babel, Mandelshtam, Pilnyak, Ivan Kataev, Artyom Vesyoly, the playwright Kirshon and the critic and literary scholar Pereverzev. Many writers not arrested were reduced to inactivity and disappeared from the literary scene for long periods: for example, Erdman, Platonov, and Bulgakov.

Ironically, while so many loyal communists perished, several writers of less than impeccable communist credentials survived and prospered: Ilya Erenburg, Alexey Tolstoy, and the former "Serapions" Fedin, Tikhonov, Kaverin, and Vsevolod Ivanov. Some writers once associated with *Lef* who ought to have been highly vulnerable as "bourgeois modernists" did very well, because Stalin had personally decreed that Mayakovsky was the greatest Soviet poet. Nikolay Aseev received a Stalin prize in 1941 for his long poem *Mayakovsky Begins* (*Mayakovsky nachinaetsya*, 1940), which celebrated Mayakovsky as a poet of the revolution and revived his memory by incorporating many direct and indirect echoes of his works.

Soviet prose of the Stalin era was dominated by the socialist realist novel, mostly of the "production" variety. Its most widely publicized work was, however, an autobiographic novel, *How the Steel was Tempered* (*Kak zakalyalas stal*, 1932–4) by Nikolay Ostrovsky (1904–36). Ostrovsky had joined the Komsomol (Communist youth organization) at fifteen and fought in the Polish campaign of 1920. He then held leading positions in the Ukrainian Komsomol. When an incurable illness blinded and paralyzed him, he dictated the story of his life (told in the third person, with the hero named Paul Korchagin), which was published as a novel. *How the Steel was Tempered* is plotless, fragmentary, cliché-ridden, and stylistically awkward. But it embodies the author's boundless devotion to his cause, his unflinching courage, and his utter lack of doubt about his values. The book has been printed in millions of copies and translated into every major world language. For generations now it has been a school text everywhere within the orbit of Soviet influence.

Another much publicized and inspirational author of the period was Anton Makarenko (1888–1939), an educator who had worked with juvenile delinquents since 1920. His *A Pedagogic Poem* (*Pedagogicheskaya poema*, in English: *The Road to Life*, 1955), serialized in 1933–5, describes, with much vivid detail, Makarenko's work at the Gorky colony for juvenile delinquents. Its leitmotif is the redemptive power of collective labor. It became an instant classic. Makarenko's *A Book for Parents* (*Kniga dlya roditeley*, 1937) was also a great success. In it, too, Makarenko's perceptive vignettes of family life and clear psychological analysis showed him to be a natural storyteller. His short novels *Honor* (*Chest*, 1937–8) and *Flags on Towers* (*Flagi na bashnyakh*, 1938) were less successful.

Meanwhile, most Soviet writers were busy grinding out more novels and short-stories of the socialist realist "production" type. *Tanker "Derbent"* (1938) by Yury Krymov (pen-name of Yury Beklemishev, 1908–41) describes how, under the leadership of a communist activist, an undisciplined tanker crew is transformed into an efficient collective. Ilya Erenburg's novels *The Second Day* (*Den vtoroy*, 1935) and *Without Pausing for Breath* (*Ne perevodya dykhaniya*, 1937), whose titles speak for themselves (the "second day of creation" is Stalin's second Five Year Plan), both deal with industrial construction in outlying districts of the Soviet Union.

Next to Sholokhov's *Virgin Soil Upturned*, Fyodor Panfyorov's (1896–1960) lengthy epic novel *Bruski* (1928–37) was the principal socialist realist work dealing with the Russian countryside. It reports how Bruski, an estate once owned by a nobleman and later by a *kulak*, is after some reverses converted into a model collective farm, mainly through the efforts of Kiril Zhdarkin, a communist activist. *Bruski*, unlike most socialist realist novels, had the one virtue of authenticity. While its characters do not come to life, least of all Zhdarkin, it presents the facts and problems of Russian village life faithfully. *Bruski* was initially a great success with the public and critics alike, but was later criticized for its poor literary craftsmanship.

Among the successful socialist realist novels of the 1930s which also earned critical praise there were some not of the "production" type at all. *Our Friends* (*Nashi znakomye*, 1936), the first novel of Yury German (1910–68), tells the story of an ordinary Soviet girl's progress through various mistakes (two bad marriages, even crime) to attain a useful and fulfilled life and a happy marriage to an officer of state security, who had crossed her path repeatedly before. The novel appealed to the public because it presented ordinary, unheroic characters (with the exception of the officer) and satisfied the critics because its moral was that political indoctrination and a work ethic cured aimlessness in life.

Solitude (*Odinochestvo*, 1936) and its sequel *Lawfulness* (*Zakonomernost*, 1937) by Nikolay Virta (1906–) mirrored actual events of the recent past: a peasant uprising against the Soviet regime in Tambov province in 1920, and the sinister activities of wreckers in the same region in the late 1920s. As in some other socialist realist works, the villains, with some historical personages among them, emerge as real human beings whose feelings and actions seem understandable and with whom many contemporary readers could secretly identify. At the same time, Soviet critics were pleased since Soviet "lawfulness" triumphed and the villains were brought to justice. *Solitude* won Virta a Stalin prize in 1941.

Another successful newcomer to Soviet fiction was Vasily Grossman (1905–64). A chemical engineer in the Donets basin mining region, Grossman began his career with stories from the life of coal miners. The support of Maxim Gorky led him to become a professional writer. His four-part epic novel *Stepan Kolchugin* (1937–40) follows the path of a young worker in a mining town through revolutionary activity, civil war, and reconstruction.

Altogether, the Stalin years were a period of long epic novels, most of which were artistically unremarkable and most probably did not accomplish much as inspirational literature either. Some of the writers who produced the most conformist socialist realist novels, such as Panfyorov, Virta, and Grossman, were among the first to take advantage of the "thaw" after Stalin's death to present an altogether different view of Soviet life. This suggests that much of socialist realist fiction of the 1930s was an exercise in mutual deception on the part of everyone involved.

Rather the same is true of the poetry of this era. Perhaps the most talented newcomer to Soviet poetry in the 1930s was Alexander Tvardovsky (1910–71). His verse epic (almost novel size) *The Land of Muraviya* (*Strana Muraviya*, 1934–6), which won him his first Stalin prize (1941), tells the story of Nikita Morgunok, a peasant who after a long journey in search of the promised land of Muraviya finally decides that his only chance for a good life is the Soviet collective farm. While the ostensible moral of the tale is the proper one, of course, the narrator's – and probably the reader's – sympathy is with the hapless Morgunok's quest for his own plot of land, and quite possibly with the plight of some other characters doomed to extinction in the land of the Soviets: exiled and dispossessed *kulaks*, an itinerant priest, and an old man who still believes in God. Tvardovsky's poem compares favorably with Nikolay Nekrasov's nineteenth-century classic *Who Can Be Happy and Free in Russia?* Its verse has the easy lilt of the village ditty, or *chastushka*. Its dialogue and often the narrative too are in a natural peasant idiom, racy and sometimes pithy. All in all, *The Land of Muraviya* is a felicitous mixture of "ethnographic" realism, folksy humor, whimsical imagination, and latent heartbreak.

Paul Vasilev (1910–37), another very talented poet who gravitated toward the epic genre and themes of peasant life, was less fortunate than Tvardovsky. Of Siberian Cossack stock, he led an unsteady life, traveling a lot, and finally perished in the purges, even though he tried to adapt his poetry to the political climate. Vasilev had a knack of writing poetry in free and quickly changing rhythms, a skill he used effectively in his epic poems on the life of Siberian Cossacks before and after the revolution: *The Salt Rebellion* (*Solyanoy bunt*, 1933–4), *Song of the Fall of the Cossack Commonwealth* (*Pesnya o gibeli kazachego voyska*, 1929–30), and *The Kulaks* (*Kulaki*, 1933–34). Critics charged Vasilev with seeing events from the kulak's rather than from the landless peasant's point of view, the former being developed with empathy and power while the latter remained lifeless. Vasilev is at his best in colorful descriptions of the joy and prosperity of village life, a strength hardly apt to endear him to party critics. Vasilev's language, imagery, and rhythms are often close to those of folk poetry. But his stylization is more complex than, say, Tvardovsky's and occasionally reminds one of Klyuev, or even of the "primitivism" of Khlebnikov. Like so many others, Vasilev was "posthumously rehabilitated," and a collection of his works appeared in 1968.

In the 1930s a general tendency toward a simple and singable lyric style emerged which carried over into the war years. Some older poets adopted it and some new names came to the fore. Mikhail Svetlov (1903–64), whose romantic revolutionary ballad "Grenada" (1926) had made this "poet of the Komsomol" a celebrity, scored another success with his "Song of Kakhovka" ("Pesnya o Kakhovke," 1935). Alexey Surkov (1899–), whose career as a literary and party functionary was more impressive than his poetry, responded to the new wave of patriotism with several collections of martial songs, such as *Attack* (*Nastuplenie*, 1932), *The Last War* (*Poslednyaya voyna*, 1934), and *Home of the Brave* (*Rodina muzhestvennykh*, 1935). Vasily Lebedev-Kumach (1898–1948), Mikhail Isakovsky (1900–73), and Stepan Shchipachov (1899–) provided the Soviet public with lyrics for popular songs about love, nature, the motherland, and Stalin. The most popular song of the 1930s, "Song of the Motherland" ("Pesnya o rodine"), which asserted that life in the Soviet Union was "getting more joyous every day" and credited the Stalin Constitution for that, was authored by Lebedev-Kumach. Isakovsky succeeded in combining old-fashioned romantic love with official patriotism: "Let the soldier watch over the Motherland, and Katyusha will watch over their love," said his song "Katyusha," one of the more popular works of the 1930s. Shchipachov actually managed an ode to the gigantic "Palace of the Soviets," which Stalin planned but never built. A profusion of such poems by these and many other poets combined the mood and the vocabulary of the prerevolutionary popular song, a combination of folk song and post-romantic poetry, with a distinctly new Soviet mentality.

The drama of the Stalin era lagged behind even the modest achievements of the other genres. This somber epoch of fear and hardship produced primarily innocuous comedies in which the most recent directives of the government, such as a new emphasis on the integrity of the family, were dramatized. The leading socialist realist playwright was Nikolay Pogodin (pen-name of Stukalov, 1900–62), who had started his career with several Five Year Plan "production plays." Pogodin's works are loosely structured, mix melodrama with unpretentious humor, and might qualify as "documentary naturalism" if they did not contain the insincere clichés of all socialist realism. Pogodin did have a stage sense, and some of his plays were genuinely popular at the Moscow Art theater and elsewhere. *Aristocrats* (*Aristokraty*, 1934) features scenes from the construction of the White Sea–Baltic canal, one of Stalin's most useless and murderous projects, which claimed countless thousands of victims. Pogodin's play describes a ragged band of convicts, identified in the playbill as "bandits, thieves, prostitutes, fanatics, kulaks, etc.," which is converted into a disciplined work force under the leadership of dedicated guards, identified as officers of the Cheka, the political police. Among Pogodin's many other plays, his trilogy on Lenin and the revolution, *The Man with a Rifle* (*Chelovek s ruzhyom*, 1937), *Kremlin Chimes* (*Kremlevskie kuranty*, 1941), and *The Third Pathétique* (*Tretya pateticheskaya*, 1959), earned him high official praise and state prizes.

Alexander Afinogenov, like other writers who had been associated with the proletarian culture movement, had trouble with the party, from which he was expelled in 1937, but unlike many others he was allowed to continue writing. His play *Distant Point* (*Dalyokoe* [a place name], 1936), the simple record of twenty-four hours at a small Siberian railway station, was a great success. Afinogenov managed to write a play about the early days of the war, *On the Eve* (*Nakanune*, 1941), before he was killed in an air raid on Moscow.

Alexey Arbuzov (1908–), actor, director, and playwright, first came to public notice with *Tanya* (1939), which has features of the "epic theater" characteristic of Arbuzov and common in the Soviet theater generally. The play consists of a sequence of scenes from the life of a Soviet woman, the first of which presents her as a callow student, and the last as a mature physician.

Leonid Leonov's plays, such as *The Orchards of Polovchansk* (*Polovchanskie sady*, 1936–8) and *The Wolf* (*Volk*, 1938), have much in common with his novels. His characters, especially the negative ones, are often complex and "Dostoevskian," certainly more interesting than those of Pogodin or Afinogenov. Also, Leonov is more consistent than other playwrights of his generation in his use of symbolic detail (after the fashion of Ibsen or Chekhov) and basing his plots on credible psychological conflicts. Leonov's stage effects are accordingly based on mood rather than on situation.

The plays of Eugene Shvarts (1896–1958) are in a very special category. Shvarts was associated with the Leningrad Children's theater and the State Children's Publishing House beginning in the 1920s. Among his more than a dozen dramatic works are some which, while ostensibly written for children or adolescents and actually staged at the Children's theater, could easily be understood as spirited satires on Stalin and the totalitarian society which he had created. *The Naked King* (*Goly korol*, 1934), *The Shadow* (*Ten*, 1940), and *The Dragon* (*Drakon*, 1943–4) are fairy tale plays, the first two based on tales by Hans Christian Andersen, and *The Dragon* on the legend of Lancelot and the dragon. However, the thrusts against Soviet reality in these plays are obvious. The dragon, in fact, has some of Stalin's mannerisms – his fondness for "enthusiastic statistics," for example – and the good burghers in all these plays behave exactly like Soviet citizens of the 1930s. The amazing fact that *The Shadow* and *The Dragon* were actually staged in Stalin's lifetime, though pulled off the boards after a few performances, may be explained by the circumstance that no censor dared to recognize the satire for what it was. Shvarts's plays are brilliant by any standards, are immensely entertaining, and have been staged with great success after Stalin's death.

Shvarts was by no means the only talented writer to devote most of his energies to literature for children. The poet Samuil Marshak (1887–1964), an excellent translator of English poetry, organized the State Children's Publishing House (*Detgiz*) and founded several children's magazines in the 1920s. He attracted many major writers and poets to this field, including such members of the OBERIU group as Kharms, Vvedensky, and Zabolotsky. Marshak himself wrote fairy tales, songs, riddles, and plays for children. Marshak's best poems for children have a lilt as well as a quaint whimsy which makes them enjoyable even to adults.

Korney Chukovsky (pen-name of Korneychukov, 1882–1969) was, like Marshak, an excellent translator of Anglo-American literature (Whitman, Mark Twain, Kipling, and many others). He also wrote a great deal on the theory of translation and was a critic of great versatility. But much of his fame rests on his verse fairy tales for children and his work in child psychology. His book *From Two to Five* (*Ot dvukh do pyati*), initially published under the title *Small Children* (*Malenkie deti*, 1928), ran through more than twenty editions and was translated into many languages.

Yet another writer of talent who wrote mostly for children and adolescents was Leo Kassil (1905–70), who had started his writing career as a contributor to *New Lef*. Kassil, who had a background in the sciences, also wrote articles on new developments in science and technology for *Izvestiya*. In his fiction he moved from stories depicting the coming of the Soviet order through the eyes of a child to stories addressed directly to children. His felicitous combining of fantasy and reality, a positive moral message, and gentle humor made him popular with generations of young readers. Yet some of Kassil's "fairy tales" can be and have been read as bold satires on Stalin and his reign of terror. For instance, one of these tales describes how the formerly happy kingdom of Sinegoriya (Bluemount) came under the rule of the stupid and wicked Fanfaron, master of all the winds. Fanfaron's winds blew into every nook and corner and reported to him every word spoken by his subjects. Previously, Sinegoriya had prided itself on its gardeners, mirror makers, and tinsmiths. Fanfaron orders the gardeners to grow nothing but dandelions. He prohibits the making of mirrors altogether, so that people cannot see their misery or Fanfaron his own ugly face. The tinsmiths are ordered to make nothing but weather vanes so that people can always tell which way the wind is blowing. People who disobey Fanfaron are punished by being thrown into a fan, where they receive a drafty ventilation treatment. As in the case of Shvarts's plays, the fact that such pieces actually saw print in Stalin's time can only be explained by the censors' reluctance to recognize their satirical subtext.

It is characteristic of Soviet literature that authors gravitate toward themes not immediately affected by or subject to ideology. In the 1930s that meant the themes of childhood, the more distant past, the world of nature, and the sphere of outright fantasy. Also, readers would be inclined to favor works of this kind as relief from the constant pressure of ideological indoctrination. Some authors who moved in these channels have been or will be discussed in other contexts, but certain ones will be mentioned here since they do not conveniently fit any classification used in this chapter.

Alexander Grin (pen-name of Grinevsky, 1880–1932) is the author of novels and short stories set in a wholly imaginary exotic world of adventure, romantic emotion, and existential alienation. Grin, who died destitute and ignored by Soviet critics, was posthumously attacked for his indifference to Soviet reality during the period of Andrey Zhdanov's stewardship of Russian literature after World War II, but his works have survived better than most socialist realist fiction of the 1920s and 1930s. Since the 1960s there has been a good deal of interest in Grin, both in the Soviet Union and in the west.

Mikhail Prishvin (1873–1954), whose stories and sketches of nature and animal life in the far north attracted favorable attention even before the revolution, continued to write in the same vein, although critics of the 1920s and 1930s accused him of "escaping" from contemporary problems. He traveled all over the Soviet Union and wrote about local life and nature in rich lyric prose. Prishvin's narrative manner vaguely resembles Remizov's: both are great masters of the lyric prose miniature. But his use of Russian folklore is more straightforward, and his entire outlook on life is simpler and more cheerful than Remizov's. The philosophy which consistently informs Prishvin's whole œuvre is a pantheist *reverentia vitae*, a serene faith in the goodness of life, and a courageous acceptance of pain and loss. In the 1920s Prishvin started his lengthy autobiographic novel *The Chain of Kashchey* (*Kashcheeva tsep*, 1923–54; from Kashchey the Deathless, a mythic figure of Russian folklore, hence "The Great Chain of Being"), on which he continued to work until his death. It is noteworthy that Prishvin's works were published all throughout the years of Stalin's reign. Their popularity suggests that an "escape" into the timeless world of nature never lost its attraction to many Soviet minds and that its strong comeback in the "country prose" of the post-Stalin period merely continued an existing strain of sensibility.

The creative profile of Konstantin Paustovsky (1892–1968) resembles Prishvin's, but Paustovsky's thematic range is broader. The title of his first novel was *Romantics* (*Romantiki*, written 1916–23, published 1935). He wrote historical and exotic fiction, and also essays on art, music, and literature. Paustovsky entered literature before the revolution but became well known only during the Soviet period. His apolitical novels, stories, and sketches reflect a romantic view of life and nature. Like Prishvin, he traveled widely and projected his impressions in his stories, such as "Kara-Bugaz" (1933) and "Colchis" ("Kolkhida," 1934). He also wrote a great deal about the simple life in and with nature. While Prishvin, himself a passionate hunter, wrote hunting sketches, Paustovsky, an angler, wrote a cycle of stories and sketches about recreational fishing, *Summer Days* (*Letnie dni*, 1937). Paustovsky came fully into his own only after Stalin's death, when he was recognized as one of the leading living Russian writers.

Stalin's great terror ended by 1939. While not many of those already arrested were released, there were few new arrests. The country was preparing for war, of which it had a brief but bloody preview in the war against Finland in the winter of 1939–40. Paradoxically, the imminence of war brought with it a general relaxation of ideological pressure. The reorientation from class struggle to patriotism, national pride, and other conservative values, which had actually begun around 1936, was a relief to most, especially after "proletarian" activists had been eliminated *en masse* in the purges. The anti-religious campaign which had peaked in the early 1930s was relaxed, and films would now show Orthodox priests praying and fighting for the Motherland.

Once the war had started, Soviet literature immediately supported the war effort, as writers became war correspondents or, if they stayed at home, concentrated on patriotic topics. As Boris

Pasternak recalls in the epilogue to *Doctor Zhivago*, to fight in the war or to contribute to the war effort in some way was for many Soviet intellectuals a relief, because for once they were engaged in a meaningful activity whose goal – the defeat of the German invaders – they could sincerely endorse. Of course the war affected the lives of many writers directly. Some fought in it, Emmanuil Kazakevich and Victor Nekrasov, for example. Some were killed in the war: Arkady Gaydar (1904–41), Yury Krymov, and Alexander Afinogenov. Some were evacuated to distant points of the Soviet Union, for example Anna Akhmatova and Marina Tsvetaeva (the latter committed suicide when she found herself alone and helpless in a small town in northeastern Russia). Some were caught in the siege of Leningrad: Olga Berggolts and Vera Inber. Some found themselves in German-occupied territory and chose to stay in the west, eventually forming the "second wave of emigration": the philosopher and critic Sergey Askoldov (1871–1945), Dmitry Klenovsky (1893–1976), Yury Ivask (1907–86), Boris Filippov (1905–), Ivan Elagin (1918–), and many others.

World War II produced a veritable flood of literature, as virtually every writer, poet, and playwright felt obliged to make some contribution, and those who ventured to publish anything not directly or positively related to the Soviet war effort were sharply attacked by reviewers. Some major writers suffered such criticism. In 1943, at the height of the war, the journal *October* published two installments of Mikhail Zoshchenko's novel *Before Sunrise* (*Pered voskhodom solntsa*) but then discontinued it without an immediate explanation. There were some angry reviews, and a few years later Zoshchenko paid dearly for his venture. *Before Sunrise* contains absolutely no anti-Soviet, or in fact any ideological material. It deals with the author's personal life, specifically with his chronic depression. Apparently, this work in the style of a confession was meant to show how the author eventually overcame his depression after rejecting Freudian psychoanalysis and applying the materialist "conditioned reflex" theory of the Russian physiologist Ivan Pavlov. What appeared in 1943 was a series of brief vignettes from the author's life which he felt contained pointers toward the solution of his problem. The outrage which the publication created was generated entirely by the fact that Zoshchenko had dared to be concerned with his personal difficulties while the nation was fighting the "Great Fatherland War."

A similar fate befell Konstantin Fedin, for the second volume of his literary reminiscences, *Vanishing St. Petersburg* (*Ukhodyashchy Peterburg*, 1944), was violently attacked for being "objective" (a derogatory term in socialist realist parlance, the opposite of "partyminded") and "detached," while the country was at war. Fedin's book was taken from bookstores and libraries, and eventually even the first volume of his reminiscences, *Gorky Amidst Us* (*Gorky sredi nas*, 1943), also came under attack for allegedly misrepresenting Gorky's views. Fedin, however, survived these difficulties much better than Zoshchenko, and his first work to appear immediately after the war, the novel *Early Joys* (*Pervye radosti*, 1946), again had nothing to do with World War II.

Other established writers did their best to support the war effort. Mikhail Sholokhov contributed a celebrated essay "The science of hatred" ("Nauka nenavisti," 1942), and published a few chapters of a war novel, *They Fought for Their Country* (*Oni srazhalis za Rodinu*), which remained unfinished, to nobody's great regret. Alexander Fadeev produced one of the better war novels, *The Young Guard* (*Molodaya gvardiya*, 1945), which deals with the underground resistance movement in a Ukrainian town. The heroes are schoolboy members of the Komsomol. The action of the novel is suspenseful, the characters, both Russian and German, are vividly drawn, and Fadeev's use of significant detail gives the whole a ring of truth. The novel received high praise when it first appeared, but later it was pointed out to Fadeev that he neglected to emphasize the leadership of the party in the resistance movement, so in 1951 he was obliged to make significant revisions in it.

Leonid Leonov contributed several war plays, to be discussed later, and a short novel, *The Taking of Velikoshumsk* (*Vzyatie Velikoshumska*, 1944), which follows the example of Leo Tolstoy in describing a battle from several different vantage points: that of the commander of the Soviet tank corps which takes Velikoshumsk, that of a tank crew which plays a decisive role in the final assault, and some local civilians who witness the action.

The war fiction based on immediate experience naturally came from writers of the younger generation who either saw action or were close to it. Several of them found their niches in Soviet literature through a war novel. Such was the novel *Days and Nights* (*Dni i nochi*, 1944) by Konstantin Simonov (1915–79), a journalist before the war and a war correspondent for *Red Star* (*Krasnaya zvezda*), the organ of the Red Army, during the war. *Days and Nights* is conventional and undistinguished as fiction, but its account of the battle of Stalingrad is vivid and apparently quite accurate. Simonov, a *littérateur* of modest gifts, went on to make a spectacular career as an author and functionary.

In the Trenches of Stalingrad (*V okopakh Stalingrada*, written in 1945, published in 1946) by Victor Nekrasov (1911–87), a much better novel than Simonov's, also launched the career of its author and brought him a Stalin prize in 1947. *In the Trenches of Stalingrad* is not only an honest account of the great battle from the viewpoint of those who fought in it, but also presents Soviet officers and soldiers as credible individuals. "Acts of heroism" are performed by patently unheroic individuals in a thoroughly unheroic manner. Nekrasov also went on to a distinguished career as a writer, but unlike Simonov's, it did not earn him the applause of the party, which he joined in 1944. Nekrasov eventually was expelled from the party and left the Soviet Union in 1974.

Emmanuil Kazakevich (1913–62) wrote in Yiddish before the war, fought in the war with distinction, and switched to Russian when he began to use his war experiences in fiction. His first Russian story, "The Star" ("Zvezda," 1947), was an immediate success, but some of his subsequent works, such as the story "Two in the Steppe" ("Dvoe v stepi," 1948), were criticized for excessive "naturalism" and "psychologizing." Kazakevich apparently took note of this criticism and avoided these elements in his novel *Spring on the Oder River* (*Vesna na Odere*, 1949), which won him a Stalin prize. Kazakevich stayed with the theme of man under extreme stress in a combat situation until the end of his life.

The war also produced a veritable flood of patriotic and martial poetry, most of it formulaic and cliché-ridden or else, whenever it described a soldier and his faithful girl back home, maudlin and pseudo-folksy. Alexander Tvardovsky once more performed the *tour de force* of producing poetry which had all these traits and yet was fresh, vigorous, and inspiring. His epic poem *Vasily Tyorkin* (serially published 1942–5) chronicles the day-to-day experiences of a simple Russian front line soldier, from the dark days of retreat, hardship, and misery to the ultimate victory. Vasily Tyorkin, a resourceful and sprightly sort, became a much beloved folk hero and earned Tvardovsky his second Stalin prize (1946). The secret of Tvardovsky's art, beside his easy rhythms, is his virtuosic command of colloquial Russian and his unerring tact in staying on the "right" side of the propaganda line of the moment without telling an outright lie, while also propounding as much of the truth as was at all possible under the current circumstances.

Several other poets also won a certain popularity during the war, though a popularity due to officially sponsored promotion. The versatile Konstantin Simonov produced several poems which were often recited and quoted during the war, for example, "Wait for me" ("Zhdi menya"), a poem in which a front line soldier addresses his beloved back home asking her to wait for him even after everyone else has given up hope of his return. Alexey Surkov (1899–1983) also produced a number of popular war songs, such as "Song of the bold" ("Pesnya smelykh") and "Song of the defenders of Moscow" ("Pesnya zashchitnikov Moskvy").

Two women poets who underwent the terrible siege of Leningrad wrote war poetry more memorable than that of either Simonov or Surkov. Vera Inber (1890–1972), a former constructivist, produced a long poem, *Pulkovo* [an astronomic observatory near Leningrad] *Meridian* (*Pulkovsky meridian*, 1942–6), portions of which are a genuinely moving evocation of the cruel suffering of the siege years. Olga Berggolts (1910–75) had published several books of poetry in the 1930s, but it was the poetry which she wrote during the years of the siege, when she also worked as a commentator with Radio Leningrad, that vaulted her into the first rank of Soviet poets. The poems of *Leningrad Notebook* (*Leningradskaya tetrad*, 1942), *Leningrad* (1944), and *Your Road* (*Tvoy put*, 1945), classical in their form and simple in their outlook, are quite literally a lyric diary of the siege, sometimes quite personal, sometimes reacting to the news of the day, sometimes inspired to praise the heroism of the defenders or the great city they were defending. Berggolts's subdued lyricism contrasts favorably with the patriotic rhetoric of most of her poetic colleagues, including Nikolay Tikhonov, who also devoted several poems to the siege of Leningrad. In his *poema Kirov is with Us* (*Kirov s nami*, 1941) he has

Kirov, head of the Communist Party of Leningrad who was assassinated in 1934, inspecting the city in spirit. The very choice of this device smacks of insincere rhetoric, since it was an open secret that Kirov had fallen victim to a power struggle within the party, and perhaps to Stalin himself, rather than to a counter-revolutionary plot, as the official version had it.

The general relaxation of ideological pressure during the war caused some poets who had fallen silent in the 1930s to appear in print again. Boris Pasternak came out with two collections of new poems, *On Early Trains* (*Na rannikh poezdakh*, 1943) and *Expanse of the Earth* (*Zemnoy prostor*, 1945), which surprised critics by their markedly new manner. As it turned out later, Pasternak had decisively turned his back upon his former "modernist" manner and was now intent upon conveying the truth of life as he perceived it in pointedly simple verse. While some admirers of Pasternak's talent regretted this shift, most reviewers welcomed it, though they still found Pasternak's reaction to the war too idiosyncratic.

Anna Akhmatova, who had been silent as a poet even longer than Pasternak, published several poems in the journal *Star* in 1940; in that same year a collection of her poetry, *From Six Books* (*Iz shesti knig*), containing some poems not previously published, also appeared. During the war Akhmatova was evacuated to central Asia, where a volume of her poetry was published (in Tashkent) in 1943. She wrote some patriotic poetry, better than most, though generally not up to her standards. Altogether, it was clear that she had lost none of her creative power. However, some of her most significant poetry would have to await more propitious times to reach an audience.

Soviet playwrights also concentrated on the war, with the prolific and versatile Simonov leading the way. His play *Russian People* (*Russkie lyudi*, 1942), set partly on the Russian side of the front and partly in occupied territory, is intended to demonstrate the self-effacing patriotism of ordinary Russian people. The plot is melodramatic and predictable. A more interesting play was Alexander Korneychuk's *The Front* (*Front*, 1942), which described a real conflict, namely that between the old and the new generation of Red Army commanders, and made the point that the tactics of the aging heroes of the civil war were outmoded and that these men had to be replaced by new leaders if the war against the German invaders was to be won. (This happened in actual fact.)

The best, though not the most popular, war plays were written by Leonid Leonov. The plots of *Invasion* (*Nashestvie*, 1942) and *Lyonushka* (1943) do not depart very substantially from the patterns found in other Soviet plays of the war years, but Leonov's characters are sharply individualized through their speech, and their actions are psychologically motivated, sometimes in an intriguing way. Nevertheless, Leonov's plays, like his fiction, ultimately ring false because all his skill and subtlety are kept on the leash of a predictable ideological message.

The victorious conclusion of the war did not bring about any positive developments in Soviet life, least of all in literature and the arts. Even those wartime relaxations allowed to stand were turned into instruments of tighter control. Thus, the *de facto* toleration, limited though it was, of at least the Russian Orthodox Church was now declared official, which made the church subservient to the communist state and a convenient tool for dealing with émigré communities and international organizations.

As a result of the unavoidable contacts with the west made in the course of the war, a more internationalist climate had developed. With the war over, the Soviet government decided enough was enough, and not a few Soviet citizens whose only crime was that they had seen too much of the west and were suspected of harboring pro-western ideas found themselves in labor camps. The fact that hundreds of thousands of Soviet citizens who in one way or another had been displaced to the west refused to return to the Soviet Union, preferring to share the fate of the émigrés "first wave," was an embarrassment, so that émigrés of the "second wave" were denounced as Nazi collaborators and war criminals at every opportunity.

A speech by Stalin on 9 February 1946 made it clear that the Soviet Union had returned to its previous position, namely that a state of irreconcilable ideological conflict existed between the Soviet Union and the west. Stalin's speech was a signal for a general "tightening of the screws" which soon led to significant developments affecting literature. On 14 August 1946 the Central Committee of the Communist Party passed a resolution, "On the

journals *Star* and *Leningrad*," which applied the principles enunciated by Stalin to literature. The wave of repression which it
initiated went under the covert name of *zhdanovshchina*, after
Andrey Zhdanov, who had supervised the proceedings of the first
Congress of Soviet Writers in 1934 and who was now again laying
down the party line in matters of art and literature.

The main content of the resolution was an emphatic reminder
that the principles of socialist realism were still in force, meaning
that "ideological neutrality," "art for art's sake," and any avoidance
of political issues were intolerable political deviations. A corollary
of this position was the rejection of all foreign influences and
punishment for authors who had in any way departed from the
canon of socialist realism. The journals *Star* and *Leningrad* were
singled out for censure on the grounds that they had published
some works by Mikhail Zoshchenko and Anna Akhmatova.
Zoshchenko himself was charged with every possible offense
against the principle of socialist realism: a lack of ideas, a fatuous
apolitical stance, and even anti-Soviet innuendoes. His story
"Adventures of a Monkey" ("Priklyucheniya obezyany"),
published in *Star* earlier that year, was called "a vulgar lampoon on
Soviet life and the Soviet people" – perhaps not altogether unjustly.
The fact that Zoshchenko had published the "disgusting" piece
Before Sunrise while the country was at war was also brought up.

Anna Akhmatova was accused of pessimism, estheticism, and
decadence. Like Zoshchenko, she was declared a harmful influence
on Soviet youth. Zhdanov subsequently said, in a widely circulated address, that Akhmatova's poetry was that of "a half-crazed
gentlewoman who tosses between the bedchamber and the chapel
[. . .] [she is] half-nun and half-harlot, or rather both nun and
harlot, her harlotry mingled with prayer."

The resolution also accused the Union of Soviet Writers and its
head, Nikolay Tikhonov, of condoning the mistakes of *Star* and
Leningrad. The resolution had far-reaching consequences. *Leningrad* ceased publication. The editor of *Star* was fired. Alexander
Fadeev replaced Tikhonov as head of the Union of Soviet Writers.
Zoshchenko and Akhmatova were expelled from the Union of
Soviet Writers, which meant that they could no longer be
published. The resolution was printed in a variety of newspapers
and journals, and some of them expanded upon it by adding more

names of authors and titles of harmful works. Pasternak, Fedin, Vsevolod Ivanov, and Vasily Grossman were among those attacked almost immediately. The Central Committee of the Communist Party then issued two further resolutions, one on the Soviet theater, the other on Soviet film. The former charged that far too many foreign (read: western) plays were being staged in Soviet theaters, to the detriment of Soviet plays dealing with contemporary events. The resolution on film singled out several films for sharp censure, among them the second part of Eisenstein's *Ivan the Terrible* for portraying the tsar as a weak and indecisive ruler and his police force, the *oprichnina*, as a band of crazed criminal degenerates. Stalin, it was known, admired Ivan the Terrible, and there was the implication that a negative image of the *oprichnina* might cast a shadow on Stalin's own political police.

As the "cold war" set in, the ideological campaign concentrated on the assertion of national pride, denunciation of the capitalist west, and a struggle against "kowtowing to the west." This situation gave birth to the term *bezrodnye kosmopolity*, "rootless cosmopolitans," which soon enough acquired anti-Semitic overtones. One of the targets of the campaign against "kowtowing to the west" was the comparative study of literature, at least insofar as it pointed to any debt Russian literature or Russian culture might owe to other literatures or cultures. The name of the great literary scholar and folklorist Alexander Veselovsky (1838–1906), the centennial of whose birth had been duly celebrated in 1938 and marked by new editions of his *Selected Essays* (*Izbrannye stati*, 1939) and *Historical Poetics* (*Istoricheskaya poetika*, 1940), now came to serve as shorthand: "Veselovskyism" for "false teachings" implying Russia's inferiority to and dependance on western culture. Ironically, at the bottom of all this there may have been a confusion of Alexander Veselovsky with his brother Alexey, a lesser literary scholar, who had indeed published a book entitled *Western Influence in Modern Russian Literature* (1879–81) in which he had emphasized Russia's "discipleship." At any rate, there were attacks, often by distinctly second-rate critics, on many distinguished scholars, critics, and writers for being guilty of "Veselovskyism." For example, Vladimir Propp's important book *Historical Roots of the Magic Tale* (*Istoricheskie korni volshebnoy skazki*, 1946), at first positively reviewed by Victor Zhirmunsky, an ex-formalist and eminent scholar in his own right, was subjected to vicious attack on the grounds that it read "more like a foreign than like a Soviet work" and that it quoted so many foreign authorities it resembled "a Berlin or London telephone directory." Other scholars and critics came under similar attacks. In April 1948 Zhirmunsky, Propp, Eikhenbaum, and other scholars and critics abjectly declared that their "comparatist" positions had been misguided and that they would correct their mistakes. Those who refused to take this step faced dire consequences. Scores of critics, editors, and scholars were purged in 1949, when the campaign against "rootless cosmopolitanism" reached its peak. An ominous new feature of these purges by comparison with the purges of the 1930s was that the real names of the purged individuals were made public whenever they had used pen-names. This revealed that many of those purged were Jewish. The campaign against "rootless cosmopolitanism" coincided with sweeping moves against Jewish organizations and cultural activities on the pretext that they were connected with Zionism.

All these ideological tendencies found expression in Soviet literature. The intellectual atmosphere was so stifling and the margin of safety so narrow that most works of the post-war period were no more than timid and tedious exercises in translating the party line into a semblance of fiction or drama. The tireless Simonov was once more at the forefront of these efforts. His plays *Someone Else's Shadow* (*Chuzhaya ten*, 1949) and *The Russian Question* (*Russky vopros*, 1947) are crude propaganda pieces. In the first, a Soviet medical scientist who believes that his discovery belongs to humanity and should be communicated to his western colleagues comes to realize that he is mistaken, for the enemy will use his discovery to destroy rather than to save lives. *The Russian Question* shows how the American press misinforms the public about the Soviet Union and how all honest voices are brutally stifled. Simonov pursued the same patriotic and anti-western themes in his fiction, as in his novels *Hearth-Smoke of the Fatherland* (*Dym otechestva*, 1948), and in verse, as in *Friends and Foes* (*Druzya i vragi*, 1948). Many other writers, poets, and playwrights produced similar works, denouncing the west, often crudely falsifying history in the process, and glorifying Russia, past and present. Some of them were generously rewarded with Stalin prizes. There was a flood of poetry extolling the wise leadership of Stalin. All these novels, plays, and poems were instantly forgotten, usually along with their authors, upon Stalin's death in 1953.

In the meantime, certain writers of the older generation were still producing works of some merit. Konstantin Fedin published *Early Joys* (1946) and *An Extraordinary Summer* (*Neobyknovennoe leto*, 1948), the first two parts of a trilogy whose third part, *The Bonfire* (*Koster*), appeared much later (1961). The trilogy tells the life story of an intellectual who makes all the right choices as he meets the challenge of historical events. While Fedin is guilty of some historical falsifications (crediting Stalin with Trotsky's achievements and making the latter a traitor), his novels are examples of careful writing in the manner of nineteenth-century "critical realism." In particular, the first part creates a vivid picture of life in a provincial city just before the outbreak of World War I.

Veniamin Kaverin's novel *An Open Book* (*Otkrytaya kniga*, 1949) eventually also led to a trilogy, completed in 1956. The heroine is a Soviet biologist whose life story the reader learns from her diary and reminiscences. As in Kaverin's other novels, elements of mystery, intrigue, and melodrama combine with what may be interpreted as serious criticism of Soviet society, in a work which ostensibly follows the canons of the socialist realist novel. Kaverin and Fedin remained fine writers even under the difficult conditions of the post-war years.

Valentin Kataev's novel *For Soviet Power* (*Za vlast Sovetov*, 1949) brought back the boy heroes of his popular novel *A Lonely White Sail Gleaming* (*Beleet parus odinoky*, 1936), set during the revolution of 1905. Middle-aged men now, they play a role in an exciting story of the anti-German underground in Odessa during World War II. Like Fadeev's *Young Guard*, Kataev's novel was criticized for minimizing the role of the party in the heroic struggle of the urban guerillas, and Kataev, like Fadeev, was forced to revise his novel.

The first parts of a major war novel by Vasily Grossman, *In a Just Cause* (*Za pravoe delo*), focused on the battle of Stalingrad, were serialized in the journal *New World* (*Novy mir*) in 1952. It received some favorable reviews, but in February 1953, as a new series of purges, directed particularly at Jews, was launched, possibly at Stalin's orders, Grossman and his novel were repeatedly denounced for their "reactionary idealism," alienation from Soviet society, and "Jewish nationalism." Grossman produced a revised version of his novel, and with the changes caused by Stalin's death it could appear in book form in 1954, winning him critical and official acclaim.

The most remarkable novel of the post-war period was Leonid Leonov's *The Russian Forest* (*Russky les*, 1953), probably the greatest achievement of socialist realism. It is set on the eve of World War II and during wartime, but plausibly reaches back to the period before the revolution when the antagonists Vikhrov and Gratsiansky, now both eminent professors of forestry, were students. Vikhrov, of humble origins, devotes all his energy to conservation, while Gratsiansky, the son of a theology professor, advocates the reckless exploitation of Russia's forests. It develops that Gratsiansky does his wrecking job because he is blackmailed by foreign agents who know that as a youth he once betrayed some revolutionaries to the tsarist police. Gratsiansky secretly indulges in decadent pastimes which have nothing to do with forestry, and is in fact writing a treatise "On suicide." He is, of course, unmasked in the end, and commits suicide. The cause of conservation triumphs. The message of *The Russian Forest* was in full accord with the contemporary position of the Soviet government, which was promoting conservation and reforestation. True to the canons of the socialist realist novel, *The Russian Forest* contains lengthy technical discussions on forestry. It was, however, criticized for an excessively mystic reverence for nature. To the western reader, and presumably to not a few Soviet readers as well, the real interest of the novel is in the character of the villain. Gratsiansky is depicted as an adolescent intellectual, vain, somewhat arrogant, rather selfish, but also capable of genuine love, artistically inclined, and possessed of great intellectual curiosity. We then observe what life under the Soviet system does to such a character. A man who would have flourished under conditions of intellectual freedom and in a congenial social atmosphere instead deteriorates morally, gradually sheds all positive human qualities, develops a death wish, and eventually commits suicide.

The post-war period also saw the emergence of new talent. Vera Panova (1905–73) scored her first success with a short novel, *Fellow Travelers* (*Sputniki*, 1946, stage version 1947), set on a hospital train during the war, which introduces some credible characters, with sympathy but without sentimentality, while focusing on their human problems and foregoing the usual patriotic rhetoric. Panova received a Stalin prize for the novel. Her next novel, *Kruzhilikha* (1947; the title is the name of a factory in the Urals), came under fire for developing a conflict on psychological rather than on social grounds, as well as for drawing an insufficiently sharp line between positive and negative characters. Panova took this criticism to heart, and her next novel, *Clear Shore* (*Yasny bereg*, 1949), depicting life on a state farm, was in full accord with the demands of socialist realism. It was in fact a fair example of the so-called "conflictless literature" widespread in Soviet culture for a few years before Stalin's death.

Galina Nikolaeva (pen-name of Volyanskaya, 1911–63), a physician who had published stories and sketches since 1939, won fame and a Stalin prize with her novel *Harvest* (*Zhatva*, 1950), set on a collective farm and describing the maturing of the heroine while her husband is away at war. Boris Polevoy (pen-name of Kampov, 1908–81), an industrial engineer turned journalist, continued to work primarily in the documentary genre after the war, in which he participated as a war correspondent. His *Tale About a Real Man* (*Povest o nastoyashchem cheloveke*, 1946) told the true story of a Soviet flyer who lost both legs when shot down but insisted on being retrained so he might fly again. It became an instant classic, was translated into many languages, and won a Stalin prize.

Soviet poetry of the post-war period was inferior to prose fiction. When the enthusiasm of the war years wore off, there were no themes available that could inspire genuine poetry and also be safe from critical attack as "subjective," "personal," or "pessimistic." Even poets who later would produce genuine poetry, or who had done so earlier came up with stillborn fabrications which, however, won critical acclaim and Stalin prizes. Such was the case with Alexander Yashin (pen-name of Popov, 1913–68), whose *poema Alyona Fomina* (1949) depicted post-war village life in rose-colored hues. (It later developed that there were some truthful strophes in it, too, which Yashin was ordered to excise.) After Stalin's death, Yashin became one of the more interesting Soviet poets.

In the last few years before Stalin's death Soviet literature had clearly reached an impasse. The theory and practice of a new "conflictless" literature were a visible symptom of this condition. The theoretical basis of "conflictless literature" was the notion, first expressed as early as 1938, after the conclusion of Stalin's second Five Year Plan, that "socialism" had been achieved in the Soviet Union and that the Soviet people were now living in a society free of class conflict. A more practical reason for its emergence was the fact that party functionaries responsible for the various branches of Soviet industry resented socialist realist "production novels" in which the condition of their particular domain was depicted as less than satisfactory or threatened by saboteurs. This meant that works dealing with contemporary Soviet life tended to become more and more celebratory and altogether removed from reality. A successful follower of this trend was Semyon Babaevsky (1909–), whose novel *The Bearer of the Golden Star* (*Kavaler zolotoy zvezdy*, 1947–8) and its sequel, *Light over the Land* (*Svet nad zemlyoy*, 1949–50), won Stalin prizes. They depict the successful rebuilding of a collective farm destroyed during the war, blatantly "prettifying reality and glossing over the difficulties of post-war reconstruction of collective farming," as the article on Babaevsky in the post-Stalin *Concise Literary Encyclopedia* has phrased it.

Even before Stalin's death, the Party became concerned about public disinterest in a literature which was neither intriguing nor challenging, had no esthetic merit whatever, and possessed none of the elements of good entertainment. As Tvardovsky would write later, all these novels "had everything just right, exactly as things were or ought to be, but were yet so unpalatable they made you howl at the top of your voice." People neither bought nor read them, and theaters which staged socialist realist plays were empty. The theory of "conflictless literature" was in trouble even before it was officially dismissed by the second Congress of the Union of Soviet Writers in 1954.

World War II was a watershed for Russian émigré literature. During the war it came to a virtual standstill. Some writers perished in German concentration camps (Yury Felzen, Mother Mariya, Yury Mandelshtam), others at the hands of the Soviets (Alfred Bem and the novelist Peter Krasnov). Some died during the war of natural causes (Dmitry Merezhkovsky, Zinaida Hippius, Konstantin Balmont, Yury Shteiger, Mikhail Osorgin) while others once again changed their country of exile. Vladimir Nabokov, Mark Aldanov, Vera Alexandrova, Vladimir Yanovsky, Gleb Struve, and many others moved to the United States, where the New York *New Review*, founded by Aldanov and M. O. Tsetlin in 1942, became the leading émigré literary organ. It was vigorously seconded by the New York daily *The New Russian Word* (*Novoe russkoe slovo*), which has always had an excellent literary section.

Most important of all, there was a "second wave" of emigrants, mostly Russians who found themselves in the west at the end of the war and chose not to return to the Soviet Union, but also several "first wave" émigrés whose home in emigration (Latvia, Estonia, Poland, Czechoslovakia, etc.) had been overrun by the Soviets. They provided émigré literature with new talent, a new set of experiences, and a whole new readership. An active life sprang up at some displaced-persons camps in Germany, and Frankfurt am Main, with a publishing house, Sowing (Posev), and a literary journal *Borders* (*Grani*, 1946–), and Munich, where a literary journal, *Lights* (*Ogni*, 1946–7), and several almanacs appeared in the years after the war, became new centers of émigré literature. Most "second wave" literati eventually emigrated to the United States or Canada (Alekseeva, Anstei, Chinnov, Elagin, Filippov, Ilinsky, Ivask, Klenovsky, Markov, Morshen, and others), joining the ranks of earlier arrivals, who had been instrumental in developing Russian studies in the United States (Roman Jakobson, Michael Karpovich, Vladimir Nabokov, Gleb Struve, and others). The poets, writers, and critics of the "second wave" developed their full powers only in America in the 1950s and after.

Meanwhile, more than a few "first wave" poets and writers resumed publishing. Vyacheslav Ivanov, who remained active as a poet and scholar until his death in 1949, experienced a surprising burst of creativity which produced the poems of his *Roman Diary* (*Rimsky dnevnik*, 1944). Georgy Ivanov reached the summit of his powers in the poems of *A Portrait Without Resemblance* (*Portret bez skhodstva*, 1950) and *Posthumous Diary* (*Posmertny dnevnik*, 1958), some of which are among the starkest expressions of human despair in all Russian poetry.

In 1947 there appeared in Paris a posthumous collection, *Poems and Verse Epics, Mystères* (*Stikhotvoreniya i poemy, misterii*), by Mother Mariya (religious name of Elizabeth Skobtsova-Kondrateva, 1891–1945), who had perished in the Ravensbrück concentration camp. Mother Mariya's religious poetry, conventional in its form, expresses a Christian's compassion for suffering humanity with great warmth.

Certain older prose writers also took up their pens again after the war. The stories of Ivan Bunin's last collection, *Dark Avenues* (*Temnye allei*, 1946), continued to deal with his former themes of death and erotic passion. He also published a volume of *Reminiscences* (*Vospominaniya*, 1950), while an incomplete but fascinating book on Chekhov appeared posthumously (1955). Mark Aldanov wrote several more novels and essays after having moved to America in 1940 and returned to France in 1947. The stylized dialogues of his *A Night at Ulm: The Philosophy of Chance* (*Ulmskaya noch: filosofiya sluchaya*, 1953) are a brilliant exercise in lucid and sophisticated philosophic prose. Aldanov was the most successful émigré writer internationally: several of his novels sold well in English and German translations.

While Nabokov was now lost to Russian literature, as was Yanovsky, who had begun writing in English, Gaito Gazdanov resumed writing Russian fiction after the war. His novels *The Specter of Alexander Wolf* (*Prizrak Aleksandra Volfa*) and *The Return of the Buddha* (*Vozvrashchenie Buddy*) were translated into English in 1950 and 1951, respectively. His post-war novels and short stories, while retaining the attractive traits of his pre-war work, are more disciplined in their descriptive and psychological detail. Gazdanov excels in creating characters and plots in which cynicism and despair remain in precarious yet convincing balance with a courageous acceptance of life and even a certain *joie de vivre*.

Alexey Remizov, who had published relatively little in the 1930s, brought several things out after the war, having worked on some of them for a long time. Though he was in ill health and going blind, he continued to practice the graphic arts and calligraphy, and some of his late writings are among his finest. *Dancing Demon* (*Plyashushchy demon*, 1949) is a quaint vision of Russia's orgiastic roots. In *With Clipped Eyes* (*Podstrizhennymi glazami*), scenes from Remizov's childhood and adolescence are transformed into a suite of strangely "atonal" surrealist composition. *The Fire of Things* (*Ogon veshchey*, 1954) is an imaginative treatment of dreams in Russian literature, while *Martyn Zadeka: A Book of Dream Interpretations* (*Martyn Zadeka: Sonnik*, 1954) is a collection of Remizov's own dreams, real or imaginary. *A Flute for Mice* (*Myshkina dudochka*, 1953) is another dreamlike surrealist composition. *In a Rosy Light* (*V rozovom bleske*, 1952) is a continuation of the life story of Remizov's wife, begun as *Olya* in 1927. Remizov's masterful late prose is quite unique in all of Russian literature, and defies assignment to any genre.

Altogether, the condition of émigré literature in 1953, when Stalin's death and the ensuing "thaw" opened the door to an intellectual rapprochement of the two Russian literatures, was not so bleak as some émigré critics had thought it before the war. There were enought talent and interest about to keep Russian literature in exile going until the "third wave" of emigration would cause it to experience another period of flowering.

10

THE TWENTIETH CENTURY: IN SEARCH OF NEW WAYS, 1953–80

The period from 1953 to 1980 saw Russian literature develop in many different directions both inside and outside the Soviet Union. With Stalin's death the intense cultural pressures which the guardians of literature had exerted after the Second World War diminished, and with some hesitation literature sought to strike out in unfamiliar channels during the period of the so-called thaw, a name adopted from Erenburg's timely novel of the day. The thaw continued through the eventual accession of Nikita Khrushchev to power, but there were clearly strict limits to it, as the controversy over Pasternak's *Doctor Zhivago* and the award of the Nobel Prize to him in 1958 showed: Pasternak finally rejected the award, and his novel was not published in the Soviet Union for nearly thirty years.

And yet the process of cultural liberalization after Stalin has never been totally reversed. The early 1960s saw the rise to prominence of Alexander Solzhenitsyn, following the publication of his *One Day in the Life of Ivan Denisovich* in 1962. Solzhenitsyn remained a central figure of the 1960s thanks to the existence of *samizdat*, since many of his further writings could not be published within the country. It is indicative that he is supremely a writer of prose, and that two mentor-poets of the older generation – Pasternak and Akhmatova – had ceased to exert very direct influence on the younger generation of writers by the early 1960s. The attitude of the authorities toward the energies of the new literature passed through certain phases. By mid-decade the government was seeking to rein in free expression through legal repression, but as the years passed and methods of informal publication enabled writers to circumvent official restrictions to a considerable degree, Soviet authorities resorted to another stratagem which unexpectedly provided Russian literature in emigration with a new impetus.

That stratagem was the expulsion from the country of many of the nation's finest writers, artists, and intellectuals, of which the most famous instance was Solzhenitsyn's involuntary exile of 1974. This Soviet policy was nearly unprecedented in world history, if one excepts the exodus of Jewish and other intellectuals from Hitler's Germany in the 1930s. The Soviet regime deliberately deprived the nation of much of the flower of its intelligentsia, and by the same token replenished Russian culture in emigration, which had been rapidly fading at the time the "third wave" of emigration began.

The "third wave" combined the characteristics of the preceding waves. Like the "second wave," its members had grown up in the Soviet period and therefore were intimately acquainted with Soviet reality, although in somewhat more normal times than those years of purge and total war which the members of the "second wave" had known. Like the writers of the "first wave," however, many "third wave" authors had established reputations before emigrating from the Soviet Union, and therefore found it easier to continue in their previous occupations upon arrival in the west. Mikhail Baryshnikov and Mstislav Rostropovich are merely two instances of non-literary artists who have accomplished this. As a consequence, Russian literature and culture abroad were even more impressive in 1980 than they had been half a century before; moreover, the linkages between Russian writers inside and outside the Soviet Union were stronger than they had been previously, as many émigré writers still think of themselves as writing primarily for an audience inside the Soviet Union.

With Stalin's death the official method of socialist realism fell into disrepute, but the social structures supporting it were sufficiently strong that it by no means withdrew from the field of battle. At the same time, other literary methods have sought to challenge or replace it. Andrey Sinyavsky went so far as to recommend fantastic literature as the only accurate means of representing the fantastic nature of Soviet reality, and although he has found some followers, most Russian prose of the last twenty years has moved along "realist" channels. Solzhenitsyn provides the example once again: he appeals to the well established traditions of nineteenth-century Russian realism in his literary approach, and also expresses through his writing the insatiable hunger of the Soviet reader for straightforward information about Soviet reality as it genuinely is. For the time being at least the leading works of Soviet literature are those which simply seek to present the unvarnished truth.

With the stimulation of intellectual curiosity and the renewed interest in the modernist traditions of the 1920s, Russian literature has lately been more experimental than before, especially in the emigration. And yet through all the vicissitudes of literary history from 1953 to 1980, the chief line of development has been realistic: from Solzhenitsyn and Shalamov through Tendryakov, Trifonov, and Rasputin to the younger writers of today, the objective has been in some way to grasp the essence of Soviet society and depict it truthfully rather than through the distorting lenses of socialist realism or the discontinuities of a modernist style. Other visions have not been excluded, but if one compares the masterful modernist prose of *Doctor Zhivago* with the approach of *Cancer Ward* or *The First Circle*, one finds that most prose writers have declined to follow the path of Pasternak, no matter how greatly they may have admired him personally and as a poet.

PERHAPS NO NATION has ever needed its literature as pressingly as did the Soviet peoples in 1953. During the preceding generation they had lived through social change, total war and political oppression on what was probably a historically unprecedented scale, yet had been prevented from attempting to absorb and digest these shattering experiences by an official censorship and cultural monopoly of unique thoroughness. The nation was both traumatized and dumb. And in the wastes ruled over by Glavlit and Agitprop, its prospects for recovering its voice did not seem bright.

Yet in the long run there proved to be countervailing forces adequate to satisfy the nation's spiritual hunger, and the result has been a particularly diverse and rewarding period of Russian literature. How did this come about?

A considerable role was played by the legacy of Russia's great literary past, a legacy which emphasized literature's civic mission, its duty not only to reveal the truth but to do so in a way which would impel the reader towards humane ideals. The authoritative tradition of literary criticism founded by Belinsky had upheld these ideals and, through the radical and Marxist critics of the second half of the nineteenth century, had laid the basis for Soviet esthetic theory. Thus the party itself recognized the rectitude of a tradition which was in potential tension with its own practice of requiring writers to conceal certain parts of Soviet reality while embellishing others. Even more than criticism, the actual *example* of the nineteenth-century writers taught to every Soviet schoolchild – Gogol, Nekrasov, Tolstoy, Chekhov – suggested that the writer had a duty to be compassionate, concerned about the individual and frank in his exposure of social evils.

Of course these writers had been depicting tsarist society, and so their strictures were *a priori* acceptable, indeed welcome, to the Soviet authorities. Yet there also existed, in semi-submerged form, an embryonic tradition which applied similar criteria to Soviet society. The prose of authors such as Babel, Zoshchenko,

Olesha, Bulgakov and Platonov contained the makings of a profound critique of the Soviet order itself. The problem was that
many of their works remained unpublished, and those which were
available had not been republished for at least twenty years and
therefore in practice reached only readers with access to special
libraries. The same applied to poets such as Khlebnikov, Pasternak, Tsvetaeva, Akhmatova and Mandelshtam, who had tried to
develop the traditions of Russian poetry in ways incomprehensible
or repugnant to their narrow-minded masters. The gradual, controversial, and still only partial publication (and republication) of
such authors was as much part of the literary history of the
post-Stalin period as the appearance of new works straight from
the typewriter. At times it all recalls the rediscovery of classical
culture in the Europe of the renaissance.

Another cultural resource gradually becoming available in the
post-Stalin period was the literature of the west, of which the
Soviet reader had received only a very limited and pre-digested
selection under the Zhdanov aegis. In 1955, as part of the party's
policy of rapprochement with the west, the monthly journal
Foreign Literature (*Inostrannaya literatura*) was founded, and soon
became highly popular with readers.

What might not have been expected was that the state-imposed
and party-controlled writers' organization should prove in certain
respects capable of making good use of these opportunities. The
Union of Soviet Writers has been a paradoxical institution. It was
structured at the outset in such a way as to enable writers to police
literature on behalf of the party. For this purpose submissive
writers had to be found and elected, through party discipline and
the lack of alternative candidates, to commanding posts within the
Union, to become, in short, literary bureaucrats. Under Stalin this
system worked unambiguously in the interests of ideological uni-
formity. Once terror ceased to be total, however, it transpired that
the Union also afforded a framework within which non-
conformist writers and editors could organize themselves and
articulate their views. Under Khrushchev's policy of reactivating
social institutions which had lain dormant under Stalin (including
the Communist Party itself), the Writers' Union both regularized
and extended its activities. Its second congress, which should
according to its charter have been held in 1937, was finally con-

vened in 1954, and provided a platform for criticism of established literary practices. During the 1950s the Union also broadened its repertoire of monthly journals. In 1955 *Youth* (*Yunost*), and in 1956 *The Young Guard*, were opened with the specific aim of providing publishing outlets for young authors, of whom there was a great need after the long-established dominance of older writers during the stagnant Zhdanov era. In Leningrad the journal *Neva* served as a kind of replacement for *Leningrad*, closed after the Central Committee decree of August 1946, though that decree itself was not revoked.

If non-conformist writers could organize themselves, then so could the conformists. In some ways their immediate need to do so was even greater, since for the first time the cultural monopoly they had hitherto enjoyed was being challenged. They reacted by establishing a new organ, the Writers' Union of the Russian Republic (RSFSR) in 1958, with its own weekly newspaper, *Literary Russia* (*Literaturnaya Rossiya*, – initially known as *Literature and Life* [*Literatura i zhizn*]), and the journals *Moscow* (*Moskva*) and *Our Contemporary* (*Nash sovremennik*). Henceforth conflict became more open, with the battle between conformists and non-conformists (or, less accurately, conservatives and liberals) being umpired by a party ideological apparatus which was no longer always automatically on the side of the conformists. Each side had its bastions in certain journals, publishing houses and local branches of the Writers' Union. The most notable was the non-conformist stronghold in the long-established organ of the Soviet Writers' Union, *New World*, under its editors Alexander Tvardovsky (1950–4 and 1958–70) and Konstantin Simonov (1954–8). Its deputy editor, Vladimir Lakshin, later called *New World* "a modest embryo of democratic socialism" and described its social impact as follows:

> The letters which came to the editorial office in huge quantities confirmed that for many people in the 1960s *Novyi mir* became a part of their personal existence: it inspired a faith in the indestructibility of the truth, it helped people to live, and it fortified a sense of human dignity in the consciousness of hundreds of thousands of our fellow citizens. The journal both reflected and formed public opinion. Its readership extended far beyond the circle of Moscow's intellectual elite or the impressionable young. *Novyi mir* was read in the corridors of power, in remote villages, and in the most distant provinces, and its readership

spanned labourers on construction sites, librarians, village school-teachers, agronomists, passionate lovers of truth and lonely seekers after faith.

The social resonance of *New World*, and of other journals, reflected the changes which had taken place in Soviet society since the 1920s. The introduction of universal primary education meant that the great majority of the population could now read, and formed part of the potential audience for literature. The nature of Soviet education ensured, moreover, that most graduates of schools and colleges had had some contact with the classics of Russian and Soviet literature, and had absorbed the elements of a systematic – however narrow – way of studying them.

The greatest transformation had taken place, however, in the nature of the creative intelligentsia. For the first time, many peasant and working-class lads were receiving a good education, and some of them were studying at the Gorky Institute and becoming writers. Peasants no longer had to look to repentant aristocrats to write sympathetically about rural life: their own sons could do so, and one or two were. If, moreover, in the nineteenth century educated young Russians had longed to merge themselves with the people, their twentieth-century counterparts had had no choice but to do so – and in conditions which were about as difficult as imaginable: on the battle front, on building sites, on the shop floor, on the collective farm, in the communal apartment, and worst of all, in the labor camps, where they lived cheek by jowl not only with the "ordinary" *narod*, but with criminals as well. This enforced intimacy had one positive result: it produced a massive cross-fertilization of Russia's cultural strata. Educated people spontaneously absorbed peasant and working-class speech, and were willy-nilly steeped in a folklore which otherwise they could only have studied with painstaking artificiality. Mihajlo Mihajlov, a Yugoslav student attending Moscow University in 1964, later recalled a dormitory party interrupted by a Siberian student singing to a guitar:

> What staggered me most of all was the actual songs. I had never imagined anything like that existed in the USSR. He sang all sorts of convict songs – happy ones, despairing ones, and cynical ones [. . .] Through them spoke the Russia we know from the works of Tolstoy and Dostoevsky; they were genuine "earthy," profoundly national

works, not stylizations – not the sort that gets broadcast on Soviet radio – but raw, sometimes naive but always profound, very melodic and profound.

This irruption of popular culture provided both an alternative language and an alternative view of the world to the officially propagated ones.

Not only songs, but also jokes and anecdotes describing the suffering of the ordinary people and directed with cheerful cynicism at their oppressors, helped to nourish the return to authenticity from the stilted banality of official Stalinist literature. As Abram Terts remarked, "The future of Russian literature, if it is destined to have a future at all, has been nourished on political anecdotes [. . .] In its pure form, the anecdote demonstrates the miracle of art, deriving as it does nothing but good from the savagery and fury of dictators."

In the 1950s, then, writers had at their disposal a great tradition from which to learn, a new and lively popular language, and institutions in which to defend one another while trying to re-animate genuine literature. Nevertheless, the obstacles were so great, and the effect of the long-enforced dumbness so profound, that the return to truth was slow, painful, and fraught with conflict. It bears all the marks, in fact, of what Freud called "the return of the repressed": a society was painfully learning to recognize what it had tried to deny and forget – in fact, had "censored" in the psychological and political sense. For that reason, understanding the recent past and integrating it into a picture of man was the dominant preoccupation – not to say obsession – of the period.

Paradoxically, non-conformism was born within the heart of the literary establishment itself, in the principal journal of the Soviet Writers' Union, *New World*. Even before Stalin's death it had published works such as Vasily Grossman's *In a Just Cause*, with its "abstract humanist" approach to the values for which the Fatherland War had been fought, and Valentin Ovechkin's *Provincial Routine* (*Rayonnye budni*), which eschewed the false picture of rural affluence currently *de rigueur*, and portrayed the collective farms as poverty-stricken and demoralized by inexpert and over-centralized management.

The man responsible for these and subsequent indiscretions was Alexander Tvardovsky. He had been a loyal member of the party

since before the war, and indeed was to sit on its Central Committee from 1961 to 1966. He accepted the party's ideology and its
literary corollary, socialist realism, but his interpretation of that
elastic doctrine displayed emphases which were not always
welcome to his colleagues among the literary bureaucrats.

The principal point at issue was how in practice to validate the
assumption, derived ultimately from Belinsky, that the good
writer, by the nature of his art, must simultaneously reveal the
truth about society, take a correct political stance towards that
truth, and also create an esthetically compelling work which
would attract, hold, and convince the reader. If that happy combination of functions was indeed intrinsic to literature, then all that
was required was to restore to literature its freedom. That was
Tvardovsky's belief: of all the elements demanded by socialist
realism, he most valued *narodnost* and the authentic description of
social reality, and he was prepared to seek and encourage them if
necessary (though it is not clear how far he acknowledged this to
himself) at the expense of ideological rectitude, "partymindedness" and "revolutionary perspectives."

But what if writers were, as much Marxist criticism seemed to
imply, mere gifted children, endowed with valuable talents and
capable of genuine insight to be sure, but also mercurial, prone to
elementary misunderstandings and irresponsible moods? The non-
conformists, with *New World* at their head, fought for the purity of
Belinsky's conception, while the newly threatened literary bureaucrats reasserted what might be termed the Leninist revision of it,
which held that writers needed to be carefully supervised and
subordinate to party discipline.

The publication of one or two non-conformist works even
before Stalin's death shows what a determined editorial collective
under able leadership like Tvardovsky's could already achieve. It
was natural, then, that in the uncertainties generated by Stalin's
death and the subsequent execution of Lavrenty Beria, *New World*
should take the lead in attempting to restore a degree of autonomy
to literature. In December 1953 a former legal expert, now
journalist, Vladimir Pomerantsev, sketched out what in the following years became virtually the esthetic program of *New
World* in his article "Sincerity in literature" ("Ob iskrennosti v
literature"). He attacked writers who do not write about what they

see and hear around them, but who force their material into stereotypes, who "embellish reality" or think in crass and over-simplified moral categories, failing to reflect life's complexity. His main message was that one should write about the *truth* as one sees it, and honestly reflect one's *feelings* about that truth. In a similar article of April 1954 Fyodor Abramov took a particular example of such literary malpractice by attacking those many novelists who had misrepresented collective farm life as flourishing and affluent, failing to reflect the collective farmers' penury and the neglect of their accumulated experience by the bureaucrats who ran their lives.

The literary work which best summed up the new mood was Ilya Erenburg's novel *The Thaw* (*Ottepel*), the first part of which was published in March 1954. It begins with a society, as it were, in deep freeze, dominated by authoritarian, plan-fulfilling factory directors and smug, insincere establishment artists. Society functions through inertia and order imposed from above: real human feelings have been drained out. People are afraid to be spontaneous, to have real feelings or to say what they think. Gradually, in the course of the novel, warmth and creativity return. Lovers discover and avow their feelings for one another. Artists regain the capacity to infuse their work with delight. That return of warmth gave the novel its name – and not only this novel, but a whole epoch.

The thrust of *The Thaw* was not, it should be noted, directed against the party or its ideology, nor even against socialist realism. Rather it disparaged a particular way of implementing that ideology. If men rediscovered spontaneity, they did so in order the better to devote themselves to the party's ideals, to the ultimate building of socialism. The vision was no longer one of a people directed from above by the party, but rather freely dedicating their energies to the ideals proclaimed by the party. The stilted language, the one-dimensional characters, the simple moral categories, the vision of a great future, all these features continued unchanged from the normal Stalinist novel. But they now served a different vision of the road to the future. That was all, but it was enough to stimulate a transformation in the literary scene, and to intensify the conflict which had already broken out. Cultural bureaucrats could not but see themselves in the figure of Pukhov, the privileged painter who fills his canvases with rosy-cheeked milkmaids and radiant young pioneers. And they feared the coming of Saburov, the poverty-stricken but genuine artist whose paintings arouse the admiration of all the visitors to his humble apartment.

During 1954, then, the literary bureaucrats initiated something of a counter-attack. Tvardovsky was removed from the chief editorship of *New World* and replaced by Konstantin Simonov. In September the journal had to admit its mistakes, and publish a resolution of the Writers' Union administrative board accusing it of "indiscriminate nihilist disdain for everything positive achieved by Soviet literature." At the Writers' Union congress in December many critical speeches were made, but the familiar nonentities, headed by Alexey Surkov, were reinstalled at the head of the organization. The party, however, in its keynote address to delegates confirmed that literature should present "the real truth of life in all its fullness and complexity," and should "reveal the contradictions and conflicts of life." Socialist realism was said to "afford ample scope for personal initiative and individual inclinations, thought and fantasy, form and content." The party, then, at this stage seemed neutral but inclined to the liberal side of the argument.

A second and deeper phase of the "thaw" began in February 1956 with Nikita Khrushchev's "secret" speech at the twentieth party congress disclosing and denouncing many of Stalin's crimes. The party's (albeit only partial and semi-public) acknowledgement of the terrible abuses of power for which it had shared responsibility stimulated a powerful reaction among writers. Thus a meeting of the Moscow branch of the Writers' Union in March heard forthright and damaging assertions: "A patron system of the Maecenas type was implanted in literature and art. The personal tastes of prominent party officials decided everything." Some speakers drew the conclusion that political steps still needed to be taken: "The personality cult still exists with regard to the Presidium of the Central Committee [. . .] We must carry through a purge of the apparatus and of the party."

Such sentiments could not be expressed in the public media, but they did prompt writers to seek ways of acquiring some degree of autonomy and a closer link with the reading public. One way to do this was through public poetry readings, or Poetry Days, organized by the Writers' Union, which began in 1955. The readings struck a chord especially among young people, and at the height of their popularity tens of thousands of listeners would gather to hear Evgeny Evtushenko or Andrey Voznesensky declaiming their verse. In 1958 the newly erected statue of Mayakovsky in Moscow became the scene of readings of new (and therefore not yet authorized) poetry. In the long run this extension of the previous practice alarmed the authorities to such a degree that they began to regard authorized readings with some suspicion as well.

Another attempt of an analogous kind was the publication of two symposia under the title *Literary Moscow* (*Literaturnaya Moskva*), put together by well-known writers under the inspiration of Konstantin Paustovsky, independently of any of the Writers' Union organizations or journals. It offered authors not published in the Soviet Union for a generation or more (Ivan Kataev, Marina Tsvetaeva, Nikolay Zabolotsky) in addition to printing the first major publications of one or two new young authors such as Naum Korzhavin. One of the items which drew greatest attention, however, was by a familiar figure, Alexander Yashin, who in the past had written his share of works "embellishing reality." In this story, "Levers" ("Rychagi"), however, he showed four collective farmers gathering for a party meeting and grumbling about the bureaucratic attitudes and ignorance of their superiors; the same four then formally begin the meeting, and use stilted official language in passing a resolution promising to fulfil the latest instructions of those same superiors. No clearer exposé of "doublethink" could be imagined: Yashin's insight that the responsibility for authoritarian mismanagement lay not only with "them" but also with "us," went to the heart of the problem.

Even conformist writers could now feel that they were being invited to contribute to the investigation of the recent past, and not only in the field of agriculture. It became clear that the methods associated with socialist realism could be turned against the party–state apparatus, portraying it as an obstacle to the building of socialism. This was the message of Vladimir Dudintsev's novel *Not by Bread Alone* (*Ne khlebom edinym*, 1956) in which an ordinary schoolmaster from among the people struggles against bureaucrats and academicians to have his progressive method of casting steel tubes adopted by Soviet industry.

The experience of the Polish and Hungarian troubles in the autumn of 1956 suggested that discontented writers could be a subversive political force, and the party intervened to regain some control over them. The authoritative party journal *Communist* (*Kommunist*) warned: "The events in Hungary have demonstrated the consequences of disregarding Leninist adherence to principle in the question of the guidance of literature and art." In May 1957 Khrushchev addressed a meeting of writers at the Central Committee. He attacked both *Literary Moscow* and *Not by Bread Alone*, accusing Dudintsev of "piling together negative facts and commenting on them tendentiously, from a standpoint hostile to us." He criticized the Moscow branch of the Writers' Union (a nonconformist stronghold) and reasserted the party's duty to exercise guidance over literature and to exclude both the "embellishers" and the "indiscriminate anti-embellishers."

As the last phrase implies, Khrushchev wanted to achieve a certain balance, and not allow literature to revert to the sugary drabness of the late Stalin years. The clearest sign of this policy was the recall of Tvardovsky to *New World* in July 1958.

A huge gulf still separated "within-system" non-conformity from the manifestations of a pre-Communist culture. This was revealed the same year in the attacks on Boris Pasternak following the award of the Nobel Prize to him in 1958. *New World* had in fact rejected the manuscript of his novel *Doctor Zhivago* two years earlier, whereupon Pasternak had arranged for its publication in Italy: foreign publication had been a regular practice in the 1920s, and he did not perhaps initially regard it as a challenge to the authorities in an era of acknowledged "thaw." Certainly there was no immediate reaction to the event, though it was the first example in nearly thirty years of a device which was about to assume the greatest importance: the publication abroad of works which had fallen foul of the censors or the literary bureaucrats at home. The Nobel award, however, galvanized into action all those who had reason to fear that good writers might find ways of eluding their control. Vsevolod Kochetov, editor of *Literary Gazette* (*Literaturnaya gazeta*), accused Pasternak of "betraying his homeland," while even the editors of *New World*, now acting in their role as defenders of the status quo, published their original rejection letter, adding that since the novel had been "taken up by the bourgeois press" Pasternak had "brought discredit on the honorable calling of a Soviet writer." The Writers' Union expelled him, and a meeting of writers even petitioned the government to deprive "the traitor Boris Pasternak" of his Soviet citizenship. In the end Pasternak backed down and sent a telegram to the Swedish Academy declining the award "in view of the interpretation put upon it in the society to which I belong." Thereupon the attacks on him abruptly halted.

The campaign showed the undignified lengths to which untalented but powerful writers would go to vilify their more gifted colleagues and to defend their own power. But the sudden cessation of the campaign also demonstrated that the party remained in charge, and that its position on literature was not as unyielding as some Writers' Union officials might have hoped. Indeed, Khrushchev is said to have privately rebuked the first secretary of the Union, Surkov, for not having properly advised him in the affair (though he seems to have been annoyed most of all at not being warned that Pasternak was a world-famous poet). It was at this time that the Writers' Union of the Russian Federation (see above) was set up to increase the organizational weight of the conservative writers.

The third and deepest phase of the "thaw" owed something both to continued pressure from writers and to party policy. It coincided with the height of Khrushchev's second wave of "de-Stalinization" in 1961–2, and with the formulation of his new party program, which emphasized popular involvement in political decisions and even raised the possibility of "the withering away of the state." But its impetus certainly also derived from the efforts of certain writers and editors, and especially of Tvardovsky, back in the saddle at *New World*. It was there that in August 1960 Erenburg commenced the serial publication of his memoirs, which would revive and make respectable the names of writers disgraced, arrested and suppressed in the Stalin period: Tsvetaeva, Mandelshtam, Pilnyak, even Pasternak. He treated their non-adherence to socialist realism as irrelevant to their literary stature, and viewed them, furthermore, as participants in a lively *European* cultural life, from which Zhdanov's "anti-cosmopolitan" campaign had isolated Russian literature.

The years 1960–2 also witnessed an upsurge of "youth prose"

and an unprecedented stream of articles, memoirs, essays and fiction, mostly but not entirely in *New World*, revealing and criticizing many aspects of Stalin's rule. The culmination of this stream was Alexander Solzhenitsyn's short novel *A Day in the Life of Ivan Denisovich*, whose publication Tvardovsky secured only by circumventing the normal censorship process and obtaining Khrushchev's personal authorization.

Eventually alarm at this opening of the floodgates spread beyond the literary bureaucracy to the highest levels of the party. Khrushchev himself was swept along by the resultant reaction, though there are indications that he may have tried to moderate its scope. In December 1962 he reviled modernist painting during a visit to the Manezh exhibition hall in Moscow, and his strictures were seized upon by party ideologists and cultural bureaucrats as the signal for a counter-offensive against "formalism," "negativism," "ideological immaturity" and "succumbing to bourgeois ideology." The offensive was led by Leonid Ilichov, Central Committee secretary for ideology, but it was not unopposed: in fact, *New World* headed a serious though ultimately unsuccessful campaign to have Solzhenitsyn awarded the Lenin Prize.

At the time of Khrushchev's fall in October 1964, then, there was open conflict in the literary world.

What followed has been widely interpreted in the west as a tightening of party policy towards literature. That interpretation is only partly correct. It is true that there was an attempt at the very top, sponsored probably by Mikhail Suslov, to restore the atmosphere of intolerance towards the west and the taboo on harsh criticism of Soviet society. This effort led to the arrest in September 1965 of Andrey Sinyavsky and Yuly Daniel, who under the pseudonyms of Abram Terts and Nikolay Arzhak had smuggled out and published in the west biting surrealist satires on Soviet society. Tried in February 1966, they were sentenced to seven and five years' imprisonment respectively for "anti-Soviet propaganda." The main point about the trial was that the prosecution's case rested exclusively on literary texts. Evidently the new leadership hoped to establish that making certain kinds of criticism of Soviet society and then evading political controls to publish them abroad were criminal activities. However, this approach provoked vehement criticism, not only in the west, but inside the Writers'

Union itself. Sixty-three Moscow writers wrote to the Supreme Soviet, dissociating themselves from the content of Terts's and Arzhak's work, but warning that "the sentencing of writers for writing satirical works creates an extremely dangerous precedent and could impede the progress of Soviet culture." As Lydia Chukovskaya (daughter of the country's most famous children's writer) wrote, "Literature does not come under the jurisdiction of the criminal courts. Ideas should be fought with ideas, not with camps and prisons."

This discrediting of Soviet justice demonstrated that the party and the KGB faced substantial problems in trying to combat ideas in a framework of less than total terror of the Stalinist type. To judge by the evidence, the party seems to have reacted by withdrawing from the immediate literary battlefield, seeking to exercise its supervisory function from a safer distance while leaving the conduct of day-by-day affairs to the literary bureaucrats themselves. They could after all be relied on to defend their privilege and power, gained less through literary achievement than through loyalty to the party. Actually Khrushchev had initiated this policy of greater party restraint, but had not himself observed it consistently.

The result was a certain shift in the constellation of conflicting forces. Two camps remained roughly as before: the nonconformists around *New World* and the dogmatists around *October*. Now, however, a third one appeared, grouped at first around the journal *The Young Guard*, later around *Our Contemporary*. The major distinguishing feature of this third school was that its members had lost much of the socio-political optimism which had hitherto been common to both sides of the argument. They were concerned about the way in which war, social upheaval and political dogma had undermined the values inherited from the past. Mostly Russian nationalists, but of an un-Stalinist kind, they lamented the devastation of Russian culture, especially as it was manifested in the poverty and demoralization of the villages. Since many of their works focused on peasant life, they were dismissed by their opponents as mere "village writers" (*derevenshchiki*). It is true that many of them were peasants by origin, and their works demonstrated the way in which peasant language could enrich literature; but for them the village was a microcosm which concentrated the symptoms of a wider spiritual disorder. In time, too, as a consequence of the party's greater restraint, these writers extended their inquiry into the field of religion, suggesting, more by hint than by detailed accusation, that the party's deliberate undermining of religious values had helped to generate the contemporary malaise.

These Russian nationalist writers proceeded cautiously and skilfully, advised no doubt by the editorial collectives through whom they published. They offered few targets for direct censorship, and their work was full of the humanity, honest realism and concern for the community which had theoretically always informed socialist realism; in one characteristic, indeed – narodnost, or "popular spirit" – they outshone their more ideologically orthodox predecessors. If attacked on literary-theoretical grounds, then, they could always be defended, and the party was reluctant to resort to extra-literary measures against them. Besides, some party leaders no doubt sympathized to an extent with the Russian nationalism which inspired them.

In another respect, too, the literary scene was transformed after Khrushchev's fall. Pasternak's example in sending his work abroad to be published now generated a much greater resonance than when it had last been practiced, in the 1920s, for many Soviet citizens now had good radio sets with short-wave receivers and could pick up foreign broadcasts. Western radio stations began to take advantage of this situation to transmit to Soviet listeners works of Russian literature which they could not obtain at home. In addition, some of the growing number of western visitors smuggled in banned works published in Paris, Frankfurt or New York to give to Soviet contacts. In this way a kind of parallel Russian literature arose, functioning both as threat and as example to Soviet writers. As Dmitry Pospielovsky has commented, "the psychological Iron Curtain became thinner and more transparent."

The possibility of foreign publication considerably enlivened the never wholly abandoned but now much more promising technique of typing out one's works in multiple copies and circulating them among friends. By analogy with the official publishing houses bearing acronyms such as Gosizdat (state-publishing), this practice became known as samizdat or "self-publishing." The first *samizdat* journal, *Syntax* (*Sintaksis*), edited by Alexander Ginzburg, appeared as early as 1959, and consisted largely of poetry. It was soon succeeded by others, like *Boomerang* (*Bumerang*), edited by Vladimir Osipov, and *Phoenix* (*Feniks*), edited by Yury Galanskov. These were part of a spate of irreverent youthful literary activity at the time originating in the frustration at the suppression of the Mayakovsky Square informal poetry readings. "Hooligans" eventually broke up these meetings, while the police searched the homes of participants, and one or two of them were arrested, including Ginzburg himself. The *samizdat* technique was later adapted for civic activity: in 1966 Ginzburg compiled a *White Book* recording the proceedings at the trial of Sinyavsky and Daniel, together with protest letters and press statements. They were circulated in typescript, and made available to western correspondents, so that they could be published in the west. This was the first use of the technique which made possible the establishment of an underground journal, *The Chronicle of Current Events* (*Khronika tekushchikh sobytiy*), in 1968 and the formation of a coherent human-rights movement, at whose birth writers thus assisted and in which they continued to play a major role.

Samizdat thus offered a possible alternative to writers whose works were persistently barred from publication. It was not, however, one to be utilized lightly. Resorting to *samizdat* channels opened one to the criminal charge of "disseminating materials defaming the Soviet state and social system." It also meant losing control over one's text, which might be sent abroad even against one's will, published there in possibly defective form and without copyright protection, and then used as a pretext for reprisals by the political authorities at home.

This was the fate of Solzhenitsyn. Even after losing the struggle over the Lenin Prize, Tvardovsky continued to champion his cause, attempting to have both *The First Circle* and *Cancer Ward* published in his journal. The first was rejected while Khrushchev was still in power, but the second was the subject of an intense debate in September 1967 in the Secretariat of the Writers' Union, where it received a largely positive response. Set up in press for *New World*, it was finally barred by the personal decision of Konstantin Fedin, first secretary of the Writers' Union. Shortly afterwards Russian texts of both novels began to appear in the west, with various publishing houses, and manifesting significant textual discrepancies.

At the same time the KGB had also intervened. As early as 1961, even at the height of Khrushchev's anti-Stalin campaign, they had "arrested" a work of literature, the second part of Vasily Grossman's novel on Stalingrad, which they had accomplished by searching his home and editorial offices with which he had dealt, removing carbon papers and typewriter ribbons as well as pages of text. Now, in 1965, the KGB confiscated *The First Circle* as well as an archive of earlier writings from Solzhenitsyn. The latter tried to retrieve his texts by private representations before taking the battle to the fourth Writers' Union congress of 1967, to which he submitted a letter charging the Union with neglecting its principal function of protecting the interests of writers. He raised not only the matter of confiscation of his own works and the Union's failure to take effective action on his behalf, but also attacked the institution of censorship, and recalled the Union's silence, indeed complicity, in the suppression and arrest of numerous writers during the Stalin period. He was supported by Georgy Vladimov and a number of other writers, but his letter was not publicly read and no mention of the matter appeared in the published record of the congress.

The Union's answer to Solzhenitsyn in effect came two years later, in the autumn of 1969, when it expelled him for "joining hands with those who speak out against the Soviet social system." Tvardovsky suffered with him. The appearance in the west of his banned poem *By Right of Memory* served as the final pretext for a campaign against him by editors of rival journals. His most independent colleagues were dismissed from the editorial board of *New World*, creating conditions under which he himself felt obliged to resign.

The final stage in Solzhenitsyn's relations with the Soviet authorities began when the KGB discovered his huge history of the prisons and labor camps, *The Gulag Archipelago* (*Arkhipelag Gulag*). Solzhenitsyn had by this time concluded that in existing conditions *samizdat* and foreign publication were a powerful weapon, if skillfully and resolutely handled. He accordingly empowered a Swiss lawyer to protect his international copyright, and prepared copies of *The Gulag Archipelago*, which he sent by underground channels to the west, with instructions that it was to be published only on his direct instructions or in the event of his sudden death. Late in 1973 the KGB discovered and confiscated a copy of *The Gulag Archipelago*, whereupon Solzhenitsyn authorized its western publication. Shortly afterwards, he was arrested and deported from the USSR.

The possibilities and dangers exemplified in Solzhenitsyn's career set the scene for the characteristic literary drama of the 1970s: a writer discovered and first published during the "thaw" gradually finds his literary explorations taking him beyond the point at which his senior literary colleagues will tolerate him and offer him publishing facilities. Sometimes the decision to ban a writer seems to be made not for purely literary reasons, but because he is involved in the civil rights movement or even for motives of personal enmity. Squeezed out of official Soviet literature, the banned writer resorts to *samizdat*, and then, voluntarily or involuntarily, to *tamizdat* (publishing "over there"), as foreign publication came to be known. This makes him a celebrity abroad and an object of scandal at home, as a result of which he attracts increasing attention from the procuracy and KGB and ends up either being arrested on a trumped up criminal charge, or else being exiled from the country. Some writers chose the latter fate under the threat of the former. Among the writers who left the country after such developments were Andrey Sinyavsky (after his imprisonment), Joseph Brodsky, Naum Korzhavin, Vladimir Maksimov, Victor Nekrasov, Alexander Zinovev, Vladimir Voynovich, Georgy Vladimov and Vasily Aksyonov.

Their arrival in the west engendered a whole "third wave" of Russian "émigré" literature – though the word "émigré" is imprecise, since the concerns of these writers remained Soviet ones, and their links with the homeland were much closer than those of earlier generations of exiles. The focus of much of their activity was in literary journals. The principal ones were *Continent* (*Kontinent*), founded in 1974 by Vladimir Maksimov in Frankfurt am Main, which adopted a neo-Slavophile political line but was broad-minded in its choice of authors; *We and Our Epoch* (*Vremya i my*), founded in Tel Aviv by Victor Perelman in 1976 to give a voice to the rich Russian Jewish tradition; and *Syntax* (*Sintaksis*), founded in 1978 in Paris as a largely critical journal by Sinyavsky, who had broken away from *Continent* with the intention of creating a more liberal and cosmopolitan forum. To these should be added a number of journals (some ephemeral) which began to appear in the late 1970s to publish young (or even not so young) writers who had emigrated before finding a niche in the Soviet literary world. Bearing titles like *Echo* (*Ekho*), *The Ark* (*Kovcheg*), *Third Wave* (*Tretya volna*) and *Twenty Two* (*Dvadtsat dva*), these journals rejected the political commitments of their elders and espoused "art for art's sake." We may in future see them as harbingers of an epoch when Stalinism and its consequences would cease to obsess writers.

Inside the Soviet Union the problem of young writers was taken up by Aksyonov. One result of the increasingly restrictive publishing policy adopted by the Writers' Union during the late 1960s and 1970s was that new young authors found it extremely difficult to publish. Literary professionals began to age to such an extent that at the seventh Writers' Union congress in 1981 only three per cent of delegates were under forty. Aksyonov, as one of the principal figures of the youth movement of twenty years earlier, sponsored in 1978 a symposium, *Metropol*, on the lines of *Literary Moscow* of 1956, to bring out works by young authors along with a few by more established figures. A key element of the initiative was that the writers themselves would do the editing, presenting a complete text to be published unchanged. At the last moment the Writers' Union blocked publication, and expelled two of its younger contributors from membership. Thereupon Aksyonov resigned from the Union in protest, and shortly afterwards emigrated from the USSR, declaring that he could see no future for himself as a writer there.

In spite of this wanton dissipation of talent, and an increasingly sclerotic leadership, not all good literature died out within the Writers' Union. Indeed, it was still possible for a determined editor to publish works of high quality and moderately controversial subject matter, even if no longer on the scale of a Tvardovsky. Thus *Friendship of Peoples* (*Druzhba narodov*), under Sergey Baruzdin and *Our Contemporary* under Sergey Vikulov (who had participated in the campaign against Tvardovsky) both established themselves as forums for good literature and serious discussion of social issues. Even *New World* was not wholly emasculated.

By the early 1980s there was thus one Russian literature in two homelands. Much of it, on both sides of the divide, was still motivated by the agenda set in the immediate post-Stalin years, that of revealing the truth about the past and of using the material of Soviet reality to achieve a fuller understanding of man's nature.

Boris Pasternak's *Doctor Zhivago*, the first serious literary attempt in the post-Stalin period to grapple with the problems of man in Soviet society, drew its resources from the pre-Soviet past, from the culture of Russia's "silver age," of which Pasternak had been a brilliant representative. Yet, as he himself was aware, that culture could not without some inner transformation adequately reflect the social and spiritual upheavals which had crushed it. As Misha Gordon pointed out at the end of *Doctor Zhivago*, Blok's statement "We are the children of Russia's terrible years" was meant to be understood figuratively; but "now everything figurative has become literal: the children are real children, and the terrors are truly terrifying . . ."

For much of his life, Pasternak was troubled by the thought that lyric poetry was inadequate to deal with the problems of the Russian twentieth century. He was haunted by the idea of writing a long novel, the genre which alone, he came to feel, could do justice to the huge triumphs and tragedies of his epoch. As he wrote once to a foreign editor, "Fragmentary, personal poems are hardly suited to meditating on such obscure, new and solemn events. Only prose and philosophy can attempt to deal with them." Nadezhda Mandelshtam thought that in this judgement he merely succumbed to the "weird gigantomania of his times," and indeed the eventual product suggests that in many ways Pasternak's talent was not well suited to the novel form. Yet he himself never wavered in his view that *Doctor Zhivago* was "the only worthwhile thing I have ever achieved."

Doctor Zhivago is a strange work. It draws a veil over the Stalin years, touching on them only in a brief epilogue. The main part of the action occurs between 1905 and 1929, and indeed most of the material is drawn from the years 1917–21, in which Pasternak, perhaps anachronistically, finds all the cardinal features of Soviet society already present. His view of it is rooted in the philosophical and religious renaissance of the early twentieth century, and especially in the neo-idealist thinkers of the *Landmarks* symposium.

The importance of these thinkers is that, though they were pre-Soviet, they were also post-Marxist: indeed, most of them had been through a Marxist period in their own lives, and then rejected Marxism for Kantian reasons, on the grounds that man was not primarily a material phenomenon bound by causality but a free spirit, creator of both history and culture.

Pasternak, who had once dreamt of being a philosopher and had studied under neo-Kantians in Germany, made this outlook the foundation of his novel. It is expounded in the early pages by Yury Zhivago's uncle, Nikolay Vedenyapin, and is then frequently reiterated in more fragmentary form by Yury, his mistress Lara and other "positive" characters, while the action and structure of the novel confirm its validity. It is also embodied in the poems composed by Yury which are an integral part of that structure. Overall, then, the novel is a kind of extended sermon.

Although in the excitement of the revolution Yury is prepared to admire the Bolsheviks as creators of history, he very soon concludes that their mode of action implies a reductionist and manipulative attitude towards human beings, born of a lack of talent for anything else. "It turns out that those who inspired the revolution aren't at home in anything except change and turmoil: that's their native element," he says. "And do you know why there is this incessant whirl of never-ending preparations? It's because they haven't any real capacities, they are ungifted. Man is born to live, not to prepare for life. Life itself – the gift of life – is such a breathtakingly serious thing!"

Yury himself, partly by design and partly by accident, lives a life diametrically opposite to that of the revolutionaries. He is a failure in almost every respect: a doctor who abandons his profession, a husband who betrays his wife, a lover who relinquishes his mistress, he ends life almost as a tramp. There is something about him of the "holy fool" (*yurodivy*) of Russian tradition. The only possible justification of his life is the slim volume of poetry which forms the last part of the novel, and is thus an indispensable part of its external action, not just of its meaning. Here Zhivago both expounds and exemplifies his concept of personality as the essence of human life and the link between that life and the structure of the universe. This is a Christian concept, since in Yury's view (and Pasternak's) only the coming of Christ put an end to the "boastful dead eternity of bronze monuments and marble columns" and inaugurated an era when "men began to live in their posterity and ceased to die in ditches like dogs – instead, they died at home in history, at the height of the work they devoted to the conquest of death . . ."

Throughout his life Pasternak had been noted for the daring metaphors in which he elaborated his vision of man and nature. In *Doctor Zhivago* metaphor ceases to be a figure of speech and becomes an outlook on life: the sensitivity to the diverse and ubiquitous inter-relatedness of human beings and the world around them. Inanimate things participate in the human drama, so that "flowers talk philosophy at night, stone houses hold meetings," and the landscape of Lara's departure forms a chorus to his grief, "as if [. . .] the trees had only now taken up their places, rising out of the ground with the purpose of offering their condolences."

It is not surprising that the editors of *New World*, members of the Soviet establishment however free-thinking, should have been alienated by this novel, which called into question everything they believed. They regarded Zhivago as "an essentially immoral man who refuses to do his duty by the people and who is interested only in his own rights, including the alleged privilege of a superman to betray with impunity." And many intellectuals who read the work in *samizdat* agreed with them, so vast was the gulf which divided Soviet from pre-Soviet culture. Yet this novel and its accompanying poems (most of which were returned to the official Soviet reader much earlier than the prose text) were to be very influential, for they helped to revive a concern with the human personality, with morality and with religion, which had been largely submerged within the majestic state-sponsored collective certainties of the Soviet era.

Pasternak's last cycle of poems, *When the Weather Clears* (*Kogda razgulyaetsya*, written 1956–9), continues the stylistic compression and simplification which the *Zhivago* lyrics had already displayed. Some critics have felt a certain impoverishment here compared with the exuberance of his early verse, while others have argued that Pasternak was now concentrating on the essentials, and doing so in a more readily comprehensible way, without loss of imaginative power. Most of the individual poems record an incident or an impression which he links with the overarching themes of the passing of the seasons, life, death and rebirth. Man and nature are linked in symbiotic unity. Indicative is "In the hospital" ("V bolnitse"), about a man suddenly rushed to hospital who, looking out of the window and realizing he is likely to die, finds new meaning in everything around him:

> There in the glare the gate glowed
> And, lit by the city, a maple
> Made with its gnarled branch
> A farewell reverence to the sick man.

The message – and Pasternak does not eschew straightforward messages – is that only the sensitive individual consciousness, and not mass movements, will change life:

> It is not revolutions and upheavals
> Which clear the way to a new life,
> But the revelations, storms and bounties
> Of someone's spirit on fire.

One young writer deeply influenced by Pasternak was Andrey Sinyavsky (1925–   ). Brought up in a family of convinced revolutionaries, his beliefs were thrown into turmoil first of all by his father's arrest in 1951, then by the revelations of Khrushchev's "secret speech." He was therefore impressed by the evocation of a renewed but traditional Christianity in the Zhivago poems, and especially for what they revealed about the way in which traditional religious yearnings had underlain and survived the secular project of the Soviet state. Sinyavsky became a personal friend of Pasternak, was later a pall-bearer at his funeral, and wrote the first serious Soviet critical survey of his poetry in a preface to the first Soviet edition of it in 1965.

Fascination with Pasternak's example did not lead Sinyavsky to Christianity: he did not exchange belief in the Soviet utopia for faith in what he saw as the Christian one. Rather he became a kind of deist, convinced of the importance of the religious urge and exhibiting a detached sympathy towards it. It was from this point of view that he wrote his witty critical essay *What is Socialist Realism? (Chto takoe sotsialistichesky realizm?*, 1956), which discerns the principal esthetic deficiency of Stalinist literature, not in the idealization of reality which it offered – for much of the finest art of the past consists in such idealization – but rather in the attempt to marry such idealization with the coolly disillusioned tone of nineteenth-century realism. One cannot simultaneously both glorify and analyze. The fault of much Soviet writing was, in his view, an incongruity internal to its genre. Sinyavsky offered a tentative prescription for a way out of this dilemma:

> Right now I put my hope in a phantasmagoric art, with hypotheses instead of a Purpose, an art in which the grotesque will replace realistic descriptions of ordinary life. Such an art would correspond best to the spirit of our time. May the fantastic imagery of Hoffmann and Dostoevskii [. . .] teach us how to be truthful with the aid of the absurd and fantastic.

Sinyavsky put this theory into practice in works like *The Court is in Session* (*Sud idet*, 1956), *Fantastic Tales* (*Fantasticheskie povesti*, 1956–61) and *The Makepeace Experiment* (*Lyubimov*, 1961–2). Like the socialist realism essay, they were smuggled out to the west and published there under the pseudonym Abram Terts – the name of a denizen of the Odessa Jewish underworld which Sinyavsky borrowed from Babel, not only to conceal his true identity, but also to signal his conviction that he could only deal creatively with Soviet life from the viewpoint of a social and ethnic outsider. The tales all invest mundane Soviet reality with elements of the grotesque, partly as a technique of *ostranenie* ("making strange") to draw attention to specific aspects of that reality, but partly also to impart a sense of the human soul as alien amid the environment which it has itself created. The atmosphere of authoritarianism, mass deceit, mistrust and fear transposes readily into a nightmare world.

The Makepeace Experiment deals directly with the utopian drive of the Soviet experiment. Its principal character, Leonid Tikhomirov, learns the secret of mass hypnosis from an old book by an ancestor, a nineteenth-century intellectual who haunts the plot. But his attempts at using his gift to create an ideal life for the inhabitants of his home town fetch up against the stolid passivity of his fellow citizens. The resulting tension generates both the comedy and the irony of the book. It is a kind of parable on Russian history, in which the tragi-comic obsessions of its rulers founder on the healthy inertia of its people.

Sinyavsky has cultivated his own private outlook on the world more directly in the aphorisms and casual jottings which make up *Unguarded Thoughts* (*Mysli vrasplokh*, 1966). Some of the themes of his stories are recapitulated here in more laconic form, especially the split within the human personality between spirit and flesh, a split given fresh, paradoxical dimensions by the Soviet experience. After his seven years in labor camp he assembled a further and much longer series of thoughts, most of them taken from letters written to his wife during that time. Published as *Voice from the Chorus* (*Golos iz khora*, 1973), they constitute a richer collection than the earlier one, not only because they are more numerous and cover a wider variety of themes – especially literature, folklore and art – but also because here the author deliberately allows his voice to merge with that of his fellow prisoners, whose pithy, demotic, sometimes vulgar comments on all manner of subjects form a fertile counterpoint to his own more leisurely and erudite obser-vations.

Overall, Sinyavsky's astringent intelligence, his sharp sense of the human strangeness of the Soviet environment, and his skepti-cism gradually yielding to religious faith based on deeply rooted cultural factors – all these features have made him a major and rather unusual witness to his times, unusual in the sense that most of his contemporaries have not followed his prescription of a "phantasmagoric art," but have thought it instead important to try first of all, in a world where reality and illusion are so closely intertwined, to re-establish a sense of the real in more traditional ways, in order to disentangle it from state-sponsored fantasy.

No one better exemplifies this project of salvaging the truth than Alexander Solzhenitsyn (1918–   ), who used his own experience of the underside of Stalinist society, acquired from eight years' imprisonment under Stalin, and drew on layers of popular consciousness hitherto excluded from Soviet literature. His short novel *A Day in the Life of Ivan Denisovich* (*Odin den Ivana Deniso-vicha*, 1962) was a challenge to official literature in more ways than one. First, of course, the subject of Stalin's labor camps had been strictly taboo, and was only now permitted through the personal intervention of Khrushchev. Second, the language of the narrator (and not only that of the characters) was the colloquial speech of what Solzhenitsyn was later to call the "nation of zeks": a language completely new to literature, derived from the murderous melting pot in which Stalin had mixed all social classes and infinitely distant from the semi-bureaucratese in which the literature of "socialist classicism" (as Sinyavsky called it) was usually couched. The persona of the narrator was himself something of an innovation. Far removed from the Olympian, all-comprehending narrator of Stalinist fiction, he hovers close to Ivan Denisovich himself, uses his language, adopts his view of the world, shares his limitations, and indeed at times merges with him in third person direct speech. His view of the world and of time and space is entirely outside the ideological mold. The narrator does not see history as going anywhere in particular: indeed, he implies that time is cyclical or at any rate repetitive (see the opening and closing lines of the story), and that the camp is merely a microcosm of a society of arbitrary authority and meaningless labor. The action does not develop in any particular direction: it consists merely of a series of daily repeated customs and devices for dealing with adversity. If there is a moral outlook in the novel, then it is expressed in old, resigned popular sayings like "groan and bend your back; if you resist, they'll break you."

When *Ivan Denisovich* appeared, the émigré critic Roman Gul wrote that it "cancels out the whole of socialist realism." György Lukács, on the other hand, called it a "significant step in the renewal of the great traditions of the Socialist Realism of the 1920s." Curiously enough, both critics were right, each in his own way. *Ivan Denisovich* did indeed expose the hollow pretensions of official Stalinist fiction; on the other hand, it also reaffirmed certain principles which official socialist realism had distorted; genuine *narodnost*, concerns with humane values, meticulous and honest reporting of the everyday life of ordinary people. Perhaps the most apposite comment was made by the writer Grigory Baklanov, who said in 1962: "We cannot write the same way again after *Ivan Denisovich*." It is certainly true that all the above-mentioned innovations were to prove enormously influential. The subject matter, action, language, narrative stance and temporal perspective of Russian fiction, were all to change radically, not least because of *Ivan Denisovich*.

Solzhenitsyn's later works do not fundamentally depart from these principles; indeed, they broaden their scope and extend their application. The novels *The Cancer Ward* (*Rakovy korpus*, first published 1968) and especially *The First Circle* (*V kruge pervom*, first published 1968) both portray the macrocosm of which *Ivan Denisovich* is a part. To reconcile the breadth of vision required for such an overview with the intense subjectivity of his narrative stance, Solzhenitsyn builds up what some critics have termed a "polyphonic novel," in which "each character becomes the central one while he is in the field of action." Probably the term "polyphonic" (at least in the sense in which Bakhtin used it about Dostoevsky) is not quite appropriate to Solzhenitsyn's method, since, for all the diversity of narrative viewpoints which he adopts, there is no real ambiguity about the moral outlook of the author himself.

The First Circle, for example, presents a moral cosmos whose structure rests on the dual poles of freedom and captivity. The co-ordinates are not, however, where they might be expected: spiritual freedom by no means corresponds to juridical freedom. Indeed, such spiritual freedom as exists in the novel dwells among those who are physically in captivity. This ironic incongruity is a basic structural feature of the novel, and is also the means by which the author, without resorting to Olympian judgments, guides us to his own conception of the truth. The setting of the special prison of Mavrino, like that of Thomas Mann's *Magic Mountain* or Albert Camus's *The Plague*, is isolated by evil from common humanity as though to encourage intense interaction among those individuals confined within it, each faced by decisions of existential importance. Dante's cosmology is suggested by the title and by certain features of the novel: the "first circle," as Rubin reminds new arrivals, is where the Christian God puts the sages of antiquity whom He cannot admit to paradise but does not wish to consign to hell. It is the least unpleasant of the circles: its denizens may rest a little from the torments of the nether regions to undertake the kind of self-examination and interaction with others which they would not bother to pursue while free and would have no strength to endure in normal camps.

Like Dante's, Solzhenitsyn's cosmos is built on moral categories. Its inhabitants must decide fundamental moral questions: whether to capitulate to the demands of a perverted system, or to retain a measure of inner freedom. The central issues revolve around *language*. The surface plot concerns the distortion of language on a telephone scrambler, and the devising of a code-breaker to decipher it, but the novel's deeper structure also turns upon the use and misuse of language. Solzhenitsyn depicts a society in which the creation and propagation of false words employs thousands of the most talented people, draining from words their real meaning, making human communication more difficult, engendering a society in which people distrust one another and keep their real selves hidden so long that they lose confidence in their own identity. This is a spiritually sick society. In contrast to the floods of spurious language vomited by the official propaganda machine stands the spare and allusive use of language between two people who know and love each other, as in the brief meeting between Nerzhin and his wife. Similarly, real literature, Esenin's poetry, Goethe's *Faust* or the verbal improvisations of Rubin, restore wholeness to human beings, and afford them deeper insight into themselves and those around them. Language, in fact, its use and misuse, carries the key to the door between the worlds of freedom and unfreedom which the characters inhabit.

In *The Cancer Ward*, the hospital corresponds to the special camp in *The First Circle*. In this case, however, both Kostoglotov, as the main character, and Soviet society in general are in transition, and the point at issue is moral responsibility. In moving from labor camp to hospital, Kostoglotov exchanges one form of deprivation of autonomy for another. In the camp the authorities, justified by ideology, exercise power over human beings whom they have deprived of the right to make their own decisions. In the hospital the doctors, justified by medical science, do precisely the same, however humane their purpose. Once again, then, we have a setting in which freedom and unfreedom are ironically juxtaposed.

The Gulag Archipelago represents Solzhenitsyn's most ambitious attempt to restore to consciousness things that have been long repressed. It is nothing less than a chronicle of that "zek nation" whose way of life its author shared for eight years. It is a mixture of personal memoir, of oral and written testimony by more than two hundred witnesses, and of straightforward documentary history. It may seem incongruous to classify it as literature, but Solzhenitsyn himself terms it "an experiment in artistic investigation," and it fulfils what he in his Nobel Prize speech of 1971 called the principal task of literature, namely the communication of human experience. It is, moreover, imbued with precisely the same moral concern which characterized his earlier works. He seeks the sources of evil not solely in social circumstances or political doctrines (though certainly there), but also in himself: "Gradually it was disclosed to me that the line separating good and evil passes not through states, not between classes, nor between political parties either – but right through every human heart [. . .]"

In a spirit of honest self-examination, Solzhenitsyn confesses that he himself, as a youthful true-believing Marxist–Leninist, was nearly recruited by the NKVD, and was only held back by a certain revulsion, which was illogical in view of his beliefs but which derived perhaps from the contempt in which nineteenth-century Russian writers held gendarmes. He recalls the arrogant self-assurance which he displayed as a young Red Army officer, treating his men as lower forms of life. All this was preparing him for the role, not of zek, but of camp commandant or intelligence officer.

Perhaps this acute awareness of how easily he could have finished up on the other side of the moral frontier imparts its agitated tone to *The Gulag Archipelago*. Much of the text is in the form of repartee, addressed to specified and unspecified antagonists. The narrator answers these antagonists' questions, anticipates their objections, unmasks their hypocrisy. The vehement language is that of a man exorcizing his own inner demons – which is of course literally the case. The most persistent of his interlocutors is in effect the youthful Solzhenitsyn, the staunch Marxist–Leninist and arrogant army officer. The anguished tone of these polemical passages alternates with the more collected and magisterial manner of the chronicler, the folklorist, the anthropologist arranging and expounding his strange material. The collective and objective are constantly interwoven with the personal, subjective and confessional. This gives *The Gulag Archipelago* its existential quality, and makes it (in the Russian sense) a novel as well as a history.

It would be wrong to attempt a judgment on the huge cycle of novels which Solzhenitsyn is writing on the Russian revolution until they are further advanced than they are now, though it is already apparent that the transition into a completely objective and historical sphere and away from personal experience carries its risks. Solzhenitsyn is now exploring the *external* roots of the evil he described in *The Gulag Archipelago*. He discerns it in a dogmatic and inhumane ideology, imported from abroad by narrow-minded, intolerant revolutionaries and implanted on a basically healthy Russian body politic because of the weakness of the last Emperor and his corrupt court. This is a perfectly tenable (though not incontestable) view of the coming of communism to Russia, but Solzhenitsyn's exploitation of the narrator's privilege of expounding it deprives his talent of its most distinctive feature: its openness and diversity. The latent guiding intelligence behind his work becomes explicit, and thereby loses its existential openness. Solzhenitsyn even inserts long passages of straight historical exposition into his novels, though set in small type as a concession to those who wish to skip them. Georges Nivat, Solzhenitsyn's most perceptive critic, once remarked that in his texts the voice of others preceded his own, which he was still in search of: "I would even say that if he is to remain Solzhenitsyn, Solzhenitsyn should not find his 'own' definite voice [. . .]" Perhaps that is what has happened. On the other hand, his language retains its demotic vigor, even when the controlling intelligence channelling it is more in evidence; and the passages in *August 1914* (*Avgust chetyrnadtsatogo*, published 1971) evoking Russian history, traditions and landscape, as in the suicide of General Samsonov and the burial of Colonel Kabanov, are among the finest he has written.

As a chronicler of the Gulag, Solzhenitsyn has one, and only one, equal. That is Varlam Shalamov (1907–82), whom he actually invited at one stage to become co-author of *The Gulag Archipelago*. Apart from recognizing Shalamov's literary talent, Solzhenitsyn had a special reason for making this offer: "Shalamov's experience in the camps was longer and more bitter then my own, and I respectfully acknowledge that to him and not to me was it given to touch those depths of bestiality and despair towards which life in the camps dragged us all." If Mavrino was the "first circle" of the Stalinist inferno, then Kolyma, where Shalamov spent seventeen years, was its nethermost region, a frozen continent separated by a thousand kilometers of trackless waste from the rest of the country, where labor camps formed a mere "archipelago."

Outwardly at least, Shalamov's work is entirely different from Solzhenitsyn's. Instead of a vast, sprawling panorama, Shalamov selects the most concise of literary forms, the short story, shaping it so carefully that his potential overall structure is like a mosaic made of tiny stones. Unfortunately, because of the way in which the stories have been published – first haphazardly in émigré journals, then in book form (*Kolyma Tales* [*Kolymskie rasskazy*, 1978]) in an order not determined by the author – we cannot be certain what this overall structure is, or even whether Shalamov intended his stories to have one. Where Solzhenitsyn is passionate, subjective and moralistic, Shalamov adopts a studiedly neutral tone, taking strict control of his discourse, conducting the narrative from a single, "objective" viewpoint, and avoiding moral statements beyond the assertion that "the camps are a negative school of life in every respect. Nobody will ever learn anything useful or necessary from them."

Most of Shalamov's stories focus on just one person or incident, and even within this narrow framework the presentation is sparing. Nature descriptions are brief and straightforward, couched in the primary colors of the taiga. Physical description of people is minimal: a face or hand seen in the dim light of a candle, a gesture glimpsed in the cold dawn. Psychological analysis and internal reflection are equally simple – though precisely traced – for human feelings are so blunted by cold, hunger and overwork as to admit of only the most basic responses. Even action is narrated parsimoniously, with essential links merely hinted at or even left unexplained, so that the reader perceives each succeeding eventuality as another element in an arbitrary design imposed by the authorities.

The overall effect is of a merciless and humiliating dissection of human nature at its basest. Shalamov deliberately strips away all the accretions of civilized life in order to understand human beings as they function under extreme stress. Yet the impact of his work is emphatically not depressing. There is something bracing about his determination to confront and report faithfully the very worst that life can offer. What he finds in human beings thus stripped down is a residual life force which manifests itself as "malice" (*zloba*). "Malice was the last feeling with which man departed into non-being, into the world of the dead. But was it dead? Even a stone didn't seem dead to me, not to mention the grass, the trees, the river."

Nor in fact does Shalamov exemplify his own assertion that prison camp life is totally corrupting and that everything experienced there is worthless. If that were so, why tell these stories at all? He comes over in his own narration as a person who reacts to adversity by retreating into inaction, while continuing to observe a minimal code of duty. His moral code is not a Christian one: perhaps indeed it is closer to that of the Stoics, the inhabitants of Dante's "first circle." Most of all, however, it resembles the wisdom of the eastern religions, especially those which enjoin the honest contemplation of everything evil in man's nature as a stage towards the abandonment of hope and indeed individuality itself. Shalamov's self-identification with rocks, stones and trees, with a basic life force, is consonant with that outlook.

For those, at any rate, who would understand what the worst of the Stalinist experience could do to human beings, it is essential to read Shalamov as well as Solzhenitsyn.

The rejection of the immediate past provoked by the Twentieth Party Congress brought many young writers into literature, bursting with determination to assert their own distinctive view of the world in opposition to that of their elders. They had their bastion, as mentioned, in the journal *Youth*. Among the writers associated with the youth trend in these years were Anatoly Gladilin (1935–), Anatoly Kuznetsov (1929–), Andrey Bitov, and Vasily Aksyonov.

The theme of the conflict of generations is familiar enough in Russian literature, but it was given a new intensity by de-Stalinization. The older generation had been intimidated, deluded or, worse still, molded by Stalin. The "sons" were therefore exceptionally raucous in their rejection of at least the externals of the preceding era. They and their literary creations dressed in jeans and sneakers, danced rock-and-roll, flaunted their reading of Sartre, Hemingway and Salinger, and spoke a language full of smart westernisms. They emphasized the subjective perceptions and emotional reactions of young people becoming acquainted with a world which was both puzzling and in many respects repellent. For that reason they cast their stories where possible in the form of dialogue or letters to a close friend, or couched their authorial narrative in the language of young people talking to one another in the jargon of sport, cars, pop music and fashion, or borrowing phrases ironically from inappropriate contexts such as classical literature or *Pravda* editorials.

The emphasis of "youth prose" was on the young person's discovery of him- or herself. This was an unusually difficult process, since the guidelines offered by the parents' generation were discredited. Young writers felt the need to cultivate a whole new mentality, to go beyond simply rejecting the externals of the immediate past. As the hero of Gladilin's story "The First Day of the New Year" ("Pervy den novogo goda") says to his father:

> You don't repair the consequences of the cult of personality by merely removing portraits and renaming cities. The cult of the personality is sluggishness of thought, fear to think for oneself, complacency and hatred of everything new.

These characters strive to avoid the fate of which the hero of Aksyonov's "A Ticket to the Stars" ("Zvezdny bilet," 1961) warns his elder brother:

> Your life, Victor, was mapped out by Papa and Mama when you were still in the cradle. Top of the class at school, distinction at college, graduate student, junior research fellow, senior research fellow, Doctor of Science, Academician, and then [. . .] the much-respected, late-lamented [. . .] Never in your life have you taken a really serious decision, never once taken a risk.

All the same, there is a sense in which "youth prose," at least during the Khrushchev period, never quite emancipated itself from the ideals of the older generation. For all their rebelliousness of style, language and outlook, these young writers and their heroes were not deeply disillusioned with Soviet society. Their personal revolt was directed towards the new and creative, and it usually culminated in re-dedication to the building of socialism, conceived in the post-Stalin spirit and therefore symbolized not only by tractors, ball bearings and hydro-electric dams, but also by sputniks, beat music and transistor radios. Aksyonov's heroes might renew themselves in the Baltic provinces, where they could pick up the latest western fashions and ideas, but they finished by heading for Siberia and honest labor on the virgin lands. Rejection of the fathers was usually mixed with a hope of some kind of reconciliation with them in mutual devotion to the common purpose.

The technical innovations and the heightened subjectivity of "youth prose" were, then, put at the service of the long familiar Soviet myth, indeed imparted to it a new sheen. But the implications of this heightened subjectivity, the rejection of the monolithic and Olympian, were, for all that, ultimately subversive. They suggested that there was perhaps not just one single Truth, in principle accessible to everyone, that search and experimentation were more valuable than submission to authority, and that each person must find their own ideal.

This search might become intensely self-centered, as in the case of the Leningrad writer Andrey Bitov (1937–), whose early stories record in conscientious, sensitive and carefully wrought prose a young man's attempt to understand himself, partly through detailed memories of childhood, partly through minute observation of his everyday reactions to events and people. Similarly, in Bitov's numerous travelogues the receptivity of the traveler serves not only to communicate a sense of place but also as a means of self-exploration. His principal work, the novel *Pushkin House* (*Pushkinsky dom*, 1978) investigates what he perceives as the betrayal of Russian culture during the Soviet period, a betrayal originating in the cowardice of the intelligentsia, to which he is conscious of belonging. The ambivalence aroused by this awareness is reflected in his experiments with narrative technique – for example the recounting of the same incident from two different viewpoints – as a means of examining the moral implications of his own and others' actions.

The implications of subjectivity and diversity also work themselves out in the successive novels of Vasily Aksyonov (1932–): the notes of individualism and subjectivity become progressively stronger, the rededication to a collective purpose ever fainter. Indeed the purpose itself, the anticipated brotherly society, assumes ever more stylized and metaphorical forms: a star-spangled square of sky seen in the shaft of a tall building (in "Ticket to the Stars"), a shipload of oranges (in "Oranges from Morocco" ["Apelsiny iz Marokko," 1963]), or a truckload of empty barrel casings (in "Excess Barrel Casings" ["Zatovarennaya bochkotara," 1968]). These images, subjective to the point of arbitrariness, flowered with baroque exuberance, while the fantasies of Aksyonov's characters clustered about them as beacons in the common quest for light, love and beauty. This many-faceted subjectivity moved Aksyonov to experiment further with his narrative viewpoint, recounting incidents through the eyes of more than one character, flashing backwards and forwards in time, merging fantasy with reality. In the process he assimilated some of the rich experimental tradition of Russian prose of the 1910s and 1920s.

As the youth writers, especially Aksyonov, were becoming bolder, the authorities were getting more restrictive. Less and less was actually getting into print. Kuznetsov (in 1969) and Gladilin (in 1976) emigrated as a result of their frustrations, and in 1980 Aksyonov followed that example.

In the United States Aksyonov published the novel which, more than any other, appraises the fate of the youth writers. This was *The Burn* (*Ozhog*, written 1969–75, published 1980). It fully divulges what had been veiled in most of his stories of twenty years earlier, the fact that Aksyonov's own mother had spent many years in the labor camps, and that he himself had grown up in Magadan, the port town for the Kolyma region. In retrospect, it now seemed that the relatively superficial *fronderie* of twenty years earlier had averted its gaze from the worst horrors committed by the older generation, perhaps in the hope of a reconciliation which would facilitate common work for a better future. The occupation of Czechoslovakia in 1968 finally destroyed any hope of such a reconciliation. The main theme of *The Burn*, therefore, is the rediscovery of the cruel father. It imaginatively recreates a generation's attempt to come to terms with this father figure and to discover a new creative starting point.

The narrator is a collective personality, at one and the same time writer, sculptor, jazz musician, surgeon and scholar, each with the same patronymic in token of their common paternity. They also share the same childhood, that of an orphaned Jewish boy, Tolya, in post-war Magadan, facing up to the consequences of his mother's arrest. The novel shows the youth culture of the late 1960s on its final drunken fling, the hope and warmth degenerating into tawdry promiscuity and betrayal, while the "fathers" (the Brezhnev generation) re-establish their grip, shaken by Khrushchev's "hare-brained schemes." Images from the past haunt the composite main character: the security police officer who once arrested his mother and beat up his best friend, a girl whom he loved at that time, and his Catholic stepfather, whose rock-like faith he always respected without wishing to imitate it. These images struggle for the soul of the adult five-fold Tolya, in an abundance of cultural, sexual and religious imagery which is never quite coherent. The novel ends with all traffic in Moscow coming to a halt in expectation of a religious revelation – which, however, fails to materialize. By 1980, at least, the "youth" generation had become disillusioned with the Soviet myth but had not yet found an alternative to it.

A different variety of "youth prose" was developed by Georgy Vladimov (1931–). His heroes care nothing for western chic. They are ordinary Russian working class lads trying to make sense of their lives and to find their own niche in a society which is rapidly changing and often unwelcoming. Like many others, Vladimov was discovered by Tvardovsky, and the first work to make his reputation, *The Great Ore* (*Bolshaya ruda*, 1961), was published in *New World*. Its main character, Victor Pronyakin, is in many respects a model socialist realist hero. At the beginning he stands looking out over the crater of a quarry near Kursk, determined to discover the layer of iron ore for which everyone is searching. In the end, despite all obstacles, he achieves this, repairing a damaged tip-up truck to out-perform everyone else in the removal of soil from the quarry floor. Working in the pouring rain, when all the others have given up, he shifts the first load of genuine ore but skids on the mud and plunges to his death, in a tragic but fitting end for a Stakhanovite hero.

The mythical element in Pronyakin is, however, minimal. The novel gives instead a psychologically searching portrait of him. He comes over as a figure driven obsessively to achievement by self-doubt, even self-hatred, and a childlike need to fulfil all his desires immediately. As his brigade leader remarks, "You're in too much of a hurry, Victor ... you want everything at once." This inner restlessness distorts his relationships with his comrades and with women. Precariously reformed alcoholic and eternal wanderer, he is unable to settle down either to family life or to routine work. In the light of the book's psychological analysis, his death looks remarkably like self-destruction.

A similar spirit pervades Vladimov's *Three Minutes' Silence* (*Tri minuty molchaniya*, 1969), a novel about the Atlantic fishing fleet.

Its hero, Senya Shalai, does achieve a more stable condition at the end, not least because of the experience of going with his comrades to the rescue of a Scottish trawler in distress in heavy seas. The experience of collective openness to the needs of others – the SOS radio silence referred to in the title – gives him a moral stability which his predecessor lacked. The shadow of the restless Pronyakin remains in this novel, however, embodied in the Legend of the Flying Dutchman, the story recounted by all Murmansk trawlermen of the lad who would never return to harbor, but would instead transfer at sea from an incoming to an outgoing ship, disdaining all the shore comforts which sailors normally yearn for: no one knew why he did it.

Although its subject is ostensibly a dog, *Faithful Ruslan* (*Verny Ruslan*) – which could only be published abroad in 1975 – also examines the enduring features of the Stalinist legacy. Sinyavsky has pointed out that the former labor camp guard dog from whose viewpoint the story is told is a true socialist realist hero. I would add that he is also a socialist realist narrator, in many ways, though he provides the reader with enough information to arrive at a totally different conclusion from his own. Ruslan observes uncomprehendingly how in 1956 the labor camp which is his physical and spiritual universe is broken up, its inmates are dispersed and he himself is abandoned to a society which bears the marks of the Gulag but nevertheless lives by different laws. Repelled by the slovenly ways of "freedom," Ruslan longs for the call, which he believes will come, to the Service which has been his life, and to the secure penitentiary environment where "people were not indifferent to one another, everyone was closely watched, and man was considered the highest value."

Ruslan has all the qualities required in a guardian of prisoners: he gets "high marks for malevolence" and "excels in mistrust towards outsiders." But he is not simply vicious. On the contrary, he finds gratuitous cruelty repugnant. The true reason for his zeal is his belief in the ideals of the Service, to which he has been trained and from which he has received his sustenance and a limited measure of affection. When he sees some of his fellow Alsatians demeaning themselves by accepting food and caresses from non-guards, "what hurt him was not so much that they had grown tired of waiting, but that they had grown tired of believing."

Vladimov calls Ruslan "poisoned by his love" – love for a system within which he has been brought up, the only one he has ever known. The parallel with the human beings who have lived by the system is plain. In this way Vladimov prepares us for the final tragedy, in which a band of enthusiastic Komsomol volunteers, marching up the road to the site of the camp, is gradually surrounded by the former guard dogs, who think they are responding to the call of the familiar Service. "Poisoned by love," a society relapses into its old shackles.

Vladimov's distinctive strength is his combination of insight into the Stalinist mentality and of detachment from it. The narrative device of adopting an animal's viewpoint enables him to fuse these two apparently incompatible attitudes in a synthesis of richly revealing irony.

In many ways, the starting point of Vladimir Voynovich (1932–) resembled that of Vladimov. His early works, published in *New World*, dealt with the working life of young people, apprentices and laborers. Narrated from a gently self-deprecating first person stance, they describe the minor triumphs and frustrations of everyday life. The characters are inexperienced, uncertain of themselves, unlike Aksyonov's heroes very unsophisticated, and appear to lack ideals, though they are groping their way towards an independent outlook on the world. They face a situation in which society's proclaimed ideals have lost their meaning – an incongruity of which everyone is aware, but which young people sense especially acutely. Some of his youthful heroes react by asserting themselves with a vehemence even they do not expect: they discover that they *do* have an authentic self underneath the inexperience and hesitation. Like Vladimov, in fact, Voynovich conducts his own re-assessment of the "positive hero," in a way which was to open up a rich vein of comedy and satire. Indeed it might be said that he tried to create a genuine as opposed to an artificial positive hero. He could only do so, however, by transgressing the bounds of what was acceptable to the authorities and resorting, at first involuntarily and then deliberately, to *samizdat* and *tamizdat*.

It was in this form that Voynovich's finest work appeared, *The Life and Extraordinary Adventures of Private Ivan Chonkin* (*Zhizn i neobychaynye priklyucheniya soldata Ivana Chonkina*, published in the west 1975–9). Its satire derives from the inauthentic existence forced on everyone in Soviet society by an overbearing system of ideology and authority, a system which endeavors, with greater or lesser success in individual cases, to remold the human personality. Chonkin himself is merely an ordinary human being in a society which lives by inhuman principles. Unlike the Good Soldier Schweik, with whom he has sometimes been compared, Chonkin is devoted to the society in which he lives and to its leadership. He is, however, incapable of the "doublethink" which most people must acquire in order to adapt to that society, and his attempt to *live* his devotion gets him into all sorts of predicaments, in the process revealing the inauthenticity of everyone else. That is one layer of the satire. Another concerns the relationship between fantasy and reality. A vital component of Soviet reality is state-sponsored fantasy, to which everyone is compelled to make at least obeisance. Some actually begin to believe it, like the collective farm chairman Golubev, who compiles figures reporting fictitious harvest yields to satisfy his superiors and then finds them so seductive that he "sometimes caught himself starting to believe them." Some, like the home-grown village scientist Gladyshev, involve themselves so enthusiastically in the official fantasy that they make life impossible for themselves and everyone around them – in Gladyshev's case by filling his home with varieties of excrement for Lysenko-like biological experiments.

Voynovich's satire has a curious twist, however, for he does not merely counterpose reality to fantasy. The author calls *Chonkin* a "novel-anecdote," and begins it with the words: "Whether all this really happened or not is difficult to say now." He thus declares that it lies on the border line between fantasy and reality, where the fantastic has itself become real, and ordinary human beings like Chonkin belong to the fairy tale. Thus it is that Chonkin, the hopelessly clumsy soldier, begins to take on miraculous qualities once he sloughs off his enforced military identity and resumes his natural existence as a peasant. In the no man's land between the fairy tale and the socialist realist epic he defeats and captures a whole platoon of NKVD troops. In the end, he even splits into two towering mythical personae: scion of the Russian nobility Prince Golitsyn (of whom Hitler dreams as the leader of an anti-Bolshevik popular rising) and the simple Russian peasant lad Ivan

Chonkin (of whom Stalin dreams as a folk hero [*bogatyr*] with flowing brown hair and clear blue eyes smiting the foes of Holy Soviet Russia). Behind both personae hovers the folk-tale image of Ivan the Fool, the humble peasant lad who won the princess's hand and had his rightful royal status restored to him. Older, deeply rooted popular fantasies replace modern, artificial, state-sponsored ones.

Despite its inconclusive ending, *Chonkin* is perhaps the most richly suggestive of all post-Stalin works of Russian fiction. Even without the mythical elements, Voynovich's satirical talent is also effectively deployed in documentary studies of Soviet society such as *The Ivankiad* (*Ivankiada*, 1976), which describes the author's struggle to assert his legitimate claim to a Writers' Union apartment against the intrigues of a powerful official of that organization; and in *The Anti-Soviet Soviet Union* (*Antisovetsky Sovetsky Soyuz*, 1985), which offers sketches of a variety of Soviet personality types, both in and outside the writers' milieu.

If the youth writers combated the past by fixing their gaze on the future, rural writers took the opposite path, seeking to return to a more distant and healthy past which had in their view been under-estimated, even disdained, during the Stalin period. This was the past of the traditional peasant village. Of course, there had been numerous depictions of the village in Stalinist fiction, but most of them operated on the assumption that it needed to be *changed*, that peasants should be dragged into the modern world, if necessary against their will, since their mentality was so backward they could not be expected to appreciate fully the advantages of modernity.

Even before Stalin's death, the approach to the peasants had begun to change. Valentin Ovechkin (1904–68), while accepting the imperative of modernization, nevertheless argued that the party and the state planning authorities should defer more to the peasant's experience, his knowledge of local climate and soil. In his *Provincial Routine* (an irregular series of sketches beginning in 1952) he portrayed frankly the atrocious conditions in the countryside, and laid the blame for them on insensitive party officials obsessed by output targets and commands from the center, and too im-patient to get the best out of the collective farmers under their charge.

Ovechkin's purpose was largely political and polemical. As writers reflected on the village, however, their tone steadily became more contemplative, even lyrical, and they started to focus less on what should change and more on what villagers had inherited from the past. Thus Efim Dorosh (1908–72), in his *Village Diary* (*Derevensky dnevnik*, published in instalments 1956–70), dwelt lovingly on private cows and garden plots, on the fretwork friezes of the peasant huts and on the local linguistic usages of the Rostov region. He saw all this as a single ecological and cultural organism whose unity could not be disrupted without economic as well as human loss.

This new and more appreciative approach to rural life established itself in part because many writers of the up-and-coming generation were themselves peasants by origin. They brought with them their memories of childhood, as well as the stories of their parents and grandparents. They offered a kind of oral history in a culture whose written history had gaping lacunae. They came to the fore, moreover, at a time when future-oriented literature looked less and less convincing, even to the "youth writers" themselves. The city was coming to seem a place not just of cultural and technical progress, but also of pollution, alienation, and even dehumanization. Khrushchev's renewal of the party's ideals had foundered first in his own chaotic personality, and then in his removal. The urge to search for a new moral anchor, and to seek it in the past, was, then, very strong.

As often, a single work crystallized the new mood: *Business as Usual* (*Privychnoe delo*), by Vasily Belov (1932–   ), published in 1966. It portrayed an ordinary peasant, Ivan Afrikanovich, who has nine children and cannot earn enough from his work on the collective farm to clothe and feed them all. Despite his devotion to the village, he is persuaded by a relative to leave for the nearest town to try his fortune there. Once out of the village, he proves to be utterly incompetent in the simplest practical matters, and never even makes it to the town. His wife, broken by their parting, suffers a heart attack and dies, so that his return to the village is marked by grief. In the manner of Solzhenitsyn, Belov adopts a third person narrative stance, using the language and outlook of Ivan Afrikanovich himself, including a dash of Vologda dialect. The strength of the novel lies in its presentation of a pantheistic unity of man and nature, a unity broken by the intrusion of urban mores and of death. The same theme is presented with idiosyncratic humour in *Vologda Whimsies* (*Bukhtiny vologodskie*, 1969), a series of episodes related in bucolic language by a *skazitel*, or folk storyteller. Contemporary mores, represented by both the town and the planned economy, are shown to be gradually undermining a way of life in which men, animals, and fairy-tale figures all lived together in harmony. The work is one of the unremarked minor masterpieces of post-Stalin literature.

The implication that politics has been a destructive force in the countryside is presented more directly in *A Carpenter's Tales* (*Plotnitskie rasskazy*, 1968) and in *On the Eve* (*Kanuny*, 1972–6), which Belov calls a "chronicle" of the prelude to collectivization in his home village. In both works he shows the way of life of the NEP village as harmonious and prosperous, while he uses diabolical language and imagery to depict the party plenipotentiaries who come to hunt out the kulaks and persuade the villagers to join the collective farms.

Belov is not the only writer who traces the contemporary troubles of the village to the manner in which the farms were collectivized. Sergey Zalygin (1913–   ) was one of the first to do so, in his novella *On the River Irtysh* (*Na Irtyshe*, 1964). This work depicts with considerable sympathy a prosperous Siberian peasant who refuses to surrender all his grain to the collective, as he wishes to be responsible for feeding his own family. He also shelters the wife and children of a neighbor who has been "dekulakized," a procedure whose arbitrary nature he amply exposes. Zalygin's use of Siberian peasant speech in his narration adds an extra touch of sympathy and drama to a well constructed story. The same qualies are evident in his longer novels, *Salty Hollow* (*Solenaya pad*, 1967) and *The Commission* (*Komissiya*, 1975), both of which portray Siberian villages during the upheavals of the civil war, when their inhabitants had to resolve questions of war, peace and political loyalty. In *The Commission*, in particular, Zalygin raises basic issues of the proper constitution of a peasant community and its relationship to the outside world, draws extensively on chronicle and legend, and gives sympathetic attention to the peasants' religious beliefs.

Fyodor Abramov (1920–84), a native of Arkhangelsk province,

was, as we have seen, the first literary critic to attack the practice of "varnishing reality" in descriptions of village life in the post-war period. He practiced what he preached in a series of four novels under the general title *The Pryaslin Family* (*Pryasliny*, 1958–78) about the far northern village of Pekashino during and after the Second World War. It is the single most sustained piece of fiction set in the Russian countryside of recent years. Couched in the dialect of Arkhangelsk, it offers a vivid picture both of work processes and of human relationships in a community under intense strain, imposed, as is made clear, both by the war and by party policies. It is especially poignant in its portrayal of the fate of the women, who bear the burden of all the agricultural work in the absence of their menfolk, even as they continue to tend house, children and private plot. Also noteworthy is the depiction of local party officials, torn between their duty to their unrelenting superiors and their identification with the desperately hard-pressed village community. Of the second novel in the series, *Two Winters and Three Summers* (*Dve zimy i tri leta*), Deming Brown has remarked "If [it] had been written by Alexander Solzhenitsyn, it would have immediately been translated in the west and proclaimed a masterpiece."

The writer who has gone furthest in developing the contemplative aspect of "village prose" is Valentin Rasputin (1937–   ), who has set nearly all his novels and short stories in the villages of the Irkutsk area of Siberia, from which he comes. His approach to his subject matter is distinct from that of the other rural writers in that, although he employs some dialect words, his narrative language is unequivocally his own, and not that of his characters. He is closely involved in their life, yet also detaches himself from them through his long and rounded periods. The opening of *Farewell to Matyora* (*Proshchanie s Materoy*, 1976) is typical.

> And so the spring came once more, just another spring in an endless series, yet the last one for the island and village of Matyora. With a ferocious crunching noise the ice floated by, piling up its floes on the banks, and the Angara opened broadly out, its sparkling current stretching away into the distance.

The first two words (simply "*i*" in Russian) ease us into the story as if we had already been listening for hours, and the action about to unfold was itself part of an eternal process. This ability to fit his characters into an all-encompassing natural rhythm is Rasputin's peculiar strength. The crux of his novels usually involves a sharp break in this rhythm, which throws his characters into turmoil and threatens their underlying spiritual strength. Thus Andrey and Nastyona, the married couple of *Live and Remember* (*Zhivi i pomni*, 1974), are in effect destroyed by Andrey's impulsive decision to desert from the army during the war in his impatience to see his wife. He has to settle secretly in a shack on the other side of the river, where Nastyona clandestinely visits him. But enforced isolation corrupts Andrey's character, secrecy undermines their conjugal relations, and in the end Nastyona, torn between her home community and her outlaw husband, commits suicide.

In Rasputin's *The Final Stage* (*Posledny srok*, 1970), the death of an old village woman, Anna, which is not in itself a disruption of natural rhythms, becomes so because of changes taking place within the village. Two of Anna's children have moved to the town, and the two who have stayed behind have become affected by urban ways. Unable to fit death into their concept of life, they make her last days more difficult, whilst she herself is helped by her own intense appreciation of ordinary natural objects around her.

In *Farewell to Matyora* a village community is faced with the ultimate crisis, its complete destruction, to be brought about by the construction of a hydro-electric power station. Rasputin lovingly evokes the performance of the last annual cycle of agricultural work as a background against which the irruption of high technology takes on the dimensions of an apocalypse, to be consummated first in the burning of all the buildings and vegetation on the island, and then in its flooding. The apocalyptic imagery accommodates itself well to the world view of Darya, most articulate of the island's elderly inhabitants, who believes that man has lost his conscience in pursuit of a technological paradise, and has delivered himself to forces over which he has no control. Her outlook is embodied in the form of a kind of earth spirit, guardian of the island and repository of the rich collective subconscious of the community, as revealed in dreams, in fairy tales, in religious ritual, and in communion with the ancestors. In the novel's last stages, the daily life of the village, earlier treated with sober and meticulous realism, gradually yields before such fantastic and other-worldly forces, and the ending is inconclusive and foreboding.

Rasputin's investigation of the threatened rural world, then, leads him to a mystical view of human nature: men are in contact with forces deep within themselves and in the natural world, from which they alienate themselves at their peril. In 1979 he was attacked by hooligans in Irkutsk and suffered a physical and spiritual trauma from which he has recovered very slowly, but stories published in 1982 confirmed and even deepened this literary trend.

A writer who stands rather to one side of the "village prose" school is Vasily Shukshin (1929–74). Like that of many of his contemporaries, his life was extremely unsettled. Born in the Altai region of Siberia, he worked on a collective farm before migrating to urban building sites and serving in the navy; his education came in fortuitous fragments. He trained in the Cinema Institute, and remained all his life an actor, and even director, as well as a writer. He was thus torn between several different worlds, and his restlessness manifested itself in his writings.

Although he did write novels, Shukshin's archetypal genre is the short story. Each one records an incident, often a *skandal*, as the Russians call a conflict which brings to the surface deep and wounding feelings. Shukshin's characters are the uprooted of Russia's whirlwind years of social change, people who are no longer at home in the village but have never quite settled anywhere else. They are truck drivers and chauffeurs, construction workers, demobbed soldiers and *shabashniki* (odd job men in the black economy). Even when his characters retain firm roots in the village, then the village itself is changing as it is invaded by urban customs and culture, imperfectly understood and reflected in distorted forms by the villagers.

In tune with his subject matter, Shukshin casts his narrative in a taut, laconic style very close to that of his characters. Indeed much of the burden of narration is borne by dialogue. People and objects are described, if at all, in the briefest of strokes. The general tone is that of a chance encounter of strangers, one of whom wishes to tell the other a story, and communicates the essentials as swiftly as possible. This abrupt manner palls in longer texts, but is well suited to the allusive framework of the short story.

In his outlook on human beings, Shukshin is about as distant from Rasputin as possible. Whereas the latter is attracted to the female principle of warmth and attachment to the hearth, Shukshin excels in the portrayal of male characters who feel a desperate yearning to escape from the regular rhythms of rural life, which they perceive as restrictive. Thus Ivan, the hero of "In Profile and Full Face" ("V profil i anfas," 1967), bemoans the lack of horizons in the village. "I don't know what I'm working for. Just so as to fill my belly? All right, it's full. What next?" This remark is quite incomprehensible to the old man with whom he is sharing a bottle of vodka, since for *him* filling his belly has been a perpetual struggle. Nor can his mother understand Ivan's urgent desire to leave the warmth she offers at home in order to better himself in the city.

This kind of conflict and mutual misunderstanding is vintage Shukshin. His characters thrash around, vaguely seeking something beyond the here and now, the familiar routine. In a sense they are engaged in the search for the transcendental, and a few of his stories contain implied religious imagery, though he does not develop it fully. In another sense, his characters yearn for the ancient peasant dream of *volya*, freedom, escape from serfdom and drudgery into the open borderlands inhabited by brigands and Cossacks. It is no accident that Shukshin's longest work is an account of the life of the seventeenth-century peasant rebel Stepan Razin: *I Have Come to Give you Freedom* (*Ya prishel dat vam volyu*, 1974).

Egor Prokudin, hero of Shukshin's "Snowball Berry Red" "Kalina krasnaya," 1973), calls what he is longing for "a festival of the soul," and perhaps this vague but evocative phrase will serve for all of Shukshin's creations. Prokudin's own failure to achieve any such "festival" is also paradigmatic. Torn from his home village as a child by the social upheavals of the 1930s, he drifted into the criminal underworld as a minimal substitute home. His attempt to "go straight" on leaving labor camp by settling down with a female pen-friend is doomed by his inability to sustain long-term personal relationships entailing any mutual commitment, as well as by his lack of practical rural skills. The criminal fraternity, with its short-term, instrumental relationships, is his natural home, and its violent reclamation of him at the end is entirely logical.

Even in his own brief lifetime Shukshin became something of a legend. He struck a chord as no other writer could, both in official circles and among dissenters.

Like Belov, Vladimir Tendryakov (1923–84) was born and brought up in the Vologda countryside, though unlike him he was old enough to fight in the war and to study at the Gorky Institute immediately afterwards. He shared the concerns of the village writers, but explored them on a broader canvas, dealing more explicitly with issues like art, education and religion. The dilemmas he poses are seen at their sharpest in *On Apostolic Business* (*Apostolskaya komandirovka*, 1969), in which an apparently successful Moscow scientist, Yury Rylnikov, decides his career and family life are meaningless, abandons them and goes off to the countryside to seek God by joining a village congregation and doing manual work on a collective farm. As often with Tendryakov, the delineation of character is somewhat schematic, and the exposition of the problems is more interesting than their resolution. The presentation of Yury's spiritual crisis – his sense that his hard-won material well-being is not fulfilling and that science does not in fact answer the ultimate questions of life – owes much to Tolstoy (especially Levin in *Anna Karenina*) and to neo-Kantian thinkers like Sergei Bulgakov, but is given heightened poignancy by the specific Soviet circumstances of the late 1960s: the feeling that the Purpose for which the Bolsheviks had sacrificed so much was receding rather than drawing nearer. Probably no Soviet work has communicated so hauntingly the sense of meaninglessness which has been a commonplace of twentieth-century western literature.

Like most writers of the preceding Stalinist period, Tendryakov deploys his characters in the context of clearly marked dichotomies. In his case, however, the dividing line is not between "progressive" and "reactionary" forces, or between different sides of the class struggle, but between good and evil seen as absolute moral categories. He concludes his story "The Court" ("Sud," 1961) with the sentence "There is no stricter court than that of one's own conscience." Under that condition, he was in favor of the "positive hero," a literary category widely considered discredited in the 1960s. But how he transformed the "positive hero" may be seen in a novel like *Spring Somersaults* (*Vesennie perever-*

tyshi, 1973), where it is the passive, easy-going characters, the dreamers, who offer a suitable model for the young people finding their way in the world rather than the practical ones whose dedication to social or technological objectives renders them insensitive to human needs. Tendryakov also has a strong sense of sheer unvarnished evil, as in the schoolboy bully, Sanka Erakhov, who delights to kill frogs by hurling them against a brick wall and forces his younger playmates to participate in this sport.

In many ways, Tendryakov's work sums up the contradictions of the age in which he lived. Although he saw early on that men could not find a complete purpose for their lives in struggling to build a perfect society, he never quite freed himself from the tense, dualistic conception of life which he learned in his youth. Even his gentle or uncertain characters usually express themselves in confident and uncompromising language. They sort their inner doubts into neat dichotomies; the rhetoric of struggle still dominates their discourse. For that reason, perhaps, Tendryakov's most characteristic work is *Death of the Boss* (*Konchina*, 1978), which recounts how a strong power-loving collective farm chairman, Evlampy Lykov, raises his farm to prosperity with the help of his accountant, a self-made, idealistic Old Bolshevik whose spine Lykov once fractured in a fight. The collaboration between the cunning autocrat and the crippled intellectual summarizes the history of the Soviet Union as a whole between the late 1920s and the early 1950s. When the chairman's death comes – significantly, in the spring of 1953 – it does not bring release, but rather leads to squabbling among his entourage and a general sense of foreboding, as if the dead man's shadow paralysed the wills of his successors, and they were incapable of liberating themselves.

The tendency of Russian writers to seek an ideal in the past has been matched by non-Russian writers. Soviet literature claims to be multi-national, and to an increasing extent that claim is becoming fact. Non-Russian intellectuals learn Russian as a matter of course, and most of them are strongly influenced by the Russian literary tradition. The Writers' Union encourages both publication in non-Russian languages, and translation into Russian, and a growing band of writers seem able to perform both functions themselves, that is, to write in their own languages and then to translate their works into Russian. In short, they view their own cultural tradition in an "all-Soviet" context.

Nevertheless the relationship is often a tense one, about which it is impossible to generalize. Some of the Soviet cultures are very old, while others date essentially from the Soviet period itself. Some nationalities have a recent history of sovereign statehood, but others do not. While Georgian or Ukrainian intellectuals sometimes express deep resentment at the political and economic domination of their nations by Russia, Moldavian ones seldom do.

Within this context, non-Russian writers have begun to make a very significant contribution to Soviet (and therefore arguably to Russian) literature. There are even signs that cultural influence now sometimes works in the historically unusual direction: that is, that the lively pre-modern culture which some non-Russian nations have preserved unusually well leaves its mark on Russian literature. Let us take just three examples of non-Russian prose writers who have achieved an acknowledged place in Soviet literature.

Vasil Bykau (Vasily Bykov) was born in 1924, in Belorussia, where he still lives. He represents a culture which is peculiarly threatened by its very closeness to the dominant Russian one, and he has sometimes spoken out bitterly against the swamping of his native language and literature by their powerful neighbor. Since modern Belorussian culture is largely a product of the Soviet period, he does not base his work on ancient legends. Rather he locates the ethnic consciousness of his people in the ordeal they experienced (even more intense than that of the other Soviet peoples) under the German occupation. In his main works, such as *The Dead Feel no Pain* (*Mertvym ne bolno*, 1965), *The Bridge at Kruglyansk* (*Kruglyansky most*, 1969), *The Ordeal* (*Sotnikov*, 1970), and *The Mark of Doom* (*Znak bedy*, 1982), he reflects the effects of war at the grass roots. He analyzes the experiences and interactions of small groups of people, whether soldiers, partisans or civilians. His approach to heroism is cool, even sceptical, though he certainly believes in moral courage. His narration is psychologically acute and morally searching as he seeks to discover the ways in which communities survive – or fail to survive – intense pressures. Especially in *The Dead Feel no Pain* and *The Mark of Doom* he shows how the heavy-handed authoritarianism of the Soviet state itself has at times weakened this communal solidarity. It could be argued that Bykov is the most penetrating of all Soviet writers on the Second World War.

Chingiz Aitmatov (1928–   ) witnessed as a small boy the forceful ending of the old tribal customs and the nomadic pastoral way of life of the Kirgiz people, of which he learnt much from his grandmother. His parents, on the other hand, were solid party members, committed to the transformation of national life on the Soviet pattern. Both strains run through Aitmatov's work, and no doubt the arrest of his father in 1937 imparted extra intensity to his awareness of the tension between them.

The Kirgiz language had no alphabet till 1928, so it was inevitable that Kirgiz written literature should bear the impress of Soviet conditions. All the same, much of Aitmatov's work incorporates legends from the oral epic tradition, and also images from the rich religious heritage of central Asia, including shamanism and animism as well as Islam. He shows with alarm how these traditions have been undermined and – even more important – not replaced by anything stable which could serve as a focus for communal identity. Thus in *The White Steamship* (*Bely parokhod*, 1970) an orphan boy is sustained spiritually by the legend of the Horned Deer-Mother, protectress of his clan, but also by the more modern vision of a distant white steamship he sees on Lake Issyk-Kul, whose captain he believes to be his lost father. His hopes of rediscovering his family are raised by the unexpected appearance of a rare mountain deer, but the local people, who have lost touch with the ancestral myths, merely shoot it for meat. Sickened, the boy throws himself into the lake in the delirious hope of rejoining his father, and is drowned.

The theme of a soulless world which has cut itself off from its past and thereby lost its community spirit is renewed in *The Day Lasts Longer than a Century* (*I dolshe veka dlitsya den*, 1980). It is condensed in the image of the *mankurt*, the slave deprived of reason and memory in fearful torture by his Tartar masters so that he may be a docile beast of burden. The action of the novel suggests Aitmatov's fear that Stalin's despotism amounted to a nearly successful attempt to achieve the same dehumanization, and that the threat is not lifted even today because of the inhuman use of science and technology. The main plot involves the attempt of a steppe stationmaster to bury an old comrade according to traditional rites, an attempt which fails because the ancestral cemetery is now occupied by a cosmodrome. A secondary plot recounts the discovery, by astronauts from this cosmodrome, of a new planet, with a more humane and progressive civilization; the terrestrial authorities decide to seal the earth off by sentry rockets from this planet. Mankind thus loses its potential future as well as its past.

Fazil Iskander was born in 1929 in Sukhumi in Abkhazia, a very distinctive region of Georgia whose people, ethnically quite separate from the Georgians, are partly Muslim and partly Christian. He has lived in Moscow for many years, and now writes only in Russian. Externally, in fact, he has completely adapted to Russian culture, but his writings still draw their content from his homeland. Although Iskander first became known for an effective satire on bureaucratic control of agriculture, "The Goatibex Constellation" ("Sozvezdie kozlotura," 1966), his most important work consists of two cycles of tales about Abkhazia. One deals with the experiences of a growing boy, *Chik's Day* (*Den Chika*, 1971); the other centers on the person of a mountain village elder and master of ceremonies (*tamada*), *Uncle Sandro of Chegem* (*Sandro iz Chegema*; Soviet publication 1973, fuller western publication 1979). This is a version of the picaresque novel, ranging from pre-revolutionary times to the post-Stalin period. Memorable chapters recount the struggles of Stalin's various Georgian henchmen, implying that the whole of Soviet politics, at least under Stalin, was an extension of a Caucasian tribal feud. Some critics have suggested that the whole Soviet project is seen in this novel as a travesty of the traditional village carnival, in which the world is "turned upside down" not joyfully and temporarily, but grimly and permanently. Stalin sometimes seems to be playing the part of a grotesque all-Union *tamada*. At any rate the contrast between the deeply rooted customs of Abkhazia and the artificial cerebral constructs of Soviet importation constitutes the core of the comedy and tragedy of Sandro's highly colored career. *Uncle Sandro* may prove one of the most durable of recent Soviet novels.

Of all writers, Yury Trifonov (1925–81) was best placed by his social position to reassess the Stalinist past and its contemporary effects. He was of the flesh and blood of the revolution: his father was one of the founders of the Cheka, and fell victim to its successor in 1937. Trifonov thus knew at first hand both the triumph and the humiliation of the old Bolsheviks. He grew up half in and half out of the elite, partaking of its privileges without being secure in their enjoyment. He knew early success himself, winning the Stalin Prize in 1951 for his novel *Students* (*Studenty*), but subsequently underwent a protracted artistic crisis during which he completely reformulated both his literary technique and his outlook on the world. As a result he became the closest approximation to a repentant aristocrat the Soviet Union has known.

When Trifonov emerged from that re-evaluation, his writing had lost the tone of magisterial certainty which characterized his first novel. It had become intensely subjective, full of anguish about moral issues. That first novel, set in post-war Moscow, had dealt with the denunciation of a literature professor for an ideological error. The narration was unproblematic, implying that the professor was simply a "survival" from a disreputable past, and that his dismissal was part of the healthy process of building the future. When he returned to this theme in *The House on the Embankment* (*Dom na naberezhnoy*, 1976), Trifonov's approach was quite different. No longer is there any moral certainty. Trifonov now sees most human beings as weak, and their moral judgments as fallible. The professor has something of the aura of the innocent victim about him, and the narration is conducted by a graduate student who has denounced him: ashamed in retrospect of what he has done, he tries to persuade himself and the reader that each step in the betrayal of his supervisor was either trivial, or inevitable, or the result of praiseworthy motives. Few novels have ever built up with such relentless logic the "banality of evil."

Trifonov's new element was the "ordeal of everyday life," or *byt*. His works of the 1970s and 1980s evoke the life of ordinary Russian professional people, their cliques and coteries, their family quarrels and love affairs, their struggles over promotion and their children's education, their intrigues over housing and foreign travel, all of which are built up into a dense and sticky web which envelops his characters relentlessly. Of course the inherited socialist realist tradition held that *byt* was unworthy of serious attention, mere trivia which the hero would crush underfoot in the advance towards the great society of the future. Trifonov rejects this point of view. "*Byt* is the great test. One should not speak slightingly of it, as if it were a base side of human life, unworthy of literature. After all, *byt* is [. . .] the ordeal of ordinary life, where the morality of today manifests itself and is put to the test," he said in 1972.

This, then, was yet another "return of the repressed," the refocusing of attention on an aspect of life ignored in the literature of the recent past. Trifonov adjusts his narrative technique accordingly, plunging in at the center of the plot, just where the vital decisions are about to be taken, and then, in a series of flashbacks, tracing the various strands which lead to this nodal moment. The technique creates a sense of ineluctability: the strands are so many tentacles of gossip, intrigue and enmity which wind round the characters and immobilize them. The details of each transaction, each intrigue, are laid exhaustively before us, piled together in long sentences often not even graced by subordinate clause connectors. Trifonov is like an inexhaustible gossipy letter writer, for whom every punctuation mark is a comma because there is so much to tell, and it is all interlinked.

Trifonov's new style was first fully revealed in three novellas dealing with the life of contemporary Moscow intellectuals: *The Exchange* (*Obmen*, 1969), *Taking Stock* (*Predvaritelnye itogi*, 1970) and *The Long Farewell* (*Dolgoe proshchanie*, 1971). Amongst the components of *byt* analyzed in these stories are the influence of the family, its history and traditions, and the way in which families coalesce, for good and evil, in marriages. Families become for Trifonov one of the strands through which the past is communicated to the present and continues to influence it, sometimes in very unexpected ways. This theme of historical forces passed down through families and individuals is the principal leitmotif of *Another Life* (*Drugaya zhizn*, 1975), and above all of *The Old Man* (*Starik*, 1978), which traces the demoralization of contemporary Soviet urban society back to the Bolshevik repudiation of morality in the name of history during the revolution and civil war. Partly because of the censorship, and partly because presumably the re-evaluation of his family's past was so painful for Trifonov, he masks the presentation of this conclusion by a good deal of surface ambiguity, as in all his novels. The positive values are expressed by individuals whose weakness and partiality are so patent that it is

difficult to take what they say seriously. As one character comments on another, we seem to see a receding series of mirrors,
none of whose images is entirely trustworthy. Yet on careful
reading, we obtain the overall impression of a writer who believes
in humane values which are not subordinate to the class struggle or
to historical expediency. In *The Old Man* Trifonov shows us how
these values were corrupted by the Bolsheviks, in spite of and
partly because of their intense idealism, with permanently demo-
ralizing effects on the society they created.

Perhaps the last of the major Russian writers for whom the
Stalinist tradition was a formative – albeit largely negative –
influence is Alexander Zinovev (1922–   ), who now lives in West
Germany. The Great Future of Stalinist myth is an overwhelm-
ingly absent presence in his first literary work, as can be sensed
from its title, *Yawning Heights* (*Ziyayushchie vysoty*, 1976). The
combination of oxymoron and bathos is entirely characteristic of
his writing, and indeed is virtually its structural foundation.

For twenty-two years Zinovev was a member of the Institute of
Philosophy, and his contributions to the field of mathematical
logic were internationally known. All the same, he was never
entirely trusted by the authorities because he had established a
record of plain speaking going back to his teenage years before the
war. As he was gradually eased out of his distinguished posts and
deprived of his students, he found himself with the leisure to
record his impressions of the society from which he was becoming
increasingly alienated. The result was *Yawning Heights*, a rambling, surrealistic presentation of that society in a variety of ten-
uously connected episodes. In a sense it is the absolute negation of
the socialist realist novel. If the Great Future no longer exists, then
the institutions of Soviet society lose their meaning, or rather
acquire a negative and sinister meaning. Soviet society is haunted
by the absence of those "magnificent prospects" which Zhdanov
used to insist were an indispensable part of Soviet culture: that is
why the distant heights no longer "gleam" (*siyayut*) but "gape" or
"yawn" (*ziyayut*).

The chaotic structure of Zinovev's work stems naturally from
that basic premise. Time has become fragmented. Plot lines are
intertwined in a confusing way. The sense of place is similarly
deranged: the setting, Ibansk, sometimes appears to cover the

whole world, at others to be merely a muddy extended village where everyone knows everyone else. Language is disordered: high and low styles alternate unpredictably, and ordinary narrative in the authorial voice is juxtaposed with theoretical discourse, doggerel verse and idle gossip. Even human beings have lost their unambiguous individuality: they are all called Ibanov (an amalgam of the commonest Russian surname with the commonest Russian obscenity) and are otherwise designated by such appellations as Thinker, Chatterer, Slanderer, Schizophrenic and so on. The narrator fragments himself among these various generic personalities, sharing their outlook and language in turn. We cannot even assign a genre to this work. "Novel" seems an inappropriate term for such a ragbag of miscellaneous items, especially since at times the author seems to aspire to write a scientific treatise.

Zinovev's purpose in writing this work and numerous later ones is illuminated by a comment of the night watchman who is the principal character of his *Notes of a Night Watchman* (*Zapiski nochnogo storozha*, 1979): "I used to think that there existed scientific studies of Ibanism [Zinovev's usual synonym for Communism], but that Ibanism itself was still far in the future. In fact it's the other way round. Full-scale Ibanism has existed for ages [. . .] But there are no scientific studies of it at all." Strictly speaking, Zinovev's only full-scale treatise on the subject is *The Reality of Communism* (*Kommunizm kak realnost*, 1981), but even this work is broken up into discrete and often quite brief sections not necessarily logically interconnected, and indeed sometimes in open tension with one another. Zinovev operates by a kind of intellectual *pointillisme*, building up his arguments in a series of snapshots. This weakens his claim to scientific accuracy, but does not necessarily detract from the literary power of his writing.

Zinovev offers a useful corrective to traditional western "totalitarian" analyses of the Soviet Union, which suffer from overconcentration on the upper reaches of the system. Zinovev's focus on the "primary collective" – the individual office, workshop, apartment block or scientific institute – enables us, as it were, to readjust our sights and to appreciate from below the human aspects of a system which otherwise appears inhuman. Perhaps Zinovev's most controversial assertion is that the political structure is appropriate to the people it dominates and enjoys their overwhelming support. Each primary collective provides the basic essentials of a social existence, including entitlement to housing and other welfare benefits, and a modest level of pay. Any other function the collective may have (such as the production of industrial goods or the education of children) is secondary. Everyone must belong to a primary collective, since otherwise one may be accused of parasitism. And within the collective the talented and eccentric will soon be either reduced to the general level of mediocrity or violently extruded. The secret police is thus in Zinovev's view only a kind of concentrated essence of the envious mistrust with which gifted individuals are regarded by their colleagues.

Zinovev has expressed this view in a dozen or so works, some of enormous length, and written in the same monotonously formless manner. His approach is both unhistorical and unscientific, and he might be dismissed altogether were it not for his powerful satirical talent. The reader who perseveres with Zinovev's works will find that he has distilled the essence of Soviet society – at least in the Brezhnev era – in a manner not found elsewhere. His account, for example, of the Ibanskian conquest of the world by the process of the Great Kissing – détente seen as a metaphorical extension of the bear-hugs which socialist dignitaries give one another on arrival at airports – has positively Rabelaisian gusto and aptness. He faithfully reflects a society which has lost its way, and in that sense his weaknesses are also his strengths.

In the early stages of the thaw, lyric poetry seemed best to answer the public need for renewed sincerity. Of all the poets of the older generation, probably Alexander Tvardovsky was best placed to reflect the popular mood during the late 1950s thanks to the fame of his verses about the simple Red Army soldier Vasily Tyorkin. He continued along similar lines with his long narrative poem *Distance beyond Distance* (*Za dalyu dal*, 1959–60), held together by the framework of a train journey from Moscow through the Urals and Siberia to the Far East. He ruminates on the ordinary Soviet people he meets, on the regions he traverses, and on the present and recent past of his country. His language is relaxed and colloquial, somewhat less demotic than in *Vasily Tyorkin*, though he retains the iambic tetrameter which he inherited from Nikolay Nekrasov, his great predecessor in the dual role of populist poet and controversial editor. In one chapter of the poem he looks back on the Stalin era, acknowledging the misjudgments that he and so many others made at the time, in worshipping a figure who turned out to be only a man-made god.

Tvardovsky's two later poems testify to the growing radicalism of his alienation from the Soviet authorities. *Tyorkin in the Other World* (*Terkin na tom svete*, 1963) returns to his wartime hero, this time in the afterlife, which, as it turns out, is divided into capitalist and socialist zones, the latter being governed by a bureaucracy markedly like the Soviet one. *By Right of Memory* (*Po pravu pamyati*, written in the late 1960s and published in the west in 1969, but in the USSR only in 1987) is a meditation on something Tvardovsky had omitted from *Distance beyond Distance*: his father's deportation as a "kulak." It is the most bitter of his poems as it evokes the memory of one who demanded that his followers deny their own mothers and fathers:

And we, proud of our unbelief in God,
In the name of our own holy places,
Peremptorily demanded that sacrifice:
Reject your father and mother.

Tvardovsky rejects the commands of the leaders of his own day to forget the past in order to concentrate on the future:

He who assiduously forgets the past
Is not likely to cope with the future.

The genre which best captured the new *narodnost* was the so-called "author's song." This genre, though simple in its appeal, was a complex synthesis derived from a variety of antecedents. There were the official mass anthems, sung by the Red Army Choir and etched into people's consciousness by blaring loudspeakers (which could not be switched off!) in every factory floor and village square in the land. These anthems' confident marching rhythms, their staunch but naive patriotism, their heroic figures striding into the glad dawn, form a kind of negative pole for the later genre, a casting which the mold no longer fits. Then there were the semi-tolerated romances and gypsy songs, with their mixture of sentimentalism and freedom-loving vigor. And as a final component, there were the strictly forbidden underworld song (*blatnaya pesnya*) and labor camp song (*lagernaya pesnya*), with their raw realism and their satirical irreverence towards the authorities and official ideology.

The first singer to draw on these sources and to achieve a synthesis powerful enough to evoke a widespread response among the Soviet public was Bulat Okudzhava (1924–   ), who by the late 1950s was carrying his guitar about to sing before groups of friends. The intimacy of the initial audience was crucial: in post-Stalin Russia, especially in the early years, it was only in such mutually trusting circles that genuine ideas and real culture could be promoted at all. And this assumed audience exists as a persona in the songs, cast in a style which would not be appropriate to a wider public. True, before long people began to record his performances on tape, so that they eventually reached a Union-wide public, but the assumption of intimacy remained an important part of their charm, as well as of their capacity to offer a subtly subversive alternative to official songs.

As perhaps befits the pioneer in the genre, Okudzhava was the romantic among the "bards." Where his successors savagely unmask, he gently deflates. He does not reject Soviet reality, but is reflectively skeptical about it. His work has a melancholy but not wholly uncomfortable irony to it. He uses children's toys and nursery rhymes to illuminate the human condition, as in "Song of the blue balloon" ("Pesenka o golubom sharike"):

Little girl crying, her balloon's flown away;
People console her, but the balloon flies on.

Young woman crying, still no beloved;
People console her, but the balloon flies on.

Grown woman crying, husband's gone to another;
People console her, but the balloon flies on.

Old woman crying, not much of a life;
But the balloon's come back, and it's sky-blue.

Similarly the song about the paper soldier who "would have liked to change the world, so everyone could be happy", and perished in the attempt, suggests the incompatibility of the fragile human frame with total idealism. The perpetual Soviet orientation towards the future is placed in perspective by the regret "that there are no hansom cabs in Moscow any longer" and by the warning that "we still dream of idols and still sometimes think ourselves slaves." Many of Okudzhava's songs simply speak affectionately of quarters of the capital city, especially the Arbat, where he grew up, and to which, with his determinedly non-teleological view of history, he expects to return:

You began your stroll from an Arbat courtyard,
And it looks as if that's where it will end.

A writer who well exemplifies the paradoxes of the "author's song" is Alexander Galich (1919–77). The first paradox in his case is that for many years he was a flourishing official Soviet dramatist, in no way distinguished from others in his artistic manner and his affluent life style. Only when a play of his was banned for painting too favorable a picture of Jews did he take up the guitar as his principal vehicle of expression, doubtless drawing on his experience as an entertainer of the troops during the war. His most characteristic songs are the songs of everyday life (*bytovye pesni*) in which he takes a typically Soviet personality or incident and describes it from inside. He renews the genre of *skaz* in the new framework provided by the hybrid form of the "author's song" and ends with a mixture of narrative and drama. As Sinyavsky has commented, "A song of Galich very often resembles a miniature play (tragedy or comedy), complete in itself, where every line is capable of replacing a whole act, and where – still more important – we constantly sense the warmth and excitement of the audience."

The element of the audience is indeed essential to Galich. His texts, like Okudzhava's, presuppose a collective "thou" whom he is addressing. An eye-witness has described a typical Galich recital thus:

In a friend's flat those invited gather; drinks and sandwiches appear on the table; tape recorders are switched on; and about ten to fifteen people, sometimes more, fall under the spell of the "famous Galich" who sings "underground songs." As he sings, he experiences everything afresh. Sometimes he finds it painful to sing, sometimes he can't help laughing. Before every song he says a few words, explains things that are obscure or tells the story of how the song came about.

This social setting is the archetypal Galich forum: a small group of people who share his background and concerns, and long to hear them filtered through the prism of the guitar song. In a sense, too, as Soviet citizens, they are accomplices in his guilt. When he pauses in the refrains to mix his own voice with that of his hero, the audience is also drawn into the mood of resigned awareness of mutual responsibility, interspersed with defiant reassertions of the right to speak out, even if from a glass house. The mood is well conveyed in "Fame is the spur" ("Zaklinanie slavy"):

I'm ashamed . . . just a fraction,
No I'm not, that's a lie.
I'll stand up for my right to
This low part that I play,
To my cheap notoriety
And my usual pain!

Galich's most extended portrait is that of Klim Petrovich Kolo-miytsev, "workshop foreman, holder of many decorations, member of the party committee bureau, and deputy to the town soviet." A series of demotic cameos depict him drinking to excess, bragging clumsily about "percentages" to West German tourists, and reading a prepared speech "in defense of peace" to an official audience so dazed with clichés that they do not even react to a line from another text which has slipped in by oversight ("As a mother and a woman . . ."). Typical is the song in which Klim Petrovich tries to get his brigade awarded the title "workshop of communist labor," taking his petition higher and higher, only to be fobbed off with routine excuses until someone points out tactfully that they produce barbed wire, and it would be bad for the Soviet Union's international reputation to decorate the producers of such a commodity. The mixture of earthy working-class Russian with the half-understood commonplaces of bureaucratese gives the whole cycle its distinctive flavor. Overall the effect is reminiscent of Zoshchenko, except that Galich's resourceful exploitation of rhyme and meter adds a touch of theatrical pungency lacking in the older writer.

Altogether, as Efim Etkind has pointed out, Galich's work constitutes a kind of miniature Soviet *Comédie humaine*. Like Balzac's larger-scale *œuvre*, it presents not merely a gallery of portraits, but also an *étude des mœurs* in which the social pathology of finance and property is replaced by that of arbitrary power, undeserved rank and crude monopolistic ideology.

Like Galich, Vladimir Vysotsky (1938–80) was an actor. Indeed, he became the most celebrated personality at that center of Soviet theatrical innovation, the Taganka theater under director Yuri Lyubimov. His guitar recitals were initially an outgrowth of his stage career, but at some time in the early 1960s they assumed an independent significance, and became part of a public image (created by rumor, not by the press) which included driving flashy cars, indulging in gargantuan drinking bouts and marrying a foreign film star. The authorities disliked many of his songs, but never rejected him altogether, as they did Galich. As Gerald Smith has commented, they "by implication acknowledged him as the most authentic voice of their historical time and their country, someone who was perhaps unruly, disrespectful, and even down-right subversive at times, but nevertheless someone who spoke to them in their own language and about their own life." It was well known that Vysotsky's songs were played at the wedding celebrations of the elite's children, whatever reservations "Papa" might have. All the same, only a small number of his songs and poems have been recorded or published in the USSR.

The persona which Vysotsky cultivated was that of the criminal and *zek*, though in fact he came from a professional family and had never been arrested. He thus deliberately fostered "the return of the repressed", focusing attention on a social stratum long disdained by Soviet literature. His songs mold the *blatnaya pesnya* into an art form capable of illuminating the lives of those whom official literature ignored or rejected. His manner is that of the lonely individual who uses the casual intimacy of an underworld binge for a spell of self-examination as frank as character and circumstances allow. From this perspective he throws a lurid light both on Russia's present and its recent past, as for example in the song "The Anti-Semites" ("Antisemity"), where he seeks to merge his criminal identity in a broader *narodnost*:

Why should I be just a common criminal?
Wouldn't it be better to join the Anti-Semites?
On their side they've got no laws, that's true,
But they have got the support and enthusiasm of millions.

581

Although he knows that Einstein, Chaplin and even Karl Marx were Jews, he nevertheless readily believes the stories of his drinking companion about "Jews drinking the blood of Christian babies." Besides:

Along the railway line from Kursk to Kazan
They've built themselves second homes, where they live like
    gods;
I'm ready for anything, for punch-ups and violence,
I'll beat up the Yids so's to save Mother Russia.

This ironic parody of popular anti-Semitism, together with the insinuation that it is considered more "respectable" than ordinary criminality, is very near the bone for most Russian listeners. So too in a different way is "Heat up the bath-house" ("Banka po-belomu"), with its portrait of a long-term Siberian *zek* who never ceased all through his grinding "spell" to believe in Stalin, but now after his release has realized that his belief was an illusion, and has "exchanged [his] dark stupidity for a life dark without end."

Vysotsky summed up his own life in the song "Horizons" ("Gorizonty"). Taking a thoroughly Soviet image, that of "pushing back horizons," he imagines himself as a racing driver whose finishing line is the horizon: on the way there he tries to break all speed records, while his enemies stretch cables across his track and fire bullets at his wheels. But it is simple mechanical failure which lets him down. His brakes fail, and the song ends enigmatically in the rationally inconceivable: he zooms right through the horizon.

The intellectual paradox seems quite appropriate as a portent of Vysotsky's end. He was a man of such hypertrophied, even hysterical dynamism that he exhausted himself. His death in July 1980, at the age of 42, generated overwhelming public reaction, so famous had his hoarse voice become through underground tapes, and so apt were his wry comments on the Soviet scene. His funeral was the occasion of perhaps the greatest outpouring of public grief since the death of Stalin.

In the late 1950s and early 1960s the greatest attention of all focused on the poets who recited their verses before huge crowds in conference halls and even sports stadiums. Evgeny Evtushenko (1933–   ) was the most conspicuous poet of a generation which seemed to symbolize the optimism of the "thaw." His style – forthright, declamatory, full of striking sound effects – was ideally suited to such occasions, as was his outgoing and generous personality. He became a kind of self-appointed spokesman of the post-Stalin generation, a tribune of the "sons" struggling against the evil "fathers" in the name of a bright future based on the original ideals of the Bolshevik revolution.

In this spirit Evtushenko wrote such long poems as *Zima Junction* (*Stantsiya Zima*, 1956), in which he utilizes encounters with ordinary people in his home town to reflect on the recent past, and on the need to recapture directness and honesty in human relations as part of a youthful faith in the future. Sharper and more controversial in tone were "Baby Yar" (1961) and "The heirs of Stalin" ("Nasledniki Stalina," 1962). The first recalled the Nazi massacre of the Jews outside Kiev in 1941, and implied that anti-Semitism was still a force in Soviet society. To this end Evtushenko rhetorically identified himself with the Jews, a gesture which attracted some disapproval, both official and unofficial. In the second poem he warned that Stalin's heirs were only biding their time, awaiting a convenient moment to reassert themselves and put a stop to the freedom and openness of the era.

> I appeal to our government
> With the request
>   To double
>   To triple
>   The guard at this slab,
> So that Stalin may not rise
>   And with Stalin
>   The past . . .

Evtushenko certainly did not lack civic courage: in a famous confrontation with Khrushchev of March 1963, when the latter attacked the modernist sculptor Ernst Neizvestni with the folk proverb "Only the grave straightens out the hunchback," he publicly replied, "I trust we have put behind us the time when the grave was used as a means of correction." Later on he protested against both the Warsaw Pact invasion of Czechoslovakia (1968) and the deportation of Solzhenitsyn (1974).

In general, however, Evtushenko's longer civic verses have a conformist ring about them. Perhaps typical in this respect is *The Bratsk Hydro-electric Power Station* (*Bratskaya GES*, 1965), which views the whole of human (and especially Russian) history through the medium of a dialogue between a static, cynical Egyptian pyramid built by slaves and a dynamic, optimistic power station built by conscious Soviet workers. Similarly *Ivanovo Calico* (*Ivanovskie sittsy*, 1976) uses the association of the name Ivan (Ivan the Fool; Ivan the Terrible; Ivan Fyodorov, the first Russian printer) with Ivanovo (home of the Russian textile industry and of the first Soviet of Workers' Deputies) to create a whole democratic parable of Russia's history: Ivan the Fool learns to read and to work with other Ivans to overthrow the tsarist regime, so that today's Ivans can study the history of their country and be worthy to rule it. Even such an impeccably acceptable concept contains, however, a drop of poison, when the author reminds his readers that "The craven empty holes of history/Create emptinesses in our children."

Evtushenko has been much criticized, and not only by Stalinists resentful of the new wave. Sinyavsky, for example, who aptly terms him both a "sharpshooter" and "choir-leader," accuses him of prolixity and superficiality, of striking attitudes and postures while lacking any rooted personality to match the mantle of heir to the classical Russian poetic tradition which he has assumed. There is justice in these reproaches. Perhaps the problem is that, from the very outset of his career, his poetic self and his civic personality were indissolubly mixed. The fluent virtuosity of his talent forced him into a public role before he had the inner resources to discharge it adequately while remaining true to himself. Some of his early poems reveal a meditative, tender and vulnerable personality, going back to mother for hot soup and homely wisdom when loneliness and aborted relationships became too much for him. Perhaps this side of his character never had time to develop properly.

Nevertheless, in his own way Evtushenko performed a genuine service for Russian literature, by reviving the sonorous traditions of Russian poetry of the first thirty years of this century, and especially those of Mayakovsky and Esenin (between whose very diverse talents Evtushenko often seemed torn), and bringing them once again into the mainstream of Russian culture.

Much of what is true of Evtushenko also holds for Andrey Voznesensky (1933–   ), who, though a slightly later developer, was his natural partner in rousing public poetry readings. He first studied architecture until a fire at his institute destroyed a design project he was due to enter for his diploma, and "I realized that architecture was burnt out in *me*. I became a poet." Pasternak encouraged him in his chosen vocation, and his early poems often recall the older poet's own experimental works, with their jagged sounds, their far-fetched metaphors and their assertion of the transcendent importance of art. From the start Voznesensky's experiments were more radical than Evtushenko's, the tone of his verse usually more strident and geometrical, as was symbolized by the image of the "triangular pear" featured on the cover of one of his books, like something straight out of a Lef poster. Mayakovsky was as important an influence on him as Pasternak.

Something of his preoccupations can be seen in "Mastera" ("Master craftsmen," 1959), which elaborates the story of the architect of St. Basil's Cathedral in Moscow, who was blinded by Ivan the Terrible so that he would never build anything to rival it. Voznesensky presents the boyars and merchants of Muscovy, like the tsar, as obtuse and envious, incapable of appreciating art but at the same time feeling vaguely threatened by it. It was an ambiguous parable of the condition of the arts in the Soviet Union at the time.

In more contemplative spirit, Voznesensky evoked, in "Treetops and roots," ("Krony i korni," 1960), the funeral of Pasternak, then disgraced, and thereby identified the poet with nature.

In his flight is his victory;
In his retreat an ascent
To pastures and planets,
Far from gilded deceit.

Forests shed their tops,
But powerfully underground
Roots twist and thrust
Like a gnarled hand.

Seeing himself as the people's tribune, Voznesensky recalled their sufferings in one of his earliest and most celebrated poems, "I am

Goya" ("Ya – Goya,", 1959). The repetition of sounds reminiscent of Goya's name (*gore, golos, golod*) recalls the insistent clang of an alarm bell. It becomes woven into a sound texture which absorbs other assonances, as in the lines

O grozdi
vozmezdiya! Vzvil zalpom na zapad –
　　　　　ya pepel nezvanogo gostya!

(O grapes of wrath! I hurled westwards a broadside of ash of the unbidden guest!)

This is but a particularly striking example of Voznesensky's ability to renew the Russian poetic language by shaking up the metric structure, using internal and approximate rhymes, parallelism and assonance to enhance his declamatory effects. Similarly, he mixes styles freely, combining elevated diction with the language of sport, technology, and newspapers, and with everyday vulgarities. His images are striking and often grotesque. In the strict sense he is probably not an innovator, since his technical devices were anticipated by poets such as Khlebnikov, Mayakovsky, Tsvetaeva and the early Pasternak. Nevertheless, his virtuoso exploitation of the potential of the modernist poetic tradition of the earlier twentieth century lent his verse a decidedly original, and even iconoclastic aspect.

Some critics have felt that Voznesensky's contribution to Russian poetry does not extend beyond such formal experiments, and that the breathtaking facade conceals an inner emptiness. This possibility has obsessed the poet himself. Appropriately, perhaps, for a man whose personality comes over most strongly at huge public readings, he feels himself to be observed, not just in body but in soul, as though he lacked all inner meaning and perhaps even minimal privacy. His "Marilyn Monroe's monologue" ("Monolog Merlin Monro," 1962) displays his obsession with nakedness leading to loss of personhood and ultimately to self-destruction, while in his "New York airport at night" ("Nochnoy aeroport v Nyu yorke," 1961) he identifies himself with a structure as bare and transparent as an airport building:

Self-portrait, neon retort, apostle or heavenly gates –
Airport!

Your duralumined plate glass darkly shines
Like an X-ray of the soul.

Voznesensky is fascinated by external structures, lines, shapes and trajectories, which he evokes with virtuoso technical effects in a way reminiscent only of Zamyatin among Russian writers. "Parabolic ballad" ("Parabolicheskaya ballada"), for example, lays before us the artist's career as not an ordinary straight line, but as a parabola, a breathtaking curve which takes him out of the sphere of ordinary people and makes it difficult for them to live with him. This theme of the artist as a creature of a different order who inevitably causes pain to his loved ones is recurrent in Voznesensky's work.

However, Voznesensky's fascination with external structures is often accompanied by a haunting fear, even as he flaunts his ego before the world, that there is nothing beyond the external structure, no inner essence. In a sense this is his fear for the whole of modern civilization, as is suggested by his long poem *Oza* (1964). Written in alternating prose and verse, with flashbacks and transitions from one imaginative plane to another, it records the progress of a love affair at the nuclear plant of Dubna. The poet's loved one, called Zoya (life), parts from him, at the same time turning her name inside out, to Oza. He fears this means that life itself is turning inside out: imagination and love are being drained from the world by the cyclotron, and the soul will have to be "removed like diseased tonsils" (much as in Zamyatin's *We*). He fears too that technology triumphant will turn human beings into cogs as effectively as Stalin did.

In spite of his exuberant anthems to modernity, then, Voznesensky expresses perhaps more effectively than any other modern Russian poet the fear that facade will triumph over essence, man's technology over man's inner world, to the general impoverishment of civilization.

Many poets have declined the role of popular tribune assumed by Evtushenko and Voznesensky in order to do what seems to them more important, especially in an era when the collective threatens to overwhelm the personal: they wish to cultivate and communicate their own awareness of the human personality and its links with the world and with God.

Among the older generation, Arseny Tarkovsky (1907–) has established himself as perhaps its leading figure. Having supported himself with translations most of his life because he could not publish his own verse, he made his debut in his fifties. His lyric poetry, concise and disciplined, is close to the acmeist tradition in its concern with this world and with the relationshp between words and things. A recurrent image is that of the poet as both "tsar" and "beggar": "tsar" because of the magnificence with which he can array the world, "beggar" because all the same he does not belong there, and can only practice his art by taking a part that which is whole:

> And from nowhere
> I have come to split
> A unified miracle
> Into spirit and flesh.
>
> Nature's sovereign realm
> I must tear asunder
> Into song and water,
> Into dry land and speech.

Of the generation just old enough to fight in the war, Boris Slutsky (1919–), David Samoylov (1920–) and Eugene Vinokurov (1925–) have the most established reputations. All of them were deeply affected by what they had seen at the front, and especially in their early work used incidents from military life to illustrate more general reflections, often of a rueful, skeptical or humane kind, rejecting the fanaticism which drives men to make war on one another. Reassessing his own youth in the light of his war experience, Vinokurov admitted

> I kept no diary. Collected no facts.
> Disdained the particular. Hated detail.
> A great light dazzled my eyes.

He came increasingly to appreciate the qualities of modesty and ordinariness. Comparing those people who have a "a thirst for great missions" with those whose ideal is to "do a spot of gardening at the dacha," he indicates a preference for the latter, confessing that with the former "here, in this life, we sometimes have real trouble."

For Naum Korzhavin (1925 –, real surname Mandel) the decisive experience was not so much war as arrest and a seven-year exile in Siberia and Kazakhstan (1947–54). A natural romantic whose early poems are full of the enthusiasm of dedication to the cause, he learnt that life was more complicated:

> From childhood I dreamt that the trumpet would sound,
> And the town would awake to the clatter of hooves,
> All would be resolved in honest battle:
> The enemy is over there, your friends are right behind you.
>
> I thought I could see, though blind as a bat.
> Among our friends, enemies scurried about,
> Right there in the midst of our columns,
> And some of them indeed were our standard bearers.

Korzhavin drew from this discovery a less militant and more humane romanticism, exemplified in "The communal cemetery in Riga" ("Bratskoe kladbishche v Rige"), which expresses compassion for Russian and Latvian nationalists, soldiers of Red Army and Wehrmacht alike, since "The various truths were as similar as tombstones." It was impossible to publish work of this kind in the Soviet Union, and in 1973 Korzhavin emigrated to the United States.

In the generation which grew up after the war there were, apart from Evtushenko and Voznesensky, so many talented poets, most of whom have published in the Soviet Union, and a few in emigration, that it seems prudent to confine oneself here to the two most generally acknowledged names, Akhmadulina and Brodsky.

Bella Akhmadulina (1937–) writes intensely personal and idiosyncratic lyrics of self-discovery. Married in turn to Evtushenko and the novelist Yury Nagibin, she suffered considerable instability both in her personal and her literary life. Her poems reflect her tentative relationships with things, people and even her own inspiration. Her love poems are tender, vulnerable and usually colored by the fear or expectation of parting. This mood communicates itself also to those poems which deal with the subject of artistic creation.

In one poem the poet appears as a lunatic, strangely affected by familiar objects:

Glimmering thus coldly and sparely,
Promising nothing in return,
My remote art draws me on
And demands my acquiescence.

Can I overcome its torments
And the charm of its tokens
And sculpt from the lunar radiance
A solid, tangible object?

At the same time, the struggle for the "solid, tangible object" brings its own rewards. Akhmadulina excels in evoking miracles out of the material of everyday life, as in "The mineral water vending machine" ("Avtomat s gazirovannoy vodoy"), in which she transforms the banal experience of putting a coin in a slot and filling a glass with water into a symbol of the secret generosity of the universe. Similarly, in "Milk" ("Moloko") she sees in the white liquid something "valuable and rare, like festivals."

The world is boundless, but there is nothing in it,
If you are not willing to notice it.

This intimacy with ordinary miracles is something which isolates Akhmadulina, and she is intensely aware of this isolation. Her most extended metaphor for it is the long poem "A fable of rain" ("Skazka o dozhde"). In a drought-parched town she is the only person soaked by rain, in fact she has her own personal shower following her about. Like a monkey or a small child, it will not leave her alone. She is both impatient with it and attached to it. It embarrasses her especially when she has to visit the apartment of a society hostess. She bids it remain outside, but then, lonely without it, summons it in desperation, causing inevitable havoc to the elegant interior. Her inspiration, her intense relationship with nature, can only cause her trouble in a society insensitive to such qualities. Unlike Evtushenko, however, she does not proudly proclaim the poet's mission: rather she is semi-apologetic about it. In other poems, such as "A chill" ("Oznob"), she sees it as an illness of which she both does and does not wish to be cured.

As the extended rain image implies, Akhmadulina senses in natural objects an intense life of their own. In "Night" ("Noch"), as she sits at her desk seized with paralysis before a blank paper, each object beseeches her:

Its soul longs to be sung
And without fail by my voice.

Even in her attacks of "dumbness," she is aware of what she calls "the eternal dialogue between nameless things and the soul which names them."

Joseph Brodsky (1940–) was brought up in post-war Leningrad, a city whose very appearance eloquently proclaimed past glory and present poverty: "those magnificent pockmarked facades behind which – among old pianos, worn-out rugs, dusty paintings in heavy bronze frames, leftovers of furniture [...] consumed by the iron stoves during the siege – a faint life was beginning to glimmer." He grew up amidst what he later saw as

> the only generation of Russians that had found itself, for whom Giotto and Mandelshtam were more imperative than their own destinies [...] Nobody knew literature and history better than these people, nobody could write in Russian better than they, nobody despised our times more profoundly [...] Poorly dressed, but somehow still elegant, shuffled by the dumb hands of their immediate masters [...] they still retained their love for the non-existent (or existing only in their balding heads) thing called "civilization."

Brodsky's work expresses the struggles, the peripeteia, and also the arrogance of a self-taught generation which had acquired, thanks to its schoolmasters, the raw materials of culture, but had to fight personally to penetrate to the culture itself. Brodsky left school at fifteen, feeling he had nothing more to learn there, and did his serious reading while working at odd jobs. It was then that he got to know western literature (particularly that of Britain and America), the Russian religious philosophers, classical mythology and the Bible. Anna Akhmatova encouraged his early attempts to write verse, but he was influenced even more powerfully by Mandelshtam, for they both saw man as in essence a cultural animal (rather than a biological product or, as Aristotle would have it, a political animal). In a world where politics had become dehumanized but the rudiments of culture were being transmitted more widely, that anthropological conception was both inspiring and fruitful. It entailed rescuing Russian poetry from the sterile

591

isolation it had endured under Stalin, and restoring its links with world culture, with what Stalin had vilified as "cosmopolitanism."

At its simplest, this conception is displayed in a poem like "A halt in the wilderness" ("Ostanovka v pustyne," 1965), which comments on the destruction of a Greek Orthodox church in Leningrad to make way for a concert hall. A "temple of art" is to replace a temple of faith. Its shape, a flat line rather than a dome, will be less pleasing, but who can say that the change is unjustified, since there are after all "now so few Greeks in Leningrad"? But it raises disturbing questions, nonetheless:

> Tonight I look out of the window
> And wonder where we are going.
> And which are we further away from,
> Orthodoxy or Hellenism?
> What are we near to? What lies ahead?
> Does not another era await us?
> And if so, what is our common duty?
> And what must we sacrifice for it?

Brodsky's attitude is much more than merely nostalgic. On the contrary, he is acutely aware of living in an era in which change is inevitable, and indeed holds forth creative possibilities. His is not a poetry of lament for lost culture, but rather an open and existential poetry, searching for the elements out of which human beings can shape a culture to sustain them in the present. In effect, words become a reality more real than the objects they denote: "By itself reality isn't worth a damn. It's perception that promotes reality to meaning." Words become even more real than the individual human beings who write them, who are likewise subject to aging and death. For Brodsky the urge to create springs from an acute sense of the passing of time or, in its concentrated form, an acute sense of nothingness. The brief life of the butterfly in "The butterfly" ("Babochka", 1972) is a parable of the precarious and beautiful incarnation of which nothingness is capable, and which is after all something.

> You are better than Nothing.
> Or rather: you are closer

And more visible. But inside
You stand in the closest possible
Relationship to it.
In your flight it took on flesh,
And therefore
In the daytime hubbub
You merit attention
As a modest barrier
Between it and me.

Nothingness, blackness, death, evil – these things are all concentrated in the chaos of things unhumanized, like the black horse of the early poem "The black horizon was lighter than those legs" ("Byl cherny nebosvod svetley tekh nog"), whose blackness Brodsky obsessively evokes in a series of ever more extravagant, and sometimes philosophically challenging, comparisons ("As black as the inside of a needle, [. . .] As the place between the ribs, As the nook beneath the earth where lies the grain"). He is black because he seeks a rider who will tame and humanize him.

The repetition of the word "black," and the accumulation of similes for blackness, are characteristic of Brodsky. Much of his work has an obsessive quality, as though he were struggling with great difficulty to make *some* sense of the materials of chaos. There is a breathlessness, too, about his rhythms: although he usually employs classical meters, he takes remarkable liberties with them, as if he wished deliberately to deform them. Some of his sentences are very long with many successive enjambements, extending even over stanzas, while in other cases individual lines are chopped up into short units. Thus in the "Great elegy to John Donne" ("Bolshaya elegiya Dzhonu Donnu," 1963), one iambic pentameter contains no fewer than nine words:

Tak beden, gust, tak chist, chto v nikh – edinstvo
(So poor and dense, so pure that in them's unity)

while earlier parts of the poem consist of long lists of objects which have fallen asleep along with Donne. It is natural, then, that Brodsky leans towards longer forms, cast, however, not usually as narratives, but as extended philosophical meditations or dialogues, in which the implications of ideas and images can be explored to their furthest reaches, and sometimes beyond the point where readers can follow him. In this he resembles the English metaphysical poets, to whom he has always felt especially close, with their protracted "conceits" combining philosophical ideas and sensuous images.

Brodsky has twice suffered exile. In 1964 he was condemned by a Leningrad court for "dronery" (which meant spending his time writing without being a member of the Writers' Union) to five years of corrective labor, later reduced to eighteen months at a state farm in the Archangel region. The second occasion was in 1972, when he was forced to leave the USSR under threat of arrest. This time he could settle in the west, whose culture he admires. As a natural citizen of the world, he has found it possible to continue writing here without loss of power, and even to produce some poems in his adopted language, English. He stands, then, as an exemplar of what his poetry rests upon: the essential unity of world culture.

A BIBLIOGRAPHY OF
RUSSIAN LITERATURE

FOREWORD

This bibliography is designed as an aid to the further study of particular points in the history of Russian literature. The limited space at the compiler's disposal has compelled him to be very selective in choosing works for inclusion. In making his selections he has followed the following general rules.

(1) The listing includes only secondary works – studies of topics, periods, individual authors.

(2) Only books have been included. No articles, no matter how seminal, have been listed.

(3) Priorities have been assigned as follows:
    (a) Works in English.
    (b) Works in Russian (including writings by émigré scholars).
    (c) Works in western European languages.

(4) Entries are listed chronologically in order to provide some notion of the historiography of Russian literatures. The final year for inclusion is 1986. In the great majority of cases I have listed secondary works in their initial editions, so far as I could determine them. If a book is not listed in its first edition, I have indicated that fact.

(5) Greater emphasis is placed upon more recent scholarly works, and more generally upon the twentieth century, but I have sought to include also certain earlier works even from the mid nineteenth century through the early twentieth century if they have become scholarly or critical "classics" even though they may now be somewhat outdated. This applies particularly to the writings of certain pioneers in the field of Russian literature in the English-speaking world.

(6) The author-listings attempt to include as many of the writers mentioned in the body of the *Cambridge History of Russian Literature* as possible where there exist individual books of some worth about them. Where writers have been the subject of extensive scholarly investigation, the listing may be quite selective. Still, in a rough way the length of each

author entry reflects the importance of that author in the history of Russian literature.

Finally, I should like to pay tribute to the achievement of Carl Proffer (1938–84), who, with his wife Ellendea, established a publishing enterprise in Ann Arbor, Michigan, which has played a unique role in the history of contemporary Russian literature. This bibliograpy reflects the secondary works which Ardis Publishers has brought out, but by its nature it cannot outline the remarkable contributions that house made to the publication of original Russian literature produced both inside the Soviet Union and in emigration – and which deserve to be remembered as well.

Charles A. Moser

ARRANGEMENT OF THE BIBLIOGRAPHY

1. Histories of Russian literature
   a. General
   b. Old Russian and eighteenth century
   c. Nineteenth century
   d. Twentieth century
2. Special topics
   Arranged chronologically to correspond to the chapters of this *History*
3. Literary movements
   Arranged alphabetically
4. Literary genres
   Arranged alphabetically
5. Comparative studies
   Arranged chronologically
6. Miscellaneous
   Arranged chronologically
7. Authors
   Arranged alphabetically

General histories

Galakhov, Aleksei, *Istoriia russkoi slovesnosti, drevnei i novoi* (2 vols., 2nd ed., St. Petersburg, 1880).

Skabichevskii, Aleksandr, *Istoriia noveishei russkoi literatury (1848–1890)* (St. Petersburg, 1891).

Pypin, A. N., *Istoriia russkoi literatury* (4 vols., St. Petersburg, 1898–9).

Tikhonravov, Nikolai, *Sochineniia* (a 3-part history of Russian literature in 4 vols., Moscow, 1898).

Waliszewski, Kazimierz, *Littérature russe* (Paris, 1900). (Translation: *A History of Russian Literature* (New York, 1900).)

Hapgood, Isabel, *A Survey of Russian Literature* (New York, 1902).

Brueckner, Alexander, *Geschichte der russischen Literatur* (Leipzig, 1905). (Translation: *A Literary History of Russia* (New York and London, 1908).)

Ovsianiko-Kulikovskii, Dmitrii, ed., *Istoriia russkoi literatury XIX veka* (5 vols., Moscow, 1910–11).

Baring, Maurice, *An Outline of Russian Literature* (London and New York, 1915).

Luther, Arthur, *Geschichte der russischen Literatur* (Leipzig, 1924).

Mirsky, D. S., *Contemporary Russian Literature 1881–1925* (New York, 1926).

Mirsky, D. S., *A History of Russian Literature from the Earliest Times to the Death of Dostoevsky* (New York, 1927).

Lo Gatto, Ettore, *Storia della letteratura russa* (7 vols., Rome, 1927–41).

Aikhenval'd, Iulii, *Siluety russkikh pisatelei* (3 vols., Berlin, 1929).

Pozner, Vladimir, *Panorama de la littérature russe contemporaine* (Paris, 1929).

Hofmann, Modeste, *Histoire de la littérature russe depuis les origines jusqu'à nos jours* (Paris, 1934).

Akademiia nauk SSSR, *Istoriia russkoi literatury* (10 vols. in 13, Moscow, 1941–56).

Stender-Petersen, Adolf, *Den russiske litteraturshistorie* (3 vols., Copenhagen, 1952).

Lettenbauer, Wilhelm, *Russische Literaturgeschichte* (Frankfurt am Main and Vienna, 1955).

Osorgina, Antonina, *Istoriia russkoi literatury (s drevneishikh vremen do Pushkina)* (Paris, 1955).

Blagoi, Dmitrii, ed., *Istoriia russkoi literatury* (3 vols., Leningrad, 1958–64).

Slonim, Marc, *An Outline of Russian Literature* (New York, 1958).

Lindstrom, Thais, *A Concise History of Russian Literature* (2 vols., New York, 1966–78).

Lavrin, Janko, *A Panorama of Russian Literature* (London, 1973).

Kolstad, Ellinor, and Ragnfred Stokke, *Russisk litteraturhistorie 1700–1970* (Oslo, 1974).

Auty, Robert, and Dmitry Obolensky, eds., *An Introduction to Russian Language and Literature* (Companion to Russian Studies 2) (Cambridge, 1977).

Terras, Victor, ed., *Handbook of Russian Literature* (New Haven and London, 1985).

Old Russian and eighteenth century

Istrin, Vasilii, *Ocherk istorii drevnerusskoi literatury domoskovskogo perioda, 11–13 vv.* (Petrograd, 1922).

Orlov, Aleksandr, *Drevniaia russkaia literatura XI-XVII vekov* (Moscow–Leningrad, 1937).

Gudzii, Nikolai, *Istoriia drevnei russkoi literatury* (Moscow, 1938). (Translation: *Early Russian Literature* (New York, 1949).)

Gukovskii, Grigorii, *Istoriia russkoi literatury XVIII veka* (Moscow, 1939).

Blagoi, Dmitrii, *Istoriia russkoi literatury XVIII veka* (Moscow, 1945).

Chyzhev'skyi, Dmytro, *Geschichte der altrussischen Literatur im 11., 12. und 13. Jahrhundert* (Frankfurt am Main, 1948).

Sazonova, Iuliia, *Istoriiia russkoi literatury: drevnii period* (2 vols., New York, 1955).

Picchio, Riccardo, *Storia della letteratura russa antica* (Milan, 1959).

Čiževskij, Dmitrij, *History of Russian Literature, from the Eleventh Century to the End of the Baroque* (The Hague, 1960).

Berkov, Pavel, *Vvedenie v izuchenie istorii russkoi literatury XVIII veka. Chast' 1: Ocherk literaturnoi istoriografii XVIII veka* (Leningrad, 1964).

Berkov, Pavel, *Literarische Wechselbeziehungen zwischen Russland und Westeuropa im 18. Jahrhundert* (Berlin, 1968).

Pereverzev, Valerian, *Literatura drevnei Rusi* (Moscow, 1971).

Fennell, John, and Antony Stokes, *Early Russian Literature* (Berkeley, 1974).

Brown, William, *A History of Seventeenth-Century Russian Literature* (Ann Arbor, 1980).

Brown, William, *A History of Eighteenth-Century Russian Literature* (Ann Arbor, 1980).

Robinson, A. N., *Literatura drevnei Rusi v literaturnom protsesse srednevekov'ia* (Moscow, 1980).

Likhachev, Dmitrii, ed. *Istoriia russkoi literatury XI–XVII vekov* (Moscow, 1980).

Nineteenth-century literature

Miller, Orest, *Russkaia literatura posle Gogolia* (St. Petersburg, 1874).

Engel'gardt, Nikolai, *Istoriia russkoi literatury XIX stolet'ia* (2 vols. 2nd ed., St. Petersburg–Petrograd, 1913–15).

Chyzhevs'kyi, Dmytro, *Russische Literaturgeschichte des 19. Jahrhunderts* (Munich, 1964). (Translation: *History of Nineteenth-Century Russian Literature*. Vol. 1. *The Romantic Period*. Vol. 2. *The Realistic Period* (Nashville, 1974).)

Duwel, Wolf, ed., *Geschichte der klassischen russischen Literatur* (Berlin and Weimar, 1965).

Kravtsov, N. I., *Istoriia russkoi literatury vtoroi poloviny XIX veka* (Moscow, 1966).

Twentieth-century literature

Nilsson, Nils Ake, *Sovjetrysk litteratur 1917–47* (Stockholm, 1948).

Struve, Gleb, *Soviet Russian Literature 1917–50* (Norman, 1951).

Slonim, Marc, *Modern Russian Literature from Chekhov to the Present* (New York, 1953).

Struve, Gleb, *Russkaia literatura v izgnanii: Opyt istoricheskogo obzora zarubezhnoi literatury* (New York, 1956).

Alexandrova, Vera, *A History of Soviet Literature* (Garden City, NY, 1963).

BIBLIOGRAPHY

Hayward, Max, and Leopold Labedz, eds., *Literature and Revolution in Soviet Russia 1917–62* (London, New York, and Toronto, 1963).

Holthusen, Johannes, *Russische Gegenwartsliteratur* (2 vols., Bern, 1963–8) (Translation: *Twentieth-Century Russian Literature: A Critical Study* (New York, 1972).)

Akademiia nauk SSSR, *Istoriia russkoi sovetskoi literatury* (4 vols., 2nd ed., Moscow, 1967–71).

Nag, Martin, *Sovjetlitteraturen 1917–1967* (Oslo, 1967).

Lathouwers, M. A., *De Sovjet-Literatuur* (Utrecht and Antwerp, 1968).

Lo Gatto, Ettore, *La letteratura russo-sovietica* (Enlarged edition, Florence and Milan, 1968).

Brown, Edward J., *Russian Literature since the Revolution* (Revised ed., New York, 1969).

Junger, Harri, ed., *Geschichte der russischen Sowjetliteratur 1941–1967* (2 vols., Berlin, 1973–5).

SPECIAL TOPICS
I. 988–1730

Budovnits, Isaak, *Russkaia publitsistika XVI veka* (Moscow–Leningrad, 1947).

Likhachev, Dmitrii, *Vozniknovenie russkoi literatury* (Moscow, 1952).

Likhachev, Dmitrii, *Chelovek v literature drevnei Rusi* (Moscow–Leningrad, 1958).

Lur'e, Iakov, *Ideologicheskaia bor'ba v russkoi publitsistike kontsa XV–nachala XVI veka* (Moscow–Leningrad, 1960).

Eremin, Igor', *Poetika drevnerusskoi literatury* (Leningrad, 1967).

Børtnes, Jostein, *Det gammelrussiske helgenvita: Dikterisk egenart og historisk betydning* (Oslo, 1975).

Likhachev, Dmitrii, *Velikoe nasledie: klassicheskie proizvedeniia literatury drevnei Rusi* (Moscow, 1975). (Translation: *The Great Heritage* (Moscow, 1981).)

Demin, Anatolii, *Russkaia literatura vtoroi poloviny XVII–nachala XVIII veka: novye khudozhestvennye predstavleniia o mire, prirode, cheloveke* (Moscow, 1977).

II. 1730–90

Nezelenov, Aleksandr, *Literaturnye napravleniia v ekaterininskuiu epokhu* (St. Petersburg, 1889).

Berkov, Pavel, *Lomonosov i literaturnaia polemika ego vremeni, 1750–1765* (Moscow–Leningrad, 1936).

Serman, Il'ia, *Russkii klassitsizm. Poeziia. Drama. Satira* (Leningrad, 1973).

III. 1790–1820

Kotliarevskii, Nestor, *Literaturnye napravleniia Aleksandrovskoi epokhi* (St. Petersburg, 1907).

BIBLIOGRAPHY

Meynieux, André, *La Littérature et le métier d'écrivain en Russie avant Pouchkine* (Paris, 1966).

Neuhäuser, Rudolf, *Towards the Romantic Age: Essays on Sentimental and Preromantic Literature* (The Hague, 1974).

Todd, William, III, *The Familiar Letter as a Literary Genre in the Age of Pushkin* (Princeton, 1976).

Al'tshuller, Mark, *Predtechi slavianofil'stva v russkoi literature (Obshchestvo "Beseda liubitelei russkogo slova")* (Ann Arbor, 1984).

IV. 1820–40

Lemke, Mikhail, *Nikolaevskie zhandarmy i literatura 1826–1855 gg.* (St. Petersburg, 1908).

Gukovskii, Grigorii, *Pushkin i russkie romantiki* (Moscow, 1965).

Brown, Edward, *Stankevich and His Moscow Circle 1830–1840* (Stanford, 1966).

Todd, William, III, *Fiction and Society in the Age of Pushkin: Ideology, Institutions, and Narrative* (Cambridge, Mass. and London, 1986).

V. 1840–55

Kuleshov, Vasilii, *Natural'naia shkola v russkoi literature XIX veka* (Moscow, 1965).

Kuleshov, Vasilii, *Otechestvennye zapiski i literatura 40 godov XIX v.* (Moscow, 1958).

Tseitlin, Aleksandr, *Stanovlenie realizma v russkoi literature (russkii fiziologicheskii ocherk)* (Moscow, 1965).

VI. 1855–80

Moser, Charles, *Antinihilism in the Russian Novel of the 1860's* (The Hague, 1964).

Lampert, Evgenii, *Sons Against Fathers: Studies in Russian Radicalism and Revolution* (Oxford, 1965).

Sokolov, Nikolai, *Russkaia literatura i narodnichestvo: literaturnoe dvizhenie 70-kh gg. XIX v.* (Leningrad, 1968).

Lotman, Lidiia, *Realizm russkoi literatury 60-kh godov XIX veka (istoki i esteticheskoe svoeobrazie)* (Leningrad, 1974).

VII. 1880–95

Volkov, Anatolii, *Ocherki russkoi literatury kontsa XIX i nachala XX vekov* (Moscow, 1952).

Bialik, B. A., ed., *Russkaia literatura kontsa XIX-nachala XX v. 1. Devianostye gody* (Moscow, 1968).

Dolgopolov, Leonid, *Na rubezhe vekov: O russkoi literature kontsa XIX-nachala XX v.* (Leningrad, 1977).

VIII. 1895–1925

Trotskii, Lev, *Literatura i revoliutsiia* (Moscow, 1924). (Translation: *Literature and Revolution* (New York, 1925).)

Nikitina, E., *Russkaia literatura ot simvolizma do nashikh dnei* (Moscow, 1926).

Oulanoff, Hongor, *The Serapion Brothers: Theory and Practice* (The Hague, 1966).

Bialyk, B. A. ed., *Russkaia literatura kontsa XIX–nachala XX veka. 2. 1901–1907* (Moscow, 1971).

Bialyk, B. A., ed., *Russkaia literatura kontsa XIX–nachala XX veka. 3. 1908–1917* (Moscow, 1972).

Keldysh, V., *Russkii realizm nachala XX veka* (Moscow, 1975).

IX. 1925–53

Eastman, Max, *Artists in Uniform: A Study of Literature and Bureaucratism* (New York, 1934).

Borland, Harriet, *Soviet Literary Theory and Practice during the First Five-Year Plan: 1928–1932* (New York, 1950).

Brown, Edward, *The Proletarian Episode in Russian Literature, 1928–1932* (New York, 1953).

Eng-Liedmeier, A. M. van der, *Soviet Literary Characters: An Investigation into the Portrayal of Soviet Men in Russian Prose 1917–1953* (The Hague, 1959).

Ruhle, Jürgen, *Literatur und Revolution: die Schriftsteller und der Kommunismus* (Cologne, 1960). (Translation: *Literature and Revolution: A Critical Study of the Writer and Communism in the Twentieth Century* (New York, 1969).)

Swayze, Harold, *Political Control of Literature in the USSR 1946–1959* (Cambridge, Mass., 1962).

Gasiorowska, Xenia, *Women in Soviet Fiction, 1917–1964* (Madison, Milwaukee and London, 1968).

Maguire, Robert, *Red Virgin Soil: Soviet Literature in the 1920's* (Princeton, 1968).

Corbet, Charles, *Une littérature aux fers: le pseudo-réalisme sovietique* (Paris, 1975).

Svirskii, Grigorii, *Na lobnom meste: Literatura nravstvennogo soprotivleniia (1946–76 gg.)* (London, 1979). (Translation: *A History of Post-War Soviet Writing: The Literature of Moral Opposition* (Ann Arbor, 1981).)

X. 1953–80

Gibian, George, *Interval of Freedom: Soviet Literature During the Thaw 1954–1957* (Minneapolis, 1960).

Rogers, Thomas, *"Superfluous Men" and the Post-Stalin "Thaw": The Alienated Hero in Soviet Prose during the Decade 1953–1963* (The Hague, 1972).

Ravnum, Ivar Magnus, *Russisk litteratur etter Stalin* (Oslo, 1973).

Mal'tsev, Iurii, *Vol'naia russkaia literatura: 1955–1975* (Frankfurt am Main, 1976).

Brown, Deming, *Soviet Russian Literature Since Stalin* (Cambridge, 1978).

Shneidman, N., *Soviet Literature in the 1970's: Artistic Diversity and Ideological Conformity* (Buffalo and Toronto, 1979).

Hosking, Geoffrey, *Beyond Socialist Realism: Soviet Fiction since Ivan Denisovich* (London, 1980).

Frankel, Edith, *Novy mir: A Case Study in the Politics of Literature 1952–1958* (Cambridge, 1981).

LITERARY MOVEMENTS
Formalism

Erlich, Victor, *Russian Formalism: History and Doctrine* (The Hague, 1955).

Ambrogio, Ignazio, *Formalismo e avanguardia in Russia* (Rome, 1968).

Pomorska, Krystyna, *Russian Formalist Theory and Its Poetic Ambience* (The Hague, 1968).

Garcia Berrio, Antonio, *Significado actual del formalismo ruso: la doctrina de la escuela del metodo formal ante la poetica y la linguistica modernas* (Barcelona, 1973).

Futurism

Chukovskii, Kornei, *Futuristy* (Petrograd, 1922). (Translation: *Les Futuristes* (Lausanne, 1976).)

Markov, Vladimir, *Russian Futurism: A History* (Berkeley and Los Angeles, 1968).

Barooshian, Vahan, *Russian Cubo-Futurism 1910–1930: a Study in Avant-Gardism* (The Hague and Paris, 1974).

Jangfeldt, Bengt, *Majakovskii and Futurism 1917–1921* (Stockholm, 1976).

Imagism (Imaginism)

Nilsson, Nils Ake, *The Russian Imaginists* (Stockholm, 1970).

Markov, Vladimir, *Russian Imagism 1919–1924* (2 vols., Giessen, 1980).

Realism

Lukács, György, *Der russische Realismus in der Weltliteratur* (3rd ed., Berlin, 1952).

Fokht, Ul'rikh, *Puti russkogo realizma* (Moscow, 1963).

Petrov, Sergei, *Realizm* (Moscow, 1964).

Fridlender, Georgii, *Poetika russkogo realizma: ocherki o russkoi literature XIX v.* (Leningrad, 1971).

Lomunov, Konstantin, ed., *Razvitie realizma v russkoi literature* (3 vols., Moscow, 1972–4).

Städtke, Klaus, *Studien zum russischen Realismus des 19. Jahrhunderts: Zum Verhältnis von Weltbild und epischer Struktur* (Berlin, 1973).

Petrov, Sergei, *Kriticheskii realizm* (Moscow, 1974).

Romanticism

Zamotin, Ivan, *Romantizm dvadtsatykh godov XIX veka* (third, revised edition, Petrograd–Moscow, 1919).

BIBLIOGRAPHY

Leighton, Lauren, *Russian Romanticism* (The Hague, 1975).
Maimin, Evgenii, *O russkom romantizme* (Moscow, 1975).
Zelinsky, Bodo, *Russische Romantik* (Cologne and Vienna, 1975).
Mann, Iurii, *Poetika russkogo romantizma* (Moscow, 1976).
Istoriia romantizma v russkoi literature. Vol. 1. Vozniknovenie i utverzhdenie romantizma v russkoi literature (1790–1825). Vol. 2. Romantizm v russkoi literature 20–30-kh godov XIX v. (1825–1840) (Moscow, 1979).
Mersereau, John, Jr., *Russian Romantic Fiction* (Ann Arbor, 1983).
Brown, William Edward, *A History of Russian Literature of the Romantic Period* (4 vols., Ann Arbor, 1986).

Sentimentalism

Orlov, Pavel, *Russkii sentimentalizm* (Moscow, 1977).

Socialist realism

Tertz, Abram, *On Socialist Realism* (New York, 1961).
Ermolaev, Herman, *Soviet Literary Theories 1917–1934: the Genesis of Socialist Realism* (Berkeley, 1963).
James, C. Vaughan, *Soviet Socialist Realism: Origins and Theory* (London, 1973).
Możejko, Edward, *Der sozialistische Realismus: Theorie, Entwicklung und Versagen einer Literaturmethode* (Bonn, 1977).
Günther, Hans, *Die Verstaatlichung der Literatur: Entstehung und Funktionsweise des sozialistisch-realistischen Kanons in der sowjetischen Literatur der 30-er Jahre* (Stuttgart, 1984).

Symbolism

Holthusen, Johannes, *Studien zur Aesthetik und Poetik des russischen Symbolismus* (Göttingen, 1957).

LITERARY GENRES
Criticism

Ivanov, Ivan, *Istoriia russkoi kritiki* (4 vols., St. Petersburg, 1898).
Lunacharskii, Antolii, and Valerii Polianskii, eds., *Ocherki po istorii russkoi kritiki* (2 vols., Moscow–Leningrad, 1929).
Gorodetskii, B. P. et al. eds., *Istoriia russkoi kritiki* (2 vols., Leningrad, 1958).
Mordovchenko, Nikolai, *Russkaia kritika pervoi chetverti XIX veka* (Moscow–Leningrad, 1959).
Steffensen, Eigil, *Nyere russisk literaturkritik. Fra Plechanov til Lotman* (Copenhagen, 1973).
Terras, Victor, *Belinskij and Russian Literary Criticism: the Heritage of Organic Esthetics* (Madison, 1974).
Stacy, Robert, *Russian Literary Criticism: a Short History* (Syracuse, 1974).
Städtke, Klaus, *Ästhetisches Denken in Russland: Kultursituation und Literaturkritik* (Berlin and Weimar, 1978).

Egorov, Boris, *Bor'ba esteticheskikh idei v Rossii serediny XIX veka* (Leningrad, 1982).

Drama

Vsevolodskii–Gerngross, V., *Istoriia russkogo teatra*. Ed. A. V. Lunacharskii. (2 vols., Moscow–Leningrad, 1929).

Varneke, Boris, *Istoriia russkogo teatra XVII-XIX vv.* (3rd. ed., Moscow–Leningrad, 1939). (Translation: *History of the Russian Theater, Seventeenth through Nineteenth Century* (New York, 1951).)

Lo Gatto, Ettore, *Storia del teatro russo* (2 vols., Florence, 1952).

Yershov, Peter, *Comedy in the Soviet Theater* (New York, 1956).

Slonim, Marc, *Russian Theater from the Empire to the Soviets* (Cleveland and New York, 1961).

Ocherki istorii russkoi sovetskoi dramaturgii (3 vols., Leningrad, 1963–8).

Roberts, Spencer, *Soviet Historical Drama: its Role in the Development of a National Mythology* (The Hague, 1965).

Welsh, David, *Russian Comedy 1765–1823* (The Hague and Paris, 1966).

Berkov, Pavel, *Istoriia russkoi komedii XVIII veka* (Leningrad, 1977).

Segel, Harold, *Twentieth-Century Russian Drama: from Gorky to the Present* (New York, 1979).

Karlinsky, Simon, *Russian Drama from Its Beginnings to the Age of Pushkin* (Berkeley, Los Angeles and London, 1985).

Folklore

Pypin, A. N., *Ocherk literaturnoi istorii starinnykh povestei i skazokh russkikh* (St. Petersburg, 1857).

Buslaev, Fedor, *Istoricheskie ocherki russkoi narodnoi slovesnosti* (2 vols., St. Petersburg, 1861).

Speranskii, Mikhail, *Russkaia ustnaia slovesnost'* (Moscow, 1917).

Skaftymov, Aleksandr, *Poetika i genezis bylin: ocherki* (Moscow and Saratov, 1924).

Sokolov, Iurii, *Russkii fol'klor* (Moscow, 1941). (Translation: *Russian Folklore* (New York, 1950).)

Stief, Carl, *Studies in the Russian Historical Song* (Copenhagen, 1953).

Propp, Vladimir, *Morfologiia skazki* (Leningrad, 1928). (Translation: *Morphology of the Folktale* (Austin, 1968).)

Propp, Vladimir, *Russkii geroicheskii epos* (Leningrad, 1955).

Alexander, Alex, *Bylina and Fairy Tale: the Origins of Russian Heroic Poetry* (The Hague, 1973).

Novel

Vogüé, Eugène Marie Melchior de, *Le Roman russe* (Paris, 1887). (Translation: *The Russian Novelists* (Boston, 1887).)

Golovin, Konstantin, *Russkii roman i russkoe obshchestvo* (St. Petersburg, 1897).

Sipovskii, Vasilii, *Ocherki iz istorii russkogo romana* (1 vol. in 2 parts, St. Petersburg, 1909–10).

Phelps, William Lyon, *Essays on Russian Novelists* (New York, 1911).

Lavrin, Janko, *An Introduction to the Russian Novel* (London, 1942).

Striedter, Jurij, *Der Schelmenroman in Russland: ein Beitrag zur Geschichte des russischen Romans vor Gogol'* (Berlin and Wiesbaden, 1961).

Bushmin A. S., et al., eds., *Istoriia russkogo romana* (2 vols., Leningrad, 1962–4).

Gifford, Henry, *The Novel in Russia: from Pushkin to Pasternak* (London, 1964).

Istoriia russkogo sovetskogo romana (2 vols., Moscow–Leningrad, 1965).

Reeve, Franklin, *The Russian Novel* (New York, 1966).

Freeborn, Richard, *The Rise of the Russian Novel: studies in the Russian Novel from Eugene Onegin to War and Peace* (Cambridge, 1973).

Piskunov, Vladimir, *Sovetskii roman-epopeia: Zhanr i ego evoliutsiia* (Moscow, 1976).

Clark, Katerina, *The Soviet Novel: history as Ritual* (Chicago and London, 1981).

Freeborn, Richard, *The Russian Revolutionary Novel: Turgenev to Pasternak* (Cambridge, 1982).

Poetry

Rozanov, Ivan, *Russkaia lirika: ot poezii bezlichnoi k ispovedi serdtsa [. . .] Istoriko-literaturnye ocherki* (Moscow, 1914).

Abramovich, Nikolai, *Istoriia russkoi poezii ot drevnei narodnoi poezii do nashikh dnei* (2 vols., Moscow, 1914–15).

Eikhenbaum, Boris, *Melodika russkogo liricheskogo stikha* (Petrograd, 1922).

Kaun, Alexander, *Soviet Poets and Poetry* (Berkeley and Los Angeles, 1943).

Sokolov, Aleksandr, *Ocherki po istorii russkoi poemy XVIII i pervoi poloviny XIX veka* (Moscow, 1955).

Poggioli, Renato, *The Poets of Russia 1890–1930* (Cambridge, Mass., 1960).

Schroeder, Hildegard, *Russische Verssatire im 18. Jahrhundert* (Cologne and Graz, 1962).

Gorodetskii, B., ed., *Istoriia russkoi poezii* (2 vols., Leningrad, 1968–9).

Grinberg, Iosif, *Puti sovetskoi poezii* (Moscow, 1968).

Hingley, Ronald, *Nightingale Fever: Russian Poets in Revolution* (New York, 1981).

France, Peter, *Poets of Modern Russia* (Cambridge, 1982).

Short story

Brang, Peter, *Studien zu Theorie und Praxis der russischen Erzählung 1770–1811* (Wiesbaden, 1960).

605

Kovalev, V. A., ed. *Russkii sovetskii rasskaz: ocherki istorii zhanra* (Leningrad, 1970).

Meilakh, Boris, ed., *Russkaia povest' XIX veka: istoriia i problematika zhanra* (Leningrad, 1973).

O'Toole, Lawrence, *Structure, Style and Interpretation in the Russian Short Story* (New Haven, 1982).

Moser, Charles, ed., *The Russian Short Story: a Critical History* (Boston, 1986).

Travelogue

Wilson, Reuel, *The Literary Travelogue: a Comparative Study with Special Relevance to Russian Literature from Fonvizin to Pushkin* (The Hague, 1973).

Comparative studies

Veselovskii, Aleksei, *Zapadnoe vliianie v novoi russkoi literature: sravnitel'-no-istoricheskie ocherki* (Moscow, 1883).

Lirondelle, André, *Shakespeare en Russie 1748–1840* (Paris, 1912).

Simmons, Ernest, *English Literature and Culture in Russia (1553–1840)* (Cambridge, Mass., 1935).

Zhirmunskii, Viktor, *Gete v russkoi literature* (Leningrad, 1937).

Setschkareff, Wsewolod, *Schellings Einfluss in der russischen Literatur der 20er und 30er Jahre des XIX Jahrhunderts* (Berlin, 1939).

Turkevich, Ludmilla, *Cervantes in Russia* (Princeton, 1950).

Brewster, Dorothy, *East-West Passage: A Study in Literary Relationships* (London, 1954).

Donchin, Georgette, *The Influence of French Symbolism on Russian Poetry* (The Hague, 1958).

Nilsson, Nils Ake, *Ibsen in Russland* (Stockholm, 1958).

Passage, Charles, *The Russian Hoffmannists* (The Hague, 1963).

Kuleshov, Vasilii, *Literaturnye sviazi Rossii i zapadnoi Evropy v XIX veke (pervaia polovina)* (Moscow, 1965).

Gronicka, Andre von, *The Russian Image of Goethe* (2 vols., Philadelphia, 1968–85).

Ingham, Norman, *E. T. A. Hoffmann's Reception in Russia* (Würzburg, 1974).

MISCELLANEOUS

Gifford, Henry, *The Hero of His Time: a Theme in Russian Literature* (London, 1950).

Matthewson, Rufus Jr., *The Positive Hero in Russian Literature* (New York, 1958).

Reilly, Alayne, *America in Contemporary Soviet Literature* (New York and London, 1971).

Chances, Ellen, *Conformity's Children: an Approach to the Superfluous Man in Russian Literature* (Columbus, 1978).

606

BIBLIOGRAPHY

INDIVIDUAL AUTHORS
Adamovich, Georgii

Hagglund, Roger, *A Vision of Unity: Adamovich in Exile* (Ann Arbor, 1985).

Afinogenov, Aleksandr

Boguslavskii, Aleksandr, *A. N. Afinogenov: Ocherk zhizni i tvorchestva* (Moscow, 1952).

Aitmatov, Chingiz

Levchenko, Viktor, *Chingiz Aitmatov* (Moscow, 1983).

Akhmatova, Anna

Eikhenbaum, Boris, *Anna Akhmatova: Opyt analiza* (Petrograd, 1923).

Vinogradov, Viktor, *O poezii Anny Akhmatovoi (Stilisticheskie nabroski)* (Leningrad, 1925).

Pavlovskii, Aleksei, *Anna Akhmatova: ocherk tvorchestva* (Leningrad, 1966).

Driver, Sam, *Anna Akhmatova* (New York, 1972).

Zhirmunskii, Viktor, *Tvorchestvo Anny Akhmatovoi* (Leningrad, 1973).

Haight, Amanda, *Anna Akhmatova: a Poetic Pilgrimage* (New York and London, 1976).

Leiter, Sharon, *Akhmatova's Petersburg* (Philadelphia, and Cambridge, 1983).

Aksakov, Sergei

Mashinskii, Semen, *S. T. Aksakov: Zhizn' i tvorchestvo* (Moscow, 1961).

Durkin, Andrew, *Sergei Aksakov and Russian Pastoral* (New Brunswick, 1983).

Aksenov, Vasilii

Dalgard, Per, *The Function of the Grotesque in Vasilij Aksenov* (Aarhus, 1982).

Możejko, Edward, ed., *Vasiliy Pavlovich Aksenov: a Writer in Quest of Himself* (Columbus, 1986).

Aldanov, Mark

Lee, C. Nicholas, *The Novels of Mark Aleksandrovič Aldanov* (The Hague and Paris, 1969).

Andreev, Leonid

Kaun, Alexander, *Leonid Andreyev: A Critical Study* (New York, 1969 [first published 1924]).

Woodward, James, *Leonid Andreyev: A Study* (Oxford, 1969).

Newcombe, Josephine, *Leonid Andreyev* (New York, 1973).

BIBLIOGRAPHY

Annenskii, Innokentii

Setschkareff, Vsevolod, *Studies in the Life and Work of Innokentij Annenskij* (The Hague, 1963).

Bazzarelli, Eridano, *La poesia di Innokentij Annenskij* (Milan, 1965).

Fedorov, Andrei, *Innokentii Annenskii: lichnost' i tvorchestvo* (Leningrad, 1984).

Arbuzov, Aleksei

Vishnevskaia, Inna, *Aleksei Arbuzov: ocherk tvorchestva* (Moscow, 1971).

Vasilinina, Irina, *Teatr Arbuzova* (Moscow, 1983).

Artsybashev, Mikhail

Dell, Sally, *Mikhail Artsybashev* (Nottingham, 1983).

Avvakum

Pascal, Pierre, *Avvakum et les débuts du raskol* (Paris, 1934).

Babel', Isaak

Stora-Sandor, Judith, *Isaac Babel': l'homme et l'œuvre* (Paris, 1968).

Carden, Patricia, *The Art of Isaac Babel* (Ithaca and London, 1972).

Falen, James, *Isaac Babel: Russian Master of the Short Story* (Knoxville, 1974).

Luplow, Carol, *Isaac Babel's "Red Cavalry"* (Ann Arbor, 1982).

Ehre, Milton, *Isaac Babel* (Boston, 1986).

Bagritskii, Eduard

Grinberg, Iosif, *Eduard Bagritskii* (Leningrad, 1940).

Bal'mont, Konstantin

Schneider, Hildegard, *Der frühe Bal'mont: Untersüchungen zu einer Metaphorik* (Munich, 1970).

Althaus-Schönbucher, Silvia, *Konstantin D. Balmont: Parallelen zu Afansij A. Fet: Symbolismus und Impressionismus* (Bern and Frankfurt am Main, 1975).

Baratynskii, Evgenii

Filippovich, P. P., *Zhizn' i tvorchestvo E. A. Baratynskogo* (Kiev, 1917).

Dees, Benjamin, *Evgeny Baratynsky* (New York, 1972).

Kjetsaa, Geir, *Evgenii Baratynskii: Zhizn' i tvorchestvo* (Oslo, Bergen and Tromsø, 1973).

Lebedev, Evgenii, *Trizna: kniga o E. A. Boratynskom* (Moscow, 1985).

Batiushkov, Konstantin

Maikov, Leonid, *Batiushkov: Ego zhizn' i sochineniia* (2nd revised edition, St. Petersburg, 1896).

Fridman, Nikolai, *Proza Batiushkova* (Moscow, 1965).

BIBLIOGRAPHY

Rossi Varese, Marina, *Batjuškov. Un poeta tra Russia e Italia* (Padua, 1970).
Fridman, Nikolai, *Poeziia Batiushkova* (Moscow, 1971).
Serman, Ilya, *Konstantin Batyushkov* (New York, 1974).

Belinskii, Vissarion

Nechaeva, Vera, *V. G. Belinskii* (4 vols., Moscow, 1949–67).
Bowman, Herbert, *Vissarion Belinsky, 1811–1848: a Study on the Origins of Social Criticism in Russia* (Cambridge, Mass., 1954).
Ambrogio, Ignazio, *Belinskij e la teoria del realismo* (Rome, 1963).
Fasting, Sigurd, *V. G. Belinskij: die Entwicklung seiner Literaturtheorie* (Bergen, 1969).

Belov, Vasilii

Seleznev, Iurii, *Vasilii Belov: razdum'ia o tvorcheskoi sud'be pisatelia* (Moscow, 1983).

Belyi, Andrei

Maslenikov, Oleg, *The Frenzied Poets: Andrey Biely and the Russian Symbolists* (Berkeley, 1952).
Mochul'skii, Konstantin, *Andrei Belyi* (Paris, 1955). (Translation: *Andrei Bely: His Life and Works* (Ann Arbor, 1977).)
Cioran, Samuel, *The Apocalyptic Symbolism of Andrej Belyj* (The Hague and Paris, 1973).
Elsworth, J. D., *Andrey Bely: a Critical Study of the Novels* (Cambridge, London, New York etc., 1983).
Alexandrov, Vladimir, *Andrei Bely: The Major Symbolist* (Cambridge, Mass., 1985).

Berggolts, Olga

Khrenkov, Dmitrii, *Ot serdtsa k serdtsu: o zhizni i tvorchestve O. Berggolts* (Leningrad, 1979).

Bestuzhev-Marlinskii, Aleksandr

Chmielewski, Horst von, *Aleksandr Bestužev-Marlinskij* (Munich, 1966).
Leighton, Lauren, *Alexander Bestuzhev-Marlinsky* (Boston, 1975).

Blok, Aleksandr

Zhirmunskii, Viktor, *Poeziia Aleksandra Bloka* (Petrograd, 1922).
Chukovskii, Kornei, *Aleksandr Blok kak chelovek i poet* (Petrograd, 1924). (Translation: *Alexander Blok as Man and Poet* (Ann Arbor, 1982).)
Bonneau, Sophie, *L'Univers poétique d'Alexandre Blok* (Paris, 1946).
Mochul'skii, Konstantin, *Aleksandr Blok* (Paris, 1948). (Translation: *Aleksandr Blok* (Detroit and London, 1983).)
Reeve, Frank, *Aleksandr Blok: Between Image and Idea* (New York, 1962).

Solov'ev, Boris, *Poet i ego podvig: tvorcheskii put' Aleksandra Bloka* (Moscow, 1965).

Bazzarelli, Eridano, *Aleksandr Blok: l'Armonia e il caos nel suo mondo poetico* (Milan, 1968).

Hackel, Sergei, *The Poet and the Revolution: Aleksandr Blok's "The Twelve"* (Oxford, 1975).

Pyman, Avril, *The Life of Aleksandr Blok* (2 vols., Oxford, London and New York, 1979–80).

Briusov, Valerii

Lelevich, Labori, *V. Ia. Briusov* (Moscow–Leningrad, 1926).

Maksimov, D., *Poeziia Valeriia Briusova* (Leningrad, 1940).

Mochul'skii, Konstantin, *Valerii Briusov* (Paris, 1962).

Rice, Martin, *Valery Briusov and the Rise of Russian Symbolism* (Ann Arbor, 1975).

Grossman, Joan, *Valery Bryusov and the Riddle of Russian Decadence* (Berkeley, Los Angeles and London, 1985).

Brodskii, Iosif

Kreps, Mikhail, *O poezii Iosifa Brodskogo* (Ann Arbor, 1984).

Bulgakov, Mikhail

Bazzarelli, Eridano, *Invito alla lettura di Bulgakov* (Milan, 1976).

Wright, A. Colin, *Mikhail Bulgakov: Life and Interpretation* (Toronto, 1978).

Riggenbach, Heinrich, *Michail Bulgakovs Roman "Master i Margarita": Stil und Gestalt* (Bern, 1979).

Ianovskaia, Lidiia, *Tvorcheskii put' Mikhaila Bulgakova* (Moscow, 1983).

Proffer, Ellendea, *Bulgakov: Life and Work* (Ann Arbor, 1984).

Natov, Nadine, *Mikhail Bulgakov* (Boston, 1985).

Bulgarin, Faddei

Mocha, Frank, *Tadeusz Bulharyn (Faddei V. Bulgarin) 1789–1859: a Study in Literary Maneuver* (Rome, 1974).

Bunin, Ivan

Zaitsev, Kiril, *I. A. Bunin: zhizn' i tvorchestvo* (Berlin, 1934).

Volkov, Anatolii, *Proza Ivana Bunina* (Moscow, 1969).

Kryzytski, Serge, *The Works of Ivan Bunin* (The Hague and Paris, 1971).

Mikhailov, Oleg, *Strogii talant. Ivan Bunin: zhizn', sud'ba, tvorchestvo* (Moscow, 1976).

Woodward, James, *Ivan Bunin: a Study of His Fiction* (Chapel Hill, 1980).

Connolly, Julian, *Ivan Bunin* (Boston, 1982).

Chekhov, Anton

Gerhardi, William, *Anton Chekhov: a Critical Study* (New York, 1923).

Garnett, Edward, *Chekhov and His Art* (London, 1929).

Toumanova, N. A., *Anton Chekhov: the Voice of Twilight Russia* (London, 1937).

Magarshack, David, *Chekhov: a Life* (London, 1952).

Zaitsev, Boris, *Chekhov: literaturnaia biografiia* (New York, 1954).

Simmons, Ernest, *Chekhov: a Biography* (Boston and Toronto, 1962).

Bitsilli, Petr, *Anton P. Čechov: das Werk und sein Stil* (Munich, 1966). (Translation (partial): *Chekhov's Art: a Stylistic Analysis* (Ann Arbor, 1983).)

Winner, Thomas, *Chekhov and His Prose* (New York, 1966).

Chudakov, Aleksandr, *Poetika Chekhova* (Moscow, 1971). (Translation: *Chekhov's Poetics* (Ann Arbor, 1983).)

Pitcher, Harvey, *The Chekhov Play: a New Interpretation* (New York, 1973).

Hingley, Ronald, *A New Life of Anton Chekhov* (New York, 1976).

Hahn, Beverly, *Chekhov: a Study of the Major Stories and Plays* (Cambridge & New York, 1977).

Peace, Richard, *Chekhov: A Study of the Four Major Plays* (New Haven, 1983).

Chernyshevskii, Nikolai

Steklov, Iurii, *N. G. Chernyshevskii: ego zhizn' i deiatel'nost'* (Second, revised edition, Moscow, 1928).

Woehrlin, William, *Chernyshevskii: the Man and the Journalist* (Cambridge, Mass., 1971).

Tamarchenko, Grigorii, *Chernyshevskii-romanist* (Leningrad, 1976).

Chulkov, Mikhail

Garrard, John, *Mixail Čulkov: an Introduction to His Prose and Verse* (The Hague, 1970).

Dal', Vladimir

Bessarab, Maiia, *Vladimir Dal'* (Moscow, 1968).

Baer, Joachim, *Vladimir Ivanovič Dal' as a Belletrist* (The Hague, 1972).

Davydov, Denis

Shik, Aleksandr, *Denis Davydov, "liubovnik brani" i poet* (Paris, 1951).

Delvig, Anton

Koehler, Ludmilla, *Anton Antonovič Del'vig: a Classicist in the Time of Romanticism* (The Hague, 1970).

Derzhavin, Gavriil

Zapadov, Aleksandr, *Masterstvo Derzhavina* (Moscow, 1958).

Serman, Il'ia, *Derzhavin* (Leningrad, 1967).

Hart, Pierre, *G. R. Derzhavin: a Poet's Progress* (Columbus, 1978).

BIBLIOGRAPHY

Dobroliubov, Nikolai

Lebedev-Polianskii, Pavel, *N. A. Dobroliubov: mirovozzrenie i literaturno-kriticheskaia deiatel'nost'* (Moscow, 1933).

Dostoevskii, Fedor

Pereverzev, Valerian, *Tvorchestvo Dostoevskogo* (Moscow, 1912).

Murry, John Middleton, *Fyodor Dostoevsky: a Critical Study* (New York, 1916).

Grossman, Leonid, *Poetika Dostoevskogo* (Moscow, 1925).

Meier-Gräfe, Julius, *Dostojewski der Dichter* (Berlin, 1926). (Translation: *Dostoevsky: the Man and His Work* (New York, 1928).)

Bakhtin, Mikhail, *Problemy tvorchestva Dostoevskogo* (Leningrad, 1929) [later editions titled *Problemy poetiki Dostoevskogo*]. (Translation: *Problems of Dostoevsky's Poetics* (Ann Arbor, 1973).)

Carr, E. H., *Dostoevsky (1821–1881)* (London, 1931)

Yarmolinsky, Avrahm, *Dostoevsky: a Life* (New York, 1934).

Grossman, Leonid, *Zhizn' i trudy F. M. Dostoevskogo* (Moscow–Leningrad, 1935). (Translation: *Dostoevsky: a Biography* (London, 1974).)

Mochul'skii, Konstantin, *Dostoevskii: zhizn' i tvorchestvo* (Paris, 1947). (Translation: *Dostoevsky: his Life and Work* (Princeton, 1967).)

Simmons, Ernest, *Dostoevsky: the Making of a Novelist* (London, 1950).

Arban, Dominique, *Dostoievski "le coupable"* (Paris, 1953).

Seduro, Vladimir, *Dostoevsky in Russian Literary Criticism 1846–1956* (New York, 1957).

Kirpotin, Valerii, *Dostoevskii i Belinskii* (Moscow, 1960).

Hingley, Ronald, *The Undiscovered Dostoyevsky* (London, 1962).

Magarshack, David, *Dostoevsky* (London, 1962).

Fridlender, Georgii, *Realizm Dostoevskogo* (Moscow–Leningrad, 1964).

Wasiolek, Edward, *Dostoevsky: The Major Fiction* (Cambridge, Mass., 1964).

Fanger, Donald, *Dostoevsky and Romantic Realism: a Study of Dostoevsky in Relation to Balzac, Dickens, and Gogol* (Cambridge, Mass., 1965).

Jackson, Robert, *Dostoevsky's Quest for Form* (New Haven, 1966).

Belknap, Robert, *The Structure of "The Brothers Karamazov"* (The Hague and Paris, 1967).

Pascal, Pierre, *Dostoievski: l'homme et l'œuvre* (Lausanne, 1970).

Peace, Richard, *Dostoevsky: An Examination of the Major Novels* (Cambridge, 1971).

Vidal, Augusto, *Dostoievski* (Barcelona, 1972).

Hansen, Knud, *Dostojevskij* (Copenhagen, 1973).

Frank, Joseph, *Dostoevsky: The Seeds of Revolt 1821–1849* (Princeton, 1976).

Jones, Malcolm, *Dostoyevsky: the Novel of Discord* (New York, 1976).

Holquist, Michael, *Dostoevsky and the Novel* (Princeton, 1977).

Catteau, Jacques, *La Création littéraire chez Dostoïevski* (Paris, 1978).
Fridlender, Georgii, *Dostoevskii i mirovaia literatura* (Moscow, 1979).
Jackson, Robert, *The Art of Dostoevsky: Deliriums and Nocturnes* (Princeton, 1981).
Leatherbarrow, William, *Fedor Dostoevsky* (Boston, 1981).
Morson, Gary, *The Boundaries of Genre: Dostoevsky's "Diary of a Writer" and the Traditions of Literary Utopia* (Austin, 1981).
Fasting, Sigurd, *Dostojevskij* (Oslo, 1983).
Kjetsaa, Geir, *Fjodor Dostojevskij: et dikterliv* (Oslo, 1986). (Translation: *Dostojevskij: Sträfling–Spieler–Dichter* (Gernsbach, 1986).)
Frank, Joseph, *Dostoevsky: the Stir of Liberation, 1860–1865* (Princeton, 1986).
Ward, Bruce, *Dostoyevsky's Critique of the West: the Quest for the Earthly Paradise* (Waterloo, 1986)

Erenburg, Il'ia

Trifonova, Tamara, *Il'ia Erenburg: kritiko-biograficheskii ocherk* (Moscow, 1952).
Goldberg, Anatol, *Ilya Ehrenburg: Writing, Politics and the Art of Survival* (London, 1984).

Esenin, Sergei

Graaf, Francisca de, *Serge Esenine, 1895–1925: sa vie et son œuvre* (Leyden, 1933).
Naumov, Evgenii, *Sergei Esenin. Lichnost'. Tvorchestvo. Epokha* (Leningrad, 1960).
Iushin, Petr, *Sergei Esenin: ideino-tvorcheskaia evoliutsiia* (Moscow, 1969).
Marchenko, Alla, *Poeticheskii mir Esenina* (Moscow, 1972).
McVay, Gordon, *Esenin: A Life* (Ann Arbor 1976).
Visson, Lynn, *Sergei Esenin: Poet of the Crossroads* (Würzburg, 1980).

Fadeev, Aleksandr

Ozerov, Vitalii, *Aleksandr Fadeev: Tvorcheskii put'* (Moscow, 1960).
Kiseleva, Liudmila, *Tvorcheskie iskaniia A. Fadeeva* (Moscow, 1965).
Bushmin, Aleksei, *Aleksandr Fadeev: cherty tvorcheskoi individual'nosti* (Leningrad, 1971).

Fedin, Konstantin

Brainina, Berta, *Konstantin Fedin* (Moscow, 1951).
Simmons, Ernest, *Russian Fiction and Soviet Ideology: Introduction to Fedin, Leonov, and Sholokhov* (New York, 1958).
Blum, Julius, *Konstantin Fedin: a Descriptive and Analytic Study* (The Hague and Paris, 1967).
Kuźnetsov, Nikolai, *Konstantin Fedin: ocherk tvorchestva* (Moscow, 1969).
Starkov, Anatolii, *Stupeni masterstva: ocherk tvorchestva Konstantina Fedina* (Moscow, 1985).

Fet, Afanasii

Gustafson, Richard, *The Imagination of Spring: the Poetry of Afanasy Fet* (New Haven and London, 1966).
Bukhshtab, Boris, *A. A. Fet: ocherk zhizni i tvorchestva* (Leningrad, 1974).
Lotman, Lydia, *Afanasy Fet* (Boston, 1976).

Fofanov, Konstantin

Michelis, Cesare de, *Le illusioni e i simboli: K. M. Fofanov* (Padua, 1973).

Fonvizin, Denis

Pigarev, Konstantin, *Tvorchestvo Fonvizina* (Moscow, 1954).
Makogonenko, Georgii, *Denis Fonvizin: tvorcheskii put'* (Moscow–Leningrad, 1961).
Strycek, Alexis, *La Russie des lumières: Denis Fonvizine* (Paris, 1976).
Moser, Charles, *Denis Fonvizin* (Boston, 1979).

Garin-Mikhailovskii, Nikolai

Iudina, Irina, *N. G. Garin-Mikhailovskii: zhizn' i literaturno-obshchestven-naia deiatel'nost'* (Leningrad, 1969).

Garshin, Vsevolod

Zelma, Ellinor, *Studien über Vsevolod Garšin* (Leipzig, 1935).
Bialyi, Grigorii, *V. M. Garshin i literaturnaia bor'ba vos'midesiatykh godov* (Moscow–Leningrad, 1937).
Parker, Fan, *Vsevolod Garshin: a Study of a Russian Conscience* (Morningside Heights, NY, 1946).
Stenborg, Lennart, *Studien zur Erzähltechnik in den Novellen V. M. Garšins* (Uppsala, 1972).
Yarwood, Edmund, *Vsevolod Garshin* (Boston, 1981).
Henry, Peter, *A Hamlet of His Time: Vsevolod Garshin, the Man, His Works, and His Milieu* (Oxford, 1983).

Gazdanov, Gajto

Dienes, Laszlo, *Russian Literature in Exile: the Life and Work of Gajto Gazdanov* (Munich, 1982).

German, Iurii

Fainberg, Rakhil', *Iurii German: kritiko-biograficheskii ocherk* (Leningrad, 1970).

Gertsen (Herzen), Aleksandr

Labry, Raoul, *Alexandre Ivanovič Herzen, 1812–1870: Essai sur la formation et le développement de ses idées* (Paris, 1928).
Putintsev, Vladimir, *Gertsen – pisatel'* (Moscow, 1952).
Ginzburg, Lidiia, *Byloe i dumy Gertsena* (Leningrad, 1957).

BIBLIOGRAPHY

Malia, Martin, *Alexander Herzen and the Birth of Russian Socialism 1812–1855* (Cambridge, Mass., 1961).

Acton, Edward, *Alexander Herzen and the Role of the Intellectual Revolutionary* (Cambridge, 1979).

Gippius (Hippius), Zinaida

Pachmuss, Temira, *Zinaida Hippius: An Intellectual Profile* (Carbondale, 1971).

Gladkov, Fedor

Brainina, Berta, *Fedor Gladkov: ocherk zhizni i tvorchestva* (Moscow, 1957).

Pukhov, Iurii, *Fedor Gladkov: ocherk tvorchestva* (Moscow, 1983).

Gogol, Nikolai

Pereverzev, Valerian, *Tvorchestvo Gogolia* (Moscow, 1914).

Slonimskii, Al., *Tekhnika komicheskogo u Gogolia* (Leningrad, 1923).

Gippius, Vasilii, *Gogol'* (Leningrad, 1924). (Translation: *Gogol* (Ann Arbor, 1981).)

Vinogradov, Viktor, *Gogol' i natural'naia shkola* (Leningrad, 1925).

Lavrin, Janko, *Nikolai Gogol* (New York and London, 1926).

Vinogradov, Viktor, *Etiudy o stile Gogolia* (Leningrad, 1926).

Belyi, Andrei, *Masterstvo Gogolia: issledovanie* (Moscow–Leningrad, 1934).

Khrapchenko, Mikhail, *N. V. Gogol'* (Moscow, 1936).

Nabokov, Vladimir, *Nikolai Gogol* (New York, 1944).

Hofmann, Modeste and Rostislav, *Gogol: Sa vie et son œuvre* (Paris, 1946).

Schloezer, Boris de, *Gogol* (Paris, 1946).

Setschkareff, Vsevolod, *N. V. Gogol: Leben und Schaffen* (Berlin, 1953). (Translation: *Gogol: his Life and Works* (New York, 1965).)

Stepanov, Nikolai, *N. V. Gogol': tvorcheskii put'* (Moscow, 1955).

Gukovskii, Grigorii, *Realizm Gogolia* (Moscow–Leningrad, 1959).

Driessen, F., *Gogol as a Short-Story Writer: a Study of His Technique of Composition* (The Hague, 1965).

Proffer, Carl, *The Simile and Gogol's "Dead Souls"* (The Hague and Paris, 1967).

Erlich, Victor, *Gogol* (New Haven and London, 1969).

Braun, Maximilian, *N. W. Gogol: eine literarische Biographie* (Munich, 1973).

Karlinsky, Simon, *The Sexual Labyrinth of Nikolai Gogol* (Cambridge, Mass. and London, 1976).

Mann, Iurii, *Poetika Gogolia* (Moscow, 1978).

Woodward, James, *Gogol's "Dead Souls"* (Princeton, 1978).

Fanger, Donald, *The Creation of Nikolai Gogol* (Cambridge, Mass., 1979).

Peace, Richard, *The Enigma of Gogol* (Cambridge, 1981).

Goncharov, Ivan

Mazon, André, *Un maître du roman russe: Ivan Gontcharov 1812–1891* (Paris, 1914).
Evgen'ev-Maksimov, V., *I. A. Goncharov* (Moscow–Leningrad, 1925).
Tseitlin, Aleksandr, *I. A. Goncharov* (Moscow, 1950).
Ehre, Milton, *Oblomov and His Creator: the Life and Art of Ivan Goncharov* (Princeton, 1974).
Setchkarev, Vsevolod, *Ivan Goncharov: His Life and His Works* (Würzburg, 1974).

Gor'kii, Maksim

Holtzman, Filia, *The Young Maxim Gorky 1868–1902* (New York, 1948).
Volkov, Anatolii, *M. Gor'kii i literaturnoe dvizhenie konets XIX i nachala XX meka* (Moscow, 1951).
Volkov, Anatolii, *A. M. Gor'kii i literaturnoe dvizhenie sovetskoi epokhi* (Moscow, 1958).
Hare, Richard, *Maxim Gorky: Romantic Realist and Conservative Revolutionary* (London, New York and Toronto, 1962).
Levin, Dan, *Stormy Petrel: the Life and Work of Maxim Gorky* (New York, 1965).
Weil, Irwin, *Gorky: His Literary Development and Influence on Soviet Intellectual Life* (New York, 1966).
Borras, F. M., *Maxim Gorky the Writer: an Interpretation* (Oxford, 1967).

Griboedov, Aleksandr

Kramareva, Olga, *Alexandre Sergiéevitch Griboiedov: sa vie, ses œuvres* (Paris, 1907).
Piksanov, Nikolai, *Griboedov i ego tvorchestvo* (Moscow, 1945).
Bonamour, Jean, *A. S. Griboedov et la vie littéraire de son temps* (Paris, 1965).
Orlov, Vladimir, *Griboedov: ocherk zhizni i tvorchestva* (Leningrad, 1967).

Grigor'ev, Apollon

Satta Boschian, Laura, *Il regno oscuro: vita e opere di A. A. Grigor'ev* (Naples, 1969).

Grin, Aleksandr

Mikhailova, L., *Aleksandr Grin: zhizn', lichnost', tvorchestvo* (Moscow, 1972).
Luker, Nicholas, *Alexander Grin: the Forgotten Visionary* (Newtonville, 1980).

Grossman, Vasilii

Markish, Simon, *Le cas Grossman* (Paris, 1983).

BIBLIOGRAPHY

Gumilev, Nikolai

Strakhovsky, Leonid, *Craftsmen of the Word: Three Poets of Modern Russia: Gumilyov, Akhmatova, Mandelstam* (Cambridge, Mass., 1949).
Maline, Marie, *Nicolas Gumilev, poète et critique acmeiste* (Brussels, 1964).
Sampson, Earl, *Nikolay Gumilev* (Boston, 1979).

Il'f, Il'ia and Evgenii Petrov

Vulis, Abram, *I. Il'f, E. Petrov: ocherk tvorchestva* (Moscow, 1960).

Inber, Vera

Grinberg, Iosif, *Vera Inber: kritiko-biograficheskii ocherk* (Moscow, 1961).

Ivanov, Viacheslav

Tschöpl, Carin, *Vjačeslav Ivanov: Dichtung und Dichtungstheorie* (Munich, 1968).
West, James, *Russian Symbolism: a Study of Vyacheslav Ivanov and the Russian Symbolist Aesthetic* (London, 1970).

Ivanov, Vsevolod

Krasnoshchekova, Elena, *Khudozhestvennyi mir Vsevoloda Ivanova* (Moscow, 1980).

Kantemir, Antiokh

Ehrhard, Marcelle, *Un ambassadeur de Russie à la cour de Louis XV: le prince Cantemir à Paris (1738–1744)* (Lyon, 1938).
Grasshoff, Helmut, *Antioch Dmitrievič Kantemir und Westeuropa* (Berlin, 1966).

Karamzin, Nikolai

Sipovskii, Vasilii, *N. M. Karamzin, avtor "Pisem russkogo puteshestvennika"* (St. Petersburg, 1899).
Nebel, Henry, Jr., *N. M. Karamzin: a Russian Sentimentalist* (The Hague and Paris, 1967).
Rothe, Hans, *N. M. Karamzins europäische Reise: der Beginn des russischen Romans* (Bad Homburg, Berlin and Zurich, 1968).
Cross, Anthony, *N. M. Karamzin: a Study of His Literary Career, 1783–1803* (Carbondale and Edwardsville, 1971).
Anderson, Roger, *N. M. Karamzin's Prose* (Houston, 1974).

Kataev, Valentin

Sidel'nikova, Tat'iana, *Valentin Kataev: ocherk zhizni i tvorchestva* (Moscow, 1957).
Skorino, Liudmila, *Pisatel' i ego vremia: zhizn' i tvorchestvo V. P. Kataeva* (Moscow, 1965).
Russell, Robert, *Valentin Kataev* (Boston, 1981).
Vogl, Josef, *Das Frühwerk Valentin P. Kataevs* (Munich, 1984).

BIBLIOGRAPHY

Kaverin, Veniamin

Piper, Donald, *V. A. Kaverin: a Soviet Writer's Response to the Problem of Commitment* (Pittsburgh, 1970).
Oulanoff, Hongor, *The Prose Fiction of Veniamin A. Kaverin* (Columbus, 1976).

Kharms, Daniil

Nakhimovsky, Alice, *Laughter in the Void: an Introduction to the Writings of Daniil Kharms and Alexander Vvedenskii* (Vienna, 1982).

Khlebnikov, Velemir

Markov, Vladimir, *The Longer Poems of Velemir Khlebnikov* (Berkeley and Los Angeles, 1962).
Stepanov, Nikolai, *Velemir Khlebnikov: zhizn' i tvorchestvo* (Moscow, 1975).
Lanne, Jean-Claude, *Velemir Khlebnikov: poète futurien* (2 vols., Paris, 1983).

Khodasevich, Viacheslav

Bethea, David, *Khodasevich: His Life and Art* (Princeton, 1983).

Kol'tsov, Nikolai

Astaurov, Boris, *Nikolai Konstantinovich Kol'tsov* (Moscow, 1975).

Korolenko, Vladimir

Shakhovskaia, N. D., *V. G. Korolenko: opyt biograficheskoi kharakteristiki* (Moscow, 1912).
Batiushkov, Fedor, *V. G. Korolenko kak chelovek i pisatel'* (Moscow, 1922).
Grigor'ev, R., *Korolenko* (Moscow, 1925).
Bialyi, Grigorii, *V. G. Korolenko* (Moscow–Leningrad, 1949).
Comtet, Maurice, *Vladimir G. Korolenko, 1853–1921: l'homme et l'œuvre* (2 vols., Paris, 1975).

Kravchinskii (Stepniak), Sergei

Taratuta, Evgeniia, *S. M. Stepniak-Kravchinskii – revoliutsioner i pisatel'* (Moscow, 1973).

Krylov, Ivan

Stepanov, Nikolai, *I. A. Krylov: Zhizn' i tvorchestvo* (Moscow, 1958).
Stepanov, Nikolay, *Ivan Krylov* (New York, 1973).
Colin, Maurice, *Krylov fabuliste: étude littéraire et historique* (Paris, 1975).
Labriollé, Francois de, *Ivan Andreevich Krylov: ses œuvres de jeunesse et les courants littéraires de son temps* (2 vols., Paris, 1975).

BIBLIOGRAPHY

Kuprin, Aleksandr

Volkov, Anatolii, *Tvorchestvo A. I. Kuprina* (Moscow, 1962).
Kuleshov, Fedor, *Tvorcheskii put' A. I. Kuprina* (Minsk, 1963).
Luker, Nicholas, *Alexander Kuprin* (Boston, 1978).

Leonov, Leonid

Kovalev, Valentin, *Romany Leonida Leonova* (Moscow–Leningrad, 1954).
Boguslavskaia, Zoia, *Leonid Leonov* (Moscow, 1960).
Fink, Lev, *Dramaturgiia Leonida Leonova* (Moscow, 1962).
Harjan, George, *Leonid Leonov: a Critical Study* (Toronto, 1979).

Leont'ev, Konstantin

Lukashevich, Stephen, *Konstantin Leontev, 1831–1891: a Study in Russian "Heroic Vitalism"* (New York, 1967).
Ivask, Iurii, *Konstantin Leont'ev: Zhizn' i tvorchestvo* (Bern and Frankfurt am Main, 1974).

Lermontov, Mikhail

Eikhenbaum, Boris, *Lermontov: Opyt istoriko–literaturnoi otsenki* (Leningrad, 1924). (Translation: *Lermontov* (Ann Arbor, 1981).)
Mikhailova, E., *Proza Lermontova* (Moscow, 1957).
Mersereau, John, Jr., *Mikhail Lermontov* (Carbondale, 1962).
Garrard, John, *Mikhail Lermontov* (Boston, 1982).

Leskov, Nikolai

Grossman, Leonid, *N. S. Leskov: zhizn', tvorchestvo, poetika* (Moscow, 1945).
Leskov, Andrei, *Zhizn' Nikolaia Leskova* (Moscow, 1954).
Cavaion, Danilo, *N. S. Leskov: saggio critico* (Florence, 1974).
McLean, Hugh, *Nikolai Leskov: the Man and His Art* (Cambridge, Mass., 1977).
Lantz, Kenneth, *Nikolay Leskov* (Boston, 1979).

Lomonosov, Mikhail

Aksakov, Konstantin, *Lomonosov v istorii russkoi literatury i russkogo iazyka* (Moscow, 1846).
Zapadov, Aleksandr, *Otets russkoi poezii: o tvorchestve Lomonosova* (Moscow, 1961).
Serman, Il'ia, *Poeticheskii stil' Lomonosova* (Leningrad, 1966).

Maiakovskii, Vladimir

Vinokur, Georgii, *Maiakovskii novator iazyka* (Moscow, 1943).
Pertsov, V. O., *Maiakovskii: zhizn' i tvorchestvo* (3 vols., Moscow, 1951–65).
Metchenko, Aleksei, *Tvorchestvo Maiakovskogo 1917–1924 gg.* (Moscow, 1954).

Ripellino, Angelo, *Majakovskij e il teatro russo d'avanguardia* (Turin, 1959).
Metchenko, Aleksei, *Tvorchestvo Maiakovskogo 1925–1930 gg.* (Moscow, 1961).
Stahlberger, Lawrence, *The Symbolic System of Majakovskij* (The Hague, 1964).
Brown, Edward, *Mayakovsky: a Poet in the Revolution* (Princeton, 1973).
Terras, Victor, *Vladimir Mayakovsky* (Boston, 1983).
Stapanian, Juliette, *Mayakovsky's Cubo-Futurist Vision* (Houston, 1986).

Maksim Grek

Ikonnikov, V., *Maksim Grek i ego vremia* (second ed., Kiev, 1915).
Denissoff, Elie, *Maxime le Grec et l'Occident* (Paris and Louvain, 1943).
Haney, Jack, *From Italy to Muscovy: the Life and Works of Maxim the Greek* (Munich, 1973).
Sinitsyna, Nina, *Maksim Grek v Rossii* (Moscow, 1977).

Mamin-Sibiriak, Dmitrii

Gruzdev, Aleksandr, *D. N. Mamin-Sibiriak: Kritiko-biograficheskii ocherk* (Moscow, 1958).
Dergachev, Ivan, *D. N. Mamin-Sibiriak: lichnost', tvorchestvo* (Sverdlovsk, 1977).

Mandel'shtam, Osip

Brown, Clarence, *Mandelstam* (Cambridge, 1973).
Baines, Jennifer, *Mandelstam: the Later Poetry* (Cambridge, 1976).
Struve, Nikita, *Ossip Mandelstam* (Paris, 1982).
Ronan, Omry, *An Approach to Mandelstam* (Jerusalem, 1983).

Merezhkovskii, Dmitrii

Spengler, Ute, *D. S. Merežkovskii als Literaturkritiker: Versuch einer religiösen Begründung der Kunst* (Lucerne and Frankfurt am Main, 1972).
Bedford, Charles, *The Seeker: D. S. Merezhkovsky* (Lawrence, 1975).
Rosenthal, Bernice, *Dmitri Sergeevich Merezhkovsky and the Silver Age: the Development of a Revolutionary Mentality* (The Hague, 1975).

Mikhailovskii, Nikolai

Billington, James, *Mikhailovsky and Russian Populism* (Oxford, 1958).

Nabokov, Vladimir

Field, Andrew, *Nabokov: His Life in Art. A Critical Narrative* (Boston, 1967).
Rowe, William, *Nabokov's Deceptive World* (New York, 1971).
Lee, L. L., *Vladimir Nabokov* (Boston, 1976).
Field, Andrew, *VN: The Life and Art of Vladimir Nabokov* (New York, 1977).

Naumann, Marina, *Blue Evenings in Berlin: Nabokov's Short Stories of the 1920s* (New York, 1978).

Pifer, Ellen, *Nabokov and the Novel* (Cambridge, Mass. and London, 1980).

Rampton, David, *Vladimir Nabokov: a Critical Study of the Novels* (Cambridge, 1984).

Clancy, Laurie, *The Novels of Vladimir Nabokov* (New York, 1984).

Nadson, Semen

Tsarevskii, Aleksei, *S. Ia. Nadson i ego poeziia "mysli i pechali"* (Kazan, 1895).

Nekrasov, Nikolai

Evgen'ev-Maksimov, V. [Vladislav Maksimov], *Zhizn' i deiatel'nost' N. A. Nekrasova* (3 vols., Moscow, 1947–52).

Corbet, Charles, *Nekrasov: L'homme et le poète* (Paris, 1948).

Kornei Chukovskii, *Masterstvo Nekrasova* (Moscow, 1952).

Peppard, Murray, *Nikolai Nekrasov* (New York, 1967).

Birkenmayer, Sigmund, *Nikolay Nekrasov: His Life and Poetic Art* (The Hague and Paris, 1968).

Risaliti, Renaldo, *Nikolaj Nekrassov (tra tradizione avanguardia)* (Paris, 1969).

Novikov, Nikolai

Makogonenko, Georgii, *Nikolai Novikov i russkoe prosveshchenie XVIII veka* (Moscow–Leningrad, 1951).

Monnier, André, *Un publiciste frondeur sous Catherine II: Nicolas Novikov* (Paris, 1981).

Jones, W. Gareth, *Nikolay Novikov: Enlightener of Russia* (Cambridge, 1984).

Novodvorskii, Andrei

Popova, Mariia, *A. O. Osipovich-Novodvorskii: Ocherk tvorchestva* (Kazan, 1970).

Odoevskii, Vladimir

Sakulin, Pavel, *Iz istorii russkogo idealizma: Kniaz' V. F. Odoevskii, myslitel'-pisatel'* (Moscow, 1913).

Cornwell, Neil, *The Life, Times and Milieu of V. F. Odoyevsky 1804–1869* (London, 1986).

Ogarev, Nikolai

Putintsev, Vladimir, *N. P. Ogarev: zhizn', mirovozzrenie, tvorchestvo* (Moscow, 1963).

Mervaud, Michel, *Socialisme et liberté: La pensée et l'action de Nicolas Ogarev (1813–1877)* (Paris, 1984).

BIBLIOGRAPHY

Okudzhava, Bulat

Ackern, Karl-Dieter von, *Bulat Okudžava und die kritische Literatur über den Krieg* (Munich, 1976).

Olesha, Iurii

Beaujour, Elizabeth, *The Invisible Land: a Study of the Artistic Imagination of Iurii Olesha* (New York and London, 1970).
Ingdahl, Kazimiera, *The Artist and the Creative Act: a Study of Jurij Olesha's Novel Zavist* (Stockholm, 1984).

Ostrovskii, Aleksandr

Patouillet, Jules, *Ostrovski et son théâtre de mœurs russes* (2nd ed., Paris, 1912).
Efros, Nikolai, *Aleksandr Nikolaevich Ostrovskii* (Petrograd, 1922).
Lotman, Lidiia, *A. N. Ostrovskii i russkaia dramaturgiia ego vremeni* (Moscow–Leningrad, 1961).
Kholodov, Efim, *Masterstvo Ostrovskogo* (Second edition, Moscow, 1963).
Shtein, Abram, *Master russkoi dramy* (Moscow, 1973).
Hoover, Marjorie, *Alexander Ostrovsky* (Boston, 1981).

Ostrovskii, Nikolai

Vengrov, N., *Nikolai Ostrovskii* (Moscow, 1952).

Ovechkin, Valentin

Vilchek, Lilia, *Valentin Ovechkin: Zhizn' i tvorchestvo* (Moscow, 1977).

Panova, Vera

Plotkin, Lev, *Tvorchestvo Very Panovoi* (Leningrad, 1962).
Ninov, Aleksandr, *Vera Panova – zhizn', tvorchestvo, sovremenniki* (Leningrad, 1980).

Pasternak, Boris

Payne, Robert, *The Three Worlds of Boris Pasternak* (New York, 1961).
Proyart, Jacqueline de, *Pasternak* (Paris, 1964).
Michelis, Cesare de, *Pasternak* (Florence, 1968).
Dyck, J. W., *Boris Pasternak* (Boston, 1972).
Hughes, Olga, *The Poetic World of Boris Pasternak* (Princeton, 1974).
Gifford, Henry, *Pasternak: A Critical Study* (Cambridge, 1977).
Fleishman, Lazar, *Boris Pasternak v dvadtsatye gody* (Munich, 1980).
Mallac, Guy de, *Boris Pasternak: His Life and Art* (Norman, 1981).
Hingley, Ronald, *Pasternak: a Biography* (New York, 1983).
Fleishman, Lazar, *Boris Pasternak v tridtsatye gody* (Jerusalem, 1984).

Paustovskii, Konstantin

Levitskii, Lev, *Konstantin Paustovskii: Ocherk tvorchestva* (Moscow, 1963).

BIBLIOGRAPHY

Pavlov, Nikolai

Vil'chinskii, Vsevolod, *Nikolai Filippovich Pavlov: Zhizn' i tvorchestvo* (Leningrad, 1970).

Pil'niak, Boris

Reck, Vera, *Boris Pil'niak: a Soviet Writer in Conflict with the State* (Montreal and London, 1975).

Damerau, Reinhard, *Boris Pil'njaks Geschichts- und Menschenbild* (Giessen, 1976).

Jensen, Petr, *Nature as Code: the Achievement of Boris Pilnjak 1915–1924* (Copenhagen, 1979).

Browning, Gary, *Boris Pilniak: Scythian at a Typewriter* (Ann Arbor, 1985).

Pisarev, Dmitrii

Plotkin, Lev, *Pisarev i literaturno-obshchestennoe dvizhenie shest'desiatykh godov* (Leningrad, 1945).

Coquart, Armand, *Dmitri Pisarev (1840–1868) et l'idéologie du nihilisme russe* (Paris, 1946).

Pisemskii, Aleksei

Moser, Charles, *Pisemsky: a Provincial Realist* (Cambridge, Mass., 1969).

Pustovoit, Petr, *A. F. Pisemskii v istorii russkogo romana* (Moscow, 1969).

Platonov, Andrei

Chalmaev, Viktor, *Andrei Platonov* (Moscow, 1978).

Geller, Mikhail, *Andrei Platonov v poiskakh schast'ia* (Paris, 1982).

Vasil'ev, Vladimir, *Andrei Platonov: ocherk zhizni i tvorchestva* (Moscow, 1982).

Pogodin, Mikhail

Barsukov, Nikolai, *Zhizn' i trudy M. P. Pogodina* (22 vols., St. Petersburg, 1888–1910).

Pogodin, Nikolai

Kholodov, Efim, *P'esy i gody: dramaturgiia Nikolaia Pogodina* (Moscow, 1967).

Polonskii, Iakov

Lagunov, Aleksandr, *Lirika Iakova Polonskogo* (Stavropol', 1974).

Prishvin, Mikhail

Khmel'nitskaia, Tamara, *Tvorchestvo Mikhaila Prishvina* (Leningrad, 1959).

Lampl, Horst, *Das Frühwerk Michail Prišvins: Studien zur Erzähltechnik* (Vienna, 1967).

BIBLIOGRAPHY

Prokopovich, Feofan

Chistovich, I. *Feofan Prokopovich i ego vremia* (St. Petersburg, 1868).
Morozov, P., *Feofan Prokopovich kak pisatel'* (St. Petersburg, 1880).

Pushkin, Aleksandr

Sipovskii, Vasilii, *Pushkin: zhizn' i tvorchestvo* (St. Petersburg, 1907).
Haumant, Emile, *Pouchkine* (Paris, 1911).
Gershenzon, Mikhail, *Mudrost' Pushkina* (Moscow, 1919).
Grossman, Leonid, *Etiudy o Pushkine* (Moscow–Petrograd, 1923).
Mirsky, D. S., *Pushkin* (New York and London, 1926).
Brasol, Boris, *The Mighty Three: Poushkin – Gogol – Dostoievsky* (New York, 1934).
Troyat, Henri, *Pouchkine* (Paris, 1936).
Lezhnev, Abram, *Proza Pushkina: Opyt stilevogo issledovaniia* (Moscow, 1937). (Translation: *Pushkin's Prose* (Ann Arbor, 1983).)
Simmons, Ernest, *Pushkin* (Cambridge, Mass., 1937).
Tomashevskii, Boris, *Pushkin* (2 vols. Moscow–Leningrad, 1956–61)
Lo Gatto, Ettore, *Puškin: Storia di un poeta e del suo eroe* (Milan, 1959).
Setschkareff, Vsevolod, *Alexander Puschkin: sein Leben und sein Werk* (Wiesbaden, 1963).
Slonimskii, Aleksandr, *Masterstvo Pushkina* (Moscow, 1963).
Vickery, Walter, *Alexander Pushkin* (New York, 1970).
Bayley, John, *Pushkin: a Comparative Commentary* (Cambridge, 1971).
Debreczeny, Paul, *The Other Pushkin: a Study of Alexander Pushkin's Prose Fiction* (Stanford, 1983).

Radishchev, Aleksandr

Makogonenko, Georgii, *Radishchev i ego vremia* (Moscow, 1956).
Lang, David, *The First Russian Radical: Alexander Radishchev (1749–1802)* (London, 1959).
McConnell, Allen, *A Russian Philosophe: Alexander Radishchev 1749–1802* (The Hague, 1964).
Babkin, Dmitrii, *A. N. Radishchev: literaturno-obshchestvennaia deiatel'nost'* (Moscow–Leningrad, 1966).

Rasputin, Valentin

Schäper, Renate, *Die Prosa V. G. Rasputins* (Munich, 1985).

Remizov, Aleksei

Kodrianskaia, Natal'ia, *Aleksei Remizov* (Paris, 1959).

Rozanov, Vasilii

Gollerbakh, Erikh, *V. V. Rozanov: Zhizn' i tvorchestvo* (St. Petersburg, 1922).
Poggioli, Renato, *Rozanov* (New York, 1962).

624

BIBLIOGRAPHY

Ryleev, Kondratii

Pigarev, Kirill, *Zhizn' Ryleeva* (Moscow, 1947).
Tseitlin, Aleksandr, *Tvorchestvo Ryleeva* (Moscow, 1955).
O'Meara, Patrick, *K. F. Ryleev: a Political Biography of the Decembrist Poet* (Princeton, 1984).

Saltykov-Shchedrin, Mikhail

Ivanov-Razumnik, *M. E. Saltykov-Shchedrin: zhizn' i tvorchestvo* (Moscow, 1930).
Kirpotin, Valerii, *Mikhail Evgrafovich Saltykov-Shchedrin: zhizn' i tvorchestvo* (Revised edition, Moscow, 1955).
Sanine, Kyra, *Saltykov-Chtchédrine: sa vie et ses œuvres* (Paris, 1955).
Risaliti, Renato, *Saltykov-Ščedrin* (Pisa, 1968).

Selvinskii, Il'ia

Reznik, Osip, *Zhizn' v poezii: tvorchestvo I. Selvinskogo* (Moscow, 1981).

Senkovskii, Iosif

Pedrotti, Louis, *Józef Julian Sekowski: The Genesis of a Literary Alien* (Berkeley and Los Angeles, 1965).

Shaginian, Marietta

Skorino, Liudmila, *Marietta Shaginian – khudozhnik: Zhizn' i tvorchestvo* (Moscow, 1975).

Shershenevich, Vadim

Lawton, Anna, *Vadim Shershenevich: from Futurism to Imaginism* (Ann Arbor, 1981).

Shestov, Lev

Wernham, James, *Two Russian Thinkers: an Essay in Berdyaev and Shestov* (Toronto, 1968).
Baranoff-Chestov, Nathalie, *Zhizn' L'va Shestova* (2 vols., Paris, 1983).
Desilets, André, *Léon Chestov* (Quebec, 1984).

Shmelev, Ivan

Aschenbrenner, Michael, *Ivan Schmeljow: Leben und Schaffen des grossen russischen Schriftstellers* (Königsberg and Berlin, 1937).
Kutyrina, Iu., *Ivan Sergeevich Shmelev* (Paris, 1960).

Sholokhov, Mikhail

Lezhnev, Isai, *Put' Sholokhova: tvorcheskaia biografiia* (Moscow, 1958).
Britikov, Anatolii, *Masterstvo Mikhaila Sholokhova* (Moscow–Leningrad, 1964).
Iakimenko, Lev, *Tvorchestvo M. A. Sholokhova* (Moscow, 1964).

625

BIBLIOGRAPHY

Stewart, David, *Mikhail Sholokhov: a Critical Introduction* (Ann Arbor, 1967).

Medvedev, Roy, *Problems in the Literary Biography of Mikhail Sholokhov* (Cambridge, 1977).

Ermolaev, Herman, *Mikhail Sholokhov and His Art* (Princeton, 1982).

Shukshin, Vasilii

Emel'ianov, Leonard, *Vasilii Shukshin: Ocherk tvorchestva* (Leningrad, 1983).

Wust, Heide, *Tradition und Innovation in der Sowjetrussischen Dorfprosa der sechziger und siebziger Jahre: zu Funktion, Darstellung und Gehalt des dorflichen Helden bei Vasilij Šukšin und Valentin Rasputin* (Munich, 1984).

Karpova, Valentina, *Talantlivaia zhizn': Vasilii Shukshin – prozaik* (Moscow, 1986).

Shvarts, Evgenii

Metcalf, Amanda, *Evgenii Shvarts and His Fairy-Tales for Adults* (Birmingham, 1979).

Simonov, Konstantin

Fink, Lev, *Konstantin Simonov: tvorcheskii put'* (Moscow, 1979).

Lazarev, Lazar, *Konstantin Simonov: ocherk zhizni i tvorchestva* (Moscow, 1985).

Siniavskii, Andrei

Dalton, Margaret, *Andrei Siniavsky and Julii Daniel': Two Soviet "Heretical" Writers* (Würzburg, 1973).

Lourie, Richard, *Letters to the Future: an Approach to Sinyavsky–Tertz* (Ithaca and London, 1975).

Sologub, Fedor

Rabinowitz, Stanley, *Sologub's Literary Children: Keys to a Symbolist's Prose* (Columbus, 1980).

Solov'ev, Vladimir

Mochul'skii, Konstantin, *Vladimir Solov'ev: zhizn' i uchenie* (Paris, 1936).

Solzhenitsyn, Aleksandr

Lukács, György, *Solzhenitsyn* (Cambridge, Mass., 1971).

Rothberg, Abraham, *Aleksandr Solzhenitsyn: the Major Novels* (Ithaca, 1971).

Moody, Christopher, *Solzhenitsyn* (New York, 1973).

Kodjak, Andrej, *Alexander Solzhenitsyn* (Boston, 1978).

Krasnov, Vladislav, *Solzhenitsyn and Dostoevsky: a Study in the Polyphonic Novel* (Athens, GA., 1980).

Curtis, James, *Solzhenitsyn's Traditional Imagination* (Athens, GA., 1984).

Scammell, Michael, *Solzhenitsyn: A Biography* (New York and London, 1984).

Song of Igor's Campaign (Igor Tale)

Mazon, André, *Le Slovo d'Igor* (Paris, 1940).
Grégoire, Henri et al., *La Geste du Prince Igor'. Epopée russe du douzième siècle* (New York, 1948).
Likhachev, Dmitrii, *"Slovo o polku Igoreve" i kul'tura ego vremeni* (Leningrad, 1978).

Sukhovo-Kobylin, Aleksandr

Grossman, Leonid, *Teatr Sukhovo-Kobylina* (Moscow–Leningrad, 1940).
Fortune, Richard, *Alexander Sukhovo-Kobylin* (Boston, 1982).

Sumarokov, Aleksandr

Bulich, Nikolai, *Sumarokov i sovremennaia emu kritika* (St. Petersburg, 1854).

Tikhonov, Nikolai

Grinberg, Iosif, *Nikolai Tikhonov: ocherk zhizni i tvorchestva* (Moscow, 1952).
Shoshin, Vladislav, *Nikolai Tikhonov* (Leningrad, 1981).

Tiutchev, Fedor

Pigarev, Kiril, *Zhizn' i tvorchestvo Tiutcheva* (Moscow, 1962).
Gregg, Richard, *Fedor Tiutchev: the Evolution of a Poet* (New York, 1965).
Pratt, Sarah, *Russian Metaphysical Romanticism: the Poetry of Tiutchev and Boratynskii* (Stanford, 1984).

Tolstoi, Aleksei Konstantinovich

Lirondelle, André, *Le poète Alexis Tolstoï: l'homme et l'œuvre* (Paris, 1912).
Dalton, Margaret, *A. K. Tolstoy* (New York, 1972).

Tolstoi, Aleksei Nikolaevich

Shcherbina, Vladimir, *A. N. Tolstoi: Tvorcheskii put'* (Moscow, 1956).
Alpatov, Arsenii, *Aleksei Tolstoi – master istoricheskogo romana* (Moscow, 1958).
Krestinskii, Iurii, *A. N. Tolstoi: zhizn' i tvorchestvo* (Moscow, 1960).

Tolstoi, Lev

Maude, Aylmer, *The Life of Tolstoy* (2 vols., New York, 1910).
Garnett, Edward, *Tolstoy: His Life and Writings* (London, 1914).
Noyes, George, *Tolstoy* (New York, 1918).
Eikhenbaum, Boris, *Lev Tolstoi* (2 vols., Leningrad, 1928–31). (Translations: *The Young Tolstoi* (Ann Arbor, 1972); *Tolstoi in the Sixties* (Ann Arbor, 1982); *Tolstoi in the Seventies* (Ann Arbor, 1982).)

Simmons, Ernest, *Leo Tolstoy* (Boston, 1946).

Hamburger, Kate, *Leo Tolstoy: Gestalt und Problem* (Bern, 1950).

Berlin, Isaiah, *The Hedgehog and the Fox: an Essay on Tolstoy's View of History* (New York, 1953).

Steiner, George, *Tolstoy or Dostoevsky: an Essay in the Old Criticism* (New York, 1959).

Lakshin, Vladimir, *Tolstoi i Chekhov* (Moscow, 1963).

Ermilov, Vladimir, *Tolstoi-romanist: "Voina i mir," "Anna Karenina," "Voskresenie"* (Moscow, 1965).

Lednicki, Waclaw, *Tolstoy Between War and Peace* (The Hague, 1965).

Christian, Reginald, *Tolstoy: a Critical Introduction* (London, 1969).

Crankshaw, Edward, *Tolstoy: the Making of a Novelist* (New York, 1974).

Wasiolek, Edward, *Tolstoy's Major Fiction* (Chicago, 1978).

Rowe, William, *Leo Tolstoy* (Boston, 1986).

Tret'iakov, Sergei

Mierau, Fritz, *Erfindung und Korrektur: Tretjakows Ästhetik der Operativität* (Berlin, 1976).

Trifonov, Iurii

Ivanova, Natal'ia, *Proza Iuriia Trifonova* (Moscow, 1984).

Tsvetaeva, Marina

Karlinsky, Simon, *Marina Tsvetaeva: Her Life and Art* (Berkeley, 1966).

Razumovsky, Maria, *Marina Zwetajewa: Mythos und Wahrheit* (Vienna, 1981).

Karlinsky, Simon, *Marina Tsvetaeva. The Woman, her World and her Poetry* (Cambridge, 1986).

Turgenev, Ivan

Haumant, Emile, *Ivan Tourguénief: la vie et l'œuvre* (Paris, 1906).

Garnett, Edward, *Turgenev: a Study* (London, 1917).

Yarmolinsky, Avrahm, *Turgenev: the Man, His Art and His Age* (New York, 1926).

Zaitsev, Boris, *Zhizn' Turgeneva* (Paris, 1932).

Granjard, Henri, *Ivan Tourguénev et les courants politiques et sociaux de son temps* (Paris, 1954).

Tseitlin, Aleksandr, *Masterstvo Turgeneva-romanista* (Moscow, 1958).

Freeborn, Richard, *Turgenev: the Novelist's Novelist. A Study* (London, 1960).

Pustovoit, Petr, *Roman I. S. Turgeneva "Ottsy i deti" i ideinaia bor'ba 60–kh godov XIX veka* (Moscow, 1965).

Gibelli, Vincenzo, *Turgheniev* (Milan, 1974).

Brang, Peter, *I. S. Turgenev: sein Leben und sein Werk* (Wiesbaden, 1976).

Schapiro, Leonard, *Turgenev: His Life and Times* (New York, 1978).

Lowe, David, *Turgenev's "Fathers and Sons"* (Ann Arbor, 1983).

Tvardovskii, Aleksandr

Vykhodtsev, Petr, *Aleksandr Tvardovskii* (Moscow, 1958).
Kondratovich, Aleksei, *Aleksandr Tvardovskii: Poeziia i lichnost'* (Leningrad, 1978).
Makedonov, Adrian, *Tvorcheskii put' Tvardovskogo: doma i dorogi* (Moscow, 1981).

Uspenskii, Gleb

Cheshikhin-Vetrinskii, V., *Gleb Ivanovich Uspenskii* (Moscow, 1929).
Prutskov, Nikita, *Tvorcheskii put' Gleba Uspenskogo* (Moscow–Leningrad, 1958).
Lothe, Jean, *Gleb Ivanovič Uspenskij et le populisme russe* (Leiden, 1963).
Prutskov, Nikita, *Gleb Uspensky* (New York, 1972).

Vasil'ev, Pavel

Mikhailov, Aleksandr, *Stepnaia pesn': poeziia Pavla Vasil'eva* (Moscow, 1971).

Venevitinov, Dmitrii

Wytrzens, Günther, *Dmitriii Vladimirovich Venevitinov als Dichter der russischen Romantik* (Graz, 1962).
Tartakovskaia, Lidiia, *Dmitrii Venevitinov: lichnost', mirovozzrenie, tvorchestvo* (Tashkent, 1974).

Viazemskii, Petr

Wytrzens, Günther, *Piotr Andreevič Vjazemskij. Studie zur russischen Literatur- und Kulturgeschichte des neunzehnten Jahrhunderts* (Vienna, 1961).
Gillel'son, Maksim, *P. A. Viazemskii: zhizn' i tvorchestvo* (Leningrad, 1969).

Vishnevskii, Vsevolod

Anastasev, Arkadii, *Vsevolod Vishnevskii: ocherk tvorchestva* (Moscow, 1962).

Voznesenskii, Andrei

Mikhailov, Aleksandr, *Andrei Voznesenskii: etiudy* (Moscow, 1970).

Zabolotskii, Nikolai

Rostovtseva, Inna, *Nikolai Zabolotskii: literaturnyi portret* (Moscow, 1976).

Zamiatin, Evgenii

Richards, David, *Zamyatin: a Soviet Heretic* (New York, 1962).
Shane, Alex, *The Life and Works of Evgenij Zamjatin* (Berkeley, 1968).

Scheffler, Leonore, *Evgenij Zamjatin: sein Weltbild und seine literarische Thematik* (Cologne and Vienna, 1984).

Zhukovskii, Vasilii

Veselovskii, Aleksandr, *Zhukovskii: poeziia chuvstva i serdechnogo voobrazheniia* (St. Petersburg, 1904).
Ellis (Kobilinsky, L.), *W. A. Joukowski, seine Persönlichkeit, sein Leben und sein Werk* (Paderborn, 1933).
Ehrhard, Marcelle, *V. A. Joukovski et le preromantisme russe* (Paris, 1938).
Zaitsev, Boris, *Zhukovskii* (Paris, 1951).
Semenko, Irina, *Vasily Zhukovsky* (Boston, 1976).

Zlatovratskii, Nikolai

Semenkin, Konstantin, *N. N. Zlatovratskii: ocherk zhizni i tvorchestva* (Yaroslavl, 1976).

Zoshchenko, Mikhail

Ershov, Leonid, *Iz istorii sovetskoi satiry: M. Zoshchenko i satiricheskaia proza 20–40–kh godov* (Leningrad, 1973).
Chudakova, Marietta, *Poetika Mikhaila Zoshchenko* (Moscow, 1979).

INDEX

This index seeks to be reasonably inclusive, although it does not contain references to literary characters. The Russian titles of works are listed where they occur in the alphabet, along with the English titles under which page references are given. This index is of such dimensions that it cannot be analytical to any great degree, but in the case of especially important authors and works the pagination of the major discussions is provided before the semicolon; less important discussions or passing references follow the semicolon.

INDEX

INDEX

665

INDEX